böhlau

KÄTE HAMBURGER KOLLEG MÜNSTER
EINHEIT & VIELFALT IM RECHT
LEGAL UNITY & PLURALISM

Edited by Ulrike Ludwig and Peter Oestmann

Volume 3

Die Reihe versteht Rechtsvielfalt als ein überzeitliches und überregionales Strukturmerkmal von Recht schlechthin. Es kann demnach von einem relationalen und historisch wandelbaren Zusammenhang von Einheit und Vielfalt im Recht gesprochen werden. Die Schriftenreihe möchte diesen Zusammenhang in seiner kulturellen Vielgestaltigkeit umfassend beleuchten: interdisziplinär, räumlich übergreifend und interepochal. Die Bände erscheinen in deutscher und englischer Sprache und sind überwiegend im Open Access zugänglich.

The book series conceptualises legal pluralism as a structural characteristic of law itself. We can therefore speak of a relational and historically changeable association between unity and pluralism in law. The book series intends to comprehensively illuminate these connections in their cultural polymorphy interdisciplinarily, transspatially and interepochally. The volumes are published in German and English and will be predominantly open access.

Die Herausgeber / the editors

João Figueiredo

Sorcery and Jurisdiction in Angola

Law and Multinormativity in Early Modern West Central Africa

BÖHLAU

This publication was made possible by the Käte Hamburger Kolleg "Legal Unity and Pluralism" at the University of Münster, funded by the Federal Ministry of of Research, Technology and Space (BMFTR).

Bibliographic information published by the Deutsche Nationalbibliothek:
The Deutsche Nationalbibliothek lists this publication in the Deutsche Nationalbibliografie; detailed bibliographic data available online: https://dnb.de.

Cover image: *"Bagi"* oath. Agnelli, Federico (illustrator) in Cavazzi: Istorica descrizione de' tre' regni Congo, Matamba, et Angola, p. 92 (Source: gallica.bnf.fr / Bibliothèque Nationale de France).

Cover design: Michael Haderer, Vienna
Typesetting: le-tex publishing services, Leipzig
Printed and bound: Hubert & Co, Göttingen
Printed in the EU

Vandenhoeck & Ruprecht Verlage | www.vandenhoeck-ruprecht-verlage.com
E-Mail: info@boehlau-verlag.com

ISBN 978-3-412-53313-7 (print)
ISBN 978-3-412-53314-4 (digital)

Contents

II. Trade Routes and Slave Fairs

III. Establishing Limits, Negotiating Belonging

Introduction

On an early morning in late November 2009, I sat half-awake in a crowded waiting room in downtown Luanda. There was no highway then, so the trip from the suburb where I lived to the city center could take two to four hours, depending on the rain, traffic, and police roadblock activity. Afraid of missing opening hours, I had arranged to stay at a nearby friend's place the night before. Exhausted from the trip and a bit anxious, I had barely managed to sleep. Distant urban noises and the constant hum of dozens of diesel generators and air conditioners kept me company through the night. Holding my Angolan personal record card, passport pictures, and a citizen card application form, I waited for my height, fingerprints, and signature to be collected. In the meantime, I struggled with mixed feelings about applying for Angolan citizenship. Born in Portugal and aware of my family's settler colonial past and 'difficult heritage' as White Africans of European ancestry, I was deeply absorbed in my thoughts. Abruptly, my bubble burst as I realized a lively discussion was happening between two young adults, a woman and a man, in the other corner of the waiting room. Both were terrific communicators, visibly thriving on the attention they were getting; they sought and often managed to provoke collective laughter and loud murmurs of approval. The thesis under debate was: "*Can Whites be sorcerers?*"[1]

---

1 Throughout this book, I capitalize Black(s), Blackness, White(s), and Whiteness while always retaining the original cases within citations. All occurrences of Black(s), in capitals or lowercase, are translations of either the Portuguese terms "*preto*" or "*negro*." From the nineteenth century onwards, the former has acquired racist and derogatory connotations, becoming a tool of White-supremacist dehumanization. At the same time, the latter has been reclaimed in Portugal, from the first decades of the twentieth century, as a positive identity marker and catalyst for progressive struggles. However, depending on context and semantics, both could be used as a slur or to 'other' somebody during the period under consideration. The difficult choice to translate all instances with the term Black thus reflects care for the present generation. It would be callous to attempt to be historically precise at the cost of reproducing symbolic violence for marginal intellectual gain (when necessary, the Portuguese original is cited). As for White(s), its capitalization is meant to signal that Whiteness was constructed as a norm during the period under study, often in opposition to Black(s) and Blackness. It can never be naively taken as a standard or a natural given. See Arlindo Barbeitos for an in-depth analysis of the history of racial relations in Angola. For an overview of the history of racial relations in the Portuguese Empire, see Charles Boxer, Francisco Bethencourt, and José Ramos Tinhorão. See Luiz Filipe de Alencastro and Patrick Wolfe for a comparison between racialization processes in Angola and Brazil All translations from Portuguese and other modern languages are my own (unless otherwise noted). Alencastro, Mulattos in Brazil and Angola, in: Bethencourt (ed.), Racism and Ethnic Relations, p. 71–96; Barbeitos, A "raça" e o racismo, p. 13–50; Barbeitos, A "raça" ou a ilusão de uma identidade definitiva, in: Gonçalves (ed.), O

I started my post-graduate studies at the University of Coimbra in 2006. At the turn of 2009, I was still undecided about the topic for my dissertation, having taken a year off to work as a lecturer at a private university in Luanda.[2] Much of my spare time was spent reading ethnographic accounts of contemporary sorcery beliefs and accusations in Sub-Saharan Africa, from Cameroon to Mozambique, Kenya to South Africa—and almost everywhere in between. Despite the seriousness of the topic, the discussion that morning proceeded in a lighter tone than I had ever anticipated. In the improvised court that the waiting room had turned into, the belonging of Whites to the post-colonial Angolan body politic and its full implications were on trial. Not only was that topic being settled, it seemed, but determining the 'truth' behind centuries of imperial exploitation and dispossession was also the order of the day. As the people in line were called forward, they would stand up and share their thoughts on these critical matters, as if casting a vote, before resuming their daily activities.

Considering both speakers' well-honed arguments, this was not their first time engaging in such a dispute. Any conclusion reached that morning would certainly be provisory. The session would soon be adjourned and resumed in other impromptu forums. The back of a crowded Toyota *Hiace* stuck in the traffic on a rainy afternoon. The terraces of the Island of Luanda, where clerks and public servants drank cold beers and ate grilled fish on lazy Sunday mornings. In 2009, it was equally impossible to escape well-informed analyses and heated debates about African witchcraft or *sorcellerie* in Anglophone and Francophone African studies journals or anthropology reviews.[3] However, in this crowded antechamber of the Angolan nation, my soon-to-be fellow citizens were framing the stakes of the discussion entirely differently. Less interested in discussing or reaffirming their 'modernity' or place within a global capitalist, neoliberal system than Western academics, they focused on history and the colonial past instead.

Eventually, the debate centered on a single crucial question: is sorcery intrinsically African, or do Whites have "*schools and universities*" in Europe devoted to teaching it? The young woman claimed to be acquainted with several Portuguese White

---

racismo ontem e hoje, p. 139–148; BARBEITOS, Angola/Portugal; BETHENCOURT, Racisms; BOXER, Race Relations; ROLDÃO, PEREIRA and VARELA, Tribuna Negra; TINHORÃO, Os Negros em Portugal; WOLFE, Traces of History.

2 I settled on the topic of sorcery accusations during the long nineteenth century, a period immediately after the one covered in this book. FIGUEIREDO, Política, escravatura e feitiçaria em Angola.

3 LUONGO, Motive Rather than Means, p. 35–57; RANGER, Scotland Yard in the Bush, p. 13–31; TER HAAR and ELLIS, The Occult Does Not Exist, p. 399–412; TONDA, La Violence de l'imaginaire des enfants-sorciers, p. 325–343; WEST, Creative Destruction and Sorcery of Construction; WEST, Sorcery of Construction and Socialist Modernization, p. 119–150.

men employed in construction firms, arguing that as soon as she got to know them better, she couldn't deny that they were as likely as anybody else to be "*feiticeiros*" or sorcerers. She speculated that they had learned their mysterious craft in Europe but that it differed from African "*feitiços*" or sorcery only because it was more potent; the men were as cruel, violent, power-hungry, and enthralling as any Angolan general or politician. These low-class Whites, however, were no match for the latter—the young man countered. In fact, like all Whites, "*they had no feitiço of their own.*" Instead, they relied on their proximity to African elites to gain access to the lion's share of the nation's natural and economic resources. Quite the opposite was true—the young woman interjected. Just like in the times of the Portuguese settler colonists, she argued, low-class Whites and Black elites shared their knowledge of sorcery: it was through *feitiço* that they genuinely bonded and enabled each other. How else could the man explain five centuries of intertwined history, "*everything that had passed before independence*"?

I couldn't hear the young man's reply as I had to proceed with my citizenship application. Perhaps this is why the young woman's question has lingered in the back of my mind and haunted me ever since. As I came to see it, it hints at the possibility of revisiting the whole colonial history of Angola, from the establishment of the hereditary Captaincy in 1571 to the final lowering of the Portuguese flag in 1975. This entire period, viewed through the prism of sorcery discourses—as if such a long, twisted narrative of pain, greed, and suffering, but also resistance, great joy, and creativity, could only make sense in this manner. How else to explain the enormity and horror of what had passed before? The centuries of the Atlantic slave trade, the incredible flourishing of Christianism in the Kingdom of Kongo, the rise and fall of a sophisticated *angolense* elite and culture, the War of Independence, and the birth of a unified Republic of Angola? Historians, of course, would never agree to such a reading, opting for other prisms to explore the rich archives of West Central Africa. Conversion, commerce, civilization, cultural innovation, and the rule of law can all be named as possible candidates for such a 'totalizing lens,' purportedly describing the goal of Portuguese expansion or the driving force and secret advantage of White conquerors, merchants, missionaries, and settlers. "*Outrageous proposals! None of these wretched illusions is any more real than sorcery,*"—I imagine the young woman enthusiastically retorting. Is it possible to write a history that considers both her view, as I briefly glimpsed it, and the perspectives of mainstream historians? Not to reconcile them and put an end to such a wonderful conversation… Not even to affirm an alternative, 'decolonial' version of Angolan history written through the prism of *feitiçaria* or a purportedly different African ontology. But, instead, to show how the dialectical interplay between these worldviews and theories about power and agency conditioned past events and shaped lasting institutions? This volume is my attempt at writing such a history. It would perhaps not have been possible without the fantastic performance of those two charismatic speakers that early morning in late November 2009.

Sorcery and the Law

This book argues that the normative cluster that can be abstracted from the beliefs, practices, and discourses related to sorcery is a prime example of a genuinely cosmopolitan form of African normative knowledge. Therefore, during the Early Modern period, the history of the relationship between jurisdiction and sorcery beliefs and practices in the Captaincy of Angola and other areas of West Central Africa under Portuguese influence (its 'dependencies') is first and foremost a legal history: the history of the concurrence and competition between two normative regimes or constellations, each centered on very different conceptual formations and practices, both including elements with a clear cosmopolitan vocation. The result of a sustained effort of transdisciplinary bricolage, this book proposes different methodological approaches and heuristics that can help us trace the evolving historical contours of the dialectic between jurisdiction, the "power to declare the law," and sorcery, the power to impose one's selfish will through (super)natural means.[4]

Over the last few decades, the anthropology of sorcery and "witchcraft studies" have generated exciting new theoretical perspectives that have yet to inform archive-driven historical analysis, at least focused on West Central Africa under historical Portuguese influence.[5] Concurrently, institutional history and the legal history of Early Modern Iberian empires have been equally dynamic fields of scholarship,

---

4 During the Early Modern period, the line between natural magic, sorcery, and supernatural agency was not clearly drawn in Europe, while the binary natural-supernatural probably made little sense in West Central Africa. Hespanha, A cultura jurídica europeia, p. 5–6; Paiva, Bruxaria e superstição; Thomas, Religion and the Decline of Magic; Walker, Doctors, Folk Medicine and the Inquisition.

5 While the term 'witchcraft' is often used in Anglophone ethnographic studies and to translate the French *sorcellerie* and the Portuguese *feitiçaria*, I will instead use the term 'sorcery.' The use of 'witchcraft,' inspired by E. E. Evans-Pritchard's choice of the term to describe the religious theories of the Azande, poses two serious problems for global historical and comparative legal studies. First, it creates a false proximity to the history of European witchcraft (*bruxaria*, not *feitiçaria* in Portuguese), which had a completely different normative framing. Second, it dissociates the history of European interactions with African sorcery discourses and beliefs from the history of the 'fetish,' directly derived from the Portuguese understanding of *feitiço* and *feitiçaria*, not *bruxaria* or witchcraft. Evans-Pritchard, Witchcraft, Oracles, and Magic; Geschiere, Sorcellerie et politique en Afrique; Geschiere, The Modernity of Witchcraft; Pietz, The Problem of the Fetish; Sansi-Roca and Parés, Sorcery in the Black Atlantic.

with most authors primarily focusing on the Latin American and Asian contexts.[6] West Central African particularities, when noted, are addressed briefly in footnotes and asides—as if too unusual to warrant attention.[7] I begin this introduction by presenting recent developments in the study of sorcery beliefs and accusations in Africa. I highlight their potential and limitations before turning to current debates about legal history, the "history of the translation of normative knowledge," and "multinormativity."[8] I conclude by presenting the methodological assemblages that

6 Benton, A Search for Sovereignty; Bethencourt, Managing Diversity in the Portuguese Empire, p. 1–23; Bicalho and Ferlini, Modos de governar; Palomo, Stumpf and Xavier, Monarquias ibéricas em perspectiva comparada; Bouza, Cardim and Feros, The Iberian World; Camarinhas, Juízes e administração; Cardim and Monteiro, Political Thought in Portugal and its Empire, p. 275–297; Cardim, Herzog, Ibáñez and Sabatini, Polycentric Monarchies, in: Cardim, Herzog, Ibáñez and Sabatini (eds.), Polycentric Monarchies, p. 3–8; Duve and Herzog, Latin American Law; Duve and Herzog, Latin American Law; Cardim, O poder dos afectos; Galdinho de Paiva, Justiça e poder; Hespanha, A cultura jurídica europeia; Hespanha, A política perdida; Hespanha, As fronteiras do poder, p. 47–105; Hespanha, Caleidoscópio do Antigo Regime; Hespanha, Como os juristas viam o mundo; Hespanha, Depois do Leviathan, p. 55–66; Hespanha, Direito Comum e Direito Colonial, p. 95–116; Hespanha, Filhos da terra; Hespanha, Governo, elites e competência social, in: Bicalho and Ferlini (eds.), Modos de governar, p. 39–44; Hespanha, Uncommon Laws, p. 180–204; Ribeiro da Silva, Dutch and Portuguese; Subtil, Atallah and Mota, Criminalidades no mundo ibérico, in: Subtil, Atallah and Mota (eds.), Criminalidades, Direito e justiça no mundo ibérico, p. 17–32; Subtil, Espaço político e organização, p. 88–116; Subtil, Estado de polícia, p. 15–40; Subtil, O terramoto político; Zeron, The Concept of Justice, in: Stephan, Mariana Dias, Roberto Hofmeister and Paulo Cruz (eds.), Current Trends in Slavery Studies in Brazil, p. 289–332.

7 The recent works of José Nafafé, José Curto, Mariana Candido, Roquinaldo Ferreira, and Vanessa Oliveria contribute to the institutional and legal history of the Captaincy of Angola. However, only Mariana Paes adopts a legal historical lens. Candido, An African Slaving; Candido, Wealth, Land, and Property in Angola; Curto, Experiences of Enslavement in West Central Africa, p. 382–415; Dias Paes, Esclavos y tierras; Dias Paes, Registro e colonialismo em Angola, in: Malaspina and Tarozzi (eds.), Historical Perspectives on Property and Land Law, p. 161–176; Dias Paes, Shared Atlantic legal culture, p. 419–440; Ferreira, Cross-Cultural Exchange; Curto, Struggling Against Enslavement, p. 96–122; Nafafé, Lourenço da Silva Mendonça; Oliveira, African Women and Commerce in the Atlantic World.

8 Duve, Legal History as a History of the Translation of Knowledge of Normativity, p. 1–12; Duve, Was ist 'Multinormativität,' p. 88–101; Herzog, What is Legal History, in: Duve and Herzog (eds.), Latin America Law in Global Perspective, p. Cambridge University Press; Herzog, Colonial Law, in: Tellkamp (ed.), A Companion to Early Modern Spanish Imperial Political and Social Thought, p. 105–127; Herzog, A Short History of European Law; Cardim, Herzog, Ibáñez and Sabatini, Polycentric Monarchies, in: Cardim, Herzog, Ibáñez and Sabatini (eds.), Polycentric Monarchies, p. 3–8; Vec, Multinormativität in der Rechtsgeschichte, p. 155–166; Duve, Historia del Derecho, p. 1–60; Duve, What is Global Legal History? p. 73–115; Duve, Legal History as an Observation, p. 1–10; Herzog, The Uses and Abuses of Legal Pluralism, p. 1–12.

are tested in each of the three parts of this book, situating the contribution of each chapter and section to the book's argument.

Peter Geschiere's ethnography of contemporary Cameroonian governmental policies, political disputes, and developmental projects has set the tone of the discussion about sorcery discourses and accusations in Africa for the last few decades, resituating the ongoing anthropological debate about the social function, structural underpinnings, and cultural significance of sorcery or witchcraft beliefs and accusations in the fields of political science and governance and accountability studies.[9] In *The Modernity of Witchcraft* (1997), Geschiere remarks that in southeast Cameroon, as in most of the continent, there is a "close conceptual link" between sorcery and power, the former being simultaneously characterized as "evil" and as offering, "thrill, excitement, and the possibility to access unknown powers."[10] Geschiere theorizes that this link allows the cultural "*imaginaire*" of sorcery to saturate both postcolonial statecraft and "popular forms" of resistance to it.[11] In Cameroon, state officials interpret non-adherence to government-backed development policies as evidence of "subversive" sorcery practices that must be eradicated to pave the way for "progress." Simultaneously, local communities perceive the interference and neoliberal entrepreneurship of outsiders and state officials as dangerous forms of "accumulative" sorcery that require ritual counteraction.[12] In both cases, members of one group seem to be equally shocked and enticed by the "occult" power of the

---

9 It is impossible to provide a comprehensive listing of the bibliography that resulted from decades of functionalist, structuralist, post-structuralist, and cultural-turn discussions of witchcraft or sorcery accusations and beliefs in Africa. The following 'classic' references have provided food for thought. Crawford, Witchcraft and Sorcery in Rhodesia; Evans-Pritchard, Witchcraft, Oracles, and Magic; Gelfand, The African Witch; Marwick, Postscript, in: Marwick (ed.), Witchcraft and Sorcery, p. 379–382; Geschiere and Fisiy, Witchcraft, Development and Paranoia in Cameroon, in: Moore and Sanders (eds.), Magical Interpretations, Material Realities; Geschiere, Kinship, Witchcraft and "the Market," in: Dilley (ed.), Contesting Markets, p. 159–179; Geschiere, Responsibility versus Responsibilization, in: Denian, Fumanti and Lynteris (eds.), Anthropology and Responsibility; Geschiere, Sorcellerie et Politique en Afrique; Geschiere, Sorcery and the State, p. 35–63; Geschiere, The (Ir)Responsible Witch, in: Rubbers and Jedlowski (eds.), Regimes of Responsibility in Africa, p. 180–198; Geschiere, The Modernity of Witchcraft; Geschiere, Witchcraft and Modernity, in: Parés and Sansi-Roca (eds.), Sorcery in the Black Atlantic, p. 233–258; Geschiere, Witchcraft as the Dark Side of Kinship, p. 43–61; Geschiere, Witchcraft, Intimacy, and Trust; Marwick, Witchcraft and Sorcery; Mary, Introduction, in: Mary (ed.), Witchcraft Confesions and Accusations, p. i–xxxviii; Mary, Witchcraft Confessions and Accusations; Turner, Witchcraft and Sorcery, p. 314–325; Wilson, Witch-Beliefs and Social Structure, in: Marwick (ed.), Witchcraft and Sorcery, p. 252–263.

10 Geschiere, The Modernity of Witchcraft, p. 1–2.

11 Bayart, The Illusion of Cultural Identity; Geschiere, Sorcery and the State, p. 35–63; Geschiere, The Modernity of Witchcraft, p. 7–8, 15–19, 98–99, 134.

12 Geschiere and Fisiy, Witchcraft, Development and Paranoia in Cameroon, in: Moore and Sanders (eds.), Magical Interpretations, Material Realities; Geschiere, Witchcraft and Modernity,

other group, being torn between the impulse to publicly tame sorcery through ritual and legal means (either within the framework of statutory laws or state-backed customary laws) or to seek ways of secretly seizing its power for their benefit.

Geschiere and Isak Niehaus argue that these dynamics impact how all perceive the post-colonial state's failure to impose the 'rule of law' and uphold transparency, also being played out in courtrooms and governmental commissions.[13] In line with Geschiere and Cyprian Fisiy's observations, in the 1980s, Cameroonian regional law courts "started convicting 'witches' often without concrete proof of aggression or confession," framing sorcery as "active resistance against modernization and development" under the Penal Code of 1967.[14] A decade later, Niehaus remarks, the establishment of the *Ralushai Commission* (1995) was a watershed moment in South Africa, signaling the post-apartheid South African state's new policy towards African normative systems and the recognition of "customary law" by accepting "witchcraft as real" and a "marker of African identity."[15] Both developments took place in the context of rising violence, as the lynching or extra-judicial killing of accused sorcerers multiplied throughout the continent, increasingly victimizing young children and older people.[16] State recognition, however, neither broke the

---

in: Parés and Sansi-Roca (eds.), Sorcery in the Black Atlantic, p. 247–247; Moore, Reflections on the Comaroff Lecture, p. 304–306.

13 Geschiere, Responsibility versus Responsibilization, in: Denian, Fumanti and Lynteris (eds.), Anthropology and Responsibility; Geschiere, The (Ir)Responsible Witch, in: Rubbers and Jedlowski (eds.), Regimes of Responsibility in Africa, p. 180–198; Niehaus, The ANC's Dilemma, p. 93–118; Niehaus, Witchcraft and a Life in the New South Africa; Niehaus, Witchcraft in the New South Africa, in: Moore and Sanders (eds.), Magical Interpretations, Material Realities; Niehaus, Witchcraft, Power and Politics; Niehaus, Witch-Hunting and Political Legitimacy, p. 498–529.

14 Geschiere and Fisiy, Witchcraft, Development and Paranoia in Cameroon, in: Moore and Sanders (eds.), Magical Interpretations, Material Realities; Geschiere, The Modernity of Witchcraft, p. 6.

15 Niehaus, Witchcraft in the New South Africa, in: Moore and Sanders (eds.), Magical Interpretations, Material Realities; Niehaus, Witchcraft, Power and Politics; Zenker and Hoehne, Processing the Paradox, in: Zenker and Hoehne (eds.), The State and the Paradox, p. 1–40.

16 According to Niehaus, in the Northern Province of South Africa, there were 389 killings related to sorcery accusations between 1985 and 1995. Meanwhile, in Sukumaland, Tanzania, 3072 purported witches were killed between 1970 and 1988, according to a government report cited by Simeon Mesaki. According to Luena Nunes Pereira, in Angola, there were "hundreds of reported cases" of sorcery accusations against children and adolescents during the 1990s, particularly in the provinces of Uíge and Zaire, neighboring the Democratic Republic of Congo. Joseph Tonda and Filip De Boeck describe how sorcery accusations increasingly focused on "sorcerer-children" in the DRC during the same period. As for "ritual murders," presumably part of sorcery rituals, Stephen Ellis accepts the estimate of 6000 having occurred in Nigeria between 1992 and 1996. Ellis also points to data suggesting the weekly incidence of "*muti* murders" related to sorcery in some South African settlements in the "late 1980s and early 1990s." De Boeck, Le «Deuxième monde» et les «enfants-

cycle of violence nor put an end to the ambiguity surrounding sorcery beliefs and accusations. Instead, it fuelled a "paradox" like those described by Olaf Zenker and Markus Hoehne regarding the normative, economic, and social impacts of state recognition of "customary law" in Africa.[17] Either by officially acknowledging or denying the existence of sorcerers, post-colonial states both alter the meaning of sorcery and get trapped in a 'Catch-22' ring of circular logic. Due to the widespread belief in Sub-Saharan Africa that one must be knowledgeable in the ways of sorcery to identify it, state officials and commissioners become suspect of being sorcerers either when they facilitate the punishment of sorcery or when they fail to act, thus tacitly siding with those accused of such anti-social practices.

In Angola, this paradoxical dynamic conditioned the discussions that led to the proposal and subsequent enactment of the new Penal Code by Law 38/20 of November 11, 2021.[18] As former Supreme Court Judge Luzia Sebastião explains, when the "*Kamutukuleno*" case involving eight men accused of lynching three purported sorcerers reached the Court in 2010, it had the immediate result of "custom being granted the status of a primary source of Angolan Law."[19] This opened the door for beliefs based on "uses and customs" to be recognized as mitigating conditions under the Penal Code of 2021, provided these beliefs align with the Constitution of Angola (2010) and respect the "dignity of the human person."[20] Such a solution, however, fails to address the normative challenges at the core of the "*Kamutukuleno*" case. As transpires from Sebastião's observations, the eight men who killed the three suspected of enslaving the spirits of the "dead" through sorcery neither believed their victims were human persons in need of state protection nor that their justified anti-sorcery violence was in any way criminal or anti-social.[21]

---

sorciers,» p. 32–57; Ellis, The Occult does Not Exist, in: Kelsall (ed.), Charlatans, Spirits and Rebels in Africa, p. 349; Mesaki, Witch-Killing in Sukumaland, in: Abrahams (ed.), Witchcraft in Contemporary Tanzania, p. 71–86; Niehaus, Witchcraft in the New South Africa, in: Moore and Sanders (eds.), Magical Interpretations, Material Realities; Pereira, Families, Churches, the State, and the Child Witch in Angola, in: Sansi-Roca and Parés (eds.), Sorcery in the Black Atlantic, p. 187–208; Tonda, La Violence de l'imaginaire des enfants-sorciers, p. 325–343.

17 Zenker and Hoehne, Processing the Paradox, in: Zenker and Hoehne (eds.), The State and the Paradox, p. 1–40.

18 Lei n.º 3820 de 11 de Novembro de 2021.

19 Sebastião, Legalidade penal, costume e pluralismo jurídico, p. 344; Sebastião, Os problemas penais do Sul e o pluralismo cultural, p. 491–546.

20 Constituição da República de Angola; Lei n.º 3820 de 11 de Novembro de 2021.

21 As Sebastião explains, the events that originated the case took place in the Southern Angolan Province of Kuando Kubando before the Constitution of the Republic of Angola of 2010 came into effect. The local community believed the three suspects to have used sorcery or "*wanga*" to force the spirits of the recently deceased to work in their fields during the night, thus explaining their high productivity. After an "*adivinhador* [diviner]" was heard, the case was taken to the "traditional authorities" of the Kingdom of Kuito Kuanavale, and a "*Mundango ya Mbunga*" or

Quite the opposite, they assumed they were executing a sentence validated by traditional authorities and in keeping with customary law. The social and political debate about the power of *feitiços*, where to draw the limits of civil society, and what constitutes a human person is thus far from settled in Angola, and contributions from all disciplinary fields are most welcome as the judicial and legislative bodies are called to address similar occurrences.

Complicating matters, in the early 1990s, if one focused on the economic, health care, and cultural fields, "sorcery themes were on everyone's lips" in post-colonial Africa, to use Mary Douglas' expression.[22] As South Africans negotiated a political end to apartheid (1990–1993), a crippling AIDS pandemic, a crushing wave of structural adjustments, neoliberal deregulation, ecological devastation, and several civil wars ravaged the continent.[23] According to Jean and John Comaroff and their associates at the Africanist circle of the University of Chicago, these large-scale historical developments and cataclysms with far-reaching global repercussions were being locally articulated and made sense of through the idiom of "witchcraft" accusations, "anti-witchcraft rituals," and "occult" gossip and imagery.[24] The Comaroffs' theoretical approach to the "modernity" of these discourses about global-local "frictions" inspired countless ethnographies, which were attentive to the "occult economies" of the continent and how neoliberalism was being critiqued through expressive narratives about vampires, cannibals, aliens, zombies, and witches.[25]

---

communitarian assembly was called for. According to Sebastião, about 2000 people decided that the penalty to be applied to the three accused sorcerers was "death" by drowning or fire. The eight men who killed them tied them to a log and threw them to the river amidst cheers and popular support. This kind of sorcery, Sebastião remarks, is referred to in Kuito Kuanavale as *Kamutukuleno* and is believed to have come from the Republic of Zambia. Similar beliefs about the power to create "*mayombola*" (Kikongo) living-dead servants through sorcery are common in Angola. See Figueiredo for information about *mayombola* or "*matumbolla*" (Portuguese). Figueiredo, Política, escravatura e feitiçaria em Angola, p. 488–492; Sebastião, Legalidade penal, costume e pluralismo jurídico, p. 22–25; Sebastião, Os problemas penais do Sul e o pluralismo cultural, p. 491–546.

22 Douglas, Sorcery Accusations Unleashed, p. 178–179.

23 Bayart, Historical Regimes of Responsibility, in: Rubbers and Jedlowski (eds.), Regimes of Responsibility in Africa, p. 21–39; Bayart, The State in Africa; Geschiere, Meyer and Pels, Introduction, in: Geschiere, Meyer and Pels (eds.), Readings in Modernity in Africa, p. 1–7; Rubbers and Jedlowski, Introduction, in: Rubbers and Jedlowski (eds.), Regimes of Responsibility in Africa, p. 1–20; Sanders, Save our Skins, in: Moore and Sanders (eds.), Magical Interpretations, Material Realities.

24 Comaroff and Comaroff, Introduction, in: Comaroff and Comaroff (eds.), Modernity and its Malcontents, p. xxiv–xxv; Geschiere, Witchcraft and Modernity, in: Parés and Sansi-Roca (eds.), Sorcery in the Black Atlantic, p. 233–235; Moore and Sanders, Magical Interpretations, Material Realities, in: Moore and Sanders (eds.), Magical Interpretations, Material Realities.

25 Apter, Atinga Revisited, in: Comaroff and Comaroff (eds.), Modernity and its Malcontents, p. 111–128; Auslander, Open the Wombs!, in: Comaroff and Comaroff (eds.), Modernity and

However, authors such as Geschiere and Sally Falk Moore became increasingly skeptical of the merits of these interventions. The former remarks that the overuse of sorcery or "witchcraft" to describe very different phenomena and comment on dissimilar power asymmetries and dynamics emptied these concepts of discernible meaning, turning them into an "empty signifier."[26] Calling for the adoption of more precise analytical terminology, Geschiere underscores the risk of academics fuelling the widespread perception that sorcery is out of control in Cameroon and elsewhere in Africa, contributing to the associated rise in anti-sorcery violence levels. The latter argues that the Comaroffs' theoretical model leaves "no place for history" and that the proposition that contemporary discussions surrounding sorcery are both an outcome, a commentary, and a constituent part of African "modernity" is neither falsifiable nor provable.[27] Simultaneously, since the early 2000s, a third strain of scholarship based on William Pietz's pioneering articles about the history of the "fetish" and James Sweet's, John Thornton's, and Linda Heywood's reconstruction of African traditions in North and South America started to pay close attention to the history of early modern Atlantic beliefs about sorcery.[28] This scholarship

---

its Malcontents, p. 167–192; Bastian, Bloodhounds Who Have No Friends, in: Comaroff and Comaroff (eds.), Modernity and its Malcontents, p. 129–166; Comaroff and Comaroff, Beasts, Banknotes and the Colour of Money, p. 107–132; Comaroff and Comaroff, Cattle, Currencies & the Politics of Commensuration, in: Adebanwi (ed.), The Political Economy of Everyday Life in Africa, p. 35–71; Comaroff and Comaroff, Occult Economies and the Violence of Abstraction, p. 279–303; Comaroff and Comaroff, Of Revelation and Revolution, Vol. 2; Comaroff and Comaroff, Transparent Fictions, in: West and Sanders (eds.), Transparency and Conspiracy; Crais, The Politics of Evil; Havik, La Sorcellerie, l'acculturation et le genre, p. 99–116; Honwana, Espíritos Vivos; West, Sorcery of Construction and Socialist Modernization, p. 119–150; Meneses, Os Saberes Feiticeiros em Moçambique; Meneses, Feitiçaria e Modernidade; Meyer and Pels, Magic and Modernity; Moore and Sanders, Magical Interpretations, Material Realities; Pels, The Magic of Africa, p. 193–209; Ranger, Scotland Yard in the Bush, p. 272–283; Schmoll, Black Stomachs, Beautiful Stones, in: Comaroff and Comaroff (eds.), Modernity and its Malcontents, p. 193–220; Shaw, Cannibal transformations, in: Moore and Sanders (eds.), Magical Interpretations, Material Realities, p. 50–70; Stewart and Strathern, Witchcraft, Sorcery, Rumors, and Gossip; Ter Haar and Ellis, The Occult Does Not Exist, p. 399–412; Tsing, Friction; West and Sanders, Transparency and Conspiracy; West, «Governem-se vocês mesmos!» p. 347–368; West, Creative Destruction and Sorcery of Construction, p. 13–31; West, Ethnographic Sorcery; West, Kupilikula.

26 Geschiere, Witchcraft, Intimacy, and Trust, p. 1–3.

27 Blair Rutherford shares a similar view. Moore, Reflections on the Comaroff Lecture, p. 304–306; Rutherford, To Find an African Witch, p. 89–109.

28 Heywood and Thornton, Central Africans; Heywood, Diáspora Negra no Brasil; MacGaffey, Twins, Simbi Spirits, and Lwas in Kongo and Haiti, in: Heywood (ed.), Central Africans and Cultural Transformations, p. 211–226; Pietz, Bosman's Guinea, p. 1–22; Pietz, The Problem of the Fetish, I, p. 5–17; Pietz, The Problem of the Fetish, II, p. 23–45; Pietz, The Problem of the Fetish, IIIa, p. 105–124; Slenes, The Great Porpoise-Skull Strike, in: Heywood (ed.), Central Africans

engages with the historiography of the Iberian Inquisitions, Afro-Brazilian and Afro-American diaspora, and religion studies, fostering a more nuanced understanding of the religious practices, beliefs, and normativities circulating in the "Black Atlantic."[29]

Nevertheless, this last strain of scholarship did not inform ongoing debates in African studies and anthropology seminars, nor did the theoretical insights of the "modernity of witchcraft" turn in ethnography and anthropological theory influence the work of historians of Africa, with very few remarkable exceptions.[30] As for the legal historians and jurists debating the institutional and normative challenges posed by contemporary sorcery accusations and anti-sorcery violence in Angola and elsewhere in Lusophone Africa, their historical horizon has remained limited to the Modern and Contemporary periods.[31] Not only is the normative regime in place during these periods more familiar but the challenges raised by sorcery discourses can also be framed by the heuristics offered by contrasting state law and

---

and Cultural Transformations in the American Diaspora, p. 183–210; Sweet, "Not a Thing for White Men to See," in: Curto and Lovejoy (eds.), Enslaving Connections, p. 139–148; Sweet, Recreating Africa; Thornton, Religião e Vida Cerimonial, in: Heywood (ed.), Diáspora negra no Brasil, p. 81–100; Thornton, Religious and Ceremonial Life, in: Heywood (ed.), Central Africans and Cultural Transformations, p. 71–90; Vanhee, Central African Popular Christianity, in: Heywood (ed.), Central Africans and Cultural Transformations, p. 243–264.

29 Bethencourt and Havik, A África e a Inquisição portuguesa, p. 21–27; Bonciani, Heresias e rebelião em Angola, p. 1–27; Calainho, Metrópole das mandingas; Castelnau-L'Estoile, Páscoa Vieira diante da Inquisição; Green, Havik and Ribeiro da Silva, African Voices from the Inquisition; Green, Inquisition; Havik, Walking the Tightrope, in: Williams (ed.), Bridging the Early Modern Atlantic World, p. 173–192; Marcocci and Paiva, História da Inquisição Portuguesa; Mott, Feiticeiros de Angola, p. 85–104; Pantoja, Inquisição, degredo e mestiçagem em Angola, p. 117–136; Ribeiro da Silva, A Inquisição nas Ilhas, p. 157–173; Sansi-Roca and Parés, Sorcery in the Black Atlantic; Sansi-Roca, Feitiço e fetiche, p. 123–153; Sansi-Roca, Fetishes and Monuments; Santos, Africans, Afro-Brazilians, p. 49–63; Santos, Bolsas de mandinga; Santos, Inquisição Portuguesa na África, p. 229–245; Schleumer, Nas bordas do Rio Kwanza, p. 13–28; Wissenbach, Práticas religiosas; Wissenbach, Ritos de magia e sobrevivência.

30 Only Rosalind Shaw and some of the contributors to the volume edited by Roger Sansi-Roca and Nicolay Parés attempt to integrate the three abovementioned strands of scholarship. The other scholars mentioned in this footnote have only used the insights from current anthropological debates to inform their historical analysis. Crais, The Politics of Evil; Geschiere, Witchcraft and Modernity, in: Parés and Sansi-Roca (eds.), Sorcery in the Black Atlantic, p. 233–258; Green, Priests, Witches and Power; Luongo, If You Can't Beat Them, Join Them, p. 451–571; Luongo, Motive Rather than Means, p. 35–57; Luongo, Witchcraft and Colonial Rule in Kenya; Shaw, Cannibal transformations, in: Moore and Sanders (eds.), Magical Interpretations, Material Realities, p. 50–70; Shaw, Memories of the Slave Trade.

31 Honwana, Espíritos vivos; Marques-Guedes and Lopes, State and Traditional Law in Angola; Meneses, Corpos de violência, linguagens de resistência, p. 161–194; Meneses, Feitiçaria e modernidade; Meneses, Os saberes feiticeiros em Moçambique; Sebastião, Legalidade penal, costume e pluralismo jurídico; Sebastião, Os problemas penais do Sul e o pluralismo cultural, p. 491–546; West, Kupilikula.

customary law and contextualized with the help of the vast existing literature on legal pluralism. My first aim in this book is to extend this horizon in time, bringing the insights of early modern African history and anthropological theory to bear on the historical archives already identified by historians of the 'fetish' and sorcery beliefs in the Black Atlantic.

Jurisdiction and Multinormativity

The ever-changing nature of *feitiços* and the inherent ambiguity of *feitiçaria* or sorcery beliefs and discourses can be challenging for ethnographers and historians of the Modern and Contemporary periods. These mercurial traits force scholars to trace sorcery discussions and practices across various fields, from medical writing to popular culture, all widely differentiated systems with their jargon and institutionalized practices and logic. From the perspective of ethnographers and modern and late modern historians, sorcery beliefs and practices are not only evidence of legal pluralism but also various other forms of pluralism, including social, cultural, economic, and religious pluralism. If the convenient reductionist heuristics of 'colonial' anthropology are dropped (e. g., the 'ethnographic present,' the 'African village,' and the bounded cultural group), a whole team of experts would be necessary to engage meaningfully with such complex phenomena.[32]

The challenges posed by these concepts for early modern historians are of a different sort. Before the revolutionary ruptures inaugurated the Modern period and the increasingly rapid differentiation of the economic, political, legal, and religious systems that occurred thereafter, the Portuguese Empire and other European polities were still governed according to a "jurisdictional paradigm."[33] While several normative orders, or spheres, overlapped in West Central Africa and metropolitan Portugal alike, sometimes concurring and often competing, legal pluralism was an unthinkable concept.[34] The law was not believed to be produced through vol-

32 These tropes and ethnographic heuristics and their connection with colonialism were extensively criticized and deconstructed in the 1980s. It is beyond the scope of this book to review this literature. See Peter Pels and Oscar Salemink for an introduction to this debate. Pels and Salemink, Introduction, p. 1–34; Pels and Salemink, Colonial Subjects.

33 Hannula, Ribeiro, Zatelli and Pihlajamäki, Comparing Early Modern Colonial Laws, p. 7; Herzog, The Uses and Abuses of Legal Pluralism, p. 1–12; Saavedra, Jurisdictional Autonomy and the Autonomy of Law, p. 325–337.

34 Lauren Benton and Adam Clulow argue that by focusing on "jurisdiction as a touchstone of legal action" and how conflict produced "legal authority," it is possible to write a global legal history of the Early Modern period that "treats legal pluralism as a valuable descriptive term rather than an analytical framework." While agreeing with Benton and Clulow that a lot can be learned by emphasizing Portuguese "jurisdictional politics," I choose to adopt 'multinormativity' as a

untaristic legislative acts of sovereigns or nation-states, then codified in statutes and applied by professionals in state courts.[35] Instead, the law was understood as an underlying, immanent dimension of a God-created and ordered cosmos, either an integral part of the whole of nature or inscribed in human hearts and made manifest through social relations. In keeping with this paradigm, jurisdiction refers to the power to declare the law or identify the aspects of the law relevant to a particular case and direct matters accordingly in a proper and just manner. While jurisdictional pluralism, meaning the coexistence of multiple offices endowed with jurisdiction, and the resulting "jurisdictional politics" could amplify the diverging tendencies found in multinormative contexts, they nevertheless preserved the social consensus about the unity of the law at a deep conceptual level.[36] Taking this fact into account, Heikki Pihlajamäki, Manuel Saavedra, Miloš Vec, Tamar Herzog, Thomas Duve, and their various co-authors and collaborators propose that the concept of "multinormativity" is more adequate for capturing the variety of forms of normative knowledge produced and acted upon during the Early Modern period.[37] Building on this argument, Duve and his colleagues call for legal historians to pay closer attention to the historical regimes of normative knowledge production and its 'glocal' (global-local) translations and circulation.[38]

---

framework because not all the "disputes" examined in this book are "disputes over legal authority" or the "capacity to declare, enforce, and reinforce laws and [legal] procedures." Some are about the capacity to find traces of sorcery and sorcerers and declare which anti-sorcery procedures and remedies are to be adopted, others about restoring balance and harmony to cross-cultural domestic spaces or determining the price of slaves or the validity of baptisms. The concept of multinormativity affords an overarching analysis of all these case studies. BENTON and CLULOW, Interpolity Law and Jurisdictional Politics; BENTON, Law and Colonial Cultures, p. 10.

35 This does not invalidate the use of legal pluralism as an analytical concept to explore early modern normative phenomena. See Peter Oestmann and Ralf Seinecke for a foray into the diverse heuristic uses of legal pluralism in legal history. See Hillard von Thiessen on the concept of "*Normenkonkurrenz*," the simultaneous concurrence and competition of norms. OESTMANN, Legal layers, legal spheres, legal systems, p. 1–51; SEINECKE, The Plural Turn, p. 1–76; VON THIESSEN, Concurrence and Competition of Norms, p. 6–51; VON THIESSEN, Das Zeitalter der Ambiguität.

36 BENTON, Law and Colonial Cultures.

37 DUVE and HERZOG, Latin American Law; DUVE, Was ist 'Multinormativität,' p. 88–101; HANNULA, RIBEIRO, ZATELLI and PIHLAJAMÄKI, Comparing Early Modern Colonial Laws, p. 1–16; HERZOG, Colonial Law, in: TELLKAMP (ed.), A Companion to Early Modern Spanish Imperial Political and Social Thought, p. 105–127; HERZOG, The Uses and Abuses of Legal Pluralism, p. 1–12; HERZOG, What is Legal History, in: DUVE and HERZOG (eds.), Latin America Law in Global Perspective, p. 39–53; SAAVEDRA, Jurisdictional Autonomy and the Autonomy of Law, p. 325–337; SEINECKE, The Plural Turn, p. 1–76; VEC, Multinormativität in der Rechtsgeschichte, p. 155–166.

38 DUVE, What is Global Legal History? p. 73–115; DUVE, Theorie und Methode der Analyse asymmetrischer Formen von Abhängigkeit, p. 1–35; DUVE, Legal History as a History of the Translation of Knowledge of Normativity, p. 1–12; DUVE, Historia del Derecho, p. 1–60; DUVE, Legal History as an Observation, p. 1–10.

Within the jurisdictional paradigm, from the point-of-view of historical actors, it makes little sense to speak of "colonial laws" or Portuguese "legal transplants" to West Central Africa, as the law was believed to be universally the same.[39] However, interpreting, translating, or actualizing a supposedly immanent 'law' into words and gestures gave rise to concrete cultural and social forms that differed according to context. These 'interpretative' practices resulted in enduring institutions, *Ius commune* doctrines, and Canon Law compilations inspired by revived Roman Law, all kinds of royal and municipal enactments (e. g., ordinances, royal decrees, orders, charters, and official letters, bylaws, and regulations), and locally binding uses, customs, and court styles. As António Hespanha remarks, some of these institutions and oral or written instantiations of normative knowledge had a universal or "cosmopolitan" vocation (e. g., Catholic monarchies, *Ius commune* doctrines, Canon Law).[40] In contrast, others remained firmly tied to their social, cultural, and spatial contexts of origin. From the fifteenth century onwards, the cosmopolitanism or universalist vocation of certain institutions and normative systems became a driving force and justification for Portuguese overseas expansion, leading to a clash between European and African juridical cultures in West Central Africa. Africans embraced different modalities of normative production structured by alternative institutions and forms of actualizing and instantiating normative knowledge with a universal vocation, such as the beliefs, practices, and discourses related to sorcery. Hence, the region's legal history was shaped by the concurrence and competition of unrelated situated universalisms.

In the "cross-cultural" context of West Central Africa, the performative act of declaring the law effortlessly coincided with the equally performative act of identifying the traces of sorcery and anti-social sorcerers, both institutive gestures being directed towards the final objective of restoring social balance and public order or harmony—all conceptualized in theological or religious terms.[41] While this coincidence allowed Portuguese officers to cut the 'Gordian knot' of an otherwise difficult, if not impossible, inter-cultural translation of normative knowledge, the conceptual and ideological issues raised by the contact of two completely alien "juridical cultures" lacking preexisting shared bridge concepts capable of serving as

39 Cardim, Herzog, Ibáñez and Sabatini, Polycentric Monarchies, in: Cardim, Herzog, Ibáñez and Sabatini (eds.), Polycentric Monarchies, p. 3–8; Hannula, Ribeiro, Zatelli and Pihlajamäki, Comparing Early Modern Colonial Laws, p. 1–16; Herzog, Colonial Law, in: Tellkamp (ed.), A Companion to Early Modern Spanish Imperial Political and Social Thought, p. 105–127.

40 Hespanha, A cultura jurídica europeia, p. 5–8.

41 Ferreira, Cross-Cultural Exchange; Fromont, Collecting and Translating Knowledge Across Cultures, in: Bleichmar and Mancall (eds.), Collecting Across Cultures, p. 134–154; Fromont, Nature, Culture, and Faith; Pietz, The Problem of the Fetish.

"channels of communication" persisted.[42] The establishment of lasting contacts and the emergence of shared "cross-cultural" or Luso-African social spaces created the need for and propelled the institutionalization of new uses, customs, styles, and various normative rearrangements and compromises.[43] This led to processes of conceptualization, abstraction, and the ideological reworking and systematization of new or locally adjusted normative knowledge.

According to Hespanha, during this period, in Europe, the "transcription of norms from one order to another" was enabled by bridge concepts such as "*pietas, natura, gratia, utilitas, usus* [piety, nature, grace, utility, custom]," or "*potestas absoluta* [absolute power]" and the fact that tight-knit communities shared an embodied "grammar of affects" expressed as a set of recognizable feelings.[44] It was these two factors that ensured that royal enactments, Canon Law regulations, domestic habits, the uses of isolated communities, the customary laws of foreigners and religious minorities, the charters or statutes that governed lay brotherhoods or corporations, or the doctrinal ruminations of legal scholars and theologians remained intelligible parts of the same European legal culture. Some of the bridge concepts and educated affects or "loves" mentioned by Hespanha, such as "piety," "filial love," or "comradeship," also had a cosmopolitan or universalist vocation. Europeans expected them to ground all normative systems they met, regardless of the religion, culture, or history of the people they encountered during their overseas travels and conquests. However, Latinate concepts were not part of the intellectual history of West Central Africa. Moreover, the educated affects and feelings that

---

42 Hespanha, A cultura jurídica europeia, p. 94, 151.

43 Throughout this book, I adopt the term Luso-African to describe the individuals, corporations, institutions, concepts, practices, and beliefs that originated in what William Pietz describes as a "cross-cultural space defined by the transvaluation of material objects moving across radically different social orders." I use 'Luso-African' instead of other possible descriptors (e. g., creole, Afro-European, intercultural) to distinguish these spaces and individuals from Dutch-African creoles and to stress that they inhabited and originated from an enduring, unique space that stood in relation, but was not reducible, to Portuguese and African ones. Pietz, The Problem of the Fetish, p. 4–5, 10; Ribeiro da Silva, Dutch and Portuguese.

44 I follow Teresa Brennan's definition of "affects" as "educated feelings," as opposed to "spontaneous" emotions, which are closer to sensations. As she describes it, "the education, beginning with the discernment, of the affects relies on the feelings, which communicate with the sensations." The latter "have a limited range of self-expression when no language or practice in their recognition is available." Since Brennan's pioneering work, much scholarly attention has been paid to what Tyrone S. Palmer defines as "grammars of affects," constituting an "affective turn" in the social sciences. See Jean Halley and Patricia Clough for an introduction to this 'turn'. Brennan, The Transmission of Affect, p. 122; Halley and Clough, The Affective Turn; Hespanha, A cultura jurídica europeia, p. 150–151; Palmer, "What Feels More Than Feeling?," p. 31–56; Palmer, Affect and Affirmation, in: Seigworth and Pedwell (eds.), The Affect Theory Reader, Vol. 2, p. 122–140; Palmer, Otherwise than Blackness, p. 246–283.

enabled normative translation in Europe were often embodied differently, becoming almost unrecognizable to Europeans who struggled to find traces of 'piety' or 'filial love.'[45] Inspired by the work of Pietz, this book argues that the solution found to these problems followed the practical one adopted by Portuguese magistrates, officers, clergy, and settlers who, when called to adjudicate, took advantage of their power to declare the law being locally understood as a form of anti-sorcery (or sorcery).[46] It proposes that in the absence of bridge concepts and a common grammar of positive affects, a shared pool of beliefs and practices regarding *feitiçaria* and its different local renditions in the Kingdoms of Kongo, Ndongo, Matamba, Benguela, and their neighboring polities enabled the translation of normative knowledge in West Central Africa. In other words, a 'cross-cultural' agreement about the phenomenology and praxeology of evil compensated for the fundamental disagreement about its theological grounding or the essence and nature of good, scaffolding the regional interpolity order.

Structure of the Volume

This book is divided into three parts, examining the institutional and legal history of the Captaincy of Angola, Benguela, and their dependencies, as well as the political and normative systems of the African polities with which the Portuguese interacted. Part One comprises three chapters that chart the principal jurisdictions, institutions, and corporate groups in West Central Africa under Portuguese influence while also examining the ideological and normative background that informed and guided their actions. Part Two includes three chapters dedicated to the principal slave-trade routes that structured the occupation of the West Central African hinterlands, delving deeper into the institutions and normative systems of independent African polities and the evolving justifications for slavery and the Atlantic slave trade. Part Three comprises three chapters that focus on the multinormative environment of Luso-African communities, exploring how concurring and competing normative frameworks influenced the handling of personal and social crises and the celebration of lifecycle events and explaining how the 'enlightened' Captain-General and Governors of Angola, along with the bishops of Angola and Congo, attempted to regulate them. This tripartite structure is inspired by the scholarship of the "modernity of witchcraft school;" each part has its general introduction detailing how

---

45 Hespanha, A cultura jurídica europeia, p. 150–151; Hufendiek, Emotions, Habits, and Skills, in: Caruana and Testa (eds.), Habits, p. 100–119.

46 Pietz, The Problem of the Fetish.

contemporary ethnography and anthropological theory have contributed to the historical analysis.[47]

As Geschiere and Jean-François Bayart remark, sorcery discourses often provide a lens through which to make sense of institutional opacity and bureaucratic despotism.[48] On the other hand, as Jean and John Comaroff stress, they seem to be intrinsically tied to market operations.[49] In this case, it is not the ambiguity associated with the production of binding normative statements without a clear rationale that is suspect but the mysterious nature of commodities, currencies, and immaterial, fungible wealth. Finally, as the more recent works of Geschiere indicate, in Africa as elsewhere, sorcery is also widely understood as connected to the dangers of proximity and intimacy, often considered the "dark side" of kinship.[50] This suggests a third lens through which to approach historical sorcery beliefs and accusations, namely by paying attention to the shifting politics of intimacy and belonging as they are renegotiated daily, giving rise to more lasting cultural, social, and normative conventions that, in time, become institutionalized. The opacity of instituted power, the oddities of market exchanges, and the dangers of intimacy and proximity are the unsettling yet constant ontological features of these fields of human experience that inspire each section at a broad conceptual level.

The first part of this book drafts an institutional history of the Captaincy of Angola and its dependencies. It not only synthesizes the scholarship of several of Hespanha's former disciples, interlocutors, and collaborators who, in the last two decades, wholly renewed the field of the institutional history of the Portuguese empire[51] but also fleshes out the Portuguese and West Central African understandings of *feitiço*, *feitiçaria*, and their African equivalents at the time of the conquest of the

47 Ashforth, Witchcraft, Violence, and Democracy, p. 117.

48 Bayart, Fait Missionnaire and Politics of the Belly, in: Geschiere, Meyer and Pels (eds.), Readings in Modernity in Africa, p. 92–98; Bayart, Historical Regimes of Responsibility, in: Rubbers and Jedlowski (eds.), Regimes of Responsibility in Africa, p. 21–39; Bayart, The State in Africa; Geschiere and Fisiy, Witchcraft, Development and Paranoia in Cameroon, in: Moore and Sanders (eds.), Magical Interpretations, Material Realities; Geschiere, Responsibility versus Responsibilization, in: Denian, Fumanti and Lynteris (eds.), Anthropology and Responsibility; Geschiere, The Modernity of Witchcraft.

49 Comaroff and Comaroff, Beasts, Banknotes and the Colour of Money, p. 107–132; Comaroff and Comaroff, Modernity and its Malcontents; Comaroff and Comaroff, Occult Economies and the Violence of Abstraction, p. 279–303; Comaroff and Comaroff, Of Revelation and Revolution, Vol. 2; Comaroff and Comaroff, Transparent Fictions, in: West and Sanders (eds.), Transparency and Conspiracy.

50 Geschiere, Witchcraft, Intimacy, and Trust.

51 Herzog, António Manuel Hespanha According to Tamar Herzog, p. 133–138; Hespanha, Entrevista a António Manuel Hespanha por Pedro Cardim, p. 430–445; Nogueira da Silva, Xavier and Cardim, António Manuel Hespanha; Xavier and Monteiro, António Manuel Hespanha, p. 473–479.

Kingdom of Ndongo and the establishment of the Captaincy of Angola. Chapter One examines how the Portuguese addressed the challenges presented by numerous royal enactments and ordinances, as well as the compilations of Canon Law and the rulings of central courts and councils, which contained orders, articles, or provisions that were not realistically applicable or enforceable in West Central Africa. As argued by Hespanha, from a contemporary analytical perspective, this happened either because the number of "official and learned jurists" was scarce at best and the "logistic apparatus" of the empire spread thin or because the "ill-prepared magistrates" that ventured to its African domains were more inclined to further their commercial interests than act as loyal subjects.[52] The same can be said of the number and preparation of soldiers, merchants, parish priests, and missionaries, as well as the ulterior motivations of canons, vicars, bishops, and other dignitaries.

However, as Tamar Herzog remarks, from the perspective of the actors themselves, who, during the period under analysis, understood ecclesiastical tribunals and royal and municipal authorities merely as "judges" and "interpreters" of an "existing legal situation" sanctioned by God, this non-applicability raised conceptual challenges.[53] While a lot has been written about the solution to similar issues found in the Spanish Empire, namely, through the employment of formulas used by magistrates and officeholders to suspend royal orders and municipal enactments while better informing the central authorities of local circumstances,[54] not enough attention has been paid to how these problems were framed and dealt with in the Captaincy of Angola, Benguela, and their dependencies.

The first section of Chapter One argues that the critics who pointed out the widespread abuses and corruption ongoing in West Central Africa under Portuguese influence often justified them due to the harshness of the climate, the deadly epidemiological environment, and an almost palpable absence of God's grace, love, and charity. Over time, these formulaic excuses evolved into a veritable 'folk doctrine,' exempting officers, judges, soldiers, merchants, and even priests and missionaries from adhering rigorously to royal orders and Canon Law regulations.[55] This 'folk

52 Hespanha, Uncommon Laws, p. 203; Hespanha, L'Administration d'une «ombre d'empire», in: François and Grenet (eds.), Raison administrative et logiques d'Empire, p. 291–335; Xavier and Nogueira da Silva, Introdução, in: Xavier and Nogueira da Silva (eds.), O governo dos outros, p. 61.

53 Herzog, Colonial Law, in: Tellkamp (ed.), A Companion to Early Modern Spanish Imperial Political and Social Thought, p. 114.

54 Namely, the proverbial "*se obedece pero no se cumple*" and "*se acata pero no se cumple*," meaning "the law is accepted but not complied" with. Anzoátegui, La ley "se obedece pero no se cumple;" Herzog, Colonial Law, in: Tellkamp (ed.), A Companion to Early Modern Spanish Imperial Political and Social Thought, p. 113–114; Irigoin and Grafe, Bargaining for Absolutism, p. 179.

55 Morton, But are they Right? p. 159–160.

doctrine' discharged them in the *foro interno* of their consciences during confession and even before their superiors and courts. As happened in Spain, this solution to the problems posed by the inapplicability of royal enactments and ordinances in extra-European spaces posed challenges to the "royal jurists" and reforming elites of the Enlightenment who began theorizing the "hypothesis that the king was sovereign."[56]

The second section focuses on these actors, explaining how a newfound optimism and a different understanding of the universality of the laws of nature undermined the 'folk doctrines' that had long excused the 'abuses' now seen as objectionable and wasteful superstitions. Highlighting the novelty of this historical situation, the third section foregrounds the conceptual implications of the hypothesis that theological natural law and *Ius gentium* were somehow suspended or bracketed in the hinterlands of Angola and Benguela. It argues that this belief barred these "cosmopolitan" concepts from functioning as "conceptual bridges" between the European and African normative systems.[57] The practical solution that emerged from the first decades of contact, conversion, and Portuguese conquest of West Central Africa, it argues, was the adoption of *feitiço* and *feitiçaria* as "cross-cultural" bridge concepts instead.[58] This meant that the translation between Portuguese and West Central African normative systems was not based on pre-existing shared concepts or 'educated' affects, which were also differently embodied, but on a concurring theory about the origin of evil.

To substantiate this claim, this section briefly traces the genealogy of *feitiço* and *feitiçaria* from the Classical period to the arrival of the first Portuguese explorers in the Kingdom of Kongo (1482–83). It also uses Jan Vansina's "word and things" method to flesh out the African "traditions" they encountered in West Central Africa, demonstrating that the core normative cluster associated with African understandings of the origin of evil remained stable for millennia, being part of a rich normative thesaurus analogous to the European *Ius commune* in terms of diffusion and influence.[59] By comparing Portuguese and West Central African understandings of sorcery, this section concludes by illustrating how a shared emphasis on eradicating evil and extreme anti-social practices grounded cross-cultural normative translations when no other cultural, moral, affective, or normative common ground could be found. The fourth and final section briefly explains how the 'folk

56 Herzog, Colonial Law, in: Tellkamp (ed.), A Companion to Early Modern Spanish Imperial Political and Social Thought, p. 114–115.

57 Hespanha, A cultura jurídica europeia, p. 5–8, 151.

58 Ferreira, Cross-Cultural Exchange.

59 Gonzales, Historical Linguistics; Pietz, Bosman's Guinea, p. 1–22; Pietz, The Problem of the Fetish, I, p. 5–17; Pietz, The Problem of the Fetish, II, p. 23–45; Pietz, The Problem of the Fetish, IIIa, p. 105–124; Pietz, The Problem of the Fetish; Vansina, Paths in the Rainforests.

doctrine' about West Central African exclusion from natural law and God's grace clashed with the enlightened program of the Captain-General and Governors of Angola of the second half of the eighteenth century.

Chapter Two examines the logistics system and the military and civil administrative layout of the Captaincy of Angola and Benguela. It gives a precise idea of what Hespanha meant when he argued that it was spread thin. It explores the two unconnected networks that branched inland from the Atlantic ports of Luanda and Benguela, providing a much-needed introduction to their multinormative framework and the institutional history of the jurisdictions and corporations that composed them. While it focuses more on institutions, royal ordinances, and municipal enactments than individuals and their personal choices and actions, it foregrounds how local circumstances shaped West Central African vernacular versions of familiar institutions such as municipal councils, *provedorias*, or lay brotherhoods. This entails a close reading and historical contextualization of royal enactments and other regulations, aided by a brief cultural history of the Luso-African normative frameworks, which cover diverse areas such as landholding, healthcare provision, religious assistance, and organized warfare.

The first section of Chapter Two lists the *presídios* and military districts that composed the Captaincy of Angola and Benguela, presenting the logistical and commercial imperatives that guided their establishment and geographical distribution. The second section then focuses on the Municipal Councils of Luanda, Massangano, and Benguela, as well as the lay brotherhoods of the *Santa Casa da Misericórdia* of Luanda and Massangano and the *Nossa Senhora do Populo* of Benguela, which were responsible for providing healthcare and various other charitable services. It frames the functioning of these institutions according to relevant ordinances and *compromissos*, showing how abstract regulations were adapted to local constraints regarding access to funding and the limited number of Portuguese *moradores*. Moreover, it foregrounds the rivalry between the municipal councils and the lay brotherhoods of Luanda and Massangano (often expressed in racialist terms) and the uniqueness of Benguela's institutions, which were the product of later absolutist reforms. The third section shifts the focus to *presídios* and districts as well as the captain majors who governed them, also paying attention to the constitution of Luso-African garrisons and the organization of second and third-line military corporations and expeditionary armies. It describes the function and normative framework of important hinterland offices such as captain major and *almoxarife da Real Fazenda*, introducing crucial local offices framed according to African norms (e.g., *golamboles, jagas, quilambas*).

The fourth section focuses on the functions, jurisdiction, ranges of competence, and privileges of the captain-general and governors of Angola. It also describes those of the subaltern governors of Benguela and their respective secretariats. This entails briefly describing the normative framing of the hereditary Captaincy of Angola granted to Paulo Dias de Novais in 1571, as well as the innovative solutions enacted by the first *donatário* to adapt it to the African economic and normative systems he encountered, which were based on the accumulation of "wealth in people," not in land.[60] It argues that these adaptations conditioned the 'normative fabric' of the Captaincy of Angola even after the hereditary captaincy was dismantled and a captain-general and governor substituted the *donatário* as its leading civil and military magistrate. The following sections explore the establishment, jurisdiction, ranges of competence, and privileges of the foremost offices of the Captaincy, beginning with the first *ouvidores* who accompanied the *donatário* to West Central Africa and then discussing the *ouvidores gerais,* ordinary judges, municipal judges, and their subordinates. The fifth section focuses on *ouvidores* and the *Ouvidores Gerais* of Luanda. It also introduces all the other offices they accumulated over the years due to the lack of personnel, from *provedores da Real Fazenda* to the judge of orphans. The sixth section introduces the municipal judges of Luanda and Benguela, as well as the ordinary judge of Massangano, completing the overview of municipal institutions begun in the second section. The seventh section concludes chapter two by explaining the workings of special courts with jurisdiction over economic matters and the jurisdiction and composition of the War Board, a commissarial board responsible for declaring just wars. As it explains, this deliberation had vast economic and fiscal implications in the Captaincy of Angola, as it resulted in the legal enslavement of countless free Africans.

Chapter Three concludes Part One by examining the ideological framework that grounded the institutional patterns described in the previous chapter, paying particular attention to how the historical transition from a jurisdictional form of government, typical of the Portuguese poly-synodal "*Antigo Regime*," to a "police state" paradigm impacted it.[61] It argues that this entailed not only a secularization of the ideological underpinning of Portuguese conquest and occupation of the Kingdom of Ndongo, from which all subsequent Luso-African institutions drew their legitimacy, but also an evolving dialectical relationship between these institutions and their 'exterior:' the West Central African institutions the Portuguese encountered already in place. This relationship was always conditioned by the jurisdictional autonomy of dispersed hinterland communities and the cruel institution of slavery. The first section explores the "Catholic Monarchy" concept, explaining how it initially provided a theological grounding to the monarch's *imperium* and Portuguese *dominium* over West Central Africa.[62] After examining the various

60 Guyer, Wealth in People, p. 83–90; Guyer, Wealth in People and Self-Realization, p. 243–265.

61 Subtil, Espaço político e organização, p. 88–116; Subtil, Estado de polícia, p. 15–40; Subtil, O terramoto político.

62 Hespanha, Como os juristas viam o mundo, p. § 77–§ 78; Hespanha, Direito comum e direito colonial, p. 95–116; Hespanha, Uncommon Laws, p. 184–185; Sánchez, Spanish Theories of

modalities of *dominium* recognized by early modern jurists, it provides a historical overview of the most important Roman Catholic institutions in the Captaincy of Angola and Benguela and the creation of the Diocese of Congo and Angola. After first introducing the Portuguese Royal Patronage rights (1455–c. 1668), it then explains how the creation of the *Propaganda Fide* (1622) and the General Missions Board (1655) of Lisbon undermined this comprehensive set of rights. The second section shifts the focus to the 'exterior' of the Captaincy, narrating the creation of the mixed-Court of the Inquisition of Lisbon (1536–1821) and describing how it exerted its jurisdiction over the Luso-African *moradores* of Luanda and the merchants and *pumbeiros* who trafficked slaves in its hinterland dependencies.

The third section of Chapter Three dives into the multinormative environment of slave compounds and slave markets, exploring the civil and Canon Law institutions that regulated and oversaw the Atlantic traffic in enslaved Africans. Special attention is paid to how the adjudication of 'freedom cases' proceeded at different hierarchical levels, from the hinterland *presídios* headed by captain majors to the "*mucano* court" of the captain-general and governor of Angola and the Missions Board of Luanda.[63] Then, the Canon Law tribunal of the enquirer of freedoms is described, as well as all the other minor offices connected with slavery. The fourth section also focuses on this peculiar institution, paying attention to the normative setting of official slave fairs, dispersed *pumbos*, and the compounds of Luso-African slave traders. It argues that contrary to what the 'folk doctrine' about West Central Africa or later doctrines of *terra nullius* might suggest, these were spaces of "jurisgenetic" abundance, not the absence of law or a lack of those willing to arbitrate or even adjudicate cases according to Portuguese doctrines, Luso-African uses and customs, or African norms and styles.[64] In other words, it reframes the constant prohibition of Whites entering the hinterlands to trade, expressed in the famous 'Article 18' of the ordinances of the captain-general and governors of Angola, as a "jurispathic" measure that sought to curtail the significant jurisdictional autonomy of White merchants and slave traders in a period when there was no "substantial" difference between their interpretation of the law and those of the Crown's deputies.[65] This section then highlights how the hinterlands' official opening to Whites was made possible by transitioning towards a police state paradigm predicated on a different understanding of royal sovereignty and the power to legislate.

The fifth section of Chapter Three focuses on this topic, explaining how the establishment of new commissarial boards in 1761, specifically the Boards of Justice,

Empire, in: Tellkamp (ed.), A Companion to Early Modern Spanish Imperial Political and Social Thought, p. 17–52.

63 Ferreira, Cross-Cultural Exchange; Santos, Esclavage africain, p. 127–148.

64 Cover, Nomos and Narrative, p. 4–68.

65 Ibid.; Saavedra, Jurisdictional Autonomy and the Autonomy of Law, p. 325–337.

Commerce, and Finance of Luanda, was instrumental in achieving this transition in the Captaincy of Angola, Benguela, and their dependencies. It situates the creation of these new institutions within the more comprehensive institutional reforms occurring throughout the Portuguese Empire, explaining how they enabled the new secretary of state of the navy and the overseas (1726) to erode the jurisdiction of the Overseas Council (1643–1833), and the dismantlement of the slave duty contract of Angola (1769). The latter reform, it explains, was also made possible by the establishment of the "*Erário Régio*" (1761–1832) that henceforward coordinated the actions of the Board of Finance of Luanda, resulting in a complete overhaul of the monetary system of the Captaincy of Angola. At this point, the creation of a Board of Commerce in Luanda enabled Lisbon-backed merchants to directly influence the decisions of captain-general and governors, bypassing the gatekeeping efforts of the Municipal Council of Luanda and other corporations better attuned to the demands of local Luso-African factions. This section concludes by exploring how the Board of Justice of Luanda equally impacted the administration of justice in Angola, Benguela, and their dependencies, curtailing the jurisdiction of the offices described in the second chapter in favor of this commissarial board that applied a summary military style justice, acting according to the dictates of a recently conceptualized "*raison d'etat*."[66]

Chapter Four inaugurates Part Two by looking at the early history of the *presídio* and slave fair network that branched inland from Luanda, reaching the easternmost hinterland slave fair of Cassange, then under the jurisdiction of the *jaga* of Kasanje, the head of an independent African Kingdom. Like the other chapters in this part, it contextualizes the "translation of normative knowledge" taking place at different West Central African markets and slave fairs within broader imperial and religious projects of cultural, religious, and economic conversion, predicated on obtaining control over what I define as the regional 'regime of commensuration.'[67] This innovative approach builds on the work of William Pietz and Cecile Fromont, highlighting that apart from being "spaces of correlation" or "cross-cultural" contact and creativity, West Central African markets and slave fairs were also the social arenas where the limits of the (in)commensurable and what constituted accounting units and different forms of currency were either politically negotiated or forcefully imposed.[68] European interpretations of African social and cultural practices, such as *feitiçaria* and African sorcery accusations, and other forms of 'othering,' were crucial to these disputes. The first section introduces Manoel Correia Leitão's mission to Cassange and the margins of the Kwango River in 1755–56, which serves as the

---

66 Subtil, Estado de polícia, p. 15–40; Subtil, O crime e o castigo, in: Subtil, Atallah and Mota (eds.), Criminalidades, direito e justiça no mundo ibérico, p. 35–64.

67 Duve, Legal History as a History of the Translation of Knowledge of Normativity, p. 1–12.

68 Fromont, The Art of Conversion; Pietz, The Problem of the Fetish.

narrative backbone of the three chapters grouped in Part Two. The second section follows Leitão's journey from Luanda to Muxima, Massangano, Cambambe, and Ambaca, starting to unpack the different layers of the history of this well-trod Luso-African trade route. It goes back to the early times of the conquest of the Kingdom of Ndongo by Dias de Novais and his followers (c. 1575–1607) to explain that their efforts were guided by an attempt to conquer existing Mbundu markets (*itanda*) to gain thereby control over a Luso-African network of *pumbos* which had already been in place for more than half-a-century but was entirely outside of the jurisdiction of the delegates and agents of the Portuguese Crown.

The third section of Chapter Four goes further back in time, explaining how this Luso-African *pumbo* network took shape during the first half-century of the Portuguese presence in the Kingdom of Kongo. It introduces the reigns of King Afonso I of Kongo (1509–1543) and King Diogo I of Kongo (1543–1561), their reception of Christianity, the political, normative, and religious underpinnings of BaKongo markets (*nzandu*), and the monetary system of the Kingdom of Kongo. It argues that its reliance on non-metallic "useful currencies" such as *nzimbu* cowrie shells and raffia cloths, and the existence of separate prestige "spheres of exchange" where only certain "social currencies" were traded for rights over women and dependents, conditioned the historical evolution of the institution of slavery.[69] Such a monetary system posed difficulties for wealth extraction, as the regional currencies had no worth in Europe, America, or mainland Asia. The solution found by Portuguese and BaKongo elites was to use enslaved Africans as an international currency, putting enormous stress on the African normative systems that tightly regulated their exchange and enslavement. The fourth section shifts back to Ndongo, explaining how the Portuguese conquerors and their Jesuit partners used their experience in the Kingdom of Kongo to inform their approach to Mbundu *itanda*. It introduces the raffia cloths and salt blocks used in the local monetary system as "general purpose money" and how the Portuguese had to adapt their institutions, resulting in the same wealth-extraction difficulties they had encountered in Kongo.[70] While using African slaves as a currency was also adopted as a solution, this section explains that in the conquered provinces of Ndongo, now under direct Portuguese jurisdiction, this solution raised the question of how the legitimacy and fairness of their enslavement was in keeping with *Ius commune* and *Ius gentium* doctrines.

The fifth section of Chapter Four introduces the ideological and normative framework that the Jesuits devised to refute early critics of the Atlantic slave trade and

---

69 Bohannan and Bohannan, The Tiv; Bohannan and Bohannan, Tiv Economy, p. 227–228; Graeber, Debt; Johnson, Cloth as Money, p. 196–197.

70 Thornton, The Development of an African Catholic Church, p. 160.

the institutions of slavery in the Captaincy of Angola. It introduces the legal conditions for enslavement, based on Second Scholasticism's revival of Roman Law and the writings of St. Thomas Aquinas (1225–1274), and how Fernão de Oliveira (1507–1681) and the Jesuit Fathers Miguel Garcia (1550–1614) and Gonçalo Leite (1546–1603) argued that slaves bought in the hinterlands of Angola and Benguela could not satisfy them.[71] It also presents two competing descriptions of the functioning of *itanda* and Mbundu institutions of slavery, those of the Jesuits Father Baltasar Barreira (1538–1612), and Luis de Molina (1535–1600). While the latter supported the criticism of Fathers Garcia and Leite, Father Barreira predicated the legitimacy of the Atlantic slave trade and the ownership of African slaves bought in the hinterlands of Angola on their supposed circulation as fungible currency in *itanda*. The sixth section concludes Chapter Four by highlighting that transforming Mbundu *itanda* into Luso-African slave fairs implied turning these spaces into sites of cultural and religious conversion and commensuration between very different normative systems and systems of value. Ensuring that enslaved Africans were exchanged as fungible currency implied dismantling preexisting African institutions and redefining the limits of (in)commensurability, transforming *itanda* from places where the social and political reproduction of Mbundu corporate kin groups and political units took place to sites where the inhumane logics of wealth extraction and the Atlantic slave trade prevailed. It argues that this shift also had religious and cultural repercussions as *itanda* went from being a place where *feiticeiros* were punished, and social harmony and an ambiance of benevolence were restored after crises, to anti-social spaces where sorcery could flourish.

Chapter Five focuses on a different, complementing aspect of Luso-African slave fairs. It argues that in addition to serving as a site of cultural and religious conversion, standardizing currencies and values, and translating normative knowledge, they also functioned as political arenas where the boundaries of what could not be compared, and thus who and what were categorized as 'other' or not fully human, were established. While earlier processes of commensuration also implied a degree of othering, this chapter explores how, during the Late Portuguese Enlightenment, religious and cultural conversion became less central to Portuguese extractivism and imperial conquest than the othering of Africans and their normative systems. The first section follows Manoel Leitão's journey from the *presídio* of Ambaca to Mbondo, the first border province of the Kingdom of Kasanje he crosses. It uses the example of how he 'othered' his Mbundu porters and the inhabitants of Mbondo to demonstrate that Africans could be marked as living outside natural law, either because they and their environment were 'unnatural' or because they lacked rationality. It then argues that, in the new epistemological environment of

71 Zeron and Dias, A Igreja e a escravidão, p. 85–106; Zeron, Linha de fé.

the second half of the eighteenth century, as the first option lost credibility, the focus of othering shifted to characterizing African uses, customs, and institutions as irrational or 'diabolical.'

The first section of Chapter Five then explains why othering processes became so crucial to the Portuguese, introducing relevant developments in the Atlantic-wide debate about the legitimacy of the institution of slavery. It explores Father Manuel Ribeiro Rocha's (1687–1745) doctrine of 'redemption contracts' that justified the 'ransom' of wrongly enslaved Africans from territories outside of civil society and natural law, describing how it proposed an innovative solution to the challenges raised by a century of criticism aimed at the doctrines of just enslavement promoted by the teachings of Second Scholasticism. It concludes by arguing that Father Rocha's doctrine, seconded by the influential jurist Pascoal José de Melo Freire (1738–1798), created the need for a neat distinction between the spheres under Portuguese jurisdiction and those beyond, posing a severe conceptual challenge to the apologists of the slave trade: how to justify the purchase of enslaved Africans at the slave markets of centralized African polities such as the Mbangala Kingdom of Kasanje.

The second section of Chapter Five recedes in time, focusing on the Portuguese and BaKongo's first contacts with the Mbangala and the warband leaders the former christened as *jagas*. This is essential to understand how almost two centuries of discursive tropes of Portuguese, Bakongo, Mbundu, and Mbangala origins allowed the Kingdom of Kasanje (established c. 1630s) to be cast in the mid-eighteenth century as a *sui generis* society, where a 'diabolical social contract' ensured that its subjects lived in a state of "natural subjection," despite their civil institutions.[72] This section begins by exploring early BaKongo accounts of the Yaka invasion of Kongo in the 1560s, describing how the Yaka came to be referred to as *jagas* and mistaken for the Mbangala. It concludes by looking at Samuel Purchas' (1575–1626) chronicle of Andrew Battel's (c. 1565–1614) adventures with a roving Mbangala warband in the 1590s, in the territory of the Ovimbundu Kingdom of Benguela. The third section focuses on the early Luso-Mbangala military alliances and their tactical, diplomatic, institutional, and economic aftermath. It explains how the groundbreaking institutional solutions found by the proto-Mbangala warbands enabled them to organize in a radically different manner, anchoring their corporate group identity on emic metaphors of 'cannibalism,' 'infanticide,' and human sacrifice that shocked their Mbundu and BaKongo neighbors, creating their enduring reputation for being cruel, inhuman warriors. Moreover, it describes how the Mbangala's acceptance of alcoholic drinks in exchange for slaves quickly made

---

72 Calafate, Estudo introdutório I, in: Calafate (ed.), A Escola Ibérica da Paz nas Universidades de Coimbra e Évora, Vol. 1, p. 17–49.

them the preferred partners of Portuguese and Luso-African merchants with access to Brazilian spirits or Portuguese wine, causing the latter's abandonment of *itanda*. It concludes by exposing all the normative and legal challenges posed by waging wars together with African groups renowned in West Central Africa and Europe for their 'cannibalism' and disrespect for *Ius gentium* just war doctrines.

The fourth section of Chapter Five focuses on the establishment of the Kingdom of Kasanje, exploring how the transition from a roving Mbangala warband to a settled kingdom was accompanied by intense ideological, political, and diplomatic spade-work David Schoenbrun defines as "groupwork."[73] It explains that two kinds of oral traditions, narrative episodes known as *malunda* and genealogical sets known as *musendo*, enabled Kasanje 'intellectuals' to create a history for the new kingdom, inserting its political titles into the lattice of regional myths and heroic narratives that scaffolded the West Central African inter-polity order. Central to these oral traditions and the regional order they enabled was the system known in Africanist literature as "perpetual kinship" and the principle of "positional succession."[74] After introducing these, this section concludes by explaining the misunderstandings caused by oral traditions that, following this system, narrated the institutional history of the Mbangala as a history of heroic individuals who embodied the offices under discussion. It argues that, from an emic perspective, tales of 'cannibalism' and 'infanticide' might signify the absorption of rival offices or the abolition of kinship-based institutions, not the actual consumption of human flesh.

The fifth section concludes Chapter Five by exploring how Capuchin's literal readings of Mbangala *malunda* and *musendo* led to the othering of the Kingdom of Kasanje as a society governed by a 'diabolical' social contract. It begins by providing the historical context of the establishment of the first Capuchin missions in West Central Africa in the aftermath of the creation of the *Propaganda Fide* (1622) and the establishment of the Apostolic Prefecture of Congo (1640). It then explores Friar Antonio Giovanni Cavazzi da Montecuccolo's (1621–1678) description of Kasanje's laws or *ijila* and his and other Capuchin accounts of the style of Mbangala courts. It concludes by arguing that, despite the Capuchins' opposition to the Atlantic slave trade and the institutions of slavery, their accounts of Kasanje's 'diabolic' social contract enabled the supporters of Father Rocha's doctrine of 'redemption contracts' to argue that all slaves bought from the fair of Cassange were justly purchased because they were being ransomed from beyond the limits of natural law and *Ius gentium*—or, in other words, literally being 'rescued' from being eaten by their cannibal countrymen. To uphold this line of reasoning, Luso-African slave

---

73 Schoenbrun, The Names of the Python.

74 Heintze, Translocal 'Kinship' Relations in: Freitag and von Oppen (eds.), Translocality, p. 179–204.

fairs could no longer be understood as spaces of conversion and commensuration but, instead, as the border or interface where Portuguese and West Central African normative systems articulated without merging, the latter being othered as beyond the pale of reason and natural law.

Chapter Six explores the conflicting attempts to gain political control over the regime of commensuration in place at the Luso-African slave fair of Cassange. It pays attention to the normative and diplomatic interventions of the captain-general and governors of Angola and the maneuvering of the *jagas* of Kasanje, framing these as conflicting attempts to gain a monopoly over disambiguation mechanisms. Concluding Part Two, it argues that since slave fairs were simultaneously places where trade goods, currencies, ideas, norms, and human beings were made commensurable and othered as radically different or incommensurable, the levels of ambiguity remained very high. From this stemmed the need to ensure the functioning of institutions capable of sorting out various categories of beings, separating sorcerers from the innocent, the wrongly from the rightly enslaved, and 'good' money from 'bad' money. Chapter Six examines how this power struggle unfolded during the second half of the eighteenth century when it was increasingly framed as a struggle to impose Portuguese sovereignty over African subjects, in line with a new absolutist paradigm. The first section describes the conclusion of Manoel Leitão's journey to Cassange, exploring the implications of one of his companions having been accused of being a sorcerer. This episode affords a brief analysis of the historical and socio-economical causes of rising anxiety levels about ambiguity in West Central Africa, resulting in similar accusations. It introduces 'anti-sorcery' ordeals as "responsibility allocation mechanisms" and forms of "situational disambiguation."[75] It concludes by explaining how Leitão addressed the accusation by claiming he was a diplomatic envoy of the captain-general and governor.

The second section of Chapter Six proposes a close reading of a list of fake diplomatic demands Leitão transmitted to the envoys of the *jaga* of Kasange as part of his attempt to pass himself off as a diplomatic envoy. It argues that they reveal a great deal about the situation at the slave fair of Cassange, illuminating the power dynamics between Luso-African merchants, *pumbeiros*, and the Mbangala ruler. The former were caught in a double bind, simultaneously depending on the authority of the *jaga* of Kasanje to ensure the reciprocity of their trading partners and resenting it because he imposed tributes and forced them to respect his *ijila*,

---

75 Geschiere, Kinship, Witchcraft and "the Market," in: Dilley (ed.), Contesting Markets, p. 159–179; Geschiere, Responsibility versus Responsibilization, in: Denian, Fumanti and Lynteris (eds.), Anthropology and Responsibility; von Thiessen, Concurrence and Competition of Norms, p. 6–51; von Thiessen, Das Zeitalter der Ambiguität; von Thiessen, Normenkonkurrenz Handlungsspielräume, in: von Thiessen and Karsten (eds.), Normenkonkurrenz in historischer Perspektive, Vol. 50, p. 241–286.

the 'laws' of Kasanje. Leitão's list of demands also reveals the prominence of the anti-sorcery ordeal, publicly held at the court of the *jaga*, known as the *ndua* ordeal. It concludes by explaining that this ordeal was so popular in Kasanje and the Captaincy of Angola that it challenged Portuguese monopolies over the arbitration of Mbundu cases and responsibility allocation mechanisms. The third and fourth sections shift the focus toward the economic situation of the Captaincy of Angola, describing how the *ad hoc* adoption of two highly problematic currencies made the need for standardized forms of disambiguation even more severe. The first of these currencies was the *banzo*, the trade goods and useful currency bundle used to buy slaves. The third section examines how failed attempts to regulate their composition sparked numerous conflicts, with this failure being viewed as an obstacle to opening the hinterlands to 'free trade.' The second of these currencies was the various types of unofficial paper money circulating in Luanda, some of which were backed by the sale of slaves in Brazil (*letras*), while others were backed by nothing more than the reputation of their private issuers (*livranças*). The fourth section explores Captain-General and Governor Francisco Inocêncio de Sousa Coutinho's efforts to reform the wealth extraction system based on these two types of paper money—a system that had evolved from the wealth extraction system using slaves as currency, as described in Chapter Four. This implied not only dismantling the Luanda slave duty contract (1769) but also reintroducing metallic currency in the Captaincy of Angola, two tasks made possible by the new commissarial boards, the Board of Commerce (1761) and the Board of Justice (1761), and the coordination of the *Erário Régio*.

The fourth section of Chapter Six then explains how these economic reforms depended on two critical pieces of police regulation: the Ordinance of the Fair Scribes of September 16, 1764, and the Ordinance of February 24, 1765, regulating the administration of justice in the Angolan hinterlands. It then analyses each article of these groundbreaking documents, explaining how they also impacted African normative systems within Portuguese jurisdictions and the 'cross-cultural' environment of the slave fair of Cassange. It concludes by highlighting how Sousa Coutinho's attempts to articulate Portuguese and Mbangala normative systems as separate, incommensurable spheres, which were perfectly adjusted to the new 'ransom' doctrines, were thwarted by the *jaga* of Kasanje's expanding influence in Portuguese jurisdictions due to the popularity of the *ndua* oath. It explains that, until the last decade of the eighteenth century, the *jaga* of Kasanje remained in control of the price ceilings of *banzos*, the payment of debts related to *letras*, and the arbitration of sorcery accusations at the slave fair of Cassange—using the latter not only as an enslaving mechanism but as a political and statecraft tool that allowed him to dispose of internal rivals and threaten Luso-African merchants.

The fifth section examines the diplomatic efforts undertaken by the captain-general and governors of the 1790s to establish, either by force or treaty, a normative environment in Cassange that was more favorable to the interests of Lisbon-backed slave traders. It presents the creation of a new office, the Director of the Fair of Cassange, as a possible compromise that enabled the *jaga* of Kasanje to retain control over the 'domestic government' of his polity, including its normative system and the *ndua* ordeal, while adding pressure for him to intervene in the repayment of goods advanced to his subjects on credit. It argues that, after more than two centuries of continuous attempts to wrestle control of the local regime of (in)commensuration from African rulers, the Portuguese settled for this compromise after being militarily defeated by the *jaga*. Meanwhile, they continued to attempt to establish direct contact with his eastern trading partners as a means of circumventing his gatekeeping. The sixth section concludes Chapter Six by analyzing how the Mbangala framed the local inter-polity order, attempting to establish how they included the Portuguese and Luso-African merchants. To do so, it analyses oral traditions collected in the early 1850s when the new liberal regime attempted to gain territorial control over the slave fair of Cassange and annex the Kingdom of Kasanje as a district. It provides an additional perspective on the exchanges in Cassange, arguing that the Mbangala understood them as upholding a regional order where the Portuguese were incorporated according to the principles of "perpetual kinship" and "positional succession."[76]

Chapter Seven opens Part Three by shifting the focus of the analysis from the Luso-African slave fairs and trade routes to the domestic spheres of West Central African households, garrisons, *arimos*, and other tightly knit corporate groups (e.g., lay brotherhoods, hunter societies, healing cults). Like the other chapters in this part, it addresses how the "intimate relations" and normative arrangements that structured these non-segregated spaces were "translated" into socially recognized uses and customs that could prove more binding than Canon Law regulations, royal enactments, or ordinances.[77] To do so, it builds on Geschiere's insight that attention must be paid to the "dark side" of kinship and intimacy, often manifested in sorcery rumors and accusations, and Romina Zamora's remark that, during the Early Modern period, the "domestic sphere" was the most "relevant" and "immediate" normative sphere for most subjects of the Iberian empires. The first section returns to the early decades of the Portuguese conquest of the Kingdom of Ndongo, exploring how the Jesuits accompanying Paulo Dias de Novais framed the spiritual dangers posed by this conquest, which opened the 'door' of Christianized villages

---

76 Heintze, Translocal 'Kinship' Relations in: Freitag and von Oppen (eds.), Translocality, p. 179–204.

77 Geschiere, The Modernity of Witchcraft; Geschiere, Witchcraft as the Dark Side of Kinship, p. 43–61; Geschiere, Witchcraft, Intimacy, and Trust, p. 23; Zamora, The Domestic Sphere, in: Duve and Herzog (eds.), Latin America Law in Global Perspective, p. 222, 231.

to African 'sorcerers.' It argues that the need to closely monitor and regulate the domestic sphere and intimate behavior of West Central Africans, rather than focusing on external manifestations of faith, became evident when the Company of Jesus first encountered Mbundu *yimbanda*. These ritual operators not only subverted the heteronormative patriarchal order introduced by the Jesuits but also interacted with spiritual entities in a performative manner instead of manufacturing 'idols,' quickly becoming the template for the 'internal' enemy of the Christian faith. This was the case because *yimbanda* forced the Portuguese to contemplate the hypothesis that even after all Mbundu 'idols' were destroyed and its public spaces were 'cleansed,' West Central Africans still abided by these "*priests of the old law*."[78]

The second section of Chapter Seven proposes revising the model of 'normative imbrication' and 'institutional cooption' created by Catarina Madeira Santos to grasp how the Portuguese polycentric monarchy accommodated African, American, and Asian "indigenous institutions" within the flexible framework provided by Portuguese *Ius commune*.[79] It argues that if we focus on the micro-scale of West Central African households and corporate groups rather than the macro-scale of the central councils of the Iberian monarchies, a broader range of modes of relating to African normative systems must be acknowledged. This is because different members of the same household or corporation could adopt radically different strategies towards equally diverse African normativities—expressing their attitudes and ambitions and manifesting these spaces' social, cultural, and religious pluralism. After discussing several sources that substantiate this argument, it adapts the interpretative grid developed by Olaf Zenker and Markus Hoehne to explore how contemporary African state officials deal with the paradoxes posed by "customary law," refining Santos' model.[80]

The third section of Chapter Seven then uses this improved model to explore what Inquisitorial sources can reveal about the "patterns of practice" adopted by Portuguese and Luso-African authorities and *moradores* of the hinterland districts

---

78 Henceforth, I will use the abbreviation "MMA" followed by a Roman numeral to identify a published document in the first series of António Brásio's source collection, *Monumenta Missionaria Africana*. The Roman numeral refers to the volume. I follow the document numbering proposed by Brásio. MMA XV, D. 101, p. 273.

79 Cardim, Herzog, Ibáñez and Sabatini, Polycentric Monarchies, in: Cardim, Herzog, Ibáñez and Sabatini (eds.), Polycentric Monarchies, p. 3–8; Sánchez, Spanish Theories of Empire, in: Tellkamp (ed.), A Companion to Early Modern Spanish Imperial Political and Social Thought, p. 17–52; Santos, Administrative Knowledge, p. 539–556; Santos, De "antigos conquistadores" a "angolenses," p. 195–222; Santos, Entre deux Droits, p. 817–848; Santos, O Império Português face às instituições indígenas, in: Palomo, Stumpf and Xavier (eds.), Monarquias ibéricas em perspectiva comparada, p. 271–303; Santos, Um governo "polido" para Angola.

80 Zenker and Hoehne, Processing the Paradox, in: Zenker and Hoehne (eds.), The State and the Paradox, p. 1–40.

and *presídios*.[81] It pays close attention to the complex interplay between "official" and "practical" modes of relating to African normative systems and institutions. It then examines how practical "recognition" or "adoption" can be accompanied by official "rejection" or "ignorance" at different levels or even by the same individuals. Focusing on sorcery accusations triggered by proximity, intimacy, and kinship, it argues that they forced the Portuguese and Luso Africans to engage with Mbundu and Mbangala institutions if they hoped to re-establish the levels of 'trust' necessary for peaceful social interaction and commerce to flourish. However, it concludes that anti-sorcery ordeals and divinations functioned as much as a "responsibility allocation mechanism," disambiguating sorcery cases from others, as a profitable enslaving mechanism.[82] This hampered their ability to restore public trust as West Central Africans became increasingly weary of the self-serving motivations of the Portuguese and Luso-African officers and African arbitrators who oversaw the administration of public and private ordeals. The fourth section concludes Chapter Seven by exploring additional factors of destabilization introduced by the Atlantic slave trade, namely the increasing popularity of the cult of 'personal' spirits associated with wealth, greed, and anti-social tendencies. It argues that this historical development generalized the suspicious stance once adopted by the Jesuits, as their rising popularity meant that even respected community members became suspects of privately worshiping dangerous anti-social entities, thus undermining its normative foundations from within.

Chapter Eight continues exploring the multinormative environment of Portuguese and Luso-African households in the Captaincy of Angola, Benguela, and their dependencies, paying close attention to seasonal and life cycle event celebrations and the "rites of passage" that accompanied and structured these "liminal periods."[83] Building on the insights of Victor Turner, it argues that these rituals afforded a critical opportunity for enlightened Captain-General and Governors of Angola and other reformers to intervene in the 'grammars of affect' that structured and grounded Portuguese and African normative regimes to "organize, arrange, and rearrange" the daily lives of West Central African subjects.[84] This was the case because, during liminal periods, norms and rules are momentarily suspended, and

81 De Herdt and Olivier de Sardan, Real Governance and Practical Norms; Zenker and Hoehne, Processing the Paradox, in: Zenker and Hoehne (eds.), The State and the Paradox, p. 24–25.

82 Geschiere, Responsibility versus Responsibilization, in: Denian, Fumanti and Lynteris (eds.), Anthropology and Responsibility.

83 Turner, Liminal to Liminoid, in Play, Flow, and Ritual, p. 56–57, 61; Turner, The Ritual Process, p. 94–95; Van Gennep, The Rites of Passage.

84 Herzog, What is Legal History, in: Duve and Herzog (eds.), Latin America Law in Global Perspective, p. 46.

"new combinatory rules may be introduced" with less resistance.[85] The first section unpacks these concepts and premises by exploring Elias Alexandre da Silva Corrêa's description of everyday life in Luanda during the 1790s. It argues that in its non-segregated urban spaces, two distinct grammars of affect coexisted, one of African and the other of European origin, structuring how feelings and affects such as love, friendship, or the sorrow associated with mourning were publicly expressed and originated biding normative obligations and social expectations. These grammars at times conflicted and at times concurred, the African one remaining hegemonic during this period. After discussing the daily rituals destined to cement friendships and assure an ambiance of peace and 'trust,' this section delineates birth, initiation, marriage, and funerary rites, as well as the payment of taxes and tribute as the primary liminal periods structuring West Central African routines. It proposes that Portuguese and African normative systems inspired different ways of handling these moments and that introducing police regulations was an attempt to discipline the affects of African and Luso-African subjects.

The second section of Chapter Eight focuses on birth rituals, introducing the West Central African institution that James Sweet claims was at the origin of one of the "most significant" misrepresentations that "plagued the relationship between Europe and Central Africans," namely, "salt baptisms."[86] After the name of the Roman Catholic sacrament was translated into BaKongo as "eating the salt" during the early years of 'cross-cultural' contact, it assumed a completely different meaning and praxeology in the Kingdom of Kongo, where preexisting anti-sorcery rituals also involved the consumption of salt.[87] From then on, these semantic and ritual associations were never lost, and 'salt' baptisms remained popular in BaKongo, Mbundu, and Ovimbundu cultural areas well into the twentieth century. This section begins exploring the normative implications of baptisms performed in these areas not being unambiguously valid under Canon Law, pointing to how the prevalence of 'salt' baptisms impacted the obligation of paying tithes, celebrating Christian marriages and funerals, keeping monogamic relations, or avoiding 'gentilic' practices which, if performed by Christians or the baptized, could be framed as heresy or apostasy. It concludes by examining the African rites of passage associated with birth that various religious orders and the bishops of Congo and Angola sought to replace with baptism. The third section analyses African, Luso-African, and Portuguese initiation, courtship, marriage, and funerary rituals, keeping in mind the ambiguity regarding the status of those who performed them, which was introduced by 'salt' baptisms. It analyses a vicious feud that erupted in 1784 between Captain-General

85 Turner, The Ritual Process, p. 56.

86 Cardoso, Comer o sal; Sweet, Recreating Africa, p. 195–197.

87 Estermann, A terminologia cristã, p. 358–364.

and Governor José de Almeida e Vasconcelos and Bishop Alexandre da Sagrada Família to highlight how this ambiguity could result in scandalous but illuminating jurisdictional conflicts between secular and ecclesiastical authorities.

The third section of Chapter Eight also explores how the police regulations imposed by the enlightened Captain-General and Governors of Angola conflicted not only with Luso-African uses and customs and the patterns of practice of captain majors but also with the ecclesiastical reforms the bishops of Congo and Angola sought to implement by establishing a more robust network of vicariates forane in the late eighteenth century. It argues that vicars forane, pastoral visitors, and captain majors all had thinly veiled economic interests in punishing Africans and Luso-Africans for practicing seasonal rituals and life cycle event celebrations in keeping with African norms and sensibilities, the latter also being invested in arbitrating the conflicts that often accompanied these rituals (e. g., separation disputes, sorcery accusations). On the other hand, the captain-general and governors were more interested in pacifying the hinterlands, maintaining 'public order' to facilitate settling debts and commerce, and ensuring that African normative systems, which dictated the extraction of slaves, were upheld. The third section concludes by providing a brief ethnographic account of the rites associated with initiations, marriages, and deaths, exploring how these were impacted by police regulations within the sphere of direct Portuguese influence. The fourth section concludes Chapter Eight by arguing that the payment of tributes and religious taxes, such as tithes, was also framed as a liminal rite. Mbundu tributes were associated with seasonal changes, epidemics, and warfare, thereby ensuring reciprocal and affective relationships between rulers and the ruled, as well as between ancestors, spirits, and the living. This section argues that by modeling their taxation and tributary systems after those of the Mbundu, the Portuguese created normative expectations that they increasingly failed to comply with, especially when the captain-general and governors of the last decades of the eighteenth century attempted to repurpose religious tithes as capitation and income taxes.

Chapter Nine focuses on three failed reform projects, arguing that despite not being implemented or successful, they had a lasting impact on the normative regime of the Captaincy of Angola, Benguela, and their dependencies. These projects were authored by Friar Alexandre da Sagrada Família, the former vicar bishop of Congo and Angola, Captain General and Governor Sousa Coutinho, and Captain General and Governor Miguel António de Mello. In common, they all proposed radical solutions to the recurring normative and social issues identified in the previous two chapters, suggesting reforms that would drastically change the multinormative environment of West Central African households and impact how belonging was negotiated and social and racial boundaries were drawn. Moreover, all projects acknowledged the fiscal and economic preponderance of the Atlantic slave trade, as well as its incredibly disruptive socio-political effects. Besides these commonalities, the three projects pointed in very different directions, constituting a thesaurus of untested possibilities that would inspire later generations. To the extent that jurisdiction meant not only 'declaring the law' but also indicating the correct way to govern domestic and public affairs, these projects express jurisprudential visions that have had a lasting normative impact.

The first section of Chapter Nine focuses on Friar Alexandre da Sagrada Família's assimilationist policies, explaining how he envisioned a network of vicariates forane capable of extending his pastoral oversight and ecclesiastical jurisdiction to the remotest hinterlands and dependencies, thus promoting conversion and the adoption of Christian values and a European grammar of affect. It also argues that he believed these new Canon Law tribunals would become self-financing by charging emoluments and imposing heavy fines on all those who adopted African norms regarding life cycle event celebrations or participated in judicial ordeal and divinations. This aspect of Friar Alexandre da Sagrada Família's project triggered conflicts with the captain-general and governors, captain majors, and local Luso-African familial factions who had opposing interests regarding arbitration disputes in the Angolan hinterlands. This section adds to our knowledge of these conflicts, concluding by listing the judicial ordeals employed in the hinterlands of Angola and Benguela and explaining how the interests of their organizers and performers conflicted with those of vicars forane. It argues that both Captain-General and Governors and Luso-African elites perceived Christian conversion and assimilation as a threat to the stability of the Atlantic slave trade, as its legitimacy now rested on the doctrine of ransom.

The second section of Chapter Nine focuses on Sousa Coutinho's attempt to segregate the social and domestic spaces of the Captaincy of Angola, Benguela, and their dependencies along racial lines. It explains that he understood the imposition of a new form of "racial patriarchy" as the best way to achieve this goal by seizing control over the "circulation of women" and their social reproductive capacities from African corporate kin groups and Luso-African familial factions.[88] It argues that if this project is considered, all police regulations proposed and implemented by Sousa Coutinho can be understood in a new light. Associating Catholic marriage with racial segregation, the captain-general and governor sought to transform this institution into a powerful political tool. This section explores how he hoped to use it to promote the White settlement of the hinterlands of Benguela, ensure that merchants and *pumbeiros* stopped defaulting on debts because they feared for their families, and reduce fears of sorcery and conflicts that resulted from the 'dark side' of kinship. It concludes by claiming that Sousa Coutinho's proposed biopolitical measures regarding the White population were accompanied by "necropolitical"

88 Doyle, Bordering on the Body, p. 5.

measures destined to increase the mortality or decrease the reproductive rate of Black and mixed-race populations.[89]

The third section concludes Chapter Nine by analyzing the legal reform projects of Captain General and Governor Mello. It introduces them by exploring an episode known in the literature as the "Socoval affair."[90] *Soba* Socoval was the most powerful Portuguese ally of the southern district of Quilengues. In the late 1790s, he was unjustly and illegally punished by the Governor of Benguela and several of his subordinates, prompting Mello to intervene, restore freedom to Socoval's subjects, and attempt to repair the damage caused by the Portuguese. This section explores Mello's proposals to prevent similar cases from occurring in the future and secure the Angolan hinterlands for commerce and the Atlantic slave trade. Unlike Sousa Coutinho and Friar Alexandre da Sagrada Família, Mello was against racial segregation and cultural and social assimilation. Instead, he argued that the uses and customs of African polities should be written, systematized, and officially recognized by the Portuguese Crown, thus reducing legal uncertainty and jurisdictional conflicts. Moreover, Mello argued in favor of reforming the *ad hoc* '*mucano*' courts that the Portuguese had developed to adjudicate freedom cases and arbitrate African conflicts. This section concludes by explaining that Mello proposed legal segregation and penal pluralism as solutions to the same problems addressed by the failed project of his predecessors.

A Note on Spellings

Readers fluent in Portuguese may notice inconsistencies in the modernized spelling of personal and place names. I chose to update the spellings of the names of the captain-general and governors of Angola, recurring characters, and key *presídios* and villages mentioned in this volume. This choice was made to help non-Portuguese speakers quickly locate related entries in the bibliography. Whenever possible, I have provided the modern spellings of African titles, names, and places in square brackets immediately following the direct transcriptions of the source materials. In other instances, I aimed to stay faithful to the source material. I paid attention to how Bantu languages use prefixes to indicate plurality. I attempted to provide the plurals and singulars of Kimbundu and Kikongo words. I sought to use these plurals instead of the Portuguese renderings, except when transcribing sources or using Luso-African coinages. This was not always easy, and some spelling anomalies might persist due to my limited proficiency with both Bantu languages.

89 Mbembe, Necropolitics.

90 Thompson, The Making of Quilengues.

I. West Central African Vernaculars

Introduction

This part presents an overview of the history of local institutions, jurisdictions, customary practices, and normative arrangements that the captain-general and governors of Angola of the second half of the eighteenth century engaged with in pursuit of their reformist goals. The first chapter begins by introducing the concept of 'folk doctrine.' It explains how the discursive formations it characterizes excused West Central African officeholders, military officers, judges, merchants, and even members of the clergy from fully obeying their ordinances, canon law regulations, and uses and customs, and even allowed them to circumvent the direct orders of their superiors. It then summarizes the social and cultural developments that impacted the "regimes of knowledge" connected with the production of normativity in the Portuguese Empire during the second half of the eighteenth century.[1] Following this, it singles out the shared belief in *feitiçaria* [sorcery] as a trans-cultural bridge concept or "channel of communication" that facilitated the alignment of the normative expectations and ideals of Africans and Europeans, beginning from the first years of European settlement in West Central Africa (1482–c. 1576).[2] This section is crucial to the chapter and this book. It argues that where and when European "cosmopolitan" concepts with a "universal vocation," such as theological natural law and *Ius gentium,* seemed contingent, these shared beliefs provided a backdrop that allowed different normative regimes to articulate and local vernaculars to emerge.[3]

The second chapter then gradually unravels the normative fabric of the Captaincy of Angola and Benguela, its southern subaltern captaincy. First, it describes the principal Portuguese civil and military institutions that structured it: municipal councils, lay brotherhoods, *presídios*, and military districts.[4] Then, its focus shifts to the officeholders with jurisdiction and their subordinates, starting from the captain-generals and governors of Angola, and including the *ouvidores* and *ouvidores gerais*, *juízes de fora*, and *juízes ordinários*. In Angola and Benguela, the latter three often accumulated several offices that different individuals in Portugal and Brazil held, namely the offices of *provedor da comarca*, *juíz dos órfãos*, *auditor da Gente de Guerra* or *provedor da Real Fazenda*. Therefore, these will be discussed

1 Saavedra et al., Historical Regimes of Normativity. Part 3.

2 Hespanha, A cultura jurídica europeia, p. 94, 151.

3 Ibid., p. 5–6.

4 According to António Hespanha, this typology was based on older "institutional templates." Municipal councils were "molded on Roman *municipia*" and medieval "municipalities," and *presídios*, military districts, and other forms of military government were "inspired by the model of the castle" as it evolved in the Iberian Peninsula. Hespanha, Uncommon Laws, p. 189.

conjointly. Next, it describes the composition and functions of the courts and *juntas* responsible for managing and intervening in specific areas of government. The third chapter then briefly focuses on the institutional layout of the different branches of the Catholic Church, as well as the functioning of the slave fairs and countless Luso-African compounds that dotted the African hinterlands. Attention is also paid to a unique feature of the Angolan institutional layout: several offices and courts dedicated to policing slaves and adjudicating freedom cases brought to them by enslaved Africans. It concludes by focusing on the transition from the more strictly jurisdictional form of government of the *Antigo Regime* to the police state political paradigm, exploring how the creation of several new commissarial boards in coordination with the secretary of state of the navy and the overseas in the 1760s reshaped the 'normative fabric' of Angola and Benguela.

While the first part does not provide an exhaustive mapping or institutional history of Angola, Benguela, and their dependencies, it seeks to situate the reader, unfamiliar with the institutional history of the Portuguese Empire, and address a gap in the literature, as similar synthetic overviews tend to focus on the South American Portuguese domains.[5] Together, the first three chapters also highlight how offices and institutions common to the Portuguese-speaking Atlantic and Indic Worlds had different local or regional inflections brought about by their specific historicity, the prevalence of different modalities of slavery, and the 'multinormative' environment of West Central Africa. An environment influenced by political and normative solutions developed by the Kingdoms of Kongo, Ndongo, Matamba, Kasanje, and many other smaller centralized polities, such as the *dembos* and Ovimbundu Kingdoms, as well as non-centralized political formations.[6] These local vernaculars are gauged by examining how ordinances, royal letters, charters, and edicts defined the duties, responsibilities, and privileges associated with the various offices that comprised the institutional structure of Angola and Benguela. This is accomplished by briefly contrasting the models that can be abstracted from these documents with archival traces and the historiography of how actual disputes were settled, jurisdictional conflicts erupted, and privileges and political belonging were brokered, denied, or abused.

---

5 Boxer, Portuguese Society in the Tropics; Salgado, Fiscais e meirinhos; Schwartz, Burocracia e sociedade; Schwartz, Sugar Plantations.

6 The title *dembo* (sing.) referred to the Mbundu ruler of an independent or semi-independent polity in the hinterlands east of Luanda. When used in the plural, it referred to the subjects of these polities, their rulers, or the polities themselves. Complicating matters, one of the districts of the Captaincy of Angola was called the Dembos—the name of the region where most of these chiefdoms were situated. I italicize *dembo* when used as a political title or to describe a political formation but not as an ethnonym or when referring to the district or region. Duve, Was ist 'Multinormativität,' p. 88–101.

This approach is inspired by critical insights of the 'law as process' turn in legal anthropology of the 1970s and 80s. Specifically, it reflects the focus scholars then placed on "processes of regularization" and the resilience and reproduction of "semi-autonomous social fields."[7] Given that, apart from Carlos Couto's pioneering work, *Os capitães-mores em Angola no século XVIII* [*Captain Majors in Angola during the 18th Century*] (1972), no institutional history of Angola, Benguela, and their dependencies is readily available, these three initial chapters begin by drafting one. However, page constraints limit the depth of their exploration of the "inconsistencies, oppositions, contradictions, and tensions" that reveal how the abstract models they enumerate played out in social life.[8] Nonetheless, this partial overview of local institutions is crucial for understanding the limitations that shape individual and collective action, as the norms and regulations that underpin them were neither infinitely malleable nor irrelevant, despite the prevailing folk doctrines regarding West Central African exceptionalism.[9]

The chapters included in this first part also aim to highlight how the admittedly complex government system in the Captaincy of Angola in the last decade of the eighteenth century was neither the result of a consciously directed, longstanding colonization plan nor the sum of purely empirical localized interventions. Rather, it resulted incrementally from several unrelated and discontinued reformist interventions that impacted the existing 'normative fabric' differently, sometimes replacing whole patterns of power relations, other times merely distorting them or adding parallel centers of power and authority. Therefore, the logic behind creating each new office and institution was neither purely additive nor subtractive. Some emptied the fields of action or greatly impinged on the jurisdictions of others, altering the overall balance while increasing the complexity of the normative system. If we accept the metaphor proposed by Hespanha, according to whom "imperial law was a lacing [machine] knotting legal threads of different colors and resistance, assisted by a disperse[d] and incoherent body of officers," we need to acknowledge that while each *morador*, missionary, merchant, soldier, and free or enslaved African contributed to weaving Angola's and Benguela's 'normative fabric,' only the powerful attempted to cut it up and patch it back together to serve their designs.[10]

---

7 Comaroff and Roberts, Rules and Processes; Moore, Law as Process, p. 3–8.
8 Moore, Law as Process, p. 3–8.
9 Couto, Os capitães-mores em Angola.
10 Hespanha, Uncommon Laws, p. 186.

1. Where Justice Suffers

1.1 A Newfound Optimism

From 1685 to 1694, Gregório de Matos e Guerra (1636?–1696) was forced into exile in São Paulo da Assunção de Loanda, a bustling Atlantic port town commonly known as Luanda.[1] Although it proved quite unhealthy for Europeans, since its founding in 1576, Luanda was the administrative hub of the Portuguese Captaincy of Angola and its most prominent establishment in West Central Africa.[2] Before being displaced, Gregório de Matos was already infamous for composing memorable satires and biting social critiques. In the late nineteenth century, after his work was first published in print in 1882, he was acclaimed as one of the greatest Portuguese-speaking Baroque poets.[3] Gregório de Matos was also an experienced lawyer, attorney, and former judge, holding a bachelor's degree in Canon Law from the University of Coimbra.[4] As customary in Luanda, despite being a *degredado*, he could make a living by offering his services as a defense attorney.[5] Being a keen observer, Gregório de Matos composed a number of poems portraying the administration of justice in Angola during his stay.[6] In his words, "*floggings*" were administered "*without mercy*," mutineers were summarily executed and cruelly

---

1 Antunes and Vos, Port Cities and Commodities, in: Curry-Machado et al. (eds.), The Oxford Handbook of Commodity History, p. 127–144; Calmon, A Vida Espantosa; Miranda, Musa Praguejadora; Peres, Gregório de Mattos e Guerra; Peres, Negros e mulatos, p. 59–75.

2 Caldeira, Dimensão sociopolítica, p. 27–59; Dias, Mudanças nos padrões, p. 43–91; Pantoja, Personagens entre mares Atlânticos, p. 136–149; Santos, Luanda, in: Brockey (ed.), Portuguese Colonial Cities in the Early Modern World, p. 249–272.

3 Calmon, A vida espantosa; Miranda, Musa praguejadora; Peres, Gregório de Mattos e Guerra.

4 Gregório de Matos was no stranger to the normative system of the Portuguese Empire. He began his academic career in the Jesuit College of Bahia, Brazil, in 1642, continuing his studies at the Jesuit College of St. Anthony the Great in Lisbon (1650–1652) and then at the University of Coimbra, where he obtained a degree in Canon Law in 1661. In 1663, after two years working as a lawyer in Lisbon, he completed the *Desembargo do Paço* exam that opened him a career as a learned judge. First, he became the municipal judge of Alcácer do Sal, Portugal. Then, back in Lisbon in 1671, he served there as *juiz do civel* (1671–1673) and *procurador* of the municipal council of Bahia (1672). Before being deported to Angola, he returned to Bahia, being appointed in 1679 as treasurer of the new Archdiocese of Bahia and *desembargador* of the *Relação Eclesiástica* of Bahia, its second instance Canon Law court. Calmon, A vida espantosa; Miranda, Musa praguejadora; Peres, Gregório de Mattos e Guerra.

5 Calmon, A vida espantosa, p. 186.

6 Süssekind, Satire and Temporal Heterogeneity, in: Valdés and Kadir (eds.), Literary Cultures of Latin America, Vol. 2, p. 241–257.

dismembered, and officers and magistrates were compulsive "*liars for reasons of state*."[7] Moreover, the sadistic practices associated with slavery, which Gregório de Matos poignantly described as the circulation of "*mulatto money*," caused great suffering and distress, debasing the Portuguese *moradores* and aggravating the plight of their African associates and dependents, who were also regularly exposed to hunger, plagues, and generalized warfare.[8] In his anguished stanzas, the poet associated all this unruliness and human suffering with the nefarious influence of the ungodly West Central African weather.

As acerbic as they might be, Gregório de Matos' verses pale in comparison to the first Portuguese-language poem known to have been written in Angola, Luís Félix da Cruz's *Nesta turbulenta terra*… [In this turbulent land] (c. the 1640s-50s), which was for long misattributed to the former.[9] Luís Félix da Cruz served as secretary to a captain-general and governor of Angola for an unknown period. He was then appointed captain major and ordinary judge of the hinterland village of Massangano in 1652 and served there for six years.[10] Like Gregório de Matos, he was familiar with how justice was administered in Angola and its dependencies. According to Félix da Cruz, West Central Africa was a place of inverted values and perverted virtues, where even feral creatures and the celestial bodies presented themselves as grotesque upside-down caricatures of their true selves. In such a "*warehouse of pain and sorrow*," the poet claimed, the "*climate wears you down*," "*exercise tears you up*," the air "*corrodes*" you, and the rain "*fertilized* [both] *meadows / and fevers*."[11] The sun, which in other places "*is a generative cause*," in Angola "*corrupts and kills*," and the moon, which elsewhere "*creates silver*," there "*sows evil deeds*." As for the locals, Félix da Cruz lamented, they boasted only of their "*thefts,*

---

7 Matos, Descreve a um amigo, in: Hansen and Moreira (eds.), Poemas Atribuídos, Vol. 2, p. 287–289; Matos, Descreve o que realmente se passa no reino de Angola, in: Hansen and Moreira (eds.), Poemas Atribuídos, Vol. 2, p. 286.

8 Dias, Famine and Disease, p. 349–378; Miller and Alden, Out of Africa, p. 195–224; Miller, The Significance of Drought, p. 17–61.

9 As Francisco Topa explains, this attribution was problematic because the poem is cited in the last volume of António de Oliveira Cadornega's (1623–1690) *História Geral das Guerras de Angola* [General History of the Wars of Angola], written four years before Gregório de Matos was deported to Angola. Topa identifies Luíz Félix da Cruz as the author and provides a critical edition of the poem. A neatly handwritten copy of *In this turbulent land*… can be found among the personal papers of Francisco Inocêncio de Sousa Coutinho (1726–1780), which were kept by his son, Rodrigo de Sousa Coutinho (1755–1812), the Count of Linhares. This version is slightly different from the ones Topa examined, suggesting that the poem continued being orally transmitted and elaborated. ANTT, CLNH, Fol. 45, D. 5; Cadornega, História geral das guerras angolanas, Vol. 3; Topa, Entre a terra de gente oprimida p. 122–147.

10 Topa, Entre a terra de gente oprimida p. 122–147.

11 Ibid., p. 150–152.

Fig. 1 Johann Theodor de Bry's Kongo. An engraving depicting the Kingdom of Kongo as a chaotic place where mythic animals existed, and wild beasts behaved in unexpected and unpredictable ways. Composed by Johann Theodor de Bry (1561–1623) and his brother Johann Israel de Bry (?–1611) to illustrate the 1598 Latin translation of Filippo Pigafetta's (1533–1604) *Relatione del reame del Congo et delle circonvicine contrade* [Report of the Kingdom of Kongo and neighboring countries] (1591). Based on Duarte Lopes' (c. 1550–16..?) accounts of the invasion of the Kingdom by the mysterious 'Giacas.' PIGAFETTA and LOPES, Regnum Congo, plate 11 (Public Domain).

malignity, / lies, falsehoods / and self-interested" acts, caring about neither their honor nor reputation. In Portuguese West Central Africa, the Captain Major concluded, "*justice suffers / lacking those capable of understanding it*," and the merciful God of the Christians revealed Himself as an Old Testament-like "*God of vengeance*." According to Gregório de Matos' and Félix da Cruz's fatalist view, in the second half of the seventeenth century, Angola seemed destined to be little more than a hunting ground for the brutal slavers who supplied the workforce to South American and Caribbean plantations, sugar cane *engenhos*, and gold and silver mines.

About a century later, Miguel António de Mello (1766–1836), Captain-General and Governor of Angola between 1797 and 1802, wrote an official letter in the same vein, headed with the line, "*on the riches of this Colony, and if it is possible or impossible to acquire them.*"[12] According to Mello, Portuguese settlers were constantly faced with the dire alternative of "*starving to death during the dry years or dying of fevers during the rainy ones.*" Therefore, the Captain-General and Governor wondered, "*What could prosper in such a land, and who would consider setting up house in it?*" Concurrently, Elias Alexandre da Silva Corrêa (c. 1738–after 1805), a Brazilian-born military officer who served in Angola between 1782 and 1799, reiterated this bleak assessment in the pages of the first academic history of Angola he began writing while serving in Luanda.[13] To him, Angola was an "*arid*" domain where the "*cruel blows of the weather*" and the "*pestiferous air of barren bushes*" mercilessly punished the "*filhos de mar em fora.*"[14] Moreover, "*vices*" immediately attracted "*popular acquiescence*" while "*virtues*" clashed with longstanding "*patriotic customs.*"[15] A "*University of evil,*" its hinterlands were a harsh domain that afforded no "*police, Charity, fear of God, faithfulness, nor the use of natural Law.*"[16] As Silva Corrêa concluded, "*the malign sicknesses of Angola, by reducing the spirit,* [and life] *force,*" did not allow "*the forwarding of the interests of justice.*"[17]

Rounding up these and many other similar references, historian Ralph Delgado argues that from the earliest stages of settlement until the Portuguese Late Enlightenment (c. 1755–c. 1804),[18] a significant degree of pragmatism, and what António Hespanha has defined as "rusticity" were officially tolerated in Angola as an integral part of the "struggle for life" in West Central Africa,[19] and understood as an accept-

---

12 Mello, Acerca das riquezas.

13 Elias Alexandre da Silva Corrêa was born in Rio de Janeiro, the natural son of councilor José Mascarenhas Pacheco Pereira de Melo, a *fidalgo* who implemented Sebastião José de Carvalho e Melo's (1699–1781) reforms in Brazil, established the *Academia Brasílica dos Renascidos* [Brazilian Academy of the Reborn] in 1759, and served on the Overseas Council. Silva Corrêa adopted the historiographic style of the Brazilian Academy of the Reborn to write his history of Angola. Oliveira, Textos militares e mercês; Santos, De "antigos conquistadores" a "angolenses," p. 205; Silva Corrêa, História de Angola, Vol. 1.

14 Silva Corrêa, História de Angola, Vol. 1, p. 13, 71.

15 Ibid., p. 15.

16 Ibid., p. 31, 44, 126.

17 Ibid., p. 77.

18 I use the Lisbon Earthquake of 1755 and the beginning of the Napoleonic Wars (1804–1815) as milestones to date the beginning and end of the Portuguese Late Enlightenment. However, I use the expression 'enlightened captain-general and governors of Angola' to refer to all those in office between 1753, when António Álvares da Cunha arrived in Luanda, and 1802 when Mello left West Central Africa. Abreu, Iluminismo e cristianismo, p. 31–61; Kury, Homens de ciência no Brasil, p. 109–129.

19 As António Hespanha explains, "rustics" were defined by the Italian jurist Alexander of Imola (1424–1477) as "*qui opere, & conversation est rusticus* [those who are rude in conversation and manners]." They were excused from knowing or understanding the subtleties of learned law because, as the jurist explained, "*in rustico est praesumptio iuris ignorantia* [in the rustic, there

able way of "adapting to the environment."[20] Yet, during the time that separated the composition of Gregório de Matos' poems from the writing of Mello's official letter and Silva Corrêa's History of Angola (the late 1790s), a lot had changed in what can be described, according to with Thomas Duve, as the "regime of normativity" and the "regimes of normative knowledge" of the Portuguese Empire.[21] In other words, in 'what' counted as binding or normative within different corporations and across rapidly differentiating social fields and 'how' this normativity was socially produced, enforced, and reproduced.[22] During the Early Modern period, theological natural law and *Ius gentium* were understood as the underlying normative frameworks that harmonized the privileges, rights, and obligations of Europeans overseas.[23] Then, 'folk doctrines' about West Central Africa's otherness and exclusion from natural law and God's grace, similar to those elaborated by Gregório de Matos, Félix da Cruz, and Silva Corrêa, locally held sway. While these doctrines did not explicitly refer to the learned discussions that had been taking place at the universities of the Iberian Peninsula since the sixteenth century, they mirrored in a distorted manner the arguments of the Second Scholastic theologians and jurists that reinterpreted *Ius gentium* and natural law after the 'discovery' and conquest of the American continent.[24] If the latter tended to agree that the origin and basis of civil power

---

is a presumption of ignorance of the law]." Hespanha remarks that the "impact of climate and landscape on rule and law" has been a "common theme" in philosophy and political thinking since Aristotle. See Lauren Benton on this topic. BENTON, A Search for Sovereignty; HESPANHA, A constituição do Império Português, in: FRAGOSO et al. (eds.), O Antigo Regime nos trópicos, p. 172–173, 179–180; HESPANHA, A cultura jurídica europeia, p. 261–262; HESPANHA, As fronteiras do poder, p. 47–105; HESPANHA, Sábios e rústicos, p. 31–60; HESPANHA, Uncommon Laws, p. 184.

20 DELGADO, História de Angola, Vol. 3, p. 14.

21 DUVE, Historia del derecho, p. 1–60; DUVE, Legal History as a History of the Translation of Knowledge of Normativity, p. 1–12; DUVE, Legal History as an Observation, p. 1–10; SAAVEDRA et al., Historical Regimes of Normativity. Part 3; SAAVEDRA et al., Why "Historical Regimes of Normativity?"

22 SAAVEDRA et al., Historical Regimes of Normativity. Part 3.

23 For an overview of this period that historicizes the emergence of theological natural law and the transition to jus-rationalism, see Tamar Herzog and Hespanha. For a more detailed discussion of sixteenth and seventeenth-century attempts to delineate the relation between theological natural law and *Ius gentium*, see Annabel Brett, Jean Porter, and the volume edited by Hochstrasser and Schröder. BRETT, Changes of State; HERZOG, A Short History of European Law; HESPANHA, A cultura jurídica europeia, p. 289–325; HOCHSTRASSER and SCHRÖDER, Early Modern Natural Law Theories; PORTER, Nature as Reason.

24 Recently, there has been an upsurge in the bibliography about the Iberian School of Peace, Spanish Second Scholastics, and some of its key figures, such as Fathers Luis de Molina (1535–1600) and Francisco Suárez (1548–1617). See the fourth chapter for more information about their doctrines on just enslavement. BRAUN, BOM and ASTORRI, A Companion to the Spanish Scholastics; BRETT, Liberty, Right and Nature; CALAFATE, Estudo Introdutório I, in: CALAFATE (ed.), A Escola Ibérica da Paz nas Universidades de Coimbra e Évora, Vol. 1, p. 17–49; FERNANDES, Luis de Molina. On

and society was God's "grace," justifying the rights of Amerindian populations, the practical men and soldiers who tacitly opposed their arguments focused precisely on its alleged absence in West Central Africa, despite St. Thomas Aquinas' claim that God's grace was open to all.[25]

Adam Morton situates "folk doctrines" at the intersection of "folk psychology, folk physics, [and] folk epistemology."[26] Expanding on this definition, Raimo Tuomela remarks that they are usually defined in philosophical literature as "belief systems that people have as a part of common folklore or common cultural heritage, not refined by science"—in other words, a "manifest image of the world."[27] Building on their insights, in this chapter, I define 'folk doctrines' as discursive formations that include impressionistic or biased theories about the minds, agency, and intentionality of others and imprecise or eccentric models of physical reality that rely on empirical knowledge that may not hold up under deeper analysis, experimental verification, and epistemological reflection. They enable the development of vernacular versions of the abstract concepts formulated, refined, and debated in philosophical, juridical, or theological discussions, thereby bridging the gap between learned discussions and local adaptations to the harsh realities of West Central Africa. In the Captaincy of Angola, folk doctrines justified behaviors that were otherwise unpardonable in the *foro interno* of Luso-African *moradores*, during confession, or in local courts. In the words of Delgado, "faced with the sad alternative of not earning enough to cover their compulsory expenses when they were honest," local authorities committed all kinds of excesses "to supplement income," being "absolved in their consciences" and facing their end of term reviews with "their heads held high" because similar practices were "longstanding and widespread."[28] However, as jus-rationalism, secularized natural law, and an instrumental understanding of royal enactments emerged,[29] 'folk doctrines' increasingly lost their footing and nor-

---

War, in: Kaufmann and Aichele (eds.), A Companion to Luis de Molina, p. 227–256; Kaufmann, Slavery between Law, Morality, and Economy, in: Kaufmann and Aichele (eds.), A Companion to Luis de Molina, p. 183–226; Salas and Fastiggi, A Companion to Francisco Suárez; Scott, The Spanish Origin of International Law.

25 Calafate, Estudo introdutório I, in: Calafate (ed.), A Escola Ibérica da Paz nas Universidades de Coimbra e Évora, Vol. 1, p. 22.

26 Morton, But are They Right? p. 159–160.

27 Tuomela, On Radical Conceptual Revolutions, p. 303.

28 Delgado, História de Angola, Vol. 3, p. 335.

29 As Herzog explains, until this period, when "kings and municipal authorities" either "discussed, explained, [or] announced the law," their actions were framed as purely "judicial rather than legislative" (if we anachronistically use today's terms). In other words, these acts discovered what the law "already contained." This situation only changed gradually during the Enlightenment. Herzog, Colonial Law, in: Tellkamp (ed.), A Companion to Early Modern Spanish Imperial Political and Social Thought, p. 113–115.

mative sway, slowly ceasing to provide an alibi for questionable uses and customs and starting to be seen as mere apologies for wasteful and superstitious behavior.[30]

Not satisfied with Gregório de Matos' and Félix da Cruz's resigned brand of fatalism, the captain-general and governors of Angola promoted queries about the root causes of the many jurisdictional conflicts that plagued the administration of justice, attempted to disentangle and clarify hierarchies, and tried their best to police even the remote corners of Angola's and Benguela's many uncharted dependencies.[31] As Captain-General and Governor Francisco Inocêncio de Sousa Coutinho (1726–1780) remarked in the preface of an ordinance he issued on February 24, 1765, regulating the competence ranges, jurisdictions, styles, duties, and privileges of captain majors, ordinary judges, scribes, and all minor-office holders involved in the administration of justice in the Angolan hinterlands, the "*times*" were markedly "*different*."[32] According to him, all previous ordinances and customary "*styles*" had become "*useless*," not only because royal orders had gradually superseded them but also because new social and economic "*needs*" had emerged.[33] As Ernst Cassirer argues was the case for Enlightenment thinkers in his preface to The Philosophy of the Enlightenment (1932), a distinctive "intellectual energy" and "enthusiasm" were the hallmarks of Sousa Coutinho's many doctrinal and normative interventions,[34] unifying his casuistic approach to the plethora of concrete issues and challenges he tackled while in office, with very different practical results.[35] In Peter Gay's words, this new outlook towards challenges previously deemed insurmountable signaled a "recovery of nerve" by the elites of the Enlightenment, characterized by their awakening to a "new sense of life," a feeling of "power over nature," and a complete

30 Bethencourt, Enlightened Reform in Portugal and Brazil, in: Paquette (ed.), Enlightened Reform in Southern Europe and its Atlantic Colonies, p. 41–44; Hespanha, A cultura jurídica europeia, p. 289–325; Nogueira da Silva, O modelo espacial do Estado, p. 23–34; Schwartz, Burocracia e sociedade; Subtil, Espaço político e organização, p. 88–116; Subtil, Estado de polícia, p. 15–38.

31 Hespanha and Santos, Os poderes num império oceânico, in: Hespanha and Santos (eds.), História de Portugal, Vol. 4, p. 351–366; Hespanha, As fronteiras do poder, p. 47–105; Hespanha, L'Administration d'une «ombre d'empire», in: François and Grenet (eds.), Raison administrative et logiques d'Empire; Santos, Entre deux Droits, p. 817–818; Santos, Luanda, in: Brockey (ed.), Portuguese Colonial Cities in the Early Modern World, p. 270.

32 AHU, CU, Angola, Box 51, D. 4624.

33 Ibid.

34 Cassirer, The Philosophy of the Enlightenment, p. xi.

35 See Delgado for a colonialist celebration of Sousa Coutinho's achievements and Ana Madalena Trigo and Crislayne Alfagali for a critical rereading of his term in office. Alfagali, Blacksmiths of Ilamba; Delgado, O governo de Sousa Coutinho em Angola I, p. 19–56; Delgado, O governo de Sousa Coutinho em Angola II, p. 49–86; Delgado, O governo de Sousa Coutinho em Angola III, p. 7–48; Trigo de Sousa, D. Francisco de Sousa Coutinho.

resignification of "change" and "innovation."[36] No longer considered the negative opposite of stability and customs reflecting a natural order sanctioned by God, both were now praised and invested with secular hope despite the "old scourges" of epidemic, famine, slavery, and war persisting.[37] However, in the minds of those not directly affected, there was reason for optimism and moderated enthusiasm.

Indeed, as the following paragraphs summarize, advances in the emerging fields of natural philosophy, jus-rationalism, and political economy radically altered how Portuguese elites framed social, juridical, and economic problems during this period. Moreover, these advances impacted rulers' and governors' perceptions of how absolutist power and royal and municipal enactments, guided by reason, could be used to remedy them, promoting the greater good of the many.[38] As José Subtil remarks, during the Late Portuguese Enlightenment, the court society typical of the Portuguese poli-synodal *Antigo Regime*[39] was gradually substituted by a "Police State" bureaucracy focused on securing and reproducing the autonomous "political space of the State" and grounded in new forms of conceiving and exercising power and authority.[40] As he remarks, this happened first gradually, with the establishment of three new secretariats of state in 1736; then, quite abruptly, when, after the Lisbon Earthquake (1755), the central bureaucratic apparatus of the kingdom had to be rebuilt almost from scratch.[41] Concomitantly, as Catarina Madeira Santos observes, establishing a "policed government" in Angola became a desirable and seemingly achievable project.[42]

---

36 Gay, The Enlightenment, Vol. 2, p. 3.

37 Ibid., p. 3–4.

38 Wehling and Wehling, Direito e Justiça, p. 174; Santos, Entre deux Droits, p. 817–848; Subtil, Espaço político e organização, p. 88–116; Hespanha, A Note on Two Recent Books, p. 1–9.

39 Cardim, "Administração" e "governo," in: Bicalho and Ferlini (eds.), Modos de governar; Cardim, A Casa Real, p. 13–57; Cardim, Cortes e cultura política.

40 Subtil's analysis of the Portuguese context is based on Michel Foucault's theorization of the 'police state' in the first two lessons of *The Birth of Biopolitics: Lectures at the Collège de France 1978–79* (2004). Complementing it, Nuno Gonçalo Monteiro remarks that this period was also characterized by continuities and even the persistence or resurgence of sixteenth-century models. Bethencourt, Enlightened Reform in Portugal and Brazil, in: Paquette (ed.), Enlightened Reform in Southern Europe and its Atlantic Colonies, p. 41–44; Foucault, The Birth of Biopolitics, p. 1–50; Monteiro, Pombal's Government, in: Paquette (ed.), Enlightened Reform in Southern Europe and its Atlantic Colonies, p. 321–338; Monteiro, The Patterns of Portuguese Politics, p. 1–6; Subtil, Espaço político e organização, p. 88–116; Subtil, Estado de polícia, p. 15–40.

41 Subtil, Estado de Polícia, p. 15–40; Subtil, O Terramoto Político.

42 Santos, Administrative Knowledge, p. 539–556; Santos, Entre deux Droits, p. 817–848; Santos, O Império Português face às instituições indígenas, in: Palomo, Stumpf and Barreto Xavier (eds.), Monarquias ibéricas em perspectiva comparada, p. 271–303; Santos, Um governo "polido" para Angola.

1.2 The Colonial Pact and its Enlightened Critics

In their poetry, Gregório de Matos and Félix da Cruz lamented the lack of charity, grace, and understanding of learned justice that plagued Angola during their time. Still, as the former pointed out, riots were effectively snuffed out, and "*mulattos*" kept circulating as currency,[43] proving that the jurisdictional form of government the Portuguese had established in West Central Africa enabled the successful extraction of slaves.[44] This, despite the ambiguities, confusion, and uncertainties that plagued it and all the pain and sorrow it caused. As Arlindo Caldeira summarizes, from the last quarter of the seventeenth century onwards, Angola had become such an essential supplier of enslaved Africans to Brazil that the illicit overreaches and abuses of governors, judges, and municipal councilors were tolerated as long as they favored the existing South-Atlantic "colonial pact."[45] Moreover, since Salvador Correia de Sá e Benevides (1594/1602–1681/1688) had reconquered Angola from the Dutch West India Company in 1648 at the helm of a fleet financed, armed, and staffed by the *engenho*-owning elites of Rio de Janeiro, the blatant disrespect the newly arrived *brasílicos* [Brazil-born] had for extant ordinances, bylaws, treaties, and the doctrines of *Ius gentium* about just war was also begrudgingly overlooked by Lisbon, Rome, and the heads of the religious orders that were present on both sides of the South Atlantic.[46] As Luiz Felipe de Alencastro remarks, the audacity of the *brasílicos* culminated in the Battle of Mbwila (1665), when a coalition of soldiers from Brazil, Mbangala mercenaries,[47] and irregular troops defeated the larger army

43 As Luiz Filipe de Alencastro remarks, this phrase was not a metaphor. Alencastro, O trato dos viventes, p. 175.

44 Boxer, Portuguese Society in the Tropics, p. 131–132; Caldeira, Dimensão sociopolítica, p. 41–43; Nafafé, Lourenço da Silva Mendonça, p. 57–60, 65.

45 Hespanha remarks that the concept of a "colonial pact" might be misleading. In keeping with his remarks, the idea of a "plurality of pacts between a plurality of institutions, resulting in a plurality and diversity of rights and duties" is more accurate. Alencastro, O trato dos viventes, p. 247–326; Caldeira, Dimensão sociopolítica, p. 53; Ferreira, Dinâmica do comércio intracolonial, in: Fragoso et al. (eds.), O Antigo Regime nos trópicos, p. 341–378; Fragoso and Florentino, O arcaísmo como projeto; Fragoso, Homens de grossa aventura; Gouvêa, Conexões imperiais, in: Bicalho and Ferlini (eds.), Modos de governar, p. 179–198; Hespanha, Uncommon Laws, p. 202; Maxwell, Pombal and the Nationalization of the Luso-Brazilian Economy, p. 608–631.

46 Alencastro, O trato dos viventes, p. 155–186, 232–234; Boxer, A Igreja militante; Boxer, Salvador de Sá; Miller, A Marginal Institution on the Margin of the Atlantic System, in: Solow (ed.), Slavery and the Rise of the Atlantic System, p. 128–129.

47 As explored in detail in the second chapter, Portuguese sources referred to the Mbangala as "*Jagas*," "*Giacas*," "*Bangalas*," or "*Imbangalas*." These same names were also used to describe several roving warbands of looting warriors that first appeared in the Portuguese records in the second half of the sixteenth century. Complicating matters, the leader of each group was also called a "*jaga*." By the first decades of the seventeenth century, Mbangala mercenaries had established the Kingdom of

of King António I of Kongo (1617–1665), *née* Nvita a Nkanga.[48] According to the historian, this 'tricontinental battle,' when the *Mwene Kongo*, an allied Christian king,[49] was decapitated by non-Christian Mbangala mercenaries commanded by *brasílicos* bent on slave-raiding, outlined the contours of the brutal, predatory relationship between Rio de Janeiro and Angola and Benguela that lasted until the 1720s.[50] Then, as discussed in the sixth chapter, the allegiances of the captain-general and governors of Angola shifted in favor of Lisbon-backed merchants and financial interests.[51]

Kasanje, headed by an elected *Jaga*. After it was dismantled in the early twentieth century, the words "*Imbangala*" or Mbangala began to describe the ethnicity of the people living in the territory of the former Kingdom of Kasanje. BIRMINGHAM, The Date and Significance, p. 143–152; BONTINCK, Un mausolée, p. 387–389; HEINTZE, The Extraordinary Journey of the Jaga, p. 67–101; HILTON, The Jaga Reconsidered, p. 191–202; MILLER, Kings and Kinsmen, p. 161–223; MILLER, Requiem, p. 121–149; MILLER, Thanatopsis, p. 229–231; MILLER, The Imbangala, p. 594–574; PINTO, Em torno de um problema de identidade, p. 193–243; THORNTON, A Resurrection, p. 223–227; VANSINA, More on the Invasion of Kongo, p. 421–429; VANSINA, On Ravenstein's Edition of Battell's Adventures, p. 321–347.

48 ALENCASTRO, O trato dos viventes, p. 287–297.

49 Jaime Gouveia claims that *Ius commune* jurists and canon law specialists framed the alliance and union between the Kingdoms of Portugal and Kongo as a "confederation" under the principle of "*aeque pricipaliter*." In keeping with these ideas, this meant that both kingdoms remained separate but were ruled by the same law. Moreover, the *Mwene Kongo* took the initiative in establishing this confederation in 1512 by requesting "a person to minister the things of justice according to Portuguese custom" and adopting "the Portuguese style." However, in practice, the political relationship between both kingdoms was always strained by Portuguese strategies of domination, as several authors remark. FROMONT, The Art of Conversion; GOUVEIA, The Creation of a Portuguese Diocese, p. 498–499; THORNTON, A History of West Central Africa, p. 78.

50 ALENCASTRO, O trato dos viventes, p. 287–297; BOXER, A Igreja militante, p. 128; FERREIRA, Cross-Cultural Exchange; SOUZA, Estruturas eclesiásticas da monarquia portuguesa, in: PALOMO, STUMPF and BARRETO XAVIER (eds.), Monarquias ibéricas em perspectiva comparada, p. 517.

51 In *Way of Death* (1988), Joseph Miller provides a definitive chronicle of how *brasílico*, *angolense*, and metropolitan Portuguese interests in the slave trade clashed and countered each other in West Central Africa. Right before the period he covers (c. 1730–1830), the 1720s were already an inflection point. At that point, the militarism of the previous generations of captain-general and governors of Angola was tempered by a royal edict that forbade their direct involvement in trade. Furthermore, as official hinterland slave fairs became more common by the middle of the eighteenth century, the military raids of *angolense* captain majors became less relevant as a source of slaves. Nevertheless, despite these changes, *brasílicos* still dominated slave shipping to the Americas and the supply of alcohol to Angola and Benguela until the 1840s, when the gradual *de facto* abolition of the Atlantic slave trade finally severed this connection. MILLER, Way of Death; MENZ, A Companhia de Pernambuco, p. 45–76; MENZ, As "geometrias" do tráfico, p. 185–222; FERREIRA, Cross-Cultural Exchange; FERREIRA, Dinâmica do comércio intracolonial, in: FRAGOSO et al. (eds.), O Antigo Regime nos trópicos, p. 341–378.

During the first decades of the eighteenth century, several isolated thinkers began to contemplate and propose reforms to the traditional ways of governing the Portuguese Kingdom and its overseas empire.[52] By the middle of the century, their critiques carried extra weight as colonial revenue began to dwindle due to the exhaustion of the Brazilian gold mines discovered in the 1690s and a decline in the price of sugar in European markets.[53] Since the nineteenth century, these thinkers have been known as the *estrangeirados* due to their cosmopolitan outlook and the unpopularity of their diagnosis of Portuguese backwardness *vis-à-vis* England and the other 'polite' Central European nations and empires.[54] Some of their modernizing ideas, influenced by Newtonian Natural Philosophy and Mercantilism, became mainstream almost overnight after the Lisbon Earthquake of 1755.[55] Then, under the reign of King Joseph I (1714–1777), Sebastião José de Carvalho e Melo (1699–1781) seized the opportunity to implement a series of sweeping reforms.[56] Carvalho e Melo was the Secretary of State for Foreign Affairs and War at the time, but he quickly accumulated additional functions and titles, including the one for which he became best known, the Marquis of Pombal. As Hespanha remarks, while often not directly involved in government or even being in personal contact with Carvalho e Melo and his aides, the *estrangeirado* elites significantly impacted the "renewal of doctrinal horizons" of the Portuguese Kingdom through their books and pamphlets.[57]

Always a divisive figure, one of Pombal's many paradoxes was his equal commitment to educational, scientific, and economic modernization, as well as the ruthless expansion of royal authority and the sadistic persecution of his personal and politi-

52 Amongst several others, Alexandre de Gusmão (1695–1753), António Nunes Ribeiro Sanches (1699–1783), Luís da Cunha (1662–1749), Luís António Verney (1713–1792), and Rafael Bluteau (1638–1734). According to Ana Carneiro, Ana Simões, and Maria Paula Diogo, these thinkers were part of a "national elite" that included "members of the clergy," a "few members of the aristocracy, often holding diplomatic positions," "physicians," and a "few military officers who established contacts with foreigners in the course of military reforms in which German and British officers collaborated." Carneiro, Simões and Diogo, Enlightenment Science in Portugal: The *Estrangeirados* and Their Communication Networks, p. 593.

53 Boxer, O Império Colonial Português, p. 183, 192; Mello e Souza, Desclassificados do ouro.

54 Cunha, Elites e acadêmicos na cultura portuguesa; Junior, Mediador das Luzes; Maxwell, Pombal; Araújo, A formação científica; Moncada, Um 'iluminista' português.

55 Boxer, O Império Colonial Português, p. 179–181; Carneiro, Simões and Diogo, Enlightenment Science in Portugal: The *Estrangeirados* and Their Communication Networks, p. 591–619; Subtil, O terramoto político.

56 Araújo, A cultura das Luzes; Maxwell, Pombal.

57 Hespanha, A Note on Two Recent Books, p. 5.

cal enemies.[58] Besides his overarching political and economic reforms,[59] the ones that proved to be of more lasting significance were the expulsion of the Jesuits from the Portuguese Kingdom and its overseas domains in 1759,[60] the law of August 18, 1769,[61] which became later known as 'The Law of Good Reason,' and the reform of the University of Coimbra, in 1772.[62] Together, these interventions imposed a hierarchy of sources of law and reorganized juridical and scientific education in the Portuguese Empire.[63] Equally important was the 'recovery of nerve' that these measures signaled, conveying to all subjects of the Crown that resignation and fatalism were to be overcome and that rusticity and adaptation to local uses and customs had their polite limits.

The law of August 18, 1769, redefined when and if customs could be applied as a source of law, forbade the subsidiary application of Canon Law in secular courts, reformed the system of standardization of jurisprudence, banned the use of the glosses of Accursius (1182–1263) and the commentaries of Bartolus de Saxoferrato (1313–1357) and Baldus de Ubaldis (1327–1400), and sought to undermine the authority of revived Roman Law.[64] As Alexander de Castro remarks, the devaluation of revived Roman Law and uses and customs, along with the restrictions imposed on the application of Canon Law, not only secured the "supremacy" of municipal enactments and *Ius regio* but also harmed the corporate interests of Portuguese jurists, thereby risking alienation of the entire class.[65] Therefore, the reform of juridical teaching at the University of Coimbra complemented the promulgation of the law of August 18, 1769, since it attempted to ensure that the next generation of jurists internalized its guiding principles and doctrines.[66] Furthermore, the univer-

---

58 Carneiro, Simões and Diogo, Enlightenment Science in Portugal: The *Estrangeirados* and Their Communication Networks, p. 591–619; Maxwell, Pombal; Monteiro, Pombal's Government, in: Paquette (ed.), Enlightened Reform in Southern Europe and its Atlantic Colonies, p. 321–338.

59 Maxwell, Pombal and the Nationalization of the Luso-Brazilian Economy, p. 608–631.

60 Boxer, O Império Colonial Português, p. 186; Rosa, O Iluminismo, p. 361–383.

61 SILVA (ed.), Colleção de legislação portugueza (1763–1774), p. 407–415; Wehling and Wehling, Direito e justiça.

62 Amorin da Costa, As Ciências Naturais na reforma Pombalina da Universidade, in: Araújo (ed.), O Marquês de Pombal e a Universidade, p. 181–208; Araújo, A Formação Científica; Carvalho, Um Iluminismo português.

63 Carvalho, Um Iluminismo Português; Castro, Enlightened Absolutism, p. 296–364; Rosa, O Iluminismo, p. 361–383.

64 Castro, Enlightened Absolutism, p. 311–328; Freire, Meneses, Instituições de Direito Civil, p. 94–104; Hespanha, A cultura jurídica europeia, p. 335–336; Neves, Ideas in Another Place?, in: Polotto, Keiser and Duve (eds.), Derecho Privado y Modernización, p. 47–81.

65 Castro, Enlightened Absolutism, p. 311–328.

66 António Hespanha and Joana Estorninho provide a detailed account of the Law and Canon Law syllabuses and the faculty's social composition before these reforms. See Mário Leite Santos for a discussion of the reformed syllabus and the jurists whose work inspired it. It was published

sity reform addressed the educational gap created by the expulsion of the Jesuits in 1759. The new *estatutos* of the University of Coimbra of 1772 introduced the study of secularized natural law, the *leis pátrias*, and Roman and Portuguese history and legal history while banning the scholastic method of teaching in favor of a new "*synthetic*" and "*compendiary*" method inspired by geometry, empirical experimentation, and jus-rationalism.[67] However ambitious these reforms were, they were less impactful than Pombal intended. Revived Roman Law and *Ius commune* glosses and commentaries continued to be *de facto* used as subsidiary law in the Kingdom of Portugal and its overseas domains,[68] conditioning the style of Portuguese courts until the dawn of liberalism.[69] Nevertheless, the university reform was a turning point, signaling the birth of a "new era in the history of *Direito* in Portugal."[70]

Simultaneously, the Paduan polymath Domenico Agostino Vandelli (1735–1816) was given a chair at the reformed University of Coimbra, being trusted with the creation of a botanical garden (1772) and with directing a series of expeditions

---

in 1773 as the second volume of the internal regulations of the University of Coimbra. The new degrees in Law and Canon Law lasted for five years and included sixteen courses, the historical ones and the course on "*Universal Natural Law of Peoples*" being taught in common. Amorin da Costa, As Ciências Naturais na reforma Pombalina da Universidade, in: Araújo (ed.), O Marquês de Pombal e a Universidade, p. 181–208; Araújo, A cultura das Luzes; Araújo, O Marquês de Pombal; Castro, Enlightened Absolutism, p. 359–360; Estatutos da Universidade de Coimbra, Vol. 2; Estorninho, A forja dos homens; Hespanha, Thirty Years of Studies, p. 22–50; Nogueira da Silva, O modelo espacial do estado, p. 28–29; Santos, Melo Freire, p. 163–190.

67 According to Manuel Paulo Merêa, the new method adopted was inspired by the methodological proposals of Christian Wolff (1679–1754) and Johann Gottlieb Heineccius (1681–1741). The authors' of the new internal regulations of the University of Coimbra attempted to synthesise the former's mathematical-demonstrative approach with the latter's axiomatic approach. As explained in vol. 2, tit. 3, chap. 1, par. 18 of the internal regulations, the result was a "*synthetic*" teaching method that strove to start, "*first of all,* [from] *the definitions and divisions of subjects that best fit the rules of good dialectics; then moving on to the first principles and general precepts that are simpler and easier to understand.*" From there, professors and lecturers were supposed to proceed to "*the more particular conclusions, formed by combining a greater number of ideas, and therefore more complicated and sublime, and more difficult to understand.*" This method was also "*compendiary*" because only "*Brief and well-organized compendiums*" were to be adopted, "*composed solely of the juice and substance of the Doctrines*" and showcasing "*the Rules and exceptions* […] *of the greatest use in law.*" Castro, Enlightened Absolutism, p. 359–360; Estatutos da Universidade de Coimbra, Vol. 2, p. 75–76; Hespanha, A cultura jurídica europeia, p. 335–336; Merêa, Lance de olhos, p. 187–214; Merêa, O ensino do Direito em Portugal, in: Loureiro (ed.), Jurisconsultos portugueses do século XIX, p. 149–190; Santos, Melo Freire, p. 163–190; Santos, Melo Freire, p. 163–190.

68 Dias Paes, Shared Atlantic Legal Culture, p. 419–440.

69 Wehling and Wehling, Direito e justiça, p. 176–181.

70 Hespanha, A cultura jurídica europeia, p. 335–336.

that became known as "philosophical journeys."[71] According to Vandelli, these expeditions had the purpose of attaining an accurate "*physical and economic description of the whole kingdom*," including its "*domains and overseas states*," mapping its "*natural, human, and technological resources*," and figuring out how to overcome the "*moral obstacles*" which stood in the way of their good use.[72] These obstacles included wasteful, superstitious,[73] and unreasonable uses and customs that had normative standing in 'rustic' jurisdictions, especially those connected with mendicancy and the management of the commons.[74] In other words, gone were the times when immemorial habits or, in the case of Angola, exposure to the unforgiving weather and epidemics, were excuses enough for the maladministration of human and natural resources. With Pombal's fall from grace after the death of King Joseph I and the accession of Queen Maria I (1734–1816), mercantilism became increasingly unfashionable, and the agrarianism and mild reformism of Vandelli and a new generation of *estrangeirados*, such as Félix de Avelar Brotero (1744–1828) and José Francisco Correia da Serra (1750–1823), offered an alternative.[75] Then, the first class of *alumni* from the reformed University of Coimbra contributed to the establishment of the Royal Academy of Sciences of Lisbon (1779) under the motto "*nisi utile est quod facimus stulta est gloria* [unless what we do is useful, glory is foolish]."[76]

---

71 Amorin da Costa, As Ciências Naturais na reforma Pombalina da Universidade, in: Araújo (ed.), O Marquês de Pombal e a Universidade, p. 181–208; Brigola, Colecções; Costa and Leitão, Portuguese Imperial Science, in: Bleichmar, De Vos, Huffine, and Sheehan (eds.), Science in the Spanish and Portuguese Empires, p. 46; Domingues, Viagens de exploração; Moutinho, Coletar, preparar, remeter, p. 125–138; Moutinho, Terra, água e ar; Raminelli, Viagens ultramarinas.

72 Vandelli, Memórias económicas inéditas (1780–1808), in: Cardoso (ed.), Memória sobre a necessidade de uma viagem, p. 33–36.

73 Book 5, tit. 3, point 3 of the *Philippine Ordinances* (1603) already listed several "*abuses*" or superstitious practices of 'rustic people' that were to be persecuted and punished during the Portuguese Late Enlightenment. However, the range of normative knowledge that could be framed as superstitious considerably broadened during this period. Ord. Fil., Book V, Tit. 3, § 3; Cosme da Cunha, Regimento do Santo Officio, p. 118–127; Walker, The Role and Practices of the *Curandeiro*, p. 223–237.

74 Subtil, Estado de polícia, p. 15–40; Vandelli, Memórias económicas inéditas (1780–1808), in: Cardoso (ed.), Memória sobre a necessidade de uma viagem, p. 33–36.

75 Carneiro, Simões and Diogo, Enlightenment Science in Portugal: The *Estrangeirados* and Their Communication Networks, p. 591–619; Santos, A nuvem por Juno, p. 423–443.

76 See Foucault for an account of how the "question of utility" provided an internal limit to the exercise of absolutist political power, mediating the transition from a police state to a liberal state grounded on a "new art of government." As I expose in the next paragraphs, in Portugal, the Royal Academy of Sciences of Lisbon was central to the creation of what Foucault defines as an "apparatus (*dispositif*) of knowledge-power:" "a regime of truth" coupled with "a set of practices" that carved out new fields of expertise and political intervention. Foucault, The Birth of Biopolitics, p. 19–20,

Henceforth, the Royal Academy of Sciences of Lisbon would provide an influential forum for discussing overseas policies and administrative reforms, as well as exploring economic and organizational solutions to the problems affecting the Portuguese Kingdom and its African domains.[77] As Subtil remarks, its socio-cultural impact was manifold. First, its scientific and economic reports enabled the consolidation of a new class of powerful bureaucrats that had emerged in the mid-1760s, the *intendentes*, *superintendentes*, and general inspectors responsible for managing specific economic activities in the Portuguese Kingdom.[78] These bureaucrats were commissioned based on their expertise and merit rather than their nobility and status, contradicting the logic of patrimonialism characteristic of the *Antigo Regime*. Second, the Royal Academy of Sciences of Lisbon forwarded the notion that scientific studies and technical reports could substitute the practical advice and jurisprudence provided by central collegiate courts such as the Overseas Council (1643–1833),[79] strengthening the position of the secretary of state of the navy and the overseas, who increasingly relied on these documents for drafting his policy proposals.[80] As discussed in the third chapter, the increasing supremacy of the secretary of the state *vis-à-vis* the Overseas Council directly impacted the Captaincy of Angola, Benguela, and their dependencies. Finally, the Royal Academy of Sciences of Lisbon promoted a new understanding of the body politic based on the ideals of physiocracy, the language of jus-rationalist contract theory, and, later, political economy.[81] No longer imagined as composed of different corporations with jurisdictional autonomy conciliated by the divinely-inspired "love" and "grace" distributed by the Crown,[82] the body politic was increasingly imagined as a cohesive

---

40–41; Rebelo da Silva, A Academia Real das Ciências de Lisboa; Santos, A nuvem por Juno, p. 423–443.

77 Rebelo da Silva, A Academia Real das Ciências de Lisboa; Santos, A nuvem por Juno, p. 423–443.

78 For instance, the general inspectorates of "agriculture" (1765), "custom houses" (1766), "factories" (1777), "the police" (1760), "the Post" (1799), and "wool making" (1769). Subtil, Estado de polícia, p. 15–40.

79 The Overseas Council was regulated by statute from July 14, 1642, and instituted on December 2, 1643. Its composition, functions, and relationship with other councils, boards, and secretariats are further discussed in the third chapter. Bardwell, The Governors of Portugal's South Atlantic Empire; Barros, Negócios de tanta importância; Boletim do Conselho Ultramarino. Legislação antiga (1446–1754), Vol. 1, p. 296–307; Caetano, O Conselho Ultramarino; Cardim, A Casa Real, p. 13–57; Myrup, To Rule from Afar, p. 63–139.

80 Subtil, Espaço político e organização, p. 88–116; Subtil, Estado de polícia, p. 15–40.

81 Nogueira da Silva, O modelo espacial do Estado; Subtil, Espaço político e organização, p. 88–116; Subtil, Estado de polícia, p. 15–40.

82 Hespanha refers to this paradigm as defined by "political pluralism." According to him, the Crown was metaphorically imagined as the "head" that governed the body but depended on all other "social organs" being autonomous to perform the specific tasks attributed to them within the economy of the whole. Hespanha, A cultura jurídica europeia, p. 62–63.

"nation" whose common good, happiness, and best interests were to be actively promoted by the monarch and policed by his delegates.[83]

The Pombaline reforms had an immediate impact on Angola and Benguela.[84] As Catarina Madeira Santos remarks, Carvalho e Melo envisaged a thorough "domestication of the colonial world" grounded on the "territorialization of the colonial state," the promotion of White settlement, the growth of agriculture and industries, and the "bureaucratization" of the administration.[85] According to Madeira Santos, this ambitious program was condensed by Carvalho e Melo in a famous *dictum* from 1760: "*Angola não é feitoria, não só é reino como pode ser império* [More than a *feitoria* or the kingdom that it now is, Angola could be an empire]."[86] Accordingly, by 1753, Carvalho e Melo had already sent to Angola the first of a series of enlightened captain-general and governors, António Álvares da Cunha (1700–1791), who was in office between 1753 and 1758.[87] The nephew of the influential *estrangeirado* Luís da Cunha (1662–1749), Álvares da Cunha was a cartographer and historian, setting the model for the "philosopher-administrators" who succeeded him.[88] As soon as he arrived in Luanda, accompanied by the cartographer Guilherme Joaquim Pais de Menezes, he began making arrangements for the statistical and cartographic surveying and description of the Captaincy of Angola and its dependencies and hinterlands, with the goal of paving the way for subsequent administrative improvements and innovations.[89]

As in the Portuguese Kingdom, centralizing reforms accelerated following the 1755 earthquake. After the expulsion of the Jesuits in 1759, their old college was occupied by the bishop of Congo and Angola as the new episcopal palace, strengthening the relative position of the secular hierarchy of the Church under the direct patronage of the Portuguese monarch.[90] As Boxer remarks, while this development

---

83 Foucault, The Birth of Biopolitics; Subtil, Espaço político e organização, p. 88–116; Subtil, Estado de polícia, p. 15–40; Subtil, O terramoto político.

84 Caetano, As reformas pombalinas, in: Baião, Cidade and Murias (eds.), História da expansão portuguesa no mundo, Vol. 3, p. 251–260; Oliveira, Textos militares e mercês; Teles, Das jóias negras.

85 Santos, Administrative Knowledge, p. 541; Santos, De "antigos conquistadores" a "angolenses," p. 197; Santos, Luanda, in: Brockey (ed.), Portuguese Colonial Cities in the Early Modern World, p. 258–259.

86 Santos, Administrative Knowledge, p. 541; Santos, Luanda, in: Brockey (ed.), Portuguese Colonial Cities in the Early Modern World, p. 249–272.

87 Santos, Administrative Knowledge, p. 544.

88 Ibid., p. 545.

89 Ibid., p. 539–556; Santos, De "antigos conquistadores" a "angolenses," p. 209.

90 Concomitantly, the Crown seized 1080 slaves owned by the Jesuits, 330 of which were distributed in several urban *senzalas* in Luanda and the remainder in the twenty *arimos* and plantations of the order. In total, they were worth 72.729$611 *réis*. Cardoso, Relação dos rendimentos, p. 541–554;

bolstered royal power, as further discussed in the following chapters, it did not wholly defuse the jurisdictional conflicts between the secular and regular branches of the Roman Catholic hierarchy that remained typical of Portuguese colonial settings.[91] Furthermore, as had happened in the Portuguese Kingdom, the expulsion of the Jesuits created an educational gap that, in this case, was filled with the establishment in Luanda of the Geometry and Fortification Class in 1769, founded as one of the many projects of Sousa Coutinho, who was in office between 1764 and 1772.[92] Madeira Santos argues that the establishment of this Class marked the beginning of a genuinely "new phase," giving rise to a generation of *angolense* administrators and military officers who were not only trained in cartography and engineering but also emancipated from the conservative pedagogy of the religious orders and better equipped and motivated to implement Carvalho e Melo's colonial policies *in situ*.[93]

In 1783, after Carvalho e Melo's forced retirement and not long after the Royal Academy of Sciences of Lisbon was established, Joaquim José da Silva (c. 1755–1810), a disciple of Vandelli, was sent by the Crown to the Captaincy of Angola on a three-year "philosophical journey" that turned into a definitive stay.[94] There, between his naturalist expeditions, he had an administrative career, first as secretary of the colonial government (1782/83–1790), then as captain major of Massangano (1790–c. 1796), and finally as captain major of the *presídio* of Ambaca (c. 1796–1810).[95] While serving as secretary in Luanda, Silva reorganized the government's archive.[96] According to Joseph Miller and John Thornton, his efforts as an archivist enabled Captain-General and Governor Miguel António de Mello to understand better the "abuses" and "disorders" perpetrated by subordinate

---

Gabriel, Os Jesuítas; Gabriel, Padrões da fé; Melo e Castro and Bettamio, Carta do Ministro Martinho de Melo, p. 561–566.

91 Boxer, A Igreja militante, p. 89.

92 Santos, De "antigos conquistadores" a "angolenses," p. 205–206; Santos, Luanda, in: Brockey (ed.), Portuguese Colonial Cities in the Early Modern World, p. 260.

93 Santos, Administrative Knowledge, p. 539–556; Santos, De "antigos conquistadores" a "angolenses," p. 198–199; Santos, Luanda, in: Brockey (ed.), Portuguese Colonial Cities in the Early Modern World, p. 249–272; Trigo de Sousa, D. Francisco de Sousa Coutinho.

94 AHU, CU, Angola, Box 67, D. 5794; Cagle and Crawford, Enlightened Reformism, in: Bouza, Cardim and Feros (eds.), The Iberian World, p. 500–519; Figueiredo and Smith, Joaquim José da Silva, p. 125–138; Simon, Scientific Expeditions.

95 AHU, CU, Angola, Box 66, D. 5750; Box 76, D. 6412; Cagle and Crawford, Enlightened Reformism, in: Bouza, Cardim and Feros (eds.), The Iberian World, p. 500–519; Figueiredo and Smith, Joaquim José da Silva, p. 125–138; Kananoja, Healing Knowledge, p. 74–76; Miller and Thornton, A crónica como fonte, p. 24; Miller and Thornton, The Chronicle as Source, p. 368; Simon, Scientific Expeditions.

96 Coimbra (ed.), Livros de "Ofícios para o Reino," p. 16–17; Mello, Relatorio do governo, p. 549.

Portuguese authorities in the Angolan hinterlands.[97] Before Mello, a series of other enlightened captain-general and governors, besides Álvares da Cunha and Sousa Coutinho, had already tried to reform the administration of justice in the hinterlands of Angola and Benguela, seeking to bring about a more polite form of centralized government and diversify the economic base of these domains.[98] These included José de Almeida e Vasconcelos (1737–1812), who was in office between 1784 and 1790, and Manuel de Almeida e Vasconcelos, who was in office between 1790 and 1797. However, with a well-organized archive, the first results from the census established in 1776, and a passion for natural philosophy and systematization, Mello was in the best position to diagnose the systematic problems afflicting the administration of justice in Angola and Benguela. As the ninth chapter argues, it was Mello who proposed that collecting and writing down African uses and customs could offer a more definitive solution to longstanding, recurring problems.[99]

1.3 *Feitiçaria* and *Feitiço* as Bridge Concepts

As soon as enlightened captain-general and governors arrived in Luanda, they were confronted with what can be metaphorically described as a varied and rich 'normative fabric.'[100] In areas of older occupation, considerable White settlement, and active missionary presence, familiar patterns might immediately catch their eye. Recognized elements drawn from Canon Law, *Ius commune* doctrines, Portuguese uses and customs, and royal enactments and ordinances resurfaced in concrete adjudications, informing the *bandos* that regulated daily life and influencing the behavior and expectations of officials, merchants, and *moradores*. These normative elements were nevertheless profoundly influenced by the multinormative environment of Angola and Benguela, each Portuguese institution in West Central Africa being, by force, a vernacular inflection of its European, Asian, or South American models.[101] Moreover, as Alfredo Margarido argues, West Central Africans kept

97 Mello, Relatorio do Governo, p. 549; Miller and Thornton, A crónica como fonte, p. 24; Miller and Thornton, The Chronicle as Source, p. 368.

98 Santos, Entre deux Droits, p. 817–848; Santos, Um governo "polido" para Angola; Subtil, Estado de polícia, p. 15–40; Caetano, As reformas pombalinas, in: Baião, Cidade and Murias (eds.), História da expansão portuguesa no mundo, Vol. 3, p. 256.

99 Santos, Entre deux Droits, p. 824.

100 Hespanha, Fazer um império com palavras, in: Barreto Xavier and Nogueira da Silva (eds.), O governo dos outros, p. 73.

101 As Catarina Madeira Santos remarks, because of the action of central councils, such as the Overseas Council, and because captain-general and governors and learned judges served in different dominions consecutively, Asian and South American institutions also made their way to Africa.

the upper hand in normative production in key social spheres well into the last decades of the nineteenth century, not only in remote hinterland slave fairs but also in Luanda's well-frequented salons where courtesans played their games of intrigue and seduction. In Margarido's words, the Portuguese were "impotent" to change the "African monetary systems" and "short-circuit" the African kinship structures that regulated the "circulation of women" at the basis of the social order.[102] Captain-general and governors, as all other military officers, civilians, and clergymen, were thus immediately forced to "Africanize" as soon as they set foot in West Central Africa, eating local food, learning Bantu languages, bartering with African currencies, and consorting with African women or men according to locally acceptable norms of engagement.[103] As Kalle Kananoja argues, this also extended to adopting local *materia medica* and healing practices, which were difficult to disentangle from African religious or spiritual practices.[104] Therefore, White *moradores* and recently arrived *filhos de mar em fora* were soon exposed to African moral and ethical values, 'grammars of feeling,' ideas about health and well-being, and beliefs about the supernatural causes of diseases and misfortune.[105]

In areas where the original African 'normative fabric' was preserved after the initial Portuguese conquest, namely the dispersed vassal Mbundu *sobados* and the semi-autonomous *dembos*, African institutions, norms, and behavior patterns were equally impacted, being reshaped by contact with European normative systems.[106] This was because, despite Pombal's groundbreaking efforts, jurisdiction was not understood and enforced according to the territorial principle until the

---

Duve, Was ist 'Multinormativität,' p. 88–101; Santos, O Império Português face às instituições indígenas, in: Palomo, Stumpf and Barreto Xavier (eds.), Monarquias ibéricas em perspectiva comparada, p. 271–303.

102 Margarido, Algumas formas da hegemonia africana in: Santos (ed.), I Reunião internacional de História de África, p. 383–406.

103 Couto, Os capitães-mores, p. 66; Dias, Angola, in: Alexandre and Dias (eds.), O Império Africano (1825–1890), p. 350–351; Dias, Estereótipos e realidades sociais, in: CNCDP (ed.), Construindo o passado angolano, p. 597–623; Pantoja, Personagens entre mares Atlânticos, p. 136–149; Santos, De "antigos conquistadores" a "angolenses," p. 195–222; Santos, Luanda, in: Brockey (ed.), Portuguese Colonial Cities in the Early Modern World, p. 249–272.

104 On July 11, 1770, Sousa Coutinho wrote a letter to Carvalho e Melo, requesting that the medical doctor Francisco Damião Cosme Vilela return with him to Portugal. According to Sousa Coutinho, the doctor risked starving to death "*because he didn't enjoy a good reputation among the curandeiros of Angola, who refused his treatment methods.*" Sousa Coutinho added that he had charitably accepted him into his household. AHU, CU, Angola, Box 55, D. 5006; Kananoja, Healers, Idolaters, and Good Christians, p. 443–465; Kananoja, Healing Knowledge, p. 26–49.

105 The concept of 'grammars of feeling' is explored in the eighth chapter.

106 Dias, Angola, in: Alexandre and Dias (eds.), O Império Africano (1825–1890), p. 355–357.

mid-decades of the nineteenth century.[107] Instead, the 'normative fabric' of West Central Africa continued to be woven out of many fine strands: the persons under civil, military, or canon law jurisdiction that mingled and interacted with the free African subjects of vassal or independent kings or chiefs. As the chapters grouped in the third part explore, the patterns emerging from their interactions were made even more complex because each of these individual strands, whether a Portuguese *morador* or a free or enslaved African, lived under the strain of "concurring and competing norms" regulating different aspects of their composite social persona.[108] Moreover, each could adopt different strategies regarding African institutions and normative systems, ranging from open "adoption" of Mbundu or other African norms and institutions to xenophobic hostility or oblivious "non-recognition."[109] Therefore, one's inclusion into the "moral communities"[110] that aggregated around Portuguese jurisdictions or autonomously organized alongside or in opposition to them was neither a straightforward nor a definitive process. Both in the garrisoned *presídios* and the Luso-African hinterland slave fairs or compounds that were part of what Hespanha defines as the "shadow empire," inclusion was part of an ongoing negotiation played out in the socio-cultural, religious, and normative fields.[111] As chapters seven to nine explore, this led to conflicting politics of inclusion and

---

107 The first topographic survey took place in Angola only in 1887. Therefore, as Jill Dias remarks, until then, the limits of Portuguese and African sovereignty coincided with the old jurisdictional boundaries of the *Antigo Regime*, framed as "customary law." Ibid., p. 355.

108 See Hillard von Thiessen on the "concurrence and competition of norms" during the Early Modern period. Von Thiessen, Concurrence and Competition of Norms, p. 6–51; Von Thiessen, Das Zeitalter der Ambiguität; Von Thiessen, Normenkonkurrenz Handlungsspielräume, in: von Thiessen and Karsten (eds.), Normenkonkurrenz in historischer Perspektive, Vol. 50, p. 241–286.

109 Zenker and Hoehne, Processing the Paradox, in: Zenker and Hoehne (eds.), The State and the Paradox, p. 1–40.

110 David Schoenbrun defines a "moral community" as one that agrees on what constitutes the acceptable "adulthoods" of its members: their duties and what sort of "actions" youths must perform to assure its social reproduction. Reflecting this view, moral communities can accommodate disagreements and tensions, being based not on the maintenance of fixed boundaries and "cultural othering" but on the social discussion of their "moral core" and its "modes of change." Neil Kodesh defines this discussion as steering "the content of a community's moral economy." Schoenbrun remarks that people can "decline the terms of the moral community," attempting to convince others to change them, remove themselves from it, or be removed. As an analytical concept, Schoenbrun's "moral community" of belonging has the advantage of not carrying the conceptual baggage of "ethnic community" or any particular ethneme (e.g., Portuguese, Mbundu, Mbangala, BaKongo), foregrounding the negotiated dimension of social life and affording more nuanced analysis of historical communities that do not presuppose cultural, religious, and normative homogeneity. Glassman, Ethnicity and Race, in: Worger (ed.), A Companion to African History, p. 206; Kodesh, Beyond the Royal Gaze, p. 173; Schoenbrun, The Names of the Python, p. 9–10.

111 Hespanha, Filhos da Terra; Hespanha, L'Administration d'une «ombre d'empire», in: François and Grenet (eds.), Raison Administrative et Logiques d'Empire.

exclusion and the need to define "secondary rules" about the norms that established and governed the limits and boundaries between different communities.[112]

In the case of the Captaincy of Angola, Benguela, and their dependencies, as the following sections describe in greater detail, the few attempts made by captain-general and governors to establish clear-cut jurisdictions, impose a hierarchy of sources of law, and regulate the relation between captain majors, Portuguese judges, and African authorities proved particularly difficult to enforce. However, contrary to what happened in the Kingdom of Portugal, where more than seigneurial justice and Canon Law, it was the application by jurists, lawyers, and judges of *Ius commune* doctrines, court styles inspired by revived Roman Law, and a Romanized interpretation of royal enactments and ordinances that threatened the reforms set in motion by Pombal, in Angola and Benguela it was the institutions of slavery and the intense pull of African normative systems that posed an actual limit to the reforms of enlightened captain-general and governors.[113]

These normative systems were very diverse, reflecting the cultural, historical, and linguistic richness of West Central Africa. However, they were grounded in shared assumptions about the origins of evil and human suffering, which historical-comparative linguistics and ethnography can help us trace back millennia into the past. Most Africans in contact with the Portuguese accepted a form of supernatural personal agency as one of the primary reasons for the occurrence of unfortunate or tragic events and afflictions.[114] If we temporarily bracket all historical and geographic contingencies, the force or power that enabled this agency can be abstractly described as sorcery. The other two shared assumptions were that mishaps could also result from breaking ritual prohibitions or angering ancestors and territorial spirits. For instance, according to Joaquim José da Silva, for the Ovimbundu, Mbundu, and neighboring "*nations*," "*nothing happens in this world that is not by*

---

112 Herbert Hart's definition informs my understanding of secondary rules despite his model being best suited to the study of British municipal law. Accordingly, I understand as secondary rules those remedying the issues he identified as the "uncertainty," "static character," and "inefficiency" of primary rules. In keeping with this model, secondary "rules of recognition" address the issues caused by uncertainty by determining what primary rules are acknowledged as bidding by the group; secondary "rules of change" regulating "legislative enactment and repeal" address the issues caused by the static character of primary rules; and secondary "rules of adjudication" afford individuals the means to "make authoritative determinations of the question whether, on a particular occasion, a primary rule has been broken" thus addressing the inefficiency of primary rules. Hart, The Concept of Law, p. 90–95.

113 Castro, Enlightened Absolutism, p. 296–364; Santos, Entre deux Droits, p. 817–848; Santos, Um governo "polido" para Angola.

114 Honwana, Espíritos vivos; Meneses, Feitiçaria e modernidade; Sansi-Roca and Parés, Introduction, in: Sansi-Roca and Parés (eds.), Sorcery in the Black Atlantic, p. 1–18; West, Ethnographic Sorcery; West, Kupilikula.

the impulse of the Indelles or Sandes, who are the souls of their deceased, or by the evil deeds of feiticeiros."[115] In other words, the ultimate cause of unfortunate events, abominations, behaviors perceived as anti-social, deviant, or evil, and significant breakdowns in the social fabric or moral order of the community could be attributed to the agency of aggravated ancestors and territorial spirits, the breaking of taboos, or sorcery, creating the need for disambiguation mechanisms such as divination rituals and ordeals. While concrete ways of appeasing ancestors, apotropaic rituals and charms, atonement rituals, and disambiguation mechanisms varied widely from one local to another, as innovation was often associated with greater ritual efficacy and potency, the general outline of this core normative cluster remained stable and easily recognizable, providing an interface with Portuguese beliefs about *feitiçaria* in the "cross-cultural spaces" of West Central Africa.[116]

Collecting historical anecdotes such as José da Silva's account, however, can hardly corroborate the claim that shared beliefs about sorcery, the origin of evil, and the power of specific ritual operators were part of a pervasive African cultural background or a rich normative thesaurus analogous to European *Ius commune* both in its widespread diffusion and lasting influence. To substantiate and support such a bold claim, it is necessary to employ "words as history," as Jan Vansina puts it, beginning from the present rather than the past.[117] The following paragraphs provide a brief overview of this historiographical approach based on Vansina's celebrated "words and things" method. This method integrates insights from historical-comparative linguistics[118] with contemporary ethnographic and archaeological data to compose an approximate history of African institutions, beliefs, values, economies, and material culture, grounded in the evolution of linguistic forms: "words" that can be associated with "things" or broadly delimited concepts.[119] In

---

115 José Da Silva, Continuação da viagem ao sertão de Benguella, continuada do N.º 2.º, p. 54.

116 Pietz, The Problem of the Fetish, p. 2; Rodrigues de Areia, Estrutura magico-religiosa.

117 Vansina, Paths in the Rainforests, p. 9–16, 258–262.

118 For an introduction to the Bantu historical-comparative linguistics field, see: Bostoen and Bastin, Dimmendaal, and Schadeberg. Bostoen and Bastin, Bantu Lexical Reconstruction; Dimmendaal, Historical Linguistics, p. 3–22; Schadeberg, Historical Linguistics, in: Nurse and Philippson (eds.), The Bantu Languages, p. 143–154.

119 As Schoenbrun summarizes it, the "words and things" method holds that when we can reconstruct the "word" for a "thing" in an earlier form of a language, then we can conclude that whenever people spoke that language, they knew something about that thing. For instance, if we can reconstruct the word for "oil palm" in "Proto-Bantu," a reconstruction of the language spoken before the Bantu expansion, then it is safe to assume that "whenever and wherever people spoke [Proto-Bantu] they knew something about oil palms." By applying the methods of historical-comparative linguistics, reconstructed shared words for things such as oil palm and lexical innovations about the same things can be distributed onto geographical maps. This distribution can ground speculations about the historical developments at the origin of observable patterns that can then be tested using archaeological and historical methods, paleo-environmental records, and the findings of ancillary

Paths in the Rainforests (1990), Vansina uses Malcolm Guthrie's hypothetical Proto-Bantu lexical roots delineated in the four volumes of the reference work *Comparative Bantu* (1967–1971)[120] to propose a reconstruction of Equatorial African "traditions" and interpret the history of Equatorial African peoples through the prism of their historical unfolding.[121] In Wyatt MacGaffey's words, these traditions consist of "cognitive patterns" and conceptual constellations that are constructed and expressed through language, thereby grounding the "cognitive reality" or "the world as the [historical] actor sees it."[122] Therefore, Vansina's "words and things" approach can turn José da Silva's generalizations about the widespread belief in the power of *feiticeiros* and *feitiços* into a falsifiable hypothesis. If such beliefs were widely shared when he wrote his reports, the words used to describe them in contemporary Angolan communities could be used to reconstruct shared traditions that predate centuries, or even millennia, the arrival of the Portuguese on the West Central African shores. The validity of this hypothesis will be verified after a concise overview of the complex historical-comparative linguistic methods that underpin it is provided.

Gerrit Dimmendaal explains that Guthrie followed a "two-stage method" to compose *Comparative Bantu*.[123] First, he created various "comparative series" that

---

linguistic disciplines such as glottochronology. Schoenberg also points to the limits of this method, for instance, its difficulties in dealing with "contact phenomena" or its uncritical assumptions about the link between "material culture and lexicalization." On these limits, see also Bostoen, Dimmendaal, and Ehret. For a more technical description of the "words and things" method, see Gonzales. BOSTOEN, Pearl Millet, p. 183–213; DIMMENDAAL, Historical Linguistics, p. 69; EHRET, History and the Testimony of Language, p. 82–104; GONZALES, Historical Linguistics; MACGAFFEY, A Central African Kingdom, in: BOSTOEN and BRINKMAN (eds.), The Kongo Kingdom, p. 42–59; SCHOENBRUN, Crafting Early African Histories, p. 99–112; SCHOENBRUN, Words, Things, and Meaning, in: DIMMENDAAL and VOSSEN (eds.), The Oxford Handbook of African Languages, p. 961–972; VANSINA, Paths in the Rainforests.

120 As Koen Bostoen clarifies, "Bantu is the prevalent language family in Central, Eastern, and Southern Africa." Gonzales remarks that it comprises more than 450 languages, stressing that a definitive account is hard to reach because there is no consensus regarding the distinction between languages and dialects. BOSTOEN, The Bantu Expansion; GONZALES, Historical Linguistics.

121 GUTHRIE, Comparative Bantu; VANSINA, Paths in the Rainforests.

122 Vansina states that these equatorial "traditions" are analogous in scope and broadness to "Confucian, Buddhist, and Judaeo-Muslim-Christian" traditions, evolving for millennia and influencing diverse historical groups. Despite defining them as predicated on "fundamental continuities," he remarks that "traditions are processes" and, therefore, "continually change to remain alive." However, Vansina argues that "basic views about ultimate reality, such as the existence of a single God and the central role witches [or sorcerers] play in disease" are "static basic principles" that once generally accepted "are never again put into question." MACGAFFEY, A Central African Kingdom, in: BOSTOEN and BRINKMAN (eds.), The Kongo Kingdom, p. 45; VANSINA, Paths in the Rainforests, p. 258–262.

123 DIMMENDAAL, Historical Linguistics, p. 68–69.

list analogous word forms, in both semantic and phonetic terms, found across several contemporary African Bantu languages. Second, he used these comparative series to identify and isolate regularities and propose speculative reconstructions of lexical root forms that, in theory, account for their origin.[124] Guthrie called these hypothetical reconstructions "starred forms" and argued they provide a model for why similar word forms occur today in geographically distant Bantu languages.[125] In other words, he reasoned that just as the degree of lexical similarity among Romance languages can be explained by their common origin in Vulgar Latin, the lexical similarity observed in contemporary Bantu languages can be attributed to their rootedness in a shared Proto-Bantu language or its later offshoots. According to Guthrie's theory, the wider the geographical distribution of analogous word forms, the contemporary "reflexes" of his starred forms, the deeper their roots can be situated in the past.[126] Almost universally distributed analogous word forms are explained as reflexes of Proto-Bantu roots, slightly less distributed ones as "reflexes" of later splits in the linguistic genealogical trees, like the one between "Eastern" and "Western Bantu languages," and regionally or locally distributed reflexes as proof that more recent splits generated regional branches.[127]

While Guthrie's circular method has been criticized by linguists and historians alike,[128] lexical root reconstruction remains central to the discipline of historical-comparative Bantu linguistics.[129] The online database *Bantu Lexical Reconstructions 3* (BLR3), edited by Thilo Schadeberg and Yvonne Bastin and based at the Royal Museum for Central Africa in Tervuren, Belgium, allows up-to-date research on reconstructed lexical root forms.[130] Despite some well-known caveats,[131] the widely disseminated lexical root forms strongly suggest that people had some understand-

124 Ibid.

125 Starred forms are conventionally notated in italics preceded by an asterisk and are dissimilar from any occurring word forms. Comparative series are referred to similarly, followed by the initials CS and a number. For instance, the starred forms **-kaca*, **-bondó*, and **-pomi* and the comparative series **-yábi* CS 1884 refer to the meaning "poison oracle" in different geographical areas. Vansina, Paths in the Rainforests, p. 301–302.

126 Bostoen, A Diachronic Onomasiological Approach, p. 113–158.

127 Ibid.

128 Flight, Malcolm Guthrie, p. 81–118; Schadeberg, Historical Linguistics, in: Nurse and Philippson (eds.), The Bantu Languages, p. 143–154; Whiteley, Xue and Wheeler, Revising the Bantu Tree, p. 329–348.

129 Dimmendaal, Historical Linguistics, p. 3–22, 68–69; Schadeberg, Historical Linguistics, in: Nurse and Philippson (eds.), The Bantu Languages, p. 143–154.

130 Bostoen and Bastin, Bantu Lexical Reconstruction; Bostoen, The Bantu Expansion.

131 Bostoen, Pearl Millet, p. 183–213; Ehret, History and the Testimony of Language, p. 82–104; Schoenbrun, Words, Things, and Meaning, in: Dimmendaal and Vossen (eds.), The Oxford Handbook of African Languages, p. 961–972.

ing of the 'things' or concepts they referred to during the "Bantu expansion" period, approximately 5,000 to 1,500 years ago.[132] It was from the geographic distribution of present-day words hypothetically related to a handful of lexical root forms that Vansina drew historical hypothesis about past African migrations, the relative chronology of technological breakthroughs and borrowings, and the location of centers of socio-cultural, political, and normative innovation—the hubs of his Equatorial African "traditions."[133]

For the case at hand, reconstructed lexical root forms can be used to ascertain whether José da Silva's statements about the generalized belief in the power of *feiticeiros* were grounded in something more than European prejudices and misconceptions about African superstition. In other words, the insights that Vansina's 'words and things' method provides can help us assess the credibility of Portuguese archival sources about this sensitive topic. The first step is to gather and systematize linguistic data and ethnographic evidence from contemporary societies that occupy the territories of the former Captaincies of Angola, Benguela, and their dependencies. Fortunately, Manuel Rodrigues Areia has taken care of this step.[134] Using contemporary borders as a reference, he has mapped the distribution of Bantu language terms related to three "magico-religious agents" in Angola, c. 1974: the "*adivinho*," the "*curandeiro*," and the "*feiticeiro*."[135] All of these, he remarks, operate in dialectical tension with political leaders or territorial chiefs;[136] the very variable terms of their relation are, however, beyond the scope of his work.[137] By synthesizing a considerable corpus, Rodrigues Areia concludes that in the three areas defined

---

132 Bostoen, The Bantu Expansion.

133 Vansina, Paths in the Rainforests.

134 Rodrigues de Areia, Estrutura magico-religiosa.

135 Ibid., p. 33.

136 In the Kingdom of Kongo, the Kikongo title "*mfumu tsi*" describes an office translated by Georges Balandier as "chief of the land" and by MacGaffey as "earth-chief" or "priest." These chiefs were distinguished from political leaders, having the ritual function of mediating between the living and the "*bakulu* [ancestors]." Their ritual functions differed from those of *nganga* (diviners/healers) because they depended exclusively on the mediation of ancestors to achieve their goals. Similarly, in the Kingdom of Ndongo, the Portuguese title *soba* hid the differences between *sobas* who were "*malemba dya ngola* [uncles of the *ngola*]" and those who were "*malemba dya ngundu* [uncles of the matrilineage]." As discussed in the eighth chapter, the former possessed a "relic" and symbol of power (the *ngola*), allowing them to relate to their ancestors differently. In contrast, some of the latter could possess "*malunga* [sing. *lunga*]" that allowed them to relate to territorial spirits. Balandier, Le Royaume de Kongo, p. 249; MacGaffey, A Central African Kingdom, in: Bostoen and Brinkman (eds.), The Kongo Kingdom, p. 46; Miller, Kings and Kinsmen, p. 46–47, 58–59, 63–70.

137 Rodrigues de Areia, Estrutura magico-religiosa, p. 33–34.

by Guthrie as linguistic zones H, K, and R,[138] sorcerers are structurally opposed to diviners and healers, who are believed to be able to counter their anti-social or evil powers.[139] Diviners do so by disambiguating the ultimate origin of specific evil deeds, abominations, or breakdowns of the social or moral order. Healers, on the other hand, offer therapeutic solutions, mediate atonement, or create apotropaic charms. Zone H encompasses the southwestern parts of the historical territory of the Kingdom of Kongo and most Mbundu polities during the time of Portuguese presence in Angola. Zone R includes the territories of the Ovimbundu polities that were in contact with the Captaincy of Benguela. Zone K comprises the Chokwe and other eastern groups who were part of the Mbangala Kingdom of Kasanje during the period covered in this monograph.

According to Rodrigues Areia's essay, in zone H, sorcerers are referred to by Kikongo-speaking BaKongo groups as "*ndoki* [pl. *bandoki*]," and the ritual practitioners who counter them can accumulate the functions of diviners and healers or exercise them separately, being referred to as "*nganga*" in either case.[140] The anti-social power of the "*ndoki*" is referred to as "*kindoki*."[141] According to him, the Kimbundu-speaking Mbundu adhere to the same conceptual scheme but refer to sorcerers as "*muloji* [pl. *aloji*]" and to diviners/healers as "*kimbanda* [pl. *yimbanda*],"[142] describing the power of the former as "*uanga*" and the ritual knowledge of the latter as "*umbanda*."[143] As for zone R, Rodrigues Areia concludes that the Umbundu-speaking Ovimbundu believe healers and diviners to be the same individuals, referred to as "*kimbanda*," while sorcerers are labeled "*onganga*."[144] Their anti-social power is called "*ouanga*" or "*wanga*."[145] Finally, in Zone K, Rodrigues Areia claims that the Chokwe-speaking Chokwe distinguish between the "*tahí*"

138 Initially, Guthrie proposed the delineation of fifteen linguistic zones, referred to by capital Roman letters (e.g., A, B, C, D…), as a convenient way of situating the comparative series under analysis. These zones were conceived and delineated according to geographic, not linguistic, criteria. "Western Bantu" languages were grouped in zones A, B, C, H, K, L, and R, and "Eastern Bantu" languages in zones D, E, F, G, M, N, P, and S. A sixteenth was later added in the Great Lakes region by researchers based at the Africa Museum, Tervuren: zone J. Bostoen and Bastin, Bantu Lexical Reconstruction; Flight, Malcolm Guthrie, p. 81–118.

139 Rodrigues de Areia, Estrutura magico-religiosa, p. 34.

140 Ibid., p. 34–36; Kananoja, Healing Knowledge, p. 39.

141 Rodrigues de Areia, Estrutura magico-religiosa, p. 38–39.

142 Ibid., p. 34–35; Marcussi, Uma "caça às bruxas," p. 1–27.

143 In 1642, the terms "*mulôgi* [*muloji*]" or "*molôgi* [*muloji*]" and "*üanga* [*uanga*]" were already used in Father Francesco Pacconio's (1589–1641) Kimbundu catechism to refer to "*feiticeiro*" and "*feitiços*," respectively. Pacconio, Gentio de Angola, p. 51–52, 60–61; Rodrigues de Areia, Estrutura magico-religiosa, p. 36–38.

144 Rodrigues de Areia, Estrutura magico-religiosa, p. 34, 48–54.

145 Ibid., p. 51.

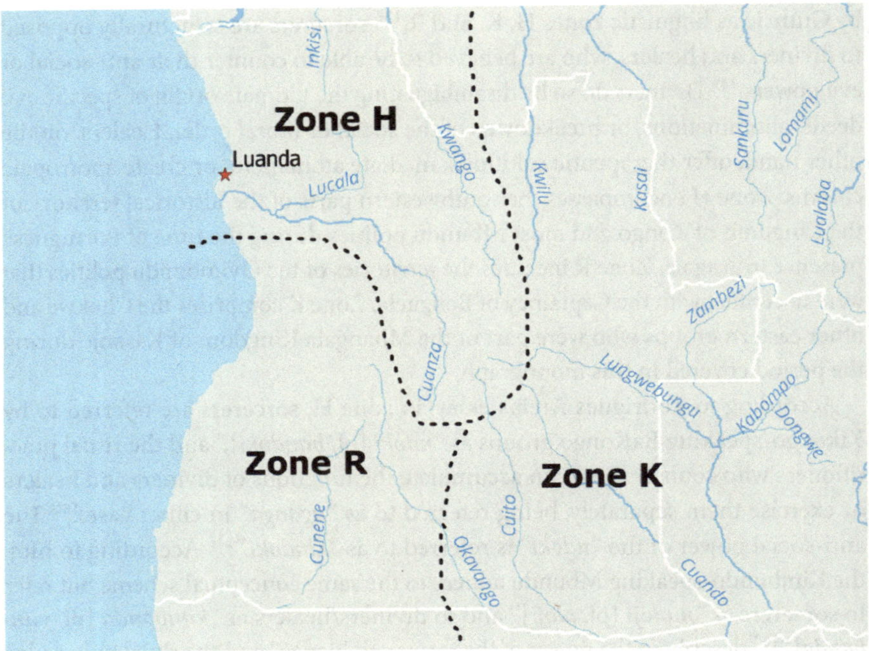

Fig. 2 Malcolm Guthrie's Fifteen Linguistic Zones H, K, and R. (Created by author with Natural Earth)

and the "*mbuke*," the former a prestigious diviner, the latter a mundane healer or surgeon, and oppose them to the anti-social "*nganga*" or sorcerer.[146] When women become healers, he remarks, the Chokwe refer to them as "*tchimbanda*" instead of *mbuke*.[147] The sorcerer's anti-social power is called "*wanga*."[148]

In *Paths in the Rainforests*, Vansina associates the terms used to describe diviners, healers, and sorcerers in the Kingdom of Kongo with Guthrie's starred forms **dogi* [witch], and comparative series *-*dòg*- [bewitch] (CS 644), *-*gàng* [to tie up] (CS 785), *-*gàngà* [religious expert/medicine man] (CS 786), *-*gàngà* [medicine/charm]

146 Rodrigues Areia makes an important caveat: while the Chokwe use the word "*nganga*" to refer to anti-social sorcerers, they refer to a series of specialized pro-social ritual operators by incorporating "*nganga*" in their titles, therefore using it in composite words with a semantic meaning like the one attributed to "*nganga*" by the BaKongo. For instance, circumcisers are referred to as "*nganga-mukanda*" and doctors as "*nganga-buka*." Portuguese and Capuchin sources suggest that the Mbundu might have done the same during the seventeenth century. Ibid., p. 41–48; Cadornega, História geral das guerras angolanas, Vol. 3; Cavazzi, Istorica descrizione de' tre' Regni Congo, Matamba et Angola.

147 Rodrigues de Areia, Estrutura magico-religiosa, p. 44.

148 Ibid., p. 48.

(CS 787) and *-*gàngà* [root] (CS 788).[149] This allows us to take the second step and project a common origin for the words related to present BaKongo beliefs into the past, proposing a model that tentatively fleshes out the traditions they were part of. Using the starred form and comparative series identified by Vansina as search parameters in BLR3, it is possible to conclude that all the designations listed by Rodrigues Areia for the BaKongo of Zone H derive from the Proto-Bantu verbs "*gàng* (tie up)," with reflexes distributed across thirteen linguistic zones, and "*dòg* (bewitch; curse)," with reflexes distributed across fifteen linguistic zones, and the Proto-Bantu name "*gàngà* (medicine-man)," with reflexes distributed across all sixteen linguistic zones.[150] This suggests that the Kikongo words for referring to diviners, healers, and sorcerers have a common origin dating back 1,500 to 5,000 years. Moreover, because the cluster of meanings they compose is predicated on the same metaphor of tying diverse elements together, the cognitive patterns associated with them are unlikely to have undergone drastic changes. Further linguistic and historical evidence suggests that this tying-up metaphor was possibly inspired by the cosmological role attributed to specific trees (e. g., the fig tree called *nsanda* in Kikongo and *mulemba* in Kimbundu [*Ficus sycomorus*]) as connectors between chthonic, watery, and celestial entities, as well as communities and their "*bakulu*" (sing. *nkulu*) [ancestors].[151] As Georges Balandier and Thornton point out, in the Kikongo-speaking areas, "*banganga*" (sing. *nganga*) are said to manipulate material elements into assemblages called "*iteke*" (sing. *kiteke*) that are capable of "capturing" or bindding "*minkisi*" (sing. *nkisi*) [spirits].[152] *Kiteke* can be anthropomorphic or

---

149 Guthrie, Comparative Bantu; Vansina, Paths in the Rainforests, p. 298–299.

150 Schadeberg and Bastin, dòg; Schadeberg and Bastin, gàngà.

151 When discussing the comparative series *-*gàngà* [medicine/charm] (CS 787) and *-*gàngà* [root] (CS 788), Vansina notes that this was a prominent association since "many medicines are made from roots." Moreover, *-*tí* [tree] (CS 1729) is closely associated by Guthrie with *-*tí* [medicine] (CS 1730) and *-*tí* [stick] (CS 1731). Note also the central cosmological role attributed to the *nsada* fig tree in the theology of the early eighteenth-century BaKongo prophet Beatriz Kimpa Vita (1684–1706). According to Thornton and Balandier, she preached that, during creation, all "blacks" had their origin in this tree, as opposed to the "whites" who originated from a white clay called "*fuma*" in Kikongo. Therefore, the *nsada* stood as a model of cosmological order, balance, and justice. Similarly, in Kinbumdu-speaking regions, the "*malemba dya ngundu* [uncles of the matrilineage]" used *nsada* trees, known in Kinbumdu as *mulemba*, to ritually access the ancestors. Balandier, Le Royaume de Kongo, p. 266; Guthrie, Comparative Bantu; Miller, Kings and Kinsmen, p. 46–48; Thornton, The Kongolese Saint Anthony, p. 160; Vansina, Paths in the Rainforests, p. 298.

152 Balandier, Le Royaume de Kongo, p. 254–255; Thornton, A History of West Central Africa, p. 45–46.

zoomorphic wooden sculptures or other compositions deemed capable of tying up or fixing spirits in place.[153]

On the other hand, as Rodrigues Areia remarks, in Zones K and R, the contemporary words "*nganga*" (Chokwe) and "*onganga*" (Umbundu), also originated from the lexical root *gàngà*, have diametrically opposite semantic meanings.[154] Moreover, the Mbundu in Zone H and the Ovimbundu in Zone R share the same word, "*kimbanda*," based on the lexical root "*bàndà* (ghost)," to describe diviner-s/healers, and the Chokwe also refer to female healers as "*tchimbanda*."[155] As for the description of the evil or anti-social power of sorcerers, despite referring to them differently, the Mbundu of Zone H and the groups from Zones R and K use the words "*uanga*" (Kimbundu), "*ouanga*" (Umbundu), and "*wanga*" (Chokwe), all arguably based on the Proto-Bantu word "*bàd* (count)," which originates from the lexical root "*bàdang* (count)" through repetition.[156] According to the BLR3 database, "*bàndà* (ghost)" has only reflexes distributed across six linguistic zones and is associated with the meaning "medicine-man" in four linguistic zones (H, K, L, and R).[157] Finally, the Proto-Bantu verb "*bàd* (to count)" has reflexes in all sixteen linguistic zones.[158] However, its semantic association with sorcery is not well attested, resting on evidence collected from languages outside of Zones H, K, and R.[159]

This data gives credence to Rodriges Areia's speculation that a more recent tradition, as opposed to the older one shared by the BaKongo, emerged from an alternative hub that influenced the Mbundu and the other groups from the southern Zones K and R.[160] According to the new tradition, the BaKongo-style *nganga* ritual operators and their herbalist knowledge and ritual practices, grounded on the tying-

---

153 Unlike Thornton, who distinguishes between "*iteke*" and "*minkisi*," Balandier and MacGaffey use the latter to describe spirits and the material assemblages they become part of. See MacGaffey on contemporary BaKongo "*minkisi*." Balandier, Le Royaume de Kongo, p. 254; MacGaffey, Aesthetics and Politics, p. 63–75; MacGaffey, Astonishment and Stickiness, p. 137–150; MacGaffey, Constructing a Kongo Identity, p. 159–180; MacGaffey, Crossing the River, in: Heintze and von Oppen (eds.), Angola on the Move, p. 221–242; MacGaffey, Fetishism Revisited, p. 172–184; MacGaffey, Franchising *Minkisi*, p. 148–157; MacGaffey, Religion and Society; MacGaffey, The Personhood of Ritual Objects, p. 45–61.

154 Rodrigues de Areia, Estrutura magico-religiosa, p. 34, 44.

155 Rodrigues de Areia, Estrutura magico-religiosa, p. 34–36, 44; Schadeberg and Bastin, bàndà.

156 Rodrigues de Areia, Estrutura magico-religiosa, p. 34–36, 45–48; Schadeberg and Bastin, bàd.

157 Schadeberg and Bastin, bàndà.

158 Schadeberg and Bastin, bàd.

159 "*Wanga*" is associated with counting or accounting, sorcery, and ache/pain in Kiswahili, a language from linguistic Zone G. TUKI, Wanga.

160 Rodrigues de Areia, Estrutura magico-religiosa, p. 45–48.

up metaphor, were associated with evil and anti-social or calculating behaviors.[161] In contrast, a new cohort of ritual operators, whose power was associated with spirit possession,[162] assumed the role of anti-sorcery experts, performing the functions of diviners and/or healers. In conclusion, based on the data gathered by Rodrigues Areia, Vansina's insights, and the BLR3 database, it is possible to argue that two parallel, conflicting African traditions existed in the territories that came to be part of the Captaincies of Angola and Benguela as well as their immediate hinterlands. Despite their differences and oppositions, which the seventh and eighth chapters explore in greater detail, the normative cluster formed by the three magico-religious agents identified by Rodrigues Areia is easily recognized and structurally stable in all the societies and groups that shared them. This lends credence to José da Silva's claims about a shared belief in the power of *feiticeiros* and *feitiços*, despite these figures and powers being referred to by different names in local languages. The question remains about what the Europeans and the Romance languages they spoke brought into the cross-cultural dialogue.

Focusing on the Portuguese side of the West Central African "cross-cultural" encounter, William Pietz argues that during the late fifteenth and early sixteenth centuries, two preexisting concepts were available to create bridges between the "radically different social orders" that came into regular contact after the first European *feitorias* were established on African shores.[163] These were the Latinate concept of *feitiço*, from which *feiticeiro* derives, and the Hellenic *ídolo*.[164] The latter term, derived from the Ancient Greek εἴδωλον [eidolon] (image, idol, double, apparition, phantom, ghost), could be straightforwardly deployed to describe the material elements of African territorial spirit shrines and representations of ancestors—the *Indelles* or *Sandes* mentioned by José da Silva.[165] Consequently, their cult was characterized by European observers as idolatry.[166] According to Pietz, this happened because figurative material elements found in these ritual spaces or in the possession of some BaKongo *nganga* and Mbundu *kimbanda* were dis-

---

161 It is worth noting that, as the fourth chapter explores, Roman Catholic priests introduced themselves in the Kingdom of Kongo as *nganga*. Later, the Jesuits uncritically adopted the Kikongo term to refer to themselves in Kimbundu-speaking former provinces of the Kingdom of Ndongo. Their militarism and association with the Atlantic slave trade might have contributed to cementing the semantic slide of *nganga* from pro-social ritual operator to anti-social, sorcerer-like ritual operator in Mbundu areas. Thornton, A History of West Central Africa, p. 86.

162 It is important to note that, on the contrary, BaKongo *banganga* did not access *bakulu* [ancestors], only manipulating spirits through *kiteke* assemblages.

163 Pietz, The Problem of the Fetish, p. 11.

164 Ibid., p. 11, 46.

165 José da Silva, Continuação da viagem ao sertão de Benguella, continuada do N.º 2.º, p. 54.

166 Bluteau, Idolatria, in: Bluteau, Vocabulario portuguez & latino, Vol. 4, p. 30–34.

cernible representations, "material signifiers referring beyond themselves."[167] The same was true of body parts (e. g., nails, hair, fur, claws, feathers, scales) that had a clear metonymical relationship to human beings and animals. Moreover, often being anthropomorphic, BaKongo *kiteke* and Mbundu ancestor figures differed from Roman Catholic statues of saints and relics only insofar as they represented unbaptized ancestors whom the Portuguese believed to be outside God's grace.[168] On the BaKongo side, this approximation was taken to an extreme during the Antonian Movement led by Beatriz Kimpa Vita (1684–1706), a precursor of later BaKongo prophetic movements, that the Portuguese brutally suppressed in 1706.[169] Amongst several other claims, which resulted in her condemnation to be burned as a heretic, Kimpa Vita demanded the veneration of "black saints" or representations of St. Anthony as a Black man, who she later claimed to embody.[170] The Portuguese elites perceived these Antonian images of Catholic saints as dangerously close to idolatrous renditions of African ancestors, having little tolerance for the continuities and ambiguity they emphasized.

The term *feitiço* has a more complex genealogy and was applied indiscriminately to describe the objects, performances, and results attributed to the actions of the ritual operators analogous to contemporary BaKongo *banganga*, Mbundu and Ovimbundu *yimbanda* or Chockwe diviners and healers as well as BaKongo *bandoki*, Mbundu *aloji*, Ovimbundo *onganga* or Chockwe *nganga* (sorcerers).[171] In other words, all three magico-religious agents who were part of the normative cluster identified by Rodrigues Areia. The activities of African diviners and healers, which differed markedly from idolatry, could be described as *feitiçaria* because their ritual performances consisted of transforming an "otherwise unconnected multiplicity" of elements "into the unity of its enduring singularity" (e. g., the *feitiço*)

---

167 Pietz, The Problem of the Fetish, p. 16.

168 Writing to his superior on January 1, 1579, the Jesuit Father Luís de Vasconcelos claims that the population of the Captaincy of Angola could be divided into three "*hominum genus* [kinds of persons]:" the Portuguese ("*Lusitanorum*") and those who came with them to trade, those who had accepted Christ and where either baptized or being catechized, and finally the "*incolarum, qui nondum Christi sacris sunt inbuti* [the inhabitants who have not yet been consecrated to Christ]." While the Portuguese had no qualms about accepting that communities were based on a tight relationship between the living and the dead, according to Father Vasconcelos' classification, unbaptized African ancestors were unredeemable others. MMA XV, D. 96; Pietz, The Problem of the Fetish, p. 35–36; Thornton, The Kongolese Saint Anthony.

169 Thornton, The Kongolese Saint Anthony.

170 Ibid.

171 Rodrigues de Areia, Estrutura magico-religiosa.

or incorporating spirits.[172] As for African sorcerers, their anti-social nature immediately approximated them with how European *feiticeiros* were framed in Canon Law and *Ius regio*, if not within the more inclusive and tolerant perspective of European folk beliefs.[173]

As Pietz argues, *feitiço*, *feitiçaria*, and *feiticeiro* all had the same Latin root, "*facticius*" or "*factitious*," an adjective formed from "*factum*" (made), the past participle of "*facere*" (to make).[174] According to him, the word form *facticius* developed in "Roman mercantile discourse" about manufactured commodities. Initially, it was employed to contrast manufactured goods with "goods produced through purely natural processes," signifying artificiality in a morally neutral manner.[175] Still, soon *facticius* came to denote "counterfeit" or "deliberately false," as opposed to genuine or unadulterated goods. Due to this second semantic value, *facticius* was adopted by the Church Fathers to adjectivize "willful alterations" of the body that were deemed unnatural, superstitious activities that damaged the soul, and non-legitimate sacramental objects.[176] All of these were understood to adulterate God's creation, but not by referring to false idols or images. By the fourteenth century, however, *feitiço* and *feitiçaria* had become topics in jurisprudence and legal doctrine, not concerns of theology or Christian dogmatics.[177] As Pietz remarks, this shift can be traced back to the publication of the *Theodosian Code* in 438.[178] Then, the normative imagination of Christian jurists and theologians was captured by the impossible task of defining "vain observances" and distinguishing between "*veneficium*" and "*maleficium*," both of which were condemned by some of the codified laws. While the second term unambiguously referred to what became known as witchcraft, the first referred to "the art of poisoning" and "sorcery exemplified by the use of herbs and magically powerful physical substances in the making of potions and philters to

---

172 As their designation's rootedness on the Proto-Bantu verb "*gàng* (tie up)" and lexical root "*bàndà* (ghost)" alludes to. PIETZ, The Problem of the Fetish, p. 16, 46–47; SCHADEBERG and BASTIN, bàndà; SCHADEBERG and BASTIN, gàngà.

173 For an overview of popular conceptions of *feitiço* and *feitiçaria* in the Black Atlantic world, see the works of Laura Mello e Souza and Luiz Mott. Daniela Calainho, Roger Sansi-Roca, and Vanicleia Silva Santos have authored more recent takes on this topic. See also the collective volume edited by Sansi-Roca and Nicolau Parés. CALAINHO, Metrópole das mandingas; MELLO E SOUZA, O diabo e a terra de Santa Cruz; MOTT, Escravidão, homossexualidade e demonologia; MOTT, Feiticeiros de Angola, p. 85–104; SANSI-ROCA and PARÉS, Sorcery in the Black Atlantic; SANSI-ROCA, Feitiço e fetiche, p. 123–153; SANTOS, Africans, Afro-Brazilians, p. 49–63; SANTOS, Bolsas de mandinga.

174 PIETZ, The Problem of the Fetish, p. 25.

175 Ibid., p. 26.

176 Ibid., p. 27–37.

177 Ibid., p. 37.

178 Ibid., p. 38–40.

achieve some specific effect on another person."[179] The semantic field of *veneficium* and the moral implications of the practices it described were thus more ambiguous than the semantic field of *maleficium*.

The distinction between *maleficium* and *veneficium* informed the *Lex Visigothorum* (642–643) of King Chindasuinth (c. 563–653) of the Visigoths, which was included in the codex his son Recceswinth (?–672) compiled and applied to all populations living under Visigothic rule.[180] After the Christian reconquest of the Iberian Peninsula, the *Lex Vesigothorum* and its technical distinction between *veneficium* and *maleficium* were revived in the *Fuero Juzgo* (1241), a codex of Castilian laws enacted by King Fernando of Castile and Toledo (1199/1201–1252).[181] About two decades later, the *Siete Partidas* (c. 1256–1265), a Castilian compilation of *Ius commune* doctrines first edited during the reign of King Alfonso X of Castile and León (1221–1284), used words derived from *facticius* to refer to forms of *veneficium* for the first time, mentioning the practice of "*fechura* [the manufacture of magical objects]," "*fechizos* [charms]" and "*fechiceros* [sorcerers]."[182] As Pietz concludes, when the *Siete Partidas* and the *Fuero Juzgo* were translated into Portuguese between 1273 and 1282, *feitiçaria*, *feitiço*, and *feiticeiro* were adopted, inheriting this complex semantic baggage.[183] By 1385, King John I of Portugal (1357–1433) used these terms in a royal charter to appease God's wrath (and counter the plague) by banishing "idolatrous sins and wicked customs" from the kingdom.[184] On March 19, 1403, he issued an enactment against "*feiticeiros*," primarily aimed at banning divination.[185] This law was compiled in the *Afonsine Ordinances* (1446) of King Afonso V (1432–1481), extant during the first Portuguese travels to West Central Africa.[186] Municipal bylaws and synodal constitutions of dioceses, such as the *Constituições* of the Archbishop of Évora (1543), further fleshed out the practices forbidden by royal enactments and ordinances under the descriptions of *feitiçaria* and *feitiço*. This normative thesaurus then informed posterior ordinances.

By the time the first ephemeral 'cross-cultural' West Central African spaces had given way to the Captaincy of Angola (c. 1576–1607), the Portuguese shared with Africans an understanding of the power of *feitiços* and *feiticeiros* that was similar to the one José da Silva attributed to his Mbundu interlopers. This is evidenced, for

179 Ibid., p. 39.
180 Ibid., p. 40.
181 Ibid., p. 40–41.
182 Ibid., p. 41; Herzog, Colonial Law, in: Tellkamp (ed.), A Companion to Early Modern Spanish Imperial Political and Social Thought, p. 115–116.
183 Pietz, The Problem of the Fetish, p. 42.
184 Ibid.; Oliveira Marques, Daily Life in Portugal, p. 227.
185 Mello e Souza, O diabo e a terra de Santa Cruz, p. 281; Pietz, The Problem of the Fetish, p. 42.
186 Pietz, The Problem of the Fetish, p. 42–43.

instance, by book 5, tit. 3 of the *Philippine Ordinances* (1603),[187] "*Dos Feiticeiros* [On sorcerers]."[188] It ordered the harshest of penalties, "*natural death*," to all those involved in stealing "*altar stones*" and "*consecrated cloths*" to use in sorcery, invoking "*diabolic spirits at crossroads*," and distributing love or hate potions.[189] Moreover, it ordered that all practices associated with divination and necromancy, such as "*seeing in water, crystals, mirrors, swords, or in any other shiny surface*" or "*guessing from the head of a dead man or animal*," were to be punished with public flogging, permanent exile to Brazil, and a 3$000 *réis* fine in favor of the denouncer.[190] When writing the first etymological dictionary of the Portuguese language, Rafael Bluteau (1638–1734) confirmed this shared understanding by defining '*feitiço*' as the "*malefic virtue*" that the "*Devil*" instilled in the charms made by European sorcerers and the "*idols*" that the "*peoples from Guinea* [Africa]" worshiped.[191] According to him, African *feitiços* could be a "*bird, a tree, a seashell, or any similar thing*," in fact, anything "*that excites the senses and captures our will*." Each African "*Province*" and "*family*" had their private *feitiço* or "*Fetiche*," and African women were adept at using them as love charms.

Considering this description and the practices singled out for prohibition in the *Philippine Ordinances* regarding sorcery, Europeans perceived no fundamental epistemological or ontological gap between Portugal and its African dominions, an outlook that Africans seem to have shared, considering that they often incorporated altar stones and material elements from Roman Catholic sacraments in their apotropaic charms[192] and worshiped Catholic images in their ancestor or territorial spirit shrines.[193] From the moment *feitiço* and *feitiçaria* provided a common ground for 'cross-cultural' understanding between Europeans and West Central Africans who shared millennial traditions where beliefs and norms associated with sorcerers, diviners, and healers constituted a stable core, new Luso-African concepts

---

187 King Philip I of Portugal (1527–1597) ordered this legal compilation during the Iberian Union (1580–1640). It superseded the *Manueline Ordinances* (1512) and was enforced in Portugal from 1603 to 1867 when the Portuguese Civil Code of 1867 was approved. Castro, Enlightened Absolutism, p. 297–298.

188 Kananoja, Healing Knowledge, p. 12; MacGaffey, Aesthetics and Politics, p. 63–75; Paiva, Bruxaria e superstição; Thornton, Religião e vida cerimonial, in: Heywood (ed.), Diáspora negra no Brasil, p. 92–95.

189 Ord. Fil., Book V, Tit. 3, § 1; Ord. Fil., Book V, Tit. 3, § 2; Ord. Fil., Book V, Tit. 3.

190 Ord. Fil., Book V, Tit. 3, § 2.

191 Bluteau, Feitiço, in: Bluteau, Vocabulario portuguez & latino, Vol. 4, p. 66.

192 Calainho, Metrópole das mandingas; Mott, Feiticeiros de Angola, p. 85–104; Sansi-Roca and Parés, Sorcery in the Black Atlantic; Sansi-Roca, The Fetish in the Lusophone Atlantic, in: Naro, Sansi-Roca, and Treece (eds.), Cultures of the Lusophone Black Atlantic, p. 19–40; Santos, Bolsas de mandinga.

193 Coimbra (ed.), Livros de "Ofícios para o Reino," p. 80, 87.

coalesced. As Pietz and Roger Sansi-Roca argue, this contact gave rise to the Creole term '*fetisso*' and then to the English "fetish" and "fetishism," the French "*féticbe*" and "*fétichisme*," and countless other European variations.[194] However, the vibrant global history of the fetish is beyond this book's scope.

1.4 Shared Beliefs Become a Source of Anxiety

Besides sharing underlying beliefs about the power of *feitiços*, during the Early Modern period, Africans and Europeans also shared an ideal of justice that was "indissociable" from "social mores" and a conception that norms should integrate "official" moral and religious principles.[195] As Nuno Camarinhas explains, according to Hespanha, this ideal was central to the "political paradigm" of the Portuguese *Antigo Regime*, structured around the Second Scholastic notion that a "Creator" God had established a "universal order" encompassing and interconnecting all beings in a tendentially harmonious whole.[196] What cemented the "kaleidoscopic" constellation of normative orders that characterized the Portuguese "*Antigo Regime*," Hespanha remarks, were several forms of love that created binding obligations and concepts such as "public utility (*publicas utilitas*)," "judicial reason (*ratio iuris*)," or "common good (*bonum communem*)" that allowed for a provisional and flexible hierarchy between normative orders to be established.[197] He concludes that it was the task of adjudicators to reach a jurisprudential and methodically deliberated decision in each concrete case presented to them, interpreting and disambiguating conflicting norms and deciding when no relevant ones existed.[198]

As for the Mbundu and Ovimbundu, according to José da Silva, as soon as they had managed, through private divination, to ascertain the ultimate cause of death of a person, they would require a "*Sova* [*soba*]" to ensure "*justice*' by having his diviner "*confirm*" or negate their findings.[199] In case both private and official divinations

---

194 Pietz, The Problem of the Fetish, II, p. 23–45; Pietz, The Problem of the Fetish, IIIa, p. 105–124; Sansi-Roca, The Fetish in the Lusophone Atlantic, in: Naro, Sansi-Roca, and Treece (eds.), Cultures of the Lusophone Black Atlantic, p. 19–40; Sansi-Roca, Feitiço e fetiche, p. 123–153; Sansi-Roca, Fetishes and Monuments; Pietz, The Problem of the Fetish; Pietz, Bosman's Guinea, p. 1–22; Pietz, The Problem of the Fetish, I, p. 5–17.

195 Wehling and Wehling, Direito e justiça, p. 9.

196 Camarinhas, Juízes e administração, p. 18–20; Hespanha, A cultura jurídica europeia, p. 62–63; Hespanha, Direito Comum e Direito Colonial, p. 95–116.

197 Chapter eight explores the implications of this fact in greater detail, foregrounding how opposing grammars of feeling clashed in West Central Africa. Hespanha, A cultura jurídica europeia, p. 149–152; Hespanha, Caleidoscópio do Antigo Regime, p. 125.

198 Hespanha, A cultura jurídica europeia, p. 152.

199 José Da Silva, Continuação da viagem ao sertão de Benguella, continuada do N.º 2.º, p. 55.

coincided, José da Silva concluded, those accused of *feitiçaria* would be "*delivered to the relatives of the deceased, to be killed or sequestered* [enslaved], *all their assets being distributed between the authors of the case, including the* [proceedings] *of the sale of the accused*" as a slave.[200] As in Portugal, where the *Philippine Ordinances* prized denouncers,[201] an easy profit could be made from a proven *feitiçaria* accusation in the Captaincy of Angola, Benguela, and their many dependencies. African and European political authorities were thus understood as responsible for maintaining and restoring a moral order in both ontologies, directly or by assisting the intervention of religious or ritual specialists. Furthermore, they were understood as deputies or indirect representatives of spiritual entities, the monotheistic Roman Catholic godhead in the Portuguese case, or the ancestors and local spirits in the African case.[202] Therefore, captain majors and ordinary judges could momentarily align with African customary practitioners when adjudicating *feitiçaria* accusations in their 'rustic' jurisdictions, and local West Central African actors came to share a common pool of practices and normative knowledge about how to handle them.[203] In the absence of a broad normative consensus based on a shared understanding of theological natural law and *Ius gentium*, an adherence to *Ius commune* doctrines, or even shared uses and customs between very diverse European and African groups, shared *feitiçaria* beliefs provided a trans-cultural point of articulation, the *feitiço* being a bridge concept that opened up political opportunities that the less scrupulous and more credulous soon explored.

As the following chapters delve into in detail, when the enlightened captain-general and governors sought to reform the administration of justice in Angola and Benguela, it became clear to them that the practices associated with sorcery beliefs and accusations were allowing the self-interested use of African uses and customs as sources of law by Portuguese captain majors, ordinary judges, and scribes.[204] Moreover, the shared belief in *feitiçaria* enabled African kings and chiefs to extend their jurisdiction and reach Portuguese subjects, as well as enslaved Africans living in Portuguese settlements and *presídios* far away from their hinterland capitals. According to the terminology of the period, these practices were framed as "abuses," stemming from individual impiousness or greed, and decried as such but seldom

200 Ibid.

201 Ord. Fil., Book V, Tit. 3, § 2.

202 Dias, Angola, in: Alexandre and Dias (eds.), O Império Africano (1825–1890), p. 329–330.

203 Honwana, Espíritos vivos; Meneses, Feitiçaria e modernidade; Sansi-Roca, Feitiço e fetiche, p. 123–153; Sansi-Roca, Fetishes and Monuments; Sansi-Roca, The Fetish in the Lusophone Atlantic, in: Naro, Sansi-Roca, and Treece (eds.), Cultures of the Lusophone Black Atlantic, p. 19–40; West, Kupilikula.

204 Santos, Entre deux Droits, p. 842–843.

punished.[205] However, as the following chapters analyze in further detail, especially after the bureaucratic reforms of the final two decades of the eighteenth century, these abuses proved to be systematic, revealing to the enlightened captain-general and governors the existence of African authorities and ritual operators who assisted the colonial administration in dealing with *feitiçaria* but stood in the way of more radical absolutist reforms and the establishment of a 'policed' government in Angola.[206] Surmounting this resistance, rather than vanquishing the adherence of an intermediary body of learned jurists and clerks to *Ius commune* doctrines or local court styles, became the focus of their reforming efforts. The underlying connection between *feitiçaria* accusations and enslavement in West Central African societies significantly hampered these efforts. As chapters four to six demonstrate, this was the case because sorcery accusations were soon coopted by profiteers involved in the Atlantic slave trade as a predatory enslaving mechanism.[207]

---

205 AHU, CU, Angola, Box 51, D. 4624.

206 Santos, Entre deux Droits, p. 817–848; Santos, Um governo "polido" para Angola; Zenker and Hoehne, Processing the Paradox, in: Zenker and Hoehne (eds.), The State and the Paradox, p. 1–40.

207 Figueiredo, Feitiçaria na Angola oitocentista, p. 21–51.

2. A Patchwork of Normative Fabrics

2.1 The Dots on the Maps

To understand the institutional and jurisdictional framework where the actions that are described in the following chapters took place, it is necessary to consider that, from the final decades of the eighteenth century until almost the middle of the nineteenth century, when the decree of December 7, 1836, first sought to reform the administrative organization of Portuguese West Central African dominions according to a territorial principle, the Captaincy of Angola consisted of six *presídios* and about nine districts.[1] The subaltern Captaincy of Benguela was split into three *presídios* (including Benguela itself) and about seven districts. Carlos Couto notes that some of these districts were only partially or nominally under Portuguese control, while others were merely "tiny hamlets." Therefore, other assessments of the number of districts have been proposed, proving that their number varies according to the criteria adopted by historians and suggesting that the number and size of actual settlements changed significantly over time. The *presídios* that constituted the Captaincy of Angola were Ambaca (1614),[2] Cambambe (1604), Encoge (1759), Massangano (1583), Muxima (1599), and Pungo Andongo (1671). The districts were the Bar of Calumbo, the Bar of Bengo, the Bar of Dande, Dande (1705), the Dembos, Golungo (1705), Icolo e Bengo, Zenza and Quilengues, and Luanda (1576), the seat of the general government of Angola.[3] As for the subaltern Captaincy of Benguela, it was composed of the *presídios* of Benguela (1617), Caconda (1680/82), and Novo Redondo (1769), and the districts of Bailundo, Bié, Dombe Grande, Galangue,[4] Huambo, Quilengues de Benguela (1781), and the Sambos.[5] Benguela was established as a separate Captaincy with an autonomous government in 1617 following the issuance of an ordinance for its governor on

---

1 Couto, Os capitães-mores em Angola, p. 102–105, 117; Ferreira, Feiras e presídios, p. 18–19.

2 Ambaca was renamed Duque de Brangança after 1839.

3 John Thornton and Linda Heywood attribute alternative dates to the establishment of Massangano, Cambambe, and Ambaca in 1582, 1602, and 1618 respectively. Ralph Delgado provides the number of slaves exported from Encoge between 1755 and 1762 (5.000 per year), suggesting that the *presídio* was established before 1759. Delgado, O governo de Sousa Coutinho em Angola III, p. 12; Heywood and Thornton, Central Africans, p. 88, 111.

4 Silva Corrêa lists Galangue as a *presídio* c. 1780. Silva Corrêa, História de Angola, Vol. 1, p. 26.

5 Couto, Os capitães-mores em Angola, p. 105, 117; Delgado, A Famosa e Histórica Benguela, p. 10; Ferreira, Feiras e Presídios, p. 18–19; Santos, Luanda, in: Brockey (ed.), Portuguese Colonial Cities in the Early Modern World, p. 254.

March 25, 1615.[6] However, after the Dutch occupation of Angola ended (1648),[7] it was administered as a regular *presídio* until 1767.[8] After 1779, the *presídio* of Benguela became the seat of a subaltern government, receiving a separate ordinance in 1796.[9]

These locations formed two unconnected networks,[10] each extending from a more densely settled Atlantic port town, Luanda and Benguela, to an unevenly occupied hinterland where dispersed slave fairs, *arimos*, Roman Catholic missions, merchant compounds, and the precarious adobe strongholds of *presídios*[11] branched out to form a loose patchwork of Portuguese or Luso-African settlements in the interior.[12] Due to the unavailability of draft animals, the expanse between these centers was traveled by foot or canoe, partially explaining the settlement pattern and the occupation of strategic positions along the navigable tracts of major rivers.[13] These navigable tracts, however, do not extend deep into the hinterlands. A mountainous plateau rises sharply after no more than a hundred kilometers from the shore, paralleling the West Central African shoreline and occasioning rapids

---

6 As noted by Carlos Couto, the decree of February 14, 1615, determined the creation of a separate government in Benguela. ANTT, MO, NU, Box 8, D. 1; Couto, Regimento de governo, p. 285; Souza, Alvará da creação do Governo p. 41–48.

7 As Filipa Ribeiro da Silva explains, the Board of Directors of the Dutch West India Company ("The Gentlemen Nineteen") had jurisdiction over the coastal regions of Angola, including Luanda and Benguela, between 1641 and 1648. Between 1641 and 1642, Dutch Angola was governed by the Central Government of the Dutch West Indies in Brazil, together with Benguela and the Dutch-occupied coasts of the Kingdoms of Loango and Kongo. In 1642, when a Southern District was created extending from Cape Lopo Gonçalves to Cape Good Hope, a separate government was created in Luanda, including two or three directors and a council. Ribeiro da Silva, Dutch and Portuguese, p. 34–36, 73.

8 Candido, An African Slaving Port; Couto, Regimento de Governo, p. 286; Delgado, O Governo de Sousa Coutinho em Angola II, p. 49–86.

9 AHU, GANG, Sr. 3, Cod. 1643, p. 59–64; Delgado, A famosa e histórica Benguela, p. 9–25; Couto, Os capitães-mores em Angola, p. 118; Couto, Regimento de governo, p. 285–294.

10 Two factors help to explain this fact. First, the South Atlantic Gyre made it challenging to sail northwards from Benguela to Luanda while facilitating the contact between Rio de Janeiro and Luanda. Second, until the early twentieth century, the Portuguese could never militarily subjugate the polities that settled in the region of Kissama and barred land communication between these two ports. Before the advent of the steam engine, it was thus more accessible for the captain-general and governor of Angola to receive news from Benguela via Rio de Janeiro. Candido, An African Slaving Port; Coutinho, Memórias do Reino de Angola, p. 189–191; Ferreira, Cross-Cultural Exchange; Silva, The Atlantic Slave Trade.

11 On December 17, 1767, Captain-General and Governor Sousa Coutinho described them as "*unfit to keep chickens*." ANTT, MR, EXP, Sr. 34, F. 605, p. 92–106.

12 Santos, Entre deux Droits, p. 817–848.

13 Santos, Luanda, in: Brockey (ed.), Portuguese Colonial Cities in the Early Modern World, p. 254–255.

and waterfalls that prevent any form of navigation.[14] As the Portuguese conquest of the Mbundu Kingdom of Ndongo progressed, the Portuguese established *presídios* next to the largest *kitanda* [pl. *itanda*, markets/fairs], hoping to secure access to slaves and control pre-existing trade routes.[15] However, as John Thornton and Linda Heywood explain, constant warfare and the intense slave-raiding practices known as "*kwata-kwata* [catch-catch]" often impacted the patterns of commerce, forcing captain-general and governors to establish new slave fairs or actively sponsor the reopening of deserted ones.[16] The reduced number of port towns resulted from geostrategy, not geography. Until the middle of the nineteenth century, the difficulty in defending Atlantic ports from European privateering and expeditionary corps justified their reduced number, which is why the Portuguese opted to expand the internal networks spreading from Luanda and Benguela instead of securing additional harbors. As Silva Corrêa put it, the Portuguese were convinced that the Dutch West India Company had been incapable of defending Luanda because it had no considerable presence in the hinterlands and could not "*mobilize the Blacks in their support*."[17] Therefore, subsequent efforts to settle Novo Redondo, Benguela a Velha (1771), and Cabo Negro (1805) with small garrisons were all motivated by the need to avoid European encroachment, with only Moçâmedes (1839), at a later date, being planned as a new Atlantic port town and entryway for the extended White settler-colonization of its hinterlands.[18]

However exhaustive, lists of names tell us little about the social and administrative organization of Portuguese West Central African dominions.[19] This is especially true when jurisdiction was understood according to the personality principle rather than the territorial one, and the porousness and extension of the borders of each socio-political unit were closely tied to the shifting military power, competence ranges, and political authority of the officers, courts, and institutions at its center. Complicating matters, the captain-general and governors of Angola and the captain majors of Angolan *presídios* and districts had jurisdiction over "vassal" Mbundu *sobas*, whose disputes they arbitrated "*according to leis gentílicas* [Gentilic laws],

---

14 Miller, Kings and Kinsmen, p. 31.

15 Cruz e Silva, As feiras do Ndongo, in: Santos (ed.), Actas do seminário, p. 405–422; Heintze, Fontes para a História de Angola, Vol. 1, p. 127.

16 Heywood and Thornton, Central Africans, p. 109–169; Pacheco, Costa and Tavares, História económico-social de Angola, p. 82–98.

17 Silva Corrêa, História de Angola, Vol. 1, p. 24–25.

18 ANTT, CLNH, Fol. 45, D. 2; Coutinho, Memórias do Reino de Angola, p. 175, 177; Delgado, O governo de Sousa Coutinho em Angola II, p. 49–86.

19 See Pedro Cardim for a historical introduction to the concept of "administration" that explains how the administration of justice, households, and municipalities was conceived during the period under consideration. Cardim, "Administração" e "governo," in: Bicalho and Ferlini (eds.), Modos de governar, p. 45–68.

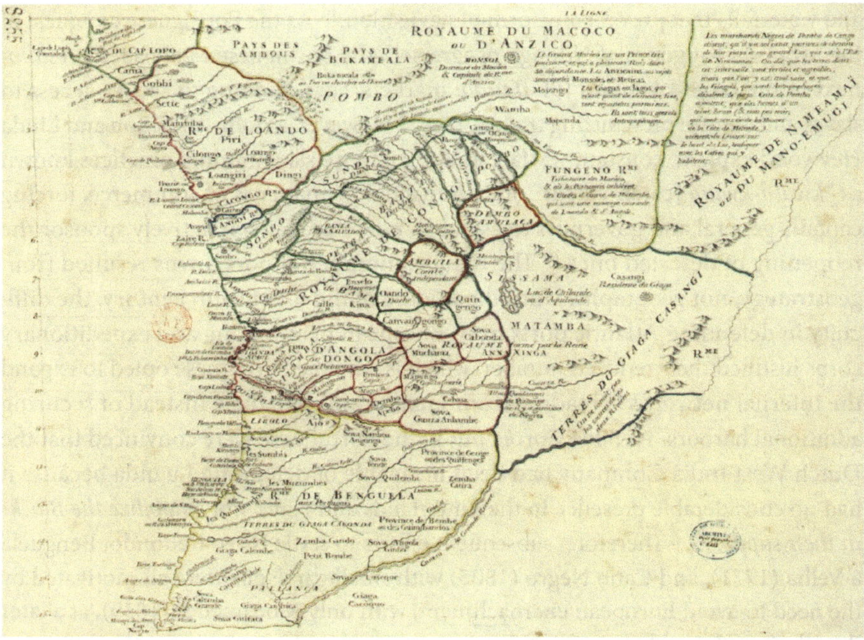

Fig. 3 Jean-Baptiste Bourguignon d'Anville's (1697–1782) *Royaumes de Loando, Congo, Angola, Benguela, c.1725* (1730). D'Anville's map depicts the Kingdoms of Kasanje, Kongo, Matamba, and Loango, Tio ("*Royaume do Macôco*"), several Dembos, and the Captainships of Angola and Benguela and their dependencies. To create this draft, d'Anville collaborated with the *estrangeirado* D. Luís da Cunha, then Envoy Extraordinary to Paris. D'Anville, *Royaumes de Loando, Congo, Angola, Benguela, c.1725* (Public Domain); Furtado, Evolving Ideas, p. 202–225.

not political ones."[20] The same was true in Benguela's "provinces," often consisting of Ovimbundu chieftainships where Luso-Africans were settled.[21] As Thornton

20 Carlos Almeida argues that the notion of "*gentio* [gentilic/gentile]" was "one of the conceptual axes that structured European thought about Africans" in areas where the agonistic pair Christian—Muslim carried no heuristic weight. According to him, in the Portuguese humanistic literature that described the first contacts with sub-Saharan Africans, "*gentios*" were defined in purely negative terms, as "neither Christians, nor Muslins, or Jews." The same negative characterization defined "gentilic laws." For an analysis of how Medieval European theology and Canon law impacted the way the encounter with 'others' was framed during the Early Modern period, see James Muldoon. Almeida, A narrativa etnográfica na literatura missionária, in: Pantoja and Thompson (eds.), Em torno de Angola, p. 25–26; Cadornega, História geral das guerras angolanas, Vol. 3, p. 238; Menezes, Memoria geografica, p. 5; MMA VIII, D. 20, p. 97; Muldoon, Popes, Lawyers, and Infidels.

21 Delgado lists 24 provinces in the late eighteenth century, including those already listed as *presídios* and districts. In a report from 1773, Sousa Coutinho suggests that the Captaincy of Angola and

describes it, the captain majors of Benguela arbitrated disputes between these provinces' "vassal" *sobas* as if they were the "principal *soba*."[22]

The free subjects of *sobados* [chieftainships] or provinces constituted most of Angola and Benguela's population.[23] In his *História geral das guerras angolanas* [General History of the Angolan Wars] (1680–1681), António de Oliveira Cadornega (1623–1690)[24] lists the African chiefs under the jurisdiction of each Portuguese authority by 1680, reminding his readers that, as "the large fish eats the small," their number, relative hierarchy, and the extension of their domains also varied greatly over time as more powerful titleholders gained ascendancy over smaller polities.[25] Furthermore, as Hespanha remarks, the distinction between "vassal" *sobas* and non-vassal ones (who could, therefore, be subjected to "just wars") was crucial, as it was contingent on shifting interests and unstable alliances.[26] The following sections focus on how the Empire's principal political and administrative institutions were locally inflected to grasp better the Portuguese patterns that marked Angola and Benguela's 'normative fabric' more permanently. As for the affective and socio-cultural construction of space, spatial attachments, and belonging, and their manifold normative implications, these dimensions will be explored in the chapters included in the second and third parts, dedicated, respectively, to the history of the caravan routes that conditioned the settlement of the Angolan hinterlands and how

---

Benguela comprised "forty provinces." However, his parameters are unclear, and it is possible that he included Rios de Senna on the East Coast of Africa. Coutinho, Memórias do Reino de Angola, p. 174–175; Delgado, O governo de Sousa Coutinho em Angola II, p. 70–71.

22 Thornton, A History of West Central Africa, p. 259–260.

23 See Maximiliano Menz and Gustavo Lopes for an estimate of each *presídio*'s population. Silva Corrêa provides a table of tithes paid by each *presídio* c. 1790, allowing for a relative comparison of their economic development (discounting their contribution to the Atlantic slave trade), as tithes were paid on harvests, cattle, and fisheries Menz and Lopes, A população do Reino de Angola, p. 1–35; Silva Corrêa, História de Angola, Vol. 1, p. 167.

24 António de Oliveira Cadornega began his career in Angola as a soldier, ascending to captain. After retiring from the military, he was elected as the ordinary judge of Massangano. He was directly involved in establishing the *Santa Casa* of Massangano in the 1660s, becoming its first *provedor*. Later in life, he moved to Luanda, where he lived for his last five years, serving as a municipal councilor. Brásio, As Misericórdias de Angola, p. 134–135; Cadornega, História geral das guerras angolanas, Vol. 1–3; Faustino, O Comércio de Escravos, p. 105–116; Heintze, António de Oliveira de Cadornega, p. 75–86; Thornton, The Art of War, p. 360–378.

25 Cadornega, História geral das guerras angolanas, Vol. 3, p. 183.

26 The former had their privileges and obligations stipulated in their "*autos de undamento*." With the latter, the Portuguese dealt with them according to a self-serving interpretation of *Ius gentium* and the doctrines of just war. Heintze, Luso-African Feudalism, p. 111–131; Hespanha, A constituição do Império Português, in: Fragoso et al. (eds.), O Antigo Regime nos trópicos, p. 170–171; Santos, Escrever o poder, in: Heintze and von Oppen (eds.), Angola on the Move, p. 173–181.

religious, cultural, and political affiliations were negotiated in the multinormative settings of West Central Africa.

2.2 Municipal Councils and Lay Brotherhoods

Of all the *presídios* and districts previously listed, only Benguela, Massangano, and Luanda had municipal councils, also called senates.[27] Municipal councils had the right to correspond directly with the monarch and were only established in populations that had achieved village status.[28] A collective body of varying size, municipal councils were usually constituted by one or two ordinary judges, several municipal councilors, a procurator, and a treasurer.[29] According to Beatrix Heintze, by the 1620s, the Municipal Council of Luanda comprised a single ordinary judge, three municipal councilors, and a procurator.[30] As further discussed in the following pages, in 1721 and 1770, the Crown introduced municipal judges in Luanda and Benguela.[31] In the case of Luanda, the municipal judge substituted the *ouvidor geral,* who had presided over the council between 1706 and 1721 (there is little evidence that the *ouvidor geral* did so in previous periods).[32] In the case of Benguela, the municipal judge substituted an *ad hoc ouvidor* appointed by and under the

27 Gastão Sousa Dias claims that Paulo Dias de Novais created the municipal council of Luanda as soon as he settled on the "hill of Luanda" because Dias de Novais' 1751 charter granted him the privilege of elevating to the status of "village" any settlement he established. However, as Arlindo Caldeira explains, we ignore the precise date of its establishment and we know little about the composition of the first councils because all municipal archives before the Dutch occupation have been lost. As for the Municipal Council of Benguela, Delgado remarks that it was established on May 1, 1771, by Pedro Nolasco Ferreira de Andrade. The Municipal Council of Massangano was established on July 18, 1658, and, as Catarina Madeira Santos remarks, had its heyday during the Dutch West India Company's occupation of Luanda (1641–1648). CALDEIRA, Dimensão sociopolítica, p. 30; DELGADO, A famosa e histórica Benguela, p. 10; DELGADO, O governo de Sousa Coutinho em Angola II, p. 58; DIAS, Os portugueses, p. 181–184; MELLO, Relação dos officios civis, p. 287; SANTOS, De "antigos conquistadores" a "angolenses," p. 256–257; TRIGO DE SOUSA, D. Francisco de Sousa Coutinho, p. 53.

28 BOXER, Portuguese Society in the Tropics, p. 142; SALGADO, Fiscais e meirinhos, p. 70.

29 Ibid., p. 69; WEHLING and WEHLING, Direito e justiça, p. 28.

30 HEINTZE, Fontes para a História de Angola, Vol. 1, p. 66.

31 CAMARINHAS, Lugares ultramarinos, p. 151; CARNEIRO, Mappa chronologico das leis, p. 536; SALGADO, Fiscais e meirinhos, p. 72.

32 ANTT, CLNH, Fol. 7, D. 1, p. 171; CALDEIRA, Dimensão sociopolítica, p. 27–59; MILLER, Way of Death, p. 548.

jurisdiction of the captain-general and governor of Angola and the *ouvidor geral* of Luanda.[33]

In the Portuguese Empire, municipal councils had judicial, legislative, and executive functions and were responsible for enforcing police regulations within their respective jurisdictions.[34] As Charles Boxer and Anthony Russel-Wood have stressed, together with lay brotherhoods, they were crucial institutions responsible for administering funds, maintaining harbors and military establishments, and celebrating annual religious feasts and festivals.[35] For its financing, the Municipal Council of Luanda relied not only on regular municipal taxes and "*fintas*" (extraordinary municipal taxes) but also on tariffs levied on imported wines and spirits, as well as the revenues generated from the export of slaves.[36] According to Boxer and Caldeira, most of its members were paid "directly or indirectly" from the profits made by exporting enslaved Africans. By 1716, the Municipal Councilors of Luanda and their direct associates had privileged access to a third of the shipping space aboard slave ships leaving the harbor.[37] The municipal council of Luanda was also responsible for branding with an R-shaped "royal mark" the African raffia cloths circulating in Angola and Benguela as currency until 1761, as official further discussed in chapters four to six.[38]

The municipal council's duties and obligations were distributed among the individual officeholders who comprised it. Every three years, usually between December 25th and January 1st, all municipal council members were elected from a local pool of *homens bons*.[39] The complex election procedure, known in the literature as the '*pelouro* system,' was tightly regulated by the *Philippine Ordinances*.[40] It is unclear how closely it was followed in West Central Africa. It involved the selection of six electors by a general assembly of *homens bons*,[41] who would then,

33 Cadornega, História geral das guerras angolanas, Vol. 3, p. 170; Delgado, O Governo de Sousa Coutinho em Angola II, p. 49–86.

34 Salgado, Fiscais e meirinhos, p. 69; Wehling and Wehling, Direito e justiça, p. 28.

35 Boxer, Portuguese Society in the Tropics, p. 141, 143–144; Ord. Fil., Book I, Tit. LXVI; Russell-Wood, Fidalgos and Philanthropists.

36 Boxer, Portuguese Society in the Tropics, p. 125; Caldeira, Dimensão sociopolítica, p. 39–43.

37 As Miller explains, this allowed them to grant the privilege of immediately shipping slaves to Luso-African merchants and associates who had paid them with *letras* backed by the sale of these slaves in Brazil. In other words, privileged access to shipping space significantly reduced the risk and, therefore, more easily secured the profit associated with investing in the slave trade. The chapters grouped in part two explore the economic aspects of the slave trade in greater detail. ANTT, CLNH, Fol. 7, D. 1, p. 204; Miller, Way of Death, p. 548.

38 Cadornega, História geral das guerras angolanas, Vol. 3, p. 195–196.

39 Salgado, Fiscais e meirinhos, p. 70.

40 Ord. Fil., Book I, Tit. LXVII.

41 In the Portuguese metropole, *homens bons* were free adult males of standing who could vote and be elected. In Angola and Benguela, this category seems to partially overlap with that of *moradores*.

in pairs, write three secret lists of candidates for all municipal positions.[42] The names mentioned in these lists would then be raffled, and those whose names were randomly selected would be appointed to serve in different roles for a year. The first two to be elected were the ordinary judges. Their jurisdictions, competence ranges, obligations, and privileges are discussed later for easier comparison with those of the captain-general and governors, municipal judges, and *ouvidores gerais*. Then, the municipal councilors were elected.[43] They also had their office regulated by the *Philippine Ordinances* and were required to convene every Wednesday and Saturday at the municipal hall.[44] Municipal councilors were involved in policing and taxing those responsible for the supply of bread[45] and meats, the construction of municipal infrastructure such as "*roads, fountains, drinking fountains, bridges, paved roads,* [and] *wells,*" and in planting trees and orchards.[46] They were also tasked with "*upholding the posturas* [municipal bylaws], *Vereações* [council rulings], *and the old customs of the city or village,*" preserving the ones they deemed reasonable and correcting those found lacking. Reunited in council with the main body of *homens bons* and the ordinary judges, municipal councilors could also propose new bylaws. If the majority approved these and they were not against the "*Fóros* [charter]" of the village or city, the new bylaws would become binding, being registered in the "*livro da Vereação* [book of municipal rulings]." Afterward, in West Central Africa, only *ouvidores* could revise these new bylaws if they found them "*harmful to the people*" or not approved according to the procedures stipulated by the *Philippine Ordinances*.[47]

It is never clear what the *Philippine Ordinances* mean when they state that the city councilors had to approve new bylaws in council with the "*homens bons que costumam andar no regimento*." Still, this passage can be interpreted as singling out only the main *homens bons* accustomed to serving in offices. Caldeira, Dimensão sociopolítica, p. 27–59; Caldeira, Luanda in the 17th Century, p. 72–104; Ord. Fil., Book I, Tit. LXVI.

42 Ord. Fil., Book I, Tit. LXVII.

43 The electoral procedures prescribed by the *Philippine Ordinances* and the *compromissos* that regulated the elections of the *Santa Casas* must be understood as a normative ideal. According to Bishop Manuel Baptista (1559–1620), appointed to the Diocese of Congo and Angola in 1609, the holders of the slave trading contract of Luanda used to "*do and undo at their pleasure the elections of the Council and the* [*Santa Casa da*] *Misericórdia, giving the offices in sale to persons without merit*." MMA VI, D. 122, p. 371.

44 Ord. Fil., Book I, Tit. LXVI.

45 In Luanda, manioc flour and beans were the staples that needed regulation. Delgado, O governo de Sousa Coutinho em Angola I, p. 22–23.

46 Ord. Fil., Book I, Tit. LXVI.

47 In the Kingdom of Portugal, *corregedores*, not *ouvidores* acting as *corregedores*, were responsible for reviewing municipal bylaws. Ibid.

The municipal council's procurator, treasurer, and scribes were elected similarly to the city councilors and ordinary judges.[48] As with the city councilors, their administrative and police functions were regulated by the *Philippine Ordinances*. The procurator was responsible for ensuring that fines were paid and for overseeing the repair of infrastructure. He could also collect money to mitigate damage caused by fires.[49] The treasurer was tasked with receiving and safeguarding the council's income.[50] In smaller places, he could be substituted by the procurator. The scribe was responsible for bookkeeping, writing the adjudications of municipal councilors in cases of injury, and swearing in the *almotacés* and minor municipal officials every month.[51] The *almotacés* were critical municipal officers responsible for imposing "*coimas* [fines]" on those who disrespected municipal bylaws or rulings, upholding the use of official weights and measures, and the regulations ordering commerce and craft associations.[52] These inspectors were appointed for a month and selected as follows: each year, the first two to serve as *almotacés* were the last two persons who had served as ordinary judges.[53] Then, the second pair of *almotacés* comprised two former city councilors, the third pair a former city councilor and the former procurator, and all subsequent teams by *homens bons* elected for this position.[54] Those fined by the inspectors could appeal to the ordinary judges, who also had the right to revise their adjudications up to $600 *réis*.[55] In cases involving higher amounts, the ordinary judges had to adjudicate appeals and revise in council with the municipal councilors. *Almotacés* were assisted by a scribe who also had the obligation to point out breaches of municipal bylaws and to check the performance of inspectors on behalf of the municipal council.[56] Finally, municipalities employed several minor, unelected officeholders responsible for policing, running infrastructure, assisting in the harbors, divulging its rulings, and capturing, transporting, and imprisoning criminals or those accused of being so. The latter included bailiffs,

48 Ord. Fil., Book I, Tit. LXVII.

49 Ord. Fil., Book I, Tit. LXIX.

50 Ord. Fil., Book I, Tit. LXX.

51 Ord. Fil., Book I, Tit. LXXI.

52 Ord. Fil., Book I, Tit. LXVII.

53 In the case of Luanda and Benguela, when the *ouvidor geral* and the captain major, respectively, served as heads of the municipal council, there is no archival evidence to suggest that they took turns serving as *almotacés*. Therefore, the allotment must have started with the last municipal councilors. Ord. Fil., Book I, Tit. LXVIII, § 11.

54 The *homens bons* who composed these pairs were appointed by the municipal council's extant members. The latter would write their names on paper and then randomly draft a team responsible for serving each month. Ord. Fil., Book I, Tit. LXVIII, § 11–§ 12.

55 Ord. Fil., Book I, Tit. LXVIII, § 2.

56 Ord. Fil., Book I, Tit. LXXII.

alcaides, *quadrilheiros*, and jailors.[57] As discussed in the following section, in Luanda and Benguela, several other minor officeholders were employed to uphold the institutions of slavery.

As Caldeira remarks, during the second half of the seventeenth century, the Municipal Council of Luanda was at the apex of its power, directly competing in influence with the captain-general and governor of Angola and asserting the jurisdiction of its members at the expense of the latter's.[58] Since September 28, 1662, its members and the *moradores* of Luanda were endowed with the same "honors, freedoms, and privileges" that the charter of the Portuguese city of Porto granted to its citizens and municipal council. In the case of council members, these privileges included the right not to be incarcerated by the captain-general and governors or *ouvidores gerais* and the right to carry weapons during the daytime. Then, on September 22, 1664, through the intervention of the senate, the monarch granted the *moradores* of Luanda privileged access to all local military, justice, and treasury minor offices.[59] In 1666, the municipal councilors managed to go so far as to expel the then-current captain-general and governor, Tristão da Cunha, and assume governance of the Captaincy of Angola for three whole years.[60] As Maria Bicalho and Nuno Monteiro note, these developments were part of an Atlantic-wide "golden age of municipal autonomy" that lasted from 1640 to c. 1704.[61] One of the aftermaths of the Portuguese Restoration War (1640–1668), this 'golden age' definitively ended when the administrative challenges posed by the Brazilian gold rush led to a wave of centralizing reforms that culminated in Luanda in the appointment of a municipal judge.[62] As discussed in the sixth section of this chapter, this judge was aligned with the Crown's interests and guided more by an empire-wide, shared normative culture influenced by the Portuguese *Ius commune* and other learned sources than the locally elected, often illiterate ordinary judges and municipal councilors.

Between 1583, when the village of Vila da Vitória de Massangano was established by Paulo Dias de Novais (1510–1589), and July 18, 1658, Massangano had

57 According to Miguel António de Mello, by 1800, the captain-general and governor of Angola appointed some of these officeholders in Benguela. The local municipal council nevertheless paid them. That was the case of the *alcaide* and the fiscal scribe. Mello, Relação dos officios civis, p. 281–293; Salgado, Fiscais e meirinhos, p. 71.

58 Caldeira, Dimensão sociopolítica, p. 27–59.

59 Ibid., p. 45.

60 See Silva Corrêa for the names of the municipal councilors who governed the Captaincy of Angola between 1667 and 1669. Caldeira, Dimensão sociopolítica, p. 27–59; Silva Corrêa, História de Angola, Vol. 1, p. 284–289.

61 Bicalho and Monteiro, As instituições civis da monarquia portuguesa, in: Palomo, Stumpf and Barreto Xavier (eds.), Monarquias ibéricas em perspectiva comparada p. 218–221.

62 Ibid.; Camarinhas, Juízes e administração, p. 122–125.

an ordinary judge and a "*public and judicial tabelião*."[63] However, António Brásio explains that it was "*customary*" for the captain major of Massangano to accumulate the office of the ordinary judge. This changed after 1658, when Captain-General and Governor João Fernandes Vieira, in office between 1654 and 1666, granted to Massangano the privilege of having a municipal council, thus electing its ordinary judge according to the '*pelouro*' system, as regulated by the *Philippine Ordinances*.[64] According to Cadornega, the "*proceedings*" of the election were then sent to the *ouvidor geral* of Angola for "*review*."[65] It took over a century for the Overseas Council to confirm this privilege on behalf of the Crown. In the meantime, the municipal councilors of Luanda often petitioned for the elimination of Massangano's municipal council, as did Captain-General and Governors António de Vasconcelos, on November 23, 1761, and Sousa Coutinho, on March 28, 1765.[66] The latter, already after the Overseas Council had finally confirmed Massangano's privileges on June 28, 1763.[67] According to Ralph Delgado, Sousa Coutinho opposed the municipal council because it "was composed of native elements," holding the prejudiced belief that they were "dedicated to spreading intrigue and discord."[68] In the end, the recognition of Massangano as a village was not framed as an acknowledgment of the size and economic development of the Portuguese settlement but as a royal act of grace to distinguish its loyalty and historical role in the resistance against the Dutch occupation of Angola.[69]

As for Benguela, its history as a municipality is more recent. According to Cadornega, by 1680, despite being the head of a separate captaincy, the *presídio* lacked basic administrative infrastructure.[70] Since 1648, when the Portuguese reconquered Benguela from the Dutch, it was headed not by a captain-general and governor but by a captain major, appointed by the captain-general and governor of Angola and confirmed by the Overseas Council.[71] Justice was "*administered by a person, referred to as an ouvidor*." His adjudications were revised and appealed to the captain-general and governor and the *ouvidor geral* of Angola. This *ad hoc ouvidor* was neither a career judge nor educated in law.[72] There was also a *provedor*

---

63 Brásio, As Misericórdias de Angola, p. 134–135.

64 Ibid.; Cadornega, História geral das guerras angolanas, Vol. 3, p. 124.

65 Cadornega, História geral das guerras angolanas, Vol. 3, p. 124.

66 Brásio, As Misericórdias de Angola, p. 146–147; Coimbra (ed.), Livros de "Ofícios para o Reino," p. 77.

67 Coimbra (ed.), Livros de "Ofícios para o Reino," p. 77.

68 See the ninth chapter for a discussion of Sousa Coutinho's racial prejudices. Delgado, O governo de Sousa Coutinho em Angola III, p. 42.

69 Ibid., p. 41–44.

70 Cadornega, História geral das guerras angolanas, Vol. 3, p. 170.

71 AHU, GANG, Sr. 3, Cod. 1643, p. 59–64; Candido, An African Slaving Port, p. 106.

72 Delgado, O governo de Sousa Coutinho em Angola II, p. 61–63.

da Real Fazenda, who accumulated the functions of *provedor*, subordinated to the *provedor* of the judicial district of Luanda, and a general treasurer and a number of scribes under the jurisdiction of the captain major of Benguela. On April 25, 1766, Sousa Coutinho created a new set of *ad hoc* offices in Benguela, the "*zeladores do bem comum* [keepers of the common good]," "*two or three men*" who were tasked with denouncing commercial abuses and the falsification of weights and measures to the captain major or the *ouvidor* of Benguela.[73] They were elected locally by an assembly of *homens bons*, confirmed by the local *ouvidor*, and had their offices regulated by a *bando*.[74] A year later, Sousa Coutinho proposed to the Crown the creation of a municipal council in Benguela, appointing a learned *ouvidor* to the *presídio* for the first time on February 3, 1767. At the beginning of 1770, he created a "*dispatch house*" to oversee the taxation of slaves and ivory at the harbor.[75] This "proto-customs house" was administered by the *ouvidor* and a merchant, the first assuming the function of *provedor da Real Fazenda* from then onwards. The municipal council of Benguela was finally established in keeping with the *Philippine Ordinances* on May 1, 1771, with the *ouvidor* assuming the position of municipal judge on April 27, 1771.[76] A year later, the first municipal infrastructure, including a "market square and an abattoir," was established. In accordance with the Ordinance of the Governor of Benguela of 1796, the municipal council was also responsible for appointing the "*salt overseer*" in charge of supervising the Crown's monopoly over the nearby salt pans.[77]

Complementing the activities of the Senate of Luanda, the *Santa Casa da Misericordia* of Luanda (1576–), the local branch of the Brotherhood of Our Lady, Mother of God, Virgin Mary of Mercy, first established in Lisbon in 1498, was the foremost charitable institution in Angola.[78] Since the first two decades of the sixteenth century, when the original *Santa Casa* of Lisbon had obtained royal patronage

---

73 ANTT, MR, EXP, Sr. 34, F. 605, p. 116–117; Coimbra (ed.), Livros de "Ofícios para o Reino," p. 92.

74 Delgado, O governo de Sousa Coutinho em Angola II, p. 58.

75 Ibid., p. 61–63.

76 Ibid., p. 58.

77 AHU, GANG, Sr. 3, Cod. 1643, p. 59–64.

78 As Lisbeth Rodrigues and Isabel dos Guimarães Sá summarize, the original *Santa Casa* was established by Queen Leonor (1458–1525), the sister of King Manuel I of Portugal, when acting as regent during her brother's trip to Spain. Together with some canons of Lisbon's cathedral, the dowager queen established this institution to assert the "crown's benevolence" in the aftermath of King Manuel's harsh measures against the Jewish and Muslim communities in 1497. Upon his return from Spain in 1498, the king promoted the creation of similar brotherhoods throughout the kingdom, a total of sixty-two being established during his reign. By 1580, 149 new *Santa Casas* had been created, 106 more by 1640, and 101 by 1834, totaling 417. Brásio, As Misericórdias de Angola, p. 106–149; Guimarães Sá and Rodrigues, Introduction, in: Guimarães Sá and Rodrigues (eds.), The Confraternities of Misericórdia, p. 3–7.

and several privileges, new branches were soon established in most Portuguese overseas dominions.[79] The *Santa Casa* of Luanda was responsible for operating and maintaining the Hospital of Luanda (1616), paying the salaries of a "learned person and a solicitor" to support destitute prisoners, and providing spiritual and material assistance to widows and orphans.[80] Furthermore, due to its philanthropic nature, the *Santa Casa* was uniquely positioned to appeal for mercy to the captain-general and governors on behalf of condemned criminals.[81] Like the municipal council of Luanda, the *Santa Casa* financed its activities by engaging in the trans-Atlantic slave trade, having been granted an annual preference on the sale of slaves in 1695.[82] A *provedor* headed it, the title given in the Portuguese Empire to office-holders responsible for the guardianship of minors, incapacitated subjects, legacies, or collective philanthropic bodies. As António Brásio remarks, the bishop of Congo and Angola and the *ouvidor geral* of Angola were often elected as *provedores* of the *Santa Casa*.[83] According to Cadornega, by 1680, the *Santa Casa* of Luanda was composed of "*about seventy brothers*," either drawn from "*the nobler*" ranks of *moradores* or "*honorable officers*."[84] *Santa Casas* differed from associations of artisans in that these corporations governed themselves according to bylaws approved by the municipal councils, whereas the former regulated their mutual assistance and charitable acts in keeping with an internal *compromisso* "based on mutual trust."[85] Therefore, these lay brotherhoods had considerable autonomy and were

---

79 Abreu, O papel das Misericórdias, p. 591–611; Brásio, As Misericórdias de Angola, p. 106–149; Guimarães Sá and Rodrigues, Introduction, in: Guimarães Sá and Rodrigues (eds.), The Confraternities of Misericórdia, p. 1–18; Russell-Wood, Fidalgos and Philanthropists, p. 18–19, 22–23.

80 Abreu, O papel das Misericórdias, p. 591–611; Brásio, As Misericórdias de Angola, p. 112; Kananoja, Healing Knowledge, p. 120–154; Russell-Wood, Fidalgos and Philanthropists.

81 Brásio, As Misericórdias de Angola, p. 109.

82 On January 29, 1695, the Crown granted to the *Santa Casa* of Luanda preference on the sale of 500 slaves per year. However, by 1699, this privilege was still not respected, and the king wrote a letter to the captain-general and governor of Angola ordering him to comply. On June 10, 1748, the preference was augmented to 700 slaves annually. Moreover, as Rodrigues remarks, in 1664, it was granted the right to receive "municipal taxes" levied "on the sale of food" for ten years. ANTT, CLNH, Fol. 7, D. 1, p. 135; Boxer, Portuguese Society in the Tropics, p. 132; Brásio, As Misericórdias de Angola, p. 118–119; Guimarães Sá and Rodrigues, Introduction, in: Guimarães Sá and Rodrigues (eds.), The Confraternities of Misericórdia, p. 70; Russell-Wood, Fidalgos and Philanthropists, p. 36.

83 Brásio, As Misericórdias de Angola, p. 106–149.

84 Cadornega, História geral das guerras angolanas, Vol. 3, p. 21.

85 Russell-Wood, Fidalgos and Philanthropists, p. 12.

entirely under the Portuguese Crown's jurisdiction, a privilege confirmed by the Council of Trent (1545–1563).[86]

While the *compromisso* of the *Santa Casa* of Luanda was likely modeled after that of the *Santa Casa* of Lisbon of 1516,[87] Cadornega's comment suggests that the institution was adapted to local constraints, as the *Santa Casa* of Lisbon was initially composed of one hundred brothers, half "noble brothers" and half "members of the mechanical trades," not seventy.[88] In accordance with the regulation of Lisbon of 1516, the *provedor* of the *Santa Casa* of Lisbon presided over a board of thirteen "*mesários* [guardians]," including himself. All were elected for a year out of the body of the brotherhood by an electoral committee of ten brothers appointed in a general meeting. The guardians included a scribe and eleven counselors, two of whom alternated serving as "*mordomos* [stewards]" for a month. It is unlikely that the *Santa Casa* of Luanda board was equally composed of twelve guardians because of the small size of the Portuguese settlement during the first years of the Captaincy of Angola when it was established. However, regardless of their number, their election probably followed the instructions provided by the *compromisso* of the *Santa Casa* of Lisbon of 1516 until the institution was secularized in 1837.[89] In Luanda, guardians often held multiple roles, including serving as municipal judges, procurators, or city councilors.[90]

From 1660, the *Santa Casa* of Luanda was forced to compete with the *Santa Casa* of Massangano for the collection of alms and providing medical assistance to the sick and injured.[91] The establishment of this second chapter of the lay brotherhood

---

86 ANTT, CLNH, Fol. 7, D. 1, p. 219–220; Guimarães Sá and Rodrigues, Introduction, in: Guimarães Sá and Rodrigues (eds.), The Confraternities of Misericórdia, p. 7.

87 The *compromissos* of new *Santas Casas* were modeled after their mother institutions. According to Russel-Wood, the "*compromisso* of Lisbon of 1516 contained nineteen chapters" and "opened with a summary of the seven spiritual and seven corporal works of charity to be practiced by all brothers." Russell-Wood, Fidalgos and Philanthropists, p. 19–20.

88 Ibid., p. 21.

89 Brásio, As Misericórdias de Angola, p. 122–136.

90 Abreu, O papel das Misericórdias, p. 591–611; Brásio, As Misericórdias de Angola, p. 106–149; Russell-Wood, Fidalgos and Philanthropists, p. 21.

91 Laurinda Abreu argues that this aggravated the first institution's financial crisis. By the middle of the eighteenth century, both *Santas Casas* were left in a disastrous state despite their privileges. As Kalle Kananoja remarks, in the case of the *Santa Casa* of Luanda, since 1693, these privileges also included the right to "approve and open the testaments of patients treated in the hospital." This privilege ensured that the legacies entrusted to the lay brotherhood were collected before other beneficiaries or the creditors of the deceased could seize them. Abreu, O papel das Misericórdias, p. 591–611; Brásio, As Misericórdias de Angola, p. 106–149; Kananoja, Healing Knowledge, p. 120–155; Russell-Wood, Fidalgos and Philanthropists, p. 36–37.

in West Central Africa was initially surrounded by scandal.[92] The brothers of Massangano initiated the process by building and operating a hospital that resorted to "local medicines," with the permission of the Chapter of Congo and Angola, then *Sede vacante*, and the *Santa Casa* of Luanda.[93] The new hospital healed the *moradores*, soldiers, and officers based in Muxima, Cambambe, Ambaca, and Pungo Andongo (after 1671).[94] When the *provedores* of the *Santa Casa* of Luanda realized that the *homens bons* of Massangano had established a new chapter of the lay brotherhood to operate the hospice, they petitioned the Crown for its prohibition.[95] Weary of losing access to the alms collected in the hinterland *presídios*, they argued that the new brotherhood lacked royal recognition and that the *Desembargo do Paço* had not confirmed the status of the village attributed to Massangano by Fernandes Vieira in 1658. While, at first, the efforts of the *provedores* succeeded, and the Overseas Council ruled against the establishment of the *Santa Casa* of Massangano in 1665, by March 15, 1676, after the municipal councilors of Massangano submitted several petitions to the Crown, this decision was revoked. The new *Santa Casa* was finally recognized, receiving royal patronage. Its *compromisso* was based on that of Luanda, but the number of its brothers and guardians was perhaps even more reduced. Lacking direct access to the revenues generated by the slave trade, by 1703, the *Santa Casa* of Massangano was in a state of significant financial decline. At this juncture, the Crown ordered the captain-general and governor of Angola to intervene, repairing the hospital and instructing its *provedor* to employ only inexpensive "local medicines."[96] This superficial intervention, however, appears to have yielded no practical results. On November 16, 1767, Sousa Coutinho, claiming the previous *provedor* had scandalously traded "a chalice and a paten for *geribita*," ordered the seizure of all the books and archives of the lay brotherhood and installed the captain major of Massangano as its de facto *provedor*.[97]

According to Brásio, a third *Santa Casa* was established in Benguela by the second half of the eighteenth century, where its lay brothers administered a military hospital.[98] Disagreeing, Kalle Kananoja argues that the *Nossa Senhora do Populo* (1765) lay brotherhood oversaw the Hospital of Benguela and that there was no

---

92 Rodrigues and Guimarães Sá claim that a third *Santa Casa* was established in São Salvador, the Christianized name of Mbanza Kongo, in 1617, but they provide no additional information about it and suggest that it might have been short-lived. Brásio, As Misericórdias de Angola, p. 134–148; Guimarães Sá and Rodrigues, Introduction, in: Guimarães Sá and Rodrigues (eds.), The Confraternities of Misericórdia, p. 3.

93 Brásio, As Misericórdias de Angola, p. 141, 145.

94 Ibid., p. 145.

95 Ibid., p. 134–148.

96 Ibid., p. 146.

97 Ibid., p. 146–147.

98 Brásio, As Misericórdias de Angola, p. 106–149; Candido, An African Slaving Port, p. 101.

Santa Casa in Benguela during this early period.[99] Contrarily to *Santas Casas*, this lay brotherhood was not under the Crown's jurisdiction, having been established by Sousa Coutinho on January 30, 1766.[100] Instead of governing itself according to a *compromisso*, the *Populo* lay brotherhood had its charter drafted by the captain-general and governor and later approved by the Crown on April 22, 1766. Therefore, it was under the jurisdiction of the *ouvidor* of Benguela, acting as *provedor*, and, after 1771, of the municipal judge who then assumed this role. In keeping with this regulation, the general board of the brotherhood consisted of a judge, a scribe, a treasurer, and several stewards responsible for ensuring the services of a doctor, surgeon, nurse, and apothecary at the hospital. Article 25 of the Ordinance of the Governor of Benguela of April 3, 1796, determined that he was responsible for ensuring that the *Populo* lay brotherhood employed the tithes collected in the district of Benguela to provide "good care for the sick."[101]

Since the *Santa Casas* were under the jurisdiction of the Crown, the medical assistance and other philanthropic activities they conducted in Luanda and Massangano were not directly controlled by the Catholic Church.[102] This gave rise to occasional jurisdictional conflicts with regular orders that administered smaller hospices and the numerous other lay brotherhoods established in these African domains, whose portfolios of charitable activities partially overlapped with those of the *Santa Casas* but remained under the jurisdiction of the bishop of Congo and Angola or the priors of religious orders.[103] In 1680, Cadornega referred to several lay brotherhoods in Angola and Benguela and their dependencies associated with churches, chapels, or the colleges of regular orders.[104] Some of these were

99 Kananoja, Healing Knowledge, p. 120–154.

100 Delgado, O governo de Sousa Coutinho em Angola II, p. 52–53.

101 AHU, GANG, Sr. 3, Cod. 1643, p. 59–64.

102 Abreu, O papel das Misericórdias, p. 593–594.

103 In keeping with Medieval Christian theology, there were fourteen works of mercy, seven corporal and seven spiritual. The corporeal were feeding the hungry, giving water to the thirsty, clothing the naked, sheltering the homeless, visiting the sick, visiting the imprisoned and ransoming the captive, and burying the dead. The spiritual included instructing the ignorant, counseling the doubtful, admonishing sinners, bearing enemies with patience, forgiving offenses, comforting the afflicted, and praying for the living and the dead. The portfolio of charitable activities sponsored by the *Santa Casas* was based on this list of fourteen works. Besides those already mentioned, they included giving "alms to the poor," burying the destitute and criminals, helping poor orphaned girls to marry, administering female retirement houses, accompanying the sentenced to the gallows, making peace between enemies, providing "occupational training for poor orphaned boys," and lending money at low interest rates. Abreu, O papel das Misericórdias, p. 591–611; Brásio, As Misericórdias de Angola, p. 106–149; Guimarães Sá and Rodrigues, Introduction, in: Guimarães Sá and Rodrigues (eds.), The Confraternities of Misericórdia, p. 11; Russell-Wood, Fidalgos and Philanthropists, p. 19–20.

104 Cadornega, História geral das guerras angolanas, Vol. 3.

composed only of Black lay brothers, such as the *Nossa Senhora do Rosário dos Homens Pretos* (1628) in Luanda. Others exclusively of White lay brothers, such as the *Nossa Senhora do Rosário dos Homens Brancos*. Most were likely mixed in their composition, especially in the hinterland *presídios*.[105] As Cadornega explains, these lay brotherhoods elected "*judges and stewards*" responsible for their administration, forwarding their charitable portfolios, assisting the brothers, and organizing religious celebrations.

2.3 *Presídios*, Districts, Military Garrisons, and Irregular Troops

Bereft of municipal councils, all *presídios* other than Benguela, Massangano, and Novo Redondo[106] were governed by a captain major. These military officers had jurisdiction as ordinary judges and disciplined their garrisons according to extant military ordinances and regulations.[107] The same was true for the districts of Dande, Golungo, Icolo e Bengo, and Galangue, where a captain major or "*captain of the moradores*" was appointed by the captain-general and governor of Angola.[108] All cases that exceeded their competence were to be sent to the *ouvidor geral* of Luanda or, in the case of the captains of Dande, Golungo, and Icolo e Bengo, to the municipal judge of Luanda (after 1721).[109] As for regents, as Silva Corrêa remarks, they had no jurisdiction, "*being fully dependent on others*."[110]

The appointment and career progression of captain majors, as well as their military duties and those of all other military officers active in Angola and Benguela, was regulated by the Ordinance of the General Inspector of the Army of August 29,

---

105 Ibid., p. 21–22, 118–122; Fonseca, Religião e liberdade, p. 70; Pereira and Henriques, História do Mutualismo, p. 42–44.

106 A regent headed Novo Redondo since its establishment.

107 Extant military laws were the Ordinance of the Captain-Majors of December 10, 1570, the Provision about the Ordinances of May 15, 1574, and the Ordinance of the Frontiers of August 29, 1645, *inter alia*. In the case of Luanda, the ordinances of the captain-general and governors of Angola also regulated some disciplinary aspects of military life. Finally, the *Philippine Ordinances* regulated the jurisdiction of ship captains sent to Africa. Book 2, tit. 47 stipulated that the "*Captains, sent by Us to our places in Africa*" when adjudicating "*crimes committed in those places*" had the competence to condemn up to, but not including, "*death and the cutting of limbs*" without appeal. In cases with penalties of death and the cutting of limbs, they had to concede an appeal to an *ouvidor*, except in cases of treason, sodomy, theft, stealing a ship, disrespecting royal protection, or jumping walls with ill intent. AHM, Div, PcE, CGR, Box 1, D. 1; AHM, Div, SENEG, Box 3, D. 31; AHU, CU, Angola, Box 51, D. 4624; Ord. Fil., Book II, Tit. XLVII; Regimento do Governo deste Reyno; Regimento dos capitães móres.

108 ANTT, CLNH, Fol. 49, D. 12, Fol. 52, D. 126; Silva Corrêa, História de Angola, Vol. 1, p. 26.

109 AHU, CU, Angola, Box 51, D. 4624; Mello, Relação dos officios civis, p. 281–293.

110 ANTT, CLNH, Fol. 49, D. 12.

1645, known as the Ordinance of the Frontiers.[111] Captain majors and most regents[112] were appointed for three years, at the end of which the former had to undergo a "*residência* [terminal review]" to be readmitted into a military career.[113] This practice was first instituted in the Ordinance of Tristão da Cunha (1666).[114] According to it, the captain-general and governor of Angola was supposed to appoint an "*idoneous*" person to review the performance of captain majors and a scribe from one of the *presídios* to write the terminal reviews and send them to the Overseas Council. The Council would then approve the readmission of each captain major or condemn him for his faults and abuses. However, by 1676, the Crown had recognized that no terminal review had yet reached the Overseas Council.[115] Therefore, the Ordinance of the Government of the Kingdom of Angola of 1676 stipulated that terminal reviews were to be adjudicated locally by the captain-general and governor and the *ouvidor geral*, with the possibility of appeal to the Overseas Council. This was regular practice until 1761. At that point, the *Junta de Justiça* [Justice Board] of Luanda assumed the function of adjudicating terminal reviews.[116] As Couto describes, they were usually elaborated by the lieutenants or *alferez* [ensigns] of the *presídios*, with most witnesses being close associates of the captain majors under correction. To avoid the inevitable irregularities and abuses that resulted from this, a ministerial letter from August 12, 1782, decreed that the newly appointed captain majors were responsible for composing the terminal reviews of their predecessors. Finally, until April 7, 1721, captain-general and governors often promoted irregular "inquiries" about the performance of individual captain majors, using these inquiries as a pretext to substitute them. However, a royal letter from this date forbade them from promoting "*inquiries of captain majors subject to terminal reviews*."

On February 24, 1765, Sousa Coutinho issued an ordinance regulating captain majors' administration of justice, abrogating all previous ordinances and uses and customs contrary to its articles.[117] This ordinance innovated because it aspired to standardize duties and obligations hitherto casuistically framed and enumerated

111 Regimento do Governo deste Reyno; AHM, Div, PcE, CGR, Box 1, D. 1; Provizão sobre a forma, p. 303–304; Regimento das Fronteiras, p. 305–308.

112 According to Dias, by 1840, the regents of the Bars of Calumbo, Bengo, and Dande were appointed for life. Dias, Angola, in: Alexandre and Dias (eds.), O Império Africano (1825–1890), p. 319–556.

113 Couto, Os capitães-mores em Angola, p. 91–98.

114 Boletim do Conselho Ultramarino. Legislação antiga (1446–1754), Vol. 1, p. 296–307.

115 Regimento do governo deste Reyno.

116 Couto, Os capitães-mores em Angola, p. 93–98.

117 AHU, CU, Angola, Box 51, D. 4624.

in the personal orders that captain majors received when appointed to their specific jurisdictions.[118] In keeping with this, captain majors were also supposed to denounce the abuses of parish priests, vicars forane, and apostolic visitors to the captain-general and governor of Angola.[119] They were also responsible for overseeing the payment of soldiers by the *almoxarife da Real Fazenda*, preventing the sale of contraband, safekeeping ammunition and gunpowder, distributing land for agricultural purposes, and registering all royal enactments and orders in a book so that their successors would have access to them. Furthermore, captain majors were supposed to collaborate in the collection of tithes by assisting and overseeing the work of tithe collectors,[120] incentivize agriculture, persecute the false imprisonment of free subjects and the non-sanctioned taking of prizes, and cooperate with the municipal judges and *ouvidores gerais* who required their assistance in connection with specific inquiries.[121] Finally, Sousa Coutinho restated that captain majors had the competence ranges determined by the *Philippine Ordinances* when acting as ordinary judges.[122] Accordingly, they could adjudicate claims concerning goods and movable properties worth less than $400 *réis* orally, but all others were to be mediated in writing with the aid of scribes. Three subordinate military officers aided captain majors in their administrative and military duties, often recruited either from the local pool of *degredados* exiled to Portuguese West Central Africa or from the ranks of *moradores*.[123]

As Couto remarks, a critical distinction between *presídios* and districts was that the captain-general and governors of Angola had the right to appoint and substitute the captain majors and regents in charge of districts.[124] In contrast, the Overseas Council appointed the captain majors who governed *presídios* on

---

118 Delgado, O governo de Sousa Coutinho em Angola I, p. 25–28; Rau, Prefácio. O "Livro de Rezão," p. 16.

119 In keeping with the ordinance, these were quite common, as clerics often extorted one or several slaves to "right the wrongs committed" by their parishioners. AHU, CU, Angola, Box 51, D. 4624.

120 As Silva Corrêa informs, in districts and *presídios* where the tax farming of tithes was not auctioned, captain majors were responsible for it. In this case, they received 12% of the collected income. This happened only in jurisdictions with no garrison, where captain majors had no fixed stipend. Abuses were common. Silva Corrêa, História de Angola, Vol. 1.

121 AHU, CU, Angola, Box 51, D. 4624.

122 These competence ranges are discussed below when considering the ordinary judge of Massangano. Ibid.

123 John Harvey remarks that at the turn of the seventeenth century, the majority or totality of the soldiers who accompanied the new captain-general and governors to Angola were *degredados*. Couto, Os capitães-mores em Angola, p. 70–71; Harvey, Politics, Commerce, and Colonization, p. 31–32; Mello, Relação dos officios civis, p. 281–293; Mello, Relatorio do governo, p. 549.

124 The royal edict of November 19, 1761, granted this privilege to the captain-general and governors. Couto, Os capitães-mores em Angola, p. 54.

behalf of the Portuguese Crown.[125] Therefore, they could not be substituted by the captain-generals and governors.[126] Furthermore, according to Couto, only the latter received a fixed stipend.[127] Since 1720, when a law of August 29 barred them from any commercial activities, this stipend was raised to 300$000 *réis* yearly.[128] Those in charge of districts were forced to make do with the emoluments they received as ordinary judges.[129] As Miguel António de Mello pointed out in 1800, this distinction led to numerous cases of "abuse" as economically precarious captain majors were incentivized to adjudicate as many cases as possible. As further discussed in the seventh and eighth chapters, this included captain majors adjudicating several kinds of *mucanos* according to Mbundu or Ovimbundu norms and arbitration styles.[130]

For each *presídio*, the captain-general and governor of Angola appointed an *almoxarife da Real Fazenda* and a scribe; the former served for a year, while the latter served for an unspecified term.[131] While the *almoxarife da Real Fazenda* received a fixed stipend paid by the general government, the scribes earned small, fixed amounts. Still, they could charge emoluments for their services, putting them in the same uncertain economic position as captain majors in charge of districts.[132] They were under the jurisdiction of Luanda's *provedor da Real Fazenda*, who revised their decisions.[133] In keeping with Sousa Coutinho's Ordinance of February 24, 1765, the scribes of *presídios* accumulated functions such as that of the scribes of the

---

125 Ibid.

126 ANTT, CLNH, Fol. 7, D. 1, p. 214.

127 Couto, Os capitães-mores em Angola, p. 54.

128 Silva Corrêa noted that this prohibition was ineffective, as captain majors figured out several ways to continue trading in slaves. Silva Corrêa, História de Angola, Vol. 1, p. 36–37.

129 Mello, Relação dos officios civis, p. 281–293.

130 The adjudication of *mucanos* was not wholly barred to captain majors. As discussed below, and in the chapters in part three, they were allowed to judge *mucanos* classified as "*freedom cases*" and disputes between *sobas*. In the former case, they were assisted by a "*scribe of freedoms*," and their decisions could be appealed to the captain-general and governor of Angola or, in the case of the districts and *presídios* of Benguela, to the subaltern governor. Mello, Carta de oficio do Governador; Santos, Esclavage africain, p. 127–148; Silva Corrêa, História de Angola, Vol. 1, p. 94.

131 Sousa Coutinho's Ordinance of February 24, 1765, stipulated that captain majors were the ones selecting the *almoxarifes da Real Fazenda* of their *presídios*. However, by 1800, Mello stated that the general government was responsible for paying their stipends, suggesting that the captain-general and governor of Angola intervened in their appointment or at least confirmed the choices of the captain majors. AHU, CU, Angola, Box 51, D. 4624; Mello, Relação dos officios civis, p. 285–286.

132 The precise amounts scribes could charge for their services were detailed by the Ordinance of February 24, 1765. AHU, CU, Angola, Box 51, D. 4624; Mello, Relação dos officios civis, p. 285–286.

133 Camarinhas, Juízes e administração, p. 105.

judges of orphans of the *presídios*, overseen by the *provedor* of the judicial district in Luanda.[134]

In keeping with a royal enactment from April 5, 1666, Luanda was to be garrisoned by eight companies, comprising a total of 800 soldiers. Benguela, by a company of 100 soldiers, and the *presídios* of Ambaca, Cambambe, Massangano, and Muxima by 25 soldiers, their garrisons composing a single company.[135] Besides these regular troops, a royal enactment from January 29, 1695, ordered the creation of 17 irregular companies of militias known as "*ordenanças*," including a "*terço* [regiment]" in Luanda, composed of the able-bodied *moradores* of the Captaincy and its dependencies.[136] During the tenure of Sousa Coutinho as captain-general and governor of Angola, the companies of regular troops were rebranded as "first-line" companies, the *ordenanças* and the irregular Africans regiments were rebranded as "third-line" companies, and a series of twenty "second-line" companies were projected to be distributed across the hinterlands.[137] This ambitious plan presupposed the existence of one first-line regiment, one cavalry squadron, and one artillery squadron in Luanda, four first-line companies and an artillery squadron in Benguela (100 men), four first-line companies in the garrisoned *presídios* (60 men each), and one artillery squadron in Caconda. These were to be assisted by a second-line regiment in Luanda, eight second-line companies in Ambaca, twenty second-line companies distributed amongst the other *presídios*, and the abovementioned third-line *ordenanças*.

However, by the final years of the eighteenth century, when Captain-General and Governor Mello attempted to reform the military administration of the Captaincy, the reality he faced was quite different.[138] As Silva Corrêa remarked, Luanda's five fortresses were always half-garrisoned, and, he stated with great irony, whenever reinforcements arrived, half of them immediately died.[139] The same was true regarding the two artillery companies that had been established in Luanda since Sousa Coutinho's time. By 1784, they had been reduced to one company, manning six

134 AHU, CU, Angola, Box 51, D. 4624.

135 Provizão da reformação da infantaria, p. 309–311.

136 Bernardino, A defesa de Angola, p. 405.

137 Ibid., p. 406.

138 Mello, Plano para a organização, p. 189–254.

139 According to Couto, by 1754, Luanda was garrisoned by 361 infantrymen, 105 cavalrymen, and 61 artillerymen, including both soldiers and officers. On June 30, 1765, Sousa Coutinho informed the secretary of state of the overseas and the navy that Luanda was garrisoned by 420 foot soldiers, half of which were "always sick or recovering," an artillery company manned by 80 *degradados* from Brazil, and two cavalry companies composed of 75 cavalrymen and 40 horses. Couto remarks that by 1773, the infantrymen were up to 476 and cavalrymen to 136. Coimbra (ed.), Livros de "Ofícios para o Reino," p. 79; Couto, Os capitães-mores em Angola; Silva Corrêa, História de Angola, Vol. 1, p. 94.

artillery pieces.[140] A first-line infantry company of 130 men garrisoned Benguela, often reduced to as few as 50 recovering soldiers, as well as an artillery company and two second-line "*Terços de Henriques* [Henriques battalions]."[141] As Roquinaldo Ferreira clarifies, the *Henriques* battalions were modeled after a famous all-Black regiment from Bahia that was essential for the Portuguese reconquest of Brazil from the Dutch West India Company in 1654.[142] In keeping with the Ordinance of the Governor of Benguela, the *Henriques* were tasked with defending its shores against smugglers, pirates, and foreign invaders.[143] Ferreira adds that they also assisted in recruiting non-regular troops and pursuing runaway slaves.[144] By 1834, Joaquim Menezes claimed that the only *Henriques* left were the officers.[145] The first and second-line garrisons of the *presídios* likely suffered even worse fluctuations due to their insalubrity, inadequate logistics, and poor healthcare. As for the districts, none had a permanent garrison, and most lacked even an adobe fortification. They could be either governed by a captain major or by a regent, as was the case of Zenza and Quilengues, and the districts situated by the bars of major rivers (the Calumbo, the Bengo, also known as Zenza, and the Dande).[146] An *ad hoc* "*sergeant major*" or "*captain of the moradores*" organized the third-line militias in these places.[147]

Salaried first-line companies and Luso-African *moradores*' militias, however, constituted a tiny percentage of the contingents of *presídios* and Portuguese armies. Silva Corrêa claimed that *presídios* were usually garrisoned by very small companies regardless of what official documents state.[148] These were composed almost entirely of Mbangala mercenaries, *quimbares*, and *empacasseiros*.[149] These groups were mo-

---

140 A document from c. 1768 lists the members of the four third-line companies that composed the regiment of *ordenanças* of Luanda. Two officers and two sergeants commanded each, consisting of 43 members (except for the fourth one, which included 35 non-disabled members and nine unfit for service). These included fishermen, lawyers, solicitors, shoemakers, tavern owners, and all active men. No information is given about their health status. ANTT, MR, EXP, Sr. 34, F. 605, p. 190–201; Silva Corrêa, História de Angola, Vol. 1, p. 94.

141 AHU, CU, Angola, Box 90, D. 7125; Delgado, O Governo de Sousa Coutinho em Angola II, p. 51; Menezes, Memoria geografica, p. 9.

142 Ferreira, Cross-Cultural Exchange, p. 207–208.

143 AHU, GANG, Sr. 3, Cod. 1643, p. 59–64.

144 Ferreira, Cross-Cultural Exchange, p. 207–208.

145 Menezes, Memoria geografica, p. 9.

146 Couto, Os capitães-mores em Angola, p. 115; Mello, Relação dos officios civis, p. 281–293.

147 Cadornega, História geral das guerras angolanas, Vol. 3, p. 30.

148 For a survey of the garrisons and military supplies of the *presídios* of Ambaca, Benguela, Caconda, Cambambe, Massangano, Muxima, and Pungo Andongo between 1684 and 1729, see Harvey. Harvey, Politics, Commerce, and Colonization, p. 21–29; Silva Corrêa, História de Angola, Vol. 1, p. 69–74.

149 Couto, Os capitães-mores em Angola, p. 256–261, 280; Thornton, The Art of War, p. 360–378; Valdez, Six Years of a Traveller's Life, Vol. 2, p. 110.

bilized, disciplined, and rewarded in accordance with African norms, Luso-African military practices, and local uses and customs. Similarly, large corps or companies of second-line "*guerra preta*" soldiers and Black militiamen were mobilized during wartime.[150] In the third volume of *General History of the Angolan Wars*, Cadornega explains that each Mbundu company of *guerra preta* was captained by an officer designated "*Quilamba*," and that several *quilambas* or larger corps were headed by a "*Golambole*," the equivalent of a "*general*."[151] As for the Mbangala, he remarked that their "*songos* [regiments]" were headed by "*quilambas*" or "*Macotas*" and that their "*captain-general*" was called "*Quiambole*."[152] Finally, Cadornega explains that the *empacasseiros* were auxiliary troops who derived prestige from their skill as large game hunters.[153] When describing each *presídio* and district, the *General History of the Angolan Wars* lists the *quilambas* and Mbangala warbands their captain majors could rally, providing a more accurate assessment of their relative military importance than the Portuguese royal decrees and personnel charts.[154]

A century later, Silva Corrêa described how expeditionary armies were raised in the hinterlands of Angola in the second half of the eighteenth century.[155] As he put it, first, the commanders would request from the captain major of *presídios* a list of possible conscripts, considering the *sobas* under their jurisdiction and the number of soldiers that should be kept in reserve to secure commerce. Then, ambassadors would be sent to independent *sobas*, presenting the motives of the upcoming war, enticing them with the prospect of looting, and requesting troops. In reply to this message, it was customary for *sobas* to offer the commander a tribute called "*Ganda*," consisting of "*one, two, or more slaves*." Silva Corrêa claimed that less scrupulous commanders also pressed "*the moradores of presídios, whites, pardos, and blacks*" for recruits, accepting bribes of "*cabeças, clocks, belt buckles, or golden rapiers, cutlery, or jewels*" to exempt them of this contribution. Then, the commander would assemble the "*jagas*" elected by the Mbangala warbands to "*administer justice, defend their people, and assist the whites*," accepting their "*sacred oath of loyalty*" as they joined the expeditionary army. According to Silva Corrêa, each "*jaga's*" army was divided into "*companies commanded by Macotas subordinated to a Golambole,*

---

150 Cruz, Militates e militarização no Reino de Angola.

151 Cadornega, História geral das guerras angolanas, Vol. 3, p. 30, 247.

152 Ibid., p. 58, 159, 164–165, 400.

153 Ibid., p. 345; Miller, Kings and Kinsmen, p. 160; Valdez, Six Years of a Traveller's Life, Vol. 2, p. 110.

154 Ambaca was the *presídio* with "*the largest number of quilambas in its term and garrison*." Furthermore, it could mobilize a "*jaga*" or Mbangala warband, "*Jaga Cabucu e Calanda*." Therefore, as Cadornega remarks, it was in Ambaca that the most prominent "*guerra preta*" corps was assembled Cadornega, História geral das guerras angolanas, Vol. 3, p. 244.

155 Silva Corrêa, História de Angola, Vol. 2, p. 48–61.

which equals a Major." Then, the commander would assemble the "*corporations of Quilambas*," an office Silva Corrêa translates as "*Corporal*." The "squadrons" led by each *quilamba* comprised "*great warriors*" that "*used rifles*" and practiced warfare as a "*trade*"—the "*Empacasseiros*."[156] Finally, the commander would accept several groups of "*Quimbares*" as freelancers. According to Silva Corrêa, the militias gathered at the *presídios* were a contingent called "*Guerra preta*." A captain major led these. The army was completed with a "*considerable*" number of porters carrying cloths for currency, ammunition, medicine, portable altars, and rations.[157]

2.4 Captain-General and Governors, Subaltern Governors, and Government Secretaries

Once the Portuguese Crown dismantled the hereditary Captaincy of Angola, which lasted from c. 1571 to 1592–93, the captain-general and governors of Angola were the highest civil and military authorities of the West Central African conquest.[158] To understand the complex institutional and 'normative fabric' that conditioned their actions, it is vital to comment on the distinctive system that Paulo Dias de Novais, the first *donatário* or title holder of the hereditary captaincy of Angola, had set in place.[159] During the hereditary captaincy period, a donation charter from September 19, 1571, granted to Dias de Novais seigneurial rights over a poorly defined stretch of land south of the Kwanza River.[160] North of the Kwanza,

156 See chapters seven and eight for more information about *empacasseiros* and daily life in Luso-African garrisons and military camps.

157 According to Silva Corrêa, the Mbangala assumed the vanguard during battles, followed by some *empacasseiro* squads. After them marched the captain major of the *guerra preta*, the artillery, and half of the first-line soldiers. The porters carrying munitions would be in the center, followed by the other half of the first-line soldiers. The rearguard would be composed of *empacasseiro* squads and the other porters. The remaining *empacasseiros* and a cavalry force of up to twenty equestrians guarded the flanks. Silva Corrêa adds that merchants usually followed these armies, buying captive slaves and cattle as soon as possible. One-fifth of the slaves and cattle were paid as tax to the Crown (the 'Royal Fifth'), but *ganda* gifts were not tributed. Silva Corrêa, História de Angola, Vol. 2, p. 51–52.

158 Alencastro, O trato dos viventes, p. 13–14; Caetano, As reformas pombalinas, in: Baião, Cidade and Murias (eds.), História da expansão portuguesa no mundo, Vol. 3, p. 254; Carvalho, Os homens do Rei em Angola; Hespanha, A constituição do Império Português, in: Fragoso et al. (eds.), O Antigo Regime nos trópicos, p. 174–177; Regimento do governo deste reyno.

159 Amaral, O consulado de Paulo Dias de Novais, p. 225–235.

160 See Ilídio do Amaral for a comparison between Dias de Novais' donation charter and those that established the captaincies of Brazil and the Atlantic islands during the previous century. Amaral, O consulado de Paulo Dias de Novais, p. 50–54; Carta de doação a Paulo Dias de Navais, p. 451–462; Heintze, Luso-African Feudalism, p. 111–131; Heywood and Thornton, Central Africans, p. 83.

Portuguese conquests were under the direct jurisdiction of the Crown, and Dias de Novais acted merely as governor.[161] As Ilídio do Amaral explains, this meant that Dias de Novais' conquests south of the Kwanza River would become his "*reguengos* [private estate]," analogous to the lands personally owned by the king, as opposed to those owned by the Crown or the State, being transmitted according to the inheritance regulations stipulated in the donation charter.[162] North of the same river, Dias de Novais was supposed to act as *sesmeiro*, the distributor of *sesmarias* [land grants], in keeping with the regulations laid down by the donation charter.[163] However, as Amaral points out, although the *sesmaria* system, developed in Portugal during the late fourteenth century, worked well in Brazil, it was not readily adaptable to the social and economic reality of the territories conquered from the Kingdom of Ndongo.

The *sesmaria* system had been created to ensure that abandoned or underused lands ('*terras devolutas*') were cultivated in Portugal, thus seeking to end recurring food shortages. *Sesmarias* were regulated by the *Manueline Ordinances* (1512–1603), which stipulated that only neglected estates could be granted in *sesmaria* and only after the *sesmeiros* sought to contact their previous holders and ensured that they had a year either to put the land and estates to good use or sell them.[164] The grant transferred the *dominium utile* of the land to the receiver, while the Crown retained the right to revoke the *sesmaria* if no improvements were made.[165] According to Dias de Novais' donation charter, those who received *sesmarias* from his hands were exempt from paying all contributions except the religious tithe and could concede smaller *aforamentos* [land leases] to the *moradores* who wished to settle in their land grants.[166] As *foreiros*, the latter would gain *dominium utile* over their small plots and a 'bundle of rights' over some of their contents (e. g., rivers, woods,

---

161 Carta de doação a Paulo Dias de Navais, p. 451–462; Heywood and Thornton, Central Africans, p. 83.

162 Amaral also explores how these regulations differed from the general principles laid down by the '*Lei Mental*' of April 8, 1434, and to what extent the inheritance of the whole captaincy was conceived in terms similar to those of the *morgados* [entailed estates]. Amaral, O consulado de Paulo Dias de Novais, p. 61–62, 216–217.

163 Dias de Novais was barred from granting *sesmarias* "*either to himself or his wife*" or his *morgados*: the first-born male successors who inherited his *reguengos* and entailed estates. He was allowed to grant *semarias* to his other children. On the *Law of Sesmarias* (1375) and its inspiration from the Roman institution of emphyteusis, see Lauren Benton and Manoela Pedroza. Benton, Possessing Empire, in: Belmessous (ed.), Native Claims, p. 24; Carta de doação a Paulo Dias de Navais, p. 451–462; Pedroza, Archaic Institutions, p. 22–44.

164 Amaral, O consulado de Paulo Dias de Novais, p. 216–218; Pedroza, Archaic Institutions, p. 29.

165 Pedroza, Archaic Institutions, p. 29.

166 Amaral, O consulado de Paulo Dias de Novais, p. 218–221; Carta de doação a Paulo Dias de Navais, p. 451–462.

wild game).[167] At the same time, the former received a *foro* [rent] in compensation, keeping the rights over their *sesmaria* conceded by the Crown and having the final say if the *foreiros* sought to alienate their leases or failed to pay the rent for more than three consecutive years or four non-consecutive ones. *Foreiros* were barred from interfering with the functioning of markets and slave fairs and, as the *sesmeiros*, could have their *dominium utile* revoked if they failed to occupy and develop their plots.[168] The problem with this landowning system, Amaral remarks, was that Mbundu lands were already cultivated and economically explored, so there was no legal basis for *sesmarias* to be granted.[169]

Aware of this limitation and familiar with Mbundu uses and customs, shortly after returning to West Central Africa in 1575, Dias de Novais developed a form of rule known in the historical literature as the '*amos* [lordships]' system.[170] Adapting the Portuguese system of emphyteusis to local institutions[171] geared towards enabling the accumulation of "wealth in people,"[172] it consisted of the *donatário* offering the vassalage of Mbundu *sobas* defeated in battle to Portuguese nobles and Jesuit priests.[173] The *sobas* were then obliged to pay '*baculamentos* [tributes]' and several other minor tributes to their new lords or protectors, equivalent to the ones previously paid to the *ngola* of the Kingdom of Ndongo.[174] Contrary to *sesmarias*

167 Pedroza, Archaic Institutions, p. 29.

168 Fernão de Sousa's Ordinance of March 20, 1624, stipulated that the captain-general and governor was responsible for distributing plots to the longer-established *moradores* who had been hitherto forced to pay rent for their housing. The ordinance regulated that the *moradores* had three years to occupy the plots and build their houses or risk losing them. Amaral, O consulado de Paulo Dias de Novais, p. 245–246; Heintze, Fontes para a História de Angola, Vol. 1, p. 148.

169 Amaral, O consulado de Paulo Dias de Novais, p. 218–222.

170 For a comparison between the *amos* system and the *encomiendas* system in Spanish South America, see Amaral. Ibid., p. 235–237; Heintze, Luso-African Feudalism, p. 111–131; Heywood and Thornton, Central Africans, p. 101–102.

171 In Father Fernão Guerreiro's yearly digest of Jesuit activities for the period 1600–1603, the *amos* system is described as "*in keeping with the custom of those people.*" According to the Jesuit missionaries who informed Father Guerreiro, "*if a soba was subjected, the first thing he did was immediately ask as for an amo* [lord]" who had to be someone "*in the Governor's court*" because "*they also* [proceeded like] *this regarding the King of Angola.*" Father Guerreiro further maintained that this system was a good choice, as "*all the security of the conquest of the kingdom of Angola*" was predicated "*in maintaining what* [the Mbundu] *were used to.*" Guerreiro, Relação anual das coisas, Vol. 1, p. 395–396.

172 See the fourth chapter for an introduction to the concept of "wealth in people." Wealth in People and Self-Realization, p. 243–265; Guyer, Wealth in People, p. 83–90; Guyer.

173 Amaral, O consulado de Paulo Dias de Novais; MMA V, D. 24, p. 51–52; Santos, O Império Português face às instituições indígenas, in: Palomo, Stumpf and Barreto Xavier (eds.), Monarquias ibéricas em perspectiva comparada, p. 292.

174 Amaral, O consulado de Paulo Dias de Novais, p. 225–242; MMA V, D. 101, p. 268; Parreira, Dicionário glossográfico, p. 27.

or other forms of emphyteusis, the *amos* system favored extracting slaves, often delivered as a tribute to the *amos* and the *donatário*, instead of productive land occupation.[175] According to the Jesuit Visitator Pero Rodrigues (1542–1603?), by 1593, all of the "*conquistadors*" of Ndongo had been granted *sobas*, some having as many as "*15, and one about 20*."[176] Nevertheless, the system failed to produce the desired fiscal and economic results.[177] Dias de Novais constantly faced difficulties financing the settlement of Angola and keeping up with the seigneurial obligations stipulated by the charter of 1571, namely the occupation of fertile lands, the discovery of mines, and the progressive conquering of Ndongo.[178]

After Dias de Novais died on May 9, 1589, his second-in-command, Luís Serrão, assumed field command over the Portuguese army while it engaged in war with Ndongo and the Kingdom of Matamba.[179] Shortly thereafter, on December 29, 1590, Serrão suffered a disastrous defeat with severe financial repercussions. In its aftermath, the Crown sent the *ouvidor* Domingos de Abreu de Brito to Angola to enquire about the state of the hereditary captaincy.[180] Displeased by Dias de Novais' administration and scandalized by Serrão's military defeat, Abreu de Brito wrote a damning report that precipitated the dismantling of the *amos* system and the end of the hereditary captaincy (c. 1593).[181] This resulted in the incorporation of all *sobas* as direct vassals of the Portuguese Crown and the establishment of a general government in Luanda, headed by a captain-general and governor with ample administrative powers, competence range, and jurisdictional autonomy.[182]

According to the Ordinance of the Governor of Angola of 1607, captain-general and governors had civil and criminal jurisdiction over everyone who lived in and

---

175 By 1630, when the *sobas* who had previously paid tribute to *amos* were already under royal jurisdiction, their *baculamentos* were registered in a book, proving that slaves still constituted a considerable share of their payments. See the eighth chapter for more details on tributes. Livro dos baculamentos.

176 MMA XV, D. 127, p. 335.

177 Brito, Um inquérito à vida administrativa, p. vi.

178 Demaret, Estratégias expansionistas.

179 Heywood and Thornton, Central Africans, p. 89.

180 Brito, Um inquérito à vida administrativa; Heywood and Thornton, Central Africans, p. 90.

181 The dismantling of the hereditary Captaincy and the *amos* system was a protracted affair, as the Ordinance of the Governor of Angola of 1607 proves. By then, Philip I of Portugal was still instructing Manuel Pereira Fojaz, in office between 1607 and 1611, to "*revoke similar donations*," forbidding him and his successors from giving *sobas* as "*serving vassals, or tribute payers to any person*." MMA V, D. 101.

182 Amaral describes that in 1620, Garcia Mendes Castelo Branco, one of Dias de Novais' companions in 1575, proposed to the Crown to create a system of *aforamento* [lease] of *sobas* as an alternative solution. This system was never applied because the Council of State rejected it. After all, vassal *sobas* were still considered free subjects. Amaral, O Consulado de Paulo Dias de Novais, p. 243–247; Brito, Um inquérito à vida administrativa; Demaret, Estratégias expansionistas.

traveled to the "*Kingdom of Angola and any of its provinces.*"[183] In criminal cases, they co-adjudicated with an *ouvidor*,[184] having the competence to absolve or condemn, up to the penalty of death, all "*pious Portuguese, as well as enslaved christãos da terra* [Christianized Africans] *and gentiles*" without appeal.[185] As for nobles with the standing of "*moços de Camara* [chamberlains]" or above, captain-general and governors could apply penalties up to "*ten years of exile and 100 cruzados* [40$000 *réis*]" except in cases of sodomy, treason, counterfeiting coins, and heresy, when the heretics were delivered to them by ecclesiastical justice. In these four cases, together with the *ouvidores*, they could condemn nobles and commoners alike to death. If they absolved anybody from the accusations of sodomy, treason, counterfeiting, or heresy, or decided to apply penalties other than death for these crimes, their decisions could be appealed to and revised by the *Casa da Suplicação* (1400s–1845) in Lisbon.[186]

Captain-general and governors could adjudicate civil cases involving up to 100$000 *réis* in movable properties or real estate without appeal.[187] Above these limits, their adjudications could also be appealed to and revised by the *Casa da Suplicação* in Lisbon. Captain-general and governors were also expected to "*augment the faith*" and "*expand the Gospel*," promote the prospecting of silver mines and of "*copper, iron, steel, plumb, pitch, and other materials*," take control of existing

---

183 MMA V, D. 101, p. 275.

184 According to the Ordinance of the Governor of Angola of 1607, the captain-general and governors were obliged to appoint an *ouvidor* until the Crown could appoint one. This happened in 1609. As further discussed below, after 1651, the *ouvidor* of Angola became known as *ouvidor geral*. Ibid.; Andrade e Silva (ed.), Collecção chronologica da legislação portugueza (1603–1612), p. 256–258; Regimento dos Ouvidores Geraez, p. 295–301.

185 MMA V, D. 101, p. 275.

186 As Nuno Camarinhas relates, the *Casa da Suplicação* was "the court of last instance of the kingdom in juridical matters," while the *Desembargo do Paço* (1521–1833) was the last instance in "matters of grace." After 1696, the *Casa da Suplicação* received appeals from the *Relação do Porto* in cases involving movable properties worth more than 100$000 *réis* or real estate worth more than 80$000 *réis*, and from the second instances of those from overseas in cases involving movable properties worth more than 3.000$000 *réis* and real estate worth more than 2.000$000 *réis*. Until the fourteenth century, the court of last instance was the *Curia Regis*, which accompanied the Portuguese King. During the reign of King John I of Portugal (1385–1433), the *Curia Regis* was divided into two courts, the *Casa da Suplicação* in Lisbon and the *Casa do Cível*, which continued to accompany the king. In 1582, the latter was abolished, the *Casa da Suplicação* was reformed, and the *Relação do Porto* was created in Porto. The first statute of the *Casa da Suplicação* was part of the *Philippine Ordinances* (1603), being reviewed in 1605. For a detailed description of these courts' internal structure, styles, and competence ranges, see Camarinhas. Ibid.; Camarinhas, Juízes e administração, p. 72–75.

187 MMA V, D. 101.

salt mines or salt pans, build municipal infrastructures such as jailhouses and abattoirs, distribute lands to the *moradores*, promote agriculture and cotton cultivation, oversee the slave trade and the Atlantic trade, and keep good diplomatic relations with neighboring African sovereigns. Crucially, as Miller remarks, initially, the captain-general and governors of Angola were allowed to trade in enslaved Africans as well as trade goods, quickly becoming significant stakeholders in the Angolan slave trade.[188] This situation officially changed after a law from August 29, 1720, barred all "*Viceroys, Captain Generals, Governors, Ministers, Officials of Justice, or the* [Real] *Fazenda*" and all military officers with "*the patent of Captain or higher*" from trading, in their name or partnership with others.[189] However, this empire-wide legislation had a negligible impact on Angola, Benguela, and their dependencies, where, for a long time, it was easy for captain-general and governors to disguise their trade partnerships.[190]

The Ordinance of the Government of the Kingdom of Angola of 1676 consolidated this new system of government after a century marked by constant Luso-Ndongo warfare.[191] The Portuguese monarch appointed the captain-general and governors after consulting the Overseas Council, almost exclusively from the higher ranks of the military nobility of the metropole.[192] Initially, it was customary for candidates to apply for the position and for the Overseas Council to review and rate these applications before the Crown proceeded with the selection.[193] Direct nominations could nevertheless occur and became more usual with time. Each captain-general and governor received an ordinance with standing instructions at the beginning of their mandates,[194] which usually lasted three years.[195] The captain-general and governors could be subjected to inquiries during their term in office and were required to undergo a terminal review upon its completion.[196] After a royal

188 Miller, Way of Death, p. 256–257.

189 Systema, ou collecção dos regimentos reaes, Vol. 5, p. 236–238.

190 As *Ouvidor Geral* Fernando José da Cunha Pereira noted on March 3, 1753, the "*raise in the salaries of captain majors and other military officials*" made to compensate for this prohibition was a waste because of the "*abuses*" they still committed. Coimbra (ed.), Livros de "Ofícios para o Reino," p. 66; Sebestyén, Vansina (eds.) and Leitão, Angola's Eastern Hinterland, p. 301–302.

191 Regimento do governo deste Reyno.

192 Cunha, Governo e governantes do Império, in: Bicalho and Ferlini (eds.), Modos de governar, p. 79–80, 87–88; Monteiro, Governadores e capitães-mores, in: Bicalho and Ferlini (eds.), Modos de governar, p. 256–267.

193 Bardwell, The Governors of Portugal's South Atlantic Empire, p. 95–187.

194 Occasionally, the captain-general and governors received additional instructions from the Overseas Council, the Board of Royal Conscience and Military Orders, and the *Desembargo do Paço*. Ibid., p. 28; Rego, Portuguese Colonization.

195 Bardwell, The Governors of Portugal's South Atlantic Empire, p. 28.

196 Ibid.; Couto, Os capitães-mores em Angola.

enactment from December 12, 1770, in case of their death, the captain-general and governors were substituted by a provisional government composed of the bishop of Congo and Angola, the colonel of the garrison of Luanda, and the *ouvidor geral* until the Crown appointed a new captain-general and governor.[197] According to Caldeira, before this enactment, the Municipal Council of Luanda used to elect an interim captain-general and governor of Angola.[198]

The governor of Benguela also had to abide by an ordinance starting after 1796, when the Overseas Council appointed Alexandre José Botelho de Vasconcelos to occupy the position.[199] As Couto remarks, until then, the five subaltern governors and the triumvirate that headed the subaltern government between 1779 and 1796 had no ordinance to "know the principles that oriented their activities or the limits of their jurisdiction, and the reach of their powers."[200] In keeping with the 1796 ordinance, the primary duties of the Governor of Benguela were similar in scope to those of his superior in Luanda but limited due to his subaltern position and the fact that the new office was created when several commissarial boards had already assumed jurisdiction over specialized domains, as discussed in the next chapter. The governor of Benguela was to "*assist in spreading the Faith*," a task the ordinance deemed difficult because of the "*attachment that all* [Blacks] *have for Polygamy, and superstitions*," promote "*the dignity of the Divine cult*," and "*ensure that the Igreja Matriz* [Mother Church] *got along with those* [established] *in the hinterlands*."[201] On the religious side, he was also to send regular reports of all baptized *sovas* to the Overseas Council. As the "*head of the military body*," the governor was responsible for repairing and maintaining the local fortress and its artillery pieces, reviewing the first and second-line troops of Benguela, including the *Henriques* battalion, and sending bi-annual statistical reports to Luanda. The governor had the highest "*economic jurisdiction*" over military affairs, was responsible for disciplining the troops according to the extant regulations, as well as for sending the "*réus* [accused]"

197 Caetano, As reformas pombalinas, in: Baião, Cidade and Murias (eds.), História da expansão portuguesa no mundo, Vol. 3, p. 251–260; Carvalho, Os homens do Rei em Angola, p. 257; Collecção das leys, Vol. 3, p. 133–135.

198 Contrariwise, a royal provision from October 30, 1733, determined that if the captain-general and governor died, the "*mestre de campo* [mestre de camp]" of the "regiment" of Luanda would substitute him or, in the absence of the latter, the highest-ranking military officer. ANTT, CLNH, Fol. 7, D. 1, p. 288; Caldeira, Dimensão sociopolítica, p. 27–59; Miller, Way of Death, p. 587.

199 AHU, GANG, Sr. 3, Cod. 1643, p. 59–64.

200 The triumvirate comprised a captain, the municipal judge, and the oldest municipal councilor, ruling Benguela between July 1788 and September 1788. Couto, Regimento de governo, p. 285–294; Delgado, A famosa e histórica Benguela, p. 9–25.

201 AHU, GANG, Sr. 3, Cod. 1643, p. 59–64.

of serious misdeeds, together with their "*judicial hearings*" to be adjudicated in Luanda by the "*War Council*."[202]

In civil cases, the Ordinance of 1796 simply states that while the governor had the "*jurisdiction that was inherent to his office*," he should not meddle with "*particular details*" because the municipal judge was "*responsible for* [overseeing] *all litigation*," accumulating the office of "*judge of orphans and provedor of the missing*" and the presidency of the Municipal Council of Benguela. Despite the municipal judge being responsible for "*policing and the economy of the city*," the governor was tasked with ensuring that the slave-shipping and salt trade regulations were abided by, taxes on exported slaves were collected, and that the royal monopoly over the ivory trade, and the rights of porters were respected. He was also responsible for overseeing the production of whitewash, tiles, and bricks and ensuring that food staples were cultivated in the nearby *arimos* of Quilengues and Catumbela. Governors were barred from interfering with commerce or the composition of the bundles of goods merchants took to the hinterlands (the *banzos*).[203] Their budgets were overseen by the Board of Finance of Angola and administered together with a "commissar *provedor*" also under the supervision of the Board. Moreover, the governors of Benguela had the privilege of appointing the "*less badly behaved*" *moradores* of the hinterlands to the positions of captain majors or ordinary judges of new populations, tasking them with "*arresting the wrongdoers*" who practiced "*homicides, thefts, and superstitions*" and sending them to be adjudicated by the Municipal Judge of Benguela, with appeal to the Justice Board.[204] Finally, as further discussed in the third chapter, the governor adjudicated *mucanos*.

At least since 1612, the captain-general and governors of Angola were assisted by a secretary known as the "*escrevente* [scribbler] of the Governor."[205] In this period, the archives of the Captaincy of Angola and the codices of the *Real Fazenda* were kept by the Municipal Council of Luanda. In 1688, a Secretariat of the General Government of Angola was created, and António Coelho Guerreiro received the first ordinance stipulating the duties and privileges of secretary of government.[206] He was appointed for three years, receiving no stipend from the *Real Fazenda*. Nevertheless, he could charge emoluments for all the "*letters patent*" of military officers as well as for the letters confirming the appointment of servants of the "*offices of Justice and the Real Fazenda*," *sesmarias*, the clearing of ships, the vassalage of *sobas*, and the certification of transcriptions of registry books. A part of these

---

202 This is a probable reference to the War Board of Luanda, further discussed in section seven. Ibid.

203 See chapters four to six for more details on these bundles of goods locally known as *banzos*.

204 Acting as a "*desembargador*," the *Ouvidor Geral* of Luanda oversaw the process before it was presented to the Board. AHU, GANG, Sr. 3, Cod. 1643, p. 59–64.

205 Coimbra (ed.), Livros de "Ofícios para o Reino," p. 9–10.

206 Ibid., p. 10; Lancastro, Regimento do Secretario deste Reino, p. 493–496.

emoluments was destined to pay for an official responsible for writing down the "*mucanos cases and registering the decisions so that certificates could be written.*" From then onwards, the Secretariat kept two books of registry, one registering the orders received from Portugal and the other those issued in Angola.[207] In 1764, Sousa Coutinho made moderate reforms to the Secretariat, ordering the reorganization of its papers and the writing of an index of existing documents.[208] Three decades later, Manuel de Almeida e Vasconcelos tasked Joaquim José da Silva with drafting a new catalog and systematizing the archive.[209] Finally, by 1796, Captain-General and Governor Mello proposed an in-depth reform of the Secretariat.[210] From then until 1836, the secretary of government was appointed by the Crown through the secretary of state of the overseas and the navy, assisted by two secretariat officers, a senior and a junior.[211] The Secretariat was responsible for keeping sixteen separate "ledgers," covering most fields of administration, keeping track of relevant orders and military, civil, commercial, and ecclesiastical jurisprudence. The 'style' of these ledgers and the models used by the Secretariat were based on the ones observed by the Secretariat of Bahia.[212] The two secretariat officers kept track of the orders and official letters sent by the Overseas Council, the Secretariat of State of the Overseas and the Navy, and other councils and courts, sending an annual report to the first two institutions.[213]

The palace of government was situated in Luanda, where the captain-general and governors presided over the *Junta de Guerra* [War Board] (c. 1611), the *Junta das Missões* [Missions Board] (1693), and several other *ad hoc* boards. These commissarial boards convened to adjudicate exceptional cases or deliberate pressing issues in a summary manner, significantly augmenting the political power and jurisdictional reach of the captain-general and governors at the expense of the other officeholders that composed them.[214] As discussed in the third chapter, after 1761, several other regular commissarial boards were established in Luanda as part of the Pombaline reforms. These were the *Junta do Comércio* [Board of Commerce] (1761), the *Junta da Fazenda* [Board of Finance] (1761), and the Justice Board (1761). Besides adjudicating and deciding urgent matters, these new boards issued jurisprudential *pareceres* [pronunciations] and, in the case of the Board of Finance, had permanent staff and the responsibility to manage and administer public funds.

---

207 Coimbra (ed.), Livros de "Ofícios para o Reino," p. 9–10.
208 Ibid., p. 11.
209 Ibid., p. 16–17.
210 Ibid., p. 12–13.
211 Ibid.; Mello, Relação dos officios civis, p. 281–282.
212 Coimbra (ed.), Livros de "Ofícios para o Reino," p. 14.
213 Ibid., p. 14–16.
214 Cardim, A Casa Real, p. 34.

For clarity, the structure and functioning of the older boards are explained only after the jurisdictions of the *Ouvidores* of Luanda (1609), Benguela (1617), Mpinda, and Mbanza Kongo, the *Ouvidores Gerais* of Angola (1651), Municipal Judges of Luanda (1721) and Benguela (1770), and Ordinary Judge of Massangano (1658) are discussed, as well as the other main offices these judges accumulated. The Pombaline commissarial boards are discussed in the third chapter because, despite assuming the same formal structure as the previous ones (except for the Board of Finance), they were predicated on an absolutist understanding of royal authority, statutory law, and sovereignty.

2.5 The *Ouvidor Geral* of Angola and other *Ouvidores*

The Portuguese Crown established the *Ouvidoria Geral* of Luanda in 1651, but *ouvidores* had been irregularly sent to Angola since the period of the hereditary captaincy.[215] As Nuno Camarinhas tells it, the creation of this institution was part of a broader strategy of progressively dismantling the remaining traces of seigneurial privileges in all Portuguese overseas dominions.[216] As he remarks, the Portuguese Crown was entitled to appoint *ouvidores* to the overseas domains of *donatários* as the monarch accumulated the offices of Grand-Master of the Military Orders of Aviz (1146–), of St. James of the Sword (1172–), and of Christ (1319–1789), retaining this privilege after the hereditary captaincies were reformed into general-governments. After 1651, *ouvidores gerais* were always learned judges appointed by the Overseas Council on behalf of the Portuguese Crown, typically for six-year terms as part of a judicial career.[217] This meant they had to hold a degree in Civil or Canon law from the University of Coimbra, the only university that conferred such degrees in the Portuguese Empire, except for the brief period of the Iberian Union, when the University of Salamanca offered an alternative.[218] It also meant that, after completing their degrees, prospective *ouvidores gerais* had to undergo the "*leitura de bacharéis* [bachelor's lecture]" exam at the *Desembargo do Paço* (1521–1833),

---

215 Carta de doação a Paulo Dias de Navais, p. 451–462; Regimento dos Ouvidores Geraez, p. 295–301.

216 Camarinhas, Juízes e administração, p. 122–123.

217 In his prosopography of Portuguese learned judicatures, Camarinhas concludes that most of the *ouvidores gerais* of Angola were naturals of the Portuguese Kingdom and that their careers often progressed to the *Relação* [second instance court] of Bahia and the *Relação* of Porto. He also notes that the *ouvidoria geral* of Luanda was usually the next step in the career of magistrates coming from São Tomé and Príncipe. Camarinhas, Juízes e Administração, p. 297–305; Subtil, Os ministros do rei, p. 37–58.

218 Camarinhas, Administração da justiça em espaços coloniais, p. 118; Camarinhas, Juízes e administração, p. 234–245.

the court responsible for examining the candidates, inquiring about their "purity of blood" and familial standing, and listing and ranking those approved.[219] The Overseas Council usually selected the names to appoint from these lists.[220] When their terms of office ended, the *Philippine Ordinances* stipulated that *ouvidores gerais* were subjected to a detailed "*juízo de residência* [final evaluation]" conducted by their successors.[221] *Ouvidores* based their adjudications on *Ius commune* doctrines, popular glosses, and other learned sources of law, besides considering municipal bylaws, local uses and customs, and relying on the *Philippine Ordinances* or, before 1603, the *Manueline Ordinances* for guidance.[222] As Camarinhas and Catarina Madeira Santos conclude, because of their peripatetic careers, elite schooling, and functions as crown judges, *ouvidores* contributed to the harmonization of the judicial administration of the empire and the transfer of normative knowledge between Portugal and its Asian, American, and African dominions.[223]

In 1571, the donation charter of Paulo Dias de Novais stipulated that "*together with his ouvidor*," the *donatário* or his successors had the right to preside over the election of the ordinary judges of all "*villages and settlements*" that they established, confirming the results, and issuing the "*charters*" to the ordinary judges and other municipal officials.[224] Furthermore, it had regulated that the *donatário* had to appoint an *ouvidor* who would "*hear new cases from within ten léguas from where he lived*" and "*apellaçois e agravos* [appeals]"[225] coming from all over the captaincy. If

---

219 Camarinhas, Juízes e administração, p. 246–266.

220 For more information about the exam, selection, and appointment process, see Camarinhas. Ibid., p. 253–266.

221 Camarinhas, As residências dos cargos de justiça letrada, in: Stumpf and Chaturvedula (eds.), Cargos e ofícios nas monarquias ibéricas, p. 161–174; Ord. Fil., Book I, Tit. LX; Wehling and Wehling, Direito e justiça, p. 37.

222 Camarinhas, Administração da justiça em espaços coloniais, p. 109–124.

223 Ibid.; Santos, O Império Português face às instituições indígenas, in: Palomo, Stumpf and Barreto Xavier (eds.), Monarquias ibéricas em perspectiva comparada, p. 271–303.

224 Carta de doação a Paulo Dias de Navais, p. 451–462.

225 As Hespanha clarifies, the Portuguese "laws of the fatherland" afforded two kinds of appeals. Canon law inspired this practice as jurists came to share the view of Canon law specialists that only the "Judgment at the end of time" was definitive. Hierarchical appeals were known as *apelos* or *apelações*. All decisions that affected the outcome of a process ("*interlocutórias mistas*") could be appealed if the value of the cause, as stated in the "*libelo* [libel]," was higher than could be adjudicated without appeal by the judge or court ("*alçada*") unless the court had the privilege of its decisions not being appealed. The latter was the case of the *Casa da Suplicação* and the *Casa do Cível* or the *Corregedores da Corte*. In seigneurial jurisdictions, first-instance decisions could be appealed to the domain lords or their *corregedores* and then to Crown courts. Canon law appeals followed the Church's hierarchy up to the Pope. In keeping with the *Philippine Ordinances*, appeals could be presented to the first-instance judges up to ten days after their rulings were known. The judges then had a month to arrange an appeal hearing within six months of the request. In the

the new settlements grew large enough to justify it, the charter specified that the *donatário* was obligated to appoint additional *ouvidores*, as was later the case in Benguela.[226] In keeping with it, the *ouvidores* were to receive appeals and revise the adjudications of ordinary judges according to the limits stipulated by the *Manueline Ordinances*. They could adjudicate civil cases without appeal up to 100$000 *réis*. In criminal cases, they had to adjudicate with the *donatário* and could condemn slaves, "*gentiles*," and "*Christian free men*" up to death without appeal. When adjudicating crimes committed by "*persons of a better quality*," the *ouvidores* had the competence to apply only penalties up to "*ten years of exile and 100 cruzados* [40$000 *réis*]" without appeal. In the cases of sodomy, treason, the counterfeiting of coins, and heresy, when the heretics were delivered to them by ecclesiastical justice, all privileges were revoked, and the charter had specified that the *ouvidores* could condemn both nobles and commoners to death.[227]

After the hereditary captaincy was dismantled, the Ordinance of the Governor of Angola of 1607 stipulated that the captain-general and governor of Angola had the obligation of appointing an *ouvidor* while the Crown was not capable of establishing an "*ouvidor Geral*" in Luanda.[228] Two years later, Manoel Ferraz Barreto was appointed the first "*Ouvidor of the Kingdom of Angola*."[229] His ordinance confirmed the competence range of previous *ouvidores* in criminal cases, stipulating that he was to co-adjudicate them with the captain-general and governor and "*adjunctos* [adjuncts]" from the Municipal Council of Luanda—possibly the ordinary judges or the oldest municipal councilors in their absence. It further clarified who were the "*persons of a better quality*" entitled to the privileges mentioned in the 1571 charter. It stipulated that in all criminal cases involving them, or when lesser penalties were applied to cases of sodomy, treason, the counterfeiting of coins, and heresy, the co-adjudications of the *ouvidor* and the captain-general and governor could be

---

meantime, their decision was suspended. In some cases, when *apelos* were impossible, there was still the possibility of *agravos*. *Agravos* followed a similar procedure to *apelos*. However, decisions that did not affect the outcome of the process could still be *agravadas*, as well as the rulings of the *Casa da Suplicação* and the *Casa do Cível* or the *Corregedores da Corte*. In addition, when first-instance judges failed to arrange an appeal hearing, an *agravo* process could be started. For brevity, henceforward, I only mention 'appeal' when discussing the competence ranges (*alçadas*) of Portuguese judges and courts. However, it always refers to both kinds of appeals (*apelo e agravo*). Hespanha, Como os juristas viam o mundo, § 2101–§ 2118; Ord. Fil., Book III, Tit. LXVIII, Tit. LXXXV.

226 In keeping with the Ordinance of Manuel Cerveira Pereira, the first Governor of Benguela, an *ouvidor* accompanied him in 1617. He adjudicated all civil and criminal matters including the "penalty of death." ANTT, MO, NU, Box 8, D. 1.

227 Carta de doação a Paulo Dias de Navais, p. 451–462.

228 MMA V, D. 101.

229 Andrade e Silva (ed.), Collecção chronologica da legislação portugueza (1603–1612), p. 256–258.

appealed to the *Casa da Suplicação* in Lisbon. Furthermore, in civil cases, it clarified that the limit of 100$000 *réis* applied to movable property and real estate and that *ouvidores* could impose penalties of up to "*fifty cruzados* [20$000 *réis*]" without appeal. As for the jurisdictional limit of the *ouvidor*, the ordinance reduced it to a five-*léguas* radius. It further stipulated that the *ouvidores* should receive appeals from the ordinary judges, the judges of orphans, and the "*ouvidor da gente branca do Reino do Congo* [*ouvidor* of the Whites residing in the Kingdom of Kongo]," and could revise their decisions acting as "*corregedores*" of the judicial district. As the *corregedores* of the Portuguese metropole, the *ouvidores* were also expected to adjudicate in public, be responsible for enforcing the municipal bylaws approved by the municipal council, and perform several other minor fiscal and judicial duties. The *ouvidores* of Angola were also to substitute the "*ouvidor da fazenda do mar* [judge of the maritime treasury]" and act as *provedores* of the judicial district. However, the captain-general and governors of Angola retained the privilege of appointing non-learned *ouvidores* to hinterland jurisdictions. On June 12, 1629, Captain-General and Governor Fernão de Sousa (c. 1563–1635), in office between 1624 and 1630, appointed António Nunes Leitão, the former *ouvidor* of Luanda, as "*ouvidor, judge of orphans, and provedor of the hinterland presídios*" as a new Crown-appointed *ouvidor* had reached Luanda in March 1629.[230]

The Ordinance of the *Ouvidores Gerais* of this Kingdom of Angola of June 23, 1651, confirmed most of these stipulations, attributing the *ouvidor geral* title to the learned *ouvidores* appointed by the Portuguese Crown, thus distinguishing them from the *ouvidores* appointed by the captain-general and governors.[231] A quarter-century later, the Ordinance of the Government of the Kingdom of Angola of 1676 determined that, since the *ouvidor geral* was by then the only learned "*Minister of Justice in the Kingdom*," he had to stay put and serve the urban population of Luanda, instead of traveling through the judicial district.[232] Furthermore, it stipulated that the *ouvidor geral* also accumulated the position of "*auditor da Gente de Guerra* [army auditor]," the highest military judicature of Angola and Benguela.[233] By then, *ouvidores gerais* had also accumulated the offices of judges of orphans and *provedor*

---

230 This is the only mention of this 'hinterland' *ouvidor* I have found in the sources. Heintze, Fontes para a História de Angola, Vol. 1, p. 94.

231 Regimento dos Ouvidores Geraez, p. 295–301.

232 Regimento do governo deste Reyno.

233 As Camarinhas relates, a law from October 20, 1763, abolished the regional army auditor office, establishing an auditor in each military unit instead. These positions were then abolished in 1789, and their jurisdictions were transferred to criminal judges (in the case of Angola, probably to the municipal judges of Luanda and Benguela). The fact that the *ouvidor geral* had military jurisdiction as army auditor was often at the root of jurisdictional disputes with the *mestre de camp* that commanded the infantry regiment of Luanda. ANTT, CLNH, Fol. 7, D. 1, p. 217, 228; Camarinhas, Juízes e administração, p. 106–107; Regimento do governo deste Reyno.

da Real Fazenda.[234] Camarinhas remarks that this also occurred in other overseas domains, where learned magistrates were scarce and often lacked training.[235] To sum up, besides acting as *ouvidores*, the *Ouvidores Gerais* of Angola also served as judges of orphans of Luanda (until 1721), *provedores* of the judicial district, army auditors, and *provedores da Real Fazenda*, often being elected *provedores* of the *Santa Casa* of Luanda. Since in Angola, the judges of orphans doubled as "judges of *defuntos e ausentes, capelas e resíduos* [deceased and absent, chapels and legacies]," the *ouvidores gerais* accumulated these functions. As mentioned above, between 1706 and 1721, the *ouvidores gerais* also presided over the Municipal Council of Luanda.[236]

As judges of orphans, *ouvidores gerais* were supposed to record all the orphans living in their district, register their legal guardians, both physical and financial, and list all their "movable properties and real estate."[237] They were responsible for guaranteeing that these assets were adequately managed and listed in "*inventories*" and presiding over the appraisal and partitioning of the estates of the deceased. In case the orphans were minors in need of "*criação* [sustenance]" or breastfeeding, the *ouvidores gerais* were to decide who was responsible for providing it to them or, in case no appropriate caretaker was found, order the municipal council to cover the expenses. They were also to oversee the marriage of orphans and keep a "*chest*" to hold their valuables. As judges of orphans, *ouvidores gerais* only had competence range to adjudicate without appeal civil cases involving orphans up to 5$000 *réis* in cases involving movable properties, 4$000 *réis* in matters involving real estate, being also able to impose penalties up to 1$000 *réis*. However, as *provedores* of the judicial district, they were paradoxically responsible for adjudicating the appeals to their own performances as judges of orphans, so in practice, their competence ranges were undoubtedly higher. Their functions as judges of the absent, chapels, and legacies were similar, focusing instead on the assets left by those missing or in the estates entrusted to chapels, hospitals, hostels, and lay brotherhoods.[238]

---

234 As Selma Pantoja explains, in keeping with the Ordinance of March 3, 1684, that regulated the shipping of slaves, as *provedores da Real Fazenda*, the *ouvidores gerais* were tasked with confirming if the number of slaves admitted aboard a slave ship was appropriate for its tonnage. This presented them with plenty of opportunities to earn a quick profit by accepting bribes from shipowners, captains, or masters. AHU, CU, Angola, Box 23, D. 2393; Coimbra (ed.), Livros de "Ofícios para o Reino," p. 58; Pantoja, Entre Luanda e Rio de Janeiro, in: Pantoja and Thompson (eds.), Em torno de Angola, p. 106.

235 Camarinhas, Juízes e administração, p. 125; Camarinhas, Lugares ultramarinos, p. 145–146.

236 ANTT, CLNH, Fol. 7, D. 1, p. 171; Caldeira, Dimensão sociopolítica, p. 27–59; Miller, Way of Death, p. 548.

237 Ord. Fil., Book I, Tit. LXXXVIII.

238 Ord. Fil., Book I, Tit. XC.

The *Philippine Ordinances* determined that a scribe of the orphans assisted them, regulating his functions.[239]

As *provedores* of the judicial district, *ouvidores gerais* headed the *Provedoria* of Luanda. This court functioned as a second instance to the adjudications of all the judges of orphans of the judicial district, overseeing the appointment and performance of the scribes of orphans and also being responsible for supervising the chapels, hospitals, hostels, and lay brotherhoods not directly administered by regular orders or under the Crown's jurisdiction.[240] In this role, the *ouvidores gerais* were under the jurisdiction of the *Mesa da Consciência e Ordens* [Board of Royal Conscience and Military Orders] (1532–1833).[241] As *provedores da Real Fazenda*, the *ouvidores gerais* of Luanda were expected to supervise the municipal procurators and tithe tax farmers and revise all courts' decisions related to fiscal and economic matters.[242] They were also entitled to levy extraordinary municipal taxes (*fintas*) to finance the building or repair of municipal infrastructure, such as the town hall, the abattoir, or the jailhouse.[243] In this role, the *ouvidores gerais* were under the jurisdiction of the *Conselho da Fazenda* [Finance Council] (1591–1833).[244] In keeping with the Ordinance of the Government of the Kingdom of Angola of 1676, as army auditor, the *ouvidor geral* adjudicated cases involving military personnel together with the captain-general and governor, except in instances where the offenses had taken place during expeditionary campaigns when the latter could judge them immediately without assistance.[245] They were also responsible

239 Ord. Fil., Book I, Tit. LXXXIX.

240 Camarinhas, Juízes e administração, p. 103–105.

241 Originally titled the "Board of Royal Conscience," this court was established by King João III as a court with jurisdiction over matters related to the king's conscience, namely those connected with religion, education, charity, and the provision of assistance to those in need. After 1551, when the Portuguese monarch became the grand master of the Military Orders of Aviz, St. James of the Sword, and Christ, this court became the last instance in all processes involving their members. Then, as Camarinhas remarks, the Board of Royal Conscience and Military Orders started acting as a "court of grace" regarding the knights of these orders, also controlling the admissions to their ranks. Ibid.; Marcocci, A Consciência de um Império.

242 Camarinhas, Juízes e administração, p. 125.

243 Andrade e Silva (ed.), Collecção chronologica da legislação portugueza (1603–1612), p. 256–258, p. 256–258.

244 As Camarinhas explains, when King Filipe I of Portugal created it, this council oversaw the financial matters of the kingdom, as the *Casa da Suplicação* had jurisdiction over the economic ones. In 1641–42, it was reformed by King João IV, assuming control over the overseas commerce, customs houses, and all the Crown's delegates and commissaries in charge of finances. As further discussed in the third chapter, after creating the *Erário Régio* in 1761, the Marquis of Pombal reformed the Finance Council, removing some of its competencies. In 1790, the Finance Council was united with the *Erário Régio*. Camarinhas, Juízes e administração, p. 62–64.

245 Regimento do governo deste Reyno.

for overseeing the payment of army salaries, which until the last decades of the eighteenth century was paid in African currencies supplied by the holders of the slave duty contract of Angola, thus being directly confronted with the unrest and conflicts resulting from late payments or the devaluation of wages due to inflation or currency changes.[246] In this role, the *ouvidores gerais* were under the jurisdiction of the *Conselho da Guerra* [War Council] (1640–1808) in Lisbon.

Like the captain-general and governors, each *ouvidor geral* of Angola received an ordinance upon appointment.[247] In principle, they could not be removed or imprisoned by the captain-general and governors or the municipal councils, and only the Overseas Council could adjudicate their criminal offenses.[248] Nevertheless, their jurisdictional conflicts with these other authorities often escalated. It was thus not unusual for them to be improperly thrown in jail before the Overseas Council had the opportunity to deliberate about the cases brought against them.[249] In case of their sudden death or incapacitation, a royal enactment from September 28, 1728, determined that the municipal judge of Luanda was to substitute them until a new magistrate was appointed.[250] However, because the Ordinance of *Ouvidor* Manoel Ferraz Barreto (1609) had stipulated that the captain-general and governor was responsible for selecting his substitute in case of illness or death, this procedure became customary, persisting even after 1728.[251] *Ouvidores gerais* worked with two scribes appointed by the captain-general and governor, being allowed to select two others to assist them in their role as *provedores*.[252] Due to a lack of resources, the first two were often shared with the municipal judges, giving rise to conflicts between the officeholders.[253] The bailiff of the *ouvidoria geral* was appointed by the captain-general and governor, but his stipend was not fixed and depended on the emoluments charged by the *ouvidoria geral*.[254]

---

246 Margarido, Algumas formas da hegemonia africana in: Santos (ed.), I Reunião internacional de História de África, p. 392; Torres, Memorias, p. 221–223.

247 ANTT, CLNH, Fol. 7, D. 1, p. 74; Cunha, Bicalho, Nunes, Fátima and Mello, Corregedores, Ouvidores-Gerais e Ouvidores, in: Fragoso and Monteiro (eds.), Um Reino e suas Repúblicas no Atlântico, p. 338.

248 Cunha, Bicalho, Nunes, Fátima and Mello, Corregedores, Ouvidores-Gerais e Ouvidores, in: Fragoso and Monteiro (eds.), Um Reino e suas Repúblicas no Atlântico, p. 338.

249 ANTT, CLNH, Fol. 7, D. 1, p. 161; AHU, CU, Angola, Box 18, D. 1930, D. 1932, D. 1936; AHU, CU, Angola, Box 19, D. 1979, D. 1990, D. 2002.

250 ANTT, CLNH, Fol. 7, D. 1, p. 263.

251 Andrade e Silva (ed.), Collecção chronologica da legislação portugueza (1603–1612), p. 256–258; Cunha, Bicalho, Nunes, Fátima and Mello, Corregedores, Ouvidores-Gerais e Ouvidores, in: Fragoso and Monteiro (eds.), Um Reino e suas Repúblicas no Atlântico, p. 338.

252 Mello, Relação dos officios civis, p. 281–293.

253 AHU, CU, Angola, Box 51, D. 4697.

254 Mello, Relação dos officios civis, p. 281–293.

Ouvidores continued to be appointed to areas outside of the Captaincy of Angola, remaining under the jurisdiction of the *ouvidor geral* of Angola, who revised their adjudications and received appeals as *corregedor* of the judicial district. Until the Ordinance of the *Ouvidores Gerais* of this Kingdom of Angola of 1651, an "*ouvidor of the Whites*" was appointed to São Salvador do Congo, or Mbanza Kongo, the capital of the Kingdom of Kongo.[255] Before this, according to a Portuguese royal edict from 1553, the *Mwene Kongo* was entitled to appoint an *ouvidor*.[256] The latter could handle cases of 15$000 *réis* without appeal in civil suits and up to death without appeal in criminal ones over persons of all statuses.[257] According to the royal edict of 1553, the *ouvidor* appointed by the *Mwene Kongo* had to be a subject of the king of Portugal and a "natural" of Portugal. Moreover, it stipulated that only one *ouvidor* could be appointed for the whole Kingdom of Kongo.[258] However, this royal edict seems to have been abrogated or ignored.[259] By 1607, the *ouvidor* of the Whites was appointed by the captain-general and governor of Angola, his

---

255 Regimento dos Ouvidores Geraez, p. 295–301; Thornton, A History of West Central Africa, p. 97.

256 A report from 12 November 1548 by the *Ouvidor* and *Provedor* Simão da Mota proves that before 1553, the *ouvidor* of Mbanza Kongo was appointed by the Portuguese Crown and accumulated the office of *provedor*. A scribe assisted him. Gouveia, The Creation of a Portuguese Diocese, p. 498; MMA II, D. 74, p. 197–198, D. 101.

257 MMA II, D. 101.

258 Thornton explains that during the first decades of Portuguese presence in the Kingdom of Kongo, the leader of the Portuguese expeditions (1491, 1509, 1512) had civil and criminal jurisdiction over the Portuguese community. The ordinance that accompanied Simão da Silva, the last of these leaders, specified that he would be assisted by a "*learned person*" in all his decisions. Furthermore, the ordinance determined that, as requested by the *Mwene Kongo*, Silva was to instruct the BaKongo about the "costumes" and styles of the Portuguese, administering justice to the Portuguese and Bakongo alike. The Portuguese monarch sent a manuscript copy of his ordinances to assist Silva. Clerical authority was in the hands of the highest-ranking missionary or, in the case of priests from São Tomé, of their superiors in the island's Church hierarchy. The stipulation that only one *ouvidor* could be appointed resulted from the conflict that pitted Alvaro Lopes, who had succeeded Silva after his untimely death in 1512, and Diogo Fernandes, a Portuguese settler in Mbanza Kongo, who got himself appointed to the position of "*corregedor*" by the *Mwene Kongo*. This resulted in a jurisdictional conflict that ended with Lopes killing Fernandes and being deported by the *Mwene Kongo* to stand trial in Portugal. MMA I, D. 65, p. 233–235, 237, 244, D. 98, D. 153, p. 531; MMA II, D. 101; Soares, O marfim nos acordos de compensação, in: Horta, Almeida and Mark (eds.), African Ivories in the Altantic World, p. 318–324; Thornton, Early Kongo-Portuguese Relations, p. 194–195.

259 A letter written by Cristóvão de Sousa to D. Catarina (1507–1578), Queen of Portugal, on November 4, 1561, suggests that the Portuguese nobles who resided in the Kingdom of Kongo and São Tomé resented the fact that the *Mwene Kongo* overlooked the "purity of blood" of his appointees, selecting new Christians to the position of *ouvidor*. This partially explains why the royal edict of 1553 was soon questioned. MMA II, D. 166.

title suggesting that more than one *ouvidor* existed in the Kingdom of Kongo.[260] Then, the office of "*captain of the Portuguese people*" or "*captain of the Whites*" who resided in the Kingdom of Kongo was also created. In the official letter from the India Council that proposed Gonçalves Pita as the first "*captain of the Portuguese people*' in the Kingdom of Kongo, the councilors refer that, until then, the *ouvidor dos brancos* often acted as an ad hoc captain major. When Gonçalves Pita assumed the office of captain of the Portuguese in 1609, his charter mentions an ordinance that specified his jurisdiction and that probably extinguished the office of *ouvidor dos brancos*, incorporating it into his captaincy.[261] Unfortunately, this document remains lost. As described above, ad hoc *ouvidores* had also been appointed to Benguela since 1617, being substituted by a learned *ouvidor* in 1767 and then by a municipal judge in 1771.[262] Primary sources further indicate that during the second half of the seventeenth century, a captain major and "*Ouvidor*" resided in Mpinda, the seaport of the Kingdom of Kongo, where a Portuguese *feitoria* was established in the late fifteenth century.[263] According to a royal letter from c. 1557, the *Mwene Kongo* was initially responsible for appointing this *ouvidor*.[264] None of these *ouvidores* were learned judges.

2.6 Municipal Judges of Luanda and Benguela and Ordinary Judges

The *juizes de Fora* [municipal judges] of Luanda and Benguela were learned judges[265] appointed for three years by the *Overseas Council* on behalf of the Portuguese Crown, having their competence ranges and jurisdiction set by the *Philippine Ordinances*.[266] As their title emphasizes (*de fora* means from abroad), they were required to be from a different community than the one they served as judges. However, their salaries were paid by the municipal councils they served in. Their outsider status could thus be perceived differently by local and central

260 MMA V, D. 100, D. 102, D. 128, D. 137, p. 386, D. 181.

261 Heintze, Fontes para a História de Angola, Vol. 1, p. 237.

262 ANTT, MO, NU, Box 8, D. 1; Delgado, O governo de Sousa Coutinho em Angola II, p. 61–63.

263 AHU, CU, Angola, Box 6, D. 676; Heintze, Fontes para a História de Angola, Vol. 1, p. 82.

264 MMA II, D. 139.

265 Since 1539, the municipal judges had to have a degree in law and undergo the *leitura de bacharéis* examination at the *Desembargo do Paço* to access their career. This career progressed along similar lines to that of the *ouvidores gerais* of Angola. Camarinhas, Administração da justiça em espaços coloniais, p. 69–70; Camarinhas, Juízes e administração, p. 253–266, 297–305; Hespanha, História das instituições, p. 234, 260; Schwartz, Burocracia e sociedade, p. 32–33.

266 Camarinhas, Administração da justiça em espaços coloniais, p. 109–124; Camarinhas, Juiz de Fora; Camarinhas, Lugares ultramarinos, p. 157; Fernandes and Rêgo, História do Direito Português, p. 249–251; Hespanha, História das instituições, p. 268–270, 432–433.

agents. In Portuguese and Brazilian jurisdictions, locals either resented their appointment as a costly interference of the Crown in their affairs and privileges or welcomed it if they felt wronged by provincial elites.[267] As for the central officials, they usually understood the outsider status of municipal judges as a guarantee of their impartiality, independence, and loyalty to the Crown.[268] As stated above, when introduced, municipal judges substituted the ordinary judges in the municipal councils, inheriting their executive, fiscal, and administrative functions and assuming the office of judges of orphans, the deceased and absent, chapels, and legacies.[269] In the case of Luanda, the municipal judge substituted the *ouvidor geral* at the municipal council and as judge of orphans. In the case of Benguela, the municipal judge replaced the *ouvidor* of Benguela, inaugurating the new municipal council in 1771.[270]

Along with all the administrative duties that came with leading the municipal councils, municipal judges accumulated civil and criminal jurisdictions.[271] According to the *Philippine Ordinances*, municipal judges could adjudicate without appeal civil cases concerning movable property worth up to 5$000 *réis*, real estate worth up to 4$000 *réis*, and criminal cases entailing penalties of up to 1$000 *réis*.[272] They were barred from leaving "*the places of their julgados* [judicatures]," had to give two public audiences per week, and also heard twice per week the prisoners brought to them by the *alcaides*, either confirming their arrest or ordering their release.[273] As was also the case with ordinary judges, municipal judges were strictly barred from receiving money, gifts, or having sexual intercourse with litigants.[274] To distinguish themselves from ordinary judges, who carried a red staff as a symbol of their office, municipal judges were required to bear a white staff whenever conducting official business.[275] Like the *ouvidores gerais*, municipal judges were subjected to a "*juízo de residencia* [final review]" at the end of their terms—in their case, not by the next municipal judge, but by the standing *ouvidor geral*.[276]

---

267 Carmo, Para a boa administração da justica, p. 85–110; Hespanha, História das instituições, p. 234, 260; Ord. Fil., Book I, Tit. LXV.

268 Hespanha, História das instituições, p. 234, 260; Carmo, Para a boa administração da justica, p. 85–110.

269 AHU, CU, Angola, Box 23, D. 2393; Wehling and Wehling, Direito e justiça, p. 31–32.

270 Delgado, O governo de Sousa Coutinho em Angola II, p. 58–61.

271 Camarinhas, Lugares ultramarinos, p. 147.

272 Ord. Fil. Book I, Tit. LXV, § 6.

273 Ord. Fil. Book I, Tit. LXV, § 4–§ 5, § 12.

274 Ord. Fil., Book I, Tit. LXV, § 10, § 39–§ 72.

275 Ord. Fil. Book I, Tit. LXV, § 1.

276 AHU, CU, Angola, Box 30, D. 2910; Camarinhas, As residências dos cargos de justiça letrada, in: Stumpf and Chaturvedula (eds.), Cargos e ofícios nas monarquias ibéricas, p. 161–174; Ord. Fil., Book I, Tit. LX; Wehling and Wehling, Direito e justiça, p. 37.

According to the *Philippine Ordinances*, municipal judges, as well as ordinary judges and "*all the judges of cities, villas, and places*" under the Crown's jurisdiction, were obliged to perform "*devassas geraes* [general inquiries]" during the first ten days of their tenure.[277] Because that fell in January, these inquiries were popularly known as "*janeirinhas*."[278] Contrary to "*devassas particulares* [specific inquiries]," general inquiries were open investigations, not triggered by any specific event or petition.[279] During these ten days, the new judges would inquire about the integrity of their predecessors and subordinates and the uprightness of other officeholders, including the municipal councilors, judges of orphans, and *almotacés*.[280] They would also inquire about church and community assets, indirectly monitoring *provedores* and procurators. The new judges had to act upon their findings if the irregularities fell within their jurisdiction or refer them to the *ouvidor geral* of Angola. Acting as a *corregedor*, the latter would also receive a full report of the general inquiries. The *Philippine Ordinances* further specified the cases that would originate specific inquiries immediately after taking place.[281] These were "*deaths, the forcing of women* [rape]," when the women complained, "*arson, the escaping of prisoners, the breaking of the jail, false coinage, resistance* [to justice], *offenses against Justice, false imprisonment, and the theft of valuables above a marco of silver* [roughly 2$800 *réis*]," and thefts below this limit if it occurred on a public way or at the request of the parties involved.[282] Furthermore, drawing weapons inside churches, during processions, or in places where the *Corpus Christi* was deposited, as well as causing wounds on the face, damaging limbs, or wounding someone with crossbows, rifles, or muskets, would also give rise to a specific inquiry.[283] A royal edict from February 20, 1743, further stipulated that cases of poisoning triggered "*devassas especiais* [special general inquiries]" because of the heinous nature of the crime.[284] Both inquiries followed an inquisitorial style directly inspired by the canonical "*ordo iudiciarius*," with the judges hearing witnesses as soon as possible, identifying the relevant facts, and then adjudicating them and sending the written records for "*correição* [revision]."[285]

---

277 Ord. Fil., Book I, Tit. LXV, § 39–§ 72.

278 Ord. Fil., Book I, Tit. LXV, § 31–§ 38, footnote 3.

279 Ord. Fil., Book I, Tit. LXV, § 31–§ 72.

280 Ord. Fil., Book I, Tit. LXV, § 39–§ 72.

281 Ord. Fil., Book I, Tit. LXV, § 31–§ 38.

282 Ibid.; Puntoni, Uma pax monetaria? p. 216–236.

283 Ord. Fil., Book I, Tit. LXV, § 31–§ 38.

284 Ibid., footnote 3; Hespanha, Como os juristas viam o mundo, § 2173.

285 Herzog, A Short History of European Law; Hespanha, Como os juristas viam o mundo, § 2173; Ord. Fil., Book I, Tit. LXV, § 31–§ 72.

The ordinary judge of Massangano was regularly elected by the *moradores* of the *presídio* from amongst their peers and adjudicated cases *ex aequo et bono* by applying a 'rustic' mixture of learned law, municipal bylaws and rulings, and local uses and customs.[286] Ordinary judges of Massangano were then either confirmed or rejected by the *ouvidor geral* of Angola, who, acting as *corregedor*, could revise their adjudications.[287] Despite the *Philippine Ordinances* stipulating that two ordinary judges were to be elected on each city council, probably due to its small size and remoteness, the *homens bons* of Massangano elected only one.[288] He was responsible for leading the municipal council, overseeing the work of all other municipal officials, from bailiffs to salt overseers and scribes, and writing the yearly "general queries."[289] According to the *Philippine Ordinances*, the competence range of ordinary judges was tied to the size of the villages they resided in.[290] However, since 1765, the office of ordinary judge of Massangano was also regulated by Sousa Coutinho's Ordinance of February 24.[291] According to it, he had the same competence range as the captain majors, regardless of the size of Massangano. In cases of "verbal injuries," the *Philippine Ordinances* stipulated that ordinary judges could adjudicate without appeal cases involving penalties of up to 6$000 *réis* but had to do so in conjunction with the city councilors.[292] They were barred from accepting money or any other form of compensation from litigants.[293] The ordinary judge of Massangano was also responsible for eradicating local uses and customs deemed

286 Camarinhas, Administração da justiça em espaços coloniais, p. 109–124; Camarinhas, Juiz de Vintena; Camarinhas, Lugares ultramarinos, p. 137–160; Fernandes and Rêgo, História do Direito Português, p. 249–251; Freire, Meneses (trans.), Instituições de Direito Civil, p. 114; Hespanha, A constituição do Império Português, in: Fragoso et al. (eds.), O Antigo Regime nos trópicos, p. 163–188; Hespanha, História das instituições, p. 259–268, 270–278; Hespanha, Sábios e rústicos, p. 31–60.

287 Camarinhas, Juízes e administração, p. 100.

288 AHU, CU, Angola, Box 28, D. 2723.

289 Ord. Fil., Book I, Tit. LXV, § 39–§ 72; Salgado, Fiscais e meirinhos; Wehling and Wehling, Direito e justiça, p. 24.

290 The *Philippine Ordinances* determined that ordinary judges could adjudicate without appeal cases worth up to 1$000 *réis* in movable property or $400 *réis* in real estate in settlements larger than 200 *moradores*. In smaller places, they could adjudicate cases worth up to $600 *réis* in movable properties or $400 *réis* in real estate without appeal. Cases involving movable properties worth up to $400 *réis* were orally adjudicated, only the final decisions being registered by a notary who was allowed to charge up to 7 *réis* for this service. In all other cases, the allegations of the parts were also registered. It is unclear if the competence range of the ordinary judge of Massangano changed as the village progressively decreased in size after the reconquest of Luanda from the Dutch. Ord. Fil., Book I, Tit. LXV, § 7.

291 AHU, CU, Angola, Box 51, D. 4624.

292 Ord. Fil., Book I, Tit. LXV, § 25.

293 Ord. Fil., Book I, Tit. LXV, § 10, § 39–§ 72.

contrary to the "*form of His Majesty's Laws.*"[294] Finally, the ordinary judge doubled as the judge of orphans, the deceased, and absent—a jurisdiction that the captain major of the *presídio* often "*usurped*" for self-serving reasons.[295] As Miller explains, since judges of orphans had jurisdiction over the assets left by deceased merchants and could order their disposal to alleged local creditors before channeling them back to legitimate heirs or creditors in Lisbon, their office was coveted as it was prone to give rise to profitable 'abuses.'[296]

2.7 Special Courts and the War Board

As Captain-General and Governor Mello related, by 1800, several special courts dealing with mercantile and maritime matters regularly convened in Luanda, these included: the "*juízo do terreiro* [Market Court]" (1764), the "*juízo da alfandega* [Customs Court]" (1784), the "*juízo das causas do mar* [Naval Court]," and the "*juízo de avarias* [Damages Court]."[297] According to him, every year, the municipal council appointed two new judges with the approval of the captain-general and governor to serve in the Market Court, as provisioned by the Royal Charter of November 13, 1761.[298] They earned fixed stipends, paid by the market's treasury, and were aided by a scribe, two guards, two measure-takers, and a porter, all appointed for equal periods and through a similar process.[299] According to a *bando* issued by José de Almeida e Vasconcelos on February 21, 1788, these judges were to use green staffs to distinguish themselves from ordinary and municipal judges.[300] They were under the jurisdiction of the captain-general and governor as head of the Justice Board. In keeping with this *bando*, the Municipal Judges of Luanda had no jurisdiction over the market or its judges, as determined by a Royal Charter of November 12, 1765. The Customs Court and its judges were tightly regulated by the Royal Charter of February 16, 1784, and the Ordinance of the Customs House of the City of Saint Paul of Luanda issued by Mello on October 21, 1799.[301] These

294 AHU, CU, Angola, Box 51, D. 4624.

295 AHU, CU, Angola, Box 28, D. 2723; Mello, Relação dos officios civis, p. 281–293; Ord. Fil., Book I, Tit. LXV, § 3.

296 Coimbra (ed.), Livros de "Ofícios para o Reino," p. 223; Miller, Way of Death, p. 308, 583.

297 Coimbra (ed.), Livros de "Ofícios para o Reino," p. 72; Mello, Relação dos officios civis, p. 281–293.

298 Delgado, O governo de Sousa Coutinho em Angola I, p. 19–56; Mello, Relação dos officios civis, p. 284–285.

299 Mello, Relação dos officios civis, p. 284–285.

300 Rocha, Administração e poder local, p. 21–23.

301 The captain-general and governor of Angola had appointed judges of the Custom House of Luanda since the government of Sousa Coutinho (1764). These were usually lawyers. However, in 1796,

judges were aided by several minor officeholders, all appointed and paid by the captain-general and governor.[302] They also had criminal jurisdiction in the customs house and its "dependencies," from warehouses to docks.[303] The Naval Court and the Damages Court were headed by the *ouvidor geral* and assisted by one of his scribes.[304]

Besides these courts, several ad hoc and conventional *juntas* had been convened in Angola since the first years of the General Government of Angola to adjudicate pressing matters in a simplified or summary style. By the 1800s, the *Junta de Guerra* [War Board] was the oldest *junta* still convening sporadically in Angola. While it is unclear when this institution was first mentioned as a *junta*,[305] since 1611, the ordinances of the captain-general and governors of Angola specified that in case they had to "*wage war to defend the presídios and the population of Saint Paul* [of Luanda]," they had to consult with the bishop of Angola and Congo, if the diocese was not *sede vacante*, the *ouvidor*, the *provedor da Real Fazenda*, and "*other ministros* [officials]."[306] After 1676, the board was enlarged to comprise representatives from the Franciscans, Carmelites, and Capuchin monastic orders as well as the General Vicar of the Cathedral Chapter of Luanda, "*the high-ranking ministers of war*," and the "*officials of the municipal council*."[307] This expanded War Board was tasked with declaring just wars according to Second Scholastic interpretations of the doctrines of *Ius gentium* and the Ordinance of the Government of the Kingdom of Angola of 1676.[308] This royal enactment specified as *casus belli* when "*Sovas, or any other Kings, or Potentates*," harassed "*Portuguese Vassals*," impeded commerce, "*favored the enemies of the Crown*," or rendered difficult "*the preaching of the Holy Gospel*."[309]

Given that the lawful enslavement of African adversaries hinged on the conflicts they were captured in being declared just wars, the War Board's decision directly impacted the livelihood of *moradores* and merchants sojourning in Angola and

---

the *Ouvidor Geral* João Álvares de Melo also accumulated the position of judge of the Custom House of Luanda. Coimbra (ed.), Livros de "Ofícios para o Reino," p. 96, 103, 108, 139; Mello, Regimento da Alfandega, p. 359–447; Mello, Relação dos officios civis, p. 283–284.

302 Mello, Relação dos officios civis, p. 283–284.

303 After adjudicating 'commercial' crimes, the judges were supposed to send a detailed account of the process to the *ouvidor geral*. After adjudicating 'blood' or violent crimes, they were supposed to send a similar report to the municipal judge of Luanda. Mello, Regimento da Alfandega, p. 443.

304 Mello, Relação dos officios civis, p. 282.

305 The Ordinance of the Government of the Kingdom of Angola of 1676 already mentions it as a "*Juncta* [Board]." Regimento do governo deste Reyno.

306 Heintze, Fontes para a História de Angola; MMA VI, D. 8.

307 Regimento do governo deste Reyno.

308 Ibid., Caldeira, Dimensão sociopolítica, p. 46–48.

309 Regimento do governo deste Reyno.

Benguela.[310] Moreover, since a tax was paid to the Crown for exported slaves, and one-fifth of the enslaved prisoners of just wars belonged to the Crown (the 'royal fifth'), the War Board's decisions also had a financial impact.[311] The same was true, for a period, about the decisions of the *Junta de Missões* [Missions Board], created in 1693. Its establishment and functions are further discussed in the following chapter, dedicated to the Catholic Church's institutional history in Angola and the institutions related to slavery. For now, it is sufficient to state that a royal letter from March 15, 1698, stipulated that the Missions Board should start receiving appeals in freedom cases when enslaved Africans had petitioned for the recognition or restitution of their free status but were sentenced in the first instance to slavery.[312] Therefore, despite its immediate field of action being the management of hinterland missions and the spreading of the Roman Catholic faith, the rulings of the Missions Board also had economic and financial impacts because of this normative entanglement with the institutions of slavery. It thus becomes clear that one of the defining local inflections of the "*junta* administrative model" is the fact that, despite having well-demarcated portfolios, West Central African commissarial boards were transversely implicated in the Atlantic slave trade, their decisions being pondered with two sets of interests in mind: the government of *moradores* and the extraction of slaves. The next chapter explores how the tension between these interests played out during the transition to a "police State" political paradigm (c. the 1760s).[313]

---

310 Couto, Os capitães-mores em Angola; Rocha, Ethiope resgatado.

311 The Ordinance of the Government of the Kingdom of Angola of 1676 stipulated that each expeditionary army would have a "person" in charge of supplying guns, gunpowder, and munitions under the jurisdiction and supervision of the *provedor da Real Fazenda*. This person would then be entitled to the royal fifth as compensation. Regimento do Governo deste Reyno; Miller, Way of Death, p. 346.

312 When this board lost most of its authority with the expulsion of the Jesuits (1759), the captain-general and governors of Angola resumed performing this function. According to Ferreira, these appeals proceeded mostly from *mucano* hearings in the *presídios*. However, since slaves were considered movable property, freedom cases could, in theory, be triggered in any judicature with jurisdiction over movable property. Ferreira, Cross-Cultural Exchange, p. 104–105.

313 Subtil, Espaço político e organização, p. 88–116; Subtil, Estado de polícia, p. 15–40.

3. From *Imperium* to Sovereignty

3.1 A Brief Overview of Roman Catholic Institutions

The Roman Catholic Church provided fundamental ideological, diplomatic, and logistical support to Portuguese overseas expansion from its very onset, validating Portuguese claims of political *dominium* and the legitimacy of the *merum imperium* of the monarch over West Central African territories.[1] As António Hespanha explains, the concepts of "*imperium*," subdivided into "*merum*" and "*mixtum imperium*," and "*dominium*" were part of revived Roman law in the Iberian Peninsula and integral to how jurists and canonists conceptualized the Portuguese and Spanish early modern composite empires.[2] In keeping with their worldview, the monarch had varying jurisdictions ("*iurisdictiones*") over the conquered provinces of the empire, having "*senhorio* [lordship]" over some territories while recognizing the pre-existing kingdoms and self-organizing communities that existed in others.[3] Moreover, the Portuguese Crown claimed to have "*senhorio do comércio* [lordship

---

1 Iberian jurists took the concept of *merum imperium* from Ancient Roman and medieval sources. It was reconceptualized during the early decades of Iberian overseas expansion to ground new understandings of the monarch's rights and describe the essence of their public power. According to Hespanha, in keeping with revived Roman law, *merum imperium* or "simple" *imperium* was subdivided into six modalities: "*imperium maximum*," which included the "supreme powers of the prince (*regalia maiora*)" such as "as making laws, convening courts, confiscating property, creating notaries;" "*imperium maius*," the power to punish; "*imperium magnum*," which included the power to deport; "*imperium parvum*," which included the power to exile; and "*imperium minus* and *minimum*," which included the power to exert minor acts of coercion. Alencastro, O trato dos viventes, p. 27; Bonciani, Poder régio em mutação; Boxer, A Igreja militante; Boxer, Four Centuries; Boxer, O Império Colonial Português; Doré, As stuações no Reino do Congo e na Costa da Pescaria, in: Doré, Lima and Silva (eds.), Facetas do Império na História, p. 227–243; Hespanha, A cultura jurídica europeia, p. 205–206; Hespanha, Como os juristas viam o mundo, § 70–§ 78, § 1036–§ 1042; Marcocci, A Consciência de um Império; Souza, Estruturas eclesiásticas da monarquia portuguesa, in: Palomo, Stumpf and Barreto Xavier (eds.), Monarquias ibéricas em perspectiva comparada, p. 513–542; Thomaz, De Ceuta a Timor.

2 Hespanha explains that, in keeping with revived Roman law, *mixtum imperium* was also conceptualized as subdivided into six modalities, ranging from the "*mixtum imperium magnum*" of the monarch to the minor forms of *mixtum imperium* of the officeholders who could only order procedural acts. While *mixtum imperium magnum* could not be delegated, the remaining five could. Hespanha, A cultura jurídica europeia, p. 205–206; Hespanha, Como os juristas viam o mundo, § 73, § 1039.

3 Hespanha, Como os juristas viam o mundo, § 73–§ 78; Hespanha, Fazer um império com palavras, in: Barreto Xavier and Nogueira da Silva (eds.), O governo dos outros, p. 80–82.

over commerce]" or over "*navigation and commerce*" in vast undefined areas such as "*Guinea*," "*Ethiopia*," "*Arabia*," "*Persia*," or "*India*,"[4] creating additional challenges to those engaged in thinking through the juridical basis of the 'Empire.'[5] Hespanha remarks that what unified the multiple political entities that composed it, at the conceptual level, was the notion of "Catholic Monarchy," or universal, all-embracing monarchy, expressed in the ideal of a single monarch having *merum imperium* over a diverse but tendentially harmonious spiritual whole and being able to delegate forms of *mixtum imperium* (*iurisdictio*) to magistrates and officeholders.[6] While this formulation of the Crown's *imperium* was purely ideological, it had practical implications on how different modalities of *dominium* were conceived, harmonized, and exercised throughout the empire. Furthermore, it firmly grounded both 'native dispossession' and the institutions of slavery, as what we today think of as individual freedom was conceptualized as a '*res*,' a 'thing' amongst many other 'things' that different persons or corporations could claim to have *dominium* over.[7] While these premises read as incredibly abstract, as this chapter explores, they provided the framework for the Portuguese conquest of the Kingdom of Ndongo and the traffic of enslaved Africans until a modern notion of royal sovereignty was formulated and began to gain traction in the second half of the eighteenth century.[8]

During the early stages of Portuguese expansion and most of the *Antigo Regime*, relationships between humans and things were conceived of as different modalities of *dominium*, each equally valid and all self-referential and autonomous.[9] In other words, while liberal notions of property are anchored in a clear-cut distinction

---

4 These terms designated broad regions without clear-cut borders, conceptualized according to a quasi-mythical worldview. Therefore, they cannot be directly equated with late modern or contemporary regions or countries.

5 Hespanha, Como os juristas viam o mundo, § 73–75; Saldanha, Conceitos de espaço e poder, in: Aubin (ed.), La Decouverte; Saldanha, Iustum imperium.

6 Barreto Xavier, Religion and Empire in Portuguese India, p. 39–42; Hespanha, Como os juristas viam o mundo, § 77–§ 78; Hespanha, Direito comum e direito colonial, p. 95–116; Hespanha, Fazer um império com palavras, in: Barreto Xavier and Nogueira da Silva (eds.), O governo dos outros, p. 70; Hespanha, Uncommon Laws, p. 184–185; Sánchez, Spanish Theories of Empire, in: Tellkamp (ed.), A Companion to Early Modern Spanish Imperial Political and Social Tought, p. 17–52.

7 Dias Paes, Esclavos y tierras, p. 6–7.

8 Marcocci, A Consciência de um Império; Russel-Wood, Iberian Expansion and the Issue of Black Slavery, p. 16–42.

9 As described by Hespanha, medieval jurists distinguished up to twenty-three different modalities, including several salvific or spiritual ones. Secular modalities of *dominium* included direct ownership ("*dominium directum*"), beneficial ownership ("*dominium utile*"), and "feudal," "usufructuary," and "mortgage" modalities of *dominium*. Hespanha, Como os juristas viam o mundo, § 1037–§ 1038.

between a willing, owning subject and an exclusively owned object, the relationship-centered notion of *dominium* afforded the recognition of co-existing claims over a 'thing,' each connoting a different spiritual, social, or personal use of it.[10] Some of the modalities of *dominium* could refer to uses directed towards achieving spiritual or salvific goals, while others were directed towards achieving temporal ones. While, as Hespanha clarifies, there was no explicit, well-defined hierarchy between modalities of *dominium*, these uses were nevertheless hierarchized.[11] The achievement of spiritual goals, forwarded by privileging specific modalities of *dominium*, was prioritized over all temporal goals. Among the latter, the achievement of community goals was prioritized over fulfilling individual ones, which could be further differentiated according to the personal status of those involved.

Within this complex ideological and normative framework, the dispossession of non-Christians of their political and personal freedom (enslavement) and lands could be framed by jurists and Canon law specialists as the privileging of modes of *dominium* that forwarded salvific goals, both stemming from and reinforcing the claims to *imperium* over West Central Africa of the Catholic Monarch.[12] Therefore, the spread of the gospel, the conversion of African potentates to Roman Catholicism, and the baptism of enslaved Africans constituted the ultimate juridical basis of early overseas conquest and expansion, lending a veneer of legitimacy to the Atlantic slave trade and its peculiar institutions even while not justifying the enslavement of freeborn non-Christianized Africans *per se*.[13] Even after the Roman Catholic Church officially discredited this reasoning, the dispossessing and genocidal practices it informed and legitimized remained constant in the Portuguese Empire.[14] The achievement of the temporal goals of the Portuguese Crown and its overseas delegates continued to be framed in salvific terms well into the mid-nine-

---

10 Dias Paes, Esclavos y tierras; Hespanha, Como os juristas viam o mundo, § 1039.

11 Hespanha, Como os juristas viam o mundo, § 1039.

12 Ibid.; Barreto Xavier, Religion and Empire in Portuguese India, p. 39–42; Dias Paes, Esclavos y tierras.

13 Giuseppe Marcocci claims the papal bull *Dum Diversas* (1452) was central to these developments. Marcocci, A Consciência de um Império, p. 46–50.

14 Hespanha explains that the Council of Constance (1414–1418) declared this line of reasoning heretical. Moreover, during the Second Scholasticism of the sixteenth and seventeenth centuries, several jurists and theologians argued that pagans could ground their *dominion* over things in natural law. Braun, Bom and Astorri, A Companion to the Spanish Scholastics; Calafate, A Escola Ibérica da Paz nas Universidades de Coimbra e Évora, Vol. 1; Calafate, Estudo introdutório I, in: Calafate (ed.), A Escola Ibérica da Paz nas Universidades de Coimbra e Évora, Vol. 1; Fernandes, Luis de Molina: On War, in: Kaufmann and Aichele (eds.), A Companion to Luis de Molina; Hespanha, Como os juristas viam o mundo; Kaufmann and Aichele, A Companion to Luis de Molina; Salas and Fastiggi, A Companion to Francisco Suárez.

teenth century when abolitionism provided an alternative ideological grounding for European conquest and African dispossession.

On a more practical note, Ângela Barreto Xavier and Fernanda Olival reckon that, until then, religious agents belonging to the secular and regular clergy or, in the earlier stages, the military orders, were often "pioneers," informally tasked with "scouting, charting, and demarcating territories" previous to their conquest and settlement.[15] As both authors describe, the clergy's institutional relationship with the Portuguese Crown were framed first by the Portuguese Royal Patronage (1455–c. 1668) and then by a less comprehensive set of "rights of patronage."[16] Initially, the Royal Patronage was an extensive set of rights and obligations conceded by the papal bull *Romanus Pontifex* on January 8, 1455.[17] It granted the Portuguese monarch the right to enslave and to wage a just war of conquest against muslins and non-Christians south of Cape Bojador, forbidding other Christian nations from visiting these African shores (the principle of *mare clausum*), and obliging the Portuguese Crown to establish and maintain there missions, churches, and monasteries. It also granted it the right to collect tithes and name the clerics appointed to the new ecclesiastical positions (the rights of *ius patronatus et praesentandi*). Soon after, the Bull *Inter coetera* of March 13, 1456, granted to the Military Order of Christ ecclesiastical jurisdiction over these *extra territorium* domains, also briefly transferring the *ius praesentandi* to the master of the Order. However, posterior bulls shifted it back to the Portuguese monarch,[18] whom the Bull *Praeclara charissima in Christo* of December 30, 1551, declared *in perpetuum* master of the Order of Christ.[19]

Concomitantly, with the creation of the Diocese of Funchal (1514) and in the aftermath of the Council of Trent, ecclesiastical jurisdiction increasingly fell into the hands of bishops, who were nevertheless appointed and closely overseen by

---

15 Barreto Xavier and Olival, O padroado da coroa de Portugal, in: Palomo, Stumpf and Barreto Xavier (eds.), Monarquias ibéricas em perspectiva comparada p. 123–160.

16 Ibid., p. 153; Gouveia, The Creation of a Portuguese Diocese, p. 497–498; Paiva, Os Bispos de Portugal p. 38–44; Silva, L'Évêche du Congo et de l'Angola p. 295–334; Silva Rego, Les Missions Portugaises.

17 Alencastro, O trato dos viventes, p. 23–25; Barreto Xavier and Olival, O padroado da coroa de Portugal, in: Palomo, Stumpf and Barreto Xavier (eds.), Monarquias ibéricas em perspectiva comparada p. 128–129; Russel-Wood, Iberian Expansion and the Issue of Black Slavery, p. 25.

18 The right to appoint bishops and archbishops was separated from the right to appoint chapter members and their privileges. Therefore, the *ius praesentandi* was often *de facto* shared by the monarch and the local bishops despite being *de jure* shared between the first and the master of the Order of Christ. Barreto Xavier and Olival, O padroado da coroa de Portugal, in: Palomo, Stumpf and Barreto Xavier (eds.), Monarquias ibéricas em perspectiva comparada p. 129.

19 Ibid., p. 128–129; Souza, Estruturas eclesiásticas da monarquia portuguesa, in: Palomo, Stumpf and Barreto Xavier (eds.), Monarquias ibéricas em perspectiva comparada, p. 515.

the Portuguese Crown.[20] The latter was still responsible for creating new religious establishments, collecting tithes, maintaining the clergy, and providing safe passage to its overseas dominions.[21] As the previous sections clarified, in West Central Africa, some of these obligations were delegated to the captain-general and governors of Angola, as well as the captain majors of the hinterland *presídios*. Spreading the Christian faith was always a priority in their ordinances, letters patent, and personal orders. In this context, the Diocese of Congo and Angola was established (1596–1940) by the Bull *Super specula* of May 20, 1596, and initially integrated into the Metropolitan Archdiocese of Lisbon.[22] A new episcopal see was established in São Salvador do Congo, the new Christian name of Mbanza Kongo, the capital of the independent Kingdom of Kongo,[23] elevating the Church of the Holy Savior of Congo (1491–1678) to the status of a cathedral.[24] Before, the Catholic population of Kongo and the hereditary Captaincy of Angola was under the bishop of São

20 Souza, Estruturas eclesiásticas da monarquia portuguesa, in: Palomo, Stumpf and Barreto Xavier (eds.), Monarquias ibéricas em perspectiva comparada, p. 516.

21 Barreto Xavier and Olival, O padroado da coroa de Portugal, in: Palomo, Stumpf and Barreto Xavier (eds.), Monarquias ibéricas em perspectiva comparada p. 135–137, 145, 148–149; Silva, L'Évêche du Congo et de l'Angola p. 3; Silva Rego, Les Missions portugaises.

22 Alencastro, O trato dos viventes, p. 71; Barreto Xavier and Olival, O padroado da coroa de Portugal, in: Palomo, Stumpf and Barreto Xavier (eds.), Monarquias ibéricas em perspectiva comparada p. 151; Brásio, Para a história do Cabido de Angola e Congo, p. 24; Gouveia, The Creation of a Portuguese Diocese, p. 495–509.

23 As John Thornton describes, the new see was created at the request of the *Mwene Kongo*, as he was weary of São Tomé vicars harassing the local New Christian Portuguese community on charges of Judaizing behaviors. Thornton, The Development of an African Catholic Church, p. 167.

24 The episcopal see was only moved to Luanda in 1716, elevating the Church of Our Lady of Remedies (1628–) to cathedral status. However, the bishops of Congo and Angola resided in Luanda from 1621–1624, abandoning the Cathedral of the Holy Savior of Congo to its chapter. In the aftermath, the *Mwene Kongo* negotiated with the *Propaganda Fide* the creation of an Italian Capuchin Mission in Kongo, which arrived in West Central Africa in 1645, despite the interference of the Portuguese Crown. Captain-General and Governor Sá e Benevides invited the Capuchins to Luanda after he reconquered Angola from the Dutch West India Company in 1648, establishing them a hospice at the hermitage of St Anthony. Brásio, Para a história do Cabido de Angola e Congo, p. 24–56; Gouveia, The Creation of a Portuguese Diocese, p. 496, 506; Mello e Souza, Alianças e embates entre religiões, in: Hermann and Martins (eds.), Poderes do Sagrado, p. 365; Silva Corrêa, História de Angola, Vol. 1, p. 269; Thornton, The Development of an African Catholic Church, p. 164.

Tomé and Príncipe (1534),[25] whose diocese had been created by the Bull *Aequum reputamus* of November 2, 1534.[26]

Oliveira and Barreto Xavier explain that the Royal Patronage was progressively undone at a second historical moment that coincided with the Iberian Union and the Portuguese Restoration War (1640–1648).[27] The establishment of the *Congregatio pro Gentium Evangelizatione* (1622–2022), better known as the *Propaganda Fide*, a congregation of the Roman Curia responsible for coordinating missionary works,[28] the ideological triumph of the *mare liberum* doctrine, and the creation of a *Junta Geral das Missões* [General Missions Board] (1655) in Lisbon, tasked with coordinating missionary activities in the overseas dominions and overseeing the activities of local, subordinated courts, all contributed equally to its erosion. In Luanda, a local Missions Board was established on March 18, 1693, composed initially of the captain-general and governor, the bishop of Congo and Angola, the *ouvidor geral*, and the *provedor da Real Fazenda*.[29] Later, the "*prelados* [priors]" of the convents that existed in Luanda were also admitted to this board.[30] In 1693, to finance its activities, the Missions Board of Luanda was granted an annual preference on the sale of slaves.[31] It became responsible for paying the "*congrua*

---

25 As Gouveia remarks, while Portuguese monarchs exercised their *Ius praesentandi* regarding the appointment of bishops, the presentation of dignitaries and canons of the cathedral of Mbanza Kongo, except for the dean and schoolmaster, and the collection of tithes soon became the responsibility of the *Mwene Kongo*. This created a permanent tension between the bishop of Congo and Angola and the Chapter of the Holy Savior of Congo Cathedral. By 1595, the Kingdom of Kongo had six churches, six lay brotherhoods, and several private chapels, which twenty priests served. Mbanza Kongo was estimated to have c. 10.000 inhabitants at the time. Gouveia, The Creation of a Portuguese Diocese, p. 505–506; MMA III, D. 145; Silva, L'Évêche du Congo et de l'Angola p. 9.

26 Brásio, Para a história do Cabido de Angola e Congo, p. 24; Gouveia, The Creation of a Portuguese Diocese, p. 501; Horta, Africanos e portugueses, p. 320.

27 Barreto Xavier and Olival, O padroado da coroa de Portugal, in: Palomo, Stumpf and Barreto Xavier (eds.), Monarquias ibéricas em perspectiva comparada p. 137.

28 For an analysis of the rivalries between the different regular orders in the Kingdom of Kongo and how the creation of the *Propaganda Fide* stoked it, see Chantal Luís da Silva and Mariana Mello e Souza. Boxer, A Igreja militante, p. 101–102; Mello e Souza, Alianças e embates entre religiões, in: Hermann and Martins (eds.), Poderes do sagrado, p. 361–382; Silva, L'Évêche du Congo et de l'Angola p. 295–334; Thornton, The Correspondence of the Kongo Kings, p. 407–421.

29 AHU, CU, Angola, Box 39, D. 3712; ANTT, CLNH, Fol. 7, D. 1, p. 93; Souza e Mello, As Juntas das Missões ultramarinas, p. 23.

30 AHU, CU, Angola, Box 39, D. 3712; Mello, Carta a D. Rodrigo de Sousa Coutinho, p. 275.

31 On March 18, 1693, the Portuguese Crown granted the Board of Missions of Luanda a preference on 700 enslaved Africans per year. According to Marcia Souza e Mello, this preference was abolished in 1758. The money raised by their public auction financed the missionary activities sponsored by the board and was administered by its treasurer. However, as Souza e Mello relates, the captain-generals and governors often usurped their jurisdiction and used the board's funds to finance other projects. Souza e Mello, As Juntas das Missões ultramarinas, p. 25–26; ANTT, CLNH, Fol.

[yearly income]" and maintaining the missionaries sent to the hinterlands, including providing African porters.[32] As further discussed in the following pages, in 1698, the board became responsible for adjudicating appeals for freedom, but lost this jurisdiction by the middle of the eighteenth century.[33] By 1755, it administered 23 missionary establishments, not counting seven missionary parishes in the *presídios* and some chapels near Luanda.[34] Of the former, all but six were regularly vacant, and, as Captain-General and Governor Miguel António de Mello noted, after the expulsion of the Jesuits (1759), the Missions Board became increasingly inefficient.[35] Also, according to him, by 1800, 25 parishes and six canonries were vacant in the Captaincy of Angola.[36] Concomitantly, on September 10, 1766, the *Propaganda Fide* established the Independent Prefecture of Congo in the Kingdom of Loango, trusting it to "French priests" and alarming the secular and ecclesiastic branches of the Portuguese administration.[37] The lack of vocations was perceived as so dire that the bishops of Congo and Angola were forced to accept the chaplains of ships as parish priests, leading to countless cases of 'abuse' because the latter were more interested in trading slaves with their former shipmates than "rescuing souls."[38]

During this later period (1660–1781), the Board of Royal Conscience and Military Orders confirmed the appointment of *extra territorium* bishops, archbishops, and holders of other canonical offices.[39] The Board of Royal Conscience and Military Orders also functioned as an appeal court in some Canon law matters.[40] In 1677, the Diocese of Congo and Angola became part of the Metropolitan Archdio-

---

7, D. 1, p. 93, 111; Boxer, Portuguese Society in the Tropics, p. 132; Russell-Wood, Fidalgos and philanthropists, p. 36.

32 AHU, CU, Angola, Box 39, D. 3712.

33 Ferreira, Cross-Cultural Exchange.

34 Souza e Mello, As Juntas das Missões ultramarinas, p. 49–69.

35 As Oliveira and Barreto Xavier point out, the decline of local missions boards was also indicated by the establishment of a Secretariat of State of the Navy and the Overseas in 1736. This secretariat eroded the authority of the Overseas Council, which was directly responsible for overseeing the non-religious dimensions of the boards' actions. Barreto Xavier and Olival, O padroado da coroa de Portugal, in: Palomo, Stumpf and Barreto Xavier (eds.), Monarquias ibéricas em perspectiva comparada p. 143; Coimbra (ed.), Livros de "Ofícios para o Reino," p. 59; Mello, Carta a D. Rodrigo de Sousa Coutinho, p. 280; Souza e Mello, Fé e Império, p. 148.

36 Mello, Carta a D. Rodrigo de Sousa Coutinho, p. 280.

37 Delgado, O governo de Sousa Coutinho em Angola III, p. 9.

38 Mello, Carta a D. Rodrigo de Sousa Coutinho, p. 280.

39 Barreto Xavier and Olival, O padroado da coroa de Portugal, in: Palomo, Stumpf and Barreto Xavier (eds.), Monarquias ibéricas em perspectiva comparada p. 131.

40 Camarinhas, Juízes e administração, p. 64–65.

cese of Bahia, created on November 16, 1676, by the Bull *Inter Pastoralis offici*.[41] After the *First Constitutions of the Archdiocese of Bahia* (1707) were approved by the synod of June 12, 1707, the *Regimento do Auditorio Ecclesiastico* [Ordinance of the Ecclesiastical Auditorium] (1704) framed the organization and administration of Canon law tribunals in Angola and Benguela.[42] By 1799, Dantas Lima, then dean and general vicar of the chapter of Luanda, remarked that there were no ecclesiastical privileges in Angola other than the canonries of the chapter and the parishes.[43] Furthermore, he noted that the monarch, who also served as master of the Order of Christ, was nominally the only patron of Portuguese West Central African domains. The chapter of Luanda was supposed to be composed of fifteen members, headed by a dean, and including an archdeacon, a "*chantre* [chanter]," a schoolmaster, a treasurer, and ten canons, who could perform specialized roles, including that of the general vicar who headed a Canon law tribunal (the ecclesiastical auditorium) where complaints were adjudicated in keeping with the Ordinance of the Ecclesiastical Auditorium of 1704.[44] However, as mentioned, most canonicate and parish positions remained vacant in Angola and Benguela for long periods due to the high mortality rates of Europeans and the Portuguese bishops' resistance to ordaining Black clergymen. Finally, the "*câmara eclesiástica*," the bishop's small council, was run by a "*provisor* [purveyor]," assisted by an irregular number of clerks and bailiffs, who also assisted the general vicar in his duties.[45]

As for the regular orders, after the expulsion of the Jesuits, there were only three religious colleges left in Luanda, belonging to the Third Order Regular of St. Francis (Franciscans), the Order of the Brothers of the Blessed Virgin Mary of Mount Carmel (Carmelites), and the Order of Friars Minor Capuchin (Capuchins).[46]

---

41 Gouveia, The Creation of a Portuguese Diocese, p. 504; Souza, Estruturas eclesiásticas da monarquia portuguesa, in: Palomo, Stumpf and Barreto Xavier (eds.), Monarquias ibéricas em perspectiva comparada, p. 538.

42 Vide, Constituições primeiras do Arcebispado da Bahia; Vide, Regimento do Auditório Ecclesiastico.

43 Lima, IV, p. 294–300.

44 In keeping with the bull that established the Diocese of Congo and Angola, the bishop received a yearly sum of 600$000 *réis* from the Crown (200$000 *réis* of stipend and 400$000 *réis* of "grace and supplement") to which 60$000 réis were added if he visited his diocese. The dean, archdeacon, *chantre*, and schoolmaster received 45$000 *réis* of stipend and each canon 40$000 *réis*. The vicar general received an extra yearly sum of 100$000 *réis*, as did the preacher. The *fábrica da Igreja* [church council] received the sum of 40$000 *réis* per year, and each of the 12 chapels initially established in the Captaincy of Angola 6$000 *réis* per year. Ibid.; Cordeiro (ed.), Estabelecimentos e resgates portuguezes na Costa Occidental de Africa por um anonymo, p. 21; Vide, Regimento do Auditório Ecclesiastico.

45 Paiva, Dioceses e organização eclesiástica, in: Azevedo (ed.), História Religiosa de Portugal, Vol. 2, p. 187–199; Rodrigues, Clergy, Society, and Power Relations in Colonial Brazil, p. 40–67.

46 Mello, Carta a D. Rodrigo de Sousa Coutinho, p. 274–281.

By 1800, Mello listed six Carmelites residing in Angola, three in the Convent of St. Thereza in Luanda, one in the parish of Pungo Andongo, one in the mission in the lands of *Soba* Bango Aquitamba, and one in jail "for very serious crimes."[47] As for Capuchins, he listed three: two managing the Hermitage of St Anthony in Luanda and one in the mission established in the lands of *Dembo* Cahenda, next to Ambaca. Finally, Mello listed six Franciscans, one residing in the Convent of St Joseph in Luanda, another serving as parish priest in Ambaca, and the remaining four living in the Bar of Dande, Massangano, Muxima, and the Bar of the Kwanza, where they lived irregular lives managing the assets of the order after having also been condemned for serious crimes.

3.2 The Mixed Court of the Inquisition

Once the Portuguese Cardinal-King Henrique (1512–1580) issued the Ordinance for the government of the Holy Office of 1552, the jurisdiction of the Court of the Inquisition of Lisbon (1536–1821) was extended to include West and West Central Africa under Portuguese influence, then under the bishop of São Tomé and Príncipe.[48] Established with the permission of the papal bull *Cum ad nihil* (1536), the Portuguese Inquisition was a mixed ecclesiastical-royal court, a "power amongst the other powers" of the poli-synodal Portuguese Kingdom, to use Giuseppe Marcocci and José Pedro Paiva's expression.[49] In the first decades of overseas expansion, it had a very ambitious agenda, seeking to extend its grasp to the Portuguese overseas domains through regular "*visitações* [visits]."[50] After the Ordinance of the Holy Office of the Inquisition of 1613, the Inquisition of Lisbon was also allowed

---

47 Mello, Relação do clero regular, p. 293–294.

48 The Portuguese Inquisition was established by the papal bull *Cum ad nil magis* issued by Pope Paul III (1468–1549) on May 23, 1536. Bishop Diogo da Silva of Évora was its first grand inquisitor, followed by the then Archbishop Henrique of Braga in 1539, who headed the mixed court for four decades. The latter gave a decisive contribution to its institutional architecture and workings. East Africa, under Portuguese influence, was soon to be under the jurisdiction of the Court of the Inquisition of Goa, established on March 2, 1560. Alencastro, O trato dos viventes, p. 25; ANTT, TSO, CG, Sr. 34, D. 331; Boxer, A Igreja militante; Horta, A Inquisição em Angola e Congo, p. 387–415; Horta, Africanos e portugueses, p. 301–321; Marcocci and Paiva, História da Inquisição Portuguesa, p. 23–48, 110–114; Ribeiro da Silva, A Inquisição nas Ilhas, p. 158.

49 Marcocci and Paiva, História da Inquisição Portuguesa, p. 15–16; Ribeiro da Silva, A Inquisição em África, in: Silva and Mateus (eds.), As Inquisições Modernas, p. 181.

50 Bethencourt, História das Inquisições; Green, Inquisition; Marcocci and Paiva, História da Inquisição Portuguesa, p. 123, 220.

to appoint officials or familiars of the Holy Office in Luanda.[51] The first visitor sent to the Captaincy of Angola was the Jesuit Jorge Pereira, who was tasked with inquiring about the "heretical tendencies" of the *moradores* of Luanda between 1596 and 1598 and focused mainly on the New Christian merchant community.[52] However, as Filipa Ribeiro da Silva describes, visits did not become regular as they were deemed too expensive after the first decades of the seventeenth century, and official representatives or familiars remained very few.[53] Therefore, the Inquisition of Lisbon relied almost exclusively on extra-official inquisitorial work performed by the agents of secular justice, such as captain majors and scribes, the regular clergy, especially the Jesuits and Capuchins,[54] and the secular clergy of local dioceses, to act in the African domains under its jurisdiction.[55]

As José Horta explains, the Inquisition of Lisbon initially had jurisdiction over accusations of practicing Judaism, Judaized Catholicism, Lutheranism, and other Christian denominations considered heretical, blasphemous, religious neglectful, simoniac, and criminalized sexual behaviors (such as male and female sodomy, and bigamy), and *feitiçaria* and spellcasting. In Angola, the court paid particular attention to accusations of the first two practices, remaining usually unconcerned with the behavior of Africans, especially those who were unbaptized.[56] This outlook was somewhat different regarding BaKongo Christian practices that Jesuit missionaries often conflated with heresy.[57] As John Thornton remarks, between 1626 and 1632, Jesuit denunciations to the Holy Office focused on the clergy that served the Kingdom of Kongo, framing their high tolerance of African religious practices as abiding "idolatry" and sorcery. Later ordinances, issued in 1613, 1640,

51 ANTT, TSO, CG, Sr. 34, D. 335; Ribeiro da Silva, A Inquisição em África, in: Silva and Mateus (eds.), As Inquisições Modernas, p. 177–234.

52 Marcocci and Paiva, História da Inquisição Portuguesa, p. 123, 525; Pantoja, Inquisição, degredo e mestiçagem em Angola, p. 118.

53 Gouveia, The Creation of a Portuguese Diocese, p. 502; Ribeiro da Silva, A Inquisição em África, in: Silva and Mateus (eds.), As Inquisições Modernas, p. 177–234; Ribeiro da Silva, A Inquisição nas Ilhas, p. 157–173.

54 As the seventh chapter explores in greater detail, since the Capuchins' mission in Angola was structured as an apostolic prefecture, therefore under the jurisdiction of the *Propaganda Fide*, Capuchin prefects acting as commissars of the Inquisition of Lisbon, often could count neither on the help nor the sympathy of the regular clergy under the jurisdiction of the bishop of Congo and Angola, nor the secular authorities. Leguzzano, Ao leitor, in: Leguzzano (ed.), Descrição histórica dos três Reinos, p. v.

55 Horta, Africanos e portugueses, p. 301–321; Horta, A Inquisição em Angola e Congo, p. 387–415; Pantoja, Inquisição, degredo e mestiçagem em Angola, p. 117–136; Ribeiro da Silva, A Inquisição em África, in: Silva and Mateus (eds.), As Inquisições Modernas, p. 177–234; Ribeiro da Silva, A Inquisição nas Ilhas, p. 157–173.

56 Horta, Africanos e portugueses, p. 301–321.

57 Thornton, Conquest and Theology, p. 258.

and 1774, expanded the inquisitorial jurisdiction to include ever more infractions, thereby increasing the power of the General Council of the Holy Office of the Inquisition and the general inquisitor over the subsidiary district branches such as the Inquisition of Lisbon.[58]

As Ribeiro da Silva explains, after 1613, the General Council headed by the general inquisitor appointed the official ministers of the Inquisition in Angola and issued some of the arrest orders. According to her, from 1553 to 1821, in all African domains except Angola, which she has yet to study in detail, accusations of the practice of *feitiçaria* adjudicated by the Inquisition remained very low.[59] When deliberating allegations from these territories, as probably those that reached them from Angola during most of this period, inquisitors always considered the place of birth and level of Christianization of the accused, African non-baptized *feiticeiros* being only decried as "bad examples" and at most confirmed by the court as non-Christians. This relative leniency of the Inquisition towards African practices contrasted with the attitude of missionaries from the regular orders, who were often paragons of iconoclasm and intolerance, as further discussed in the seventh chapter.[60] During the eighteenth century, however, the Inquisition of Lisbon increasingly relied on local officials, and more familiars and even commissars were appointed to the African domains, including Angola.[61] The latter were called "overseas commissars," the first of whom was appointed to Luanda in 1719.[62] As Luís Oliveira argues, this tendency was probably a sign of the decreased influence of the court, and the local elites took on these positions merely as signs of social prestige or bases for petty power struggles.[63] What complaints to the Inquisition can tell us about how belonging to a local "moral community" was locally negotiated is also explored in the seventh chapter.[64]

---

58 Ribeiro da Silva, A Inquisição em África, in: Silva and Mateus (eds.), As Inquisições modernas, p. 186–187.

59 Ibid., p. 177–234.

60 MMA V, D. 24.

61 Bethencourt, História das Inquisições; Cabral de Oliveira, "He homem pardo, mas para com os nacionaes he branco da terra," p. 169–202.

62 According to Marcocci and Paiva, João Calmon was the first 'overseas commissar' based in Luanda. He was given the power to 'carry out judicial investigations and ratify witnesses, to speed up proceedings and reduce the dangers arising from the distance from Lisbon." Marcocci and Paiva, História da Inquisição Portuguesa, p. 319.

63 Bethencourt, História das Inquisições.

64 Kodesh, Beyond the Royal Gaze; Schoenbrun, The Names of the Python.

3.3 The Institutions of Slavery

Given that the Captaincy of Angola, Benguela, and their dependencies held a unique position in the economic organization of the Portuguese Empire as providers of slaves to the plantations and mines of South America and that the taxes levied over exported slaves were the Crown's primary source of revenue in West Central Africa,[65] by the nineteenth century, several institutions were in place to guarantee the legal enslavement of Africans according to Second Scholastic doctrines of just enslavement and *Ius gentium* principles of just war and justice in war.[66] Judicial processes known as 'freedom cases,' in theory, if seldom in practice, allowed those who had been wrongly enslaved to reclaim their original freedom.[67] The genealogy of these institutions can be traced back to the third edition of the *Manueline Ordinances* (1521–1603) and the *Extravagant Laws* (1569) edited by Duarte Nunes do Leão (1530–1608), which A. Saunders argues provided a "slave code capable of meeting most of the contingencies arising in a slave-owning society" contrary to the previous *Afonsine Ordinances* (c. 1448).[68] However, in the Captaincy of Angola,

---

65 The eighth chapter explores taxation in greater detail.

66 The chapters in the second part will discuss the Second-Scholastic doctrines of just enslavement and their historical evolution from the sixteenth to the eighteenth century. See Pedro Calafate for an introduction to the Iberian School of Peace and Portuguese and Spanish thinking about the doctrines of just war and justice in war in the context of their empire's overseas expansion. AHU, CU, Angola, Box 87, D. 6986; Calafate, A Escola Ibérica da Paz ; Calafate, A Escola Ibérica da Paz nas Universidades de Coimbra e Évora,Vol. 1; Fernandes, Luis de Molina: On War, in: Kaufmann and Aichele (eds.), A Companion to Luis de Molina.

67 In his 1802 report, Mello explains that he usually restored freedom to all enslaved Africans who claimed that they had been sold by their parents or had sold themselves as slaves to escape starvation. However, the captain-general and governor also admits that captain majors such as José Nogueira da Rocha, the captain major of Muxima at that time, got rich overnight by buying "*innumerable blacks*" for a "*fistful of manioc*" during periods of extreme hunger. See José C. Curto for an analysis of several cases of enslaved Africans who managed to recover their "*original freedom*" through judicial means, including the *mucano* hearings. Candido, African Freedom Suits, p. 447–459; Candido, An African Slaving Port, p. 191–236; Curto, Experiences of Enslavement in West Central Africa, p. 382–415; Curto, Struggling Against Enslavement, p. 96–122; Curto, The Story of Nbena, in: Lovejoy and Trotman (eds.), Trans-Atlantic Dimensions of Ethnicity, p. 43–64; Curto, Un butin illégitime, in: Sala-Molins and Henriques (eds.), Déraison, esclavage et droit, p. 314–327; Ferreira, Cross-Cultural Exchange, p. 52–125; Mello, Relatorio do Governo, p. 548–564; Santos, Esclavage africain, p. 127–148; Santos, O Império Português face às instituições indígenas, in: Palomo, Stumpf and Barreto Xavier (eds.), Monarquias ibéricas em perspectiva comparada, p. 292–298.

68 As Saunders explains, the *Afonsine Ordinances* were inadequate to cope with the advent of mass-scale African slavery, being primarily concerned with the handling of Muslim slaves. Moreover, many of the relevant norms regulating the institutions of slavery during this earlier period were found in local uses and customs, *posturas municipais*, Canon law, and revived Roman Law. By

institutions related to slavery were significantly impacted by Mbundu institutions dating from before the Portuguese conquest of the Kingdom of Ndongo.[69]

According to Cruz e Silva, in the *itanda* [fairs/markets] of Ndongo, the *ngola* appointed officers to inquire about the fairness of the enslavement and the status of the enslaved persons traded there.[70] In the early seventeenth century, after the Portuguese occupied some of the main *itanda* and turned them into slave fairs supplying the Atlantic markets, a "*mani quitanda* [lord of the market]" was appointed by the captain-general and governors of Angola to direct them. Still, it is unclear if he inherited the functions of these preexisting Mbundu officers.[71] By the late eighteenth century, it was captain majors acting as ordinary judges and the ordinary judge of Massangano who were supposed to hear and adjudicate *mucanos* regarding wrongful enslavement, following the same summary style applied to arbitrate other *mucanos*.[72] In Ambaca, Cambambe, Encoge, Massangano, and Pungo Andongo, they were assisted by the official scribes who accumulated the functions of "*escrivães de liberdades* [scribes of freedoms]," being tasked with writing down the decisions

---

1514, King Manuel of Portugal ordered the baptism of enslaved Africans within half a year of their landing in Portugal, noting that slaves older than ten years of age could opt to decline baptism. This regulation created the need to appoint clergy responsible for hearing and baptising willing slaves. However, as Saunders notes, by 1568, most slave masters still ignored the command, and the archbishop of Lisbon reinforced it with a pastoral order. In the aftermath of the Council of Trent, the baptism of slaves became predicated on their knowledge of fundamental Roman Catholic dogma and prayers (e. g., the Paternoster, the Ave Maria, the Ten Commandments, and the Articles of the Faith), creating the need for new offices responsible for catechising the enslaved. In an ordinance from 1519, D. Manuel also regulated the marking or branding of African slaves brought to São Tomé with a "*cross on their right arm*," a brand later changed to a "*G*" for Guinea. For an exhaustive list of all royal enactments and other normative sources regarding slaves from 1211 to 1876, including a breakdown of all the articles of the *Manueline Ordinances* related to slavery, see Margarida Seixas. Saunders, A Social History of Black Slaves, p. 13, 41, 113–114; Seixas, Pessoa e trabalho no Direito Português, p. 787–871.

69 Santos, Esclavage africain, p. 127–148.

70 As further discussed in the fourth chapter, not all enslaved or servile Mbundu could be freely alienated from the villages of the corporate kin groups who held rights over them, thus creating the need to monitor their trade. Cruz e Silva, As feiras do Ndongo, in: Santos (ed.), Actas do seminário, p. 405–422; MMA III, D. 54.

71 Heintze, Fontes para a História de Angola, Vol. 1, p. 127; Sousa, O extenso relatório do governador a seus filhos, in: Heintze (ed.), Fontes para a História de Angola, Vol. 1, p. 217–362.

72 The ninth chapter explores the different kinds of *mucanos* adjudicated by captain majors and Captain-General and Governors Sousa Coutinho's and António de Mello's attempts to typify and regulate them. ANTT, CLNH, Fol. 7, D. 1, p. 114; Santos, O Império Português face às instituições indígenas, in: Palomo, Stumpf and Barreto Xavier (eds.), Monarquias ibéricas em perspectiva comparada, p. 292–298.

in a ledger.[73] A local "*tendala*" would serve as an interpreter in these hearings.[74] On March 14, 1698, a royal charter instituted a dedicated scribe of freedoms in Luanda responsible for keeping a master ledger registering all the decisions reached by captain majors in freedom cases.[75] When the captain majors adjudicated against the petitioners' freedom, the latter could still appeal to the *mucano* hearing held by the captain-general and governor of Angola at no cost.[76]

Roquinaldo Ferreira argues that, by the middle of the seventeenth century, *mucanos* regarding the conditions of enslavement, appeals, and the *mucano* hearings that adjudicated them became so common that they came to be conceived of as customary Portuguese institutions, the juridical action of the petitioners being known as "*apelidar liberdade* [appeal/plea for freedom]" and the hearing of appeals held by the captain-general and governor of Angola as the "*tribunal de mucanos* [*mucanos* court]" or "*tribunal de liberdades* [freedom court]."[77] In this 'court,' by the end of the eighteenth century, adjudication was often grounded on revived Roman law and *Ius gentium* doctrines regarding just enslavement.[78] However, Catarina Madeira Santos argues that all *mucano* hearings remained firmly rooted in African norms because the evidence and testimonies brought before the adjudicator related to past arbitrations and conflicts were framed according to the principles of

73 Mello, Relação dos officios civis, p. 281–293; Santos, Esclavage africain, p. 127–148.

74 AHU, CU, Angola, Box 51, D. 4624; Parreira, Dicionário glossográfico; Santos, Entre deux Droits, p. 839; Santos, Esclavage africain, p. 127–148.

75 Unfortunately, as Catarina Madeira Santos remarks, the *mucano* ledgers of the Captaincy of Angola have been lost. However, the *dembo* archives that have been preserved provide several examples of cases that were adjudicated under the heading of *mucano* by these semi-autonomous African potentates. Namely, as Santo's relates, cases regarding the "possession and use of insignia of power, payment of debts, exchange of gifts, circulation of women, possession of land, lineage rights and regulation of African slavery issues." Some of their *mucano* adjudications can be found transcribed in the source volume edited by Paula Tavares and Santos, *Africæ monumenta* (2002). The archives of *Dembos* "Caculo Cacahenda [*Kakulu ka Kahenda*], and probably Ngombe Amuquiama, Quibaxe, [and] Mufuque" were incorporated by the Overseas Historical Archive (AHU) in Lisbon in 2006 and 2009, being registered in the 'Memory of the World Programme' by UNESCO in 2011. They have been progressively digitized and publicized online. Couto, Os capitães-mores em Angola, p. 157; Dembos (1677–1920); Santos, Écrire le pouvoir en Angola, p. 767–795; Santos, Esclavage africain, p. 127–148; Tavares and Santos, *Africæ Monumenta*.

76 Originally, this ledger was to be undersigned and revised by the oldest ordinary judge of Luanda. However, when the ordinary judges were substituted by municipal judges in 1721, it is unclear whether one of the new judges 'inherited' this responsibility or if the scribe of freedoms became the only one responsible for the ledger. AHU, CU, Angola, Box 88, D. 7031; Couto, Os capitães-mores em Angola, p. 157, 161; Santos, O Império Português face às instituições indígenas, in: Palomo, Stumpf and Barreto Xavier (eds.), Monarquias ibéricas em perspectiva comparada, p. 292–298.

77 Ferreira, Cross-Cultural Exchange, p. 99–100.

78 AHU, CU, Angola, Box 88, D. 7031.

African normative systems.[79] She contends that, according to a Mbundu normative understanding, "compensations" negotiated between the corporate kin groups of individuals involved in severe misdeeds, such as "violent deaths, sorcery, non-payment of a debt, theft, [or] injuries," took the place of the individual sanctions and penalties usually applied in Europe to anti-social wrongdoings conceptualized as crimes.[80] Therefore, *mucano* hearings were also framed by contemporary Portuguese observers as forms of debt settlement between *sobas*.[81] This was the case because the compensations agreed to "repair the crimes" of the offender were often estimated in slaves that their corporate kin group needed to offer to the kin group of the offended to "reestablish equilibrium and peace."[82]

According to Santos, it was only during the seventeenth century that Mbundu "*mukano*" and Luso-African *mucano* hearings became increasingly associated with the "judgments of freedoms," the latter remaining, however, a "kind of *mucano* amongst others." As the following chapters discuss in greater detail, the legal implications of *mucano* hearings by captain majors or captain-general and governors remaining rooted in African normative systems were historically perceived and constructed differently. While at first, this was considered a worrying source of illegitimacy that even threatened to delegitimize the *dominium* over the freedom of enslaved Africans that South American plantation owners and slave masters acquired from Atlantic slave merchants, eventually, several doctrinal and normative innovations came to predicate this legitimacy precisely on West Central Africans having been condemned to slavery according to African normative systems.

As Ferreira discusses, until 1698, appeals for freedom were orally adjudicated by captain-general and governors, with no appeal, another hallmark of their sig-

---

79 AHU, CU, Angola, Box 88, D. 7031; Santos, Esclavage africain, p. 127–148; Santos, O Império Português face às instituições indígenas, in: Palomo, Stumpf and Barreto Xavier (eds.), Monarquias ibéricas em perspectiva comparada, p. 271–303.

80 Heeding the criticism of Claude Meillassoux, Igor Kopytoff, Laura Doyle, and Wyatt MacGaffey, I use the more neutral term corporate kin group instead of 'lineage' or 'matrilineage' to avoid reifying "membership by birth" as the privileged or the only criterium of membership in West Central African groups organized using the conceptual language of kinship and descent. I will still use the concepts of 'lineage' or 'matrilineage' when citing authors or their translations of African concepts (e. g., translating *malemba dya ngundu* as uncles of the matrilineage, in keeping with Joseph Miller). Similarly, I opt to use David Schoenbrun's concept of "communities of moral belonging" to refer to Miller's "cross-lineage" or "extra-lineage" groups, except when these concepts appear in quotations or when directly discussing the latter's work. Doyle, Bordering on the Body, p. 5; Kopytoff, Introduction, in: Kopytoff (ed.), The African Frontier, p. 41–43; Meillassoux, The Anthropology of Slavery, p. 23–26; Miller, Kings and Kinsmen; Santos, Esclavage africain, p. 127–148; Schoenbrun, The Names of the Python.

81 See, for instance, the Ordinance of the Government of this Kingdom of Angola of February 12, 1676. Regimento do governo deste Reyno.

82 Santos, Esclavage africain, p. 127–148.

nificant jurisdictional autonomy.[83] However, when a dedicated scribe of freedoms was appointed in Luanda in 1698, a royal charter of March 15 transferred the right to adjudicate appeals for freedom to the Missions Board of Luanda.[84] Despite this board being equally headed by the captain-general and governor and following the same oral and summary style as the *mucanos* court, due to its collegiate nature, it was supposed to be less prone to adjudicating freedom cases self-interestedly or according to Mbundu norms. However, with the decline of the Missions Board, the captain-general and governors of Angola regained their old privilege of deciding *mucanos* without assistance or appeal, which was extended to the subaltern governor of Benguela.[85] In the words of Captain-General and Governor José de Almeida e Vasconcelos, in office between 1784 and 1790, by then, freedom "*rulings were oral, nothing was written, except for* [a] *short record of the decision, after hearing a lengthy speech in Kimbundu by the parties.*"[86] However, soon after, Captain-General and Governor Mello complained of precisely the opposite.[87] This leads Ferreira to conclude that, with time, the hearing of appeals for freedom and other *mucanos* posed an administrative challenge to enlightened captain-general and governors, not only because the plaintiffs and the first-instance adjudicators or arbiters of the cases presented to them had framed their cases according to Mbundu or Ovimbundu norms but also because of their vast number.[88] As further discussed in the ninth chapter, Mello attempted to solve this problem by transferring the adjudication of appeals of freedom to the *ouvidoria geral* and other *mucanos* to civil courts.[89]

In Luanda, there was also the Canon law court of the *inquiridor de liberdades* [enquirer of freedoms], presided over by a canon of the Chapter of Luanda who was aided by two "*catechisadores de liberdades* [catechists of freedoms]," one stationed in Luanda, the other in Benguela.[90] These catechists were presbyters of the chapter in charge of interviewing all slaves about the fairness of their enslavement before they were baptized and shipped overseas.[91] They were also tasked with baptizing

---

83 Ferreira, Cross-Cultural Exchange, p. 99–100.

84 Ibid., p. 102–104.

85 AHU, CU, Angola, Box 88, D. 7031; Ferreira, Cross-Cultural Exchange, p. 104–105.

86 Ferreira, Cross-Cultural Exchange, p. 104.

87 AHU, CU, Angola, Box 88, D. 7031.

88 Ferreira, Cross-Cultural Exchange, p. 110–111, 116–118.

89 Ibid., p. 110–111.

90 On March 22, 1690, the Crown first ordered that "*two clerics were to assist the exame* [inquiry] *of the mucanos* [freedom causes]," probably referring to the cases brought before the enquirer of freedoms. ANTT, CLNH, Fol. 7, D. 1, p. 75; Couto, Os capitães-mores em Angola, p. 165; Lima, IV, p. 294–300; Santos, Luanda, in: Brockey (ed.), Portuguese Colonial Cities in the Early Modern World, p. 269.

91 Couto, Os capitães-mores em Angola, p. 157.

those who accepted their bondage and referring those who contested it to the enquirer's court. Despite being clerics, the enquirer of freedoms and the catechists of freedoms were appointed by the captain-general and governor of Angola, preferably from amongst those capable of understanding Kimbundu or any other African language.[92] Finally, the statute that created a new government in Benguela on April 3, 1796, determined that its governor had appellate jurisdiction over the "freedom cases" adjudicated in the dependencies of the former captaincy.[93] In the case of Benguela, however, no ledger of freedoms was kept. After 1796, the officeholder responsible for 'branding' the slaves became responsible for interviewing them about their status and referring those who contested their enslavement to the governor. According to Ferreira and Santos, the appellants who sought a hearing with the governor of Benguela had to "pay a cow" in less critical cases or a "young female or male young slave" in more important ones.[94] While the Ordinance of the Governor of Benguela of 1796 does not confirm these privileges, it refers to the "*cases of mucanos*," framing them exclusively as freedom cases.[95] Furthermore, according to the ordinance, the governor of Benguela had the "*same jurisdiction*" over *mucanos* as the captain-general and governor of Angola. He was supposed to "*process them summarily*," condensing the "*interlocutory hearings*" and the "*reading of the final sentence*," and be assisted by a neutral "*learned adviser*."

Complementing the *mucano* and the enquirer of freedom's courts, "*capitães das marcas* [captains of the brands]" were appointed by the captain-general and governors of Angola to some of the hinterland *presídios* and districts, tasked with policing the enslaved and sending runaway slaves back to Luanda.[96] Their name was derived from the system of slave branding developed in Angola and Benguela. As Ferreira and Jill Dias summarize, enslaved Africans were branded on their chests with hot irons at different moments, marking their progressive transition from African regimes of asymmetric dependency to the mercantilist one that underpinned the Atlantic slave trade.[97] In a lecture he presented to the Royal Academy of Sciences of Lisbon in 1793, Luís António de Oliveira Mendes (1750–1817) explained that slaves were first branded with "*the private signal of Certanejo* [hinterland trader], *who takes them into slavery so that they can be known and found if they escape*."[98]

92 Ibid., p. 165; Lima, IV, p. 294–300; Santos, De "antigos conquistadores" a "angolenses," p. 214.

93 Couto, Os capitães-mores em Angola, p. 167–168.

94 Ferreira, Cross-Cultural Exchange; Santos, Esclavage africain, p. 127–148.

95 ANTT, MO, NU, Box 8, D. 1.

96 ANTT, CLNH, Fol. 52, D. 77, D. 111; Ferreira, Cross-Cultural Exchange, p. 122; Ofícios para o Reino do Governdor D. Fernando António de Noronha, p. 12.

97 Dias, Angola, in: Alexandre and Dias (eds.), O Império Africano, p. 319–556; Ferreira, Cross-Cultural Exchange; Winnebeck et al., On Asymmetrical Dependency.

98 Mendes, Memória a respeito dos escravos, Vol. 4, p. 8.

Then, Oliveira Mendes continued, when "*they arrive at the seaport where they are to be taken on board, they are branded on their chests with the arms of the king and the nation, whose vassals they are.*" This second brand was made "*with a silver instrument when paying the duties, and this mark is called a Carimbo* [stamp; from the Kimbundu *kirimbu* for signal]."[99] A third brand, Oliveira Mendes claimed, was made "*by their private master, under whose name and negotiation they are transported to Brazil*" being placed "*either on their left breast or on their arm, so that they may also be known in the event of their escape.*"[100] All these '*carimbos*,' Oliveira Mendes argues, were made on top of a series of other markings which the enslaved Africans had voluntarily made on their faces, each scar, he claimed, "*indicating the family, Kingdom, Presídio, and place where they were born and were moradores.*"[101] The officers who were responsible for branding the enslaved Africans in Luanda and Benguela were the "*marcadores de escravos* [slave branders]," appointed by the captain-general and governor but paid by the local municipal councils as part of the staff of the custom houses.[102] Captains of the brands were tasked with inspecting these markings on all suspected slaves and returning wayward ones to their masters.

3.4 Official Slave Fairs, *Pumbos*, and Merchant Compounds

Official slave fairs, or unofficial ones known in West Central Africa as *pumbos*,[103] complemented Angola and Benguela's institutional infrastructure. As mentioned above, from the time of the earlier occupation of the Kingdom of Ndongo, the Portuguese Crown sought to control the flow of trade in the Angolan hinterlands, occupying preexisting fairs known as *itanda* and adapting Mbundu institutions, a process analyzed in more detail in the next chapter.[104] Official fairs were either established next to the *presídios* and thus under Portuguese military control or remained under the protection of African authorities.[105] Their number and precise

99 Ibid., Parreira, Dicionário Glossográfico, p. 56.

100 According to Silva Corrêa, Captain-General and Governor José de Almeida e Vasconcelos proposed to brand all hinterland army recruits with a small "*AR*" or "*FR*" silver brand between their index finger and thumb to avoid desertion. Mendes, Memória a respeito dos escravos, p. 8; Silva Corrêa, História de Angola, Vol. 1, p. 71–72, Vol. 2, p. 118.

101 Mendes, Memória a respeito dos escravos, p. 8.

102 ANTT, CLNH, Fol. 47, D. 91.

103 Heintze, Fontes para a História de Angola, Vol. 1, p. 124; Parreira, Dicionário Glossográfico, p. 96; Sousa Coutinho, Para o Secretario de Estado Francisco de Mendonça.

104 Cruz e Silva, As feiras do Ndongo, in: Santos (ed.), Actas do seminário, p. 405–422.

105 Couto, Os capitães-mores em Angola, p. 194; Fernandes, A feira de Cassanje, p. 30–41; Hespanha, L'Administration d'une «ombre d'empire», in: François and Grenet (eds.), Raison administrative et logiques d'Empire, p. 291–335.

location varied greatly, as successive Luso-African wars and skirmishes, as well as African dynastic conflicts, made commerce impossible, and fairs had to be constantly relocated, reopened, or established anew by the captain-general and governors.[106] After half a century of conquest, by the 1630s–40s, several significant *pumbos* and a couple of official slave fairs remained entirely outside Portuguese military control. Adriano Parreira lists those in the Kingdoms of Matamba and Kasanje and the *pumbo* of Okanga, north of the Kingdom of Kongo, as the most significant ones, mentioning that several other smaller slave fairs and markets were also held in the independent Kingdoms of Kongo and Loango.[107]

In 1624, when Fernão de Sousa became captain-general and governor of Angola, it was customary for *mani quitandas* to be appointed to direct Portuguese-controlled fairs, with the assistance of bailiffs and other unspecified officials, who likely exercised the functions of interpreters and *almoxarifes*.[108] According to Beatrix Heintze, the *mani quitandas* were *quimbares* and often themselves slaves. Therefore, they were directly overseen by the captain-general and governors, who tasked them with managing the slave trade and collecting tributes.[109] Already by 1618, Captain Major Baltazar Ribeiro de Aragão denounced to the Crown that many 'abuses' resulted from this system, claiming that, by then, slave fairs were deserted and no "*houses, nor factories*" bearing the "*royal coat of arms*" existed in either Luanda or the hinterland *presídios*.[110] As Ribeiro de Aragão described, "*governors impose*[d] *a tyrannical tribute on fairs*," their "*bailiff*" or *mani quitanda* picking "*one in every ten slaves*" as a political tribute to the captain-general and governor and then allowing his personal "*buyer*" to choose first which slaves to purchase. Next, the captain major continued, the "*black bailiff of the Ouvidor*" of Luanda would pick which slaves to buy for his master, followed by the representative of the secretary of the

---

106 Cordeiro (ed.), Terras e minas africanas segundo Rebello de Aragão, p. 13; Heywood and Thornton, Central Africans, p. 109–169.

107 Parreira, Economia e sociedade, p. 118–123.

108 Sousa, O extenso relatório do governador a seus filhos, in: Heintze (ed.), Fontes para a História de Angola, Vol. 1, p. 217–362.

109 Heintze, Fontes para a História de Angola, Vol. 1, p. 122.

110 According to Luciano Cordeiro, Ribeiro de Aragão was born in Portugal and reached Angola in 1593. In 1599, he established the *presídio* of Muxima at his own expense and, by 1607, was tasked by the captain-general and governor of Angola to attempt to reach the Eastern Coast by land. Besides denouncing these abuses, Ribeiro de Aragão also lamented that vassal *sobas* were "*stolen and mistreated*" because captain-general and governors and captain majors insisted that their tributes were to be paid in slaves, accepting no other "*produce of their lands*." Cordeiro (ed.), Terras e minas africanas segundo Rebello de Aragão, p. 12–13; Cordeiro (ed.), Estabelecimentos e resgates portuguezes na Costa Occidental de Africa por um anonymo, p. 5–8.

captain-general and governor, and those of "*many other persons to whom the said governor has granted the varas* [staffs] *of bailiffs*."[111]

In the end, Ribeiro de Aragão concluded, all "*good slaves were picked*" before *moradores* could have a choice, and only the "*refuse*" was left for the "*miserable people*" to buy—the "*elderly Blacks and children*." According to him, this system resulted in Luso-African merchants traveling to "*where the tyrannical jurisdiction* [of captain-general and governors] *doesn't reach*" and Black slave merchants known as "*guenze*" abandoning official slave fairs in favor of distant *pumbos*.[112] The solution to the economic problems caused by this abandonment, Ribeiro de Aragão argued, would be to avoid governors having such ample jurisdiction in matters of "*justice and finance*," establishing a "*juiz dos feitos de El-Rei* [judge of the royal deeds]" in Angola responsible for overseeing and adjudicating all matters related to the royal treasury and finance, including the taxation of the commercial transactions taking place at slave fairs.[113] While his request was partially heeded,[114] according to Couto, official slave fairs remained mostly abandoned up until the middle of the eighteenth century for, as Ribeiro de Aragão also pointed out, unscrupulous captain-general and governors quickly obtained slaves through raids and warfare, thus losing interest in maintaining them.[115] As Miller explains, until 1720, when captain-general and governors were forbidden to trade in slaves, South American planters simply "worked through militaristic governors in Angola to raid for slaves."[116] Entrepreneurial *angolense* captain majors did the same on a smaller scale, offering warlord-like services to interested Atlantic partners when neither the captain-general and governor nor the Municipal Council of Luanda were strong enough to oppose them.

From the outset, establishing a network of official fairs was also predicated on restricting the free movement of White *moradores* and Luso-African merchants sojourning in the Angolan hinterlands.[117] While the need for this restriction, which

---

111 Cordeiro (ed.), Terras e minas africanas segundo Rebello de Aragão, p. 13.

112 Ibid., p. 13–14; Heintze, Fontes para a História de Angola, Vol. 1, p. 118.

113 Cordeiro (ed.), Terras e minas africanas segundo Rebello de Aragão, p. 13–14; Freitas, A burocracia do "eloquente," p. 72.

114 In 1623, Ribeiro de Aragão was appointed *provedor da Real Fazenda* of Angola for six years. AHU, CU, Angola, Box 2, D. 130.

115 Cordeiro (ed.), Terras e minas africanas segundo Rebello de Aragão, p. 13–14; Couto, Os capitães-mores em Angola, p. 216–218; Systema, ou collecção dos regimentos reaes, Vol. 5, p. 236–238.

116 Miller, Way of Death, p. 530–531.

117 As the sources cited in the following pages help clarify, the Whiteness of White *moradores* was constructed according to a West Central African understanding often regarded as alien or unreasonable by external observers. For instance, the Rio de Janeiro-born Silva Corrêa noted with irony that "*brancos certanejos* [whites from the hinterlands]" were all those who were "*not puritan* [sic] *blacks*," explaining that "*in the Hinterlands of Angola, they call whites, those Blacks, whose*

was always more of an aspiration than a reality, had evident economic and fiscal roots, it also stemmed from the jurisdictional form of government of the Portuguese Empire.[118] As Manuel Saavedra summarizes, during the *Antigo Regime*, the Iberian empires, "normative activity was by definition interpretative."[119] Therefore, in principle, there was no "substantive difference" between the normative interpretations of "the prince, of the community through custom, of the judge in the administration of justice, or in the conceptual construction of the jurist."[120] In the many dependencies of Angola and Benguela, the significant jurisdictional autonomy this normative ordering conceded to the heads of dispersed Luso-African communities was quickly perceived as a threat by captain-general and governors, *ouvidores gerais*, and other learned officeholders.[121] They constructed it as the origin of countless cases of 'abuse' against Christendom, the Crown's fiscal rights, and the dignity of Mbundu or Ovimbundu vassals framed as *miserabiles personae* or other free African populations.[122] As explored in the first chapter, these complaints and fears contributed to the growing thesaurus of narratives that coalesced into the 'folk doctrine' of Portuguese West Central African domains being outside of God's grace and beyond the pale of natural law and *Ius gentium*.

However, even in keeping with this 'folk doctrine,' the *pumbos* and Luso-African compounds dispersed in the hinterlands of Angola and Benguela were not lawless environments but a context where the perverse normative impulses of *moradores* and slave traders could only be kept in check by curtailing their freedom of movement and sphere of action to where the rectifying jurisdiction of learned judges

---

manners, and distinction allow them to wear shoes." As described by Arlindo Barbeitos, by the mid-nineteenth century, Whiteness was still constructed in Angola in the same manner, often startling European observers. Barbeitos, A "raça" ou a ilusão de uma identidade definitiva, in: Gonçalves (ed.), O racismo ontem e hoje, p. 139–148; Silva Corrêa, História de Angola, Vol. 1, p. 120.

118 Couto, Os capitães-mores em Angola, p. 194–215.

119 As Tamar Herzog explains, the king was regarded as a "judge," a privileged interpreter of the underlying normative order of the universe—not someone endowed with legislative power as we now understand it. Herzog, What is Legal History, in: Duve and Herzog (eds.), Latin America Law in Global Perspective, p. 39–53; Hespanha, Fazer um império com palavras, in: Barreto Xavier and Nogueira da Silva (eds.), O governo dos outros, p. 91–92; Saavedra, Jurisdictional Autonomy and the Autonomy of Law, p. 325–337.

120 Saavedra, Jurisdictional Autonomy and the Autonomy of Law, p. 325–337.

121 As described by Hespanha, the same was true in South America and West Africa, where communities of "*bandeirantes*" and "*lançados*," respectively, were perceived as "archipelagos of loose colonists" with a "remarkable legal and political agency" that the Crown often faced with distrust. Hespanha, Filhos da terra; Hespanha, L'Administration d'une «ombre d'empire», in: François and Grenet (eds.), Raison administrative et logiques d'Empire, p. 291–335; Hespanha, Uncommon Laws, p. 181.

122 Hespanha, A cultura jurídica europeia, p. 291.

could reach them. Focusing on religious communities, Robert M. Cover proposes a theoretical framework that can help frame what was truly at stake in the Portuguese Crown's attempts to reign in these wayward communities.[123] As Cover explains, "tight communities" are created by a "process of juridical mitosis" that can be described as a form of "jurisgenesis."[124] Cover argues that "new law is constantly created through the sectarian separation of communities" and is a manifestation of their "jurispotence" or ability to produce norms for their self-regulation. Hespanha argues that "creole" or "raw laws" proliferated at the edges of the Iberian empires due to similar jurisgenetic processes.[125] Jurisgenesis also encompasses what Saavedra describes, following Paolo Grossi, as the "creative function" that jurists, community heads, and other jurisconsults and "interpreters" of the law played in *Antigo Regime* Iberian empires.[126] According to Cover's model, jurisgenerative processes are countered and balanced by "jurispathic" processes that prune the normative excess resulting from such communities' and experts' unbridled jurispotence.[127] Cover identifies official jurisprudence and the "courts of the state" as prominent jurispathic institutions during the Late Modern period. In the context at hand, the jurisdiction of captain-general and governors, captain majors, *ouvidores gerais*, and municipal judges can also be understood as jurispathic, especially concerning African normative systems and the uses, customs, and informal norms that resulted from the jurisgenerative actions of *moradores* and Luso-African merchants.[128]

In conclusion, contrary to what later tropes of colonized lands being framed as *terra nullius* might suggest, officeholders with jurisdiction were perfectly aware that what challenged them was the immense vitality of normative production in Angola and Benguela and their dependencies, not the lack of pre-existing normative frameworks, institutions, conflict resolution mechanisms, experts and arbitration courts.[129] Chapters four to six will explore how the Portuguese authorities dealt with West Central African jurispotence in the context of slave fairs; chapters seven

---

123 Cover, Nomos and Narrative, p. 4–68.

124 Ibid., p. 15.

125 Hespanha, Uncommon Laws, p. 183–184, 203–204.

126 Grossi, El orden jurídico Medieval, p. 168; Saavedra, Jurisdictional Autonomy and the Autonomy of Law, p. 325–337.

127 Cover, Nomos and Narrative, p. 40.

128 However, captain majors and ordinary judges, being what Santos has identified as "in-between" judicatures, also forwarded jurisgenetic processes, giving rise to local vernaculars, a trait also shared by royal magistrates, albeit perhaps to a lesser degree. These are further explored in the seventh and eighth chapters. Santos, Entre deux Droits, p. 817–848; Santos, O Império Português face às instituições indígenas, in: Palomo, Stumpf and Barreto Xavier (eds.), Monarquias ibéricas em perspectiva comparada, p. 271–303.

129 Hespanha, Fazer um império com palavras, in: Barreto Xavier and Nogueira da Silva (eds.), O governo dos outros, p. 91–92; Hespanha, Uncommon laws, p. 180–204.

to nine focus on how they dealt with it in the domestic and intimate spaces of *presídios*, *arimos*, and households. The outcomes of the unrestrained normative production that occurred in these spaces were frequently characterized as heretical, illegitimate, or perverse interpretations of the fundamental normative order of the universe, reinforcing the belief that neither natural law nor God's grace could be found in the Captaincy of Angola, Benguela, and their dependencies. In other words, the normative imagination and creativity of Luso-African *moradores* and slave merchants contributed to reinforcing the 'folk doctrine' that justified some of the local vernaculars at the expense of some of the Crown's jurisdiction.

To counter this, by 1607, the Ordinance of the Governor of Angola had already instructed the captain-general and governor to forbid "*white men*" from attending fairs, "*even if they claim to be keeping justice and setting* [things] *in order*."[130] According to the ordinance, this prohibition was due to the "*great loss to the common good*" they caused when arbitrating cases *ex aequo et bono*. About sixty years later, the Ordinance of Captain-General and Governor Tristão da Cunha, briefly in office between September 1666 and February 1667, ordered him to put an end to the habit of granting the military "*insignia of Captain*" to "*white men*" bent on trading in the hinterlands as a way of circumventing this prohibition.[131] According to this ordinance, these illegitimate captains committed "*injustices in the lands they crossed*," forcing the *sobas* to buy their wares and provide them porters, and acting as "*judges of mucanos*," adjudicating the 'debts' that African chiefs had amongst themselves. Due to this practice, the ordinance added, "*the captivity of many freedoms ensued* [sic], *without any consideration being paid to the fear of God*" or *Ius gentium*. In other words, many were wrongly enslaved. Ten years later, the Ordinance of the Government of the Kingdom of Angola of 1676 still lamented the fact that "*white men*" as well as "*mulattoes, and blacks with trousers or staffs*" had the habit of entering the "*hinterland*" and "*pumbos*," where they caused "*significant damage*" by passing as "*judges of mucanos*."[132] There, they continued to arbitrate cases between *sobas* that involved 'debts,' resulting in the enslavement of many free Africans as judicial payments. According to the Ordinance of 1676, these 'abuses' were so bad that official fairs where Whites could not go and "*keep justice*" were devised to solve the revolts and uprisings caused by their self-interested rulings. To complement this jurispathic strategy, in 1703, a royal letter from June 9 ordered the "*pseudo-captain majors*" to return to Luanda, where they were told to remain, and, in 1704, a royal letter from February 10 forbade the captain-general and governors of Angola

130 MMA V, D. 101, p. 274.

131 Andrade e Silva (ed.), Colleção chronologica da legislação portugueza (1657–1674), series 2, p. 110–117, p. 113.

132 Regimento do Governo deste Reyno.

to trade in the hinterlands, restricting their business to Luanda.[133] Finally, by 1720, all authorities were prohibited from trading in slaves.[134] The efficacy of all these measures, however, was questionable.

Until 1758, when a royal edict from January 11 ended the restriction on White men entering the West Central African hinterlands, the ordinances of the captain-general and governors always included a clause known as 'clause 18,' which ordered them to enforce this prohibition.[135] The dropping of clause 18 in 1758 signaled the adoption of new mercantile practices, as Miller has carefully detailed, and, crucially, a new approach to the problems posed by the jurispotence of Luso-African communities and White merchants.[136] As the royal edict from January 11 noted, the privilege of trading in the hinterlands was granted to all royal "*vassals of these kingdoms and their Dominions*." If the merchants remained "*under the protection*" of the "*king's laws*," no "*magistrate*" had the right to bar them henceforward.[137] In other words, the opening of the hinterlands to free trade was predicated on accepting a new hierarchy of sources of law that privileged statutory law and curtailed the jurisdictional autonomy of White *moradores* and Luso-African merchants in a new way. Now, their worst jurisgenetic excesses were not to be casuistically pruned by the adjudications of learned judges and military officers but by police regulations that strove to codify the normative content of disperse ordinances and royal decrees and write down local uses and customs.[138] This momentous policy change entailed that commissarial boards assumed the jurispathic vigilance hitherto assumed by captain-general and governors, *ouvidores gerais*, municipal judges, and captain majors.[139] As the last pages of this chapter argue, the three commissarial boards established in 1761 assumed this role, becoming instrumental in policing

133 Couto, Os capitães-mores em Angola, p. 74, 198.

134 Ibid., p. 198.

135 Couto, Os capitães-mores em Angola, p. 194–215; Ley para ser livre, e franco o commercio de Angola, p. 531–535.

136 Cover, Nomos and Narrative, p. 4–68; Miller, Way of Death, p. 577–578, 586–587.

137 Ley para ser livre, e franco o commercio de Angola, p. 531.

138 Heikki Pihlajamäki defines early modern police laws and regulations as "the legislative activity of an early modern state, which organizes its administration with statutes, decrees, ordinances, and other pieces of legislation." According to him, these laws were legitimated by the ideology of "good government, *Staatsräson* or *raison d'Etat*." Miguel, Que se abram os sertões; Pihlajamäki, The Westernization of Police Regulation, in: Pihlajamäki and Duve (eds.), New Horizons in Spanish Colonial Law, p. 97–124; Santos, Um governo "polido" para Angola; Subtil, Estado de polícia, p. 15–40.

139 Hespanha argues that introducing new commissarial boards, paradoxically, "far from being a decisive factor of centralization and standardization," was "the source of unlimited context-sensitive political casuistry." In other words, it exacerbated jurisgenetic tendencies. While this is true if we focus on the macro level, commissarial boards had a clear jurispathic impact on local jurisdictions and communities. Hespanha, Uncommon Laws, p. 186.

the hinterlands according to the new police state paradigm.[140] Immediately before they were created, António de Vasconcelos, the first captain-general and governor tasked with opening the hinterland trade to Whites, was openly critical of the royal edict from January 11, noting in a *bando* from 1759 that the reason why "*the price of Slaves has excessively Risen in the conquistas* [conquered territories]" was due to the "*ambition of white men*" who traveled there "*each one Being a Superior in Himself, and governing his actions according to his Costumes.*"[141] His solution was to reform the administration of official fairs, fixating the prices of '*banzos*,' the commodity bundles exchanged for a standard slave.[142] Until such reforms were undertaken, the captain-general and governor refused to publish the royal edict from January 11, 1758, in Angola, arguing that it would "*facilitate the disorders that* [Roma] *gypsies and New Christians and other depraved peoples want to commit in the hinterlands.*"[143] António de Vasconcelos justified his non-compliance by concluding that these persecuted groups "*had never been regarded favorably by* [His Majesty's] *Laws*" but always depended "*on their severity, to be restrained.*"

As soon as Sousa Coutinho assumed his office in 1764, he immediately undertook the reform of the administration of slave fairs suggested by António de Vasconcelos, finally opening the Angolan hinterlands to free trade—a measure that amounted to

---

140 Two weeks after the hinterland trade was opened to all merchants, a royal edict from January 25, 1758, reformed the taxation system of the Portuguese-controlled Atlantic ports in West Central Africa. Moreover, the royal edict from January 11, 1780, also modified several essential details of how slave ships were loaded and how permission to leave the harbor was granted. As Miller describes, all these had a profound economic and fiscal impact on the Captaincy of Angola, preparing the ground for the progressive abolition of the Angola slave contract after 1769. The Board of Commerce and the Board of Finance were instrumental in enforcing these reforms. Ley para ser livre, e franco o commercio de Angola, p. 531–535; Ley sobre a arrecadação dos direitos dos escravos, p. 537–540; MILLER, Way of Death, p. 586–588, 590–597.

141 In a note annexed to the copy of this *bando* sent by the captain-general and governor to the secretary of the navy and the overseas, António de Vasconcelos argues that the vassal Blacks deserted the hinterlands near Encoge because of the "*irreparable insolence of White merchants.*" Furthermore, he explains that in the fair next to the court of *Dembo* Ambuela, this African chief charged the tax of 4$000 *réis* for each slave sold there. To remedy these situations and several frauds committed by *pumbeiros* and seeking to divert the trade the *dembos* made with other European powers, António de Vasconcelos created an official fair next to the new *presídio* of Encoge. ANTT, MR, EXP, Sr. 34, F. 605, p. 5–15.

142 The composition and functioning of *banzos* are further explored in the chapters grouped in the second part. In keeping with Carlos Couto, this designation was already employed to designate the commodity bundles exchanged for slaves during the first decades of the seventeenth century. It cannot be mistaken with the *banzo* disease, a depressive or melancholic state that befell slaves taken away from their homelands and that often led to suicide or death by inaction. ANTT, MR, EXP, Sr. 34, F. 605, p. 1–3; COUTO, Os capitães-mores em Angola, p. 223; KANANOJA, Healing Knowledge, p. 179–180.

143 COUTO, Os capitães-mores em Angola, p. 206.

a *de jure* recognition of a *de facto* reality.[144] Apart from reshaping the structure and function of the existing commissarial boards, and experimenting with the creation of a "*Conferência do Comércio* [Conference of Commerce]," as described in the following pages, Sousa Coutinho reorganized the structure of official slave fairs and promoted the establishment of several new ones.[145] All the while assuming that it was impossible to administer them according to the regulations governing European fairs due to their remoteness and isolation.[146] According to him, the "*hinterlands were full of degredados of perverse habits*," who, together with Blacks who were considered "*whites as soon as they stopped wearing thongs and put on shoes*," acted as "*ministers of justice*," convening "*courts, hearing litigants, and arbitrating*" cases.[147] In simpler terms, the jurispotence linked to Whiteness posed an even more significant threat in West Central Africa because racial fluidity was typical during this period, and the adoption of European mores often sufficed to be considered White. Furthermore, in the vicinity of the slave fairs, it was usual for *degredados* to enslave their Black trading partners, or "*their wives and children*," in reprisal for missing payments or unpaid debts.[148]

Nevertheless, in a circular letter of July 12, 1764, Sousa Coutinho ordered that the captain majors of Ambaca, Cambambe, Encoge, Massangano, and Pungo Andongo were to refrain from interfering in the internal functioning of existing fairs, allowing the merchants to govern themselves.[149] This order was then confirmed by the sixth article of the Ordinance of February 24, 1765, that further regulated that captain majors were to refrain from meddling in commerce, interfering with the "*economy*" of the fairs, or issuing orders to the merchants.[150] These measures were then complemented by a September 16, 1764, ordinance regulating the scribes of the fairs elected by the merchants and delimiting their jurisdiction.[151] The ordinance decreed that they should limit themselves to economic management and only adjudicate commercial disputes, cooperating in all other jurisdictional matters with the captain majors, who acted as ordinary judges and provided military backup. As the following paragraphs clarify, these reforms were only understood as possible

---

144 Ibid.

145 Ibid.; Delgado, O governo de Sousa Coutinho em Angola I, p. 20–25; Miller, Way of Death, p. 582–585.

146 Sousa Coutinho, Para o Secretario de Estado Francisco de Mendonça.

147 AHU, CU, Angola, Box 51, D. 4624.

148 According to Sousa Coutinho, *moradores* also used to "*lash them, oust them* [of their rights], *and rob them*" and exposed Black merchants to the sun in "*aspas* [X-shaped crosses] *loaded with irons*" or tied them to trees until they died of exposure and insect bites. Ibid.

149 Ferreira, Feiras e presídios, p. 24.

150 AHU, CU, Angola, Box 51, D. 4624.

151 AHU, CU, Angola, Box 50, D. 4585.

because a reformed Board of Justice started acting against the jurisdictional 'abuses' of White merchants and Luso-African *moradores*.

By the end of the eighteenth century, a new wave of reforms attempted to reorganize the administration of slave fairs and increase the control captain-general and governors had over Luso-African merchants, especially by introducing the office of slave fair director.[152] According to José Joaquim Lopes de Lima (1797–1852), by the beginning of the nineteenth century, larger slave fairs had directors who acted as a "*kind of judge, who policed and guaranteed the good faith* [needed] *for transactions* [to take place]," adjudicating minor cases "*in a summary manner*."[153] The captain-general and governors of Angola appointed the directors who, in the case of the slave fairs of Beja, Dondo, and Lucamba, were allowed to choose a scribe from amongst the merchants established at the fair.[154] According to Mello, by 1800, the captain-general and governor appointed the scribes of all other fairs, who remained their highest civil authority.[155]

In 1765, Sousa Coutinho attempted to establish official slave fairs in Gollo, Bende, and next to the court of *Soba* Calandula.[156] Three years later, he ordered the captain major of Benguela to establish several smaller fairs in the hinterlands of Benguela and Caconda.[157] While the fairs at Gollo, Bende, and Calandula were intended to deviate northern trade routes away from the seaports controlled by the independent kingdoms of the Loango Coast, the new slave fairs in Benguela were designed to fix in place the itinerant merchants and *pumbeiros* who traded with the Ovimbundu of the southern hinterlands of Portuguese West Central African domains.[158] In both instances, however, Sousa Coutinho's efforts were not crowned with lasting success.[159] During the tenure of Mello, fairs were held at

---

152 Couto, Os capitães-mores em Angola, p. 211–215; Miller, Way of Death, p. 308–312, 363, 499–500, 619–620.

153 Lopes de Lima and Bordalo, Ensaios sobre a statistica das possessões portuguezas, Vol. 3, p. 63–64.

154 Couto, Os capitães-mores em Angola, p. 216; Mello, Relação dos officios civis, p. 287.

155 Mello, Relação dos officios civis, p. 289.

156 Ferreira, Feiras e presídios, p. 24–26; Sousa Coutinho, Para o Secretario de Estado Francisco de Mendonça.

157 Sousa Coutinho proposed to establish these smaller fairs in Huila, Quipungu, Bejé, Catatu, Galamgue Grande, Ivagando, Benguela a Velha, and Gunza Cabolo. Ferreira, Feiras e presídios, p. 24–26; Sousa Coutinho, Bando sobre as feiras que devem haver nos certoes.

158 ANTT, MR, EXP, Sr. 34, F. 605, p. 5–15; Ferreira, Feiras e presídios; Parreira, Dicionário glossográfico, p. 95; Sousa Coutinho, Bando sobre as feiras que devem haver nos certoes; Sousa Coutinho, Para o Secretario de Estado Francisco de Mendonça.

159 Ralph Delgado notes that while Sousa Coutinho failed to fix slave fairs, he established eleven villages and seven corporalships in the hinterlands of Benguela that lasted at least from 1769 to 1800. Namely, the villages of Contins, Salvaterra de Magos, Borba, Nova Golegã, Amarante, Alba-Nova, Passo de Sousa, Sarzedas, Linhares, Novo-Belém and Vila Viçosa, which an elected judge

Lucamba (next to Ambaca), Beja (next to Pungo Andongo), Cassange, Dondo (next to Cambambe and Massangano), Haco, Encoge (next to the *presídio* of the same name), and Libollo.[160] Furthermore, Mello confirms that, by 1800, official scribes were appointed to the courts of *Soba* Calandula, *Dembo* Ambuila [Ndembu Mbwila], and *Soba* Quitexi to adjudicate cases involving Luso-African merchants residing there.[161] In 1768, Sousa Coutinho had already sent a scribe to the court of the king of Matamba to perform the same duties.[162] Despite all reformist efforts, still in the 1790s, Silva Corrêa claimed that the slave masters, White merchants, and Luso-African *pumbeiros* who sojourned in the hinterlands still acted as "*soberanitos* [little sovereigns]," having the "*abominable*" custom of condemning persons "*to death for no good reason*."[163]

3.5 The Boards of Justice, Commerce, and Finance

Captain-General and Governors Manuel de Almeida e Vasconcelos and Sousa Coutinho used the new commissarial boards established by consecutive royal decrees in 1761, the Board of Commerce, the Board of Finance, and the Board of Justice, to profoundly reshape the 'normative fabric' of Angola and Benguela. Their efforts were initially coordinated with Francisco Xavier de Mendonça Furtado, Secretary of State of the Navy and the Overseas, between 1760 and 1769.[164] Therefore, they need to be contextualized within the Empire-wide transition from the polisynodal, jurisdictional form of government of the *Antigo Regime* to a new paradigm of government, both of the metropole and its overseas territories, that was in line with what was then happening throughout most of 'civilized' or 'policed' Europe.[165]

---

with military and administrative authority and unspecified jurisdictional limits and competence ranges headed. A minor military officer headed the corporalships of Catumbela, Dombe, Sapa, Quiaca, Quibula, Bumbo, and Quipungo. While the villages' toponomy replicated that of the Portuguese Kingdom, the toponym of the corporalships reflected pre-existing African ones. This choice, and the supposed transitoriness of military-ruled corporalships, is in keeping with the ideological framework of Sousa Coutinho's White settler-colonial project, which is further analyzed in the ninth chapter. Delgado, Ao Sul do Cuanza, p. 117–118.

160 Mello, Relação dos officios civis, p. 281–293.

161 Ibid., Sousa Coutinho, Para o Secretario de Estado Francisco de Mendonça.

162 ANTT, MR, EXP, Sr. 34, F. 605, p. 290–292.

163 Silva Corrêa, História de Angola, Vol. 1, p. 94–95.

164 Coimbra (ed.), Livros de "Ofícios para o Reino," p. 71–112.

165 Barreto Xavier and Nogueira da Silva, O governo dos outros, p. 21–31; Foucault, The Birth of Biopolitics; Santos, Administrative Knowledge, p. 539–556; Santos, Entre deux Droits, p. 817–848; Santos, Luanda, in: Brockey (ed.), Portuguese Colonial Cities in the Early Modern World, p. 249–272; Santos, O Império Português face às instituições indígenas, in: Palomo, Stumpf and Barreto Xavier (eds.), Monarquias ibéricas em perspectiva comparada, p. 271–303;

As in the Portuguese Kingdom, this socio-political reorganization was predicated on three interrelated processes in Angola, Benguela, and their dependencies. First, on the gradual "deconstruction of jurisdictional autonomy."[166] Second, on the new instrumental understanding of royal enactments and statutory law described in the first sections of this chapter and a decisive shift in the ideological grounding of the authority and political power of the monarch, no longer conceived in vague theocratic terms (*imperium*) but according to a precise secular framing (political sovereignty).[167] Third, on the creation of secretariats staffed not according to the principles of patrimonialism but bureaucratic "meritocracy:" the Secretariat of State of the Navy and the Overseas in Lisbon, and the reformed Secretariat of the General Government of Angola in Luanda.[168]

When the Secretariat of State of the Navy and Overseas was created by the Royal Edict of July 28, 1736, it did not immediately assume the preponderance it would have in the 1760s.[169] At the start, together with the two other new Secretariats of State, it was part of a superficial reform that substituted three inefficient Secretariats established after the Restoration of Independence (1640) still according to a patrimonial principle.[170] From the onset, to function properly, the secretary of state who headed it had to assert his political authority at the expense of the jurisdiction of the Overseas Council.[171] As Maria Fernando Bicalho argues, establishing new commissarial boards in overseas domains was crucial to this process, as it enabled the creation of "alternative circuits" of government and the circulation of administrative information that simultaneously reinforced the authority and power of secretaries of state and captain-general and governors.[172] As she describes, by 1714, the Overseas Council had achieved a decadent stage, a tendency that,

---

Santos, Um governo "polido" para Angola; Subtil, Espaço político e organização, p. 89–92; Subtil, Estado de polícia, p. 15–40; Subtil, O terramoto político.

166 Subtil, Espaço político e organização, p. 89–92.

167 Foucault, The Birth of Biopolitics, p. 5–6.

168 Coimbra (ed.), Livros de "Ofícios para o Reino," p. 11; Subtil, Estado de polícia, p. 24.

169 Bicalho, Os Conselhos da Índia e Ultramarino; Simões Junior, A Secretaria de Estado do Ultramar, p. 73–92; Subtil, O terramoto político.

170 The other two Secretariats of State were: the Secretariat of Internal Affairs of the Kingdom and the Secretariat of Foreign Affairs and War. Together with the Secretariat of State of the Navy and the Overseas, they substituted the Secretariat of Mercies, the Secretariat Expedient, and the Secretariat of the Signature. Subtil explains that the latter were exclusively comprised of archivists, notaries, and solicitors. Until 1736, only one secretary of state was responsible for enabling political communication between the Crown and the councils and corporations constituting the body of the poly-synodal monarchy. Simões Junior, A Secretaria de Estado do Ultramar, p. 75; Subtil, Espaço político e organização, p. 96–97.

171 Bicalho, Os Conselhos da Índia e Ultramarino; Miller, Way of Death, p. 572; Simões Junior, A Secretaria de Estado do Ultramar, p. 73–92.

172 Bicalho, Os Conselhos da Índia e Ultramarino.

according to Miguel Dantas da Cruz, culminated in the early 1760s when it lost some of its old prerogatives and rights of appointment.[173] The Overseas Council had been established in 1643, modeled after the *Conselho da India* [India Council] (1604–1614).[174] It financed itself with the revenues collected overseas, accumulated administrative functions in the treasury, justice, and war domains, and regulated the movements of ships.[175] The council was also responsible for appointing most of the personnel sent to Angola and Benguela, subject to the Crown's approval, except the bishops and clerics who were appointed by the Board of Royal Conscience and Military Orders (1532–1833).

The Overseas Council was initially comprised of four voting members: a president, three councilors, and a secretary.[176] Two councilors were selected from the military nobility and expected to be men of "*capa e espada* [sword and cape]," and the third had to be a "*letrado* [man of letters]."[177] All presidents of the Overseas Council were drawn from the ranks of the "*fidalgos*."[178] Members of the Overseas Council served for an indefinite period and were expected to have had first-hand experience of the Portuguese overseas domains.[179] When it was abolished in 1833, it included a president, seven councilors, a secretary, and twenty-four other officials, having greatly varied in size and composition.[180] Despite the Overseas Council's *de jure* preponderance until the first decades of the nineteenth century, the polisynodal government of the Portuguese Kingdom was replicated on a smaller scale in Angola and Benguela, where, in practice, each officeholder countered and balanced the power of all the others. As Camarinhas notes, all local offices were characterized not only by a strong connection with the metropole's councils and courts responsible for appointing and confirming their titleholders but also with those responsible for reviewing their performance, revising their adjudications, receiving appeals to their decisions, and issuing orders in specific fields of government, such as the *Desembargo do Paço* (1521–1833), the War Council, the Finance Council, and the

---

173 Ibid.; Cruz, Um império de conflitos, p. 382–386.

174 Bicalho, Os Conselhos da Índia e Ultramarino.

175 Bardwell, The Governors of Portugal's South Atlantic Empire; Barros, Negócios de tanta importância; Bicalho, Os Conselhos da Índia e Ultramarino; Caetano, O Conselho Ultramarino; Cardim, A Casa Real, p. 13–57; Cruz, Um império de conflitos; Gouvêa, Conexões imperiais, in: Bicalho and Ferlini (eds.), Modos de governar, p. 179–198; MMA V, D. 70; Monteiro, Governadores e capitães-mores, in: Bicalho and Ferlini (eds.), Modos de governar, p. 93–115; Myrup, To Rule from Afar, p. 63–139.

176 Bardwell, The Governors of Portugal's South Atlantic Empire.

177 Ibid.; Cruz, Um império de conflitos, p. 168–169.

178 Bardwell, The Governors of Portugal's South Atlantic Empire.

179 Bicalho, Os Conselhos da Índia e Ultramarino.

180 Bardwell, The Governors of Portugal's South Atlantic Empire.

Casa da Suplicação.[181] Therefore, the Overseas Council was not the only central court with jurisdiction over the Portuguese officers and *moradores* of Angola and Benguela, and the typical balance of a kaleidoscopic poly-centric society was kept in West Central Africa.

As described by Nuno Gonçalo Monteiro, by the middle of the eighteenth century, this balance was wholly altered by the concentration of political power in the hands of captain-general and governors at the expense of all other offices and judicatures.[182] The new commissarial boards established in 1761 enabled this by allowing the captain-general and governors who presided over them to curtail the criminal, economic, and financial jurisdictions of *ouvidores gerais*, *provedores*, *provedores da Real Fazenda*, municipal judges, ordinary judges, and captain majors. This deconstruction of their jurisdictional autonomy proceeded in tandem with the economic reforms that opened the door of the Angolan hinterlands to 'free trade,' contributing to the progressive differentiation of the economic system as an "autonomous system."[183] Foucault conceptualizes this differentiation as the transition from a paradigm in which the market was understood as another "site of jurisdiction" or a "site of distributive justice" to one in which "the market becomes a site of truth."[184] In Angola and Benguela, this historical transition had the particularity of being centered on slave fairs—markets where the primary transitioned 'merchandise' was the *dominium* over the freedom of enslaved Africans (or, as the Africans themselves probably understood it, rights over persons and dependents). While this exchange was prosaically understood as the trade in slaves, by the mid-eighteenth century, it was still juridically predicated on privileging modalities of *dominium* oriented towards achieving spiritual goals, not on the commodification of human beings.[185] In keeping with this ideological framing, the Portuguese monarch was obliged to forward the salvation (baptism) of the slaves and guarantee the equitable access of his subjects to their "*resgate*"—literally ramson, but in practice, purchase.[186]

---

181 Aidar, Governar a Real Fazenda, p. 163–217; Camarinhas, Administração da justiça em espaços coloniais, p. 109–124; Camarinhas, As residências dos cargos de justiça letrada, in: Stumpf and Chaturvedula (eds.), Cargos e ofícios nas monarquias ibéricas, p. 161–174; Camarinhas, Juízes e administração; Regimento do governo deste Reyno; Salgado, Fiscais e meirinhos.

182 Bicalho and Monteiro, As instituições civis da monarquia portuguesa, in: Palomo, Stumpf and Barreto Xavier (eds.), Monarquias ibéricas em perspectiva comparada p. 209–236; Monteiro, The Patterns of Portuguese Politics, p. 1–6.

183 Polanyi, The Great Transformation; Saavedra, Jurisdictional Autonomy and the Autonomy of Law, p. 325–337.

184 Foucault, The Birth of Biopolitics, p. 30–31.

185 Hespanha, Como os juristas viam o mundo, § 1039; Rocha, Ethiope resgatado.

186 As discussed in the chapters grouped in the second section, the notion that slaves were ransomed was central to both the Dominican and Jesuit Neo-Thomist justifications of legitimate enslavement and the ransom doctrine that came to substitute them during the second-half of the eighteenth

At the core of Ribeiro de Aragão's 1618 critique of how slave fairs operated in the Angolan hinterlands was the claim that captain-general and governors 'abused' their financial jurisdiction to forward their interests at the expense of equity and justice.[187] Then, Ribeiro de Aragão understood the slave market as a place where even the "*miserable people*" of Angola and Benguela were entitled to a share of the 'ransomed' slaves.[188] In other words, his critique was predicated on the notion that the theocratic *imperium* of the Portuguese Crown over West Central Africa obliged the monarch to secure equity and promote harmony amongst the different corporations and groups that constituted the Portuguese "Catholic Monarchy."[189] According to this worldview, the mechanisms set in place to assure that no wrongly enslaved Africans were exchanged at slave fairs, the need for the War Council's recognition of a given war as 'just' for it to yield legitimately enslaved Africans as booty, the offices that oversaw and reviewed the adjudications of captain majors, and the inclusion of 'clause 18' in the ordinances of captain-general and governors were all concurring remedies, intended to restore slave fairs to sites of "distributive justice," and curtail perverse uses and customs motivated by greed and the unforgiving African environment.[190] In sum, the economic system was not yet autonomous. It was still subordinated to the religious and normative systems, and the trade in African slaves, if they had been rightly enslaved according to Second-Scholastic doctrines of legitimate enslavement, was predicated on promoting social harmony and spiritual salvation.[191]

The elimination of 'clause 18' and the subsequent *de jure* opening of trade in the West Central African hinterlands (1758), the simplification of the taxation and shipping system of slaves (1758), the Royal Edict of August 5, 1769, ending the Angola slave duty contract, and, concomitantly, the establishment of the chartered companies of *Grão Pará and Maranhão* (1755–1778) and *Pernambuco and Paraíba*

century. In keeping with the theologians and jurists of Second Scholasticism, the ransom of war prisoners or criminals condemned to death was one of the four "*condiciones legitimas* [legitimate conditions]" that validated the 'title' or *dominium* of enslavers over the freedom of enslaved persons. McManus, Martín de Azpilcueta on Trade and Slavery, in: Bragagnolo (ed.), The Production of Knowledge of Normativity, p. 363; Zeron, Les Jésuites et le commerce d'esclaves, in: Hebrard (ed.), Brésil quatre siècles d'esclavage, p. 82; Zeron, Linha de fé, p. 206.

187 Cordeiro (ed.), Terras e minas africanas segundo Rebello de Aragão, p. 13.

188 Ibid., Foucault, The Birth of Biopolitics, p. 30–31.

189 Hespanha, Como os juristas viam o mundo, § 77–§ 78; Hespanha, Direito Comum e Direito Colonial, p. 95–116.

190 Foucault, The Birth of Biopolitics, p. 30–31.

191 Second-Scholastic doctrines regarding the conditions of just enslavement are further discussed in the fourth and fifth chapters. Saavedra, Jurisdictional Autonomy and the Autonomy of Law, p. 325–337.

(1759–1780),[192] obeyed to a radically different logic.[193] When the Board of Commerce was established during the government of António de Vasconcelos by a Royal Charter of November 14, 1761, it was immediately tasked with adjudicating trade disputes in the Angolan hinterlands, fixing the price of the *banzos* paid for "*blacks and wax*," and licensing and policing the Luso-African merchants who were now allowed to sojourn there.[194] As António de Vasconcelos had already noted in 1759, the intervention in the price of *banzos* was deemed necessary because the "*ambition of white men*" and countless cases of business fraud had utterly distorted the functioning of the market in the hinterland slave fairs.[195] Ensuring that the market revealed its truth,[196] instead of guaranteeing an equitable distribution of ransomed slaves, became the mission of the Board of Commerce, which determined its field of intervention at the expense of the jurisdictions previously connected with the slave fairs.[197] It was composed of the captain-general and governor of Angola, the *ouvidor geral* and one of the municipal judges of Luanda, and the colonel, lieutenant-colonel, and sergeant-major of the garrison of Luanda.[198] Furthermore, it consulted two procurators appointed by the merchants of Luanda and the secretary of the colonial government, who acted as "*tutor and curador* [guardian] *of the Blacks*." Crucially, this guardian was tasked with safeguarding Black merchants in their capacity as trade partners and suppliers of slaves, not guaranteeing that adequate measures were set in place to avoid illicit enslavement. False enslavement remained a serious issue while slavery was juridically predicated on the salvific *dominium* over the freedom of the enslaved. However, during this transition period, it was increasingly seen as a fiscal, not a commercial matter.[199]

---

192 For an overview of the impact of both companies on the Angolan slave trade, see Miller. MILLER, Way of Death, p. 573–579.

193 MAXWELL, Pombal and the Nationalization of the Luso-Brazilian Economy, p. 622–623, 626–627.

194 COUTO, Os capitães-mores em Angola, p. 206–207; FERREIRA, Feiras e presídios, p. 22–24.

195 The sixth chapter explores the composition of *banzos*, how they relate to African and European currencies, and Portuguese attempts to regulate them. ANTT, MR, EXP, Sr. 34, F. 605, p. 1–3.

196 As Miller notes, during this period, the "truth" of the market was conceived in mercantilist terms, not liberal political economy ones. Therefore, rhetoric about economic freedom and open markets paradoxically coexisted with monopolistic chartered companies, state monopolies, and tightly controlled official fairs during this period, as the third section of the second chapter explores. Nevertheless, Miller confirms that the 'market' and slave fairs were no longer understood as primarily "jurisdictional sites." FOUCAULT, The Birth of Biopolitics, p. 30–31; MILLER, Way of Death, p. 586–587, 594.

197 FOUCAULT, The Birth of Biopolitics, p. 30–31.

198 FERREIRA, Feiras e presídios, p. 22–23.

199 On June 10, 1762, the members of the Board of Finance commented about the *mucano* hearing system. As slaves circulated as currency, they appeared worried the circulation of the wrongly enslaved had the same impact on the royal treasury as the circulation of counterfeit currency. FERREIRA, Cross-Cultural Exchange, p. 112.

On July 12, 1764, unsatisfied with the performance of the Board of Commerce, Sousa Coutinho created a "*Conference of Commerce*" that absorbed some of the competencies of the Board of Commerce and also included "*the best businessmen*" of Luanda and deputies from the chartered companies of *Grão Pará and Maranhão* and *Pernambuco and Paraíba*.[200] As Delgado describes, in its first meeting on June 10, 1764, its members decided to eliminate all taxes on slave transactions in the hinterland fairs, shift the place of the official fair of Ambaca, prepare a set of regulations limiting the intervention of captain majors in commercial operations, and conceding to the scribes of fairs jurisdiction in matters related to the testamentary execution of deceased merchants, at the expense of the jurisdiction of local scribes and judges of orphans.[201] Overall, as Miller remarks, the Board and the Conference of Commerce effectively transferred control over the hinterland slave trade to the representatives of Lisbon-backed merchants and the delegates of the chartered companies, allowing the captain-general and governor of Angola to access these merchants' needs better and act accordingly.[202] Substituting the Municipal Council of Luanda and ignoring some of its acquired privileges, these boards appointed the scribes of fairs, ordered them to enforce fixed prices, exclude goods imported by merchants not backed by Lisbon from *banzos*, and policed Luso-African merchants. By the early eighteen hundreds, when the previous commercial

---

200 Coimbra (ed.), Livros de "Ofícios para o Reino," p. 80; Ferreira, Feiras e presídios, p. 24–26; Miller, Way of Death, p. 586; Trigo de Sousa, D. Francisco de Sousa Coutinho, p. 44.

201 According to a letter to the secretary of state of the navy and overseas undersigned by the main Lisbon and Brazilian-backed merchants established in Luanda on May 31, 1803, one of the greatest threats to their business operations was the jurisdiction judges of orphans had over the assets of their deceased commercial envoys and partners who travelled in the West Central African hinterlands. In an earlier attempt to rectify this issue, the 18th point of the 17th chapter of the statutes of the Board of Commerce of the Kingdom of December 12, 1756, and the Royal Edict of June 17, 1766, had determined that the partners of the deceased could administer their assets for up to two years without the interference of judges of orphans, giving them the time to pay outstanding debts and conclude business transactions. As determined by the Board of Commerce of Angola, the appointed scribes would oversee this process. However, by 1803, the merchants claimed that the *ouvidor geral* was attempting to reassert his jurisdiction as *provedor* of the judicial district and those of the judges of orphans. In their undersigned letter, the merchants argued that the Crown had "*the right inherent to the Sovereignty of Prices*" to decree and "*abolish laws when it was convenient to public utility*." No "*Court, or Magistrate, no matter how wide their power, and broad their jurisdiction*," they argued, had the right to object. Therefore, they petitioned the captain-general and governor to uphold the Royal Edict of June 17, 1766, further considering that some fairs convened in "*the hinterlands and places of several Potentates, where the Empire of Justice cannot enter*," but merchants could still self-organize. ANTT, MR, EXP, Sr. 34, F. 605, p. 420–443; Delgado, O governo de Sousa Coutinho em Angola I, p. 19–56; Silva (ed.), Colleção da legislação portugueza (1750–1762), p. 458–479; Silva (ed.), Colleção de legislação portugueza (1763–1774), p. 253–254.

202 Miller, Way of Death, p. 586–587.

system had been mostly dismantled, only the Board of Commerce still convened, but it was highly dysfunctional.[203]

Concomitantly, the Board of Finance was created by the Royal Charter of November 18, 1761, also during the tenure of António de Vasconcelos.[204] Composed of the captain-general of Angola, the *ouvidor geral*, the *provedor da Real Fazenda*,[205] and a municipal judge of Luanda, acting as procurator, this board also had a dedicated treasurer, an overseer, and a scribe, all appointed for three years.[206] As Bruno Aidar has noted, establishing this board was part of an Atlantic-wide series of reforms that gave captain-general and governors a prominent role in administrating public finance, offering them more power to draft and implement local fiscal policies.[207] Contrarily, focusing only on South America, Miguel Dantas Cruz argues that the Boards of Finance actually restricted the jurisdiction of the captain-general and governors because, from their establishment onwards, almost all payments had to be processed and approved by their members.[208] Both perspectives complement each other instead of being mutually exclusive. In Angola and Benguela, the Board of Finance expanded the reach of the captain-general and governors' financial jurisdiction and limited their previous autonomy regarding payments. Still, arguably, the regional centralization of payments and bookkeeping mainly impacted the jurisdiction of ordinary judges, municipal judges, and city councilors, which the establishment of the Board of Commerce and the Board of Justice had already circumscribed.[209]

Like other boards of finance created during this period, the Board of Finance of Angola was under the jurisdiction of the *Erário Régio* [Royal Treasury] (1761–1832), a centralized institution created by Sebastião José de Carvalho e Melo on December 22, 1761, according to the new police state paradigm and a new understanding of royal sovereignty and the Crown's 'legislative' functions.[210] The Royal Treasury

---

203 Couto, Os capitães-mores em Angola, p. 207–215.

204 Trigo de Sousa, D. Francisco de Sousa Coutinho, p. 20.

205 Up until then, the *provedor da Real fazenda*, who was often the *ouvidor geral*, was responsible for gathering all the accounting documents of the *almoxarife da Real Fazenda* and municipal treasurers of Angola and Benguela, as well as the "*recebedores da Fazenda Real* [receivers of the *Real Fazenda*]" of Benguela and sending it to the Overseas Council. This Council would then forward it for revision to the *Casa dos Contos do Reino e da Casa Real* [Counting House of the Kingdom and the Royal House] (1627–1761). Balanço geral da receita e despesa da Fazenda Real no Reino de Angola.

206 Trigo de Sousa, D. Francisco de Sousa Coutinho, p. 20.

207 Aidar, Governar a Real Fazenda, p. 163–217.

208 Dantas da Cruz, Pombal e o Império Atlântico, p. 1–24.

209 Miller, Way of Death, p. 587.

210 On December 17, 1790, the Royal Treasury absorbed the Finance Council, assuming part of its jurisdiction in 1761. In the 1760s, it had substituted the Counting House of the Kingdom and the

was presided over by a powerful general inspector, a position immediately assumed by Carvalho e Melo. For the first time, a single court collected all the incomes of the Crown, now labeled 'public' revenues, approved and processed the expenditure of almost all other councils, courts, and boards, and oversaw the auctioning of tax farming contracts and commercial monopolies.[211] The general inspector managed four general accountants, including the general accountant of West Africa, Maranhão, and Bahia, responsible for Angola and Benguela, with the aid of a "*tesoureiro-mor* [high treasurer]" and his secretary.[212] Therefore, from 1761 onwards, not only the accounting documents collected by the *provedor da Real Fazenda* in Luanda were sent to the Royal Treasury instead of the Overseas Council,[213] but also all the public revenues collected in Angola, Benguela, and their dependencies.[214]

As Miller carefully details, this significant fiscal overhaul allowed Sousa Coutinho to tackle one of the most critical challenges of the administration of West Central Africa, namely, curtailing the economic and financial stranglehold that the slave duty tax farming contract holders had on the Captaincy of Angola and its

---

Royal House. As Subtil remarks, it inaugurated a new system of accounting enabled by double-entry bookkeeping using "*folhas de caixa* [diaries]," "*livros Mestre* [balance sheets]," and "*livros auxiliaries* [auxiliary sheets]." It was responsible for producing two yearly reports, one per semester. The *Aula do Comércio* [Class of Commerce] (1759) trained bureaucrats to implement these reforms. Benavente, A extinção do Erário Régio, p. 238–246; Contadoria da Junta da Fazenda Real do Reino de Angola; Dantas da Cruz, Pombal e o Império Atlântico, p. 1–24; Rau, A Casa dos Contos; Rodrigues, Os homens do Erário Régio, p. 59–81; Subtil, Estado de polícia, p. 23.

211 Benavente, A extinção do Erário Régio, p. 238–246; Contadoria da Junta da Fazenda Real do Reino de Angola; Dantas da Cruz, Pombal e o Império Atlântico, p. 1–24; Rodrigues, Os homens do Erário Régio, p. 59–81.

212 Each of the four General Accountings had a diary and a balance sheet, undersigned by the general inspector, and a variable number of auxiliary sheets. In the case of West Africa, Maranhão, and Bahia, there were 27 auxiliary sheets, each undersigned by a general accountant of another General Accounting. The General Accounting of West Africa, Maranhão, and Bahia was extinguished in 1807, but then reinstated in 1809. From the 1820s until 1832, when the Royal Treasury was abolished, it underwent several institutional makeovers. Benavente, A Extinção do Erário Régio, p. 238–246; Contadoria da Junta da Fazenda Real do Reino de Angola; Dantas da Cruz, Pombal e o Império Atlântico, p. 1–24; Rodrigues, Os homens do Erário Régio, p. 59–81.

213 One of the defining traits of the Royal Treasury was secrecy. Only the general inspector, the high treasurer, his scribe, and the monarch had access to all information gathered by the institution, having a complete overview of the financial situation of the Empire. Even general accountants only had access to information about their jurisdictions. This system completely sidestepped the Overseas Council, severely limiting its ability to produce relevant deliberations. Balanço geral da receita e despesa da Fazenda Real no Reino de Angola; Rodrigues, Os homens do Erário Régio, p. 59–81.

214 Dantas da Cruz, Pombal e o Império Atlântico, p. 1–24; Rodrigues, Os homens do Erário Régio, p. 59–81.

dependencies.[215] The first tax farming Contract of Angola dates from 1587, and was approved by a royal edict on July 28, 1587.[216] It extended for six years, detailed all the contract holders' privileges, duties, and obligations, and guaranteed that the privilege of taxing the trade of slaves in Angola was separated from the privilege of taxing the slave trade from São Tomé.[217] As Miller describes, after 1607, the Contract of Angola was auctioned every three years until 1769, extending to the ports of "Angola, Congo, Loango, and Benguela."[218] Unlike Spanish *asientos*, Portuguese "*contractos* [contracts]" did not entail owning slaves but only the levying of taxes over their exportation and extraordinary rights and privileges regarding importing and exporting commodities to West Central Africa.[219] These rights and privileges were more attractive than tax farming, even after a fiscal reform changed the tax system in 1723. Therefore, contracts were taken mainly by merchants who soon flooded the local markets with Asian and Brazilian goods they sold on credit to Luso-African merchants in exchange for *letras* backed up by the sale of slaves in Brazil.[220] As analyzed in the next chapter, most currencies circulating in Angola and Benguela and their dependencies had no value outside West Central Africa.[221] Hence, these *letras* were to be repaid in bullion after the slaves bought with the trade goods received on credit in Luanda were transported to and auctioned in South America.[222]

This system obliged contract holders to employ representatives on both sides of the Atlantic but had the advantage, from the point of view of the former, of keeping all liabilities connected with slave-owning on the Luso-African slave supplier's side.[223] As for the taxes, they were paid in particular bills of exchange known as *letras dos direitos* that conferred to their holders the right over the first 15 to 25 percent of the proceeds of slaves auctioned in Brazil. After collecting, the tax farming revenue was paid to the Portuguese Crown in Angola in cloth, military uniforms, flour, and other military rations destined to provide for the captaincy's garrisons and first-line

---

215 Miller, Way of Death.

216 MMA IV, D. 116, D. 117.

217 Amaral, O consulado de Paulo Dias de Novais, p. 194–202.

218 Miller, Way of Death, p. 555–556.

219 For a comparison between Portuguese *contratos* and Spanish *asientos*, see Amaral. Amaral, O consulado de Paulo Dias de Novais, p. 194–202; Miller, Way of Death, p. 552–553; Newson and Minchin, From Capture to Sale.

220 Miller, Way of Death, p. 552–553.

221 Ibid., p. 558.

222 Ibid., p. 564–565.

223 Ibid., p. 558–560.

companies.[224] Because these cheap wares were accounted for in *réis* or *cruzados*, their value was inflated in Luanda, where they were scarce, providing another source of profit for the contract holders. Besides extending credit through goods advancement, contract holders also issued *livranças*, unofficial bills of exchange that circulated as paper money in the hinterlands.[225] As Miller concludes, whenever any officeholder with fiscal jurisdiction sought to curtail contract holders' privileges or a captain-general and governor entered trade disputes with them, their first reaction was to threaten to withdraw the payment of their unofficial bills of exchange, collapsing the regional economy and causing widespread social unrest.[226] After 1769, the Board of Finance faced this challenge by substituting *livranças* for officially-backed *letras do tesouro*, framing the former as counterfeit currency.[227]

Finally, the Board of Justice was established by a Royal Charter of November 14, 1761.[228] Also referred to as the Criminal Board, it was comprised of the captain-general and governor of Angola, the *ouvidor geral* and the municipal judge of Luanda, and "*the colonel, lieutenant colonel, and sergeant major of the garrison*" of Luanda.[229] It had jurisdiction over cases of murder, robberies in the streets of Luanda, thefts if they were carried out with coaction or forced entrance, and all violence committed against travelers on public highways.[230] According to the royal letter, an emergency state analogous to what Giorgio Agamben defines as a "state of exception" warranted the creation of the new board.[231] The document explained

224 The goods and currencies used by contract holders to fulfil their obligations varied greatly during the almost two centuries the slave duty tax farming contract lasted. See the chapters grouped in the second part for more details. Ibid., p. 558.

225 Ibid., p. 592–593.

226 Ibid., p. 567–569.

227 Ibid., p. 596.

228 A royal edict from January 18, 1765, created a second kind of "*juntas de justiça* [justice board]" in the Portuguese Empire. Local *ouvidores gerais* headed these, and they included two "*learned ministers*" or, in their absence, "*two graduates appointed by the ouvidor*." While Captain-General and Governor Sousa Coutinho published this royal edict in Angola on July 1, 1766, it is unclear if this second kind of commissarial board ever convened in Angola and Benguela. On the contrary, the one created in 1761 resumed its meetings immediately after the royal edict was issued. Coimbra (ed.), Livros de "Ofícios para o Reino," p. 82–83; Collecção da Legislação Portugueza (1763–1774), p. 143–144; Galdinho de Paiva, Justiça e poder, p. 191–202; Silva (ed.), Supplemento à collecção de legislação portugueza (1750–1762), p. 833–834.

229 Abrahão, A conjuração dos degredados, p. 69–110; AHU, CU, Angola, Box 47, D. 4365; Caetano, As reformas pombalinas, in: Baião, Cidade and Murias (eds.), História da expansão portuguesa no mundo, Vol. 3, p. 258; Silva (ed.), Supplemento à collecção de legislação portugueza (1750–1762), p. 833–834; Silva Corrêa, História de Angola, Vol. 1, p. 23–25.

230 AHU, CU, Angola, Box 47, D. 4365; Silva (ed.), Supplemento à collecção de legislação portugueza (1750–1762), p. 833–834.

231 Agamben, State of Exception, p. 1–31.

that the new commissarial board was needed due to the exceptional climate of "*debauchery, in which we can find the most atrocious vices in the lands of* [the] *Kingdom* [of Angola], *inhabited by so many facinorous convicts, and corrupted by so many, and so abominable abuses*."[232] The proposed solution was substituting the customary "*delays and tergiversations of the ordinary style* [of court proceedings]"[233] with a simplified, martial, oral summary style.[234] Suspects were to be "*arrested, verbally, and summarily heard and sentenced*." Penalties were applied that day, even if the sentence was "*death*." These dispositions, the royal letter clarified, were to be obeyed regardless of "*any Laws, Royal edicts, Dispensations, Orders, Ordinances, and styles contrary to it*" because the monarch had decided "*by his Mottu proprio, certain Science, Plenary, and Supreme Royal Power, to derogate these*" norms and jurisprudence.[235]

With the creation of the Board of Justice, the Portuguese Crown thus signaled the transition from the *Antigo Regime*'s jurisdictional form of government grounded on a theological conception of the monarch's *imperium* to a new paradigm predicated on a secular understanding of sovereignty, no longer constrained by previous normative arrangements but capable of mobilizing a state of exception to overrule them and decree new laws according to the dictates of "*raison d'etat*."[236] However, as with

232 AHU, CU, Angola, Box 47, D. 4365; Silva (ed.), Supplemento à collecção de legislação portugueza (1750–1762), p. 833–834.

233 As Hespanha clarifies, civil and criminal processes followed a similar style, differing only in a few aspects. While a petition started civil procedures, criminal ones were formed either by a "*devassa* [inquiry]" or a "*denúncia ou querela* [complaint or quarrel]." These triggered a "*citação* [court summons]." The *Philippine Ordinances* determined who could be summoned and regulated different summons and their deadlines. After the summons, a "*libelo* [libel]" was produced describing the "factual situation" that had triggered the process and determining its value. The libel was then articulated and could not be substantially altered afterward. After it was presented to the accused, they could bring forward "*exceções* [exceptions]" that contested the validity of the original petition or complaint ("*exceção perentória*") or the competence of the court ("*exceção dilatória*") before providing their take on the facts alleged in each article of the libel. The authors of the libel would then be able to reply. Several means of proof were accepted, from documents to witnesses, oaths, confessions, and presumptions. Hespanha argues that there was an implicit hierarchy of evidence during most of the *Antigo Regime*. Confessions were the gold standard, except if resulting from torture, which jurists shunned, then came written documents, the statements of renowned witnesses, those of less reputable ones, and, finally, oaths both parties took. Once the sentence was announced, appeals could be made within the prescribed deadlines. Hespanha, Como os juristas viam o mundo, § 2013–§ 2083; Ord. Fil., Book III, Tit. LXVIII, Tit. LXXXV.

234 AHU, CU, Angola, Box 47, D. 4365; Silva (ed.), Supplemento à collecção de legislação portugueza (1750–1762), p. 833–834.

235 AHU, CU, Angola, Box 47, D. 4365; Silva (ed.), Supplemento à collecção de legislação portugueza (1750–1762), p. 833–834.

236 Agamben, State of Exception, p. 1–31; Foucault, The Birth of Biopolitics.

any other ambitious political or administrative reform, such a radical transformation was easier idealized than implemented in West Central Africa and proceeded in stages. Soon after the new commissarial board was created, a Royal Charter of November 22, 1761, stipulated that the Board of Justice could also adjudicate, in a "*verbal and summary manner*," the acts of captain majors who "*disobeyed the orders*" they received from the Overseas Council.[237] During António de Vasconcelo's tenure, the Board of Justice was instrumental in the brutal repression of the "*conjuração dos degredados* [mutiny of the convicts]" of 1763.[238] In this instance, the board condemned to death 22 individuals, including José Álvares de Oliveira, the supposed leader of the rebellion, who was dismembered and publicly burned.[239] All their bodies were "reduced to ashes by fire," then scattered by the wind, sending a powerful message to all Luso-African *moradores* that still echoed in Silva Corrêa's times.[240] Given its effectiveness in disciplining first-line troops and efficacy in quelling rebellions, the Board of Justice allowed the introduction of metallic currency in the Captaincy, substituting the cloths and uniforms distributed by the contract holders to military men as salaries, also contributing to the curbing of the power of the holders of the slave duty tax farming contract.[241]

As soon as Sousa Coutinho assumed office, he reformed the Board of Justice, further expanding its jurisdiction. On May 31, 1764, he informed Mendonça Furtado, the secretary of state of the navy and the overseas, that he had already ordered all criminal processes to be delivered to the board in Luanda to be quickly adjudicated.[242] However, by June 27, Coutinho was forced to recognize that their adjudication had been halted because the *ouvidor geral* had doubts about the range of competence and jurisdiction of the board.[243] Six days later, Sousa Coutinho informed the secretary of state that the *ouvidor geral* was quarreling with the municipal judge of Luanda because both shared a scribe, mutually distrusting his discretion and loyalty.[244] Sousa Coutinho reported both incidents to the Overseas Council, who would give an opinion about them almost two years later. In April 1766, it confirmed that there was nothing to be done since the scribe's was a patrimonial position, arguing that "*to change this form of serving*" would "*entail examining*" the scribe's office "*since its origin* [...] *so that the entitlements and*

237 AHU, CU, Angola, Box 51, D. 4624; Couto, Os capitães-mores em Angola, p. 68.

238 Abrahão, A conjuração dos degredados, p. 69–110; Silva Corrêa, História de Angola, Vol. 2, p. 23–28.

239 Abrahão, A conjuração dos degredados, p. 96.

240 Ibid.; Silva Corrêa, História de Angola, Vol. 2, p. 28.

241 Miller, Way of Death, p. 558.

242 Coimbra (ed.), Livros de "Ofícios para o Reino," p. 71.

243 Ibid., p. 72.

244 Ibid., p. 73.

mercy through which it had been produced" were not breached.[245] Similar incidents showcase why commissarial boards and the new secretariats, staffed according to meritocratic principles, gained Sousa Coutinho's preference. In his original report to the Overseas Council, the captain-general and governor had also asked it to approve the extension of the board's jurisdiction to non-serious offenses, and those under $400 *réis*. Regarding this request, the council's reply was inconclusive. If Sousa Coutinho sought confirmation of the council's limitations within the new police state paradigm, he had to look no further.

Continuously faced with these delays and tergiversations, Sousa Coutinho simply pressed on, ordering on July 6, 1764, that all criminal processes were to be delivered to the board and using it as a second instance court where the adjudications, appeals, and *embargos* of the municipal judge of Luanda and the ordinary judge of Massangano were reviewed in a summary style.[246] In September 1764, to assist him and the military delegates of the board in their quarrels with the learned commissars, Sousa Coutinho requested Mendonça Furtado's permission to hire a lawyer.[247] By February 25, 1765, he asked the secretary of state to approve an Ordinance of February 24, 1765, regulating the captain majors' and the ordinary judge's administration of justice, as described in the previous chapter.[248] This new ordinance also stipulated that the Justice Board would adjudicate their final reviews according to its articles.[249] On June 23, 1766, Sousa Coutinho requested of Mendonça Furtado that the board start to adjudicate "*summarily*" all the "*crimes of the Blacks*" and that he himself, as its "*Regent*," started visiting the jails for correction.[250] As Santos describes, the Board of Justice also adjudicated cases against independent African chiefs if these could be framed according to the royal charter that instituted it.[251] In her view, this allowed the captain-general and governors to simultaneously extend their juridical protection to the Black subjects of the hinterlands, now framed as

245 AHU, CU, Angola, Box 51, D. 4697.

246 In this regard, he acted according to a previous jurisprudential deliberation of the Board of Justice, from January 8, 1763, which collectively decided in favor of the board's right to receive appeals from the adjudications of the *ouvidor geral* against the vote of the latter. ANTT, MR, EXP, Sr. 34, F. 605, p. 14, 33–44, 190–201; Coimbra (ed.), Livros de "Ofícios para o Reino," p. 73.

247 Coimbra (ed.), Livros de "Ofícios para o Reino," p. 74.

248 AHU, CU, Angola, Box 51, D. 4624; Coimbra (ed.), Livros de "Ofícios para o Reino," p. 77.

249 AHU, CU, Angola, Box 51, D. 4624; Coutinho, Documento N.° 6, in: Couto, Os capitães-mores em Angola, p. 332; Couto, Os capitães-mores em Angola, p. 68–70.

250 Coimbra (ed.), Livros de "Ofícios para o Reino," p. 83.

251 Santos, Entre deux Droits, p. 819–820.

"*personae miserabilae*,"[252] and subtract the arbitration of disputes between *sobas* from the jurisdiction of captain majors.[253]

In conclusion, the Board of Justice allowed Sousa Coutinho to police each jurisdiction of Angola, Benguela, and their dependencies, providing a new political and normative solution to the problems posed by the *de jure* opening of the African hinterlands to White merchants. It was no longer predicated on a jurisdictional form of government nor a theological framing of the monarch's *imperium*. On the contrary, it rested on a despotic, enlightened conception of royal sovereignty and the privileged legislative powers attributed to the monarch during a state of emergency. While ideals such as 'public peace' and the 'greater good of the many' played a part in legitimizing the state of exception, which afforded the Crown the possibility to issue laws that summarily abolished previous uses and customs, ordinances, styles, and procedural guarantees in West Central Africa, in practice, these abstractions were always subordinated to the cruel imperatives of the Atlantic slave trade. The next three chapters trace the history of the main trade route of enslaved Africans to the port of Luanda up until this transition moment. The last three explore how local groups used their jurisdictional autonomy to create and negotiate the shifting borders of their "moral communities" during the second half of the eighteenth century.[254] It focuses not only on the challenges posed when co-existing in a tense social environment fraught with violence and anti-social behaviors brought about by conquest and the Atlantic slave trade but also on the clash between African and European 'grammars of feelings' and the lasting impact of Mbundu institutions.[255] Therefore, both sections explore the limits of this new totalizing conception of political power.

---

252 Sousa Coutinho used the expression "*miseráveis* [miserable persons] *who trembled without Remedy*." ANTT, MR, EXP, Sr. 34, F. 605, p. 326–328.

253 Santos, Entre deux Droits, p. 819–820, 830.

254 Schoenbrun, The Names of the Python.

255 Hespanha, A cultura jurídica europeia, p. 65.

II. Trade Routes and Slave Fairs

Introduction

Part two of this work focuses on the history of the 'regimes of commensuration' that enabled the traffic of enslaved Africans along the most important West Central African trade route under partial Portuguese control, connecting Luanda to the hinterland slave fair of Cassange in the Kingdom of Kasanje. It adopts this heuristic to situate the "translation of normative knowledge" that occurred in these multinormative spaces within broader Portuguese projects of conquest and conversion that impacted several dimensions still undergoing the early stages of their differentiation into separate fields, from the religious to the economic, and the cultural one.[1] This heuristic approach affords an analysis that remains open to concurrences and synergies while also foregrounding the importance of paying attention to the shifting limits of (in)commensurability and processes of "othering" and exclusion.[2] The fourth chapter focuses on attempts to convert the BaKongo and Mbundu markets into slave fairs where Portuguese jurisdiction and the rules of the Atlantic slave trade dictated who and what objects and ideas could be made commensurable or exchanged. The fifth chapter centers on how these contested spaces were also crucial to the othering of cultures, normative systems, and specific human subjects and groups. Considering both aspects as sides of the same coin, the sixth chapter explores how retaining control over regional regimes of commensuration enacted in markets and slave fairs became a political imperative, foregrounding how the clash of opposing claims by captain-general and governors of Angola and the *jaga* of Kasanje impacted the normative framework and functioning of the Luanda-Cassange trade route.

Wendy Espeland and Mitchell Stevens define commensuration as comparing different entities according to a common metric or scale.[3] As both authors stress, this act is not merely descriptive but also transformative since it turns qualities into quantities and shapes "difference into magnitude." Accordingly, commensuration is a profoundly symbolic and inherently political gesture, serving as a technology

---

1 Duve, Legal History as a History of the Translation of Knowledge of Normativity, p. 1–12; Saavedra, Jurisdictional Autonomy and the Autonomy of Law, p. 325–337.

2 See Francisco Bethencourt and the essays in Angêla Barreto Xavier and Cristina Nogueira Silva for an overview of different forms of 'othering' in the Portuguese Empire from the fifteenth to the twentieth century. For a comparative analysis of how different empires approached "religious and cultural difference," see Frederick Cooper and Jane Burbank. Barreto Xavier and Nogueira da Silva, O governo dos outros; Bethencourt, Managing Diversity in the Portuguese Empire; Bethencourt, Racisms; Burbank and Cooper, Empires in World History.

3 Espeland and Stevens, Commensuration as a Social Process, p. 316.

of power and a means to model societies and marginalized groups. It differs from other standardization mechanisms, such as censuses or surveys, as it is predicated on "aggregations" of seemingly fundamentally different things. Therefore, it affords the integration of valuing, aesthetic, moral, and normative systems into a coherent regime. In practical terms, commensuration is what allows us to attribute a monetary value to 'things' as different as human suffering, biodiversity, artwork and cultural heritage, and public goods such as education, water, and sewage utilities.[4]

As Martha Nussbaum and Cass Sunstein remark, several political thinkers, from Plato to Jeremy Bentham (1748–1832), have attempted to develop a "monistic theory of value" that supports a total commensuration regime.[5] Such a hypothetical regime would be predicated on "reducing" different kinds of valuation to standardized scales that use "super concepts" such as the common good, happiness, utility, or pleasure as benchmarks.[6] However, as Nussbaum and Sunstein explain, commensuration is always linked to the delimitation of what remains or is excluded as incommensurable.[7] Excluded elements, dimensions, or fields of social life can be framed positively as sacred, precious, or vital for social reproduction. In contemporary societies, this kind of positively valued incommensurability is at the heart of child labor regulations, heritage preservation, or environmental protection laws.[8] It also explains why some exchanges are socially shunned, such as bans on

4 Espeland and Sauder, Rankings and Reactivity, p. 1–40; Espeland and Vannbo, Accountability, Quantification, and Law, p. 21–43; Karpik, Valuing the Unique; Fourcade, Cents and Sensibility, p. 1721–1777; Ng and He, The Institutional and Cultural Logics of Legal Commensuration, p. 1104–1143.

5 Nussbaum, Plato on Commensurability and Desire, p. 55–96; Sunstein, Incommensurability and Valuation in Law, p. 781–785.

6 Martha Nussbaum explores the Platonic dialogue *Protagoras* to exemplify the pitfalls of such reductions. In this dialogue, Plato has Socrates arguing with Protagoras about the need for an "ethical science of measurement" to avoid *akrasia* or lack of self-control. The problem under discussion is framed as follows: "A can do either *x* or *y*. A knows that *x* is better (overall), but chooses *y*, because she is overcome by pleasure." By adopting a monistic theory of value that allows him to reduce "pleasure" to a form of good, making both commensurable, Plato's Socrates claims to have proven the behavior of subject A to be absurd, as it amounts to choosing a lesser quantity of good over a larger one. Explanations for this absurdity can then be rationalized as "the result of a mistaken judgment" by subject A. As Espeland, Stevens, and Sunstein remark, similar reductions are not only inadequate descriptions of "actual valuations," implying the loss of significant information, but also "impair predictive accounts" of how real actors behave in concrete situations. Espeland and Stevens, Commensuration as a Social Process, p. 330; Nussbaum, Plato on Commensurability and Desire, p. 58–61; Sunstein, Incommensurability and Valuation in Law, p. 784–785.

7 Espeland and Stevens, Commensuration as a Social Process, p. 328; Sunstein, Incommensurability and Valuation in Law, p. 828.

8 Fourcade, Cents and Sensibility, p. 1721–1777; Karpik, Valuing the Unique.

selling public offices and human organs or forms of prostitution.[9] What remains incommensurable can also be negatively framed. Things that cannot be measured, quantified, scaled, or weighted against each other have been associated with the irrational, the absurd, dangerous passions, and political mayhem since the Pre-Socratics.[10] Therefore, as Espeland, Stevens, and Sunstein conclude, disputes over the limits of (in)commensurability or what can become fungible (e. g., transitive or tradable) are often found at the center of political strife, indicating shifting power relations and the emergence of new religious, normative, cultural, or legal paradigms.[11] The provisional equilibrium between different valuation frameworks and the legally, socially, normatively, or religiously sanctioned limits of what remains incommensurable is what I define in this section as a historical regime of commensuration.

In their study of nineteenth-century Protestant evangelism in South Africa, Jean and John Comaroff examine one such historical regime, pointing out that struggles to set the terms and limits of commensuration were central to missionary efforts.[12] For the Nonconformist missionaries in South Africa, converting Tswana "heathens" into Christians not only required changing their systems of moral valuation and understanding of the sacred but also quite prosaically "teaching" them how to use metallic currencies, how to commodify and sell their labor and land, and to accept the primacy of market exchanges over gift-giving and barter.[13] By introducing per-

9 Espeland and Stevens, Commensuration as a Social Process, p. 328; Gregory, Gifts and Commodities p. xl; Sunstein, Incommensurability and Valuation in Law, p. 779–861.

10 Nussbaum, Plato on Commensurability and Desire, p. 55–96.

11 Sunstein, Incommensurability and Valuation in Law, p. 799; Espeland and Stevens, Commensuration as a Social Process, p. 323.

12 Comaroff and Comaroff, Beasts, Banknotes and the Colour of Money, p. 107–132; Comaroff and Comaroff, Cattle, Currencies & the Politics of Commensuration, in: Adebanwi (ed.), The Political Economy of Everyday Life in Africa, p. 35–71; Comaroff and Comaroff, Of Revelation and Revolution, Vol. 2, p. 166–217.

13 It is impossible to provide a comprehensive overview of the anthropological literature on gift exchange, a core topic of the discipline since Bronislaw Malinowski, Lévi-Strauss, and Marcel Mauss wrote foundational monographs on the subject. Debates about the difference between gifts and commodities, the nature of this distinction, and how commercial valuation frameworks based on "exchange value" and 'traditional' systems based on "rank value" interact have also originated a large corpus of bibliography. Christopher Gregory's new preface to the 2015 reedition of *Gifts and Commodities* (1982) introduces the most relevant discussions since the late 1970s (previous ones having been addressed by its first two chapters). Marilyn Strathern's *The Gender of the Gift* (1988) has shifted the terms of the debate, calling into question the strict opposition between gift and commodity as a Western projection and pointing to the subjectivizing nature of exchange. It remains actual. Bronislaw, Argonauts of the Western Pacific; Comaroff and Comaroff, Beasts, banknotes and the colour of money, p. 107–132; Comaroff and Comaroff, Of Revelation and Revolution, Vol. 2, p. 168–171; Gregory, Cowries and Conquest, p. 201; Gregory, Gifts and

fectly fungible (e. g., transitive, exchangeable) metal coins or tokens, the Comaroffs explain, European missionaries hoped to disassemble the existing economic system in which cattle exchange allowed the social and material reproduction of the political power of Tswana elders and chiefs.[14] This was the case because junior or client Tswana males relied almost entirely on the herds of their elders or patrons to access the cattle necessary to pay judicial fees, blood money, political tributes, or bridewealth.[15] As the Comaroffs remark, pursuing wealth was inherently tied to constructing enduring social and kinship ties for the Tswana.[16] Cattle embodied the "living connections" between persons or groups, and beasts were highly exchangeable but not fungible.[17] The "magnitude" of the worth of individual beasts, recognizable by their gender, age, color, size, and markings, was a function of the "density" of relations they had constructed through being exchanged.[18] As such, cattle served the functions of a "social currency."[19] As David Graeber describes

---

Commodities; Gregory, Savage Money; Lévi-Strauss, The Elementary Structures of Kinship; Mauss, The Gift; Strathern, The Gender of the Gift.

14 Comaroff and Comaroff, Beasts, Banknotes and the Colour of Money, p. 107–132; Comaroff and Comaroff, Of Revelation and Revolution, Vol. 2, p. 171; Ferguson, The Bovine Mystique, p. 647–674.

15 Comaroff and Comaroff, Cattle, Currencies & the Politics of Commensuration, in: Adebanwi (ed.), The Political Economy of Everyday Life in Africa, p. 43, 60, 64.

16 Ibid., p. 43.

17 Comaroff and Comaroff, Of Revelation and Revolution, Vol. 2, p. 174.

18 Ibid.; Piot, Of Persons and Things, p. 405–424.

19 David Graeber's concept of "social currency" builds on Gregory's and Strathern's work to recover some of the insights of previous theories about "special purpose money" without being hindered by the conceptual and historiographic problems that mired them. In the late 1960s, 'substantivist' anthropologists and 'formalist' economists clashed over the distinction between "general purpose money" and special purpose money. Following Karl Polanyi, the former claimed that although 'primitive' forms of money serve only one or two of the four purposes served by "general purpose money" (which is a mode of payment, standard of value, means of exchange, and store of wealth), they should still be accounted for in economic models as forms of "special purpose money." This distinction dovetails nicely with Paul and Laura Bohannan's work on separate "spheres of exchange," further discussed in the fourth chapter. By merging their model with Polanyi's theory, substantivists argued that in non-capitalist, pre-industrial societies, a sphere of direct barter co-existed with higher "spheres of exchange" where special-purpose money was used to sustain and nurture reciprocity-based relationships. If these societies used general-purpose money, the substantivists reasoned, they reserved it for the lower spheres of exchange. The formalists completely disregarded the distinction between "primitive money" and general-purpose money in their economic models and numismatic theories, only focusing on the latter and denying the importance, or even existence, of separate spheres of exchange. Substantivist theories became increasingly unfashionable as their abstract models about pre-colonial economic systems proved empirically unverifiable, and leading Africanist historians drew inspiration from formalist models to analyze non-metallic currencies such as cotton cloth, cowries, or commodity bundles. As Marion Johnson and Jan Hogendorn exhaustively documented, despite being hitherto considered "primitive currencies," shell and cloth

them, social currencies are used to "create, maintain, and otherwise reorganize relations between people."[20] Due to the fact that for the Tswana, cattle were inextricably connected to the social relations they constructed and embodied, their exchange posed limits to the extraction or alienation of wealth by colonial or conquering powers.[21] The substitution of social currencies for perfectly fungible ones that afford a "violent separation of value from context" and the reduction of the values they embody to commensurable quantities was, therefore, understood as a prerequisite of imperial expansion and the extraction of wealth.[22] It was also welcomed by those previously excluded from trading in prestigious social currencies, ensuring that many disenfranchised male Tswana were sympathetic to the European missionaries' cause.

Moreover, as the Comaroffs aptly demonstrate, religious conversion also hinged on enforcing a new regime of commensuration.[23] Social currencies allowed Tswana elders and chiefs to accumulate "wealth in people" instead of "wealth in things," grounding an economic system European missionaries framed as wasteful and

---

currencies had served as general-purpose money for centuries. They could ground value extraction at the core of mercantilism and the slave trade. With his concept of social currency, Graeber highlights that some currencies are deeply embedded in the social relations that they maintain without insisting on the existence of separate spheres of exchange being only a feature of pre-capitalist, pre-industrial societies or associating social currencies exclusively with gift economies. See Enrique Martino and Mario Schmidt's introduction and Michael Hudson's foreword to the latest translation of Heinrich Schurtz's *An Outline of the Origins of Money* (2024 [1898]) for a discussion on the recent comeback of some of the ideas dismissed by formalists. Bohannan and Bohannan, The Tiv; Bohannan and Bohannan, Tiv Economy; Bohannan, The impact of money, p. 491–503; Bohannan, The impact of money, p. 491–503; Dalton, Primitive, Archaic, and Modern Economies; Graeber, Debt; Graeber, Towards an Anthropological Theory of Value, p. 130; Gregory, Cowries and Conquest, p. 195–217; Gregory, Gifts and Commodities; Gregory, Savage Money; Hogendorn and Johnson, The Shell Money; Hudson, Foreword, in: Schurtz, An Outline of the Origins of Money, p. xv–xxviii; Johnson, Cloth as Money, p. 193–202; Johnson, Cotton Imperialism in West Africa, p. 178–187; Lovejoy, Interregional Monetary Flows, p. 563–585; Lovejoy, Polanyi's "Ports of Trade," p. 245–277; Martino and Schmidt, Introduction, in: Schurtz, Heinrich, An Outline of the Origins of Money, p. 1–24; Pallaver, Introduction, in: Pallaver (ed.), Monetary Transitions, p. 1–30; Piot, Of Persons and Things, p. 405–424; Strathern, The Gender of the Gift; Webb (Jr.), Toward the Comparative Study of Money, p. 455–466.

20 Graeber, Debt, p. 130.

21 Comaroff and Comaroff, Beasts, Banknotes and the Colour of Money, p. 107–132; Comaroff and Comaroff, Of Revelation and Revolution, Vol. 2, p. 166–217.

22 Comaroff and Comaroff, Of Revelation and Revolution, Vol. 2, p. 174; Gregory, Savage Money; Maurer, Primitive and Nonmetallic Money, in: Battilossi, Cassis and Yago (eds.), Handbook of the History of Money and Currency, p. 8.

23 Comaroff and Comaroff, Cattle, Currencies & the Politics of Commensuration, in: Adebanwi (ed.), The Political Economy of Everyday Life in Africa, p. 35–71.

sinful because it put a prize on polygamy and male indolence.[24] Moreover, cattle reified and stored the cultural, social, and aesthetic values European missionaries wished to substitute by providing the topic for epic poetry, countless stories, and normative ruminations.[25] Therefore, its reduction to a commodity was considered a prerequisite for converting the Tswana to Christian values. In reaction to Methodist interventions and the spread of European trading posts, attempts to retain control of the limits of (in)commensurability became central to the chiefs' and elders' resistance against colonial encroachment.[26] This turned South African marketplaces into sites where political and economic control was imposed and contested and where bids for social, cultural, and normative reform through the imposition or adoption of a new regime of commensuration were materially and ideologically played out.[27] Similar dynamics have been analyzed by James Scott in Southeast Asia and Clifford Geertz in Indonesia, where attempts to retain control over the regime of commensuration and uphold the existence of separated markets for prestige goods were at the heart of peasant rebellions in the first half of the twentieth century.[28] It seems, therefore, that not only disgruntled elites play a part in contesting and subverting imposed regimes of commensurability, but also subaltern groups whose livelihood is threatened by the expansion of the free market. The following three chapters explore how similar dynamics played out in Early Modern West Central Africa, where the history of local regimes of commensuration is inextricably tied to the history of the Atlantic slave trade and the institutions of slavery.

---

24 The concept of "wealth in people" was proposed by Suzane Miers and Igor Kopytoff and adopted for the study of Ndongo and Mbangala groups by Miller and Vansina. As Vansina remarks, it signals that "whenever possible, wealth in goods was […] converted into followers" through their circulation as social currency. Miller argues that adopting this strategy stemmed from the fact that "human dependence was the most efficacious means of increasing production" in areas where access to land was not a limiting factor and the capital investment needed to enter the most lucrative industries was negligible. For a critique of the concept's limits, see Jane Guyer and Samuel Belinga. Guyer and Belinga, Wealth in People as Wealth in Knowledge, p. 91–120; Guyer, Wealth in People and Self-Realization, p. 243–265; Guyer, Wealth in People, p. 83–90; Miers and Kopytoff, Slavery in Africa; Miller, Way of Death; Vansina, Paths in the Rainforests, p. 251.

25 Comaroff and Comaroff, Beasts, Banknotes and the Colour of Money, p. 107–132; Comaroff and Comaroff, Of Revelation and Revolution, Vol. 2, p. 166–217.

26 Comaroff and Comaroff, Of Revelation and Revolution, Vol. 2, p. 174; Graeber, Debt, p. 148–164.

27 As the Comaroffs remark, not all changes were exteriorly imposed. Younger Tswana cohorts, women, migrants, and city dwellers might welcome and precipitate changes, as the new regime of commensurability proposed by the missionaries offered them advantages vis-à-vis the one controlled by elders and chiefs. Comaroff and Comaroff, Beasts, Banknotes and the Colour of Money, p. 107–132; Comaroff and Comaroff, Of Revelation and Revolution, Vol. 2, p. 166–217.

28 Geertz, Agricultural Involution; Scott, The Moral Economy of the Peasant.

4. Sites of Conversion and Commensuration

4.1 A Journey to the Margins of the Kwango

On August 31, 1755, the slave trader Manoel Correia Leitão left Luanda on a secret mission.[1] Captain-General and Governor António Álvares da Cunha (1700–1791), in office between 1753 and 1758, had personally selected him for the job. A practicing cartographer, Álvares da Cunha had decided to promote the surveying and mapping of Portuguese establishments in West Central Africa to provide a more rational and quantifiable basis for the governing of the Captaincy of Angola.[2] In 1755, Leitão occupied the position of sergeant major of the third-line militia of *moradores* of the district of Dande. He was born in Luanda, experienced in traveling in the Angolan hinterlands, and was fluent in Kimbundu and some of the other "*languages of* [those] *bushes*."[3] His official task was to travel east to the Kingdom of Kasanje through the Portuguese *presídios* of Massangano, Cambambe, and Ambaca and, once he reached the Luso-African slave fair of Cassange, explore the margins of the nearby Kwango River in greater detail. He was to measure the "*width, depth,* [and] *quality of the water*" of the Kwango, observe and register its fords, and find a safe way to cross it.[4] Furthermore, he was to locate a nearby "*height where one could build a fortress*," considering the availability of drinking water and fertile lands to plow capable of sustaining a small garrison.

Leitão's was a delicate mission because since the Kingdom of Kasanje had been established c. 1620–30, its *kulashingo*, an elected sovereign who was titled *jaga* by the Portuguese, successfully barred them and their representatives from crossing the Kwango. This prohibition effectively frustrated Portuguese efforts to penetrate inland slave markets directly and find a land route to their East African innermost settlements in Rios de Senna.[5] Leitão was also to contact the kingdom's northern neighbors, the Holo, and report their uses, customs, religion, and possible contacts

---

1 I use Éva Sebestyén and Jan Vansina's English translation of Leitão's report. Sebestyén, Vansina (eds.), and Leitão, Angola's Eastern Hinterland, p. 333.

2 Santos, Administrative knowledge, p. 545; Santos, De "antigos conquistadores" a "angolenses," p. 198, 209; Santos, Entre deux Droits, p. 817–818; Santos, Um governo "polido" para Angola.

3 Sebestyén, Vansina (eds.), and Leitão, Angola's Eastern Hinterland, p. 330.

4 Ibid., p. 332–333.

5 Fernandes, A Feira de Cassanje, p. 30–41; Ferreira, Cross-Cultural Exchange, p. 48–49; Madeira Santos, Em busca dos sítios do poder na África Centro Ocidental, in: Heintze and von Oppen (eds.), Angola on the Move, p. 30–31; Miller, Kings and Kinsmen, p. 191–192; Miller, Kings, Lists, and History in Kasanje, p. 52–53.

with rival European traders and caravans from the "*other coast of the Ocean*."[6] More importantly, he was to identify their trade preferences, a piece of information precious to Luanda-based slave merchants and their commercial associates. By then, the internal slave trade of Holo, an "independent lordship" that had broken away from Kasanje at the end of the seventeenth century, was also closely monitored by the *jaga* of Kasanje, who might not have a say on his neighbors' taste for cloths but definitively interfered in the redistribution of enslaved people in Holo markets.[7] The Pilot Antonio Roiz Grizante accompanied Leitão, tasked with fixing the latitude of the Cassange slave fair and performing additional astronomical measurements that would allow these hinterland *presídios* and market spaces to be more precisely pinpointed on Portuguese maps. At that point, distances were still measured in traveling days, which could change drastically according to season and individual march rhythms, making planning business and military expeditions more challenging. Moreover, as Joseph Miller remarks, river crossings had to be negotiated with ferrymen, countless toll stations were set up by the "local gentry," and rumors about nearby "highwaymen" stopped caravans on their tracks for days, resulting in no more than 10 kilometers ever being covered on a good day's march.[8] At its largest, Leitão's party was comprised of about 150 men, including porters, slaves, and, perhaps, a tiny irregular militia.[9]

Contrary to Álvares da Cunha, who trusted Leitão's capabilities and loyalty, António de Vasconcelos, the captain-general and governor of Angola who succeeded him in office between 1758 and 1764, described Leitão as a habitual drunkard and a compulsive liar, framing the whole affair as a thinly disguised slave-trading business venture, unofficially sponsored by his predecessor.[10] Upon completing his mission on August 15, 1756, Leitão was ordered to write a report that Jan Vansina and Evá Sebestyén estimate he concluded by May 1757, only after borrowing notes from Grizante and including additional details retrospectively at the request of Álvares da Cunha. Because Leitão neither kept a journal nor wrote daily itineraries during his journey, Vansina and Sebestyén conclude that he wrote the report from memory, often synthesizing conflicting gossip and rumors.[11] With all its limitations, and even though Leitão mentioned nothing about the Luso-African merchants and *pumbeiros* who had been based in the fair of Cassange since the early seventeenth

---

6 Sebestyén, Vansina (eds.), and Leitão, Angola's Eastern Hinterland, p. 332–333.

7 For an account of previous attempts by the captain-general and governors of Angola to establish direct trade connection with the Holo, see Roquinaldo Ferreira. Ferreira, Cross-Cultural Exchange, p. 20–51; Miller, Way of Death.

8 Miller, Way of Death, p. 192.

9 Ibid., Sebestyén, Vansina (eds.), and Leitão, Angola's Eastern Hinterland, p. 299.

10 Sebestyén, Vansina (eds.), and Leitão, Angola's Eastern Hinterland, p. 301–302.

11 Ibid., p. 303–304.

century, his account is still a precious source about the Kingdom of Kasanje and the administration of justice at this slave market operating entirely outside of Portuguese military control.[12] As the previous chapter introduced, slave markets such as Cassange were crucial to the livelihood of Luso-African *moradores* and merchants and the financial stability of the Portuguese Crown and local corporations, from lay brotherhoods to missionary religious orders and the Municipal Council of Luanda. Álvares da Cunha's orders and Leitão's report, document that they were also sites where the institutions of slavery became deeply ingrained within competing valuing systems and different forms of othering.[13] There, norms and practices related to the ownership and trade of slaves, the valuing systems that grounded what Paul and Laura Bohannan define as "spheres of exchange," and various forms of segregating and discriminating formed a regime of commensuration that was politically contested and normatively framed both by royal enactments and ordinances, *Ius commune* doctrines, and African norms.[14] The chapters in this part focus on its *longue durée* history, tracing its development from its inception in the 1560s to the 1800s. Moreover, they explore how analogous beliefs about what the Portuguese conceptualized as *feitiçaria*, the BaKongo as *kindoki*, and the Mbundu and other Kimbundu speakers as *uanga* came to be at the center of the political and ideological disputes over its control.

In the 1950s, the Bohannans coined the concept of "spheres of exchange" to distinguish between the three economic arenas that the Tiv of Nigeria recognized before colonization (c. the 1920s).[15] According to them, each sphere was a "different universe" of commensurable objects governed by a "different set of moral values and different behavior." Items exchanged in the 'lowest' sphere comprised fresh produce, tools, and utensils; items exchanged in the 'middle' sphere included cattle, brass rods, slaves, magic items, and cloth; and only rights over free women and children were exchanged in the 'top' prestige sphere.[16] According to the Bohannans, exchanges within each sphere ("conveyances") tended to be considered morally neutral by the Tiv. In contrast, exchanges between spheres ("conversions") tended to be

12 Ibid., p. 304; Fernandes, A feira de Cassanje, p. 30–41; Ferreira, Feiras e presídios.

13 Barreto Xavier and Nogueira da Silva, Introdução, in: Barreto Xavier and Nogueira da Silva (eds.), O governo dos outros, p. 21–31.

14 Bohannan and Bohannan, The Tiv; Bohannan and Bohannan, Tiv Economy, p. 227–228.

15 The concept of spheres of exchange has been applied to the study of several other African and Melanesian societies. Graeber, Debt, p. 36–37; Gregory, Gifts and Commodities p. 48–49; Piot, Of Persons and Things, p. 405–424.

16 These 'rights' were probably understood by early modern Portuguese observers in terms of *dominium*, if not over the freedom of women and dependents, at least over some of their 'functions' (e.g., reproductive functions, reproductive labor, productive labor). See the third chapter for more on different modalities of *dominium*.

morally charged and highly regulated.[17] Upward conversion was deemed desirable, while downward conversion was rare and taboo. Paul Bohannan further argued that exchange spheres collapsed with the introduction of colonial currencies.[18] However, a consensus has emerged that contrary to Paul Bohannan's assessment, the introduction of colonial currencies did not necessarily collapse existing spheres of exchange—as this and the next chapters demonstrate.[19]

Leitão's secret mission to the fair of Cassange, and from there eastwards to the Kwango River and northwards to the Holo slave markets, was part of a systematic effort orchestrated by Álvares da Cunha to integrate further these distant socio-geographical spaces, African polities, and the valuation frameworks that underpinned their prestige spheres of exchange into a commensuration regime more firmly controlled by the Portuguese Crown. This entailed not only fixing latitudes and measuring the depth and width of the river, noting the fashion preferences of the Holo, and reporting on the uses and customs of the Mbangala, but also imposing on the *jaga* of Kasanje a Portuguese understanding of the limits of the (in)commensurable. While the *jaga* might have been open to further integrating his polity into the Atlantic slave trade and accepting the considerable degree of commensuration between different valuation frameworks and spheres of exchange that this assimilation imposed, as discussed in the following sections and chapters, he was keen on retaining the last word when delimiting what remained incommensurable and invested on integrating European norms and valuation frameworks into a historical regime of commensuration of Mbangala design.[20] Understanding disputes over commensuration and its limits as a "calculus of power" at this regional level allows us to pay attention to its "constitutive power" in connection with legal, normative, and socio-cultural categories.[21] In other words, be sensitive to their centrality in the 'politics of conversion' and the evolution of Portuguese legal and normative frameworks. As Wendy Espeland and Mitchel Stevens summarize, while "strategic commensuration" and resistance to it are tied to the capacity to "create numbers that reflect our will," constitutive commensuration is always in dialectic tension with the limits of the incommensurable.[22] Measuring the Kwango or identifying

---

17 Bohannan and Bohannan, The Tiv; Bohannan and Bohannan, Tiv Economy, p. 227–228.

18 Bohannan, The Impact of Money.

19 Graeber, Debt, p. 36–37; Gregory, Gifts and Commodities p. 48–49; Piot, Of Persons and Things, p. 405–424.

20 Eltis, Precolonial Western Africa in: Solow (ed.), Slavery and the Rise of the Atlantic System, p. 97–119; Ferreira, Dinâmica do comércio intracolonial, in: Fragoso et al. (eds.), O Antigo Regime nos Trópicos, p. 341–378.

21 Espeland and Stevens, Commensuration as a Social Process, p. 331.

22 James Scott has thoroughly explored how strategic commensuration and resistance to measurement and comparison are central to how "individuals are made governable" or resist statecraft

the latitude of Cassange are examples of strategic commensuration; determining or contesting the price for enslaved persons and who could be sold at hinterland fairs are constitutive operations with more profound cultural, normative, and personal impacts.

Joseph Miller explains that by the time of Leitão's journey, the fair of Cassange was of particular interest to the Portuguese Crown.[23] According to him, there were three major commercial trade routes in West Central Africa during this period, each with marked specificities.[24] Cassange was situated upstream of the central one that reached Luanda and was traversed by large Lisbon-financed slave caravans known as *libambos*.[25] The other two were not fully integrated into the Portuguese mercantilist system.[26] One, to the north, was entirely controlled by the BaKongo, Teke, Vili, and other African diaspora traders who sold slaves to the French and British at a considerable profit at the ports of the coast of Loango.[27] To the south, the other channeled Ovimbundu war prisoners to the mostly *brasílico* [Brazilian-born] merchants based in Benguela or the European ships that frequented its southern shores.[28] Merchants and *pumbeiros* operating in the central trade route experienced significant losses of slaves during the long trek of their coffles to Luanda. This was due to poor nutrition, the hostile epidemiological environment, the roughness of the terrain, and the fact that large caravans took time to assemble, and the waiting debilitated the first enslaved persons to be rounded up for transport.[29] These long waiting periods were due to the fact that the enslaved Africans traded in the central trade route were obtained from relatively unpopulated areas at the rim of equatorial rainforests that could not sustain dense settlements. Furthermore, slave merchants

---

in contemporary times. Ibid.; Scott, Seeing Like a State; Scott, State Simplifications, p. 42–85; Scott, Weapons of the Weak.

23 Miller, Way of Death, p. 214.

24 Ibid., p. 207–208.

25 As Luís António de Oliveira Mendes reports, the half-inch-thick iron chains that bound slaves were also known as *libambos*. Some could chain thirty persons, others up to one hundred. Female and male slaves were chained in different *libambos*. Usually, their right hands were bound, and children would accompany their mothers unchained. Before joining a coffle, enslaved Africans were kept in wooden shackles known as *troncos*. Mendes, Memória a respeito dos escravos, p. 20–21.

26 Miller, Way of Death, p. 208.

27 According to Cecile Fromont, the geographical term "Coast of Loango" was used to refer to the strip of land extending from Cape Lopez in present-day Gabon to Luanda. Phyllis Martin argues that the term was used to describe the coastal regions between "southern Gabon and the Zaire River." This included the Loango Kingdom and the neighboring Kingdoms of Ngoyo and Kakongo. Fromont, Common Threads, p. 842; Miller, Way of Death, p. 208; MacGaffey, Crossing the River, in: Heintze and von Oppen (eds.), Angola on the Move, p. 221–242; Martin, Power, Cloth and Currency, p. 1–12.

28 Miller, Way of Death, p. 208.

29 Ibid., p. 583; Ferreira, Cross-Cultural Exchange, p. 26.

operating this trade route were forced to deal with Portuguese bureaucracy and taxation. They thus operated their business ventures with a considerable handicap *vis-à-vis* the agents that worked in the northern and southern trade routes.

To overcome these hindrances, Miller argues, Lisbon-backed merchants and *pumbeiros* developed a system based on offering trade goods on "ruinously liberal terms of credit" to their African partners, creating the need for a robust judiciary system capable of enforcing the payment of debts and overseeing the inheritance of the assets, debts, and the credit of deceased merchants and *pumbeiros*.[30] Such a need did not arise in the northern routes, where non-state-centered African normative systems described by Europeans as cults or secret societies regulated the trading diasporas and the (re)integration of their members into local "moral communities."[31] In the southern hinterlands of Benguela, the relative cheapness of war-prisoner slaves allowed many small-scale merchants and *pumbeiros* to establish themselves entirely outside Portuguese jurisdiction, presenting different challenges to the Portuguese Crown.[32] However, the fact that the credit practices of Luanda-based merchants created the need for a robust judiciary does not mean that this need was equally addressed between the early seventeenth and mid-nineteenth centuries or fully addressed at all. On the contrary, this *desideratum* kept conditioning the projects and practices of successive captain-general and governors, merchants, and Luso-African *moradores* and traders.[33] Considering that, in the Luanda-Kasanje trade route, difficulties in collecting debts and managing credit were evergreen, one of the unstated objectives of Leitão's trip to Cassange, Vansina and Sebestyén argue, could have been to attempt to settle a loan advanced by Álvares da Cunha's trading associates in Luanda to merchants or *pumbeiros* established at the fair.[34]

This chapter explores the complex political and normative arrangements that emerged and consolidated in the slave fairs that dotted the Luanda-Kasanje route, understanding them through the prism of evolving historical regimes of commensuration. In other words, it pays close attention to the deployment of strategic and constitutive forms of commensuration, religious, cultural, and legal debates about

---

30 Miller, A Marginal Institution on the Margin of the Atlantic System, in: Solow (ed.), Slavery and the Rise of the Atlantic System, p. 138–139, 142–143; Miller, Way of Death, p. 208, 307.

31 Graeber, Debt, p. 148–164; Harms, River of Wealth, River of Sorrow; Janzen, Lemba, 1650–1930; MacGaffey, Crossing the River, in: Heintze and von Oppen (eds.), Angola on the Move, p. 236–237; Miller, Way of Death, p. 674; Olivier and Armore, Medieval Africa, p. 165; Schoenbrun, The Names of the Python, p. 8–9.

32 In 1792, a group of merchants established in Benguela complained that twenty-two French and two British vessels had visited the region in the previous year, eclipsing the number of Portuguese ones. ANTT, MR, EXP, Sr. 34, F. 605, p. 404–411; Vansina, Long-Distance Trade-Routes, p. 383.

33 See the ninth chapter for more on the historical impact of unfinished or failed projects in the Captaincy of Angola and Benguela.

34 Sebestyén, Vansina (eds.), and Leitão, Angola's Eastern Hinterland, p. 299.

the limits of (in)commensurability and the ideologies and normative frameworks that grounded the Portuguese and African regimes. Leitão's journey from Luanda to the Cassange fair provides the narrative backbone of this and the following two chapters. At critical moments, his narrative recedes to the background for us to explain how the various layers of history that marked the social and normative landscape he was traveling through had settled.

4.2 Conquering Mbundu *Itanda*

About two weeks after departing Luanda, Manoel Leitão arrived at the small garrison town of Muxima, where a Portuguese fortification oversaw the Kwanza River from the top of a natural hill that dominated its left margin.[35] He had first travelled by foot from Luanda to Calumbo, on the right bank of this same river, and then navigated upstream to Muxima by canoe. On September 19, 1755, still water-bound, Leitão reached the historical town of Massangano, which he described as being "*reduced* [...] *to a depopulated village, almost without settlers*." Captain Major António Gonçalves de Carvalho provided him with porters to proceed, as ordered by Álvares da Cunha. A few days later, Leitão left Massangano on foot, continued following the river until he reached Cambambe on September 29. From there, he climbed the trails that led to the central plateau, leaving the Kwanza Valley behind. Once atop, Leitão marched northwards to Ambaca, the last "*of the dominions of Portugal*" at the edge of the inner highlands. He reached the *presídio* there on October 22. While waiting for Captain Major Apolinario Francisco de Carvalho to provide him with fresh porters, Leitão assembled "*provisions of dry meat and various sorts of flour*," which he kept in leather bags to preserve them from the rain.[36]

After Carvalho managed to "*fetch*" porters from "*all over the vast* [area] *of his jurisdiction*," Leitão departed eastwards, still traveling a couple of days more through highland chieftainships belonging to the jurisdiction of Ambaca before finally reaching the valleys of "*Muene Bondo* [*ndala quissua*]," a "*vassal of the Emperor and Jaga Casangi* [Kasanje]."[37] Leitão described his trek through "*such wild and rustic forests*" according to the travel-writing conventions of his times. During the day, he had to face all kinds of "*wild beasts*," and his porters were terrorized by "*appalling claps of thunder*" and lightning that turned "*huge trees* [...] *into slivers*." At night, his camp was attacked by "*lions*" and ruthless "*highway robbers who* [were] *always*

35 Ibid., p. 334.
36 Ibid., p. 335.
37 Ibid., p. 335–336.

stealing and killing traders." Maintaining that he would prefer to face great "*perils at sea*" than repeat this trying and dangerous journey, in his report, Leitão inflated the dangers he faced and emphasized his deeds as an explorer seeking to secure the Crown's favor. Nevertheless, he traveled along a well-trodden path, retracing the steps of early Portuguese conquerors, traders, and missionaries.[38]

Shortly after starting the first campaign of the Luso-Ndongo wars in 1580, Paulo Dias de Novais (1510–1589) had also sailed up the Kwanza, hoping to secure the assistance of dissenting Mbundu *sobas* in his fight against Njinga Ngola Kilombo kia Kasenda, the *ngola* or sovereign of Ndongo between 1575 and 1592.[39] Then, Dias de Novais' army comprised 290 soldiers, accompanied by 200 slaves, aboard "*two galiots, a caravelão,*[40] *and other smaller vessels*."[41] Muxima Kitangonge was one of the most powerful *sobas* to join the Portuguese at this early stage of the conquest of Ndongo.[42] After Muxima became a vassal of the Portuguese Crown, providing a secure riverine harbor in his domains,[43] Dias de Novais pressed on towards Cambambe, establishing his headquarters in Mocumbe.[44] According to Father Baltasar Barreira (1538–1612), then superior of the Jesuits in West Central Africa, Dias de Novais was stalled in Mocumbe for almost two full years, raiding neighboring chieftains for slaves and awaiting backup before attempting to resume the conquest eastwards.[45] The Jesuit priest personally brokered these reinforce-

---

38 Heywood and Thornton, Central Africans, p. 87–89.

39 Heywood and Thornton, Central Africans, p. 87–89; MMA III, D. 46; MMA IV, D. 132; Leitão, A missão do P.e Baltasar Barreira, p. 43–91.

40 A *caravelão* [pl. *caravelões*] was a smaller version of the caravel measuring 20 to 25 tons. As A. Saunders describes, they were the "*duty boat for the* [Portuguese] *factories in Africa*." Saunders, A Social History of Black Slaves, p. 11.

41 MMA III, D. 46, p. 199–200; MMA IV, D. 132, p. 566.

42 Heywood and Thornton, Central Africans, p. 87–88; MMA III, D. 46, p. 200; Thornton, A History of West Central Africa, p. 86.

43 According to José Leitão, Muxima Kitangonge joined the Portuguese after being terrorized by the atrocities committed by the troops accompanying Dias de Novais. Describing the campaign in 1583, Father Baltasar Afonso boasted that from one of the "*wars* [the Portuguese army] *had brought 619 noses from the heads that they decapitated, and in another, the dead were so many, that they say it was impossible to walk without stepping on them*." In a previous letter, Father Afonso described how the Portuguese army sustained itself and the merchants and missionaries that accompanied it by looting while mercilessly raiding for slaves. John Thornton and Linda Heywood argue that political dissent against Njinga Ngola Kilombo kia Kasenda drove Muxima Kitangonge to join the Portuguese. According to this interpretation, based on a letter from Father Diogo da Costa, the *ngola's* violence pushed *sobas* to join Dias de Novais.Cordeiro (ed.), Terras e minas africanas segundo Rebello de Aragão, p. 10; Heywood and Thornton, Central Africans, p. 85–86; Leitão, A missão do P.e Baltasar Barreira, p. 55; MMA III, D. 46, D. 63, D. 87, p. 339; MMA V, D. 86.

44 MMA III, D. 65, p. 256.

45 MMA III, D. 47.

ments. They consisted of a large army of "*gente da terra* [locals]" sent by the *Mwene Kongo* and soldiers, gunpowder, and other military supplies from Luanda.[46]

Soon after receiving reinforcements, Dias de Novais advanced up to a place named Nova Gaza, near where the mobile "*Cabaça* [*kábàsà*—capital]" of the *ngola* was at the time.[47] On February 2, 1583, he won the Battle of Talandongo against kia Kasenda, managing to route his larger army.[48] Nevertheless, Dias de Novais abandoned Nova Gaza, retreated half a day's march westwards, and established a strategic base at Massangano, overseeing a large natural island in the Kwanza.[49] He would die there on May 9, 1589, leaving his field Captain-Major Luís Serrão, in command of the Captaincy of Angola.[50] From Massangano, the Portuguese slowly expanded eastwards, seeking to conquer the mythical silver mines of the hills of Cambambe and southwards, to intercept the salt trade route from Kissama.[51] By 1599, the *presídio* of Muxima had been established by Baltazar Ribeiro de Aragão after his successful campaign against the *sobas* of Kissama.[52] At that point, it occupied a place known as Casenga, further inland than the hilltop fortress later built in 1655. By 1604, Manuel Cerveira Pereira, captain-general and governor between 1603 and 1607, had finally managed to build a *presídio* in Cambambe, realizing, however, that its bountiful silver mines were nothing but a mirage.[53]

Between 1583 and 1607, Massangano remained at the center of the many Luso-Ndongo wars and skirmishes that allowed the Portuguese to militarily enslave Africans and expand their dominium over critical passageways and the fertile margins of the Kwanza.[54] During this period, as Rosa da Cruz e Silva argues, they followed a double strategy, relying on siphoning captured war prisoners to the emerging Atlantic sugar plantations and conquering the sites of Mbundu *itanda*

---

46 Leitão, A missão do P.e Baltasar Barreira, p. 54–57.

47 Ibid., p. 59–60; Coelho, Em busca de Kábàsà, in: Santos (ed.), Actas do seminário, p. 443–478; MMA III, D. 56; Parreira, Dicionário glossográfico, p. 143.

48 MMA III, D. 65; MMA IV, D. 132, p. 567–568.

49 Heywood and Thornton, Central Africans, p. 87–88; MMA III, D. 65; Thornton, A History of West Central Africa, p. 92–93.

50 Heywood and Thornton, Central Africans, p. 89.

51 Ibid., p. 91; Cordeiro (ed.), Terras e minas africanas segundo Rebello de Aragão, p. 9–17; Leitão, A missão do P.e Baltasar Barreira, p. 43–91; MMA V, D. 101, p. 264–265; Thornton, A History of West Central Africa, p. 93.

52 Cordeiro (ed.), Terras e minas africanas segundo Rebello de Aragão, p. 5–8, 12–13.

53 Couto, Os capitães-mores em Angola, p. 105, 117; Ferreira, Feiras e presídios, p. 18–19; MMA V, D. 86.

54 Thornton, A History of West Central Africa, p. 92–93; Vansina, Long-Distance Trade-Routes, p. 382.

(sing. *kitanda*) [markets/fairs] to establish control over pre-existing trade routes.[55] The donation charter of Dias de Novais even established that the *donatário* was entitled to a third of what was "*traded or negotiated*" in the "*resgates* [slave fairs] *and tratos* [markets]" that he "*opened or found*" as an enticement, a privilege that was almost immediately revoked.[56] These thirds would have been considerable sums. For instance, on July 4, 1585, Father Diogo da Costa, who accompanied and assisted in the healing of Portuguese troops together with Father Barreira, said that as they advanced towards Cambambe, they heard about a "*fair*" that convened nearby.[57] Deciding to halt the march eastwards to sack it, Father Costa remarks that the Portuguese were able to capture 500 slaves, 500 "*capões* [castrated chickens]," and 2.100$000 *réis* worth of "*fazenda da terra* [local movable property]."

In the meantime, New Christians, crypto-Jews, Gypsies, and other persecuted groups took the same riverine route as Leitão and Dias de Novais, escaping the harassment of the Portuguese Inquisition and participating in a half-a-century-old Luso-African network of *pumbos* or *resgates*, slave trading centers situated entirely outside of the Portuguese Crown's jurisdiction.[58] Understanding past Portuguese experiences with this *pumbo* network that extended as far north as Nsundi, one of the northern provinces of the Kingdom of Kongo, and Malebo Pool (Lake Nkunda), is crucial to understanding the strategic decisions taken by Dias de Novais and his Jesuit companions in the Captaincy of Angola.[59] It also sheds light on these wayward subjects' animosity towards Dias de Novais, the Jesuits, and other deputies of the Crown and ecclesiastical authorities.[60] As the following pages explore, this previous experience was deeply conditioned by the resilience of the *Mwene Kongo* and the capacity of the BaKongo elites to incorporate Portuguese institutions, accept and

---

55 Cruz e Silva, As feiras do Ndongo, in: Santos (ed.), Actas do seminário, p. 405–422; Klein, The Atlantic Slave Trade to 1650, in: Schwartz (ed.), Tropical Babylons, p. 206; Schwartz, A Commonwealth within Itself, in: Schwartz (ed.), Tropical Babylons, p. 158–200; Schwartz, Sugar Plantations, p. 65–72.

56 The charter stipulated that Dias de Novais's successors would have been entitled to a fourth. Nevertheless, as Ilídio do Amaral remarks, this privilege was revoked still during Dias de Novais' lifetime, despite his constant complaints. Amaral, O consulado de Paulo Dias de Novais, p. 68–69.

57 MMA III, D. 81.

58 On the persecution of New Christians in the Portuguese Kingdom during this period, see Giuseppe Marcocci and José Pedro Paiva. Hilton, The Kingdom of Kongo, p. 57–66; Marcocci and Paiva, História da Inquisição Portuguesa, p. 49–76; Miller, A marginal Institution on the Margin of the Atlantic System, in: Solow (ed.), Slavery and the Rise of the Atlantic System, p. 125–126, 140–141; Parreira, Dicionário glossográfico, p. 176; Salvador, Os Cristãos-Novos e o Comércio; Thornton, A History of West Central Africa, p. 96; Thornton, The Development of an African Catholic Church, p. 147–167.

59 Miller, Angola in the Sixteenth Century, in: Hower and Preto-Rodas (eds.), Empire in Transition.

60 Amaral, O consulado de Paulo Dias de Novais, p. 126–127.

shape Roman Catholic dogma and practices, and engage in the emerging Atlantic slave trade without losing complete control over the division between different spheres of exchange and the commensuration regime that underpinned it.[61]

4.3 The Kongo Experiment

According to Anne Hilton, the establishment of the abovementioned Luso-African *pumbo* network, which spanned from the Loango Coast to Lake Nkunda, coincided with the strengthening of Christianity and the centralization of royal authority within the Kingdom of Kongo in the early sixteenth century.[62] Hilton maintains that BaKongo cosmologies had facilitated the conversion of D. João I of Kongo, *née* Nzinga a Nkuwu, the *Mwene Kongo* between 1470 and 1509.[63] Although Wyatt MacGaffey has criticized Hilton's use of contemporary ethnographic material to interpret early Portuguese and Kongo sources, he agrees with her overall reading of Nzinga a Nkuwu's conversion, adding the caveat that local cosmologies were not part of an "established doctrine" but of an ongoing political discussion.[64] To this

---

61 Thornton, Conquest and Theology, p. 247–248; Thornton, Early Kongo-Portuguese Relations, p. 183–204; Thornton, King Afonso I of Kong, in: Robert (ed.), African Christian Biography, p. 107–111; Thornton, The Origins and Early History p. 89–120.

62 Balandier, Le Royaume de Kongo, p. 130–131; Hilton, The Kingdom of Kongo, p. 57–66; Thornton, A History of West Central Africa, p. 96.

63 Hilton, The Kingdom of Kongo, p. 49.

64 As Thornton puts it, the BaKongo believed in the existence of a "constellation of Other Worldly beings." While Hilton and MacGaffey agree with him on this point, none of them accept the typology proposed by the other. Hilton bases her classification of Kongo otherworldly powers on the division between three categories of entities: ancestor spirits, the "*mbumba* dimension" spirits (earth and water spirits), and the "*nkadi mpemba* dimension" spirits (air spirits). Each ancestor spirit had its domestic cult, while *Mbumba* spirits and associated powers were handled by "*kitome*" priests. One of the duties of *kitome* priests was to enthrone chiefs, including the *Mwene Kongo*, and *mbumba* cults could even come to constitute "extra-lineage" chiefdoms. The *nkadi mpemba* dimension and its techniques could be appropriated by chiefs and sorcerers (*kindoki*). MacGaffey not only disagrees with Hilton's reconstruction of Kongo "matrilineal lineages" (the "*kanda*"), claiming that matrilinearity was a later "invention," but argues that these separate spirit dimensions are her fabrication. According to him, the relevant classificatory distinction must be made at the level of "experts" in otherworldly power. Basing himself on Vansina's *Paths in the Rainforest*, he argues that these were the "headman," the "witch [sorcerer]," the "earth-chief" or priest, and the "healer." While earth chiefs and priests operated "in the sphere of production," headmen and sorcerers competed to control "social reproduction." The headmen and earth-chiefs were public figures, "acting for the community" according to a "redistributive" logic. Sorcerers and healers were private individuals, acting for their gain according to a "market exchange" model. Distancing himself from these abstract models, Thornton argues that a "transcendent spiritual force" connected "all the Other Worldly entities," "human souls while living," and ancestors. He defines this force

remark, Thornton adds that an "inclusive" attitude on the side of the Portuguese missionaries, who were aware they were guests in a powerful African kingdom, not conquerors, further eased the adoption of Christianity in West Central Africa.[65] Moreover, contrary to Hilton and MacGaffey, Thornton upholds that the conversion of Kongo was grounded on genuine religious motivations on both sides and cannot be reduced to a cynical power-grabbing maneuver on the part of the *Mwene Kongo* or the Portuguese.[66] Building on their scholarship, Cecile Fromont concludes that this African-led conversion opened a unique "space of correlation" that allowed BaKongo cosmological categories to be made commensurable with Roman Catholic beliefs, giving rise to various social and cultural innovations but also grounding the subsequent trans-Atlantic traffic in human beings.

When Diogo Cão (c. 1452–1486) first landed at Mpinda in 1482–83, the BaKongo made sense of the unprecedented event by cautiously associating the Europeans with categories of spirits believed to be white and known to reside across a great body of water.[67] Upon the return of the Portuguese in 1491, Nzinga a Nkuwu enthusiastically accepted baptism as D. João I and consolidated his internal power by monopolizing access to the new source of legitimacy brought by the cult of these intriguing other-worldly entities and their priests, which he perceived and respected as *nganga* (pl. *banganga*), local ritual specialists.[68] Concomitantly, he ordered the burning of old

---

as "*nkisi*" and claims that entities could be divided as "ancestors," "supernatural entities" tied to "territorial units," and "minor" spiritual entities who could be "malicious." *Nkisi* could be captured by physical objects called "*iteke* (sing. *kiteke*)." HILTON, The Kingdom of Kongo; MACGAFFEY, A Central African Kingdom, in: BOSTOEN and BRINKMAN (eds.), The Kongo Kingdom, p. 42, 48–49, 56–57; MACGAFFEY, A Note on Vansina's Invention of Matrilinearity, p. 269–280; MACGAFFEY, Constructing a Kongo Identity, p. 171, 177; MACGAFFEY, Dialogues of the Deaf, in: SCHWARTZ (ed.), Implicit Understandings, p. 249–267; THORNTON, A History of West Central Africa, p. 45–46; VANSINA, Paths in the Rainforests.

65 When Thornton states that the missionaries carried "an inclusive conception of the religion," he means that they considered all aspects of Kongo culture that were not "directly contrary to the fundamental doctrine of the Church" acceptable. THORNTON, The Development of an African Catholic Church, p. 152–153.

66 Ibid., p. 147–167; FROMONT, The Art of Conversion; FROMONT, Under the Sign of the Cross, p. 109–123.

67 HILTON, The Kingdom of Kongo, p. 50–51; MACGAFFEY, Dialogues of the Deaf, in: SCHWARTZ (ed.), Implicit Understandings, p. 255.

68 Thornton remarks that the Franciscan missionaries that accompanied the first Portuguese expeditions to Kongo referred to themselves as "*nganga*" and performed all public roles expected of these ritual specialists, namely "initiation ceremonies (baptism)," creating "charms for luck (religious medals)," "protecting the fields," "performing ceremonies to appeal to earth spirits in case of drought (with penitent processions, and self-flagellation)," and consecrating the *Mwene Kongo*. In 1491, the Secular Canons of St John the Evangelist arrived in Kongo, substituting the Franciscans as missionaries and taking charge of education and all these ritual functions. ALMEIDA, Christianity in Kongo; HILTON, The Kingdom of Kongo, p. 50–51; MACGAFFEY, A Central African

"*minkisi* [sing. *nkisi*],"[69] which the Portuguese associated with sorcery or idols, and D. João I saw as a potent but dangerous power source outside his immediate control.[70] Hilton remarks that by doing so, the *Mwene Kongo* alienated most of the *mwisi Kongo*, the aristocratic residents of the capital Mbanza Kongo, who resented the exclusivity of the new Christian cult and remained faithful to the old *minkisi*.[71] In no time, the Portuguese and their faith were associated with anti-social *kindoki* by the *Mwene Kongo*'s rivals.[72] When D. João I died in 1506, and his son D. Afonso I, *née* Mvemba a Nzinga, seized power, he sensed the opportunity the connection with the socially ambiguous European *banganga* offered.[73] Fully embracing Christianity as a form of state religion, D. Afonso I, *Mwene Kongo* between 1509 and c. 1543, tightened the alliance with the Portuguese and launched a systematic campaign

---

Kingdom, in: Bostoen and Brinkman (eds.), The Kongo Kingdom, p. 57; Thornton, A History of West Central Africa, p. 37–39; Thornton, The Development of an African Catholic Church, p. 157.

69 In 1984, Thornton defined a "*nkisi*" as a charm or "material object which houses spiritual forces." More recently, he has argued that the translation of "*nkisi*" as "holy" is a "sound one theologically." MacGaffey prefers the spelling *n'kisi*, arguing that the term is "untranslatable" and can refer to "talismans or protective devices" of all sizes and kinds. He also highlights that *n'kisi* are obtained from *banganga* and impose taboos on their 'owners.' MacGaffey, A Central African Kingdom, in: Bostoen and Brinkman (eds.), The Kongo Kingdom, p. 47; Thornton, The Development of an African Catholic Church, p. 157–158; Thornton, The Kingdom of Kongo and the Counter Reformation, p. 44.

70 According to Hilton, *kindoki* was the term used for "all malevolent action." It included the activities of those born *ndoki*, those possessed by evil spirits, and those who "cursed or bewitched" through their "superior spiritual power." In the latter case, Hilton adds that "elders and chiefs" could legitimately practice *kindoki* within their "lineages." While she translates *kindoki* as "witchcraft" and *ndoki* as "witch," in Portuguese, these terms were translated to *feitiçaria* and *feitiço*. MacGaffey translates *kindoki* as "occult forces" or "witchcraft," remarking that it was an essential component of the power not only of "witches" or sorcerers but also of chiefs and the *banganga* tasked with finding them. Hilton, The Kingdom of Kongo, p. 17, 50–51; MacGaffey, A Central African Kingdom, in: Bostoen and Brinkman (eds.), The Kongo Kingdom, p. 48–49; MacGaffey, Dialogues of the Deaf, in: Schwartz (ed.), Implicit Understandings, p. 249–267; Thornton, The Development of an African Catholic Church, p. 147–167.

71 Hilton, The Kingdom of Kongo, p. 52; MacGaffey, A Central African Kingdom, in: Bostoen and Brinkman (eds.), The Kongo Kingdom, p. 57; MacGaffey, Constructing a Kongo Identity, p. 159–180; Olivier and Armore, Medieval Africa, p. 170–171.

72 Hilton, The Kingdom of Kongo, p. 52; MacGaffey, A Central African Kingdom, in: Bostoen and Brinkman (eds.), The Kongo Kingdom, p. 57; Thornton, A History of West Central Africa, p. 39–40.

73 Almeida, Christianity in Kongo; Fromont, The Art of Conversion, p. 26–32; Thornton, A History of West Central Africa, p. 40–41; Thornton, Early Kongo-Portuguese Relations, p. 183; Thornton, King Afonso I of Kong, in: Robert (ed.), African Christian Biography, p. 107–111.

against the "houses" of the old "*nkisi*-fetishes."[74] This involved sending "*officials of justice*" to burn the 'idols' that existed throughout the provinces, arresting the persons who possessed them or made them, and denouncing the belief in their powers as superstition and their handling as sorcery.[75] The atmosphere of social ferment and cultural upheaval caused by the arrival of Europeans thus resulted in a 'witch-hunt' that exacerbated local conflicts, aggravating the violence of the succession war.

The Portuguese, armed with unknown weapons such as crossbows and muskets, their terrifying horses, and unheard-of military tactics, played a crucial role in helping D. Afonso I secure his claim to the throne.[76] Despite being ineffective in the sub-equatorial African battlefields, because of their novelty and shock value, Portuguese guns and tactics had a significant impact on morale.[77] Moreover, by offering a convenient ideological alternative, Portuguese priests facilitated the removal of the *minkisi* at the base of the political and ritual power of the BaKongo elites who might oppose D. Afonso's legitimacy.[78] However, the co-option of the *mwisi Kongo* and provincial BaKongo elites with the luxury items brokered by the Portuguese proved even more critical for consolidating D. Afonso's political power than the European's military and moral support.[79] Ultimately, the ability to incite greed emerged as the decisive factor in the succession war. If the new *Mwene Kongo* could initially secure Portuguese luxury items as gifts, they would soon be exchanged as commodities, and obtaining them would require more than symbolic offerings of ivory and public displays of religious fervor on his part.[80] Aware of this fact,

74 Fromont, Under the Sign of the Cross, p. 109–123; Hilton, The Kingdom of Kongo, p. 62–65; MacGaffey, Dialogues of the Deaf, in: Schwartz (ed.), Implicit Understandings, p. 258–259; Mello e Souza, Alianças e embates entre religiões, in: Hermann and Martins (eds.), Poderes do sagrado, p. 361–382.

75 Fromont, Under the Sign of the Cross, p. 109–123; Hilton, The Kingdom of Kongo, p. 62–65; MacGaffey, Dialogues of the Deaf, in: Schwartz (ed.), Implicit Understandings, p. 258–259; MMA I, D. 23., p. 96.

76 Heywood and Thornton, Central Africans, p. 57–68; Thornton, A History of West Central Africa, p. 42–43.

77 Thornton, A History of West Central Africa, p. 42–43.

78 MacGaffey, A Central African Kingdom, in: Bostoen and Brinkman (eds.), The Kongo Kingdom, p. 55–56; Thornton, A History of West Central Africa, p. 43; Thornton, The Development of an African Catholic Church, p. 157–158.

79 For a detailed list of the luxury goods and animals sent from Lisbon to Mbanza Kongo in 1512, see: MMA I, D. 66. Thornton, A History of West Central Africa, p. 42–43; Vansina, Paths in the Rainforests, p. 200–201.

80 Ana Lucia Araujo explores the *longue durée* impact this gift-giving pattern followed by commodity trading had in the broader region. Araujo, The Gift; Hilton, The Kingdom of Kongo; Soares, O marfim nos acordos de compensação, in: Horta, Almeida and Mark (eds.), African Ivories in the Altantic World, p. 317–338.

D. Afonso I of Kongo appointed his cousin Pedro to the governorship of the Nsundi province. There, Pedro secured access to a supply of high-quality copper from the Mindouli and Boko-Songo areas in the Niari Valley, west of Malebo Pool, enabling the *Mwene Kongo* to trade it with the Portuguese.[81] When the Portuguese started demanding slaves instead of copper in the late 1520s,[82] Pedro supplied D. Afonso I with war prisoners captured during the ongoing skirmishes with a neighboring Teke polity—the Tio Kingdom.[83] This development would have significant historical consequences, first bringing the destabilizing influence of the Atlantic slave trade to the Central African hinterlands. Soon, the Teke began brokering the local slave trade, creating a slave fair in Mpumbu, Malebo Pool, where the Portuguese *pumbeiros,* meaning Mpumbu dwellers, and their agents, could settle and trade.

A stable network of *pumbos* or *resgates* connecting Mpumbu to Mpinda and Mbanza Kongo emerged and consolidated during the tenures of D. Afonso I and D. Diogo I, *Mwene Kongo* between c. 1543 and 1561, also extending to the Atlantic seaports of the Kingdoms of Loango, Kakongo, and Ngoyo, respectively Loango, Molembo, and Cabinda.[84] Initially, these *pumbos* were likely modelled after the BaKongo "*nzandu* [market]."[85] As Georges Balandier and Manuel Martins describe, *nzandu* were ritually warded spaces where violence was bracketed off, and peace, security, and freedom of transaction were ensured by a "chief of the market" sponsored by the notables who had established the market.[86] Large BaKongo markets were very well-organized places, with a precise temporal and spatial disposition, testifying not only to the "vigorous economy" of the Kingdom of Kongo but also to

---

81 For an overview of the significance of the copper trade in precolonial Africa, see Eugenia Herbert. Toby Green explores the "spiritual place of copper" in the societies of West Central Africa, including the Kingdoms of Kongo, Ndongo, Matamba, and Kasanje. GREEN, A Fistful of Shells, p. 224–227; HERBERT, Red Gold of Africa; HILTON, The Kingdom of Kongo, p. 54; RADEMAKERS et al., Copper Production and Trade in the Niari Basin, p. 1251–1270.

82 As Vansina remarks, after the Portuguese settled the Island of São Tomé in 1486 and started producing sugar, the demand for slaves immediately increased. VANSINA, Paths in the Rainforests, p. 200.

83 Linda Heywood remarks that wars against Ndongo and some of the *dembos* also provided D. Afonso I with slaves. ARAUJO, The Gift, p. 19–20; HEYWOOD, Slavery and Its Transformation, p. 5; OLIVIER and ARMORE, Medieval Africa, p. 159.

84 ARAUJO, The Gift, p. 12; THORNTON, Early Kongo-Portuguese Relations, p. 191; THORNTON and HEYWOOD, The Treason of Dom Pedro Nkanga a Mvemba, in: MCKNIGHT and GAROFALO (eds.), Afro-Latino Voices; OLIVIER and ARMORE, Medieval Africa, p. 165.

85 BALANDIER, Le Royaume de Kongo, p. 129; THORNTON, The Kingdom of Kongo, p. 32.

86 Martins notes that the Kikongo word *nzandu* also translates as "neutral place," "joyful place," or a "*lugar de igualdade*"—a place where all are equal. BALANDIER, Le Royaume de Kongo, p. 129; MARTINS, Contacto de Culturas no Congo Português, p. 99; THORNTON, The Kingdom of Kongo, p. 32.

the "rigor of its laws."[87] This was the case, Balandier explains, because the BaKongo *nzandu* was a "*lieu d'asile* [place of asylum]," the arena where political and matrimonial negotiations took place, the stage where the public part of initiations was performed, and the court where "criminals" and "sorcerers" were publicly executed. In sum, in BaKongo *nzandu*, different spheres of exchange co-existed but remained differentiated, one pertaining to the exchange of fresh produce, others to the exchange of prestige goods, political tributes, religious and magical services, and offices, and, finally, an upper-most one where rights over free women and dependents were brokered. When the Portuguese entered these complex African spaces or established alternative *pumbos*, they converted an institution whose economic dimensions were "partly destined for subsistence, partly at the service of the State and the aristocracy" into an "inhumane" one, focused exclusively on the mercantilist extraction of slaves.[88] Moreover, the economic reshaping of *nzandu* went together with the creation of alternative places of asylum and political and matrimonial negotiation, the Christian churches and schools, and Portuguese-style courts.[89] In the wake of D. Afonso's iconoclastic campaigns, alternative scapegoats for *kindoki* or *feitiçaria* also emerged—the politically unfavored *minkisi* and their ritual operators and adepts.[90] These suspects would likely be judged according to new procedures in Christianized spaces. Together, these developments represented a significant challenge to one of the central institutions of BaKongo polities, where their social, cultural, and political continuity was ensured through public performances and negotiations: the *nzandu*.

At first, D. Afonso I retained control over the currency used in the Luso-African *pumbos* under BaKongo and Teke jurisdiction, thus managing to exert a modicum of economic control over Portuguese caravans and those of the Vili from Loango, the Kotchi from Kakongo, and the Woyo from Ngoyo.[91] However, as an exchange of letters between D. João III of Portugal (1502–1557) and D. Afonso I of Kongo proves, the *Mwene Kongo*'s control over who could be legitimately sold as a slave in these markets was being fast eclipsed by entrepreneurial Luso-African *pumbeiros* and the agents of sugar-cane planters from São Tomé.[92] On November 18, 1526, the Kongo monarch complained that many of his countrymen, "*because of the great*

---

87 Balandier, Le Royaume de Kongo, p. 129.

88 Ibid., p. 131.

89 MMA I, D. 65; Thornton, A History of West Central Africa, p. 59.

90 MMA I, D. 23., p. 96; Fromont, Under the Sign of the Cross, p. 109–123; Hilton, The Kingdom of Kongo, p. 62–65; MacGaffey, Dialogues of the Deaf, in: Schwartz (ed.), Implicit Understandings, p. 258–259.

91 Araujo, The Gift, p. 13–15; Balandier, Le Royaume de Kongo, p. 122–131; Hilton, The Kingdom of Kongo, p. 57–66; Vansina, Paths in the Rainforests, p. 200–201.

92 MMA I, D. 147, D. 153.

desire they have for the trade goods and things from those Kingdoms [Portugal]," were kidnapping "*forros* [free] *and isemtos* [exempt]" persons to satisfy their "*unruly appetites*," including "*fidalgos*" and the *Mwene Kongo*'s "*relatives*."[93] These exempt persons, the *Mwene Kongo* continued, were being taken to "*white men*" during the night so that they would not be publicly recognized and immediately branded with hot irons as slaves. To do them "*Justice*," D. Afonso I decreed that "*by law*," any "*white men*" acquiring slaves had to present them before "*Pedro Manipunzo*," "*Dom Manuel Manissaba*," the *Mwene Kongo*'s bailiff, and Gonçalo Pires, the "*armador mor* [chief supplier]" in charge of the Port of Mpinda. In 1529, D. João III of Portugal replied, signaling to D. Afonso I his lack of interest in controlling or even regulating the *pumbos* and explicitly stating that if the *Mwene Kongo* halted the flow of slaves, he would cut the supply of luxury items.[94] By D. Diogo I's reign, Teke suppliers and Vili middlemen began accepting Portuguese wares instead of Kongo currencies. The *Mwene Kongo* had to resort to taxing the *pumbeiros*,[95] fixing the measures and weights used in official transactions,[96] and doubling the official price of slaves, in an attempt to retain control over long-distance trade and redistribution.[97] However, the export of slaves remained stable despite these measures.[98]

It is, therefore, during this period that the Portuguese had their first West Central African experience with the politics of commensuration, being made aware of how the ability to dictate and impose the terms of conversion, and cultural and institutional translation, was deeply entangled with the capacity to regulate measures and standards, control the monetary system, and set the limits of (in)commensurability by defining the normative framing of different spheres of exchange. This entailed determining which *minkisi* were considered *feitiços* or idols, a crucial aspect of

---

93 MMA I, D. 147.

94 Ibid., p. 526–527.

95 According to Father Cornélio Gomes, by 1553, D. Diogo I taxed "white men" that frequented *pumbos* between "fifteen thousand *maravedises* [405$000 *réis*]" and "eight" thousand *maravedises* [216$000 *réis*]. These values might be inflated, as Father Gomes, a Jesuit, had an axe to grind against D. Diogo. See also Thornton. MMA II, D. 98, p. 306; Thornton, Early Kongo-Portuguese Relations, p. 189–190.

96 On February 18, 1549, Francisco de Barros de Paiva, captain of São Tomé, complained to D. João III of Portugal that D. Diogo I of Kongo adopted a "*vara* [yardstick—1,10 m.]" and "*covado* [0,66 m.]" that were larger than the official Portuguese ones used until then. Hilton, The Kingdom of Kongo, p. 66; MMA II, D. 81, p. 234.

97 By the early decades of the seventeenth century, the *Mwene Kongo* had also established a "series of toll booths" along the main trade routes from Mpumbu to Luanda. Heywood, Slavery and Its Transformation, p. 9; MMA II, D. 81, p. 234; Vansina, Paths in the Rainforests, p. 158.

98 As Paul Lovejoy describes, during the first two decades of the sixteenth century, slave exports from Mpinda totaled about 2.300–2.500 slaves per year, with the rate rising to 5.400 in 1521 and stabilizing at that level until mid-century. This trade collapsed in 1568. Lovejoy, Transformations in Slavery, p. 38–41.

religious conversion and inter-polity alliances. Additionally, it involved deciding who could be traded as a slave, by whom, where, and on what occasions, and determining the type of counter-gifts that could be exchanged, thus framing the space of correlation where economic conversions took place. The Portuguese had a limited understanding of the social, political, legal, religious, and cultural significance of the BaKongo *nzandu*. However, they were very aware of the *Mwene Kongo*'s efforts to control the markets and the new *pumbos* by supervising and regulating the exchanged currencies. Therefore, as the following paragraphs detail, they soon waged a veritable currency war with Kongo, with disastrous results for their West Central African allied kingdom. While this economic dispute seemingly focused on one of the many normative layers overlapping in BaKongo *nzandu*, it inadvertently impacted all others, having a profound social impact.

As Duarte Pacheco Pereira (c. 1460–1533) noted in *Esmeraldo de situ orbis* (1506), "*small shells*" of the "*size of pine-nuts*" called *nzimbu* [*Olivancillaria nana* Lam.] and collected in the Island of Luanda were "*used as money*" in the Kingdom of Kongo.[99] According to the geographer, "*fifty of them* [would] *buy a hen, and three hundred a goat and so forth.*"[100] When the *Mwene Kongo* conferred a "*favor on one of his nobles or reward*[ed] *a service done to him*," he gave them a certain number of cowries, "*just as* [Portuguese] *princes bestow money of these realms on those who deserve it.*" Since the *nzimbu* were understood as the official currency of Kongo,[101] they were soon commensurate with the Portuguese currency of account—ten medium-sized shells from the Island of Luanda being worth a Portuguese *real.*[102] Conventional accounting units were used to count *nzimbu*: *funda* (1.000 shells), *pistole* (3.500 shells), *lufuku* (10.000 shells), *kofu* (20.000 shells), or *bondo* (100.000 shells).[103]

---

99 According to Heywood, Rui de Pina is the first to mention *nzimbu* in his *Relazione del Regno di Congo* when summarising the statements of members of the 1491 mission to Kongo. Heywood, Slavery and Its Transformation, p. 10; Radulet, O cronista Rui de Pina, p. 116; Pacheco Pereira, Kimble (trans.), Esmeraldo de situ orbis, p. 145.

100 Pacheco Pereira, Kimble (trans.), Esmeraldo de situ orbis, p. 145.

101 As the next section discusses, raffia cloth currencies circulated as general-purpose money in some of the provinces of the Kingdom of Kongo and the Kingdoms of Ndongo, Kakongo, and Ngoyo.

102 Simões, De Garcia Simões para o Provincial de São Paulo de Loanda, p. 340.

103 The worth of *nzimbu* would drop drastically during the seventeenth century. According to Parreira, by 1540, a *kofu* was worth 13$300 *réis*; by 1615, 10$000 *réis*; by 1619, between 1$600 and 2$300 *réis*; by 1622, 2$000 *réis*; and by 1653, 1$000 *réis*—less than 10% of its original worth. As Green remarks, despite this "spiraling devaluation," the *nzimbu* remained the official currency of Kongo until the eighteenth century. As for Angola and its hinterlands, Silva Corrêa claimed that it was still accepted as currency in the last decades of the eighteenth century, a *bondo* being worth 5$000 *réis*, a *lifuco* 500 *réis* and a *funda* 50 *réis*. Green, A Fistful of Shells, p. 222, 227, 229–231; MMA I, D. 98., p. 357; Parreira, Economia e sociedade, p. 86–87; Silva Corrêa, História de Angola, Vol. 1, p. 135.

According to Kongo regulations, a *kofu* weighed about 30 kilograms, the maximum weight a porter could carry.[104] The *Mwene Kongo* regularly received *nzimbu* from his nobles as a tribute[105] and used them to pay for the upkeep of local clergy and the stipends of the Portuguese specialists residing at his court.[106]

Thornton remarks that despite this general-purpose money being an "international currency" with a "wide circulation in Africa and Asia," it posed a problem of "non-convertibility" to the Portuguese.[107] In other words, *nzimbu* were not accepted as currency in America and Europe. As it becomes clear from a letter D. Afonso I of Kongo wrote to D. Manuel I of Portugal on November 5, 1514, this problem was momentarily fixed by using two of the social currencies that circulated in the prestige spheres of exchange of the Kongo and neighboring kingdoms, copper manillas

---

104 Balandier, Le Royaume de Kongo, p. 123–126.

105 Contrary to MacGaffey, who frames the transaction of *nzimbu* in ritual terms, Thornton argues that the shells were "general purpose money" and that the governors of provinces used them to pay "*rendas*" to the *Mwene Kongo*. These *rendas*, which Thornton translates as "revenue assignments," were a percentage of the taxes they farmed in their provinces. Balandier remarks that *nzimbu* did play a part in rituals, being used to create "amulets and charms" and "intervening in ordeals." However, like Thornton, he claims that the governors of Kongo provinces paid taxes in *nzimbu*, extracting them from local nobles according to an arrangement analogous to European tax farming. Balandier, Le Royaume de Kongo, p. 123–125, MacGaffey, A Central African Kingdom, in: Bostoen and Brinkman (eds.), The Kongo Kingdom, p. 55–56; Thornton, A History of West Central Africa, p. 34, 40; Thornton, The Development of an African Catholic Church, p. 160.

106 In 1514, D. Manuel I of Kongo paid between one and two *lufuku* (10.000 or 20.000 shells worth 6$500 or 13$000 *réis*, respectively) for each stone that the Portuguese stonemasons residing at his court laid for his new house. A century later, in 1622, Pedro II of Kongo made the provision of one hundred *kofu* (2.000.000 shells worth 200$000 *réis*) to maintain the first chaplain of his royal chapel of St James, forty *kofu* (800.000 shells worth 80$000 *réis*) to support the dean, and three hundred *kofu* (6.000.000 shells worth 600$000 *réis*) to sustain the other nine chaplains and the treasurer. Heywood, Slavery and Its Transformation, p. 9–11; Hilton, The Kingdom of Kongo, p. 80–81; MMA I, D. 83, p. 306; Parreira, Economia e sociedade, p. 87; Randles, L'Ancien Royaume du Congo, p. 75–78; Thornton, A History of West Central Africa, p. 33–35.

107 Thornton argues that Portugal and Kongo had "general-purpose monies," gold and silver in the Portuguese case, *nzimbu* and raffia cloth in the BaKongo one. Thornton also remarks that both kingdoms had "international currencies, in that gold and silver were widely accepted worldwide, while cowrie shells [...] had a wide circulation in Africa and Asia." However, he concludes, both kingdoms faced a "problem of the non-convertibility" of their "international currencies" because their spheres of acceptance did not overlap. Balandier complicates this picture by noting that *nzimbu* were not 'true' cowries—meaning the *Cypraea moneta* that circulated in East Africa and Asia—and that when the latter began circulating in Kongo, they were called *mbési*. This raises questions about the worth of BaKongo *nzimbu* in other regional contexts (e. g. West or East Africa). Balandier, Le Royaume de Kongo, p. 124; Thornton, Early Kongo-Portuguese Relations, p. 187.

and slaves,[108] as if they were general-purpose money in inter-polity transactions.[109] This precarious solution entailed handling social currencies ritually exchanged as political tribute or gifts (e. g., copper manillas, ivory, and slaves) as if they were lowly commodities or the currencies used to purchase them. From the perspective of the *Mwene Kongo*, however, if these precious goods and slaves were exchanged for European luxury goods according to the norms that regulated their prestige spheres of exchange, and if his loyalists monopolized the trade with the Portuguese Crown, the worst disruptive effects of using social currencies in an anti-social way could be avoided. Controlling the exchange of copper, ivory, and slaves for luxury goods also implied not allowing them to be used locally as general-purpose money[110] and ensuring that the Portuguese did not conflate the exchanges of rights over free women and children with the buying of slaves.[111] As the following pages unpack,

---

108 As described by Balandier, copper manillas served "as ornaments, clan treasures and marks of social importance." Their production was tightly controlled by the smiths, who formed an aristocratic group within BaKongo society. Both their manufacture and exchange were under male control, suggesting that women were excluded from their sphere of exchange and that manillas could be used to temporarily compensate for an "unequal exchange" in the sphere where rights over women and dependents were brokered. In other words, it was offered as a temporary counter-gift by a group that received women until the 'right' counter-gift of women could be offered back. Balandier also refers to how slaves captured in war were exchanged similarly. On copper manillas, see also Herbert. BALANDIER, Le Royaume de Kongo, p. 99–102, 105, 112–121; HERBERT, Red Gold of Africa.

109 MMA I, D. 83.

110 For this reason, successive *Mwene Kongo* kept making local payments in *nzimbu*, as noted above, only offering slaves as counter-gifts to high officers about to depart. This division is also signaled by the distinction that is always made between slaves and money in official letters. For instance, in his letter to D. Manuel I of Portugal, D. Afonso I reports that he promised to offer Cristóvão de Aguiar on his return to Portugal "*some peças* [slaves] *or money for him to buy them*" in exchange for the "*blue blanket*" and 15 *covados* [30 palms] of Portuguese cloth he had received from him. In the same letter, the *Mwene Kongo* informs the Portuguese monarch that he had offered a "*thousand manillas and some slaves*" to his "*cousin*" Fernão de Mello, as well as "*four masked palm civets*," a local prestige good. Ibid., p. 303; PARREIRA, Economia e sociedade, p. 96; BALANDIER, Le Royaume de Kongo, p. 106.

111 According to Vansina, this was precisely what happened in the Tio Kingdom, where "a trade in slaves had not existed," and the Portuguese *pumbeiros* initially bought rights over free Teke dependents and proceeded to treat them as alienable slaves. Vansina argues that this is proven by the fact that in the local languages, slaves are known as "persons of *nzimbu*" or as "persons acquired with Kongo shell money." MacGaffey also claims that until the institutionalization of the Luso-Teke slave trade, BaKongo corporate kin groups had to exchange women either directly or across generations—a practice that was known as "*sompa n'kento* [to borrow a woman]." MACGAFFEY, A Central African Kingdom, in: BOSTOEN and BRINKMAN (eds.), The Kongo Kingdom, p. 51; VANSINA, Paths in the Rainforests, p. 201.

D. Afonso lost his wager, soon realizing that the disruptive effects of the Atlantic slave trade could not be so easily kept at bay.[112]

The Portuguese, the planters from São Tomé and their agents, and Luso-African *pumbeiros* actively sought to convert BaKongo slaves into a "commercial currency" that would allow them to separate "value from context" because only in this manner would they be able to freely transfer wealth from West Central Africa to other regions of the Empire where copper manillas or ivory were almost as worthless as *nzimbu*.[113] In the ordinance of King Manuel I of Portugal to Simão da Silva, leader of the 1512 Portuguese expedition to Kongo, he orders the latter to remind the *Mwene Kongo* "*of the great expense made by sending these ships, Friars and clerics and the things we send him*,"[114] as well as by maintaining and educating his sons in Lisbon, pressing him to return those ships as soon as possible and "*above all, well supplied with slaves*."[115] Moreover, D. Manuel instructed Silva to determine what "*things*" could be traded, "*from whose hands they could be received*," and if "*slaves, copper, and ivory*" were only exchanged by the *Mwene Kongo* or if he could also find BaKongo "*merchants*" that traded them.

By 1540, it was Afonso I of Kongo who suggested to D. João III of Portugal the use of slaves as a means of indirectly converting between Portuguese *cruzados*

---

112 As described by the anonymous author of *Report on the Coast of Guinea* (1607), after the establishment of the Portuguese settlement in Luanda, a Portuguese captain was appointed to oversee the 'mining' of *nzimbu* on behalf of the *Mwene Kongo*. Concomitantly, the Portuguese began shipping in cowry shells from all over the Atlantic and Indian Ocean, immediately causing significant inflation and leading to what Toby Green describes as "currency wars." Green analyses the economic impact the occupation of Luanda had on the Kingdom of Kongo and how its kings sought the assistance of the Dutch West India Company to recover their monopoly of the *nzimbu* 'mined' on the Island of Luanda, concluding that this inflation played an essential part in eroding the power of Kongo monarchs. Christopher Gregory disagrees with this interpretation, arguing that the inflation of shell currencies was the aftermath, not the cause, of the decay of African polities. After the Battle of Mbwila (1665), the Portuguese assumed total control of the mining of *nzimbu* on the Island of Luanda. As Silva Corrêa tells it, three kinds of cowries from Bahia were sold in Luanda at the end of the eighteenth century: "*zimbo cascalho*," "*cascalho escolhido*," and "*Buzios*." A *cazonguel* [14 litres] of *cascalho* was sold for 2$000 *réis* in Bahia and worth 5$000 *réis* in the Angolan hinterlands; a *cazonguel* of *cascalho escolhido* was sold for 3$000 *réis* or 4$500 *réis* in Bahia and worth 5$000 *réis* in the Angolan hinterlands. An *arroba* (14.7 kg) of *buzios* was sold for 4$000 *réis* in Bahia and worth 12$000 *réis* in Angola. GREGORY, Cowries and Conquest, p. 195–217; BALANDIER, Le Royaume de Kongo, p. 122–125; GARCIA, Descrição das moedas de Angola, p. 179–215; GREEN, A Fistful of Shells, p. 219–231; MMA V, D. 137., p. 389; SILVA CORRÊA, História de Angola, Vol. 1, p. 136–137.

113 BALANDIER, Le Royaume de Kongo, p. 127, 133; COELHO, Em busca de Kábàsà, in: SANTOS (ed.), Actas do seminário, p. 8.

114 For the complete list of objects, see MMA I, D. 66.

115 MMA I, D. 65, p. 239–240.

(gold or silver coins) and *nzimbu*.[116] To finance his embassy to Rome, the *Mwene Kongo* offered fifty *kofu* of *nzimbu* (1.000.000 shells) to be used locally to buy slaves in *pumbos* sponsored by himself. In exchange, he requested that five thousand *cruzados* were to be delivered to his ambassadors in Europe by the Portuguese Crown. Complex financial arrangements such as this one are not only evidence that slaves were used to ease the transfer of wealth out of West Central Africa but also that, during this period, they were not a fungible currency or commodity directly commensurate with *cruzados* or *réis*. In other words, the *Mwene Kongo*'s request only presupposes the existence of two fungible but non-convertible currencies, *cruzados* and *nzimbu*, and the possibility of using persons rightfully enslaved according to BaKongo norms, and traded in *pumbos* he had jurisdiction over, as an ad hoc means of extracting wealth to Europe. The exchange of slaves thus remained embedded in local normative systems under African control. One episode that took place during the turbulent reign of D. Diogo I can attest to this fact, also evidencing how, on the Portuguese side, the taxation policy of the Crown set limits on reducing BaKongo slaves to fungible money.

D. Diogo I of Kongo had secured his claims as *Mwene Kongo* at the end of a prolonged civil war against his uncle D. Pedro I of Kongo, who was D. Afonso's son and had been *Mwene Kongo* from c. 1540 to c. 1543.[117] As Thornton explains, already during the last years of D. Afonso's long rule, different BaKongo factions, in collusion with Portuguese clerics, sought to take direct control of the succession to the throne, going as far as plotting against the life of the elderly *Mwene Kongo* in 1540.[118] While the "*Kibala* [Court]" faction of D. Pedro managed to secure his coronation, D. Diogo launched a successful but prolonged military campaign against the *mwisi Kongo* and provincial elites loyal to D. Pedro, accompanied by critical ideological and economic interventions.[119] On the ideological battlefront, D. Diogo sought the approval of the pope by framing his feud with D. Pedro as a fight against "*bad Christians, and many infidel heathens*" bound on returning to the worship of idols.[120] Concomitantly, he invited the Jesuits to the Kongo in 1548, adding another faction to the local clerical community that was already split between those loyal to the Portuguese Crown and the secular hierarchy of the Diocese of São Tomé and all regular and secular clerics residing in Mbanza Kongo

116 MMA II, D. 38, p. 102.

117 Thornton, A History of West Central Africa, p. 58; Thornton, Early Kongo-Portuguese Relations, p. 197.

118 Thornton, A History of West Central Africa, p. 58–59; Thornton, Early Kongo-Portuguese Relations, p. 197; Vansina, Kingdoms of the Savanna, p. 51–58.

119 Thornton, A History of West Central Africa, p. 58–59; Thornton, Early Kongo-Portuguese Relations, p. 197; Thornton, The Development of an African Catholic Church, p. 147–167.

120 MMA XV, D. 63.

who attempted to escape both.[121] When the Jesuits aligned with the faction from São Tomé instead of the local one, whom D. Diogo hoped they would support, the *Mwene Kongo* cut his backing of the Company of Jesus, resulting in its abandonment of the first Jesuit mission in Kongo (c. 1555).[122] On the economic front, as already mentioned, D. Diogo imposed several restrictions on the trade of slaves.[123]

These economic measures dovetailed with D. Diogo's religious strategy, as the best way to curtail the agency of the factions from São Tomé or Portugal was to restrict their ability to extract wealth by exporting slaves, rendering them dependent on BaKongo *nzimbu*. As Father Cristóvão Ribeiro complained in 1548, because there was "*no money*" in Mbanza Kongo they could send to Portugal, and it was impossible to transfer slaves, clerics under the patronage of the Crown lived "*barefoot and ragged*."[124] In this tense environment, as Thornton notes, bitter denunciations and accusations between different factions became the norm, and, in 1571, Gaspar Cão (?–1574), Bishop of São Tomé at the time, faced multiple accusations of illicit slave trading and gross neglect of his pastoral duties.[125] In the "*libelo* [indictment booklet]" of the case against him that was adjudicated by Cardinal Henrique (1512–1580), the bishop was accused of receiving "*many slaves*" from Kongo, whom he supposedly "*sold and through which he made much and heavy money*," meaning *cruzados*, he then transferred to a niece he used as a front for his slave trading business.[126] In his defense, the bishop argued that "*the slaves that came to him from Kongo were the product of the rights of the Church*," paid in "*shells they called ygos*,[127] *which are not current money, and therefore*" the rights were transferred to São Tomé "*as slaves*" as had been the "*use of his predecessors*."[128] Moreover, the bishop claimed he had the privilege of not paying duties over the "*slaves produced by the Church of Kongo*" and preference over the shipping space on vessels traveling to the island.[129] While Cardinal Henrique absolved Bishop Cão of all accusations,

---

121 MMA II, D. 81; Thornton, A History of West Central Africa, p. 61–62; Thornton, Conquest and Theology, p. 245–259; Vansina, Kingdoms of the Savanna, p. 61–63.

122 Hilton, The Kingdom of Kongo, p. 66; MMA II, D. 76; Thornton, A History of West Central Africa, p. 61–62; Thornton, The Development of an African Catholic Church, p. 149; Vansina, Kingdoms of the Savanna, p. 59–63.

123 Hilton, The Kingdom of Kongo, p. 66; MMA II, D. 81, p. 234.

124 MMA XV, D. 64.

125 MMA II, D. 79, D. 81, D. 104; MMA III, D. 3; Thornton, Early Kongo-Portuguese Relations, p. 183–204.

126 MMA III, D. 3, p. 11.

127 According to a letter from 1553 denouncing the bishop of São Tomé for allowing the clergy established in Kongo to have concubines as long as they paid him a "*pair of slaves*," the term *ygos* or "*iguoos*" referred specifically to the *nzimbu* paid as a tithe to the Church. MMA II, D. 104.

128 MMA III, D. 3, p. 26.

129 Ibid., p. 27.

he did not confirm the latter's privileges, which an "*assento* [deliberation]" of the Board of Conscience from February 10, 1561, had explicitly denied, decreeing that all slaves that exited Kongo, "*even if bought or resgatados* [ransomed] *with the fruits of rents and tithes or any episcopal rights*" had to pay duties to the Crown.[130] This example perfectly illustrates to what extent both the Portuguese monarch's and the *Mwene Kongo*'s power rested on controlling the regime of commensuration, resisting attempts to reduce BaKongo slaves to a perfectly fungible currency.

4.4 Describing Mbundu *Itanda*

The Jesuits accompanying Dias de Novais in his early diplomatic mission to the Kingdom of Ndongo penned the first European descriptions of Mbundu markets no more than a couple of years after the Company of Jesus abandoned the Kingdom of Kongo.[131] Despite the novelty of their reports, by then, Portuguese slave traders from São Tomé had frequented the Island of Luanda and its bay for decades, having helped the *ngola* consolidate his power locally and attain political autonomy from the *Mwene Kongo*.[132] According to one of the Jesuits, lay Brother António Mendes, mineral salt from Kissama was the general-purpose currency used in the daily *itanda* where crops and livestock were traded.[133] In these markets, a tubular piece of mineral salt three palms long and one palm wide at its base circumference was worth three capons or six chickens, three salt pieces were worth a goat or a castrated buck, and 14 or 15 salt pieces were worth a cow.[134] Brother Mendes also stated

130 MMA II, D. 164.

131 Paulo Dias de Novais first arrived at the mouth of the Kwanza on May 3, 1560. He had been sent to the capital of the Ngola as an ambassador by Cardinal-King D. Henrique. He was accompanied by Father Francisco de Gouveia, the superior of the Jesuits, Father Agostinho de Lacerda, and two lay brothers, António Mendes and Manuel Pinto. When he returned as *donatário* in 1574, he brought 700 soldiers aboard: "*two galleons, two caravels, two pataxes and a galiot.*" Four Jesuits accompanied him this second time: Father Garcia Simões, acting as superior, Father Baltasar Afonso, and the Brothers Cosme Gomes and Constantino Rodrigues. MMA II, D. 156, D. 157, D. 162; MMA IV, D. 132., p. 552–553; Vansina, Kingdoms of the Savanna, p. 62–63.

132 Thornton argues that the influence of the Portuguese in the consolidation of the power of the *ngola* and his growing autonomy from the Kingdom of Kongo was not decisive. Amaral, O consulado de Paulo Dias de Novais; Cruz e Silva, As Feiras do Ndongo, in: Santos (ed.), Actas do seminário, p. 405–422; Mello e Souza, Alianças e embates entre religiões, in: Hermann and Martins (eds.), Poderes do sagrado, p. 361–362; Olivier and Armore, Medieval Africa, p. 170–172; Rodrigues, Between West African and America, p. 58–59; Thornton, Early Kongo-Portuguese Relations, p. 193–194; Vansina, Paths in the Rainforests, p. 200.

133 MMA II, D. 173, p. 511.

134 As Vansina describes, the salt used in Ndongo as currency was 'mined' in Kissama, while in the Kingdom of Kongo, salt was harvested in the salt pans of Ambriz and Mpinda. Writing

that cloth was accepted as currency in smaller purchases, mentioning that he and the other Jesuits often cut small "*strips of cloth*" from their robes to buy "*corn flour*."[135] Finally, writing in 1575, when Dias de Novais was returning to Ndongo as a conqueror, Father Garcia Simões mentioned that "*emponda*," a kind of *palmilha* used for loin-cloths, and "*margarideta*" trade-beads were also used as money.[136] As Hilton remarks, *nzimbu* were conspicuously absent from the list of currencies accepted in Luanda's *itanda*,[137] confronting Dias de Novais, the Portuguese Crown, and the Jesuits with a serious problem of 'non-convertibility' as their attempts to conquer Kissama floundered.[138] Cloths, however, were highly regarded as a social currency, as becomes clear from the report of Brother Mendes.[139] The Jesuit explained that the *ngola* had the royal privilege of using certain kinds of "*blue*"

---

in 1618, Baltazar Rebelo de Aragão claims that the mines in Kissama were in a place called "*Adenda* [Ndemba]," twelve "*léguas*" from the shoreline and that each "*stone*" was worth $200 *réis*. Parreira briefly explains the process of mining salt in Kissama, adding that Ndemba was under the jurisdiction of a local ruler, *Kakulu Kakimone*. In Ndemba, circular holes one palm wide and three palms deep were first dug in the ground. These holes would naturally fill with a thick, watery paste that, once dried, would crystalize in that tubular shape. After that, the salt miners would dig around the salt tubes, extract them, scrap them clean, and smoke them for better preservation. These tubes would then circulate as currency. As Parreira mentions, sea salt was also obtained in Benguela, circulating in the southern trade routes, and the Mbangala produced an inferior quality of salt in the hinterlands from the water of the Luminhi River. CORDEIRO (ed.), Terras e minas africanas segundo Rebello de Aragão, p. 11–12; MMA II, D. 173, p. 511; PARREIRA, Economia e sociedade, p. 64–65; VANSINA, Long-Distance Trade-Routes, p. 378.

135 Jan Vansina remarks that maize was first introduced into the Kingdom of Kongo between 1548 and 1583. Therefore, Brother Mendes is most likely referring to millet. MMA II, D. 173, p. 511; VANSINA, Long-Distance Trade-Routes, p. 376–390.

136 As A. Saunders describes, colourful *palmilha* cloths were used by Portuguese Black slaves, suggesting that early expeditions to Ndongo carried goods in keeping with their tastes. Amaral remarks that by then, *margarideta* beads were manufactured in Augsburg and Nuremberg, being central to the slave trade in the Portuguese Fortress of St George of Mina, where they were shipped via Antwerp or Venice. The *Manueline Ordinances* tightly regulated their trade. AMARAL, O consulado de Paulo Dias de Novais, p. 83–86, 166; PARREIRA, Dicionário glossográfico, p. 42; SAUNDERS, A Social History of Black Slaves, p. 94; SIMÕES, De Garcia Simões para o Provincial de São Paulo de Loanda, p. 340.

137 In 1610, António da Silva, then the Duke of Bamba, remarked to the Dominican vicar stationed in Luanda that he had refrained from sending him the *kofu* of *nzimbu* that the *Mwene Kongo* had attributed him because "*they were worthless in Luanda*." MMA V, D. 232.

138 In his donation charter, the Portuguese Crown had conceded to Dias de Novais the monopoly over "*taking cowries from under the sea*" south of the Dande River. This privilege was extended to the Island of Luanda (then under the jurisdiction of a deputy of the *Mwene Kongo*), signaling the intention of disrespecting the rights of the Kongo monarch. AMARAL, O consulado de Paulo Dias de Novais, p. 67; HILTON, The Kingdom of Kongo, p. 75; THORNTON, Early Kongo-Portuguese Relations, p. 187.

139 MMA II, D. 173, p. 501.

and "*stripped*" cloth and that the Mbundu nobility "*highly esteemed*" all black and blue "*stripped cloths*."[140] Consequently, the Portuguese adopted this social currency as an ad hoc alternative to local general-purpose money.[141] At first moment, this meant introducing raffia cloths from Mpinda and other northern ports instead of the *nzimbu* obtained by trade in Kongo. Soon, the *Mwene Kongo* figured he could earn an additional income by taxing the lucrative new European-mediated trade in raffia cloth from the Kongo to Ndongo.[142]

Previous to Portuguese arrival in Luanda, the raffia cloths that were exchanged in the prestige exchange spheres of Ndongo were brought by African "merchant-brokers" from specialized producing centers situated on the rim of Central African equatorial rainforests, reaching the Mbundu from as far away as the Loango Coast, the Nkisi Valley and even north of the Kasai River.[143] Raffia cloths were woven with fibers from endogenous palm trees, known in Kikongo as "*ntombe* [*Raphia vinifera*]" or "*nteva* [*Hyphaene guineensis*]."[144] Other types of cloth were woven out of fibers produced from pineapple, "*embondeiro* [*Adansonia digitata*]," and "*mulemba* [*Ficus sycomorus*]" bark.[145] The Mbundu prized these latter two for their ceremonial and prestige value, while the BaKongo depreciated them because of the rudimentary process employed to weave them.[146] While there is no doubt that all these different cloths functioned as social currency, Phyllis Martin and Marion

140 Ibid.; Fromont, Common Threads, p. 838–867.

141 Vansina, Raffia Cloth in West Central Africa, in: Mazzaoui (ed.), Textiles, p. 279–280.

142 Hilton, The Kingdom of Kongo, p. 75.

143 Adriano Parreira claims that some of the *Dembos* were also raffia cloth production centers. Fromont, Common Threads, p. 838–867; Hilton, The Kingdom of Kongo, p. 6–7, 33, 40–41; Martin, Power, Cloth and Currency, p. 1; Martin, The Kingdom of Loango, in: Lagamma (ed.), Kongo, p. 47–86; Parreira, Economia e sociedade, p. 53–54; Santos, Escrever o poder, in: Heintze and von Oppen (eds.), Angola on the Move, p. 173–181; Thornton, A History of West Central Africa, p. 94; Vansina, Long-Distance Trade-Routes, p. 378; Vansina, Raffia Cloth in West Central Africa, in: Mazzaoui (ed.), Textiles, p. 261–282; Vieira, As cartas do Dembo Caculo Cacahenda, p. 41–54.

144 Brother Mendes describes only one species of domesticated palm tree in Ndongo which was used to produce palm fruits, palm oil, and timber but no cloth. Martin, Power, Cloth and Currency, p. 1; MMA II, D. 173, p. 510; Vieira, As cartas do Dembo Caculo Cacahenda.

145 Parreira, Economia e sociedade; Vansina, Raffia Cloth in West Central Africa, in: Mazzaoui (ed.), Textiles, p. 271; Amaral, O consulado de Paulo Dias de Novais, p. 22; Cadornega, História geral das guerras angolanas, Vol. 3, p. 368; Martin, Power, Cloth and Currency, p. 1–12.

146 According to Parreira, baobab cloths were used by the *nganga-ya-kimbanda*, one of the ritual specialists of the Mbangala *kilombo*, and *mulemba* fabrics were prestige symbols amongst the Mbundu because the tree was "sacred" to them. Baladier describes how *nsanda* (as *mulemba* was called in Kikongo) and baobab cloths were considered "vulgar" in the Kongo. However, the followers of BaKongo prophetess Beatriz Kimpa Vita (1684–1706) attributed to them sacramental value and political symbolism. António de Oliveira Cadornega remarks that baobab bark cloths were called "*licondos*" and were used by widows during mourning, as explained in the eighth chapter. Balandier, Le Royaume de Kongo, p. 108, 266; Cadornega, História geral das guerras angolanas,

Fig. 4 A Raffia Cloth Cushion Cover from Kongo. Acquired by the Armoury of the Swedish Royal Palace in the early seventeenth century, it was likely a diplomatic gift offered by a Portuguese embassy to Queen Christina of Sweden (1626–1689). ETNOGRAFISKA MUSEET, Dyna (inventory number: 1889.04.4166) (CC). Stockholm, 2025.

Johnson also explore their properties as a "self-regulating currency,"[147] a currency that maintains its value through being widely accepted and useful even though no centralized state or powerful sovereign can vouch for its worth or exchange rate.[148] These properties of raffia cloths would significantly impact subsequent Portuguese policies and deeply condition the trading environment of Luanda's hinterlands.

In keeping with Martin, palm trees were so common in the Kingdom of Loango and its immediate neighbors that the region was known locally as "the land of palms."[149] She argues that until Europeans started introducing imported textiles during the sixteenth century,[150] cloth production in this region was a common household industry and "part-time occupation," in the case of plain cloth, and a

Vol. 3, p. 266, 368–369; PARREIRA, Economia e sociedade, p. 54; THORNTON, The Kongolese Saint Anthony, p. 160–161.

147 Miller disagrees with this reading, arguing that West Central African long-distance exchange was based on bartering goods for their "use-values rather than on currency equivalents." He argues that "quantity and quality of concrete goods that were maintained at fixed use-value equivalencies assumed all the adjusting function that variation in abstract currency prices performs in capitalist economies." For a critique of the 'myth of barter' that questions Miller's interpretation, see Graeber. GRAEBER, Debt, p. 21–41; MILLER, Way of Death, p. 62–70.

148 As Johnson remarks, another property of currencies whose value is predicated on usefulness, as opposed to "state authentication" or by "demand in an external market," is that they are better "stores of value" than the latter and less prone to inflation. However, she admits that cloth currencies' sturdiness limited their capacity to store value over long periods. As Fromont remarks, shifting aesthetic tastes and the introduction of cheap European fabrics, which stripped African cloths of much of their practical use, also limited raffia cloths' ability to store value. FROMONT, Common Threads, p. 838–867; JOHNSON, Cloth as Money, p. 193–202; MARTIN, Power, Cloth and Currency, p. 1–12; VANSINA, Raffia Cloth in West Central Africa, in: MAZZAOUI (ed.), Textiles, p. 261–282.

149 MARTIN, The Kingdom of Loango, in: LAGAMMA (ed.), Kongo, p. 48.

150 David Eltis argues that, by the 1680s, only the African elites could afford to wear imported cloth, and even when these became more common in the eighteenth century, the domestic industry remained competitive. According to him, this pattern only shifted when the price of English fabrics dropped drastically in the nineteenth century. ARAUJO, The Gift, p. 11–28; ELTIS, Precolonial Western Africa in: SOLOW (ed.), Slavery and the Rise of the Atlantic System, p. 108.

specialized craft in the case of more elaborate fabrics.[151] Vili women wove mats and baskets while the cloth and clothing industry remained in the hands of men, who passed their specialized knowledge to younger male family members.[152] Noble houses patronized the production of prized fabrics, and the *maloango* [ruler of Loango] sponsored royal weaving workshops in his "*mbanza* [capital]," where cloths of exclusive design and quality were produced.[153] Anne Hilton situates the Nkisi Valley production centers in the Kongo provinces of Mbata and Mpangu, remarking that the centers north of the Kasai were also tributaries of the *Mwene Kongo*.[154] As both she and Balandier agree, in these regions, there was also a strict division of labor between genders, with BaKongo men producing all tree-related products, from palm oil and palm wine to raffia and bark cloths.[155] Despite being made commensurate by European merchants, at this stage, different kinds of cloth circulated in separate and gendered exchange spheres, with precious prestige fabrics, like the blue "*stripped cloth*" Brother Mendes described the *ngola* using being reserved for rulers, according to what Martin defines as the local "politics of costume."[156] She further explains how in Loango, raffia cloths were also "essential" to several significant life events, from births to initiation ceremonies, courtship rituals, funerals, and the payment of "legal fees."[157] Moreover, Vili elders and wealthy patrons "manipulated power" by controlling cloth circulation, using it to accumulate dependents, celebrate political alliances, and pay tribute.[158] The same was true in the Kongo provinces, where

151 Martin, Power, Cloth and Currency, p. 2.

152 Martin explains that specialized craftspersons wove high-quality cloths, coloring the fibers by exposing them to the sun or infusing them with red "*takula* [redwood]," white *mpemba* kaolin, or black charcoal. While several basic plain cloths could be woven in one day using a loom, finer royal cloths could take more than two weeks to produce. Fromont notes that the colors red, white, and black are still central to local cosmologies and symbolic systems, as MacGaffey concludes in his analysis of baKongo political thought. However, Fromont cautions us not to project contemporary ethnographic accounts too hastily back into the sixteenth century. Fromont, Common Threads, p. 848; MacGaffey, Kongo Political Culture, p. 85; Martin, Power, Cloth and Currency, p. 2; Martin, The Kingdom of Loango, in: Lagamma (ed.), Kongo, p. 48.

153 Martin, Power, Cloth and Currency, p. 2; Olivier and Armore, Medieval Africa, p. 163–164.

154 Hilton, The Kingdom of Kongo, p. 40.

155 Vansina remarks that women participated in the embellishment of Kongo cloths by the last decades of the eighteenth century. Balandier, Le Royaume de Kongo, p. 82–109; Hilton, The Kingdom of Kongo, p. 5–6; Vansina, Raffia Cloth in West Central Africa, in: Mazzaoui (ed.), Textiles, p. 273.

156 For a detailed description of the 'politics of taste' in Kongo, Loango, Kakongo, and Ngoyo, see Vansina and Fromont. Fromont, Common Threads, p. 846; Martin, Power, Cloth and Currency, p. 2, 4–5; MMA II, D. 173, p. 501; Thornton, A Cultural History of the Atlantic World, p. 354–356; Vansina, Raffia Cloth in West Central Africa, in: Mazzaoui (ed.), Textiles, p. 261–282.

157 See the eighth chapter for information on Mbundu life cycle celebrations. Fromont, Common Threads, p. 838–867; Martin, Power, Cloth and Currency, p. 3.

158 Martin, Power, Cloth and Currency, p. 3.

raffia cloth was also used as a social currency. According to Vansina, it was used to buy "manufactured goods," "rights over persons," and "settled dues of any sorts," but never to buy produce, "wage labour, land, or even houses," as there was no market for these last three goods to be exchanged.[159]

Due to the fact that salt circulated in Mbundu *itanda* as general-purpose money, raffia cloths were probably reserved for the same kind of prestige exchanges and were thus central to acquiring slaves, ritual offices, and rights over free dependents and women.[160] Salt from Kissama would be reserved for more mundane exchanges. Raffia cloths came to be known in Ndongo as *libongo* [pl. *mbongo*], if from the Loango Coast, and *kundi* or *endebo*, if from the Kongo.[161] According to Martin, a *libongo* was about "14 inches [c. 35.56 cm] square," the size of a "handkerchief," while Vansina estimates that *libongo* measured forty centimeters square and *kundi* fifty-two centimeters squared.[162] Ten *mbongo* or *kundi* were counted as a "*makuta*," a local currency of account.[163] Some of the raffia cloths produced in Kongo were so sturdy that the Portuguese sailors used them to fix the sails of their seafaring ships.[164] *Mbongo* could also be quite durable, and Portuguese soldiers who received their salaries in cloth soon discovered they could sew them together to "*make tents which could withstand the wind and rain*."[165] Nevertheless, passing from hand to hand as currency and constantly being cut and resewn together seems to have quickly deteriorated circulating cloths, which were better stores of value if kept treasured in trunks or worn as adornments.[166] In an address of the Municipal Council of Luanda from May 24, 1679, the ordinary judge and councilors complained that as soon as a *makuta* left "*the hands of the* [slave duty] *contractors*," it dropped from being worth 150 *réis* to being worth 40 *réis* because the *mbongo* that composed it

159 Vansina, Raffia Cloth in West Central Africa, in: Mazzaoui (ed.), Textiles, p. 279.

160 Cordeiro (ed.), Terras e minas africanas segundo Rebello de Aragão, p. 11–12; Vansina, Paths in the Rainforests, p. 201–203.

161 Cadornega, História geral das guerras angolanas, Vol. 3, p. 55–56, 184, 195; Green, A Fistful of Shells, p. 231; Heintze, Fontes para a História de Angola, Vol. 1, p. 117; Parreira, Economia e sociedade, p. 53–54.

162 Martin, Power, Cloth and Currency, p. 2; Vansina, Raffia Cloth in West Central Africa, in: Mazzaoui (ed.), Textiles, p. 276.

163 *Makuta* of different raffia cloths varied in worth. According to Martin, on the Loango Coast, ten *mbongo* also formed a '*makuta*,' but units of four, ten, twenty, forty, or a hundred *mbongo* also circulated. Parreira, Economia e sociedade, p. 86–87; Martin, Power, Cloth and Currency, p. 4.

164 Parreira, Economia e sociedade.

165 Martin, Power, Cloth and Currency, p. 4; Vansina, Raffia Cloth in West Central Africa, in: Mazzaoui (ed.), Textiles, p. 270.

166 Hilton points out that by 1648, when Luanda was restored to the Portuguese, the *mbongo* circulating there since before Dutch occupation had lost half their value due to being so ragged. Hilton, The Kingdom of Kongo, p. 77.

were "*too small, made of rotten straws, too thin, and badly woven,*" crumbling in the hands of the receivers.[167] Parreira remarks that daily usage fabrics were known in Ndongo as "*mpusu,*" "*urila,*" "*bungu,*" and "*maxize,*" being differentiated from *mbongo* and *kundi.*[168] These cloths were used to make clothes, bags, mats, pillows, and blankets and were probably freely exchanged by men and women alike.

Johnson argues that a critical aspect of useful currencies such as raffia cloths is that their value fluctuates as they flow through the economic system from producing centers toward eventual consumers, contrary to non-useful currencies, where this fluctuation is less pronounced.[169] In the case at hand, this explains why the *nzimbu* collected in the Island of Luanda were practically worthless in Ndongo while becoming more valuable as they moved northwards, towards Kongo and Loango, the same being true for raffia cloths flowing southwards from the raffia belt or salt eastwards and northwards from Kissama.[170] Considering this effect, Hilton predicates her account of the emergence of the Kingdom of Kongo as a centralized polity on the stabilization of a regional commercial or tribute network composed of the trade routes that spontaneously emerged between the different "ecological zones" were raffia cloths, salt, and shells were produced.[171] According to her, previous to European arrival, the *Mwene Kongo* explored the spontaneous value

---

167 MMA XIII, D. 203.

168 Parreira, Economia e sociedade.

169 Bullion currencies, such as gold or silver coins, were affected by similar processes. Both metals are useful (e.g., in altars, jewellery, and religious paraphernalia) and extracted only in specific areas. For instance, Green vividly describes how gold geographically fluctuated in value in his account of the impact of *Mansa* Musa's (c. 1312–c. 1337) pilgrimage from the Mali Empire to Mecca in the 1320s. Green, A Fistful of Shells, p. 39–40; Johnson, Cloth as Money, p. 196–197; Webb (Jr.), Toward the Comparative Study of Money, p. 455–466.

170 The physical circulation of commodity bundles ("assortment bargaining"), and their adoption as a currency of account, was one of the measures devised to counter this "one-way effect." As explored in the sixth chapter, by combining different styles of cloths, shells, beads, iron utensils, alcohol, and salt in the commodity bundles referred to in the Captaincy of Angola as *banzos*, merchants could guarantee that the value of this composite currency was relatively stable no matter where they travelled, as decreases of value in one of its elements were compensated by increases of value in another, without the need for political or legal regulation. ANTT, MR, EXP, Sr. 34, F. 605, p. 1–3; Hilton, The Kingdom of Kongo, p. 31–35; Johnson, Cloth as Money, p. 197; Webb (Jr.), Toward the Comparative Study of Money, p. 455–466.

171 Vansina argues that a "centralized government," a "system of rotating markets," a "standard national currency," and "institutions for the transport of goods overland" existed in the Kingdom of Kongo before European arrival, but the establishment of purely commercial caravans, "modeled after parties of tribute bearers," was a later development. In keeping with this reading, after 1491, the pre-existing politico-religious tribute network gradually became a commercial network. Hilton, The Kingdom of Kongo, p. 31–35, 40–41; Vansina, Long-Distance Trade-Routes, p. 376–390; Vansina, Paths in the Rainforests, p. 200; Vansina, Raffia Cloth in West Central Africa, in: Mazzaoui (ed.), Textiles, p. 261–282.

fluctuation of these items by receiving tributes from governors of the coastal areas in salt and shells (e. g., *nzimbu* from the Island of Luanda) and tribute from governors of the eastern provinces in raffia cloths (e. g., *kundi* from the Nkisi Valley), and then redistributing these as gifts to clients and dependents residing in different ecological areas, including Ndongo.[172] As Vansina explains, from 1491 to the 1660s, when the Battle of Mbwila (1665) and the consolidation of the Kingdom of Kasanje as a settled Mbangala polity profoundly altered the power relations in this region, European merchants also explored the properties of this economic system, making huge profits. Since African elders and political leaders used their luxury wares to increase their political power, prestige, and network of clients and dependents, the demand for European imports was "self-sustaining."[173]

Writing in 1611, Pedro Sardinha provides an insight into the volume of trade achieved during the first decades of the conquest of Angola in the regional market that comprised the Portuguese Captaincy and the Kingdoms of Kongo and Loango.[174] By then, the *moradores* of Luanda sent their slaves to "*Congo de Batta*" or Ngongo Mbata, the center of the Mbata province of Kongo, to acquire the cloths used as money in Luanda and the hinterland "*resgates* [slave fairs]."[175] He mentions that these cloths were also used to clothe slaves and for day-to-day expenses.[176] By 1611, they were classified into five categories according to their origin and quality. Annually, large amounts came from the Kongo: between 12.000 to 15.000 "*panos pintados* [painted cloths]," being worth 640 *réis* each and totaling 8.000$000 *réis*; between 40.000 and 50.000 *songas*, which were taxed and controlled by the Municipal Council of Luanda,[177] being worth 200 *réis* each and totaling about 9.000$000; and about 35.000 "half *cundes* [half-*kundi*]," that were worth approximately a "*tostão* [100 *réis*]," totaling 3.500$000 *réis*.[178] Therefore, Sardinha estimated that about 20.500$000 worth of cloth that had "*no value or acceptance in any other place*" entered the Captaincy of Angola from Kongo alone.[179] Furthermore, a total of 3.000$000 *réis* worth of "*exfula*" cloths and 400$000 *réis* worth of "*ensaca*" cloths

172 Hilton, The Kingdom of Kongo, p. 31–35, 40–41; Miller, Way of Death, p. 60–62.

173 Vansina, Paths in the Rainforests, p. 198, 203.

174 MMA VI, D. 15.

175 Clist et al., African-European Contacts in the Kongo Kingdom, p. 464–501; MMA VI, D. 15, p. 52.

176 MMA VI, D. 15, p. 52.

177 According to Cadornega, by 1680, the treasurers of the Municipal Council of Luanda used an R-shaped brand to mark twice each "*cundi* [*kundi*]" and once each "*libongo*." Cadornega, História geral das guerras angolanas, Vol. 3, p. 195.

178 Vansina remarks that "*cundes*" got their name because they were produced in Kundi, while "*songos*" came from Songo. Vansina, Raffia Cloth in West Central Africa, in: Mazzaoui (ed.), Textiles, p. 261–282; MMA VI, D. 15, p. 52–53.

179 MMA VI, D. 15, p. 52–53.

arrived annually by sea from the harbor of Loango, where a monopoly contract had been established.[180]

All these cloths were bought with "*fazendas* [wares]" or "*droguas* [drugs]" exported from Angola that had paid no customs to the Portuguese Crown when leaving Luanda.[181] According to a report by Sardinha a year later, the profits made by moving these different useful currencies around were enormous.[182] Anne Hilton estimates that cloth merchants made 800% profits by 1611 and still 500% by the 1630s.[183] Even the very high profit margins made by legally exporting slaves (approximately 200%) paled in comparison. As Vansina remarks, even if Sardinha was exaggerating the margins, in 1680, António de Oliveira Cadornega confirmed that before the 1640s, the profits of trading raffia cloths far exceeded those of selling slaves.[184]

However, from the point of view of merchants and the Portuguese Crown, the problem of efficiently extracting wealth from this regional economic system persisted, as slaves were the only social currency that had worth outside of it.[185] Nevertheless, their exchange in prestige spheres of exchange was still embedded in African normative systems and regulated by royal enactments and ordinances, Canon law, and *Ius commune* doctrines. In other words, the historical commensurability regime in place still limited the fungibility or transitiveness of slaves between different regional economic contexts. Despite these limitations, an Atlantic-wide system of wealth extraction and taxation soon consolidated, as proved by the Royal Edict of June 26, 1588, determining the way the legacies of those deceased in Angola were to be transferred to their rightful heirs.[186] According to the edict, Diogo da Fonseca, the general treasurer of the legacies of those deceased in Brazil and Guinea, had complained to the Crown that he was not able to receive any valuables from Angola because "*no credits exist in this Kingdom or other forms to transfer fazendas* [wealth] *or money*."[187] In reply, the Crown determined that all the assets

180 According to Vansina, a merchant in Lisbon usually held the monopoly contract, which lasted from c. 1611 until 1692. Ibid., p. 53–54; Vansina, Raffia Cloth in West Central Africa, in: Mazzaoui (ed.), Textiles, p. 15.

181 For a price conversion between *makuta* of different raffia cloths, measures of *nzimbu*, Portuguese *reais*, European bullion coins, and slaves that are valid for the mid-seventeenth century, see Parreira. Parreira, Economia e sociedade, p. 86–89; MMA VI, D. 15, p. 53–54, D. 30, p. 104–105.

182 MMA VI, D. 30.

183 Hilton, The Kingdom of Kongo, p. 77.

184 Cadornega, História geral das guerras angolanas, Vol. 3, p. 273–275; Vansina, Raffia Cloth in West Central Africa, in: Mazzaoui (ed.), Textiles, p. 277.

185 Vansina, Raffia Cloth in West Central Africa, in: Mazzaoui (ed.), Textiles, p. 279.

186 MMA III, D. 99.

187 During this time, the term 'Guinea' in Diogo da Fonseca's title referred to all of West Africa, including West Central Africa. Ibid., p. 368.

that composed these legacies would be auctioned in Luanda for the highest bid in *nzimbu*. The shells would then be employed to buy slaves, which would then be sent to Brazil for auction and paid for in bullion currencies.[188] All the taxes, shipping expenses, and upkeep of these slaves would be deducted from the total sum of the legacy, paid in *nzimbu* in Luanda and bullion in Brazil.[189] The liquid remainder would then be transferred to Lisbon, either in bullion or colonial goods, where the general treasurer of the legacies of the deceased would distribute it.[190] Slightly modified versions of this pattern of wealth extraction would persist well into the mid-nineteenth century.

4.5 Converting Mbundu *Itanda*

When Father Barreira arrived in Luanda on February 23, 1580, appointed as the new superior of the Jesuits, he was aware of the recent conflicts between members of his order and D. Diogo I of Kongo, which had resulted in the abandonment of the Jesuit mission to Mbanza Kongo.[191] He was also aware of the difficulties in transferring wealth outside the regional exchange circuit formed by São Tomé, the Kingdom of Kongo, its neighboring African polities, and the Captaincy of Angola. Highly educated, both at the University of Coimbra and the University of Évora (1559–1779),[192] and of an aggressive, militaristic bent, he quickly became Dias de Novais' energic right arm, being instrumental not only in securing the backup that allowed him to establish New Gaza and win the Battle of Talandongo but also obtaining military supplies from São Tomé that helped fortify Massangano.[193] As José Leitão remarks, together with Ribeiro de Aragão, Father Barreira was also crucial to the conquest of Cambambe, having been convinced by reports of the existence there of silver mines.[194] Moreover, his constant logistical support was essential to securing the Portuguese rearguard as, for religious reasons, "*rebellious*"

188 Ibid., p. 368–369; MMA III, D. 26.

189 MMA III, D. 26; D. 99., p. 368–369.

190 MMA III, D. 99., p. 368–369.

191 Bonciani, "Minas de almas," p. 7; Leitão, A missão Do P.e Baltasar Barreira, p. 50.

192 The University of Évora was established in 1559 by Cardinal Henrique under the aegis of the Jesuits and confirmed by Pope Paul IV (1476–1559). It was abolished by Sebastião José de Carvalho e Melo in 1779 when the Jesuits were expelled from the Portuguese Kingdom and Empire. Calafate, Estudo introdutório I, in: Calafate (ed.), A Escola Ibérica da Paz nas Universidades de Coimbra e Évora, Vol. 1, p. 17–49; Mauricio, A Universidade de Évora e a escravatura, p. 153–200.

193 Alencastro, O trato dos viventes, p. 170–171; Amaral, O consulado de Paulo Dias de Novais, p. 172–173; Leitão, A missão Do P.e Baltasar Barreira, p. 54–57, 61–63; MMA III, D. 65.

194 Cordeiro (ed.), Terras e minas africanas segundo Rebello de Aragão, p. 5–8, 12–13; Leitão, A missão Do P.e Baltasar Barreira, p. 55–57; MMA III, D. 86.

sobas still allowed the Jesuit '*banganga*' and their entourages to transit through their lands.[195]

The Jesuit superior also had to administer a fast-growing number of slaves. On December 22, 1581, Dias de Novais rewarded Father Barreira a *sesmaria* [land grant] 2.500 *braças* [c. 5.5 km.] wide and two *léguas* long, south of the Kwanza River and seven *sobas* as rewards for his service. He continued to grant privileges to the Jesuits as the conquest of Ndongo proceeded.[196] Each *soba* paid tribute to Father Barreira in slaves, cattle, cloths, and salt.[197] When the Jesuit provincial superior from Brazil visited Angola in 1594, the Jesuits were paid an average of 300 slaves per year in tribute, also receiving many slaves as legacies.[198] Of these, they catechized, converted, and manumitted about forty, kept a hundred employed as domestic labor, and exchanged the remaining for the local currencies or goods that allowed them to buy food and supplies. As Alencastro remarks, being highly skeptical of the results achieved by the conversion of the Kingdom of Kongo and any form of "Constantinism" centered on African monarchs, Barreira advocated for a "total war of economic, territorial, and ideological conquest" of Ndongo.[199] As the following pages discuss, this entailed ensuring that Portuguese conquerors and the Jesuits assumed complete control of the local regime of commensuration, not only conquering *itanda* and converting them into slave markets according to the model of *pumbos* or *resgates* but also manipulating the limits of incommensurability. This meant misrepresenting Mbundu rules of enslavement, setting less-tolerant limits for religious syncretism, and redetermining which human groups were within the fold of theological Natural law and *Ius gentium*.

At this precise historical juncture, the ongoing Atlantic debate about the legal and moral legitimacy of buying and owning enslaved Africans in Brazil, Peru, and New Granada was reaching a climax, forcing Father Barreira to intervene.[200] As

---

195 Leitão, A missão Do P.e Baltasar Barreira, p. 55–57.

196 Two other *sobas* were donated by other "*conquistadores* [conquerors]" of Ndongo to the Jesuits as legacies. Each of the nine *sobas* that came to be under the lordship of the Jesuits had other minor *sobas* under his rule, three being especially powerful. See the second chapter for more information on the '*amos*' system and the normative framework of landowning and land grants in the Captaincy of Angola. Ibid., p. 57, 66–67; MMA XV, D. 99, D. 101, D. 102.

197 Leitão, A missão Do P.e Baltasar Barreira, p. 66–67.

198 Ibid., p. 71–72.

199 Alencastro, O trato dos viventes, p. 170.

200 Alencastro, O trato dos viventes, p. 171; Cagle, Imperial Tensions, Colonial Contours, in: Martínez-San Miguel and Arias (eds.), The Routledge Hispanic Studies Companion to Colonial Latin America and the Caribbean, p. 215–230; Sweet, Black Robes and "Black Destiny," p. 87–133; Zeron and Dias, A Igreja e a escravidão, p. 85–106; Zeron, Les Jésuites et le commerce d'esclaves, in: Hebrard (ed.), Brésil quatre siècles d'esclavage, p. 65–83; Zeron, Linha de fé.

Alencastro, Carlos Alberto Zeron, David Sweet, and Mattias Kaufmann summarize, by the second half of the sixteenth century, Jesuit scholars took a juridical approach to justify the 'peculiar institution,' sidelining theological and philosophical considerations central to the debate since the times of Aristotle.[201] In short, this meant that, in keeping with a Second-Scholastic understanding of the precedence of Natural law over royal ordinances and municipal enactments, the Society recognized several "*condiciones legitimas*" or titles of just enslavement, each validating the *dominium* of slaveowners over the freedom of enslaved persons.[202] The four main conditions were: the slaves being captured in a just war, having obtained their status in commutation of the death penalty, having sold themselves as slaves because of extreme necessity (e.g., to avoid starvation), or having inherited their condition from their mother.[203] These conditions were grounded on a reading of *Ius gentium* that reinterpreted elements from revived Roman law through the prism of Natural law, affording their application to all extra-European peoples and contexts.[204] Moreover, as Tomás Tassinari remarks, they were meant to discern the legitimacy of the *dominium* of slave owners over slaves obtained in any part of the world, having the global reach of the Society of Jesus and the Iberian Catholic monarchies in mind.[205] In other words, they allowed African, American, Asian,

201 For a brief account of Classical Greek and Roman attitudes towards slavery, early philosophical theories of slavery, and the debates of early theologians and the Church Fathers about the institution see Peter Garnsey. Mary Sommar provides an overview of these debates from the first century until 1582 when Pope Gregory XII promulgated a new *Corpus Iuris Canonici*. See also Russell-Wood. ALENCASTRO, O trato dos viventes, p. 171–172; GARNSEY, Ideas of Slavery from Aristotle to Augustine; KAUFMANN, Slavery between Law, Morality, and Economy, in: KAUFMANN and AICHELE (eds.), A Companion to Luis de Molina, p. 194–201; MCMANUS, Martín de Azpilcueta on Trade and Slavery, in: BRAGAGNOLO (ed.), The Production of Knowledge of Normativity, p. 352–370; RUSSEL-WOOD, Iberian Expansion and the Issue of Black Slavery, p. 34; SOMMAR, The Slaves of the Churches; SWEET, Black Robes and "Black Destiny," p. 93–94; ZERON, Linha de fé, p. 190.

202 CALAFATE, A Escola Ibérica da Paz nas Universidades de Coimbra e Évora; KAUFMANN, Slavery between Law, Morality, and Economy, in: KAUFMANN and AICHELE (eds.), A Companion to Luis de Molina, p. 194–201; MCMANUS, Martín de Azpilcueta on Trade and Slavery, in: BRAGAGNOLO (ed.), The Production of Knowledge of Normativity, p. 363; PIMENTA DE BRITO, Fernão Pérez (1531?–1595?); ZERON, Les Jésuites et le commerce d'esclaves, in: HEBRARD (ed.), Brésil quatre siècles d'esclavage, p. 82; ZERON, Linha de fé, p. 206.

203 ALENCASTRO, O trato dos viventes, p. 171–172; HESPANHA, Luís de Molina e a escravização dos negros, p. 937–960; SWEET, Black Robes and "Black Destiny," p. 87–133; ZERON, Les Jésuites et le commerce d'esclaves, in: HEBRARD (ed.), Brésil quatre siècles d'esclavage, p. 82; ZERON, Linha de fé, p. 206.

204 HERZOG, What is Legal History, in: DUVE and HERZOG (eds.), Latin America Law in Global Perspective, p. 39–53; ZERON, Linha de fé, p. 190.

205 For a discussion about the global reach of Father Luis de Molina's and Father Martín Azpilcueta's writings on legitimate enslavement, see McManus. As he explains, the latter's *Manual de Confes-*

European, and Pacific vernacular modalities of "extreme asymmetric dependency" that were deeply embedded in local historical, cultural, and social backgrounds to be made commensurable and slaves from these disparate regions to become fungible—at least in abstract juridical terms.[206]

When Father Barreira was forced to enter the debate about the legitimacy of owning African slaves in Brazil in the 1580s, a parallel discussion about the legitimacy of enslaving Amerindians was reaching a tipping point, with a consensus emerging in favor of substituting the forced labor of "*escravos da terra* [slaves of the land]" or "*negros da terra* [Blacks of the land]," as enslaved Amerindians were then referred to, for that of "*negros da Guiné* [African Blacks]" or African slaves.[207] Questioning the possibility of Amerindians and Africans being commensurate was central to this shift and to Jesuit arguments in favor of importing African slaves.[208] However, as the limits of incommensurability were redrawn to accommodate the exceptionality of Amerindians and the abolition of Amerindian slavery,[209] the whole "Jesuit theory of slavery" faced a moment of crisis as two professors from the Jesuit College of Bahia raised a serious juridical objection to it.[210]

Robin Blackburn highlights Fernão de Oliveira's (1507–1581) *The Art of Maritime Warfare* (1555) as an influential, early critique of Portuguese participation in the

---

sores y Penitentes (1566), where the four legitimate conditions for enslavement were discussed, was particularly influential in Portuguese India, South East Asia, and Japan. McManus, Martín de Azpilcueta on Trade and Slavery, in: Bragagnolo (ed.), The Production of Knowledge of Normativity, p. 352–370; Tassinari, Notas sobre a justificativa da escravização de ambundos.

206 Tassinari, Notas sobre a justificativa da escravização de ambundos; Winnebeck et al., On Asymmetrical Dependency; Zeron, Linha de fé, p. 190.

207 Schwartz, Sugar Plantations, p. 52; Monteiro, Negros da terra; Schwartz, A Commonwealth within Itself, in: Schwartz (ed.), Tropical Babylons, p. 158–200; Alencastro, The Apprenticeship of Colonization, in: Solow (ed.), Slavery and the Rise of the Atlantic System, p. 152; Alencastro, O trato dos viventes, p. 117–154; Thornton, A Cultural History of the Atlantic World, p. 299–301; Kaufmann, Slavery between Law, Morality, and Economy, in: Kaufmann and Aichele (eds.), A Companion to Luis de Molina, p. 192–193.

208 Cagle, Imperial Tensions, Colonial Contours, in: Martínez-San Miguel and Arias (eds.), The Routledge Hispanic Studies Companion to Colonial Latin America and the Caribbean, p. 215–230; Schwartz, Sugar Plantations, p. 52; Sweet, Black Robes and "Black Destiny," p. 87–133.

209 As Russell-Wood remarks, in 1570, a law had already forbidden the enslavement and traffic of enslaved Japanese people by the Portuguese, and in 1624, that prohibition would be extended to the Chinese, rendering enslaved Chinese and Japanese incommensurable with enslaved Africans. Nevertheless, as Russel-Wood adds, the de facto enslavement of Japanese and Chinese persisted until the middle of the eighteenth century. Russel-Wood, Iberian Expansion and the Issue of Black Slavery, p. 40–41; Schwartz, Sugar Plantations, p. 52.

210 Cagle, Imperial Tensions, Colonial Contours, in: Martínez-San Miguel and Arias (eds.), The Routledge Hispanic Studies Companion to Colonial Latin America and the Caribbean, p. 216.

Atlantic slave trade that paved the theoretical ground for this crisis.[211] According to Oliveira, a former Dominican friar who had been recently appointed the director of the University of Coimbra Press, his countrymen had been "*the inventors of an evil trade*" by "*buying and selling peaceable, free men, as one buys and sells animals*."[212] Moreover, he claimed that it was "*no excuse to say that* [the Africans] *sell one another because he who buys what is wrongly sold is still guilty, and because the laws of this land and others condemn him*."[213] Amongst those who took up Oliveira's critique were Father Alonso de Sandoval (1576–1652) and the two abovementioned Jesuit professors, Father Miguel Garcia (1550–1614) and Father Gonçalo Leite (1546–1603).[214]

By the early 1580s, Father Garcia, then professor of theology at the Jesuit college of Bahia, had become utterly convinced that it was impossible to establish with reasonable certainty the modality of enslavement of any imported slave and that, therefore, Brazilian slave owners had no legitimate *dominium* over the freedom of their slaves.[215] Consequently, he and Father Gonçalo Leite, a professor of philosophy at the same college, refused to confess anybody who owned slaves, including their

211 Blackburn, The Making of New World Slavery, p. 120–121; Russel-Wood, Iberian Expansion and the Issue of Black Slavery, p. 36–37.

212 Blackburn, The Making of New World Slavery, p. 120–121; Monteiro, A Pioneering Treatise on Naval Strategy, p. 94–107.

213 Blackburn argues that Oliveira's views influenced the Dominican Friar Martin de Ledesma's (c. 1509–1574) *Secunda Quartae* (1560), also published in Coimbra, and subsequent Dominican and Jesuit critics of the slave trade. For an overview of Spanish critiques of the Portuguese slave trade, see David Sweet. Blackburn, The Making of New World Slavery, p. 120–121; Calafate, A Escola Ibérica da Paz nas Universidades de Coimbra e Évora; Sweet, Black Robes and "Black Destiny," p. 87–133.

214 Father Sandoval was the Rector of the Jesuit College of the port of Cartagena, New Granada, where he administered the last sacraments to enslaved Africans while enquiring of them about the conditions of their enslavement. Despite accepting the legitimacy of slavery, Father Sandoval questioned the possibility of ascertaining the fairness of all individual enslavements and, therefore, the legality of mass captivity and the Atlantic slave trade. By then, the debate had moved on and was focused on how to frame and enforce masters' appropriate behavior toward their slaves, so he was removed from his position without causing too much scandal. Alencastro, O trato dos viventes, p. 162–168; Blackburn, The Making of New World Slavery, p. 120–121; Cagle, Imperial Tensions, Colonial Contours, in: Martínez-San Miguel and Arias (eds.), The Routledge Hispanic Studies Companion to Colonial Latin America and the Caribbean, p. 220; Marquese and Joly, Panis, disciplina, et opus servo, in: Dal Lago and Katsari (eds.), Slave Systems, p. 87–133; Sweet, Black Robes and "Black Destiny," p. 87–133; Zeron, Les Jésuites et le commerce d'esclaves, in: Hebrard (ed.), Brésil quatre siècles d'esclavage, p. 65–83.

215 Cagle, Imperial Tensions, Colonial Contours, in: Martínez-San Miguel and Arias (eds.), The Routledge Hispanic Studies Companion to Colonial Latin America and the Caribbean, p. 215–230; Sweet, Black Robes and "Black Destiny," p. 87–133; Zeron, Les Jésuites et le commerce d'esclaves, in: Hebrard (ed.), Brésil quatre siècles d'esclavage, p. 65–83; Zeron, Linha de fé, p. 499–504.

superiors, Jesuit priests, and lay brothers, because they reasoned slaveowners were "*living in sin*" until they freed their illegitimately held slaves and compensated them for their forced labor.[216] The scandal this caused resulted not only in Father Garcia being recanted back to Portugal by a decision of the Board of Royal Conscience but also in the Provincial Visitator of Brazil requesting the opinion of renowned jurists and Jesuit theologians on the matter, including Father Fernão Perez (c. 1531–1595), Father Gaspar Gonçalves (1528–1599), Father Luis de Molina (1535–1600), and Father Martín de Azpilcueta (1491–1586).[217] They concluded that if doubts about the legitimacy of the enslavement of a concrete slave arose, owners were obliged to inquire them about it, restituting their original freedom and compensating the enslaved for their past labor if their enslavement proved illegitimate. However, the theologians agreed that when it was impossible to conduct a serious investigation, the *dominium* over the slave's freedom was legitimate.[218]

Faced with the need to obtain more precise information about the origins of Angolan slaves to put an end to the crisis created by Fathers Garcia and Leite, Father Cristóvão de Gouveia (1542–1622), then the visitator responsible for overseeing the Jesuit missions in Brazil, contacted Father Barreira and the bishop of São Tomé.[219] In reply to Father Gouveia's inquiries, the former wrote a manuscript titled *Information About the Slaves of Angola*.[220] In this document, Father Barreira builds upon previous descriptions of Mbundu *itanda*, strategically redefining the local regime of commensuration. According to Alencastro, Father Barreira's report was not only addressed to the visitator but also to the theologians and jurists of the Universities of Coimbra, Évora, and Salamanca, allowing them to consolidate the "Jesuit theory of slavery" against Fernão de Oliveira's and Fathers Garcia's and

---

216 MMA XV, D. 103; Sweet, Black Robes and "Black Destiny," p. 93; Zeron, Les Jésuites et le commerce d'esclaves, in: Hebrard (ed.), Brésil quatre siècles d'esclavage, p. 70–72; Zeron, Linha de fé, p. 159–160.

217 Father Molina's *Tractatus de iustitia et de iure* [Treatise on Justice and Law] (1593) is further discussed in the following pages. Alencastro, O trato dos viventes, p. 170–171; Capela, Éthique et représentation de l'esclavagisme, in: Henriques and Sala-Molins (eds.), Déraison, esclavage et droit, p. 340; McManus, Martín de Azpilcueta on Trade and Slavery, in: Bragagnolo (ed.), The Production of Knowledge of Normativity, p. 352–370; MMA XV, D. 103; Sweet, Black Robes and "Black Destiny," p. 93; Zeron, Les Jésuites et le commerce d'esclaves, in: Hebrard (ed.), Brésil quatre siècles d'esclavage, p. 75; Zeron, Linha de fé, p. 499–504.

218 Bonciani, "Minas de almas," p. 24; Capela, Éthique et représentation de l'esclavagisme, in: Henriques and Sala-Molins (eds.), Déraison, esclavage et droit, p. 340; Tassinari, Notas sobre a justificativa da escravização de ambundos; Zeron, Linha de fé, p. 168.

219 MMA XV, D. 103.

220 MMA III, D. 54.

Leite's criticisms and helping to overcome the uneasiness about the Jesuits owning slaves expressed by successive general superiors of the Society of Jesus.[221]

According to *Information About the Slaves of Angola*, by the early 1580s, a salt tube from Kissama could buy two capons or four chickens, two salt tubes could buy a castrated buck, and ten salt tubes could buy an ox or one of the enslaved persons that the Portuguese called "*peças*."[222] Writing in the final decade of the eighteenth century, Elias Alexandre da Silva Corrêa explains that an ideal "*Peça da India*" was a male "*young slave, tall, robust, and without any disability*."[223] By then, the price for all other slaves, either female, older or younger, frail, or disabled, could be calculated as fractions of this abstract *peça*, which was commensurate with African cloth and shell currencies, commodity bundles, European bullion currencies, and the Portuguese currency of account, the *real*.[224] Silva Corrêa naturalized this historical regime of commensuration, noting it as an ancient custom in Angola and Benguela.[225] However, when Father Barreira wrote his report, it was still in its ideological infancy,

---

221 As Alencastro explains, Father Barreira's letters and reports were considered "edifying" and, therefore, were read aloud during mealtimes at Jesuit colleges and seminars. This made his views highly influential despite their contrast with those of the general superiors of the Society of Jesus. Francis Borgia (1510–1572), superior general of the Jesuits between 1565 and 1572, had not only restricted the involvement of priests in all commercial transactions, including the trade in slaves, but also expressed his disapproval of Jesuits owning slaves. Previously, Ignatius of Loyola (1491–1556) and Diego Laynes (1512–1565) also had expressed unfavorable opinions about the ownership of slaves, which were reiterated by Superior Generals Everard Mercurian (1514–1580) and Claudio Acquaviva (1543–1615). Alencastro, O trato dos viventes, p. 168–180, 170–172; Marquese and Joly, Panis, disciplina, et opus servo, in: Dal Lago and Katsari (eds.), Slave Systems, p. 214–230.

222 MMA III, D. 54, p. 227.

223 According to Estevam Thompson, originally, "*peças d'India*" were the premium slaves sold by the Portuguese in the Spanish Indies, the "*Índias de Castella*." Silva Corrêa, História de Angola, Vol. 1, p. 54; Thompson, The Making of Quilengues, p. 234.

224 The Ordinance of the Customs House of Luanda of 1799 used the accounting unit "*Cabeça* [head]" instead of *peças da índia*. According to this ordinance, all enslaved children, referred to as "*Crias* [cubs]," were taxed as fractions of a *Cabeça*, according to their height. If they measured more than four palms according to the measuring *Vara* [stick] used in Lisbon, they would be taxed as *Cabeças*; if less, they would be taxed as *cria de pé* [walking cubs]. Breastfeeding babies would be taxed together with their mothers as one *Cabeça*. Miller claims that the *cabeça* system was adopted after the Restoration (1640) and differed from the *peça* system because *cabeças* were accounted as undivided units. However, the ordinance of the customs house suggests otherwise—at least regarding children. As Martin describes, the mid-eighteenth century, on the Loango coast, a standard unit of account emerged called "*piéce*," an apparent pidgin version of *peça*. This was, however, a genuinely abstract currency of account or "ghost-money," in Marion Johnson's terms, with cloth currencies, commodity bundles, and slaves being valued in or reduced to *pieces*. Johnson, Cloth as Money, p. 193–202; Martin, Power, Cloth and Currency, p. 8; Mello, Regimento da Alfandega, p. 411; Miller, Capitalism and Slaving, p. 44; Vellut, Le Royaume de Cassange, p. 120.

225 Silva Corrêa, História de Angola, Vol. 1, p. 54.

and the Jesuit superior significantly contributed to its formation and consolidation by including slaves in the same sphere of exchange as fresh produce and cattle.[226] Moreover, Father Barreira commented on the origins of the legal status of the enslaved. By doing so, he distorted the Mbundu normative framework in which local relations of extreme asymmetric dependency were embedded to make local norms commensurable with the *condiciones legitimas* that grounded the Jesuit theory of slavery.

According to Baltasar Barreira's manuscript, the enslaved persons traded at *itanda* were either the descendants of slaves taken in wars, prisoners of war, or those condemned of "*delictos* [offenses], *for which they deserved death.*"[227] The first kind of slave, he added, was rightfully enslaved because independent sobas had enslaved their ancestors before the *ngola* conquered the provinces of Ndongo. In other words, before the current political society was established—and, presumably, the Mbundu lived closer to a state of nature or war of all against all. The second kind of slave, he stated, was rightfully enslaved because the *ngola*, as a *princeps*, assured that they were captured in just wars.[228] The third kind of slave, he concluded, was rightfully enslaved according to the uses and customs of Ndongo. Previously, in 1576, Father Garcia Simões had remarked that after inquiring about the origin of the 12.000 slaves traded annually from Luanda, he had formed the opinion that almost all of the Mbundu were "*slaves of the King* [*ngola*]," either because they had been previously condemned for "*adulteries or theft*," the penalty of death usually applied

226 Focusing on the emergence of the Atlantic system, Miller points to the strategic advantages of the commensuration of enslaved Africans with relatively cheap merchandise (either the secondary products of sugar and tobacco processing or the rudimentary output of early mass-production processes) and non-bullion currencies (cowrie shells and cloth). This allowed European businessmen "at the edge of bankruptcy" to enter the Atlantic slave trade and produce commodities exchangeable in Europe for hard currency with recourse to only a small amount of capital. Both Miller and Toby Green explore the long-term implications of this historical regime of commensuration, the first arguing it contributed to the increasing peripheral status of Portugal and Brazil within the rising European world system, the latter focusing on its impacts in 'underdeveloping' Africa. ALENCASTRO, O trato dos viventes, p. 168–180; CANDIDO and GREEN, How Europe Underdeveloped Africa by Walter Rodney—50 Years On, p. 1–3; GREEN, A Fistful of Shells; MILLER, A Marginal Institution on the Margin of the Atlantic System, in: SOLOW (ed.), Slavery and the Rise of the Atlantic System, p. 145; RODNEY, How Europe Underdeveloped Africa.

227 MMA III, D. 54, p. 228.

228 This assumption is in keeping with the doctrines of the Iberian School of Peace. Father Molina claimed that God's grace was at the origin of "civil power," following St Paul in the conclusion that there was "no king that does not come from God." From this stemmed the presupposition that, being a *princeps*, the *ngola* would act in keeping with Natural law. CALAFATE, Estudo introdutório I, in: CALAFATE (ed.), A Escola Ibérica da Paz nas Universidades de Coimbra e Évora, Vol. 1, p. 22; KAUFMANN, Slavery between Law, Morality, and Economy, in: KAUFMANN and AICHELE (eds.), A Companion to Luis de Molina, p. 183–226.

in these cases being reduced to enslavement, or because the *ngola* had defeated them in battle.[229] Moreover, Father Simões argued that it was a crime punishable by death or enslavement to sell a free person, so few dared to commit it. However, contrary to Father Barreira, he did not claim slaves were exchanged for salt and bucks at *itanda* or that the *ngola*'s war of conquest had been just. Nevertheless, both Jesuits omitted all additional information about the emic 'legal' statuses associated with these three forms of asymmetric dependency.[230]

According to Aida Freudenthal, Beatrix Heintze, Catarina Madeira Santos, and Heywood and Thornton, in Ndongo, the first kind of enslaved persons identified by Father Barreira was referred to as "*ijiku* [pl. *kijiku*]" in Kimbundu and contrasted both to "*murinda* [free commoners]" or "*ana murinda* [children of the *murinda*]," and the aristocratic *makota* (sing. *dikota*) and *sobas*.[231] However, *kijiku* were more of a servile class than slaves, rights over their services probably being exchanged in the prestige spheres of exchange where rights over free women were brokered.[232] They remained bound to "*nhundu*" or "*ngundu*" corporate kin groups, the diffuse populational unit ruled by *sobas*, usually consisting of one to several villages.[233] They could not be sold or alienated and were inherited as part of the chiefly 'estate' but could be gifted as political tribute.[234] Moreover, as Santos remarks, they were headed by an officer titled "*mopolo*," who represented them at the *ngola* of Ndongo's court

229 MMA III, D. 23, p. 146.

230 Heywood and Thornton, Central Africans, p. 72–79; Winnebeck et al., On Asymmetrical Dependency.

231 Heywood and Thornton use the term *kijikos* instead of *ijiku* and *kijiku*, as proposed by Freudenthal and Santos. Moreover, instead of referring to Mbundu corporate kin groups as *nhundu* (Freudenthal) or *ngundu* (Miller), they refer to them as *murinda*, who, according to Freudenthal and Santos, were the free commoners that composed kin groups. According to Santos, the translation of *murinda* as free commoners is further authorized by António da Silva Maia's *Portuguese-Kimbundu-Kikongo* (1964) and António de Assis Júnior's *Dictionary of Kimbundu-Portuguese…* (1949) dictionaries, which translate it, respectively, as "*livre* [free person]" and "he who can dispose of himself, he who is free, the inhabitant of a region or a place, the vassal who cannot be sold." Heintze remarks that *murinda* were also referred to as "*morinda*" or "*morindas*" in Portuguese sources, while *kijiku* were referred to as "*quizicos*." Assis Júnior, Dicionário de Kimbundu-Português; Freudenthal, Sobas, conquistadores e peças d'Índias, in: Pantoja and Thompson (eds.), Em torno de Angola, p. 71; Heintze, Fontes para a História de Angola, Vol. 1, p. 123–124; Heywood and Thornton, Central Africans, p. 72–79; Maia, Dicionário complementar; Santos, Esclavage africain, p. 127–148.

232 Freudenthal, Sobas, conquistadores e peças d'Índias, in: Pantoja and Thompson (eds.), Em torno de Angola, p. 71; Heywood and Thornton, Central Africans, p. 72–79.

233 Heywood and Thornton, Central Africans, p. 72–79; Miller, Kings and Kinsmen, p. 46–48.

234 Freudenthal, Sobas, conquistadores e peças d'Índias, in: Pantoja and Thompson (eds.), Em torno de Angola, p. 71; Heywood and Thornton, Central Africans, p. 72–79.

and participated with the *sobas* and *makota* in the latter's election.[235] The second and third kinds of enslaved persons were known as "*abika* [sing.]" or "*mubika* [pl.]." This class comprised war captives and those who had been judicially enslaved for severe offenses.[236] *Mubika* could be freely alienated from the *ngundu* and exchanged for prestige goods or rights over free persons by their owners. According to *Information About the Slaves of Angola*, some slaves were used by *sobas* to "*cultivate their lands*" and help "*in their toils and hardships*" (probably the *mubika*), while others to pay the "*tributes they paid to their King*" (the *kijiku*). Barreira also mentions that the *ngola* appointed an official to each *itanda* in charge of ascertaining the fairness of each enslavement and that selling a free person was considered a significant infringement. Heywood and Thornton maintain that the same ban applied to selling *kijiku* or alienating them from their *ngundu*.

Other Jesuit sources provide additional details about the political administration of Ndongo, advancing more precise claims about how its judicial system supposedly produced slaves. In a letter from 1575, Father Simões adds that the Kingdom of Ndogo was divided between "*ten or twelve Sobas* [...] *who are like Dukes and great lords, and each one of them in their lands has jurisdiction to sell and kill his vassals, when the kind of offense they are involved in calls for it*."[237] More significant than the *ngundu*, these units were called *kandas* and ruled over by nobles claiming a privileged connection with *ngola* titleholders.[238] From Simões' testimony alone, sobas administered justice and were responsible for enslaving guilty parties as *mubika*—a later source, however, nuanced Father Simões' claims. According to the information collected in a chronicle of the Jesuit presence in Angola written in 1594, Ndongo was divided into the territories of 736 individual *sobas*. The jurisdictions of these *sobas* often intersected and nested, as *sobas* in charge of *kandas* had jurisdiction over several smaller *ngundu*. In keeping with this document, all *sobas*, "*from the King* [*ngola*] *to the smallest Soba have a Governor to whom they call Tendala, that hears both parts and gives them justice*."[239] In Ndongo, Heywood and Thornton remark, the *tendala* was drawn from the *kijiku* class.[240] According to the

235 Santos, Esclavage africain, p. 127–148.

236 Heywood and Thornton, Central Africans, p. 72–79; MMA III, D. 54, p. 228.

237 Simões, De Garcia Simões para o Provincial de São Paulo de Loanda, p. 341–342.

238 Heywood and Thornton, Central Africans, p. 75–76; MMA IV, D. 132, p. 559.

239 MMA IV, D. 132, p. 559.

240 The other Mbundu officer mentioned both in early and later sources is the "*Chiambole*" or "*Angolá Ambole* [*Ngola Ambole*]," described as the "*captain major of war*" or the "*lieutenant-general*" of the *sobas*' troops. In time, the Portuguese would adopt and adapt both offices, appointing *tendalas* as interpreters and *ngola amboles* as majors of the second-line detachments. Carvalho, Os homens do rei em Angola, p. 50–51; Cruz, Militates e militarização no Reino de Angola, p. 62, 80–87; Heywood and Thornton, Central Africans, p. 75–76; MMA IV, D. 132, p. 562; MMA X, D. 228, p. 235; Parreira, Dicionário glossográfico.

Jesuit chronicle from 1594, by then, most of the slaves obtained by the Portuguese were bought at *itanda*, not enslaved in wars. These had been condemned to slavery because one of their relatives had "*betrayed their Lord and wanted to rebel* [and] *take his estate or* [had] *committed a crime* [adultery] *with the women of the Lord* [*soba*]."[241] In such cases, the chronicles state that the perpetrator would be killed, and all their "*generation*" would be enslaved by the *tendala*. While all these sources suspiciously align Mbundu norms with Jesuit doctrines regarding just enslavement, leaving one to wonder about their integrity, they don't address the fulcrum of Father Garcia's objection. How could Brazilian slave owners be sure that their specific slaves had been rightfully enslaved, considering that not all African wars were just and not all Mbundu norms were in keeping with a theological understanding of Natural law?

Father Barreira addressed this issue by claiming that the Africans used "*certain things that have their usual and fixed prices, amongst which slaves*" instead of "*gold coins or of any other metal*."[242] Because slaves were used as a fungible currency, he claimed, the "*three kinds of peças* [slaves] *circulate from fair to fair*" to the extent that "*it is impossible to determine what is the title by which our* [countrymen] *buy them.*" Moreover, Father Barreira claimed that obtaining additional information from Mbundu sellers was impossible, as they merely "*laughed*" and kept the origin of their "*peças*" a "*secret*."[243] In conclusion, he argued, from nowhere "*in Guinea* [Africa] *were peças*" shipped "*that could be more safely bought*" because of this impossibility of obtaining any credible information about their pasts. In his opinion, this absolved slave masters in their *foro interno*, providing a solid basis for their *dominium* over the freedom of all enslaved Africans coming from the Captaincy of Angola. As Alencastro remarks, this went beyond reading local institutions through an *Ius gentium* lens.[244] Father Barreira innovated by defining African slave markets as the places where the legal and moral legitimacy of the *dominium* slave owners claimed over the freedom of their slaves was determined and confirmed. In a way, this was the historical culmination of the tendency to turn social currencies used in African prestige spheres of exchange into general-purpose money and of the century-old project of converting BaKongo and Mbundu slaves into fungible assets that enabled the extraction of wealth from the West Central African context. Like Bishop Cão and countless merchants from Portugal and São Tomé and *pumbeiros* before him, Father Barreira sought to commensurate *peças*, a perfectly fungible

---

241 MMA IV, D. 132, p. 561.

242 Alencastro, O trato dos viventes, p. 168–180; MMA III, D. 54, p. 227–228.

243 MMA III, D. 54, p. 228.

244 Alencastro, O trato dos viventes, p. 168–180.

currency of account, with *mubika, kijiku,* and all the free women and dependents whose reproductive labors were brokered by male elders and political leaders.[245]

When a Jesuit college was established in Angola in 1593, Father Pero Rodrigues (1542–1603?), the Jesuit visitator in Angola at the time, endorsed Father Barreira's theory about Mbundu slavery, guaranteeing its continuity.[246] As Roberto Pich remarks, probabilism, the Catholic moral doctrine according to which it is legitimate to follow an authoritative opinion regarding the morality of an action even if an opposite opinion is available that seems more probable, played a crucial role in this, enabling Jesuits and merchants to follow Father Barreira's lead instead of heeding the opinions of those critical of the Atlantic slave trade.[247] By then, Father Barreira had returned to the Iberian Peninsula, as his support for the *amos* system, in the process of being dismantled by the Portuguese Crown, had turned him into a *persona non grata*.[248] In his report to the superior general, Father Rodrigues claimed that it, "*was no scandal the priests of Angola pay their debts with slaves*" because, he reasoned, "*as in Europe the money that circulates is gold, and silver coins, in Brazil is sugar, and in Angola and neighboring kingdoms are slaves*."[249] Moreover, he continued, some of the slaves obtained by the Society were received as tribute, tithes, alms, or as part of legacies. Finally, since the Jesuits had the privilege of being exempt from the taxes paid on exported slaves and sugar, the "*peças* that would be sold in Angola by standard prices" could be sold with high profits in Brazil, where they were worth more than double. Father Rodrigues concluded that just as "*whoever sells wheat or other things not needed in his household, does so where they have more worth*," it was only reasonable and legitimate to sell slaves where they would fetch higher prices.

Father Rodrigues' option to side with Father Barreira did not proceed from a lack of more detailed information about Mbundu *itanda* and West Central African enslaving mechanisms and normative systems or the lack of opposing authoritative opinions within the Society of Jesus.[250] That same year, Father Molina published *Tractatus de iustitia et de iure* [Treatise on Justice and Law] (1593) in Cuenca,

245 MMA III, D. 3.

246 Alencastro, O trato dos viventes, p. 172–176; MMA XV, D. 127.

247 Pich, Probabilismo e escravidão negra, p. 17–67; Pich, Second Scholasticism and Black Slavery, p. 1–13; Pich et al., Second scholasticism and Black slavery, p. 3–15.

248 Alencastro, O trato dos viventes, p. 172–176; Amaral, O consulado de Paulo Dias de Novais, p. 229–242; Bonciani, Heresias e rebelião em Angola, p. 3–4; MMA XV, D. 127.

249 MMA XV, D. 127, p. 337.

250 Calafate, Estudo introdutório I, in: Calafate (ed.), A Escola Ibérica da Paz nas Universidades de Coimbra e Évora, Vol. 1, p. 17–49; Kaufmann, Slavery between Law, Morality, and Economy, in: Kaufmann and Aichele (eds.), A Companion to Luis de Molina, p. 183–226; Pich, Probabilismo e escravidão negra, p. 17–67; Pich, Second Scholasticism and Black Slavery, p. 1–13; Pich et al., Culleton and Storck, Second scholasticism and black slavery, p. 3–15; Pimenta de Brito, Fernão Pérez (1531?–1595?).

Spain, with a total of nine disputations dedicated to the Angolan slave trade.[251] As Hespanha, José Capela, and Pedro Calafate explain, the treatise was based on Father Molina's class materials from when he taught at the University of Coimbra (1563–1567) and the University of Évora (1568–1583), so its content already circulated in Portugal before its publication in 1593.[252] In *Tractatus de iustitia*, Father Molina argued that considering the four classic prerequisites for just enslavement was not enough, as most slaves bought by the Portuguese had been previously enslaved according to African normative systems.[253] Attention should thus be paid to these systems because, as Hespanha summarizes, if a "European buyer could not buy something that the seller did not possess; and if the latter was not the legitimate proprietor of the slave, the European buyer was not their legitimate proprietor as well."[254] Therefore, contrary to Father Barreira, who predicated the legitimacy of the slave owners' title or *dominium* over the freedom of their slaves on them being used as fungible currency in *itanda*, a fact that foreclosed any further inquiries into the slaves' past, Father Molina insisted on the need to inquire about the past of each slave casuistically.[255]

Moreover, Father Molina argued that if the death penalties that had been commuted to slavery had been unfair, then it was the "charitable" obligation of the Portuguese to ransom those who had been unfairly punished.[256] This graceful

---

251 Hespanha, Luís de Molina e a escravização dos negros, p. 937–938; Molina, On Slavery and the Slave Trade.

252 Calafate, Plano da obra, in: Calafate (ed.), A Escola Ibérica da Paz nas Universidades de Coimbra e Évora, Vol. 1, p. 13–15; Capela, Éthique et représentation de l'esclavagisme, in: Henriques and Sala-Molins (eds.), Déraison, esclavage et droit, p. 337; Hespanha, Luís de Molina e a escravização dos negros, p. 937–938.

253 I interpret Father Molina's argument based on Pedro Calafate's and Hespanha's translations of key passages from *Tractatus de iustitia et de jure*. Daniel Schwartz and Jorg Telkamp are editing an English translation of disputations 32 to 40. See Matthias Kaufmann for an introduction to Father Molina's thinking about slavery and the slave trade and Maria Pimenta de Brito on the impact of Father Fernão Perez's teachings on Father Molina's work. Calafate, Estudo introdutório I, in: Calafate (ed.), A Escola Ibérica da Paz nas Universidades de Coimbra e Évora, Vol. 1, p. 17–49; Hespanha, Luís de Molina e a escravização dos negros, p. 940; Kaufmann, Slavery between Law, Morality, and Economy, in: Kaufmann and Aichele (eds.), A Companion to Luis de Molina, p. 183–226; Molina, On Slavery and the Slave Trade; Pimenta de Brito, Fernão Pérez (1531?–1595?).

254 The next chapter explores how Father Manuel Ribeiro Rocha's *Etíope resgatado, empenhado, sustentado, corrigido, instruído e libertado* [Ethiopian Ransomed, Indentured, Sustained, Corrected, Educated, and Liberated] (1758) provided a different doctrinal solution to this issue. Hespanha, Luís de Molina e a escravização dos negros, p. 940; Rocha, Ethiope Resgatado.

255 Pich, Probabilismo e escravidão negra, p. 17–67; Pich, Second Scholasticism and Black Slavery, p. 1–13; Pich et al., Second Scholasticism and Black Slavery, p. 3–15.

256 Kaufmann, Slavery between Law, Morality, and Economy, in: Kaufmann and Aichele (eds.), A Companion to Luis de Molina, p. 197–201.

act could not be the basis for fair enslavement.[257] The need to know more about Mbundu normative systems led Father Molina to inquire about them directly to Mbundu "*sobas*," his overall description of Mbundu political organization being close to Heywood and Thornton's historical reconstruction.[258] As Father Molina described it, each Mbundu *soba* ruled over a "*mirinda* [*murinda*],"[259] where four species of persons resided: "*mocotas* [*makota*]" nobles, the freeborn "sons of the *mirinda* [*murinda*]," and "*quisico* [*kijiku*]" and "*mobicas* [*mubika*]" slaves.[260] While the last two classes of persons were unfree, according to Father Molina, only "*mobicas*" could be rightfully sold by the *sobas* to the Portuguese, as the "*quisico*" belonged to the "*mirinda*." By analogy to the norms regulating the Portuguese land-owning system, he explained that the possession and alienation of "*quisico*" were framed in terms similar to those regulating "*morgados* [entailed estates]." In contrast, the possession and alienation of "*mobicas*" were framed in terms similar to those regulating "*reguengos* [private estates]." While "*quisico*" inherited their status, "*mobicas*" were often prisoners of war. Nevertheless, Father Molina concluded these wars were not just wars because they resulted from the escalation of "*mochanos* [*mucanos*]" or legal disputes between *sobas*, being more akin to feuds. Basing himself on these premises, he concluded that neither "*mobicas*" nor "*quisico*" could be legitimately purchased by Portuguese or Luso-African merchants, the first because their sale was against Mbundu norms, the second because they had not been captured in just wars.

Father Molina then assessed if it was legitimate to buy *sobas*, "*mocotas*," and "sons of the *mirinda*," who had been condemned to death and had their punishment commuted to enslavement.[261] Reflecting on this, he concluded that West Central African normative systems had what Hespanha defines as several "justice deficits." First, Father Molina argued that the Mbundu "administered [Justice] under the shade of some trees by the king and some elders, [deciding] by a vote [...] and condemning some to perpetual enslavement instead of death" for very slight offenses, such as "the theft of chickens or something even smaller."[262] Second, these condemnations were often based on nothing but "signs." If a *soba* had perceived "signs" that someone planned his death, Father Molina argued, he would "reduce [the suspects] to slavery, confiscate all their assets, as well as those of their family,

257 Hespanha, Luís de Molina e a Escravização dos Negros, p. 946.

258 Ibid., p. 950; Heywood and Thornton, Central Africans, p. 72–79.

259 According to Freudenthal, Father Molina mistakes the *murinda* and *ana murinda* that composed a corporate kin group for the group itself (*nhundu*). Freudenthal, Sobas, conquistadores e peças d'Índias, in: Pantoja and Thompson (eds.), Em torno de Angola, p. 71.

260 Hespanha, Luís de Molina e a Escravização dos Negros, p. 950.

261 Ibid., p. 950–952.

262 Ibid., p. 948.

appropriating himself of all that belonged to them, without any investigation or form of judgment." Moreover, as Father Molina related, if someone pressed charges against a third person, and the validity of these was "denied" by the *soba*, the accuser suffered the same fate. Third, one could be condemned for crimes committed by their relatives and other members of the *ngundu*.[263] Considering all these "justice deficits," Father Molina concluded that, contrary to what Father Barreira argued, the buying of enslaved Mbundu could not be considered legitimate, except, perhaps, when there was the danger of them being killed by their owners to "obtain a profit in the market with their flesh." As the next chapter explores, the specter of cannibalism would provide a solid grounding for future doctrinal interventions in favor of the 'ransom' of slaves.

Finally, Father Molina argued that the captain-general and governors of Angola understood local Mbundu normative systems, going so far as to use them to condemn and get rid of opposing *sobas*.[264] In his words, "When they want to condemn a *soba*, they use the styles of his fatherland, gathering in a huge military assembly the *sobas* and presenting the accusations against the one charged before judges appointed for that role." If the "accused was guilty of lese-majesty, they not only killed him but included in the conviction those who were dependent on him as soldiers, be they nobles, be they sons of the *mirinda*, killing a lot of these and reducing others to slavery." Then Father Molina continued, the *soba* accused by the captain-general and governor would be "dismembered, and all the members of his family would be reduced to slavery, including his wife and children." As for the *ngola*, whom Father Molina understood as a sort of "emperor" who had in the recent past subjugated several *sobas*, his rules were no less capricious in the Jesuit's opinion. Father Molina reported that he had 'laws' condemning to death or enslavement anyone who took feathers from his "peacocks" and those who obtained palm wine from palm trees using siphons.[265] In conclusion, Father Molina was convinced that the title slaveowners had over the freedom of slaves bought in West Central Africa was most likely illegitimate. However, as Hespanha remarks, he was not concerned with the political or normative problems raised by this fact but only with its moral and religious consequences at the *foro interno* of slaveowners and during confession.[266] It is thus difficult to assess the impact of Father Molina's doctrinal intervention in Angola and Benguela, considering the moral leeway afforded by probabilism and Father Rodrigues' endorsement of Father Barreira's opposing readings of Mbundu institutions. Nevertheless, it is safe to assume that his and similar interventions by his peers at the Universities of Coimbra, Évora, and Salamanca,

---

263 Ibid., p. 951–952.
264 Ibid., p. 949, 951.
265 Ibid., p. 951.
266 Ibid., p. 938.

informed the deliberations of the Board of Conscience, as they were also at the basis of the institutions set in place in West Central Africa to ascertain the legitimacy of enslavement, from the *mucano* hearings to the enquirers of freedoms and the catechists of freedoms operating in the Atlantic port towns.[267]

4.6 The 'Birth' of the Angolan Slave Market

Father Barreira's ideological spadework was not restricted to an apology of slavery and the Atlantic slave trade. If we accept that Mbundu *itanda* were spaces where justice was served and economic, religious, political, and social transactions took place, just like BaKongo *nzandu*, converting and reducing them to slave markets implied interfering with the prestige spheres of exchange where religious or magical services and rights over free women and dependents were brokered. In other words, it meant intervening in the normative spheres of the institutions the Portuguese reconceptualized as idolatry, *feitiçaria*, and African marriage. When he wrote his report on the slaves bought in Angola, Father Barreira also penned a *Report on the Marriages of Angola* (1582–1583).[268] In this report, the Jesuit focuses on the prestige sphere of exchange where rights over women were brokered, using this exchange as an argument in favor of the non-existence of the institution of "*legitimate marriage according to Natural law*" in Angola.[269] He reasoned that, since rights were exchanged multiple times, women circulated accordingly, and elders and political leaders accumulated several wives and unfree "*Quicumbas* [concubines]" as a form of "*estate*," there was no such thing as a Mbundu marriage. In this case, the incommensurability of a Mbundu institution was predicated on the circulation of

267 Domingos Mauricio and José Capela mention the works and teachings of Father Fernão Perez, Father Fernão Rebelo (c. 1547–1608), Father Estêvão Fagundes (1577–1645), and Father João Baptista Fragoso (1559–1639) as especially influential in the Portuguese context. For a discussion of each's positions on the institutions of slavery and the slave trade, see Mauricio and Calafate. The specialized bibliography on Second Scholastics, the 'School of Salamanca' (which also included Neo-Thomist scholars from the Universities of Alcalá [1293], Coimbra, Évora, and Valladolid [1241]), is too vast to be fully reviewed here. Braun, Bom and Astorri, A Companion to the Spanish Scholastics; Brett, Liberty, Right and Nature; Calafate, A Escola Ibérica da Paz nas Universidades de Coimbra e Évora; Calafate, A Escola Ibérica da Paz; Capela, Éthique et représentation de l'esclavagisme, in: Henriques and Sala-Molins (eds.), Déraison, esclavage et droit, p. 329–348; Hill and Lagerlund, The Philosophy of Francisco Suárez; Kaufmann and Aichele, A Companion to Luis de Molina; Mauricio, A Universidade de Évora e a escravatura, p. 153–200; Salas and Fastiggi, A Companion to Francisco Suárez; Schweighöfer, Die Begründung der normativen Kraft von Gesetzen; Scott, The Spanish Origin of International Law.

268 MMA III, D. 55.

269 Ibid., p. 230–231.

rights over people in the market, having the demeaning effect of only recognizing Christian wedlock as binding.

As for "*idols*," Father Barreira often bragged about "*burning so many Idols on one side and the other of the Kwanza River that one would not believe*."[270] In his reports, which include extensive transcriptions from Father Baltasar Afonso, to whom Father Barreira claimed "*God has given a particular talent against the idols of the land, and the instruments of their idolatry*," the "*cremation of idols*" and the "*places and houses where they resided*" went hand-in-hand with the religious conversions signaled by baptisms.[271] With the non-recognition of African marriage, the Jesuit's monopoly over conversion terms was meant to ensure that, contrary to what had happened in the Kongo, no "space of correlation" was left under African control.[272] However, the presence of the "*heretics*," New Christians, Jews, and crypto-Jews who composed the *pumbo* network established since the earlier days of contact with the Kongo threatened this project.[273]

According to Rodrigo Bonciani, the merchants from São Tomé, their agents, and the Luso-African *pumbeiros* who frequented BaKongo and Mbundu markets often traded in 'counterfeit' "relics" such as "saint's bones," pieces of certificates of indulgencies granted on account of crusading bulls (*bulla cruciata*), adorned copies of the Torah, images of saints and "Our Lady and baby Jesus," crucifixes, and Roman Catholic sacramental elements.[274] These exchanges threatened Father Barreira's conversion project in two ways. First, they ensured that *itanda* and *nzandu* remained arenas where religious and magic services were brokered, competing with the alternative *fora* provided by Catholic churches and missions. Second, they evidenced that African and Luso-African agents remained in control of the local regime of commensuration. Their open disrespect for Roman Catholic limits of (in)commensurability resulted in the exchange of sacramental and sacred items that the Jesuits deemed intrinsically incommensurable and intransitive. For instance, Manuel da Silveira, a Portuguese merchant known locally as "*Quitingo* [the limp],"

---

270 MMA III, D. 47, D. 65.

271 See the seventh chapter for a detailed account of Father Afonso's iconoclasm and the eighth chapter for a discussion of how the sacrament of baptism was adapted to West Central African preexisting belief systems. MMA III, D. 65; MMA XV, D. 127, p. 272–273.

272 Fromont, The Art of Conversion; Fromont, Under the Sign of the Cross, p. 109–123.

273 Bonciani, Heresias e rebelião em Angola, p. 1–27; Bonciani, Inquisição, tráfico de escravos e circulação, in: Pérez, Megiani and Alonso (eds.), Redes y circulación en Brasil durante la Monarquía Hispánica, p. 265–289; Bonciani and Silveira, Um pombeiro nas origens do Atlântico, p. 520–591; Horta, A Inquisição em Angola e Congo, p. 387–415; Horta, Africanos e portugueses, p. 301–321.

274 Bonciani, Inquisição, tráfico de escravos e circulação, in: Pérez, Megiani and Alonso (eds.), Redes y circulación en Brasil durante la Monarquía Hispánica, p. 273–277, 283–285.

sold copies of "papal Bulls of Our Lady of Victory" in the Kongo province Mbata.[275] As Bonciani relates, Silveira obtained these copies from the bishop of São Tomé and tasked "his Black women" with peddling them in *itanda* for "five *songo* or one *pintado* cloth" per page.[276] Like the pages of the "bull of the crusades," which were then considered very powerful "*textos com feitiço* [texts with *feitiço*]," these pages were probably used in anti-sorcery rituals or to create protective charms.[277] The same happened with Jewish ritual objects and texts, and Silveira also peddled the physical elements of Roman Catholic sacraments, such as the salt administered before baptism.[278] While these practices were then framed as heresy, crypto-Judaism, and simony, they can also be understood as evidence that even if 'idols' were burned, shared beliefs in *ndoki*, *uanga*, and *feitiçaria* guaranteed the existence of a space of correlation outside of Jesuit control. Its physical locus was the markets where accusations of *ndoki* and *uanga* were adjudicated, and Portuguese, BaKongo, and Mbundu religious and magical items and services were made equivalent and exchanged.

By 1580, the Portuguese and Spanish Crowns had been united (1580–1640), opening the vast slave markets of the Spanish Indies to Portuguese merchants.[279] Fifteen years later, Philip I (1527–1598) created the *Asiento*, a master contract to deliver enslaved Africans to the Spanish Indies.[280] As Heywood and Thornton describe, most *asientos* were soon held by persons with privileged connections to the Angolan slave trade.[281] Simultaneously, the Crown promoted the establishment of official slave markets where Portuguese merchants were obliged to reside and trade so that they could be more easily taxed.[282] From the 1590s to the 1620s, Thornton estimates, the *Asiento* went from 50% supplied by Angolan slaves to 80%.[283] The economic viability of *asientos*, Bonciani remarks, depended on the

---

275 Bonciani explains that these bulls had been issued by Pope Pious V (1504–1572) in celebration of the victory of Christian troops against the Ottomans at the Battle of Lepanto (1571). In 1573, Pope Gregory XIII (1502–1585) renamed the Feast of Our Lady of Victory the Feast of Our Lady of the Rosary. Ibid., p. 271.

276 Ibid., p. 278; ANTT, TSO, CG, Sr. 20, D. 776.

277 Santos, Escrever o poder, in: Heintze and von Oppen (eds.), Angola on the Move, p. 173–181; Bonciani, Inquisição, tráfico de escravos e circulação, in: Pérez, Megiani and Alonso (eds.), Redes y circulación en Brasil durante la Monarquía Hispánica, p. 265–289; Bonciani and Silveira, Um pombeiro nas origens do Atlântico, p. 520–591; Bonciani, Heresias e rebelião em Angola, p. 1–27; Bonciani, "Minas de almas," p. 1–29.

278 The use of salt in Roman Catholic baptisms will be further discussed in the eighth chapter.

279 Miller, Kings and Kinsmen; Thornton, A History of West Central Africa.

280 Newson and Minchin, From Capture to Sale; Thornton, A History of West Central Africa, p. 93.

281 Heywood and Thornton, Central Africans, p. 39–40.

282 Thornton, A History of West Central Africa, p. 95–96.

283 Ibid., p. 113.

"*feitores* [foreman]" sent by the contract-holders to the principal Atlantic harbors being able to establish and maintain their private networks of hinterland merchants and *pumbeiros* in direct competition with pre-established ones.[284] By 1607, as discussed in the first chapter, a slave duty contract was created in Angola, its holders being granted the monopoly over importing *mbongo* cloths to Luanda.[285]

As the economic stakes rose, the Inquisition of Lisbon promoted a visit to Angola between 1593 and 1596 and an inquiry between 1596 and 1598.[286] Spurred by the Jesuits, the mixed-court cracked down on the New Christians and their *pumbeiros*, asserting control over these wayward subjects and their parallel network of *resgates* to better control the flux of trade in raffia cloths and enslaved Africans.[287] In this context, captain-general and governors started appointing a *mani quitanda* to oversee slave fairs, guaranteeing that taxes were paid.[288] These developments closed the cycle opened by the arrival of Diogo Cão in the Kongo, as the *pumbeiros* and insubordinate European merchants loyal to the *Mwene Kongo* or São Tomé were brought under relative control.[289] While Mbundu *itanda* probably continued to be spaces where African agents kept the upper hand in determining what could be made commensurable and exchanged and what remained off-limits, Portuguese slave fairs matured as a separate institution, were a different regime of commensurability was imposed and daily enacted. As the next chapter discusses, a new historical cycle was about to begin based on the cooperation between the Portuguese and Mbangala warbands. Incidentally, Father Barreira also played a minor role in setting the ideological framing of this relationship.

---

284 Bonciani, Inquisição, tráfico de escravos e circulação, in: Pérez, Megiani and Alonso (eds.), Redes y circulación en Brasil durante la Monarquía Hispánica, p. 265–289.

285 Miller, Way of Death, p. 555–556; MMA XIII, D. 203.

286 Horta, Africanos e portugueses, p. 96; Horta, A Inquisição em Angola e Congo, p. 387–415; Thornton, A History of West Central Africa.

287 Thornton, A History of West Central Africa, p. 95–96; Bonciani, Inquisição, tráfico de escravos e circulação, in: Pérez, Megiani and Alonso (eds.), Redes y circulación en Brasil durante la Monarquía Hispánica, p. 265–289; Bonciani, Heresias e rebelião em Angola, p. 1–27; Bonciani, "Minas de almas," p. 1–29.

288 Heintze, Fontes para a História de Angola, Vol. 1, p. 127; Sousa, O extenso relatório do governador a seus filhos, in: Heintze (ed.), Fontes para a História de Angola, Vol. 1, p. 217–362.

289 Bonciani, Inquisição, tráfico de escravos e circulação, in: Pérez, Megiani and Alonso (eds.), Redes y circulación en Brasil durante la Monarquía Hispánica, p. 265–289; Bonciani, "Minas de almas," p. 1–29.

5. Sites of *Othering* and Redemption

5.1 The Road from Conversion to Redemption

Manoel Correia Leitão reached the "*gloomy and mountainous forests*" of Mbondo in early February 1756.[1] Situated "mid-journey between Ambaca and Cassange," Mbondo was by then a province of the Kingdom of Kasanje.[2] As the previous chapter describes, Leitão had left Luanda in August 1755, sent by the captain-general and governor of Angola, António Álvares da Cunha, on a secret mission to this Mbangala kingdom. There, he was supposed to help Antonio Roiz Grizante find the exact latitude of the Luso-African slave fair of Cassange, explore the margins of the nearby Kwango River, and obtain precious commercial information about the kingdom's northern neighbors, the Holo.[3] As Leitão notes, in Mbondo, "*wild negroes*" lived in isolated "*caves and dens*" amidst vicious raiders and wild beasts.[4] Although it was possible to barter for foodstuff with them, he remarked that "*the buyer must remain armed so that they don't take him and harm him.*" If anyone could be said to be living in a Hobbesian state of nature on the well-trodden path to Cassange,[5] by then the busiest slave fair of the Angolan hinterlands, it would be these cave-dwellers—or at least according to Leitão's report.[6] The small vignette he dedicates to them alerts us that plotting the limits of "civil society" was as crucial

---

1 Sebestyén, Vansina (eds.), and Leitão, Angola's Eastern Hinterland, p. 336.

2 As John Thornton and Jean-Luc Vellut remark, the province of Mbondo was often disputed between the Kingdom of Kasanje and the Kingdom of Matamba. In 1681, Kingo a Hanga, then *ndala quissua* [ruler] of Mbondo, contested the election of the new *jaga* of Kasanje, appointing his son as a puppet ruler and allying himself with Matamba to raid the *kilombo* of his opponent. Kingo a Hanga also raided the fair of Cassange in the process, pillaging the cloths and slaves of Luso-African *pumbeiros*. The army sent by the Portuguese in retaliation was routed, and its captain was killed. The ensuing conflict with Mbondo and Matamba lasted until 1683. See Vellut for an account of the fraught relationship between the *ndala quissua* of Mbondo and the *jaga* of Kasanje from Leitão's visit until 1810. Ibid.; MMA XIII, D. 203; Sousa Coutinho, Carta para Ioaquim Iozê Roiz, p. 297–298; Thornton, A History of West Central Africa, p. 181, 208–209; Vellut, Le Royaume de Cassange, p. 117–136.

3 Sebestyén, Vansina (eds.), and Leitão, Angola's Eastern Hinterland, p. 332–333.

4 Ibid., p. 336.

5 As Annabel Brett explains, Hobbes' state of nature presupposed a "brutalization" of "human nature outside the sovereign state," where "man is a wolf to man." While Leitão was probably ignorant of Hobbes' writings, he brutalized the cave dwellers of Mbondo accordingly. Brett, Changes of State, p 5.

6 Hespanha, A cultura jurídica europeia, p. 319; Miller, Way of Death, p. 214; Sebestyén, Vansina (eds.), and Leitão, Angola's Eastern Hinterland, p. 336.

for the Portuguese as surveying the Kwango, collecting trade information, and gathering astronomical data.[7] As stressed in the previous chapter, establishing the limits of (in)commensurability, including defining and negotiating the boundaries of humanity or civil society, was a central aspect of controlling the regime of commensuration that underpinned the intercultural "spaces of correlation" opened by the arrival of the Portuguese in West Central Africa.[8] As this chapter discusses, Leitão's framing of Kasanje and its provinces as an abode of savagery and unnatural abominations had a clear ideological purpose and far-reaching normative implications.

By the mid-eighteenth century, Luso-African slave fairs were no longer seen merely as places where different economic systems, religious and cosmological worldviews, and normative orders were made commensurable as a prerequisite for conversion, and African slaves were used as fungible currency. They were also the sites where certain African groups and their sovereigns were othered, not because of living in a "state of nature" utterly destitute of institutions, but because their social and normative systems were deemed un-natural and against *Ius gentium*, being based on what came to be framed as a 'superstitious' or 'diabolic' social contracts.[9] This form of othering afforded a new basis for doctrines justifying the institutions of slavery, allowing them to persist during the Enlightenment. To start unpacking its specificities, it is helpful to contrast it with how the cave-dwellers of Mbondo were dehumanized, bearing in mind that by the time Leitão described them, theological Natural law was broadly understood in two contrasting forms.[10] As Cătălin Avramescu remarques, one way of understanding Natural law was as if

---

7 Hespanha, A Cultura Jurídica Europeia, p. 319.

8 Fromont, The Art of Conversion; Fromont, Under the sign of the cross, p. 109–123.

9 Hespanha, A cultura jurídica europeia, p. 319; Pietz, The Problem of the Fetish, p. 140–141.

10 These two generic approaches to Natural law do not consider the Augustinian tradition, which tended to equate it with the content of the book of Revelation. It is worth noting that, as Jon Miller remarks, considering the richness and diversity of Natural law jurisprudence and the fact that the thinkers who have contributed to it, "from the Stoics to Aquinas" and up to the present day, have addressed radically different problems, discussions, and contexts, any form of classification is perforce reductionist and arbitrary. For a more detailed discussion of the many different strands of natural jurisprudence of the sixteenth and seventeenth centuries, including Protestant and Humanist, and their impact on later political thought, see Annabel Brett, Brian Tierney, Jean Porter, Perez Zagorin, and the volume edited by Tim Hochstrasser and Peter Schröder. This chapter will not focus on the learned discussions of jurists, theologians, and humanists about the nature and limits of Natural law except when they are directly relevant to discussing the legitimacy of Portuguese institutions of slavery in West Central Africa. Brett, Changes of State; Brett, Liberty, Right and Nature; Hespanha, A Cultura Jurídica Europeia, p. 209–212, 289, 303; Hochstrasser and Schröder, Early Modern Natural Law Theories; Miller, Spinoza and Natural Law, in: Jacobs (ed.), Reason, Religion, and Natural Law, p. 201–221; Porter, Nature as Reason; Tierney, Natural Rights; Zagorin, Hobbes and the Law of Nature.

it was "inscribed on the human heart by the finger of divinity."[11] As the first book of the Digest had defined it, in keeping with Ulpian's *Manual*, Natural law was "*that which nature has taught to all animals; for it is not a law specific to mankind but is common to all animals—land animals, sea animals, and the birds as well.*"[12] From this understanding of Natural law, it followed that to 'other' a human group as existing outside of it, it was necessary to characterize the bodies or lifeworld of its members as grotesque or monstrous inversions of proper nature, where even the elements acted unlawfully (see the 'folk doctrines' discussed in the first chapter).[13]

The Mbondo, Leitão claimed, dwelt in "*wild and rustic forests*" populated by "*wild beasts*" and "*highway robbers,*" where "*detonations of appalling claps of thunder*" resounded and lightening constantly fell for no apparent reason.[14] Living as wolves to other men where nature was "*evil,*" and grotesque, othered them as not fully human—as untouched by God's grace.[15] However, during the Portuguese Late Enlightenment, 'folk doctrines' based on the pre-modern notion that "an inverted world" existed beyond the pale of the city or predicated on the existence of contingent laws of nature lost most of their rhetorical appeal and normative sway. By then, enlightened captain-general and governors such as António Álvares da Cunha would be suspicious of high tales of miracles, diabolic interventions, and natural wonders. As Cardinal and Grand Inquisitor João Cosme da Cunha (1715–1783) would state twenty years later in the new Ordinance of the Portuguese Inquisition of 1774, the latest consensus amongst the elites was that neither "*evil spirits*" nor the "*pacts*" made by "*Feiticeiros, Sortilegos* [cursers], *Diviners, and Judicial Astrologists*" could impact the "*Fundamental Laws of Nature's order, that the Providence of the Supreme Author of said Nature made inviolable, and immutable for the conservation*

---

11 Avramescu, An Intellectual History of Cannibalism, p. 15.

12 In the original: '*Ius naturale est, quod natura omnia animalia docuit: nam ius istud non humani generis proprium, sed omnium animalium, quae in terra, quae in mari nascuntur, avium quoque commune est*' (D. 1.1.1.3 *Ulpianus libro primo institutionum*), *apud* Jakob Urbanik. Hespanha, A cultura jurídica europeia, p. 303–304; Urbanik, On the Uselessness of it All, p. 947; Watson (trans.), The Digest of Justinian, Vol. 1, p. 1.

13 Hespanha, Fazer um império com palavras, in: Barreto Xavier and Nogueira da Silva (eds.), O governo dos outros, p. 71–72.

14 Sebestyén, Vansina (eds.), and Leitão, Angola's Eastern Hinterland, p. 335.

15 This description approximates them of the "natural slaves" theorized by Aristotle. However, Second-Scholastic theologians and jurists of the School of Salamanca had discredited this theory since the debate of Valladolid between Friar Bartolomé de las Casas (1484–1566) and Father Juan Ginés de Sepúlveda (1550–1551) surrounding Amerindian enslavement. Avramescu, An Intellectual History of Cannibalism, p. 9; Calafate, Estudo introdutório I, in: Calafate (ed.), A Escola Ibérica da Paz nas Universidades de Coimbra e Évora, Vol. 1, p. 29; Urbano, The Debate of Valladolid, in: Tellkamp (ed.), A Companion to Early Modern Spanish Imperial Political and Social Thought, p. 222–251.

of the World."[16] In other words, while 'folk doctrines' about West Central Africa's exclusion from Natural law continued to circulate in Angola and its hinterlands, they could not convince learned officials or ground doctrinal or theological apologies for the slave trade.

Another way of conceiving of Natural law, Avramesco explains, was as a "kind of universal agreement between human beings" or, as Cicero put it in the third book of *De re publica* (54 BCE–51 BCE), as "*right reason in agreement with nature* [...] *of universal application*."[17] In keeping with this Stoic conception, as Cicero concluded in *De legibus*, "*this reason, when firmly fixed and fully developed in the human mind, is Law*."[18] Since the advent of Second Scholasticism, a different way of othering African groups originated from this understanding of Natural law. This mode followed St. Thomas Aquinas, perceiving Natural law as a *recta ratio* closer to *Ius gentium* than to the physical laws of nature.[19] As Annabel Brett remarks, the School of Salamanca's Dominican scholars Francisco de Vitoria (1483–1546) and Domingo de Soto (1494–1560) reworked St. Aquinas' doctrines of Natural law to argue that *Ius gentium* derived from natural reasoning, finding the source of its "positivity in the consensus of all mankind."[20] In de Soto's words, this consensus did not require "all human beings to gather together into one place" to agree on Natural law "because reason teaches it to individuals."[21] In keeping with Dominican Neo-Thomist doctrines, later elaborated and reworked by the Jesuits, it was reason (*ratio*), more precisely the "ability to reason towards an end," that generated both "natural rights" and *Ius gentium*, even grounding 'pagan' or 'gentilic' *princeps' dominium* over their realms, which was withheld from animals acting out of mere "natural instinct."[22]

When discussing the behavior of the Mbundu porters who accompanied him to the forests of Mbondo, Leitão claimed that when faced with danger, they sought the "*salvation of their lives in flight*," climbing "*trees with the same nimbleness as*

---

16 Cosme da Cunha, Regimento do Santo Officio, p. 122.

17 In the original, "*recta ratio naturae congruens, diffusa in omnes*." Avramescu, An Intellectual History of Cannibalism, p. 15, 266; Cicero, Keyes (trans.), De Re Publica. De Legibus, p. 210–211.

18 In the original, "*eadem ratio cum est in hominis mente confirmata et confecta est lex*." Cicero, Keyes (trans.), De Re Publica. De Legibus, p. 316–317; Hespanha, A cultura jurídica europeia, p. 304–305.

19 Porter, Nature as Reason.

20 Brett, Changes of State, p. 12–13, 23; Brett, Liberty, Right and Nature, p. 94–95; Calafate, Estudo introdutório I, in: Calafate (ed.), A Escola Ibérica da Paz nas Universidades de Coimbra e Évora, Vol. 1, p. 17–49; Koskenniemi, Vitoria and Us, p. 119–138; Pich, Probabilismo e escravidão negra, p. 17–67.

21 Brett, Changes of State, p. 23.

22 Calafate, Estudo introdutório I, in: Calafate (ed.), A Escola Ibérica da Paz nas Universidades de Coimbra e Évora, Vol. 1, p. 17–49.

apes or monkeys" and running "*naked without fear of rains or winds.*"[23] Because they lacked "*the judgment to distinguish between the bigger and the lesser peril,*" Leitão concluded, sometimes they "*put themselves in the mouth of the animals*" they were trying to escape. In the case of the Mbundu porters, therefore, it was their apparently 'irrational' reactions that marked them as absolute 'others' to Leitão. However, although they were on par with the cave dwellers of Mbondo, this was not due to their supposed existence in a Hobbesian state of nature where even nature was outside of God's grace. Rather, their 'otherness' stemmed from their lack of reason (*ratio*). Both forms of othering, the one directed at the cave-dwellers of Mbondo and the one directed at the Mbundu porters, co-exist in Leitão's narrative, the first based on a 'folk physics' that was hard to sustain in learned circles, the latter on a 'folk psychology,' a theory about the other's capacity for rational agency and motivation, that remained convincing.

As Avramesco describes, during the Enlightenment, countless thought experiments about the limits of Natural law were penned and intensely debated, most figuring an extreme cast of tropes, such as the "anthropophagous cannibal," the cruel "Oriental despot," or the incestuous "princely monster."[24] The growing "encyclopedia of bizarre customs" or 'list of aberrations" they were based on, he concludes, was to serve as a laboratory for thought experiments that would allow European jurists, political philosophers, and theologians to distill the "new ingredients" of an emerging body of positive, "political laws" out of this "irrational" substratum.[25] In other words, while European scholars lost interest in rustic accounts of miracles and natural prodigies, assuming that the laws of nature were everywhere the same, they became avid consumers of outlandish descriptions of African uses and customs.[26]

In the Portuguese case, however, when similar aberrations or bizarre customs were described as taking place in West Central Africa, the narrators often had more prosaic concerns in mind. At the time of Leitão's trip, the "Jesuit theory of slavery" that had underpinned the slave trade in the Lusophone Atlantic for the last two centuries was fast losing influence.[27] Moreover, the Neo-Thomist understanding that a "natural order" established by God provided the underlying framework that fastened together the "kaleidoscopic" normative constellation of the Portuguese

---

23 Sebestyén, Vansina (eds.), and Leitão, Angola's Eastern Hinterland, p. 335.

24 Avramescu, An Intellectual History of Cannibalism, p. 3, 17, 31, 44–45, 50.

25 Ibid., p. 14–40.

26 For an account of how this interest drove the creation of a "colonial library" and the cementing of an "idea of Africa," see Valentin Mudimbe. Mudimbe, The Idea of Africa; Mudimbe, The Invention of Africa.

27 Cagle, Imperial Tensions, Colonial Contours, in: Martínez-San Miguel and Arias (eds.), The Routledge Hispanic Studies Companion to Colonial Latin America and the Caribbean, p. 216.

"Old Regime" was also declining.[28] After years of anti-Jesuit agitation, the Society of Jesus was about to be expelled from the Portuguese Kingdom and Empire, including the Captaincy of Angola (1759). Moreover, Portuguese *leis pátrias* [laws of the fatherland] and royal enactments and ordinances were quickly ascending to the top of the new hierarchy of sources of law pushed by royalist jurists and enlightened reformers, as discussed in the first chapter.[29] This chapter explores how the transition from a regime of normative knowledge about slavery, grounded in Second-Scholastic doctrines and methodologies, to a new post-Enlightenment normative framework, impacted the institutions of slavery and their justification within the Portuguese Empire.[30] Moreover, it explores how West Central Africans were othered when claims that they lived in an inverted world outside of God's grace were no longer reason enough to justify the 'abuses' committed against them or acceptable according to a naturalistic framing of nature.[31] As Natural law was secularized under the impact of jus-rationalism and natural philosophy, the foundations of the othering of Africans shifted accordingly, now focusing on 'aberrant' social contracts and despotic or cannibalistic sovereigns.

This transition is already signaled by Carl von Linnaeus' account of different human races in *The System of Nature* (1735). In this influential treatise, he claimed that a lack of rationality (*recta ratio*) marked even the Africans he did not consider "*monstrous*."[32] This is evidenced by Linnaeus' description of their social, political, and normative systems being "*governed by caprice*."[33] William Pietz explains that

28 Hespanha, A cultura jurídica europeia, p. 149–152, 212.

29 Boxer, O Império Colonial Português, p. 186; Carvalho, Um Iluminismo português; Castro, Enlightened Absolutism, p. 296–364; Hespanha, A cultura jurídica europeia, p. 335–336; Rosa, O Iluminismo, p. 361–383; Wehling, Uma solução setecentista, p. 146–164.

30 As Brett and José Eisenberg remark, Dominican opinions about the legitimacy of the Portuguese slave trade did not differ radically from Jesuit ones. Both dialogued with St. Thomas Aquinas' synthesis of Aristotelian philosophy and Christian theology. Brett, Changes of State, p. 94–95; Duve, Historia del Derecho, p. 1–60; Duve, Legal History as a History of the Translation of Knowledge of Normativity, p. 1–12; Duve, Legal History as an Observation, p. 1–10; Eisenberg, Cultural Encounters, Theoretical Adventures, p. 375–396; Saavedra et al., Historical Regimes of Normativity. Part 3; Saavedra et al., Why "Historical Regimes of Normativity"?

31 As Calafate explains, in their lessons at the University of Coimbra, Friar Martín de Ledesma (1509–1574) and Father Fernando Pérez (1530–1595) argued that all "men that lived like beasts" could be forced to obey orders, but not so those men who respected the "laws" of an instituted civil power. In this, the Dominican and Jesuit followed the arguments of Friar Domingo de Soto's *De iustitia et iure* (1556). Calafate, Estudo introdutório I, in: Calafate (ed.), A Escola Ibérica da Paz nas Universidades de Coimbra e Évora, Vol. 1, p. 28–29.

32 Linnaeus, Race and the Enlightenment, in: Eze (ed.), The God-Given Order of Nature, p. 13.

33 Linnaeus divided the species *Homo sapiens* into five sub-species or races: the "*four-footed, mute, hairy*" "*Wildman*;" the "*copper-colored, choleric, erect*" "*American*," "*regulated by customs*;" the "*fair, sanguine, brawny*" "*European*," "*governed by laws*;" the "*sooty, melancholy, rigid*" Asians, "*governed*

Linnaeus' "paradoxical idea of Africans generating a social order out of a chaotic principle" was derived from earlier Portuguese and Jesuit accounts of their use and faith in *feitiços*, signaling the emergence of a perverse feedback loop. As a "general theory of fetichism" was synthesized by Charles de Brosses in 1757 and adopted by Central European *philosophes* and naturalists, Portuguese *estrangeirado* elites, oblivious to the fact that their countrymen's prejudiced descriptions had provided the evidence for its construction, adopted it as a heuristic.[34] As discussed in the first chapter, in his pioneering etymological dictionary of the Portuguese language, the *estrangeirado* Rafael Bluteau (1638–1734) traced the genealogy of *feitiço* to "*Fetiche*," inverting the history of the concept and thus reifying prejudices about West Africans' lack of rationality as a factual description.[35] In the meantime, as the following pages and the next chapter explore in greater detail, African anti-sorcery ordeals and the rationale behind the exchanges made in prestige spheres of exchange were mobilized to justify the redemption as slaves of freeborn Africans from African polities ruled by cannibals or despots.[36] As Pietz summarizes, while, at a first historical moment, these ordeals and commercial practices were accepted as central to the functioning of the slave trade in slave fairs controlled by Africans, at a second one, they became central to justifying the trade itself.[37]

As Judith Spicksley explains, by the middle of the eighteenth century, two of the titles of just enslavement put forward by Jesuit theologians and jurists were particularly contested by Portuguese magistrates, secretaries of the state, and other high-ranking officeholders.[38] Namely, voluntary enslavement, including debt bondage

---

by opinions;" and the "*Black, phlegmatic, relaxed*" Africans, "*governed by caprice.*" Besides these, Linnaeus identified several "*Monstrous*" variants, according to "*climate or art:*" the "*Mountaineer,*" the "*Patagonian,*" the "*Hottentot,*" the "*American,*" the "*Chinese,*" and the "*Canadian.*" According to his system, neither the "*wildman*" sub-species nor "*monstrous*" variants of *Homo sapiens* had a form of government. Ibid., p. 13–14.

34 Pietz, The Problem of the Fetish, p. 5–7, 140–141.

35 Bluteau, Feitiço, in: Bluteau, Vocabulario Portuguez & Latino, Vol. 4, p. 66.

36 As Calafate makes clear, this line of defense of just enslavement also had its roots in Second-Scholastic doctrines of just war. For instance, as Calafate's translations of Father Pérez *De bello* (1588) shows, the Jesuit considered it was "*against Natural law to kill innocent people, whether indigenous or foreign, either to eat them or to sacrifice them to idols.*" Therefore, those who committed these acts were "*committing an extremely grave injustice*" and could be "*defeated by us, who are part of the human race, as the most unjust aggressors of the human race.*" Calafate, Estudo introdutório I, in: Calafate (ed.), A Escola Ibérica da Paz nas Universidades de Coimbra e Évora, Vol. 1, p. 32.

37 Pietz, The Problem of the Fetish, p. 141.

38 Mattias Kaufmann remarks that the title of "selling oneself or being sold" by one's parents due to extreme necessity was already questioned by Father Luís de Molina. Kaufmann, Slavery between Law, Morality, and Economy, in: Kaufmann and Aichele (eds.), A Companion to Luis de Molina, p. 197–201; Spicksley, Contested Enslavement, p. 247–275; Zeron, Les Jésuites et le commerce d'esclaves, in: Hebrard (ed.), Brésil quatre siècles d'esclavage, p. 82; Zeron, Linha de fé, p. 206.

and even in cases of extreme necessity (e.g., to obtain food in times of hunger or safety during wars and epidemics), and enslavement in the aftermath of a just war.[39] As Russell-Wood explains, the latter condition was predicated on St. Aquinas' doctrine of "just war," which determined the basic requirements for a conflict to be considered just, i. e. "right authority, sufficient cause, and right intention."[40] While these prerequisites left no margin for doubts about the legitimacy of unprovoked wars against Muslins and, after the papal bull *Dum diversas* (June 18, 1452), against all "enemies of Christianity;" in Angola, in theory, military campaigns against Mbundu or BaKongo states or Ovimbundu chieftains had to be endorsed as just wars by the War Council to yield legitimate slaves.[41] As Captain-General and Governor Francisco Inocêncio de Sousa Coutinho (1726–1780) remarked in a letter to José Vieira de Araújo, captain major of Benguela in 1772, it was impossible to "*heal barbarity with barbarism*," so he reminded him that wars had to have a "*just cause*," be the last resort, and be commanded by "*Generals, who know how to lead troops, but also know the limits of just offense, and necessary defense, Regulated by Divine Laws, and the customs of all Nations*."[42] Given their lack of 'right' authority, legitimate intention, and minimal knowledge of Canon law, it was always dubious whether wars between non-Christian African rulers could result in legitimate slaves.[43]

As for voluntary enslavement, as José Eisenberg remarks, after two centuries of legal and theological debates about the institution of voluntary slavery in Brazil, a vast corpus of jurisprudence about the voluntary enslavement of Amerindians had accumulated.[44] Already in 1694, Jesuit Father António Vieira (1608–1697) argued that, concerning Amerindians, "*any pact which entails perpetually forfeiting one's liberty is invalid, for even though one is master of his liberty, nobody is the owner of his body*."[45] While the extent to which he intended this indictment to impact the West Central African context is debatable, given Father Vieira's apology for the African slave trade, it eroded the institution's legitimacy.[46] In the case of debt bondage, Spicksley claims that, as it became obsolete in most of Europe, Portuguese observers of African judicial systems grew increasingly weary of it, eventually framing debt enslavement as a barbarous infraction against Natural law, now reconceived

39 Spicksley, Contested Enslavement, p. 250.
40 Russel-Wood, Iberian Expansion and the Issue of Black Slavery, p. 23.
41 Ibid., p. 24–25; Marcocci, A Consciência de um Império, p. 46–50.
42 Sousa Coutinho, Carta para Iozê Vieira de Araujo, p. 379–382.
43 Russel-Wood, Iberian Expansion and the Issue of Black Slavery, p. 23.
44 Eisenberg, Cultural Encounters, Theoretical Adventures, p. 375–396.
45 Ibid., p. 395.
46 Zeron, Vieira em movimento, p. 171–192.

according to a jus-rationalist paradigm.[47] Case in point, in 1771, for instance, Sousa Coutinho issued a *bando* expressly "*forbidding, that Freeborn Blacks be pawned, or mortgaged for Civil debts*."[48] As Joseph Miller suggests, an alternative explanation for Sousa Coutinho's diligence might be that the persistence of African-controlled prestige spheres of exchange, where rights over free women, dependents, and slaves were brokered, constituted a challenge to the increasingly differentiated Portuguese economic system.[49] In other words, African-controlled debt-peonage offered an economic and normative alternative to Portuguese-controlled credit systems (as either a pawn or their corporate kin group mortgaged their freedom instead of becoming indebted), and, as such, needed to be dismantled for purely economic reasons.[50] As explored in the next chapter, the mid-eighteenth-century push against what was perceived as debt enslavement can also be read as an attempt to harmonize the protracted temporalities of African gift exchange and debt-peonage with the faster pace of the Atlantic credit-based markets.[51]

In any case, when Leitão reached Kasanje, having obtained the slave status in commutation for the death penalty or execution was the better-accepted justification for the enslavement of the Africans 'ransomed' in the Angolan hinterlands (the doctrine of *partus sequitur ventrem* never being questioned).[52] James Duffy remarks that the term "*resgates*" was already used for Portuguese slave markets in West Africa during the late fifteenth century.[53] This term always marked slave fairs as places where slaves were supposedly redeemed or ransomed to avoid death penalties or being killed as captured war prisoners, being a crucial ideological tool for justifying legitimate enslavement. After a century of internal criticisms leveled against the Portuguese slave trade, in the mid-eighteenth century, the legal foundations of the theory of *resgate* or redemption were elaborated in a more sophisticated manner, becoming predicated on the laws of the fatherland instead of Second-Scholastic doctrines.[54]

---

47 Spicksley, Contested Enslavement, p. 247–275; Spicksley, The Decline of Slavery for Debt in Western Europe, in: Cavaciocchi (ed.), Serfdom and Slavery in the European Economy, p. 465–486.

48 AHU, CU, Angola, Box 55, D. 5058; Sousa Coutinho, Carta para Ioaquim Iozê Roiz, p. 297–298.

49 Miller, Way of Death, p. 69–70.

50 Antunes and Vos, Port Cities and Commodities, in: Curry-Machado et al. (eds.), The Oxford Handbook of Commodity History, p. 135.

51 Miller, Way of Death, p. 49–53, 58.

52 Alencastro, O trato dos viventes, p. 171–172; Sweet, Black Robes and "Black Destiny," p. 87–133; Zeron, Les Jésuites et le commerce d'esclaves, in: Hebrard (ed.), Brésil quatre siècles d'esclavage, p. 82; Zeron, Linha de fé, p. 206.

53 Duffy, Portuguese Africa, p. 140.

54 Fragoso, Na Bahia setecentista, p. 68–105; Silva, A escravidão no discurso de Manoel Ribeiro Rocha, p. 1–42; Wehling, Uma solução setecentista, p. 146–164.

Father Manuel Ribeiro Rocha's (1687–1745) *Etíope resgatado, empenhado, sustentado, corrigido, instruído e libertado* [Ethiopian Ransomed, Indentured, Sustained, Corrected, Educated, and Liberated] (1758) exemplifies the renewed wave of criticism of the period and its almost immediate dialectical sublation.[55] A priest and lawyer born in Portugal but residing in Bahia, Rocha's critique of the institutions of slavery echoed Father Miguel Garcia's.[56] Just like Father Garcia and Father Luis de Molina, Father Rocha had no qualms with the extant modalities of "*justos titulos* [just titles]" that grounded the slave owners' *dominium* over the freedom of their slaves: being captured in "*public wars*" if these were "*just*" and pitted "*one Prince against another*;" being condemned to "*privação da liberdade* [loss of freedom]" for committing a "*serious offense*;" or being sold by "*the father, for extreme indigence and need*."[57] Father Rocha even argued that contrary to the opinion of Father Molina, wars between African "*Princes*" were just, even if they did not observe the "*Law of the Gospels because* [Princes] *observe Natural law and the law of peoples*" as they could have only attained the exalted rank of *princeps* through God's grace and will.[58] However, as with both the other two critics of the Portuguese slave trade, he believed that most slaves sold in Brazil were illegitimate because "*thousands and thousands of African Blacks* [had been] *barbarously captured by their countrymen, stolen by acts of piracy, mischief, hoaxes, and other similar means*"[59] in regions that

---

55 Fragoso, Na Bahia setecentista, p. 68–105; Rocha, Ethiope resgatado; Russel-Wood, Iberian Expansion and the Issue of Black Slavery, p. 38; Silva, A escravidão no discurso de Manoel Ribeiro Rocha, p. 1–42; Spicksley, Contested Enslavement, p. 253; Wehling, Uma solução setecentista, p. 146–164.

56 According to the inquisitorial license annexed to *Ethiopian Ransomed…*, Father Rocha had been born in Lisbon and studied Canon law at the University of Coimbra. Besides this license, the book also includes a note of approval from the Society of Jesus and other congregations. In all, these very approving notes prove that Father Rocha's criticism was not considered as revolutionary as Father Garcia's. Rocha, Ethiope resgatado; Wehling, Uma solução setecentista, p. 146–164.

57 Rocha, Ethiope resgatado.

58 This last claim was rooted in Augustinian theology. In *The City of God* (426), St. Augustine of Hippo (354–430) builds on the passage "*by me kings reign, and tyrants possess the land*" (Proverbs 8:15) to advocate for the legitimacy of constituted powers. In his words, "*power and domination are not given even to such men* [tyrants] *save by the providence of the most high God, when He judges that the state of human affairs is worthy of such lords*." Ibid.; Augustinus, Evans and Bettenson (trans.), City of God, p. 102.

59 Arno Wehling remarks that Father Rocha grounds his list of "*unjust customs*" in a work published by the Jesuit Father Fernão Rebelo in 1608. In keeping with it, "*violence, fraud, offenses committed by the parents, descendants, relatives, wife or husband, unjust wars, assaults*" and "*hoaxes*" could not be the basis of just uses and customs. According to this doctrine, as Spicksley remarks, African notions of corporate responsibility, or the corporate ownership of rights over free women, dependents, and slaves, cannot be the basis of sound normative claims as their exchange as a social currency would be framed by the Portuguese as punishing the wives or children for the "sins" of the father, husband, or other relative. Spicksley concludes that this misunderstanding created a lot of tension

were "*uncultured, rude, barbarous, and inhumane,* [...] *where neither Natural law, nor the laws of nations, nor even the laws of humanity were observed.*"[60] By 1758, the Kingdom of Kasanje was considered a quintessential example of the latter, as the Mbangala had been othered as non-human cannibals for over a century.[61]

According to Father Rocha, however, the solution to the problem posed by the indeterminacy of the legitimacy of the *dominium* slaveowners had over the freedom of their slaves was not, as Father Garcia had advocated, to abandon the institutions of slavery completely, but rather to reshape their legal and moral foundations. In his words, there was a way of "*legitimately continuing to trade and possess captive Blacks.*"[62] While Father Rocha agreed that wrongly or dubiously enslaved Africans should be immediately liberated as "*ingenuos* [freeborn]," he argued against Father Molina that Catholic merchants were entitled to "*resgatar* [redeem] *by commerce*" slaves whom Africans had wrongly enslaved and that those "*redeemed*" in this manner "*contracted*" a debt with their purchasers.[63] Therefore, even those liberated as freeborn because the wrongness of their enslavement was subsequently established in court were still to serve "*as slaves*" until they "*paid the sum spent for their redemption*" and maintenance.[64] However, the hold over their freedom could not be

---

between African and Portuguese normative systems from the late eighteenth century onwards. SPICKSLEY, Contested Enslavement, p. 247–275; WEHLING, Uma solução setecentista, p. 146–164.

60 Moreover, as Father Barreira had argued in 1583, Father Rocha stated that Africans would not "*consent*" to the "*examination of the justice*" of the title they had over their slaves. ROCHA, Ethiope resgatado, p. 19–20; WEHLING, Uma solução setecentista, p. 151.

61 Miller argues that the exaggeration or fabrication of Mbangala cannibalism was a cover for their illicit trade with slave smugglers. According to this interpretation, merchants who complained to Portuguese officials about losing slaves to the cannibals avoided the custom house in Luanda and traded them directly with *brasílicos*, São Tomé planters, or merchants of other European nations. HEINTZE, Contra as teorias simplificadoras, in: SANCHES (ed.), Portugal não é um país pequeno, p. 215–228; HENRIQUES, A invenção da antropofagia africana, p. 51–80; MILLER, Kings and Kinsmen, p. 199–200; SOUZA CORREA, A antropofagia na África Equatorial, p. 9–41; THOMPSON, The Making of Quilengues, p. 81–87; THORNTON, Cannibals, Witches, and Slave Traders, p. 273–294.

62 ROCHA, Ethiope resgatado, p. 107.

63 Roberto Pich notes that Father Molina had already developed his analysis of the institutions of slavery as a critique of its "commutative justice." This shifted the focus of the debate from discussions about just war doctrines or Aristotelian natural slavery to the slave trade. Ibid., p. 47–57, 139–140; PICH, Probabilismo e escravidão negra, p. 17–67.

64 Father Rocha stipulated that the price paid "*during the first sale at the Customs House or the merchants*" door should be considered a benchmark. Taking into consideration that, by the middle of the eighteenth century, slaves were still bought in Angola with local general-purpose money, such as cloth, salt, and bundles of commodities, and first sold for bullion currencies in Brazil, this would amount to making the enslaved responsible for guaranteeing the profit made by using their transference as a form of wealth extraction. Moreover, Father Rocha stipulated that "*redeemed*" Africans had to pay for any expenses made teaching them "*an art or craft*" and that their offspring would have to serve their redeemers as slaves until the age of 25. As for the redeemed, Father

conceptualized as a form of *dominium* but as a "*jure pignoris*," a temporary "*pledge and retention rights*" over their freedom.[65] This was the case, Father Rocha argued, because, at the precise moment of purchase, slave dealers unwittingly entered a "*contrato de redenção* [redemption contract]" with the slaves they were buying.[66] This contract, he continued, was a "*minor part*" of the "*major*" contract celebrated during the purchase of enslaved Africans.[67] It remained valid even if the latter was nullified because the 'just' enslavement of slaves bought from Africans could not be sufficiently proved. If, as Father Molina had argued, the contract of purchase was not "*constitutive of the state of slavery*," Father Rocha concluded that it was constitutive of a state of extreme asymmetric dependency analogous to it that could still provide the basis for the plantation economy of Brazil and the Atlantic trade in human beings.[68]

At the *foro interno*, Father Rocha argued that Portuguese merchants and slave owners committed a great "*sin*" by trading in the services and rights over pledged persons as if they "*were true, legitimate slaves*" because by doing so, they recognized as "*just, legitimate, rational, and human*" African normative systems he deemed outside of "*Natural law*" and *Ius gentium*.[69] While it was probably true that Luso-African merchants and *pumbeiros* consistently traded in rights over persons considered dependents and pawns by their African partners as if they were trading in slaves, by condemning this practice, Father Rocha's aim was not to advocate for respecting the limits on enslavement imposed by African normative systems, as Father Molina had argued in 1593.[70] Rather, his point was to condemn African normative systems for allegedly enabling Africans to do what the Europeans were doing, i. e. trading illegitimately enslaved persons as commodities or currencies. In other words, instead of recognizing centuries of self-interested misrepresentation of African institutions and pleading for their normative limits on enslavement to be respected or for wrongly enslaved Africans to be gracefully rescued, Father Rocha deepened this misrepresentation. He claimed that African normative systems' unjust, illegitimate, and irrational nature enabled Europeans to base their institutions on the brokerage of redemption contracts.[71] African prestige spheres of exchange

---

Rocha set the limit of 20 years for their services. Rocha, Ethiope resgatado, p. 79, 94–95, 99–103, 124–134.

65 Ibid., p. 74–75.

66 Ibid., p. 124–129, 131.

67 Ibid., p. 124–134.

68 Hespanha, Luís de Molina e a escravização dos negros, p. 940; Rocha, Ethiope resgatado, p. 72–74.

69 Rocha, Ethiope resgatado, foreword.

70 Hespanha, Luís de Molina e a escravização dos negros, p. 937–960; Miller, Way of Death, p. 69–70.

71 Father Molina's *Tractatus de iustitia et de iure* (1593) paved the ground for this solution. While he argued that, in theory, ransomed persons should be gracefully freed if the death punishment

where rights over people were exchanged were thus misconstrued as forums where the sale of unfairly enslaved Africans as commodities took place, warranting the 'ransom' of these de jure free persons who could nevertheless be de facto forced to provide services to Europeans "*as slaves*."[72]

Father Rocha's "innovative solution" must be framed considering the rising popularity of the "language or vocabulary of contract" during the Enlightenment.[73] As Carole Pateman and Charles Mills have demonstrated, by then, several "political fictions" about the "original" social contract not only provided "an account of the creation of the public sphere of civil freedom" but also allowed "the sphere of natural subjection" to be "separated out as [a] non-political sphere," creating a "juridical space for non-Europeans as a separate category of beings."[74] Considering these reflections, Father Rocha's most significant and enduring innovation was not his attempt to reduce all problematic slave-purchase contracts to morally and legally unimpeachable redemption contracts, remedying the challenges posed by the slave trade to commutative justice. Instead, it was grounding the legitimacy of a new modality of extreme asymmetric dependency on the delimitation of African spheres of sociability and normativity that Europeans now framed, in keeping with the increasingly popular theories about African fetichism, as being governed by "the superstitious equivalent of the laws of contract found in civilized societies."[75]

In theory, this "superstitious equivalent" would allow groups to be bound by social norms and civil institutions that paradoxically kept them in a state of natural subjection.[76] By 'redeeming' Africans from beyond the outer limits of Natural law and *Ius gentium* and bringing them into 'true' civil society, merchants were to acquire, through "*redemption contracts*," temporary rights over their freedom and

---

they had been saved from had been unfair, he conceded that "*considering men were jealous of their possessions*," and, therefore, needed economic incentives to act morally, it was permissible to allow the ransoming of those wrongly condemned to death in exchange for their services. Hespanha, Luís de Molina e a escravização dos negros, p. 946.

72 Rocha, Ethiope resgatado, p. 132, 134.

73 Wehling and Charles Boxer remark that Father Rocha's juridical innovation was transforming the "enslavement bond into a contractual one." His comments about how redeemed slaves were to be sustained, corrected, and educated were either based on the *First Constitutions of the Archdiocese of Bahia* (1707) or the Jesuit Jorge Benci's (1650–1708) *Christian economy of masters in the government of slaves* (1705). As for Father Rocha's arguments in favor of 'just' slavery and against the legitimacy of owning slaves whose legitimate enslavement was not sufficiently proved, they followed Father Fernão Perez, Father Gaspar Gonçalves, and Father Luis de Molina's replies to Father Garcia. Boxer, Um panfleto raro; Höpfl and Thompson, The History of Contract as a Motif, p. 927; Wehling, Uma solução setecentista, p. 146–164.

74 Mills, The Racial Contract, p. 26; Pateman, The Sexual Contract, p. 3, 10–11; Pateman and Mills, Contract and Domination, p. 82.

75 Pietz, The Problem of the Fetish, p. 141.

76 Pateman, The Sexual Contract, p. 3, 10–11.

services based on a *jure pignoris*.[77] If Father Molina had argued against Aristotelian notions of natural slavery, claiming that African societies were within the pale of theological Natural law and *Ius gentium*, Father Rocha incorporated folk doctrines about African societies' otherness into his apology of ransom, firmly situating them outside of civil society.[78] He achieved this by emphasizing African normative systems' supposed unfairness, unreasonableness, and illegitimacy, building on Father Molina's proto-ethnographic accounts and doctrinal arguments to reach diametrically opposite conclusions.[79] In keeping with Father Rocha's doctrine, slave fairs were the interface between two normative spheres that no longer had to be made commensurable for the slave trade to flow but had to be articulated in their incommensurability.

In practical terms, this meant that the 'redemption' or 'ransom' of Africans would have to occur in areas outside of Portuguese jurisdiction or those of Christian African sovereigns such as the *Mwene Kongo* or vassal Mbundu *sobas* because these *Princeps*' domains would be within reach of Natural law and *Ius gentium*. As Sousa Coutinho explained to the captain majors of Benguela and Caconda, the regent of Novo Redondo, and the ordinary judges of the new settlements he established in the 1770s, problematic forms of enslavement according to African norms were to be prohibited only within the jurisdiction of the Portuguese or their vassals, as interfering with the normative systems outside of that sphere would "*drain the means of Commerce in this Kingdom*" and "*expose the unfortunate to die eaten by those who cannot sell them*."[80] In other words, the morality and legality of slave extraction became predicated on the existence of areas under the direct jurisdiction of 'cannibals' or African 'despots,' whose superstitious social contract perverted Natural law and whose leaders could not be mistaken for graceful *Princeps*.

In spaces entirely within civil society, the jurist Pascoal José de Melo Freire (1738–1798) concluded in 1791 that "*Black slaves*" were illegitimate and no more than "*tolerated*" according to the laws of the fatherland.[81] There was no legal or normative basis whatsoever to keep "*them as slaves in true ownership*" or have *dominium* over their freedoms. However, Melo Freire reasoned, the "*direito de resgatar* [right to redeem]" and the contractual obligation those who had been "*redeemed*" incurred towards their redeemers were venerable institutions of "*Portuguese Civil Law*," received from *Ius commune* and Visigothic codes, and later confirmed by

---

77 Rocha, Ethiope resgatado, p. 124–134.

78 Calafate, Estudo introdutório I, in: Calafate (ed.), A Escola Ibérica da Paz nas Universidades de Coimbra e Évora, Vol. 1, p. 17–49; Hespanha, Luís de Molina e a escravização dos negros, p. 958; Pich, Probabilismo e escravidão negra, p. 17–67.

79 Rocha, Ethiope resgatado, foreword.

80 Sousa Coutinho, Carta para Ioaquim Iozê Roiz, p. 297–298.

81 Freire, Meneses (trans.), Instituições de Direito Civil, p. 18.

statutory laws and royal ordinances.[82] Melo Freire had been appointed substitute lecturer of the chair of "*Direito Pátrio* [Law of the Fatherland]" after the Pombaline reform of the University of Coimbra in 1772.[83] Soon, he became its chair (1781) and a member of the Royal Academy of Sciences of Lisbon (1780). His four-volume *Institutiones Juris Civilis Lusitani, cum Publici tum Privati* [Portuguese Civil Law Institutions, both Public and Private] (1789–1794), where he made the above comments, was written in as part of the statutory requirements of his chair and served as its official textbook from 1805 to 1841, having a considerable impact on Brazil where it inspired the first systematizations of Civil law after independence (1822).[84] Although Father Rocha's *Ethiopian Ransomed…* was not widely circulated, Melo Freire's authoritative comments contrasting the illegitimacy of slavery to the legitimate right redeemers had over the services of the slaves they redeemed prove that Father Rocha's argument had captured the spirit of the times, indicating a major doctrinal shift.[85] For slavery to survive as a 'tolerated' institution after the 1750s, an outside sphere governed by norms incommensurable with Natural law and the 'law of the fatherland' had to be delineated. This is the space that Manoel Correia Leitão had just entered, where tropes about the *jagas*' cannibalism and shared beliefs about *feitiçaria* and anti-sorcery ordeals turned the Luso-African slave market of Cassange into a site of othering and 'redemption.' It is to the historical construction of these tropes that we now turn.

5.2 The *Jagas*' Debut as Historical Actors

In 1567, King Bernardo I of Kongo (1534–1567) was killed during a war of conquest he was waging in the rich raffia textile-producing lands east of his core provinces.[86] This mishap was but a prelude to the upheavals that his kingdom was about to suffer at the hands of his slaughterers. Soon after, the "*Jaguas*," which was how the Portuguese first referred to the warriors who had defeated the *Mwene Kongo* in battle, launched a brutal full-scale attack against the Kingdom of Kongo, as graphically described by Filippo Pigafetta (1533–1604) in his *Relatione del Reame*

---

82 Ibid., p. 14–15.

83 Fernandes, Freire, Pascoal de Melo.

84 As Paulo Manuel Merêa remarks, Melo Freire's "admirable work" was true "to the spirit of the Law of Good Reason and the Pombaline Statutes" of the University of Coimbra, reducing "the country's legislation to a regular and easy-to-understand plan, [and] exposing it in a compendium form" that was as accessible as it was influential. Fernandes, Freire, Pascoal de Melo; Merêa, Resumo das lições de História do Direito Português, p. 164; Santos, Melo Freire, p. 163–190.

85 Boxer, Um panfleto raro; Wehling, Uma solução setecentista, p. 146–164.

86 MMA VI, D. 101, p. 294–295; Thornton, A History of West Central Africa, p. 74.

del Congo et delle circonvicine contrade [Report on the Kingdom of Kongo and neighboring countries] (1591).[87] Pigafetta's informant was Duarte Lopes, a New Christian of Portuguese origin who had been sent by Bernardo's successor, King Álvaro I of Kongo (1530–1587), to Rome as ambassador.[88] As Lopes' accounts describe, the *Jagas* or "*Giacas*" followed "*the style of the Arabs and the old Nomads,*" "*feeding on human flesh,*" and "*stealing all the countries through which they pass.*"[89] An astute diplomatic intervention, Pigafetta and Lopes' report not only framed the questionable enthronization of Álvaro I of Kongo as legitimate but struck all the right chords to plea for European reinforcements and establish the war against the "*Giacas*" (whom Thornton identifies as the Yaka) as just.[90] Meanwhile, forced by the Yaka invaders to flee his capital to the islets on the Congo River next to the Port of Mpinda, Álvaro I had also asked for the help of King Sebastião of Portugal (1554–1578).[91] The young king assisted him promptly with an expeditionary force of 600 soldiers commanded by Francisco de Gouveia Sottomaior, then captain and governor of São Tomé.[92] From the Portuguese perspective, Sottomaior's campaign (1571–1576) was a tremendous military, political, and economic success.[93] After defeating the Yaka and reconducting Álvaro I to his *mbanza* or capital, the governor of São Tomé not only secured his permission to collect enough *nzimbu* from the Island of Luanda to cover his war efforts (a privilege the Portuguese soon abused)[94] but also secured the *Mwene Kongo*'s support in conquering the Kingdom of Ndongo

---

87 José Matias Delgado provides an additional list of Portuguese manuscript sources about this attack in footnote 1 to the first volume of António de Oliveira Cadornega's *General History of the Wars of Angola*. Cadornega, História geral das guerras angolanas, Vol. 1, p. 12–13; Pigafetta and Lopes, Relatione del Reame di Congo, p. 59–61; Thornton, A History of West Central Africa, p. 74–76.

88 Thornton, A History of West Central Africa, p. 75–76.

89 Pigafetta and Lopes, Relatione del Reame di Congo, p. 59.

90 Thornton, A History of West Central Africa, p. 75–76.

91 Green, A Fistful of Shells, p. 217–218; MMA III, D. 17; Thornton, A History of West Central Africa, p. 76–77; Thornton, Firearms, Diplomacy, and Conquest in Angola, in: Lee (ed.), Empires and Indigenes, p. 167–192.

92 MMA III, D. 17; Thornton, A History of West Central Africa, p. 76–77; Thornton, Firearms, Diplomacy, and Conquest in Angola, in: Lee (ed.), Empires and Indigenes, p. 167–192.

93 As Toby Green remarks, the Yaka invasion had already proportioned the sale of hundreds of cheap slaves to planters of São Tomé before his intervention. Green, A Fistful of Shells, p. 218; MMA III, D. 17, D. 23; Thornton, Firearms, Diplomacy, and Conquest in Angola, in: Lee (ed.), Empires and Indigenes, p. 173–174.

94 According to Jesuit sources, after the Yaka invasion, "*forty rich Portuguese men lived*" on Luanda Island under Kongo jurisdiction. They had moved there to escape the "*fierce barbarians who sustained themselves with human flesh and had destroyed and eaten all the kingdom*" of Kongo. Amaral, O consulado de Paulo Dias de Novais, p. 76–77; Heintze, Fontes para a História de Angola, Vol. 1, p. 148–149; MMA IV, D. 132, p. 554; Thornton, Firearms, Diplomacy, and Conquest in Angola, in: Lee (ed.), Empires and Indigenes, p. 173–174.

and a permanent seat for Portuguese ecclesiastical advisors on the electoral council of Kongo.[95]

Nevertheless, the incredible historical journey of the terms '*Jaga*,' referring to a people, or '*jaga*,' referring to a ruler, did not end with the defeat of the Yaka armies at Sottomaior's hands—it had just started.[96] By associating the Yaka with the Arabs, ancient nomads, cannibals, and the enemies of all men, Lopes and Pigafetta created a powerful discursive trope that soon outlived this very localized West Central African conflict. The *Relatione del Reame del Congo* was quickly translated into Latin and several European vernaculars. Concomitantly, the title *Jaga* began being applied to describe all African groups whom the Europeans had a reason to other more radically.[97] The Jesuit Father Baltasar Barreira, Dias de Novais' former right-hand man, pioneered this usage.[98] As Estevam Thompsom remarks, after being sent to "*Serra Leoa*" in 1604, in what is today Sierra Leone, Father Barreira tried to persuade the Portuguese Crown to conquer the territory by suggesting that the local "*Sumbas*" or "*Manes*" had the same origin as the "*Jacas*" in the Kingdom of Kongo and several other African and Asian groups.[99] His reasoning was clear. A war of conquest against these groups and a subsequent occupation of the territory would be economically and spiritually rewarding because when fighting against cannibals, the enslavement of captured enemies and the buying of their prisoners were both justified. The first, according to *Ius gentium*, and the latter, according to the doctrine of ramson (as cannibals supposedly eat their dependents, buying

---

95 GREEN, A Fistful of Shells, p. 219; THORNTON, A History of West Central Africa, p. 76–78; THORNTON, Firearms, Diplomacy, and Conquest in Angola, in: LEE (ed.), Empires and Indigenes, p. 175–176.

96 HEINTZE, Contra as teorias simplificadoras, in: SANCHES (ed.), Portugal não é um país pequeno, p. 215–228; HEINTZE, The Extraordinary Journey of the Jaga, p. 67–101; MACEDO, Jagas, canibalismo e "guerra preta," p. 53–78; MILLER, The Imbangala, p. 549–574; PINTO, Em torno de um problema de identidade, p. 193–243.

97 Thompson remarks that the original Jagas have been compared with the Zulu, the Anziku, the Teke, the Mayaka, the Baga, the Azande, the Fang, the Ashanti, the Fanti, the Dahomeans, the Beninese, the Chaga, and the Masai. THOMPSON, The Making of Quilengues, p. 88.

98 GUERREIRO, Relação anual das coisas que fizeram os padres da Companhia de Jesus, Vol. 3, p. 255.

99 In one of his reports (1607–1609), Father Barreira argued that "*about sixty years ago* [c. 1548], *a certain nation of barbarians because they could no longer fit into the lands where they were born and raised, left to look for others to live in.*" According to him, these nomads were known "*as jacas in Kongo, and in Angola, gindas; in India, zimbas; in Preste João's Ethiopia, galas; and in this region* [Sierra Leone] *çumbas.*" Their food was "*human flesh, which they boiled with palm hearts or palm sprouts, thus depopulating the lands they passed through of their inhabitants and destroying the palms, that are like vineyards and olive groves.*" In war, "*to astonish and frighten the people,*" they carried a "*foot or hand or other* [severed] *human limb between their teeth, pierced through the mouth; the sight of which was enough to send great armies fleeing.*" Ibid.; THOMPSON, The Making of Quilengues, p. 85–86.

them would be equivalent to commutating a death penalty). The next step in the consolidation of the '*Jaga*' trope was the association of the term with the Mbangala warbands and their leaders whom, regardless of their emic titles, the Portuguese had started referring to as '*jagas*' ever since they first encountered them in 1601.[100]

These groups were culturally, historically, and linguistically unrelated to the Yaka people despite, as Miller and Toby Green remark, also being the outcome of a century of intense slave-raiding and the steady inland expansion of a predatorial credit-backed Atlantic economy.[101] However, until Miller firmly contested this association in 1972, most historiographies on the *Jagas* reiterated versions of the myth that the Yaka warriors and the Mbangala were a similar kind of group or even the same migrating population.[102] If the bibliography on the origin of the first *Jagas* and their possible association with the Mbangala was already quite extensive by 1972, the secondary literature tracing the ensuing debate between Africanist historians soon followed.[103] By 1976, Miller published *Kings and Kinsmen* (1976), providing a still unsurpassed account of the emergence of the Central and West Central African institutions, titles, and political innovations that constituted the normative framework of the Mbangala war bands, settling the discussion regarding the origin of the West Central African groups that were referred to as the *Jagas* by the Portuguese from the seventeenth century onwards.[104]

---

100 As Vansina notes, the *ouvidor* Domingos de Abreu de Brito, who was sent to Angola in the 1590s to enquire about the state of the hereditary captaincy, already mentioned the "*Guindas and Yaguas*" as neighbors of Ndongo. However, there is no evidence the Portuguese had had direct contact with these "*Yaguas*" at this point. Brito, Um inquérito à vida administrativa; Green, A Fistful of Shells, p. 220; Heywood and Thornton, Central Africans, p. 90; Miller, Kings and Kinsmen, p. 177–178; Vansina, Foundation of the Kingdom of Kasanje, p. 369.

101 According to Beatrix Heintze, by the early seventeenth century, the Kikongo term *mfuka* [debt, credit, loan] had given origin to the creoles "*infuca*" and "*emfuca*," which described the practice of extending liberal credit to Mbundu *sobas* and demanding its sudden repayment. When the *sobas* were unwilling or incapable of paying, Portuguese merchants, *moradores*, and their Luso-African accomplices took their "wives and children" as collateral, selling them as slaves in Luanda. Green, A Fistful of Shells, p. 220–221; Heintze, Fontes para a História de Angola, Vol. 1, p. 118; Miller, Kings and Kinsmen, p. 176.

102 Carvalho, O Jagado de Cassange; Heintze, Contra as teorias simplificadoras, in: Sanches (ed.), Portugal não é um país pequeno, p. 215–228; Heintze, The Extraordinary Journey of the Jaga, p. 67–101; Macedo, Jagas, canibalismo e "guerra preta," p. 53–78; Miller, The Imbangala, p. 549–574; Pinto, Em torno de um problema de identidade, p. 193–243.

103 Bontinck, Un mausolée, p. 387–389; Green, A Fistful of Shells; Heintze, The Extraordinary Journey of the Jaga, p. 67–101; Hilton, The Jaga Reconsidered, p. 191–202; Macedo, Jagas, canibalismo e "guerra preta," p. 53–78; Miller, Requiem, p. 121–149; Miller, The Imbangala, p. 549–574; Pinto, Em torno de um problema de identidade, p. 193–243; Thompson, The Making of Quilengues; Thornton, A Resurrection, p. 223–227; Vansina, More on the invasion of Kongo, p. 421–429.

104 Miller, Kings and Kinsmen, p. 151, 161–162, 167–168, 175.

As Miller describes, the Mbangala war bands originated "sometime in the sixteenth century" when, escaping from the Luba, holders of Lunda titles migrated towards the hinterlands of Benguela from the areas to the far northeast of the Portuguese Captaincy of Angola.[105] During this migration, they came under pressure from the centralized Mbundu states and Ovimbundu chieftaincies of the West Central African coast, such as Ndongo and Benguela. Given that they were the heads of "lineageless" bands precariously held together by Lunda, Chokwe, and Luena "nonlineage" institutions when facing these larger, better-organized states, the proto-Mbangala were forced to adjust and devise more robust political solutions.[106] When they reached the hinterlands of Benguela, they came into contact with and adopted a "cross-cutting"[107] Ovimbundu institution that fit this description—a male initiation society focused on establishing a tightly regulated *kilombo* [war camp] where rituals bringing together unrelated males of the same age group occurred.[108] As further discussed in the following sections, the adoption of the *kilombo* normative framework allowed the original proto-Mbangala bands to incorporate dispersed Mbundu corporate kin groups successfully, eventually enabling the emergence of large-scale, slave-raiding Mbangala warbands and then centralized states, such as the Kingdoms of Kasanje and Matamba.

As Miller explains, from the Mbundu perspective, the political solution found by the Mbangala was a complete abomination, soon described in terms of cannibalism and *uanga* or sorcery.[109] In his words, the Mbundu defined humanity in ethnocentric terms, understanding sedentary farming, the occupation of ancestral lands, and political organization according to "matrilinear lineages" or corporate kin groups as central aspects of being human.[110] The Mbangala not only disregarded all these revered institutions but also actively embraced the tactical advantages of the terror caused by their alleged non-humanity, building "their rituals and symbolism of non-humanity on ideas already present in the cultures of western Central Africa"—cannibalism and sorcery.[111] Moreover, while the Mbundu associated the birth of children sired by uncircumcised, un-initiated men as a manifestation of *uanga*, the Mbangala considered circumcision and initiation into "matrilineages" a

---

105 Ibid., p. 151, 161–162.

106 Ibid., p. 161–162, 167–168.

107 Miller defines these as institutions that "cut across existing lineage divisions," allowing for "supralineage political organization." In keeping with the terminology adopted in this book, "cross-cutting" institutions are those that enable the political articulation of different corporate kin groups. Ibid., p. 160.

108 Ibid., p. 151, 161–162, 167–168, 175.

109 Ibid., p. 244–245; Rodrigues de Areia, Estrutura magico-religiosa, p. 34–35.

110 Miller, Kings and Kinsmen, p. 242.

111 Ibid., p. 244; Thornton, Firearms, Diplomacy, and Conquest in Angola, in: Lee (ed.), Empires and Indigenes, p. 181.

tabu, selling or killing all Mbundu war prisoners who had already undergone it.[112] According to colonial ethnographers and folklorists, contemporary Mbundu of the early twentieth century believed that "*muloji* [sorcerers]" consumed the flesh of their victims during elaborate night-time ceremonies, equating them with wild beasts.[113] Based on this, Miller speculates that seventeenth-century Mbundu also understood the "cannibalistic rituals" of the Mbangala as evidence of their sorcerer-like non-humanity.[114] Moreover, the practice of incorporating war prisoners into the *kilombo* could have been metaphorically framed in terms of the Mbangala 'eating' the Mbundu corporate kin groups through "ritual death" and the transformation of their members into "non-human beings," adding an extra layer to the trope.[115] In conclusion, Miller argues that adopting the symbolism and practice of ritual cannibalism might also have allowed the Mbundu incorporated into the *kilombo* to navigate their own normative and cosmological anxieties. Without access to an ancestral land connected to ancestors, the newly made Mbangala had to figure out new apotropaic rituals to ward themselves against the interference of the spirits of slain enemies and deceased comrades. By ritually burying their corpses in their "bellies," a practical solution was found.

The English sailor Andrew Battel (c.1565–1614) provided one of the first oral descriptions of the Mbangala, with whom he lived for about twenty months during the first years of the seventeenth century.[116] His memories and recollections were transcribed by an unknown scribe and then included by his neighbor and editor Samuel Purchas (1575–1626) in his *Purchas his Pilgrimage* (1613) and *Samuel Purchas His Pilgrimes* (1625), before being re-edited by E. Ravenstein in *The Strange Adventures of Andrew Battell of Leigh* (1901).[117] Vansina remarks that Purchas' volumes were highly influential as soon as they were published, contributing to the widespread acceptance that the Yaka who had invaded the Kingdom of Kongo,

---

112 Miller, Kings and Kinsmen, p. 229, 232–233.

113 Ibid.; Redinha, Etnossociologia do Nordeste de Angola; Ribas, Ilundo; Ribas, Uanga (Feitiço); Rodrigues de Areia, Estrutura magico-religiosa, p. 34–35.

114 Debates about the realism of the accounts of Mbangala anthropophagy and the political and economic strategising beyond the spread of 'gourmet' cannibalism myths have also produced a great deal of literature. Heintze, Contra as teorias simplificadoras, in: Sanches (ed.), Portugal não é um país pequeno, p. 215–228; Macedo, Jagas, canibalismo e "guerra preta," p. 53–78; Miller, Kings and Kinsmen, p. 244–249; Shaw, Cannibal Transformations, in: Moore and Sanders (eds.), Magical Interpretations, Material Realities, p. 50–70; Thornton, Cannibals, Witches, and Slave Traders, p. 273–294

115 Miller, Kings and Kinsmen, p. 246–249.

116 Ravenstein, The Strange Adventures of Andrew Battell; Thornton, Firearms, Diplomacy, and Conquest in Angola, in: Lee (ed.), Empires and Indigenes, p. 18; Vansina, On Ravenstein's Edition of Battell's Adventures, p. 321–347.

117 Vansina, On Ravenstein's Edition of Battell's Adventures, p. 321–347.

Fig. 5 Johann Theodor de Bry's *Jagas*. PIGAFETTA and LOPES, Regnum Congo, plate 12 (Public Domain).

referred to by Purchas as "*Anzichi*," the "*Giacchi*" mentioned by Lopes, and the Mbangala described by Battel were all offshoots of the same original group.[118] Purchas' volumes were also a vital source of the growing "encyclopedia of bizarre customs" mentioned by Avramesco.[119] In *Purchas his Pilgrimage*, Purchas claimed that the "*Anzichi strecht from Zaire to Nubia*," being the "*cruellest Cannibals which the Sunne looketh on*," not only eating their "*enemies, or their dead*" but also "*their Kinsfolkes and Country-folkes*" and slaves.[120] Some, Purchas remarked, even offered "*themselves to the Butcherie, as faithfull subjects unto their Princes.*" As for the group called "*Iagges by the Portugall*," and "*by themselves Imbangolas* [Mbangala]," Purchas claimed that these were the '*Giacchi*' mentioned by Lopes' account of the invasion of Kongo, originating from "*Sierra Liona*"—information he might have gleaned from Jesuit sources.[121] However, quite confusingly, he also states that the "*Giacchi*" called themselves "*Agag*" according to Lopes and that they lived on "*both sides of*

118 Ibid., p. 329; PURCHAS, Purchas his Pilgrimage, p. 701.

119 AVRAMESCU, An Intellectual History of Cannibalism, p. 14–40.

120 PURCHAS, Purchas his Pilgrimage, p. 701.

121 Ibid., p. 699.

Nilus," meshing details about the Yaka, the '*Jagas*' trope,' and the Mbangala into a single incoherent narrative.

Following Battel, Purchas continued, Mbangala "*weapons are Darts*," and "*their food humane flesh, without all humanitie devoured*."[122] They "*wander in an unsettled course*" and "*neither Plant nor Sowe, nor breede up Cattell*," nourishing "*none of their owne children*," but commit infanticide by burying their newborn babies alive. Finally, Purchas stated that, according to Battel, the Mbangala had no "*Fetisso's* [*feitiços*, charms], *or idols*," the "*great Iagge, or Prince*, [being] *the matter of all their Ceremonies, and* [...] *a great Witch*." Accordingly, their most important ritual was a "*sacrifice*" known as "*Kissembula*," which Battel was never allowed to witness, when the leader of the *kilombo* was presented with "*his Kissengula, or Warre-Hatchet*" by a "*Ganga*," and proceeded to sacrifice four slaves, goats, and dogs and ritually consume their flesh in a banquet. In *Samuel Purchas His Pilgrimes*, Purchas describes the Mbangala in greater detail, referring to them as "*Gagas, or Gindes*" and relating them to Lopes' "*Giacchi*."[123] Following this second rendition of Battel's accounts, the latter met the "*Gagas*" and their "*Generall*," the "*great Gaga*," while preparing to fight the Kingdom of Benguela. By then, Battel was a crewmember of a Portuguese trading vessel sailing the coast near the mouth of the Cuvo River in search of untapped slave markets.[124]

The crew made a deal with the "*great Gaga*," Imbe Kalandula, transporting his army across the Cuvo in exchange for a business partnership; they would be granted preference over buying the enemies enslaved in upcoming battles.[125] Consequently, after the Mbangala were victorious over the Ovimbundu *osoma* "Hombiangymbe [Hombi a Njimbe]" of Benguela,[126] the traders bought many cheap slaves.[127] Promptly selling the slaves acquired from the Mbangala for a significant profit in Luanda, the crew soon returned to the mouth of the Cuvo River in search of their new partners. According to Purchas, not finding the mobile war band there, they explored the hinterlands, where they were soon arrested by an *osoma* called "Mofarigosat [Mufari Ngosato]" who forcefully enlisted them as military advisors

---

122 Ibid.

123 Purchas, Purchas His Pilgrimes, Vol. 6, p. 377–378; Vansina, On Ravenstein's Edition of Battell's Adventures, p. 324.

124 Purchas, Purchas His Pilgrimes, Vol. 6, p. 377–378; Miller, Kings and Kinsmen, p. 177–178.

125 Purchas, Purchas His Pilgrimes, Vol. 6, p. 377–378; Thornton, A History of West Central Africa, p. 104.

126 According to Thornton, Hombi a Njimbe was said to command "some 100 chief lords," referred to by the Portuguese as *sobas* or *sobetas* if they were the heads of smaller groups. As he further explains, this was a mischaracterisation, as the Ovimbundu would refer to them in the Umbundu language as *osoma* and conceived of their office in dissimilar terms. Thornton, A History of West Central Africa, p. 103.

127 Purchas, Purchas His Pilgrimes, Vol. 6, p. 378–380.

and mercenaries.[128] Eventually, the slave traders brokered their release, leaving Battel as a hostage. Realizing his Portuguese crewmates would probably not risk their lives to come and redeem an Englishman, Battel escaped to search for and try to join the Mbangala "*Caniball people*" he had previously met. In the remainder of his account of Battel's journeys, Purchas confirms most of the information already published in 1613, claiming that there was "*no Image among*" the Mbangala, that their women were allowed to "*enjoy none of their children*," and that they ate all the "*men and women they kill*," only permitting boys and girls under "*thirteene of fourteene yeares of age*" to join the *kilombo*.[129] However, in this version of Battel's exploits, some crucial details about the economic life of the Mbangala and the *Kissembula* ritual are added.

In keeping with *Samuel Purchas His Pilgrimes*, the "*Divell* [devil]" appeared to the Mbangala during the *Kissembula* ceremony, suggesting it was a possession ritual.[130] An anonymous description of the "*hinterlands of Benguela*" written between 1617 and 1622 confirms this interpretation, its author claiming that the "*Jagas*" had "*neither law nor sect, except the devil talking to them a lot of times, entering some of them without causing them harm and expressing itself with a very soft voice that is almost impossible to hear*."[131] As for the economic life of the Mbangala *kilombo*, Purchas remarked that according to Battel, the "*Gagas delight in no Countrie, but where there is great store of Palmares, or Groves of Palmes*."[132] However, contrary to Mbundu *sobas* and *dembos*, or the *Mwene Kongo* and his provincial governors, the Mbangala coveted palm groves not because of their capacity to produce exchangeable raffia cloths or edible palm oil but because they could be tapped to produce alcoholic palm wine. The way Mbangala extracted this wine, Purchas remarked, was "*contrarie to the Imbondos* [Mbundu]," killing the plants and thus forcing the Mbangala to be constantly on the move in search of new groves to sustain their addiction.[133] While the destructive extractivism of the Mbangala war bands contributed to the perception the Mbundu and BaKongo had of them not being fully human, their fondness for alcohol made them the ideal trade partners for Portuguese merchants and *moradores* who had access to Portuguese wine or Brazilian spirits.[134] Moreover,

128 Ibid., p. 379–380; Thornton, A History of West Central Africa, p. 104.

129 Purchas, Purchas His Pilgrimes, Vol. 6, p. 383–386.

130 Ibid., p. 387–388.

131 The anonymous author adds that these ceremonies were called "*xaquetar*" and were accompanied by the sacrifice of "*cows, rams, and other animals*" or "*blacks*" so that the "*devil*" would answer the audience's questions. After, the sacrifices would be consumed. Cordeiro (ed.), Benguella e seu sertão por um anonymo, p. 18.

132 Purchas, Purchas His Pilgrimes, Vol. 6, p. 383.

133 Ibid., p. 383–384.

134 In 1620, Garcia Mendes Castelo Branco submitted to the Portuguese Crown a project for the complete reform of the Captaincy of Angola. In it, the companion of Dias de Novais remarked

from the Crown's perspective, there were fiscal advantages in disrupting the Luso-African-controlled *pumbo* networks, which traded in raffia-cloths, *nzimbu*, copper, and salt by introducing alcoholic beverages as part of the commodity bundles that were increasingly being adopted as the standard price of slaves, as discussed in the following chapter. Moreover, the fact that the Mbangala were universally othered, even embracing this as their core corporate identity trait, meant that the slaves bought from them or their enemies could always be considered rightfully enslaved, either according to the Jesuit doctrines of just enslavement or the ransom doctrine that was slowly gaining ascendency.[135] In ideological terms, as the following pages discuss, all that was needed was for the heads of settled Mbangala kingdoms, such as Kasanje, to be neatly distinguished from Mbundu or BaKongo *Princeps*.

5.3 The Birth of the Luso-Mbangala Alliance

In the long run, simultaneously raiding and warring for slaves and establishing or controlling pre-existing slave fairs, a practice pioneered by the first captain-general and governors of Angola, didn't yield good results for the Portuguese Crown.[136] Thornton and Heywood remark that constant warfare could not but disrupt the trade flow and often left the conquered Mbundu *itanda* deserted.[137] As Captain Major Baltazar Ribeiro de Aragão would denounce to the Crown in 1618, the reason why the Captaincy of Angola was in "*bad shape, and there are no fairs, was that we made war in the same province, where we have our city and presídios, waging it so close to home that, instead of destroying the enemies we destroyed ourselves.*"[138] Moreover, the heavy taxes and downright extortions imposed by captain-general and governors on those that frequented conquered *itanda* disincentivized Portuguese *moradores* or Luso-African *pumbeiros* from visiting the slave fairs of vassal Mbundu *sobas*.[139]

---

that the "*Jagas who assist* [the Portuguese]" were "*very fierce*" and "*effective in scaring the gentios* [non-Christians]." Therefore, Castelo Branco argued that the monarch should "*concede them the grace of three* [500 liters] *barrels of wine per year*" during the "*major festivities*," as they desired "*nothing else*." He concluded that it was necessary to keep them as friends and that the investment would "*result in pessas* [slaves] *that would cover the expense and more*." CURTO, Jeribita, p. 301–325; MILLER, Kings and Kinsmen, p. 196–198; MMA VI, D. 136, p. 451; THORNTON, A History of West Central Africa, p. 113.

135 HEINTZE, Fontes para a História de Angola, Vol. 1, p. 115.

136 CRUZ E SILVA, As feiras do Ndongo, in: SANTOS (ed.), Actas do seminário, p. 405–422.

137 Due to these difficulties, the administrative solution of clustering merchants in official slave fairs under close Portuguese scrutiny was only retried by the middle of the eighteenth century. HEYWOOD and THORNTON, Central Africans, p. 123; MILLER, Way of Death, p. 583–584.

138 CORDEIRO (ed.), Terras e minas africanas segundo Rebello de Aragão, p. 18.

139 Ibid., p. 13.

By 1625, Fernão de Sousa (c. 1563–1635), captain-general and governor of Angola between 1624 and 1630, concluded that the war against the Kingdom of Ndongo, because of its "*duration, that outlasted two continuous years*," had caused so much death and destruction that "*all fairs were over, and all those who escaped* [had] *spread to different parts*" of the kingdom.[140] Meanwhile, the commerce of raffia cloths and salt continued in the *restages* and *pumbos* networks outside the Crown's control.[141] Faced with this reality, King Philipp II of Portugal ordered Manuel Pereira Forjaz, captain-general and governor of Angola from 1607 until 1611, to focus on strengthening commerce and fostering peaceful relations with the Mbundu.[142]

Cambambe became a vital slave trade center during this period.[143] However, when Bento Banha Cardoso succeeded Forjaz, becoming interim captain-general and governor between 1611 and 1615, he defied the royal orders given to his predecessor. Joining forces with several Mbangala war bands, he launched a violent campaign against Ndongo and formerly allied Mbundu *dembos*.[144] Álvaro II of Kongo immediately complained to Philipp II, demanding the Portuguese stop using the "*Jaga*" as auxiliaries because they were "*heathens and cannibals*."[145] These complaints were reiterated by Álvaro III of Kongo (1595–1622), who wrote to Pope Paul V (1560–1621) in 1617 complaining about Banha Cardoso's unlawful wars, stressing that his abuses were aggravated by his alliance with "*a nation of people that is very brutal, called Giagas and Iagas, that live off human flesh and bodies*."[146] The two *Mwene Kongo* thus sought to capitalize on the misguided association between the Mbangala and Lopes' *Jagas*, which was 'common knowledge' by then.[147] Diplomatically, their campaign was a success. Philipp II of Portugal was soon forced

---

140 Sousa, História das relações entre a Angola Portuguesa e o Ndongo, in: Heintze (ed.), Fontes para a História de Angola, Vol. 1, p. 197.

141 Silva Corrêa notes that salt kept circulating as currency in the Angolan hinterlands until the end of the eighteenth century. Then, despite the royal monopoly over the salt pans near Benguela and all the attempts to regulate the circulation of salt in Luanda and Massangano, the salt from Kissama continued to be freely extracted outside of Portuguese jurisdiction, being exchanged for cloths by Luso-African merchants. Silva Corrêa also claims that, due to its alleged medicinal virtues, this salt was even exported to Brazil. Heywood and Thornton, Central Africans, p. 110–114; Silva Corrêa, História de Angola, Vol. 1, p. 127–129; Thornton, A History of West Central Africa, p. 95–97.

142 MMA V, D. 101; Thornton, A History of West Central Africa, p. 94.

143 Heywood and Thornton, Central Africans, p. 113; Thornton, A History of West Central Africa, p. 107.

144 Thornton, A History of West Central Africa, p. 114; Miller, Kings and Kinsmen, p. 181–183.

145 Vansina, Foundation of the Kingdom of Kasanje, p. 370.

146 MMA VI, D. 100.

147 Pigafetta and Lopes, Relatione del Reame di Congo, p. 59.

to appease the Pope by assuring Cardinal Gaspar de Borja y Velasco (1580–1645) that he had issued "*very tight orders, so that neither the governors of Angola nor any other of* [his] *vassals*" sought the military assistance of "*Jagas, who eat human flesh and have destroyed the lands of the King of Congo.*"[148]

Nonetheless, in the aftermath of Banha Cardoso's rogue military adventures, the potential of Luso-Mbangala alliances to completely change the tactical course of events was obvious to all.[149] By then, the Portuguese had failed to conquer Kissama and gain military control of its salt mines, and the raffia-cloth trade escaped the Crown's supervision.[150] The Mbangala, however, gladly accepted imported alcohol in exchange instead of salt and raffia cloths, and soon, just as Battel's crew had done, Portuguese merchants and Luso-African *pumbeiros* followed their war bands around, buying enslaved war prisoners with Portuguese wine and Brazilian spirits.[151] Therefore, despite Álvaro II's and Álvaro III's protests and Philip II's precise orders, Luís Mendes de Vasconcelos, captain-general and governor between 1617 and 1621, enlisted three major Mbangala war bands to renew the offensive against Ndongo during an ongoing dynastic conflict.[152] After a series of striking military successes, in 1618, Mendes de Vasconcelos built the fortress of Ambaca,[153] situated in the lands of *Soba* Kaita ka Balanga, with the support of *Soba* Mubanga, one of the contenders for the Ndongo throne.[154] Ambaca remained the easternmost foothold of the Portuguese Crown for half a century until Pungo Andongo, the last independent *kabasa* [capital] of Ndongo, was conquered in 1671.[155] During this period, the network of official fairs was all but abandoned, not only because of the significant increase in violence and warfare but also because it was cheaper to buy the slaves captured by the roving Luso-Mbangala armies than to trade for them with cloths.

Bishop Manuel Baptista (1559–1620), appointed to the Diocese of Congo and Angola in 1609, composed a disheartened account of this period and the maladministration of justice in Luanda.[156] As a report from 1619 related, successive

---

148 MMA VI, D. 111.

149 Thornton, A History of West Central Africa, p. 123.

150 Ibid., p. 113.

151 Ibid.; Curto, Jeribita, p. 301–325; Miller, Kings and Kinsmen, p. 196–198.

152 Thornton, A History of West Central Africa, p. 117; Thornton, Firearms, Diplomacy, and Conquest in Angola, in: Lee (ed.), Empires and Indigenes, p. 180; Miller, Kings and Kinsmen, p. 196–198.

153 The new *presídio* was built where Banha Cardoso had established the *presídio* of Ango Akikoito, near the Lukala River, c. 1611. Vansina, Foundation of the Kingdom of Kasanje, p. 369.

154 Miller, Kings and Kinsmen, p. 199–200; Thornton, A History of West Central Africa, p. 117.

155 Heywood and Thornton, Central Africans, p. 75; Thornton, A History of West Central Africa, p. 187.

156 MMA VI, D. 122.

captain-general and governors took advantage of the fact that the Crown's "*courts*" were very distant to "*molest and steal from the naturaes* [natives], *and moradores, regularly starting unjust wars, capturing, killing, and oppressing the innocent, and provoking unspeakable vexations*."[157] To aggravate matters, Manuel Cerveira Pereira, who had been captain-general and governor first between 1603 and 1606 and then between 1615 and 1617, had expelled the *ouvidor* appointed by the Crown, appointing another *ouvidor* of his liking so that "*no justice* [could] *take place*" outside of the dictates of his "*own will*." Like his predecessors, the bishop lamented, he used the military services "*of Jagas*," a "*cruel but warlike people* [...] *much feared by the naturaes*." Bishop Baptista confirmed that the "*Jagas*" lived "*only from theft and eating human people*." They did "*not raise children, because they kill them at birth*" and turned into "*Jagas, the young ones they take in the wars they are always involved in*." Moreover, he continued, the "*Jagas*" had no "*fixed dwellings*," "*used public feitissos* [*feitiços*], *and invocations of the devil*," and "*sacrificed to the devil people and animals before their undertakings*"—all in the presence of the Portuguese "*who accompany them*," including the captain-general and governors. Cerveira Pereira, Bishop Baptista remarked, had expressed his remorse in associating with such a group, but "*risking losing wars*," instead of letting the "*Jagas go,* [he] *embraced them*," "*killing by their* [side], *and capturing countless innocents, not only against the law of God, and Natural* [Law] *but also against the written ordinances*" of the Crown.

Bishop Baptista also claimed that because of the newly found Mbangala allies, all "*wars were riskless*."[158] While a clear exaggeration, this remark might reflect that Luso-African armies under Portuguese command had started adopting the disciplinary framework of the Mbangala *kilombo*.[159] By the 1620s, Luso-Mbangala armies were also referred to as a "*quilombo* [*kilombo*]," as the ordinance provided by Captain-General and Governor Fernão de Sousa to Captain Major Paio de Araújo de Azevedo evidences.[160] Moreover, this ordinance suggests that the Mbundu officeholders that composed them were subjected to a tighter form of discipline. In keeping with the twelfth article of Azevedo's ordinance, he was to ensure that in the *kilombo* he was appointed to lead, the "*captain of the Black people*" was to be a "*quiambolle* [*ngola ambole*]," and not a "*tendalla*." While, in keeping with Mbundu

157 Ibid., p. 366–368.

158 Ibid., p. 368.

159 Thornton argues that Mbangala war bands offered "no particular military innovations, in either weapons or tactics" other than the "terror" caused by their deployment. However, the tactic advantages offered by the streamlined discipline of the *kilombo* must be considered. Thornton, Firearms, Diplomacy, and Conquest in Angola, in: Lee (ed.), Empires and Indigenes, p. 181.

160 Sousa, Regimento de Fernão de Sousa a Paio de Araújo de Azevedo, in: Heintze (ed.), Fontes para a História de Angola, Vol. 1, p. 207–208.

norms, the "*tendalla*" had ample jurisdictional powers, the *ngola ambole* was a purely military commander associated with hunting expeditions.[161] Therefore, this reform suggests an attempt to centralize the authority of expeditionary commanders and simplify the administration of military justice during campaigns. Fernão de Sousa also ordered Azevedo to reduce the number of Mbundu "*officials*" under the *ngola ambole*, thus avoiding jurisdictional conflicts and disciplinary breaches.[162] While Fernão de Sousa's apparent attempt to reform Luso-African armies according to stricter *kilombo* disciplinary frameworks failed, it hints at Mbangala tactics' lasting impact on Luso-African warfare.[163]

In any case, Bishop Baptista continued, due to the avarice stoked by the military successes occasioned by the Luso-Mbangala alliance, captain-general and governors were soon fabricating *casus belli*.[164] Moreover, Luso-Mbangala armies conquered "*the lands that God had made the King of Kongo the natural lord of*," thus committing a great injustice and endangering the lives and wealth of the Portuguese "*resgatadores* [redeemers]" of slaves that had established themselves there.[165] The BaKongo, the bishop informed the Portuguese king in another letter, came to fear the "*Jagas*" so much that "*they ran*" when their name was spoken.[166] Soon, Bishop Baptista concluded, Mbundu "*slave markets were closed, all commerce and ramsons stopped*," the Kongo "*pathways were closed*," and merchants were "*dying of starvation*."[167] Moreover, the "*Jagas that were once amicable*," finding themselves without loot, rebelled, sacking Luso-African compounds and "*taking as many black porters, resgatadores* [slave traders] *and fato* [wealth]" as they could find.

At the beginning of his tenure as captain-general and governor of Angola, Mendes de Vasconcelos expressed his disgust with the "*Jagas*" to the Crown, just as his predecessor Cerveira Pereira had done.[168] In his words, previous captain-generals and governors, as well as moradores, used these "*Blacks that nourish themselves with human flesh and are the enemies of all living things*" as "*bloodhounds, to unjustly fetch them slaves*."[169] The "*Jagas*," he continued, were so cruel that "*they ate more* [slaves] *than the ones they delivered alive*" and would surely "*in no time devour the naturaes*

161 Heintze, Fontes para a História de Angola, Vol. 1, p. 125–128; MMA IV, D. 132., p. 559.

162 Sousa, Regimento de Fernão de Sousa a Paio de Araújo de Azevedo, in: Heintze (ed.), Fontes para a História de Angola, Vol. 1, p. 207–208.

163 Heintze, Fontes para a História de Angola, Vol. 1, p. 125.

164 MMA VI, D. 122, p. 368.

165 Ibid., p. 368–370; Thornton, Firearms, Diplomacy, and Conquest in Angola, in: Lee (ed.), Empires and Indigenes, p. 167–192.

166 MMA VI, D. 123, p. 378.

167 MMA VI, D. 122, p. 370.

168 MMA VI, D. 98.

169 Ibid., p. 283–285.

of this Kingdom," destroying it as they had destroyed the Kingdom of Benguela. In fact, as Mendes de Vasconcelos, related, when he assumed his office, there were no slaves in Benguela, and the local slave fair was closed "*because the Jagas had eaten them*." Moreover, several Portuguese captains roamed the Angolan hinterlands, "*stealing, killing, capturing and feeding to the Jagas the vassals*" of the Portuguese Crown, governing themselves through the "*answers that the devil gives to the Jagas*." The new captain-general and governor vouched to uproot the treasonous behavior of these Portuguese who followed the divinations of Mbangala possession cults. However, soon after, Mendes de Vasconcelos enlisted the services of the Mbangala warbands himself.[170]

Jaga "*Dom João Casanze* [Kasanje]" commanded one of the Mbangala warbands enlisted by Mendes de Vasconcelos between 1617 and 1621.[171] According to Fernão de Sousa, by the early 1620s, Casanze deserted the Portuguese amidst the war waged by Mendes de Vasconcelos against the Mbundu Kingdom of Matamba, taking "*80.000 archers*."[172] João Casanze moved between the Rivers Kwanza and Kwango and began independently pillaging the middle and upper Kwango Valley, raiding Matamba and Ndongo.[173] Other Mbangala groups, such as the warbands led by Kaza ka Ndongo and Donga, even turned against the Portuguese, joining the Ndongo army and sacking Ambaca.[174] Due to this treasonous behavior, Fernão de Sousa would later claim that all "*wars waged against the Jaga* [Mbangala] *were justissimas* [most fair] *because they were impious persons, enemies of all, ferocious and diabolic*."[175] For as he said, the Mbangala neither "*till the land nor saw nor seek to leave posterity*," only caring "*for those who are soldiers*" and eating "*everybody else*." However, since in their "*public human slaughterhouses*," those "*who are not eaten are sold,*" the Portuguese felt justified in buying their captives. In contrast, already by 1630, Fernão de Sousa remarked that the other "*wars of Angola* [were] *not all just, and when they are, that does not imply that the peças of slaves captured*

170 Miller, Kings and Kinsmen, p. 196–198; Thornton, A History of West Central Africa, p. 117.

171 According to Thornton, Mbangala allies, most notably the Mbangala band Kakonda, were also crucial to Benguela's economic welfare. Moreover, unable to establish a foothold in the southern highlands, the Portuguese adopted similar raiding tactics. Sousa, A Angola portuguesa e regiões circunvizinhas, in: Heintze (ed.), Fontes para a História de Angola, Vol. 1, p. 210–216; Thornton, A History of West Central Africa, p. 158–159.

172 Sousa, A Angola portuguesa e regiões circunvizinhas, in: Heintze (ed.), Fontes para a História de Angola, Vol. 1, p. 210–216.

173 Heywood and Thornton, Central Africans, p. 114–123; Thornton, A History of West Central Africa, p. 118–119.

174 Thornton, A History of West Central Africa, p. 118.

175 Sousa, A Angola portuguesa e regiões circunvizinhas, in: Heintze (ed.), Fontes para a História de Angola, Vol. 1, p. 210–212.

in them are justly captured because the necessary prerequisites for them to be justly captured are not met."

5.4 The Permanent Settlement of Kasanje

Until the 1650s, it is unlikely that *Jaga* Casanze or his successors managed to turn a roving band of Mbangala mercenaries into a fully settled kingdom.[176] As Beatrix Heintze remarks, war, famines, and instability remained endemic in West Central Africa, first because of the Luso-Ndongo wars and then because of the aftermath of the Dutch occupation of Luanda (1641–1648).[177] However, by the middle of the seventeenth century, the Kingdom of Kasanje, through the slave fair of Cassange, emerged as a major supplier of slaves to the Portuguese Lisbon-backed merchants.[178] Therefore, Thornton convincingly argues that from the 1640s to the 1660s, intensive state-building must have occurred in Kasanje.[179] As he explains, during these decades, the *Jagas* remained 'true' to the Mbangala normative principles that governed life in the militarized *kilombo* while incorporating members of different corporate kin groups into their emerging polity and adopting and adapting some of their institutions.[180] This involved military campaigns, diplomatic interventions, the incorporation of Mbundu norms, uses and customs, ritual innovation, and other forms of the ideological and political spade-work that David Schoenbrun defines as "groupwork."[181]

According to Schoenbrun and Neil Kodesh, groupwork encompasses all intellectual and material labor conducted to create and maintain communities of "moral belonging."[182] These can be small face-to-face groups, like the smallest Mbundu *ngundu*, where technologies such as writing and bureaucratic forms of statecraft played little or no part in convincing individuals that they shared a "future and a past with others," or larger ethnic groups, states, and the "cults" and "secret societies" that structured the trading diasporas of the northern trading routes.[183] In the case of Kasanje, it is helpful to adopt groupwork as a neutral, analytical concept because it allows us to explore the discursive and performative elements that afforded its

---

176 Heintze, The Extraordinary Journey of the Jaga, p. 81–82.

177 Thornton, A History of West Central Africa, p. 156.

178 Heintze, The Extraordinary Journey of the Jaga, p. 83; Heywood and Thornton, Central Africans, p. 155–156; Thornton, A History of West Central Africa, p. 179–181.

179 Thornton, A History of West Central Africa, p. 156, 189–193.

180 Ibid., p. 155–156, 179–181.

181 Ibid., p. 156, 189–193; Schoenbrun, The Names of the Python, p. 3–12.

182 Kodesh, Beyond the Royal Gaze; Schoenbrun, The Names of the Python, p. 3–12.

183 Miller, Way of Death, p. 204–205; Schoenbrun, The Names of the Python, p. 3–4.

settlement and that Europeans described as a 'diabolic' or 'superstitious' form of social contract. These new tropes helped rationalize why a settled kingdom was no different from roving Mbangala warbands when justifying buying its slaves and war prisoners. In other words, they explained why a *jaga* was not a *Princeps* and why the Kingdom of Kasanje remained outside of *Ius gentium* and theological Natural law. Before turning to how the Capuchin Friar Antonio Giovanni Cavazzi da Montecuccolo (1621–1678) described Mbangala groupwork, this section briefly accounts for the emic political metaphors and regional "political *imaginaires*" used by the Mbangala to shape their political institutions, anchor their normative system, and integrate regional inter-polity constellations.[184]

Thornton mentions that, according to Pasqual Fernandez Quemba, who served as a "notary in Kasanje's court" c. 1655, to perform his job, he had to know the languages of the "Congo [BaKongo], Abundo [Mbundu], Cotintinem [?], of Quiâca [Chokwe], Ambundo [Ovimbundu] and the language of Cassange," a dialect of Kimbundu.[185] To accommodate all this linguistic and cultural diversity, the *jaga* of Kasanje not only employed officers capable of translating between these different African languages and the Luso-African pidgin used in Cassange but also fostered the work of "Kasanje intellectuals" who, as Thornton remarks, soon "fashioned a history for themselves." In formal terms, this history was expressed through two main styles of oral tradition, "narrative episodes," referred to as *malunda*, and "genealogical sets," referred to as *musendo*.[186]

According to Miller, who collected large sets of both in the 1960s, *musendo* are either "lineage genealogies," which relate historical and political information about existing corporate kin groups or bloodlines, or "political genealogies," organizing political offices in a hierarchical structure that offers some information about their institutional history.[187] Conventionally, both kinds of *musendo* trace the genealogy of existing political titles or "lineage" titles back to a family tree of mythical ancestors and heroic founders. Miller defines this mythic layer of *musendo* as an "overriding aetiological level" that is distinguishable from the narrative layers

184 Jean-François Bayart argues that the local "political *imaginaire*" always conditions African groups' constitutive imagination. In the case of the Mbangala, Miller remarks that the "images, metaphors, clichés, or plots" of different oral traditions can inform us about the "complex fund of Mbundu artistic and intellectual themes" that are part of this "*imaginaire*." Therefore, their tropes and images cannot be read as factual historical descriptions. Bayart, The Illusion of Cultural Identity; Miller, Kings and Kinsmen, p. 23–24.

185 Thornton, A History of West Central Africa, p. 189.

186 Miller also refers to other forms of Mbangala "oral art," including "*jisabu* [proverbs]" and "*kumbu* [praise names]," songs, and unspecified "didactic performances." Although these oral performances were undoubtedly part of forms of groupwork, Miller argues that *musendo* and *malunda* were the "primary modes of historical performance." Miller, Kings and Kinsmen, p. 16, 21.

187 Ibid., p. 21.

containing historical information about existing institutions, corporate kin groups, or past title-holders. At the aetiological level, he explains, common ties with mythic ancestors and founders shared with neighboring polities can be elaborated in a performance of cross-regional groupwork.[188] In other words, the mythical strata of *musendo* genealogies afford connections with local, historical corporate kin groups and individuals to a regional framework of empires and kingdoms that share a matrix of cultural heroes and legendary ancestors. In this regard, *musendo* are like European chronicles and sagas that trace the genealogy of medieval kings to the Homeric heroes mentioned in the Iliad or connect the founding of bishoprics or chapels to the lives of renowned saints. By offering an interface between local histories and regional myths, *musendo* enable groupwork on a macro scale.

Malunda are the narratives tied to specific offices or positions, explaining their origins, privileges, rights, duties, and responsibilities.[189] According to Miller, *malunda* "refer selectively" to "certain parts of the past, those which have evident analogues in the present." In other words, Kasanje historians "view past centuries through the prism of social and political conditions of their own time" and "explicitly view their history as concerned with the present." Accordingly, *malunda* and *musendo* were constantly refashioned to accommodate new incoming groups and allies into the complex lattice of corporate kin groups and political offices that constitute the institutional underbelly of the Kingdom of Kasanje and the broader regional order.[190]

By 1655, as Thornton claims, Kasanje intellectuals were primarily concerned with incorporating different groups into their emerging polity and the permanent settlement of their once-roving warband at Polongolo.[191] Later, they would produce *malunda* and *musendo* adjusted to the growing importance of commercial ties with the Lunda and their neighbors.[192] Therefore, Kasanje oral traditions tell the origin story of Kasanje, which reflects these shifting worries and priorities and is entirely at odds with Portuguese records and the oral traditions of neighboring polities.[193] As Manuela Palmeirim argues,[194] this discrepancy led to several historiographic

---

188 Ibid.; Thornton, A History of West Central Africa, p. 188–189.

189 Miller, Kings and Kinsmen, p. 12–13, 21.

190 Heintze, The Extraordinary Journey of the Jaga, p. 67–101; Heintze, Translocal 'Kinship' Relations in: Freitag and von Oppen (eds.), Translocality, p. 179–204.

191 Thornton, A History of West Central Africa, p. 188–189.

192 Heintze, The Extraordinary Journey of the Jaga, p. 67–101; Heintze, Translocal 'Kinship' Relations in: Freitag and von Oppen (eds.), Translocality, p. 179–204; Hoover, The Seduction of Ruwej; Thornton, A History of West Central Africa, p. 328; Vansina, Foundation of the Kingdom of Kasanje, p. 372; Vansina, It Never Happened, p. 387–403.

193 Vansina, Foundation of the Kingdom of Kasanje, p. 255–374.

194 See also Estevam C. Thompson for an account of this debate. Palmeirim, Do "Culture Heroes" Exist; Thompson, The Making of Quilengues, p. 95–101.

and methodological debates in the 1960s, launched by a series of groundbreaking articles by Vansina and David Birmingham.[195] As she explains, Vansina pioneered the notion that oral traditions such as *malunda* and *musendo* could be used as historical sources, influencing a whole generation of historians to either interpret them as literal descriptions of past events or, as Miller later suggested, to tackle them with a "more metaphorical and analytical approach."[196] In contrast, structuralist anthropologists, headed by Luc de Heursch, argued that the same oral narratives should be interpreted as myths and, therefore, as ahistorical sources that can only allow researchers to grasp the "models used by society to think [about] itself."[197] Combining both perspectives, as suggested by the later work of Miller, Thornton, and Vellut, it is possible to argue that Kasanje's oral traditions are historically situated enunciations of the structural models that allowed the Mbangala to think, organize, and comment about their society's and culture's values, doubling as cultural epics and an emic form of institutional history.[198] In other words, each recorded oral tradition provides a snapshot of Mbangala groupwork in the making, providing clues to its internal logic.

According to Miller, through *musendo* and associated *malunda*, the Mbangala and neighboring Mbundu, Chokwe, and Lunda peoples "visualized their society as a set of named roles" or offices which "personalized social statuses associated with defined rights and obligations."[199] The relationship between roles or offices was conceptualized and described using the metaphorical language of kinship (e. g., father-son, uncle-nephew, brother-brother, or husband-wife) and regarded as immutable, despite being historically contingent.[200] This system is common in Central and West Central Africa and is known in Africanist literature as "perpetual kinship." In keeping with this system, as soon as concrete individuals assume a temporary office, they are immediately situated *vis-à-vis* all the other officeholders related to

---

195 Birmingham, Speculations on the Kingdom of Kongo, p. 1–10; Birmingham, The Date and Significance, p. 143–152; Birmingham, The Mbundu and Neighbouring Peoples; Vansina, De la Tradition Orale; Vansina, Foundation of the Kingdom of Kasanje, p. 255–374; Vansina, Kingdoms of the Savanna; Vansina, Oral Tradition

196 Miller, The African Past Speaks; Palmeirim, Do "Culture Heroes" Exist; Vellut, Notes sur le Lunda, p. 61–166.

197 De Heusch, Le Roi Ivre; De Heusch, Rois Nés d'un Coeur de Vache; Sarró, Manuela Palmeirim, p. 225–226; Vansina, Bantu in a Crystal Ball, p. 293–325; Vansina, Is elegance proof? p. 307–348; Willis, Translator's introduction, The Drunken King, p. vii–xiv; Wrigley, Myths of the Savanna, p. 131–135.

198 Miller, Kings and Kinsmen; Thornton, A History of West Central Africa, p. 188–189; Vellut, Notes sur le Lunda, p. 61–66.

199 Miller, Kings and Kinsmen, p. 45.

200 Ibid.; Heintze, Translocal 'Kinship' Relations in: Freitag and von Oppen (eds.), Translocality, p. 179–204.

their new positions. For instance, if a given political office is conceptualized as the nephew of a given "lineage title," it means that its titleholder will have to act accordingly regarding the holder of the latter (e.g., with deference and respect). As Heintze explains, according to Central and West Central African political ontologies, when an individual assumed a new office, they "literally" became their "predecessor," taking their "predecessor's name, his wife (or wives) and children, his social roles and part of his property."[201] This principle is called "positional succession." It also applied to offices that were gendered female. Moreover, as Miller points out, the biological sex and adopted gender of individual incumbents might not coincide with the gender attributes of the perpetual kinship offices they temporarily occupy.[202] For instance, in Mbundu *musendo*, holders of political titles are gendered male. In contrast, all holders of "lineage titles" are gendered female, despite Mbundu corporate kin groups often being headed by elder uncles who otherwise identified as male.

Heintze remarks that extensive networks established by perpetual kinship and positional succession structured the relations between corporate kin groups part of different ethnic groups (i.e., Mbangala, Mbundu, Chokwe, Lunda) and between polities (i.e., the Kingdom of Kasanje, the Kingdom of Matamba, the Kingdom of Ndongo), scaffolding what can be analogically described as the West Central African regional inter-polity order.[203] These networks could establish ties "that would serve as the basis for becoming privileged trading partners, opening trade routes or minimizing conflicts." From the middle of the seventeenth century onwards, Kasanje intellectuals were busy reshaping these networks, laying down the ideological and material infrastructure of the Mbangala-controlled half of the central West Central African slave trade route that siphoned enslaved Africans from the Lunda Empire and its southern tributaries, the region Vansina describes as the wider "Lunda Commonwealth," to the Portuguese controlled port of Luanda.[204] Crucially, as mentioned above, the political *imaginaire* they drew from was saturated with the imagery of cannibalism and sorcery.[205] This meant that Mbangala *musendo* and *malunda* often described the acts of cannibalistic or sorcerer-like mythic ancestors or cultural heroes as a way of conveying information about their political and institutional history, further confirming the myths and biases about the *Jaga* that

201 Heintze, Translocal 'Kinship' Relations in: Freitag and von Oppen (eds.), Translocality, p. 184.

202 Miller, Kings and Kinsmen, p. 19–20.

203 Heintze, Translocal 'Kinship' Relations in: Freitag and von Oppen (eds.), Translocality, p. 179–204.

204 Vansina, Government in Kasai before the Lunda, p. 1–22.

205 Bayart, The Illusion of Cultural Identity; Miller, Kings and Kinsmen, p. 23–24, 244–245; Rodrigues de Areia, Estrutura magico-religiosa, p. 34–35.

had been in circulation since the late sixteenth century and providing fertile ground for theories about diabolical social contracts.

5.5 Of Diabolical Pacts and Social Contracts

Constant slave-raiding by Luso-Mbangala armies within the borders of the Kingdom of Kongo resulted in a complete breakdown of trust between the *Mwene Kongo* and the Portuguese Crown.[206] As Thornton and Fromont remark, by 1619, Álvaro III of Kongo had become highly resentful of the patronage rights the Portuguese monarch had over the local bishops and of his command over the military orders, requesting from the pope directly, priests and missionaries that were neither Portuguese nor under Portuguese jurisdiction.[207] This request resonated with Rome. Soon after, eager to circumvent the privileges his predecessors had granted to the Iberian Crowns, Pope Gregory XV (1554–1623) established the *Propaganda Fide* (1622) and offered to create an apostolic prefecture of Italian missionaries of the Franciscan Order of Friars Minor Capuchin in the Kongo under its jurisdiction.[208] Due to constant Portuguese interference,[209] the missionaries first requested by Álvaro III would arrive more than two decades later, amidst the Thirty Years' War (1618–1648), and when the Dutch West India Company controlled the coasts of Loango and Angola from the port town of Luanda (1641–1648).[210] The Kingdom

---

206 Thornton, A History of West Central Africa, p. 128–129; Thornton, The Kingdom of Kongo and the Counter Reformation, p. 40–58.

207 Fromont, Collecting and Translating Knowledge Across Cultures, in: Bleichmar and Mancall (eds.), Collecting Across Cultures, p. 136; Thornton, A History of West Central Africa, p. 127; Thornton, The Kingdom of Kongo and the Counter Reformation, p. 40–58.

208 Bontinck, Introduction, p. xii–xiii; Thornton, A History of West Central Africa, p. 127–128.

209 For a detailed account of Portuguese attempts to prevent Italian and Spanish missionaries from reaching Kongo, see Bontinck. Until 1639, the *Real e Supremo Conselho de Portugal* [Royal and Supreme Council of Portugal] (1582–1639), created by Philip I of Portugal to assist him in governing the Kingdom of Portugal, provided a platform for Portuguese interference with the plans of Rome (from 1639 to 1640 it was substituted by the *Junta de Inteligências de Portugal*—Board of Portuguese Information). After the Brigantine Dynasty restored Portuguese independence (1640), the Overseas Council was established (1642), resuming the negotiations with the *Propaganda Fide* and the Capuchin order. During the Luso-Spanish war (1640–1668), the Capuchins' main challenge was navigating the anti-Spanish feelings of their Portuguese interlocutors while relying on the Spanish Atlantic armada to assure their safe passage to Kongo through the coastal regions controlled by the Dutch West India Company. After the Portuguese regained control of Luanda (1648), the Friars had to reconsider their alliances, becoming more cooperative with the Portuguese Crown. Bontinck, Introduction, p. xi–xx.

210 For a detailed period account, see Filipa Ribeiro da Silva. Ibid., p. xv–xix; Ribeiro da Silva, Dutch and Portuguese.

of Kongo had been recently made part of the Apostolic Prefecture of Congo, created by the *Propaganda Fide* on June 25, 1640, and entrusted to the Capuchins.[211] Because of the war with the Dutch, the twelve Spanish and Italian Capuchins that composed the first mission sent by the *Propaganda Fide* to the Prefecture of Congo were transported aboard a small commercial Genoese vessel, arriving in Mpinda on May 25, 1645.[212]

The West India Company's control of the Angolan coast had been made viable by an inter-denominational Dutch-BaKongo alliance.[213] This strained alliance was first proposed by *Mwene Kongo* Pedro II (?–1624) in 1623, in the aftermath of a series of Luso-Mbangala incursions in the Kongo.[214] Two years earlier, Captain-General and Governor João Correia de Sousa, in office between 1621 and 1623, had mobilized a Luso-Mbangala army to besiege the marshes known as "*Ensaca of Cassanze* [Kasanze]," on the left bank of the Kwanza River and immediately to the interior of Luanda.[215] At the time, Kasanze was a safe harbor for enslaved Africans who managed to escape being shipped to Brazil. Its rulers, the "*mani Cassanze* [Kasanze]" and the *sobas* "*Manigonge* [*Mani* Guengue] *and Manicorinha* [*Mani* Corimba]" were vassals of the Duke of Mbamba, and thus tributaries of the Kingdom of Kongo.[216] In the aftermath of the brutal siege of the Ensaca, *Mani* Kasanze, Gunegue, and Corimba were beheaded, their lands were distributed to Portuguese soldiers, and twenty-six Mbundu *sobas* and their free subjects and dependents were enslaved and shipped to Brazil.[217] Then, Pedro Afonso, soon

---

211 Bontinck, Introduction, p. vii–xxviii.

212 For the background of each friar and their many adventures and clashes with the Dutch before finally meeting the *Mwene Kongo*, see Jean-François de Rome's report and Leite de Faria's biography of Friar Cavazzi. Ibid., p. xvii–xix; Faria, João António Cavazzi, in: Leguzzano (ed.), Descrição Histórica dos Três Reinos, p. xi–lviii; Jean-François de Rome, La Fondation de la mission des Capuchins, p. 24–44.

213 For an account of the Dutch's failed attempts to convert the *Mwene Kongo* to Calvinism, see Thornton. Bontinck, Introduction, p. xv; Postma, The Dutch in the Atlantic Slave Trade, p. 60; Thornton, The Kingdom of Kongo and the Counter Reformation, p. 40–58.

214 Thornton, A History of West Central Africa, p. 129–132.

215 Sousa, Mapa das regiões circunvizinhas de Luanda, in: Heintze (ed.), Fontes para a História de Angola, Vol. 1, p. 158–165.

216 The title *mani* is the Portuguese adaptation of the Kikongo word *mwene* [lord]. Ibid.; MMA VII, D. 7, p. 20.

217 According to Correia de Sousa, Kasanze had only "*16 Sovas* [*sobas*]" under his "*jurisdiction*." In a letter written on June 2, 1622, the captain-general and governor brags to the Marquis of Frecilha that he had first requested Pero de Sousa Coelho, the captain of the Luso-Mbangala *kilombo* that besieged Kasanze, to escort to Luanda all these *sobas*, as well as their "*macotas* [*makota*]," "*tendalas*," "*maculuntos* [foremen]," and "*war ministers*," because he wanted to confirm them as Portuguese vassals in a ritual called *undamento*. He also requested the presence of "*four gingos, which are the heirs and contenders of Casange* [Kasanze]" under the pretext of electing the new *Mani* Kasanze.

to be Pedro II of Kongo, who had been recently appointed Duke of Mbamba and, as such, was sent to Luanda to negotiate the boundary between Angola and Kongo and disentangle the loyalties and jurisdictions of local Mbundu *sobas*.[218] However, Correia de Sousa accused him of assisting *Mani* Kasanze and demanded that Álvaro III of Kongo arrest and execute his diplomatic envoy upon his return to Kongo. Not only were Correia de Sousa's demands not heeded, but Duke Pedro Afonso was appointed the successor of Álvaro III after he unexpectedly died in 1622. Faced with this turn of events, while insisting on imposing unreasonable requests to the BaKongo, the captain-general and governor of Angola launched a full-scale invasion of Mbamba, now ruled by Duke Paulo Afonso.[219] This invasion resulted in the beheading of Duke Paulo, Marquis Cosme of Mpemba, and countless other Christian BaKongo nobles who, according to a Jesuit observer, were "*all buried in the bellies of the barbarous iagas*."[220]

However, soon after this initial victory over unprepared adversaries, a BaKongo army raised by Pedro II of Kongo routed the Luso-Mbangala forces.[221] As a result, the Luso-African merchants and *pumbeiros* residing in Kongo or operating along the northern trade routes immediately suffered heavy retaliations, despite the *Mwene Kongo* extending them his protection, many being killed and losing up to a total of "800,000 cruzados [about 320.000$000 *reis*] in merchandise." As Thornton explains, because of the magnitude of this loss, the Municipal Council of Luanda sided with Pedro II against Correia de Sousa, vocally declaring that further military interventions in Kongo were against the interests of Luso-African *moradores* and merchants. Before, the *ouvidor* and the Jesuits had already condemned the wrongful enslavement of the subjects of Kasanze and declared the invasion of Mbamba to be "against the law of nations."[222] Isolated and forced to flee Luanda on May 2, 1623,

---

However, as soon as these men arrived, Correia de Sousa arrested them all and requested the presence of their entire corporate kin groups, including women and children. Once they arrived in Luanda, all these unsuspecting subjects were sold off as slaves to Brazil, filling five slave ships. Heintze, Fontes para a História de Angola, Vol. 1, p. 120; MMA VII, D. 7, p. 21, D. 30; MMA XV, D. 190, p. 508–529; Sousa, Mapa das regiões circunvizinhas de Luanda, in: Heintze (ed.), Fontes para a História de Angola, Vol. 1, p. 158–165; Thornton, A History of West Central Africa, p. 129.

218 Thornton, A History of West Central Africa, p. 129.

219 Correia de Sousa demanded to Canon André Cordeiro, whom Pedro II had sent to Luanda as a peace negotiator, that the *Mwene Kongo* concede the copper mines of Mpemba and the *nzimbu* fisheries of the Island of Luanda to the Portuguese as compensation for his alleged assistance to the *Mani* Kasanze. MMA VII, D. 30, p. 191–192, 293–294.

220 Ibid.

221 Thornton, A History of West Central Africa, p. 131–132.

222 BaKongo diplomacy would reclaim a thousand prisoners wrongly enslaved during Correia de Sousa's unlawful invasion. MMA VII, D. 30; MMA XI, D. 166, p. 293; MMA XV, D. 190, p. 512; Thornton, The Kingdom of Kongo and the Counter Reformation, p. 42–43, 51.

the former captain-general and governor of Angola was arrested, eventually dying destitute and disgraced in the Limoeiro Prison in Lisbon.[223] Pedro II first proposed an alliance with the Dutch West India Company in this turbulent political context, paving the ground for the Dutch occupation of Angola.[224]

The first Capuchin mission arrived in Kongo during the reign of Garcia II, *Mwene Kongo* from 1641 to 1661. While the BaKongo elites expected the friars to provide them with the much coveted Christian sacraments, especially baptisms, the Capuchin, who had barely escaped the Calvinist Dutch, embarked on a quest to reform Kongo's Church up to Counter-Reformation standards following the decrees and canons of the Council of Trent (1545–1563).[225] While, as discussed in the previous chapters, BaKongo Christians, Portuguese secular priests, Carmelites, and Jesuits alike equated the non-Christian elements of BaKongo ritual life they wished to abolish to *feitiços* and idols, by 1645, this analogy was not predicated on notions of diabolical pacts or intentional contacts with the devil that were popularized only during the Counter-Reformation.[226] The Italian Capuchins, however, shared the Central European *imaginaire* of diabolical pacts and conscious contacts with the devil that were never popular in Portugal.[227] Soon, as Thornton remarks, they were framing BaKongo institutions such as the *kimpasi* anti-*kindoki* apotropaic cult as "diabolic," as well as circumcision and menstruation rituals, consultations with *nganga*, and all forms of divination.[228] In the words of Father António Brásio, after the euphoria of the initial cross-cultural shock subsided, the Capuchins produced an avalanche of "inexhaustible and vast documentation" about West Central African uses and customs.[229] Some of these were detailed lists of "inappropriate customs."[230]

---

223 Thornton, A History of West Central Africa, p. 131–132.

224 Thornton, The Kingdom of Kongo and the Counter Reformation, p. 41–42.

225 Ibid., p. 40–58; Jean-François de Rome, La fondation de la mission des Capuchins, p. 24–44; Thornton, A History of West Central Africa, p. 168.

226 Fromont, Nature, Culture, and Faith; Fromont, The Art of Conversion; Fromont, Under the Sign of the Cross, p. 109–123; Thornton, Afro-Christian Syncretism, p. 53–77; Thornton, Early Kongo-Portuguese Relations, p. 183–204; Thornton, Religião e vida cerimonial, in: Heywood (ed.), Diáspora negra no Brasil, p. 81–100; Thornton, The Development of an African Catholic Church, p. 147–167; Thornton, The Kingdom of Kongo and the Counter Reformation, p. 55.

227 Fromont, Collecting and Translating Knowledge Across Cultures, in: Bleichmar and Mancall (eds.), Collecting Across Cultures, p. 141; Paiva, Bruxaria e superstição.

228 For more information about the anti-sorcery and healing *kimpasi* public cult, see Thornton's monograph on Beatriz Kimpa Vita. Thornton, Afro-Christian Syncretism, p. 73; Thornton, A History of West Central Africa, p. 168; Thornton, The Kingdom of Kongo and the Counter Reformation, p. 55; Thornton, The Kongolese Saint Anthony, p. 42–44, 54–56, 71–75, 85–90, 114–118.

229 MMA XI, Introdução, p. viii.

230 MMA X, D. 135; Thornton, The Kingdom of Kongo and the Counter Reformation, p. 56.

Documents such as Friar Giovanni Francesco Romano's *Breve relatione del successo della missione de frati minori Capuccini del serafico padre san Francesco al regno del Congo* [Brief report of the success of the mission of the Capuchin Friars Minor of the seraphic Father Saint Francis to the kingdom of Congo] (1648), were immediately published by the *Propaganda Fide* in Rome and became highly influential,[231] while others, such as Friar Boaventura de Alessano's 1649 memorandum about BaKongo uses and customs, were meant for internal distribution.[232]

Friar Romano concludes his account of the Capuchin's mission to Kongo by providing a brief history of the West Central African kingdom and a description of its uses and customs. The latter, he divided into several headings, a couple dealing with "*some very harmful customs observed by the natives of the Congo*" and "*how much they are given to superstitions*."[233] Under the first heading, Friar Romano included BaKongo marriage arrangements, which he framed as the habit of "*taking women on a tryout*," condemning the habit of future husbands paying the "*dowry*," the freedom each partner had of terminating the provisional arrangements, and the expensive celebrations that marked the end of the "*tryout*" period through the celebration of a "*marriage according to the Roman Church*."[234] Moreover, he lamented BaKongo elites' fondness for noble titles, including BaKongo women.[235] Under the second heading, Friar Romano condemned the ritual performances of *banganga* as the workings of "*devilish sorcerers operating by diabolic artifices*." He reported that while their divinations were supposed to be therapeutic, *banganga* just extorted money from their clients, "*summoning the devil by talking to a calabash*." Writing about four years later, Friar Boaventura de Alessano gave his superiors at the *Propaganda Fide* a more comprehensive nine-point list of uses and customs deemed reproachable.[236] According to this list, the BaKongo: had orgies in "*places specially prepared, adorned with statues of idols, where they invoked the devil*" and committed incest; they manufactured "*several idols*" to help them with "*illnesses and other needs*" and practiced circumcision and polygamy. Moreover, Friar Alessano identified two "*sects*" or societies, one composed only of men and the other only of women, who performed ritual functions. The masculine society was entrusted with

231 Bontinck lists seven Italian editions between 1648 and 1651 (Rome 1648, Naples 1648, Milan 1649, Rome and Parma 1649, Rome 1649, Trent 1650, Milan 1651), followed by a first French translation in 1649 (Lyon) and a German one by Friar Ignatius von Rheinfelden, published in Contanz (1664). This first German translation had four editions (1664, 1666, 1667, 1699), and a second translation was published in 1912. Bontinck, Introduction, p. xi–xii.

232 Ibid., p. vii–xxviii; MMA X, D. 135.

233 Jean-François de Rome, La Fondation de la mission des Capuchins, p. 117–123.

234 Ibid., p. 118–119.

235 Ibid., p. 119–120.

236 MMA X, D. 135.

keeping a remote shrine where two fireplaces were "*constantly lit*," and a cult of earth spirits was worshiped. These men, the Capuchins explained, were "*considered the custodians of the land*." The feminine society was comprised exclusively of "*pure*" women or "*maidens*" who were considered the custodians "*of the homesteads*."

Finally, Friar Alessano described the *banganga* as "*magicians, charmers, sorcerers*," lamenting that when someone "*suffered a mishap with another person*" or "*lost some small thing*," they were called to settle the matter, "*adjudicating the accused and prizing his children, relatives and all they have, selling them as slaves, either to Catholics, or to heretics* [Calvinists], *or gentios* [i. e., non-Christian]."[237] This description clashes with how Friar Romano described the way justice was delivered in Kongo. According to him, palavers were the norm for civil cases, all "*criminal*" ones being "*rigorously*" punished by the *Mwene Kongo* with the death penalty.[238] During palavers, a "*judge*" would sit on a stool atop a "*large carpet*" in a "*public square*" with a "*staff in his hand*." Both adversaries would choose their "*lawyers*" amongst the audience's most "*intelligent*" members and take turns making their arguments. Then, "*according to Natural law*," all disputes were solved "*in no time*." The distinction Friars Romano and Alessano made between justice administered publicly under the auspices of the *Mwene Kongo*, the *Princeps* who guaranteed its full accordance with Natural law, and the private adjudication of other cases by the *banganga*, according to superstitious or diabolic divinations, would remain central to Capuchin and Portuguese understandings of West Central African normative systems until the late eighteenth century. Moreover, it paved the way for Father Rocha's ramson doctrine.[239] Given that two forms of adjudicating cases coexisted in Kongo, one perceived as based on Natural law, the other on diabolical superstitions, no legal certainty could be had about the just enslavement of BaKongo slaves. However, all adjudications of *feitiçaria* or *kindoki* by judicial ordeal or oath could be safely described as 'diabolical,' justifying the ransom of the accused.

The Capuchins, however, remained vocal opponents of slavery and its institutions, never subscribing to Second-Scholastic doctrines of just enslavement.[240] Moreover, being mendicants, they refused to own personal property, depending on free Africans to serve them as porters and personal assistants.[241] Nevertheless, their accounts of West Central African uses and customs would provide the basis for the doctrines that justified slavery or similar forms of extreme asymmetrical dependency during the Enlightenment. These accounts were not limited to the Kingdom

---

237 Ibid.

238 Jean François de Rome, La Fondation de la mission des Capuchins, p. 131–132.

239 Rocha, Ethiope resgatado.

240 Cagle, Imperial Tensions, Colonial Contours, in: Martínez-San Miguel and Arias (eds.), The Routledge Hispanic Studies Companion to Colonial Latin America and the Caribbean, p. 216.

241 Thornton, The Kingdom of Kongo and the Counter Reformation, p. 58.

of Kongo and its BaKongo and Mbundu vassals. During the three months of the dry season of 1660, Friar Cavazzi collected Kasanje's oral histories in situ.[242] He included elements from them in the printed monograph *Istorica Descrizione De' Tre' Regni Congo Matamba Et Angola* [Historical Description of the Three Kingdoms of Kongo, Matamba, and Angola] (1687),[243] edited posthumously by Father Fortunato Alamandini, and the three manuscript volumes known as *Manoscritti Araldi, A, B, C* [Araldi Manuscript, A, B, C] (1668).[244] Friar Cavazzi had been sent to Kasanje by the Portuguese Crown to advance the missionary efforts of his fellow Capuchin Friar António da Serravezza,[245] who had managed to do little more than baptize Jaga Kasanje ka Kinguri as Dom Pasqual Machado in 1657 after two years of failed evangelization attempts.[246] Volume A of the Araldi Manuscript is titled *Missione evangelica del Regno de Congo* [Evangelical Mission to the Kingdom of Kongo].[247]

242 Miller, Kings, Lists, and History in Kasanje, p. 55.

243 This primary source is explored in the chapters included in the third section.

244 I follow Thornton's English translation of this manuscript. Henceforward referred to as MSS Araldi, Modena. Cavazzi, Thornton (trans.) MSS Araldi, Modena; Levi, Padre Giovanni Antonio Cavazzi, p. 29–47; Thornton, New Light on Cavazzi's, p. 253–264.

245 According to Captain-General and Governor Luís Martins de Sousa Chichorro, in office between 1654 and 1658, the *jaga* of Kasanje had requested the missionary himself, after having "*dreamt*" that he would "*submit to the law of their* [the Portuguese's] *God*." MMA XI, D. 166, p. 515–516.

246 Before baptising *Jaga* Kasanje ka Kinguri as Dom Pasqual Machado, Friar António da Serravezza made him a series of demands. According to a letter of July 9, 1657, transcribed by Friar Cavazzi, Friar Serravezza requested that the *jaga* professed his belief in "*one true God*," the "*Most Holy Trinity*," and other articles of Roman Catholic faith, "*renege*[d]" "*all the idols and devils enemies of God*" and "*prohibit*[ed] *all sorts of Witch-doctors*;" and adopted monogamy. Moreover, he demanded that the *jaga* frequent the "*Church on Sunday*," be buried "*there, or in the cemetery outside the Church*," and build a church next to "*whatever place*" he situated his *kilombo*. The capuchin also demanded that "*no Christian*" be allowed to "*eat human flesh*," nor would the *jaga* "*allow men or women to be killed by Witch-doctors, nor let their blood be taken, nor let them be eaten, to hold funeral and sacrifices for any dead person*." Friar Serravezza further stipulated that "*any woman*" who killed her child was to be "*publicly whipped with the sum of 39 or 40 lashes*," the same penalty applied to those who tore "*their children to pieces*" or forbade them "*to be baptized until they have teeth*." Finally, he demanded as a condition for the baptism of the *jaga* that "*public*" oathtaking was abolished and that the oath "*Priest*" be "*condemned to slavery*" if he failed to convert to Christianity. Friar Cavazzi considered Friar Serravezza's missionary efforts a failure because, in his view, he had been unable to convince the *jaga* to deliver any of these requests. As discussed in the following paragraphs, most of these demands react to the *ijila* or "*laws*" of the *kilombo*, mistakenly taking them at face value. Cavazzi, Thornton (trans.) MSS Araldi, Modena, Book 3, Chap. 2, 4; Thornton, A History of West Central Africa, p. 192.

247 According to Thornton, Friar Cavazzi started writing *Missione evangelica* in Luanda c. 1666–7. Besides his notes and memories, he used the archive of the Capuchin hospice in Luanda, as well as "recollections of the fellow missionaries resident there." He returned to Europe and completed this draft c. 1671 after engaging with "extensive archival research." Thornton argues that one of Friar Cavazzi's most critical European sources was a "very detailed report" of Friar Giacinto Brugiotti

The first and third of its books describe Kasanje, shaping Mbangala *musendo* and *malunda* into a European-style chronicle that narrates the institutional history of Kasanje titles as a realist account of the deeds of historical individuals.

Friar Cavazzi starts by narrating a *musendo* genealogical set, connecting the contemporary *Jagas* of Kasanje with mythical ancestors and 'lineage title' holders. According to the first chapter of the first book of *Missione evangelica del Regno de Congo*, Kasanje was founded by "*Zimbo*," who had sent "*Dongij*," one of his captains, to marry a local woman called "*Mussasa*."[248] From this union, Friar Cavazzi narrates, "*Tembo Andumba*" was born, who in turn married "*Zimbo*" and mothered a daughter also called "*Tembo Andumba*." According to the Araldi manuscript, this second Tembo Andumba was "*the mother*" and "*legislator*" of all the Mbangala warbands, introducing the *ijila* [laws; sing. *kijila*] that regulated their *kilombo* or war camps.[249] According to the third chapter of the first book, after "*legislating*," the second Tembo Andumba married a "*soldier*" named "*Culemba*," who eventually murdered her with poison (perhaps a reference to an anti-sorcery ordeal), assuming total control of the original Mbangala warband. The Capuchin friar then claims that Culemba subsequently married "*Bomba Ignacha*" and appointed several "*captains*" as his delegates in the warband, including the ones named "*Casa, Calanda, Cabucco,* [and] *Caimba*." After Culemba's death, the Capuchin friar continues, he was succeeded by "*Chingurij*," then by "*Golaximbo*," and finally by "*Cassange, Caimbe, Cabuco, Casa*" and "*others* [who] *took up the government* [of Kasanje] *in turn*." Friar Cavazzi further related that the last two *Jagas* of Kasanje, "*Cassange Calunga* [Kalunga ka Kilombo]," who had dealt with Salvador Correia de Sá e Benevides, captain-general and governor of Angola between 1648 and 1651, and "*Cassange Canquigurij* [Kasanje ka Kinguri]," who had been baptized by da Serravezza in 1657, were the last two in this succession line.[250]

After conveying this *musendo*, Friar Cavazzi narrates a *malunda* episode describing how the second Tembo Andumba cemented the Mbangala *kilombo* by celebrating a diabolical social contract. According to him, Tembo Andumba bequeathed the *ijila* to the Mbangala after sacrificing her baby daughter, crushing her alive in a "*great mortar*" called "*quino*" to produce a "*holy oil*" known as "*Maggi*

---

da Vetralla, the Prefect of the Capuchin mission from 1652 to 1657, titled *Infelicitá felice o vero mondo alla roversa* [Happy unhappiness or the real world upside down]. According to Thornton, Friar Brugiotti's thesis that the "world was «upside down» in the Kingdom of Kongo" strongly influenced Friar Cavazzi's writings. Thornton, New Light on Cavazzi's, p. 253–264.

248 Cavazzi, Thornton (trans.) MSS Araldi, Modena, Book 1, Chap. 1; Thornton, A History of West Central Africa, p. 189.

249 Cavazzi, Thornton (trans.) MSS Araldi, Modena, Book 1, Chap. 2–3; Thornton, A History of West Central Africa, p. 189.

250 Miller, Kings, Lists, and History in Kasanje, p. 79.

Fig. 6 Tembo Andumba Prepares the *Maji a Samba* Ointment. CAVAZZI, ALAMANDI (trans.), Historische Beschreibung Der In dem untern Occidentalischen Mohrenland ligenden drey Königreichen, Congo, Matamba, und Angola, p. 293 (Source: gallica.bnf.fr / Bibliothèque Nationale de France).

ÿa Samba [*maji a samba*]."[251] After reducing her child to a pulp, Tembo Andumba mixed it with herbs, roots, and coal and stored the "*precious ointment or liquor*" in "*gourds.*" This oil, the Capuchin friar continued, was believed by Mbundu and Mbangala alike to grant magical powers to warriors of the *kilombo*. Anointing herself with it, Friar Cavazzi described, Tembo Andumba became a fierce male warrior and, by dispensing it to the other soldiers, gained ascendancy over them. This, he concluded, allowed Tembo Andumba to reform the Mbangala warband, whose military prowess now depended on their magic, by giving it "*particular laws to keep and observe which their ancestors neither had nor observed.*" Emboldened by the *maji a samba*, the Capuchin friar remarked, Mbangala warriors quickly subdued the neighboring kingdoms, turning "*their flesh*" into "*food*" and "*their blood*" into "*drink.*"

The mythical genealogy attributed by Friar Cavazzi to the last two historical *Jagas* of Kasanje can be understood as his rendering of the mythic level of the *musendo* he collected from Mbangala intellectuals or their Mbundu neighbors while conducting

251 CAVAZZI, THORNTON (trans.) MSS Araldi, Modena; MILLER, Kings and Kinsmen, p. 165–167, 232.

his mission in Kasanje. Tembo Andumba can thus be identified as a 'lineage title' rather than a historical person.[252] Accordingly, this passage metaphorically recounts how its incumbents came to sacrifice their authority over their corporate kin group (e. g., the sacrificed daughter) to have jurisdiction over the warriors of the *kilombo*, establishing the laws that ruled this 'cross-lineage' political institution.[253] In other words, such a reframing suggests that the *malunda* at the root of Friar Cavazzi's biased description of Mbangala 'customs' narrated a political innovation of great consequence, namely the establishment of the *maji a samba* warrior cult. As Miller explains, this cult enabled a form of groupwork that allowed members of very diverse 'lineages' and ethnic groups to come together under the leadership of the warband commanders and identify as a novel community of 'moral belonging,' the militaristic *kilombo*. This reframing allows us to move past literal interpretations of descriptions of infanticide and cannibalism and accept these tropes as emic metaphors for political assimilation (cannibalism) and the transfer of legitimacy from the *sobas* and *makota* who ruled Mbundu *ngundu* [corporate kin groups] to appointed political leaders (infanticide).[254]

As Miller argues, "in a figurative sense," the preparation of *maji a samba* was a "symbol for the enormity of a ruler's power over his people" and the abolishment of "lineages" through the "denial of the social significance of a physical birth" and a refusal to recognize the role of motherhood in the social reproduction of the group.[255] Furthermore, to thoroughly understand the political impact of the *maji a samba* cult, Miller continues, it is crucial to contrast the power exerted by *jagas* with that wielded by Mbundu political title holders.[256] Miller explains that Mbundu political title holders only had "temporal" authority over their subjects, leaving the mediation with "the supernatural" to "lineage title" holders (*makota*), diviners, and other specialized agents in charge of shrines.[257] This distinction is not always clear in Portuguese primary sources because of the indiscriminate use of the title *soba* to describe Mbundu political and "lineage title" holders and the dismissal of other ritual agents (all dismissed as *feiticeiros*). Contrary to what happened in Mbundu territories or independent polities, after the *maji a samba* cult became part of the

252 Miller, Kings and Kinsmen, p. 232–236.

253 In this reading, Tembo Andumba's mythical gender swap signifies the transition of the title 'Tembo Andumba' from being a corporate kin group title (female) to being a political one (male).

254 Heywood and Thornton, Central Africans, p. 72–79.

255 Miller, Kings and Kinsmen, p. 165–166.

256 Ibid., p. 232–236.

257 For an opposite opinion, see Wyatt MacGaffey. MacGaffey argues that in Central Africa and other contexts that borrowed political models from it, "the distinction between political and ritual roles, so important to those for whom the separation of church and state seems obvious, cannot be made." MacGaffey, Crossing the River, in: Heintze and von Oppen (eds.), Angola on the Move, p. 226–227.

kilombo institutional matrix, the Mbangala *jaga* assumed "dual competence in both the temporal and supernatural spheres," completely centralizing authority in their office.[258] Therefore, the adoption of the *maji a samba* cult offered to Mbangala *jagas* the same kind of political leeway that the conversion to Roman Catholicism had provided to the *Mwene Kongo*, enabling them to wield political as well as spiritual power and undermine the opposition of competing title holders who tied their legitimacy to the latter. Purchas corroborates this interpretation, claiming that Battel described the *Jagas* as having no "*Fetisso's* [*feitiços*, charms], *or idols*" other than the "*great Iagge, or Prince,*" who was "*the matter of all their Ceremonies, and* [...] *a great Witch*."[259] However, from the BaKongo, Mbundu, Capuchin, and Portuguese perspectives, adopting the *maji a samba* cult could not be equated with converting to Roman Catholicism or any other form of organized religion. For the Africans, this cult provided insufficient normative framing for their daily lives and the social reproduction of the settled *kilombo*; for the Europeans, it evidenced that the Mbangala predicated their social contract on a 'diabolical' pact.

In the third and fifth chapters of the first book of Evangelical Mission to the Kingdom of Kongo, Friar Cavazzi describes the 14 "*diabolical quixillas*" or "*laws*" of Tembo Andumba fleshing out how a settled Mbangala polity could still be said to live close to a Hobbesian state of nature due to the diabolical contract that held it together.[260] He begins by contrasting *ijila* with the "*Divine laws*" of the Christians, finding them "*barbarous and inhuman*" in comparison and wanting in "*Majesty and Kindness*."[261] Friar Cavazzi then equates their normative weight to the recommendations that "*fathers and mothers give their children*," adding that Mbangala "*priests equally give quixillas* [*ijila*] *in occasions of sickness or death, traveling, business and* [bad] *weather conditions*," and that they were all "*faithfully observed and such is the fear of transgressing them that in many it causes death*." When describing these "*priests*" in the eighth chapter of the first book, Friar Cavazzi uses the expression "*Ganga* [*nganga*]," situating them in opposition to the "*Singhili* [*xinguilas*—spirit mediums]" whom he describes in the ninth chapter of the same book as "*bishops*."[262] Before enumerating different kinds of *nganga* and *xinguilas*, Friar Cavazzi claims that these offices were common to both Mbangala and "*non-Giagas*" peoples (i. e., Mbundu and BaKongo), whom he understood to be all arranged in "*congregations*" headed by the "*parish priests*" of "*their idols*."[263] At the

---

258 Miller, Kings and Kinsmen, p. 232–236.

259 Purchas, Purchas his Pilgrimage, p. 699.

260 Cavazzi, Thornton (trans.) MSS Araldi, Modena, Book 1, Chap. 3, 5.

261 Ibid., Book 1, Chap. 3.

262 Ibid., Book 1, Chap. 8–9; Parreira, Dicionário glossográfico, p. 84, 113.

263 According to Miller, while the Mbangala incorporated some of the "lineage titles" and ritual specialists of the Mbundu, at first, there needed to be a marked contrast between the way they

same time, he continued, "*the summation of all* [Mbangala] *laws, rites, customs and heathen ceremonies*" rested in the "*hands*" of *xinguilas* capable of incorporating and thus speaking for "*idols*" or the spirits of deceased *jagas*. This confirms the claims about the centrality of possession rituals mediated by *xinguilas* made by Purchas and Battel, Bishop Baptista, and Captain-General and Governor Mendes de Vasconcelos.[264]

As Thornton notes, Friar Cavazzi's choice to contrast Tembo Andumba's *ijila* with the "*Divine laws*" of the Christians certainly impacted his rendering of these prohibitions, influencing his decision to list them in a format that echoed, albeit in a 'diabolical,' deeply misogynous manner, that of the Ten Commandments.[265] By doing so, the Capuchin friar not only reified what was probably a diffuse set of oral prohibitions into a written, enumerated list of laws of the *kilombo* but also made a case for a settled polity to be ruled by laws contrary to Natural law, defined either in theological or jus-rationalist terms. The first *kijila* Friar Cavazzi mentions was "*Quixilla Variangue*," which prohibited Mbangala women from giving birth inside the *kilombo*.[266] The second *kijila* he mentions was "*Quixilla Quiari*" or "*Quÿari quixilla*." A variation on the first, it also prescribed infanticide in specific cases and described some of the rituals that incorporated children captured in war.[267] According to Friar Cavazzi, this *kijila* stipulated that children born in the *kilombo* were to be sacrificed to produce *maji a samba*. Further norms for incorporating

---

operated as part of the *kilombo*. This contrast is easily explained by the fact that the *kilombo* was a "cross-lineage institution," built on the incorporation of "lineages" through forms of groupwork that denied significance to matrilineal ties and connections both to matrilineal ancestors and territorial spirits (Friar Cavazzi's "*idols*"). Therefore, while the *xinguilas* described by Friar Cavazzi could also be found in Mbundu polities, Miller explains that in Kasanje, they incorporated the spirits of deceased *jagas*, not Mbundu ancestors or other spirits. As for the *banganga* tied to local shrines or ordeals, they would have been useless to a roving band of mercenaries. Nevertheless, Miller concludes, as the Kasanje warband settled, "older, non-Imbangala, political titles and symbols" were incorporated by the emerging polity, and by the middle of the seventeenth century, the Mbangala came to venerate Mbundu "local spirits." The next chapter returns in greater detail to the contrast between Mbangala and Mbundu ritual operators. Cavazzi, Thornton (trans.) MSS Araldi, Modena, Book 1, Chap. 8–9; Miller, Kings and Kinsmen, p. 235–238, 257.

264 MMA VI, D. 98, p. 285, D. 122., p. 367; Purchas, Purchas His Pilgrimes, Vol. 6, p. 387–388.

265 Cavazzi, Thornton (trans.) MSS Araldi, Modena, Book 1, Chap. 3.

266 According to Friar Cavazzi, this *kijila* stated that "*if anyone gives birth she should kill the child or leave it where she gave birth or throw it into a river*." It further stipulated that "*for children, they should keep those they captured in war*." Ibid., Book 1, Chap. 3, 5.

267 According to Friar Cavazzi, this *kijila* ordered Mbangala to have their "*two middle upper teeth pulled out*" to differentiate them from the non-Mbangala. Furthermore, it stipulated they were to be branded with an iron called "*quirimbo*," which the Capuchin describes as like the one used to brand enslaved Africans with "*the mark of the whites*." Ibid., Book 1, Chap. 5.

children into the *kilombo* are provided in the sixth *kijila*, "*Quixilla Samano*."[268] The third *kijila* Friar Cavazzi mentions was "*Quixilla Gitatu*" or "*Quitatu quixilla*." It concerned preparing and using the *maji a samba* oil during warfare. According to Friar Cavazzi, war was also regulated by the fourth, "*Quixilla Givana*," eighth, "*Quixilla Naque*," and thirteenth *ijila*, "*Quixilla Cuim*" or "*Quixilla Cuim ne quitatu*."[269] These, respectively, stipulated that the Mbangala were to "*make sacrifices killing men and animals imploring their dead ones*" for favor before starting a war, interrupt the campaigns when the commander's first concubine was menstruating, and "*make sacrifices and abstain from intercourse*" for "*two months before war*." According to Friar Cavazzi, "*Quixilla Givana*" also stipulated that the Mbangala were "*to bury those who were killed in the war in their own bellies*." The seventh *kijila*, "*Quixilla Sambuari*," further regulated cannibalism. The fifth *kijila* Friar Cavazzi mentions was "*Quixilla quitanù*" or "*Quixilla quitanu*," the tenth was "*Quixilla Cuim*," and the eleventh was "*Quixilla Cuim ne moxi*."[270] Together, they regulated the human sacrifices that were to take place at the burials of "*valorous soldiers*" and the disposal of the remains of "*dead lords*." The twelfth *kijila*, "*Quixilla Cuimaijari*" or "*Quixille Cuim ne aÿari*," regulated the offers due to these dead lords when they possessed *xinguilas*. The ninth *kijila* Friar Cavazzi mentions was "*Quixilla Vua*," regulating the rituals associated with the menarche of Mbangala women, and the fourteenth *kijila* was "*Quixilla Cuim ne vana*," prescribing the enthronement rituals of the *jagas*.

Whether we interpret them literally or figuratively, these fourteen *ijila* seem all geared towards turning the Mbangala *kilombo* into an effective warband, unencumbered by the presence of young children and unconstrained by any dependency or allegiance ties between its members and the heads of corporate kin groups or any other authorities except the living and deceased commanders (i. e., ancestors) of the warband.[271] As such, the normative ideals expressed by the *ijila* allowed for a radically different form of groupwork, based not on the Mbundu and BaKongo conceptual idiom of bloodlines, uterine descent, and connection with ancestral territories but in incorporation through impressment, military training, and martial valor. As for the normative elements related to women's reproductive cycles, these seem to fill the void left by the non-existence of groups like the feminine BaKongo 'sects' described by Friar Alessano, which probably regulated the socially appropriate gendered behavior of women in Kongo during menstrual periods, menarche, or menopause.[272] Similarly, possession rituals and forms of ritual cannibalism not only

268 Ibid., Book 1, Chap. 3, 5.

269 Ibid., Book 1, Chap. 3.

270 Ibid., Book 1, Chap. 3, 5.

271 Miller, Kings and Kinsmen.

272 MMA X, D. 135.

stand in for ancestor cults and cults of territorial spirits, assuaging Mbundu cosmological anxieties, as Miller argues, but also seem to contribute to the centralization of the *jagas*' power.[273]

Regardless of how the Mbundu and BaKongo perceived the conversion of the normative knowledge that grounded their corporate kin groups into the *ijila* that provided the normative framework of the Mbangala *kilombo*, the Capuchin and Portuguese observers perceived it as marking the transition from a form of government based on Natural law to one based on despotism, irrational "laws," and the 'diabolic' social pact established by Tembo Andumba.[274] On the one hand, if Natural law is understood as "*that which nature has taught to all animals*," by killing their offspring, eating their fellow men, and refusing to procreate, the Mbangala seemed bent on acting against it.[275] On the other, if Natural law is understood as being grounded on *recta ratio* and *Ius gentium*, their alleged superstitions, capricious behavior, and refusal to accept Mbundu and BaKongo normativities situated Kasanje firmly outside its limits.

Regarding the administration of justice at the court of the *jaga* of Kasanje, Friar Cavazzi mentioned the existence of a political office that accumulated functions similar to those of the Mbundu *tendala* and *ngola ambole*, namely the "*Colambolo*" or "*Golombolo*."[276] As the Capuchin friar reported, the office of "*Colambolo*" was one of the most prestigious, "*meaning Sergeant General, an office which among the Giaga people is only given to belligerent, inhuman and cruel soldiers*." Furthermore, it was the *colambolo*'s "*responsibility to pass sentence and define the reason*," having the "*power of sanction before his Lord even if he is the King*." Friar Cavazzi added that his "*sentences were punctually and quickly executed*" and that he sat "*in the public square in his tribunal as sentencing judge*." As all others in charge of "*the administration of temporal justice*," the Capuchin friar explained, the *colambolo* was only "*able to pass sentence*" after putting on "*some cloth of their dead predecessor*" and rubbing his "*arms and chest with chalk, they call Pemba*."[277] It was as if these clothes, he wrote ironically, "*had taught him knowledge and the opinions of doctors and lawyers*." According to Adriano Parreira and Catarina Madeira Santos, both rituals were also

273 Miller, Kings and Kinsmen, p. 246–249.

274 In the third chapter of the third book of Evangelical Mission to the Kingdom of Kongo, Friar Cavazzi narrates his attempt to convert the *jaga* of Kasanje. He describes how he sought to forbid the observance of *ijila* but was told by different Mbangala officeholders that they were central to the government of the *kilombo*. Friar Cavazzi paraphrases these dialogues as apologies for cannibalism and human sacrifice. Cavazzi, Thornton (trans.) MSS Araldi, Modena, Book 1, Chap. 3; Book 3, Chap. 3.

275 Hespanha, A cultura jurídica europeia, p. 303–304; Watson (trans.), The Digest of Justinian, Vol. 1, p. 1.

276 Cavazzi, Thornton (trans.) MSS Araldi, Modena, Book 3, Chap. 1; MMA XII, D. 118.

277 Cavazzi, Thornton (trans.) MSS Araldi, Modena, Book 1, Chap. 5.

central to Mbundu investiture ceremonies and, therefore, seem to be related to taking a political office conceived in perpetual kinship terms and not specifically with the ability to adjudicate.[278] As they explain, by the seventeenth century, the Portuguese had incorporated both in the "*undamento*" rite that formalized vassal relations between *sobas* and *dembos* and the Portuguese Crown.[279]

To give his readers an idea of the style followed by Mbangala courts, Friar Cavazzi narrated three judgments supposedly passed by *Jaga* Kasanje ka Kinguri when he was still named "*Gongo quitulla*" and occupied the office of *colambolo*.[280] Likely, these are adapted from *malunda* and cannot be understood as literal accounts of Mbangala justice in action or the deeds of historical individuals. In the first case, Friar Cavazzi claims that acting as "*iniquitous judge*," Gongo quitulla ordered an unspecified "*ruling official*" to decapitate five persons "*without trial*" to "*satisfy his appetite and desire to feed off their flesh*." In the second case, he affirms that Gongo quitulla killed one of his "*blood*" brothers when he was captured as a slave by the Mbangala. In keeping with the Capuchin friar, Gongo quitulla had been initially captured by Kalunga ka Kilombo in "*Dambi aquitulla* [Ndambi a Kitula]" and condemned to death in the *kilombo*. However, because of his cruelty and cannibal appetite, Friar Cavazzi adds, he was nevertheless spared, eventually ascending to the Mbangala throne. According to the Capuchin friar, because Gongo quitulla had this life trajectory, it was doubly scandalous that he showed no mercy to his captured brother. In the third case, Friar Cavazzi describes that acting as *colambolo*, Gongo quitulla accused "*Giaga Tembanzo*," *Jaga* Kalunga ka Kilombo's "*principal Concubine*" of practicing sorcery, condemning her to be burned alive. While a Mbundu *tendalla* would require the confirmation of a diviner to act in similar cases, the *colambolo*'s spiritual connection with the ancestors seems to have allowed him to circumvent this need.[281]

---

278 In other words, the ritual signaled the new incumbent 'becoming' their predecessor, symbolically having access to their accumulated wisdom and knowledge. Parreira, Dicionário glossográfico, p. 106–107; Santos, Escrever o poder, in: Heintze and von Oppen (eds.), Angola on the Move, p. 176.

279 The *undamento* also resulted in a written document, an "*auto de vassalagem* [bill of vassalage]," that listed the privileges and obligations of both parties. After the *amos* system was abolished at the beginning of the seventeenth century, these bills could be signed between *sobas*, *dembos*, *jagas*, or other African authorities and captain-general and governors, captain majors, or other Portuguese officers acting as delegates of the Crown. Until the late nineteenth century, the wording of these bills was still inspired by the "*formulário de homenagens* [homage formular]" instituted by D. João II of Portugal in the *Cortes* of Évora (1481). Heintze, Luso-African Feudalism, p. 111–131; Mello, Carta de oficio do Governador; Santos, Um governo "polido" para Angola, p. 116–117; Ximenes, Bahia e Angola, p. 106–109.

280 Cavazzi, Thornton (trans.) MSS Araldi, Modena, Book 3, Chap. 1.

281 Heintze, Fontes para a História de Angola, Vol. 1, p. 125.

According to Friar Cavazzi, in Kasanje, it was "*a great ignominy and opprobrium to be a magician* [sorcerer], *and they are convinced magicians are* [to be] *condemned to the flames because they hold that nobody can die except from witchcraft.*"[282] Friar Cavazzi approved of this custom, saying that the Mbangala means of killing sorcerers by fire could be turned into a "*good*" inquisitorial practice if only "*the rigor of the law did not make* [an] *exception for anyone.*" In that case, he continued, a "*general judgment*" of the "*Lords who govern*" could occur, perhaps under his direction. However, the Capuchin friar lamented, "*nobody* [was] *called to an office or to public appointment unless* [...] *experienced in several arts and especially those of witchcraft* [sorcery]," and of the powerful, "*nobody speaks, and the rigor of the law is only executed against some poor unfortunate.*"

Interpreting these three narratives as Friar Cavazzi's adaptation of Mbangala *malunda* affords us a better understanding of the functions, privileges, and obligations of the office of *colambolo*, casting doubts regarding their accuracy regarding the styles adopted at his court. From this perspective, this Mbangala officer seems to have overseen the sorting and integration of enslaved persons, deciding their fate. The first case alludes to the *colambolo*'s responsibility to choose war prisoners to be incorporated first as slaves, then as members of the *kilombo* (expressed through the trope of cannibalism).[283] The second case alludes to his role in alienating the war prisoners who were not selected as slaves (expressed through the trope of fratricide and sacrifice). These first two cases thus refer to how the Mbangala, like the Mbundu, conceptualized the distinction between alienable and inalienable slaves.[284] The centrality of sorcery beliefs and accusations evidenced by the third case testifies to another normative overlap between both groups, suggesting the possibility that the emerging polity incorporated Mbundu practices and norms related to sorcery accusations, divination, and ordeals. Confirming this hypothesis, Cavazzi claims that both Mbangala and Mbundu employed the services of a "*Ganga ya Bulungo*," or "*Priest of the ordeal*," responsible for administering the *mbulungo* ordeal or 'oath.'[285] Besides this incorporation, as the following chapter describes, between the settlement of Kasanje and the visit of Leitão in 1756, the *jagas* of Kasanje encouraged the development of a court specialized in adjudicating sorcery accusations. This court allowed them to enslave their subjects and extend their

282 The term "witchcraft" is used in Miller's translation, but it is unclear what word Friar Cavazzi used and whether sorcery would be a better fit. Cavazzi, Thornton (trans.) MSS Araldi, Modena, Book 3, Chap. 1.

283 See Miller for an analysis of the Mbangala institution translated as "slavery" by European observers. Miller, Imbangala Lineage Slavery (Angola), in: Miers and Kopytoff (eds.), Slavery in Africa, p. 205–234.

284 In the case of the Mundu, the distinction between *kijiku* and *mubika*.

285 Cavazzi, Thornton (trans.) MSS Araldi, Modena, Book 1, Chap. 8.

jurisdiction to Portuguese *presídios*, turning the fair of Cassange into a site of normative disambiguation where the aporias that resulted from two normative systems overlapping while being articulated as incommensurable could be economically exploited.

6. Clashing Monopolies on Disambiguation

6.1. Rumors Spread of a Sorcerer Coming to Cassange

Soon after Manoel Correia Leitão left the forests of Mbondo beyond, Antonio Roiz Grizante, the pilot who accompanied him to the Kingdom of Kasanje with instructions to fix the latitude of the Luso-African slave fair of Cassange, was rumored to be a "*sorcerer*."[1] As Leitão's report describes, in February 1756, news that their "*coming to trade was fictitious, because in reality* [he] *had a sorcerer with* [him] *to bewitch their lands*" spread like wildfire. Grizante, a sailor and probably not an experienced hinterland traveler, "*had publicly made observations of the sun*" in Cambambe and Ambaca using his navigational instruments. According to Leitão, the purpose of these measurements puzzled their Mbundu porters, and gossip about Grizante soon preceded the caravan. Aware of the severe implications of letting this rumor escalate into a formal accusation arbitrated by the *jaga*, Leitão quickly devised a plan. Sending the Mbangala ruler a notice stating that he brought an official "*diplomatic message*" from the Captain-General and Governor António Álvares da Cunha, Leitão demanded that, in keeping with "*the Right of nations*," the *jaga* grant him passage and protection. According to Leitão's narrative, the plan worked perfectly, allowing him to conclude his secret mission. After consulting the state oracles, the ruler of Kasanje sent a delegation to meet Leitão in a place called "*Magile*"[2] because he never talked "*in person with a white person*" on account

---

1 Sebestyén, Vansina (eds.), and Leitão, Angola's Eastern Hinterland, p. 337.

2 According to Vansina and Sebestyén, "*Magile*," also glossed by Leitão as "*maGille*," means "the roads" or "crossroads" and probably refers to a place near the fair of Cassange. Then, the *jaga*'s *kilombo* was still distant from the Luso-African fair. As Vellut describes, this changed in 1795, when the *jaga* felt the need to oversee the transactions at the fair, if not directly because of the *ijila* that barred him from doing so, at least from a closer distance, through appointed officeholders. In the 1850s, according to a report published by Sergeant António Rodrigues Neves in 1854, Cassange was separated from the capital of Kasanje only by a small stream called "*Njue*." By then, Fernandes Soares explains, the slave fair was no longer held where it first convened in 1624, in the aftermath of a military operation led by Captain Roque de São Miguel against the original Mbangala warband that was to give origin to the Kingdom of Kasanje. According to a topographic report by Captain António Maria Ribeiro published in 1863, the fair was initially situated in Macúria and later moved to Cassanza. Soares concludes that Macúria was located between the Angolan towns of Tala Mungongo and Cafuxe (nowadays Cafuchi). In contrast, Cassanza was located next to the old Portuguese administrative post of Xamuteba in the municipality of Quela. Unfortunately, Leitão did not include Grizante's measurements in his report. Fernandes, A feira de Cassanje; Neves, Memória da expedição a Cassange p. 124; Sebestyén, Vansina (eds.), and Leitão, Angola's Eastern Hinterland, p. 331, 337; Vellut, Le Royaume de Cassange, p. 129–130.

of his "*relevant rules and omens*," the *ijila* that governed the *kilombo*. At Magile, Leitão transmitted a made-up "*diplomatic message*" to the envoys and seized the opportunity to "*enter the lands*" of Kasanje and "*investigate*" the margins of the Kwango River and contact the neighboring Holo while awaiting an official reply.[3]

Leitão's list of false diplomatic demands discloses a lot about the state of Cassange at the moment of his visit and the fraught relationship between local Portuguese authorities, the Luso-African merchants who frequented the slave fair, and the *jagas* of Kasanje. This chapter concludes Part II, exploring how the multiple ambiguities that resulted from the historical development of the regime of commensuration described in the previous two chapters were resolved. It analyses the attempts of the Portuguese authorities and the *jagas* to retain a monopoly on mechanisms of disambiguation and associated forms of legitimate violence. As Grizante's predicament proves, the "space of correlation" that allowed African and European beliefs and values to be made commensurable and the slave trade to flourish, also resulted in high levels of uncertainty regarding practices whose ulterior purpose was challenging to discern across cultural, social, or religious divides.[4] From the times of Father Baltasar Barreira (1538–1612) and Bishop Gaspar Cão (?–1574) to the mid-1750s, the Atlantic slave trade had moved from being a form of transferring accumulated wealth in people out of the region to become a truly global economic enterprise at

3 Sebestyén, Vansina (eds.), and Leitão, Angola's Eastern Hinterland, p. 337–339.

4 Fromont, The Art of Conversion; Fromont, Under the Sign of the Cross.

the cutting edge of technological and financial development.[5] New financial instruments, such as *letras* and *livranças*, now mediated wealth extraction from Angola to Portugal.[6] Concomitantly, a veritable overflow of mass-produced North European and Asian trade goods and guns, imported through African-controlled Atlantic ports of Cabinda, Molembo, and Loango, was destabilizing African kingdoms like Kasanje.[7] This influx fueled the spread of African trading diasporas organized as corporate kin groups or "cross-lineage associations," while new shrines or cults attempted to 'domesticate' the most anti-social aspects of the trade (e.g., the high levels of distrust, greed, violence, and trauma).[8] Finally, as discussed in the first

---

5 Since Eric Williams published *Capitalism & Slavery* (1944), many scholars have explored the connections between the Atlantic and Indic Ocean slave trades and the twin processes of capitalist financial innovation and technological development. Recently, a consensus has been reached regarding periodization. As Dale Tomich, Michael Zeuske, and Robin Blackburn explain, from the mid-1770s onwards, the familiar patterns of what they define as 'the first slavery' were progressively overthrown by the economic, political, technological, and cultural revolutions of the long nineteenth century. However, plantations and the Atlantic slave trade had a 'second wind,' prospering during the period these authors define as "second slavery" (c. 1776–1888). For an overview of the financial and economic innovations that afforded or resulted from the transition from the mercantilist institutions of "first slavery" to the capitalist ones of "second slavery," see Caitlin Rosenthal, David McNally, and Ian Baucon. See Daniel Rood for an overview of the main technological innovations associated with the productive spaces of second slavery. For a pioneering and still unsurpassed analysis of the financial and economic impact of the Atlantic and Indic Ocean slave trade on the Portuguese bourgeoisie during the period of "second slavery," see José Capela. Baucon, Specters of the Atlantic; Berg and Hudson, Slavery, Capitalism and the Industrial Revolution; Blackburn, The Overthrow of Colonial Slavery; Blackburn, The Reckoning; Candido, African Businesswomen, in: Tomich and Lovejoy (eds.), The Atlantic and Africa; Capela, A burguesia mercantil do Porto; Capela, O tráfico de escravos; Laviña and Zeuske, The Second Slavery; McNally, Blood and Money; Rood, The Reinvention of Atlantic Slavery; Rosenthal, Accounting for Slavery; Tomich and Lovejoy, The Atlantic and Africa; Tomich, Slavery and Historical Capitalism; Williams, Capitalism & Slavery.

6 As Joseph Miller explains, *livranças* were personal bills of credit issued by reputable merchants or the holders of the Angolan slave duty contract, often backed with "nothing more substantial than the prestige of their association with creditworthy patrons." By the mid-eighteenth century, *livranças* circulated as fiduciary paper money in Luanda, where they were exchanged for trade goods and useful currencies. *Letras* were the bills of exchange Lisbon-backed merchants and Luso-African slavers used to pay for the trade goods and useful currencies they obtained from Lisbon on credit. Delgado, O governo de Sousa Coutinho em Angola I, p. 37–40; Dias, Os portugueses, p. 185–187; Menz, A Companhia de Pernambuco; Menz, As "geometrias" do tráfico; Miller, Way of Death, p. 299–300, 310–312, 442.

7 Delgado, O governo de Sousa Coutinho em Angola III, p. 14; Ferreira, Documento N.º 4, in: Couto, Os capitães-mores em Angola, p. 316; Miller, Way of Death, p. 102, 214–215.

8 See John M. Janzen for an account of the *Lemba* cult, which provided the normative framework for the trading diasporas in the triangle between Loango, Cabinda, and Malebo Pool; and Zdenka Volavka for a description of the *Lusunzi* shrine in Ngoyo. According to Wyatt MacGaffey, the BaKongo corporate kin groups that came to be erroneously described as "matrilineages" and their

chapter, reorganized archives, professionalized secretariates, and new surveying and planning technologies allowed the captain-general and governors of Angola to envisage more ambitious administrative reforms.[9] Together, these developments had profound social and cultural impacts, resulting in higher levels of social complexity and system differentiation, which made the economic, financial, and administrative spheres more opaque to African and Luso-African commoners. In Kimbundu-speaking areas, as Grizante's example proves, the language and tropes of *feitiçaria* or *uanga* were available to express the uneasiness associated with this increase in opacity and ensuing ambiguity.[10]

Moreover, as John Thornton and Joseph Miller remark, enslaved Mbundu and BaKongo, on their way to the Americas, understood their agonizing experience in highly ambiguous terms, being afraid their White captors were sorcerers, cannibals, or both.[11] In the words of Jose Monzolo, a BaKongo slave testifying before an ecclesiastical inquest in Cartagena in 1659, they believed their captors would kill them "to make the flags for the ships from their remains."[12] Miller begins his history of the slave trade, *Way of Death* (1988) by explaining that the "*Mwene Puto*," as the Portuguese monarch was vernacularly known in West Central Africa, was also considered a "great Lord of the Dead."[13] Reports abound that West Central Africans believed the Portuguese "pressed" the dead bodies of slaves to extrude their "cooking oil," bled them to produce their "deep red wine," used their brains to make "cheeses," and "burned the bones of the blacks to yield the ashlike, lethal gray powder that, when placed in iron tubes, transformed itself back into the flames it had come" from. As Thornton concludes, following Miller's and William Pierson's analysis of popular narratives of 'white cannibals', the tropes of 'cannibalism' and sorcery were used by Africans to make sense and speak of the terrors of the middle passage, being a kind of "folk wisdom" that informed a "folk ideology" which persisted in the Caribbean and the Americas.[14] As Wyatt MacGaffey defines it, "folk opinions" such as these

---

"marriage politics" evolved in tandem with the emergence of trading diasporas and the slave trade. JANZEN, Lemba, 1650–1930; MACGAFFEY, Kongo Political Culture, p. 154–156, 215–216; MILLER, Way of Death, p. 281–282, 441; VOLAVKA, Crown and Ritual.

9 Especially after the establishment in Luanda of the Geometry and Fortification Class in 1769, as described in the first chapter. SANTOS, De "antigos conquistadores" a "angolenses," p. 205–206; SANTOS, Luanda, in: BROCKEY (ed.), Portuguese Colonial Cities in the Early Modern World, p. 260.

10 RODRIGUES DE AREIA, Estrutura magico-religiosa, p. 36–38; THORNTON, Cannibals, Witches, and Slave Traders.

11 MILLER, Way of Death, p. 4–5, 157–158; THORNTON, Cannibals, Witches, and Slave Traders.

12 THORNTON, Cannibals, Witches, and Slave Traders, p. 273.

13 MILLER, Way of Death, p. 4–5.

14 Rosalind Shaw argues that what Thornton defines as "folk wisdom" or "folk ideology" persisted in Africa as embodied or ritually performed memories of the slave trade. See Janzen on the persistence in America and Africa of *Lemba* and other "drums of affliction" tailored to the therapeutic needs of

"do not undergo testing by debate among specialists" but are "constantly argued by diviners, politicians, and public assemblies," being tested "by correspondence with experience."[15] Moreover, they can also be seen as clear indexes of the ambiguity surrounding the novel mass-produced goods circulating in the Atlantic economy and the Atlantic slave trade itself, an increasingly complex economic and financial enterprise whose final purpose eluded the enslaved.[16]

As Leitão was surely aware, uneasiness quickly turned into fast-spreading gossip in the African hinterland. As soon as vague gossip coalesced into more precise rumors that started to circulate openly, it was only a matter of time before a formal sorcery accusation was brought before the *jaga* of Kasanje or any other political authority, putting them in charge of setting in motion disambiguating mechanisms such as ordeals and divinations to test the validity of the charges and arbitrate the compensations and punishments required to settle matters. Exploring similar dynamics in contemporary Cameroon, Peter Geschiere argues that sorcery in Africa is always perceived as a politically ambiguous force as it is said to either serve as a "support for the [...] elites" or a "weapon of the weak against the state."[17] Moreover, Geschiere remarks, it is also perceived as a morally ambiguous force, as it can be put to legitimate, socially affirming use, for instance, to "protect oneself or reinforce

---

those traumatized by the Atlantic slave trade. HEYWOOD and THORNTON, Central Africans; JANZEN, Lemba, 1650–1930; PIERSEN, White Cannibals, Black Martyrs; SHAW, Cannibal Transformations, in: MOORE and SANDERS (eds.), Magical Interpretations, Material Realities; SHAW, Memories of the Slave Trade; THORNTON, A Cultural History of the Atlantic World; THORNTON, Africa and Africans in the Making of the Atlantic World; THORNTON, Cannibals, Witches, and Slave Traders, p. 275.

15 MACGAFFEY, Kongo Political Culture, p. 3.

16 As Miller neatly summarizes, during a transition period which he situates between 1730 and 1770, in Luanda, "power ceased to be a function of how many slaves one owned and the extent to which one could control supplies of food to the city." Henceforth, power hinged on "the ability to distribute imports on credit and on how reliably one could cover a bill of exchange payable in Lisbon." This shift not only impacted local allegiances, as captain-general and governors of Angola stopped cooperating with Luso-African slavers and captain majors and started championing the interests of Lisbon-backed merchants, but also made the ultimate purpose of the Atlantic slave trade unclear to African interlopers who had no difficulties understanding the previous pattern of power relations (e. g., as a variation of the strategy of accumulating wealth in people). Moreover, during the later period, since the interests of Lisbon-backed merchants remained in "selling goods and collecting debts," the levels of neglect and violence towards slaves soared, resulting in countless deaths in coastal slave pens. While these deaths and violence made economic sense, as Miller notes in the conclusion of *Way of Death*, they were undoubtedly hard to witness and impossible to make human sense of. MILLER, Way of Death, p. 312, 392, 657–667; THORNTON, Cannibals, Witches, and Slave Traders, p. 274–275.

17 For a brief account of the consequences of this ambiguity in Portuguese Guinea, see Shaw. GESCHIERE, The Modernity of Witchcraft, p. 9–10, 16; SHAW, Memories of the Slave Trade, p. 213–215.

authority and, more generally, to succeed in life" or to illegitimate, anti-social use.[18] In this regard, his ethnography of contemporary Cameroon describes a social metaphysics of power and an ontological understanding of the origin of evil and mishaps analogous to those tentatively described by eighteenth-century Portuguese sources and systematized by Anne Hilton, Georges Balandier, John Thornton, and Wyatt McGaffey when exploring the historical context of the Kingdom of Kongo, by John Janzen when studying the three historical Kingdoms of the Loango Coast, and by Manuel Rodrigues Areia when reviewing the anthropological literature on contemporary Angola (c. 1970s).[19]

The "polyinterpretability" of sorcery, Geschiere continues, is also a reflex of political actors' embeddedness in preexisting kinship, social, and cultural networks, which situate them in overlapping and often competing normative and value systems that are not fully transparent even to themselves.[20] When acting according to a set of norms or values (e. g., social, legal, economic) implies neglecting or breaking others (e. g., cultural, kinship, religious), any act is inherently ambiguous and can be interpreted in Cameroon as upholding the norms said to govern the 'occult' dimension of sorcery.[21] Therefore, on the one hand, sorcery is perceived as morally and politically ambiguous, on the other, the language of sorcery and sorcery accusations provides a venue to express anxieties about ambiguity and affirm the need for disambiguation. It follows that ordeals, divinations, and anti-sorcery remedies can be framed not only as "responsibility allocation mechanisms," as Geschiere convincingly argues, but also as what Hillard von Thiessen defines as forms of "situational disambiguation" that address the ambiguity caused by the concurrence and competition of social roles and cultural, social, religious, or other

---

18 Geschiere, The Modernity of Witchcraft, p. 12–13.

19 Balandier, Le Royaume de Kongo; Hilton, The Kingdom of Kongo; Janzen, Lemba, 1650–1930; MacGaffey, A Central African Kingdom, in: Bostoen and Brinkman (eds.), The Kongo Kingdom; MacGaffey, Fetishism Revisited; MacGaffey, Kongo Political Culture; MacGaffey, Religion and Society; Rodrigues de Areia, Estrutura magico-religiosa; Thornton, Afro-Christian Syncretism; Thornton, Religious and Ceremonial Life, in: Heywood (ed.), Central Africans and Cultural Transformations; Thornton, The Development of an African Catholic Church.

20 Geschiere, The Modernity of Witchcraft, p. 10–11.

21 Ibid., p. 23.

kinds of norms.[22] As different social and cultural fields and normative and religious systems overlap and are made commensurate at slave fairs, the concurrence of norms caused by this process leads to rising levels of ambiguity and the need for forms of disambiguation. The same occurs when African normative systems and cultures are othered at slave fairs, forcing actors to choose between upholding conflicting norms or value systems. Combine these twin dynamics with high rates of mortality, open displays of anti-social greed, and naked violence to obtain the perfect combination for the exponential increase in sorcery accusations.

As public or official forms of disambiguation, anti-sorcery ordeals and divinations became central to political disputes over the control of the regime of commensuration in place in Cassange.[23] As this chapter explores, concomitantly, as responsibility allocation mechanisms, they quickly turned into a political tool and enslaving mechanism. In the arbitration of sorcery charges at courts of centralized African kingdoms such as Kasanje, disambiguation was followed by the imposition of penalties, including death or enslavement, to those found guilty of sorcery and the redistribution of their belongings, including their rights over people and dependents, as judicial fees and compensation to the wronged parties.[24] Due to this fact, the political interests of Portuguese officials trying to wrestle the monopoly on disambiguation from the *jaga* did not coincide with the economic interests of Luso-African merchants and slave traders who purchased Africans enslaved by the *jaga*'s court (although they often overlapped, as the former usually had direct or vested interests in the slave trade).[25] Matters were complicated as the doctrine of ransom explored in the previous chapter became hegemonic during the Portuguese Late Enlightenment, and the legitimacy of the titles slaveowners had over the freedom

---

22 A third and equally valid perspective on anti-sorcery ordeals and divinations is to frame them primarily as therapeutic performances, as Janzen describes the members of the *Lemba* cult. This angle is explored in the next chapters. Janzen, Lemba, 1650–1930; Geschiere, Responsibility versus Responsibilization, in: Denian, Fumanti and Lynteris (eds.), Anthropology and Responsibility; Geschiere, Kinship, Witchcraft and "the Market," in: Dilley (ed.), Contesting Markets; von Thiessen, Concurrence and Competition of Norms, p. 34–35; von Thiessen, Das Zeitalter der Ambiguität; von Thiessen, Normenkonkurrenz Handlungsspielräume, in: von Thiessen and Karsten (eds.), Normenkonkurrenz in historischer Perspektive, Vol. 50.

23 As Shaw remarks, it is common anthropological knowledge that ordeals and divinations also have a private dimension, helping individuals navigate life crises and intersubjective conflicts. This chapter, however, focuses only on the political and normative implications of public or official ordeals and divinations, such as the anti-sorcery ordeal of the Kingdom of Kasanje. See Martin Chanock for an account of how Central African "conquest" and "slaving" states of the nineteenth century adapted local ordeals previously specialized in disambiguating private matters into political and statecraft tools. Chanock, Law, Custom, and Social Order; Shaw, Memories of the Slave Trade, p. 3.

24 Seabra da Silva, Carta de José de Seabra da Silva.

25 Figueiredo, Feitiçaria na Angola oitocentista.

of their slaves was now predicated on them being bought from African polities that would otherwise execute or 'sacrifice' them.

As anti-sorcery ordeals were potentially lethal, together with cannibalism, they soon provided one of the key tropes in apologies for the persistence of the slave trade. This created a conflict of interests for Portuguese authorities, who simultaneously framed the ordeals as a threat to Portuguese sovereignty, as they were a political tool of the *jaga*, and as a cornerstone of the Angolan economy, as they justified the ransom of slaves.[26] Ambiguity reigned as captain majors, fair scribes, and Luso-African merchants engaged with African ordeals self-interestedly. Therefore, after almost three centuries of contact—as Leitão's list of mock diplomatic demands also suggests— Portuguese, Luso-Africans, and West Central Africans alike experienced an acute need for disambiguation, not only regarding matters connected with sorcery but also regarding the limits and nature of sovereignty and jurisdiction at the hinterland borders of the Captaincy of Angola and regarding the legitimacy of the institutions of slavery. This chapter focuses on the political and legal remedies that came to be implemented in the Luanda-Kasanje connection, exploring how the patchworked nature of its normative fabric called for the implementation of different, often clashing forms of disambiguation. The chapters then included in Part III explore how personal belonging and the shifting limits of the West Central African communities were negotiated and redefined.

6.2 A Revealing List of Diplomatic Demands

According to Leitão, the first demand he transmitted to the envoys of the *jaga* of Kasanje, supposedly on behalf of Captain-General and Governor Álvares da Cunha, was that the *jaga* resume paying tribute to Luanda, as he claimed his "*predecessors had always done as* [Portuguese] *vassals*."[27] Regardless of the claim's veracity, this demand suggests that Leitão needed to clarify the nature of the political relationship between the Kingdom of Kasanje and the Portuguese Crown.[28] The second demand

26 The ransom of Africans condemned to death after being accused of sorcery accusations became the main argument for the Angolan apologists of slavery during the transition to abolition that took the greater part of the nineteenth century. Figueiredo, A Questão das "Ouvidas;" Figueiredo, Feitiçaria na Angola oitocentista; Figueiredo, Política, Escravatura e feitiçaria em Angola.

27 Sebestyén, Vansina (eds.), and Leitão, Angola's Eastern Hinterland, p. 337–338.

28 According to a Mbangala *musendo* collected by the German Engineer Benedictus Otto Schütt in 1881, a *jaga* he identifies as "*Culachingo*," the "*nephew*" of the first *jaga* of Kasanje (who Otto Schütt identifies as "*Quinguri*"), had promised the Portuguese a "*tribute in ivory and etc.*" if they agreed to establish a slave fair and factory at his *kilombo* (c. 1620). Following Miller, "*Culachingo*" and "*Quinguri*" refer to the Lunda appointive titles of "*kinguri*" and "*kulashingo*," suggesting that this *musendo* does not narrate a historical episode but conveys a mythical account that justifies the

he transmitted was that the *jaga* either behead or capture and send to Luanda the many "*refugees* [...] *clustered together in those vast forests of Bondo* [Mbondo]."[29] These "*refugees*" were escaped slaves who had "*absconded*" from Portuguese *arimos* and *presídios*. The third demand Leitão transmitted to the envoys was that the *jaga* guaranteed that the roads under his jurisdiction were "*freed of the cruel robbers, for the common good*" of Portuguese and Mbangala alike. These requests can be understood as a plea for the *jaga* to assert his sovereignty over Mbondo, securing it for Lisbon-backed caravans. While, as discussed in the previous chapter, Leitão framed the province as a liminal space outside civil society, the fact was that its ruler, the *ndala quissua*, often shifted alliances between the Kingdom of Matamba and Kasanje. This partly explains why the inhabitants of Mbondo repeatedly sided with the subjects of Matamba, then known as *Gingas*, to raid Luso-African caravans heading to the fair of Cassange or slave coffles returning to Luanda.[30] These first three demands signal that Leitão envisaged the possibility of the *jaga* acting as a proxy for the interests of Lisbon-backed merchants in the mid-Kwango valley if he accepted to act as a 'loyal' vassal of the Portuguese Crown and was able to fully impose his sovereignty over the semi-independent provinces on his borders. As Leitão reported, the Portuguese could then force the Mbangala sovereign into submission because "*if he relied on guns, he would see that* [the Portuguese] *could reduce them to worthless sticks, by totally withholding gunpowder from him*."[31] The question remained if the Mbangala ruler could impose his sovereignty over distant vassals and corporate kin groups who might be more interested in trading directly with the independent Atlantic ports of the Loango Coast than with the Portuguese through Cassange.

Complicating matters, in Leitão's view, the lack of jurisdictional clarity precluded this cooperation. The fourth demand Leitão transmitted to the envoys was for the

---

1881 status quo. This leaves the question open regarding the tribute that the *jagas* of Kasanje may have offered before Leitão's visit, as the *musendo* might reflect the outcome of the vassalage treaty imposed on Kasanje on December 19, 1789. Even if the oral tradition recorded by Schütt referred to a status quo ante 1756, it does not refer to the tribute being a recognition of vassalage. Moreover, in the letter from July 26, 1789, that encouraged the *jaga* to sign this treaty, the annual tribute is referred to as "*ganda*" instead of "*loanda*," the tribute paid by *sobas* to the *ngola* of Ndongo, which the Portuguese continued receiving as a sign of vassalage. The *ganda*, as further explained in the following sections, was a military tribute usually paid in slaves. Couto, Os capitães-mores em Angola, p. 222; Heintze, Der Portugiesisch-Afrikanische Vasallenvertrag in Angola; Heintze, Exploradores alemães em Angola, p. 370; Heintze, Fontes para a História de Angola, Vol. 1, p. 119; Miller, Kings and Kinsmen, p. 191–192; Vansina, Foundation of the Kingdom of Kasanje; Vellut, Le Royaume de Cassange, p. 120.

29 Sebestyén, Vansina (eds.), and Leitão, Angola's Eastern Hinterland, p. 337–338.

30 Vellut, Le Royaume de Cassange, p. 130.

31 Sebestyén, Vansina (eds.), and Leitão, Angola's Eastern Hinterland, p. 341.

jaga to respect the jurisdiction of the scribes whom the merchants of Cassange regularly elected as "*the heads*" of the fair.[32] He added that the *jaga* should "*abandon his bad behavior*" of "*robbing*" the merchants "*when it pleased him, with the menace that he would eat them cooked.*" Threats which were accompanied by an elaborate pantomime, as the *jaga* had his servants "*carry pots, wood, and water*" in front of the merchants "*to bully them even faster.*" While this demand makes the *jaga*'s refusal to accept any competing jurisdiction plain, the alleged extortion and 'cannibalism' threats warrant further unpacking, considering Leitão's fifth demand. This fifth demand concerned "*the goods*" taken from the Luso-African merchants "*on credit.*" The *jaga* of Kasanje was to order the debts to be settled immediately. Moreover, he was to "*shun the barbarism of forbidding the sale of food*" to the merchants and of them fetching water "*from the rivers and wells.*" On first reading, this latter demand seems related to a single issue, i. e. the financial stress put on Luso-African merchants waiting for the goods they had advanced on credit to be repaid with slaves.[33] However, it also touches on jurisdictional matters. The need to harmonize the protracted rhythms of African prestige spheres of exchange where rights over women and dependents were brokered with the faster-paced cycles of interest-generating debt was at the heart of Leitão's insistence on having "*debts*" settled.[34] Due to the fact that the exchanges in African prestige spheres of exchange aimed to establish lasting relationships and not generate profit like the Atlantic slave trade, slow reciprocation rhythms were understood as a positive feature, not a drawback. The opposite was true from the perspective of slave traders choking with debt.

Leitão's fourth and fifth demands suggest that, by the 1750s, the Lisbon-backed merchants whose interests he represented understood payment delays not as a way of investing in wealth in people, as their Mbangala partners or previous generations of Luso-African merchants might have interpreted them, but as a heavy financial burden. However, the Portuguese could not directly influence the spheres of exchange where rights over women and dependents were exchanged according to

---

32 Ibid., p. 337–338.

33 As Miller explains, similar practices were standard in other hinterland slave fairs under African kings' direct control or jurisdiction. In his words, "Kings often prohibited agriculture or stock-keeping within the marketplaces and deliberately restricted the immigrant traders to their confines to increase their dependence on foodstuffs." MILLER, Way of Death, p. 177, 583.

34 According to Stuart Schwartz, legal interest rates remained stable, even decreasing during this period: 6.25% until 1757 and 5% afterward. However, as Miller remarks, "concealed" interest rates were rapidly increasing. These were "phrased instead as higher nominal sales prices for the goods borrowed." Therefore, he concludes that, by 1801, "concealed implicit interests" were up to 30% at compound rates for loans averaging two years and four months, 50% for loans of a year and a half, and 70% for loans of a year. SCHWARTZ, Sugar Plantations, p. 205–206; MILLER, Way of Death, p. 102, 184, 308–309, 392, 667.

African norms using social currencies.[35] This meant they depended on the *jaga*'s centralized authority and ability to issue binding *ijila* backed by legitimate physical and spiritual violence to enforce the quick counter-gifting of slaves for the goods they had offered their African trading partners in advance and avoid bankruptcy.[36] The *jaga*, however, aggravated their troubles by issuing *ijila* prohibiting the sale of supplies and demanding tribute in exchange for excusing merchants from observing the *ijila* of the *kilombo* (thus allegedly 'robbing' them).[37] This left the Luso-African merchants in a double bind between escaping the immediate oversight of the *jaga* to avoid being subjected to prejudicial *ijila* or welcoming it to ensure that their exchange partners upheld their end of the bargain within a reasonable time frame. In Leitão's opinion, the best solution was not to limit the *jaga*'s jurisdiction over his subjects but to clarify that the scribe of Cassange had jurisdiction over Luso-African merchants and African traders. As this chapter explores, from the 1760s onward, several captain-general and governors attempted to implement this solution by imposing treaties on the Kingdom of Kasanje and drafting ordinances regulating the functions and jurisdiction of scribes and other Portuguese officeholders.

The sixth demand Leitão transmitted was that the *jaga* should close "*the two houses of charms, called Emduás, where, under the pretext of finding the truth,*" witnesses "*argued with each other*" and many claimants and suspects "*died from the poison given to them.*"[38] These "*houses*" were also referred to in Portuguese sources as the *indua* or *ndua* oath or ordeal, the public anti-sorcery ordeal of the Kingdom of Kasanje to which Grizante would probably have been subjected if Leitão had not interfered in the course of events.[39] Thus, Leitão requested the *jaga* to relinquish his monopoly on the disambiguation of sorcery accusations in his court. The seventh and final demand was that the *jaga* embrace Christianity so the "*catholic Princes would not punish him*" without just cause.[40] These two last demands read as *pro forma* requests, as the abolition of the *ndua* ordeal and the adoption of Christianism as the official religion of Kasanje would probably have paralyzed the slave trade at Cassange or as proof of Leitão's lack of full understanding of the complex normative constellation in which the Cassange slave fair was embedded. As discussed below, subsequent captain-generals and governors adopted a different approach

35 Margarido, Algumas formas da hegemonia africana in: Santos (ed.), I Reunião internacional de História de África.

36 Miller, Way of Death, p. 205, 234–237.

37 Sebestyén, Vansina (eds.), and Leitão, Angola's Eastern Hinterland, p. 337–338.

38 Ibid.

39 Miller, Way of Death, p. 223.

40 Vansina and Sebestyén interpret this passage differently, arguing that Leitão claimed that the captain-general and governor had ordered the *jaga* to declare himself a Portuguese vassal. Sebestyén, Vansina (eds.), and Leitão, Angola's Eastern Hinterland, p. 339.

to anti-sorcery ordeals and conversion in their official diplomatic demands, never interfering with the internal government of Kasanje.

Together, Leitão's demands show that the Portuguese and Luso-Africans felt an acute need for disambiguation regarding the limits of the *jaga*'s jurisdiction and sovereignty, the normative weight of *ijila*, the nature of economic transactions and their normative framing (e. g., differentiating gifts and prestige exchanges from commercial loans and credit advances), and the structure of the regional inter-polity order. Moreover, they indicate that on the Mbangala side, an adaptation of the normative system that was previously geared toward the militaristic lifestyle of the *kilombo* had taken place, aligning it with the new social pressures and economic opportunities presented by the Atlantic slave trade. Further, Leitão's report does not mention the *colambolo*, or any similar Mbangala officer in charge of justice, or the *ganga ya bulungo* responsible for administering the *mbulungo* ordeal but only the "*houses of charms, called Emduás*."[41] These lacunae suggest that the *ndua* ordeal's prominence might also be an adaptation to the new economic environment. This chapter first explores how some of the ambiguity resulting from the increasing economic and financial complexity of the slave trade was dealt with in West Central Africa. It then focuses on Captain-General and Governor Francisco Inocêncio de Sousa Coutinho's (1726–1780) attempt to sort some of the jurisdictional, hierarchical, and normative causes of ambiguity Leitão identifies, tracing how his successors built on his measures until the last decades of the eighteenth century. It explores West Central African's need to disambiguate sorcery rumors and accusations, examining how it allowed the *jaga* of Kasanje to provide an alternative regional normative framework and contest the Portuguese monopoly on disambiguation. It concludes by exploring a Mbangala oral tradition which explains how Kasanje elites envisioned the regional inter-polity order and the place of the Portuguese and Luso-African merchants in it.

6.3 Failed Attempts to Regulate Free Trade

Less than two years after the conclusion of Leitão's journey, during the tenure of Captain-General and Governor António de Vasconcelos (1758–1764), the Royal Edict of January 11, 1758, reformed commerce in "*Angola, Kongo, Loango, and Benguela,* [and] *the adjacent Ports and hinterlands*" in keeping with the Pombaline doctrine of "*freedom of trade*."[42] Apart from significantly curtailing the privileges of

41 Ibid., p. 337–338.

42 Ley para ser livre, e franco o commercio de Angola; MAXWELL, Pombal and the Nationalization of the Luso-Brazilian Economy.

the holders of the Angolan slave duty contract, which was entirely abolished in 1769, this law opened up commerce to all those willing to send their representatives "*to the Hinterlands and general Fairs with all sorts of sanctioned Fabrics to* [proceed to] *the resgate* [ransom] *of Slaves*."[43] Concomitantly, the Royal Edict of January 25, 1758, greatly simplified the taxation of exported slaves, streamlining the fiscal revenues produced by the iniquitous trade.[44] Tasked with implementing both laws, António de Vasconcelos immediately pointed out to his superiors in Lisbon that the Crown had inadequate means to police trade in the hinterlands, as Leitão's requests for the assistance of the *jaga* of Kasanje in policing the roads in Mbondo underlined, and that the upholding of "*freedom of trade*" would have the consequence of flooding the interior with "*Jews, gypsies, and criminals*."[45] António de Vasconcelos, who might have had vested personal interests in keeping access to the interior slave trade restricted, lamented the proposed opening because he argued that this "*flood*" would result in countless cases of abuse against free Africans and the defrauding of Luanda-based creditors.[46] Moreover, he complained that Lisbon-backed merchants and slave duty contract administrators refused to acknowledge the edicts, relying on local customs and jurisdictional autonomy to trump police laws unsupported by military might.[47]

Establishing new regulated slave fairs where a 'free' trade in slaves was to take place was one of the paradoxical solutions to the problems posed by the liberalization of the internal slave trade envisioned by António de Vasconcelos and subsequently pursued by his successor Sousa Coutinho.[48] Shortly after both royal edicts were issued, taking advantage of the disruption in European trade caused by the Seven Years' War (1756–1763), António de Vasconcelos reformed the network of Portuguese fairs in an attempt to assert control over commerce and intercept the slave trading caravans that usually traded with rival Europeans in the independent ports of Cabinda, Molembo, and Loango and smaller unsupervised anchorages

---

43 Ley para ser livre, e franco o commercio de Angola; Miller, Way of Death, p. 578, 590–597.

44 Ley sobre a arrecadação dos direitos dos escravos.

45 Miller, Way of Death, p. 578; Sebestyén, Vansina (eds.), and Leitão, Angola's Eastern Hinterland, p. 337–338.

46 An "*Opinion on the Trade of Angola*" undersigned by the councilors António de Azevedo Coutinho, Alexandre Metello de Souza Menezes, and Ignacio Ferreira Souto in Bahia, January 3, 1758, had already addressed similar concerns. Reaching an opposite conclusion, the councilors stressed that free trade in the Angolan hinterlands was in keeping with "*Natural, and Theological Law, and the interests of State*," remarking that it was "*libelous to argue that Blacks would behave better* [as hinterland traders] *than Whites*"—as António de Vasconcelos concerns suggested. Coutinho et al., Documento N.º 3, in: Couto, Os capitães-mores em Angola, p. 306–309; Miller, Way of Death, p. 578; Vellut, Le royaume de Cassange, p. 118.

47 Miller, Way of Death, p. 578.

48 Silva Corrêa, História de Angola, Vol. 2, p. 22.

along the Loango Coast.[49] First, in 1759, he established the *presídio* of Encoge in the territory of a vassal *dembo*, intended to intercept the flow of slaves from the middle Kwango Valley up to the ports visited by French and British ships.[50] By the 1760s, an inverse flux of BaKongo, Vili, and Teke "*quibucas* [caravans]" threatened Luanda's merchants' predominance as suppliers of imported trade goods in that section of the valley, enabling *pumbeiros* and Luso-African slave traders to operate outside of the official fair network and also eroding the trade monopolies of West Central African kings.[51] Second, he established regulated fairs in Beja, near the *presídio* of Pungo Andongo, and Ndala Jinga, near the *presídio* of Ambaca, seeking to control the trading practices of the Luso-Africans based in these settlements.[52] Concomitantly, on July 7, 1762, António de Vasconcelos issued a *bando* ordering merchants to live no farther than "*30 leagues*" (roughly 120 kilometers) from regulated fairs.[53] Finally, the captain-general and governor placed a tax on all slaves brought to Luanda from the hinterlands.[54]

This first wave of measures was insufficient to counter the disruptive impact of *quibucas* bringing trade goods from the Loango Coast.[55] While a steady flow of 5.000 slaves per year was dispatched from Encoge to Luanda for the duration of the Seven Years War, as soon as the conflict ended and rival European vessels returned in strength to Loango, these numbers nosedived.[56] Moreover, the epidemiologic environment of the *presídio* proved to be particularly lethal to European troops and horses, turning it into a constant resource drain. Aggravating matters for the Lisbon-backed merchants and the Crown, in the aftermath of a jurisdictional conflict, the *jaga* of Kasanje banned all Whites and the Portuguese scribe from Cassange for two years (1760–1762) and, in 1765, the *Propaganda Fide* established its first independent mission in Loango, staffed exclusively by French priests.[57] Official fairs remained deserted, making the situation seem even more desperate for

---

49 Couto, Os capitães-mores em Angola, p. 207; Maxwell, Pombal and the Nationalization of the Luso-Brazilian Economy, p. 612; Miller, Way of Death, p. 573.

50 According to Silva Corrêa, the captain-general and governor was advised to do so by a "*private board*" of merchants. Couto, Os capitães-mores em Angola, p. 207; Delgado, O governo de Sousa Coutinho em Angola III; Miller, Way of Death, p. 583–584; Silva Corrêa, História de Angola, Vol. 2, p. 15–19.

51 Delgado, O governo de Sousa Coutinho em Angola III; Miller, Way of Death, p. 184–185; Vellut, Le royaume de Cassange, p. 118–119.

52 Delgado, O governo de Sousa Coutinho em Angola I, p. 21; Miller, Way of Death, p. 583–584.

53 Ferreira, Cross-Cultural Exchange, p. 33.

54 Delgado, O governo de Sousa Coutinho em Angola I, p. 21.

55 AHU, CU, Angola, Box 51, D. 4639; Delgado, O governo de Sousa Coutinho em Angola III.

56 Delgado, O governo de Sousa Coutinho em Angola III, p. 11–12.

57 Delgado, O governo de Sousa Coutinho em Angola III, p. 9; Vellut, Le Royaume de Cassange, p. 118.

those dependent on the Atlantic slave trade. In an official report submitted by João Alvarez Ferreira, a wealthy Luanda-based merchant, to the Board of Commerce of Luanda on June 26, 1762, the reasons why the slave fairs were abandoned are clearly stated.[58] First, the captain majors and scribes overseeing them interfered in the transactions, coercing the African partners to exchange the better-appraised slaves only with their associates.[59] Second, according to Ferreira, since the "*Blacks are not guided by reason*," they terminated their sale contracts if they felt jealous of other traders getting better deals. This led to countless disputes, often escalating to physical violence. Nevertheless, as he assumed office, Sousa Coutinho reopened the fair at Cassange, moved the fair of Ndala Jinga to Lucamba, where water and timber were more plentiful, and attempted to complete his predecessor's network of fairs, establishing regulated fairs in Gollo, Bende, and next to the court of *Soba* Calandula.[60] Moreover, despite remaining doubtful about the high-maintenance costs of the new *presídio*, Sousa Coutinho launched a series of successful military operations from Encoge, targeting independent or 'rebel' African polities that backed the Luso-African merchants' trade rivals.[61]

From the point of view of both captain-general and governors, if assembled in regulated fairs, Luso-African merchants and *pumbeiros* were more easily subjected to the "legal proceedings" of their creditors.[62] Moreover, they would be under the jurisdiction of captain majors or scribes who, acting as judges of orphans, could dispose of the assets that composed their estates in case they died, favoring the repayment of debts to Lisbon-backed merchants instead of other business partners and inheritors.[63] From an African perspective, however, besides excessive taxation and the problems already identified by Ferreira, African trade partners and their

---

58 Ferreira, Documento N.º 4, in: Couto, Os capitães-mores em Angola, p. 310–317; Miguel, Que se abram os sertões, p. 115–116.

59 Ferreira, Documento N.º 4, in: Couto, Os capitães-mores em Angola, p. 313–315.

60 AHU, CU, Angola, Box 51, D. 4639; Delgado, O governo de Sousa Coutinho em Angola I, p. 21–22; Ferreira, Feiras e presídios, p. 24–26; Sousa Coutinho, Para o Secretario de Estado Francisco de Mendonça; Vellut, Le Royaume de Cassange, p. 118–119.

61 For a detailed account of the military operations against the "*quipaca* [fortified villages]" of opposing BaKongo Dukes, Mbundu *sobas*, and *dembos*, see Delgado. AHU, CU, Angola, Box 51, D. 4677, Box 52, D. 4804; Delgado, O governo de Sousa Coutinho em Angola III, p. 10–11, 18–23; Vellut, Le Royaume de Cassange, p. 118–119.

62 As Miller argues, when Domingos Dias da Silva, the holder of the last contract on slave export duties (1766–1771), was faced with Pombal's intention to cancel it in 1769, he flooded Luanda and its hinterlands with bad *livranças*, provoking a series of credit defaults. In the aftermath of this event, Sousa Coutinho was particularly invested in keeping merchants and *pumbeiros* under Portuguese jurisdiction so that the courts could reach them in case of default. Miller, Way of Death, p. 590–597.

63 Captain-general and governors then faced the challenge of regulating the actions of scribes and captain majors acting as judges of orphans, as discussed in the following paragraphs. Ibid., p. 308–309.

slaves and dependents were exposed to sorcery attacks and accusations in slave fairs, a danger exacerbated by the reigning "atmosphere of malevolence," sickness, and greed.[64] Ferreira noted that "*some blacks*" were afraid even to enter them because they believed that "*the whites*" assembled there "*would cause them harm*."[65] When exploring the root cause of these widespread fears, Miller feels tempted to predicate them on the epidemiological conditions of slave pens and trading compounds, where the ideal conditions for contagious diseases to incubate and spread existed.[66] However, as he concludes, agreeing with Janzen, it is impossible to disentangle the "social," "moral," and physiological roots of the ailments that Africans thought originated from these spaces, which were often referred to or made sense of through the ambiguous language of sorcery.[67] A language that, as Geschiere and Janzen highlight, could also be used to make sense of the quick, anti-social enrichment of some African traders or to express feelings of jealousy and disaffection.[68] As discussed below, the *jagas* took advantage of this fact to extend their jurisdiction to slave fairs and other Luso-African milieus, pushing the *ndua* ordeal as a much-needed form of disambiguation and thus contesting the dominance of Luso-African captain majors and even the jurisdiction of captain-general and governors.[69]

One other solution immediately proposed by António de Vasconcelos was to attempt to regulate the price of *banzos*, the commodity bundles that paid for "*blacks and wax*," and later ivory, in the Angolan hinterlands.[70] As Marion Johnson explains, one of the traits of useful currencies, such as the cloths, salt, and *nzimbu* circulating in the Angolan hinterlands and the Kingdom of Kongo, was that their value fluctuated as they flowed from producing centers toward consuming centers.[71] This posed a problem to itinerant Luso-African merchants and *pumbeiros*, who might find their currencies' value fluctuating drastically as they traveled. Assortment bargaining, or adopting commodity bundles as a currency of accounting or composite currency, was one of the measures devised to counter the "one-way effect" identified by Johnson.[72] By carrying bundles composed of different styles of cloths, shells, beads, iron utensils, alcohol, and salt, slave traders guaranteed that

64 Chanock, Law, Custom, and Social Order, p. 88–89.

65 Ferreira, Documento N.º 4, in: Couto, Os capitães-mores em Angola, p. 319.

66 See Silva Corrêa and Luís António de Oliveira Mendes for an eyewitness account of these terrible conditions. Mendes, Memória a respeito dos escravos, p. 24–28; Miller, The Significance of Drought; Miller, Way of Death, p. 186; Silva Corrêa, História de Angola, Vol. 1, p. 35–57, 80.

67 Janzen, Lemba, 1650–1930; Miller, Way of Death, p. 186, 202, 206.

68 Geschiere, The Modernity of Witchcraft, p. 12–13; Janzen, Lemba, 1650–1930.

69 Miller, Way of Death, p. 223.

70 ANTT, MR, EXP, Sr. 34, F. 605, p. 1–3; Couto, Os capitães-mores em Angola, p. 206–207; Ferreira, Feiras e presídios, p. 22–24; Foucault, The Birth of Biopolitics, p. 30–31.

71 Johnson, Cloth as Money, p. 196–197.

72 Ibid., p. 197; Webb (Jr.), Toward the Comparative Study of Money.

the total value of their currency reserves was relatively stable no matter where they traveled, as decreases of value in one of their elements were likely compensated by increases of value in another.[73] As Carlos Couto remarks, attempts to regulate the content of *banzos* were at the center of several policy reforms during the eighteenth century.[74]

While attempts to regulate *banzos* date from at least a century before,[75] they always yielded unsatisfactory results as commodity bundles did not depend on police regulation or royal enactments to work but on the free interplay of economic 'one-way effects' that resulted from different regional rates of supply and demand of useful currencies and, in the case of currencies with an associated aesthetic component, such as cloths and beads, also on shifting African tastes and fashions. This often left slave traders at the mercy of African tastes and shifting fashions, as António de Vasconcelos dryly remarked in a July 9, 1762, letter.[76] The complexity and opacity of the dynamics that affected the value of self-regulating composite currencies guaranteed that the prices of slaves in the hinterland markets were always uncertain and that Luso-African merchants, *pumbeiros*, and Portuguese officers alike experienced much ambiguity regarding the motives of their instability, often attributing it to the caprice of their African partners or the corruption of local authorities. Attempts to fix the composition of *banzos* always occasioned coercion backed by violence as local authorities misunderstood the mysterious economic tendencies that foiled them. They can be seen as an effort to monopolize the disambiguation of the price of slaves, which would otherwise occur on a case-by-case basis (e. g., whenever and wherever a slave was purchased, according to the local supply and demand of useful currencies, fashions, and tastes).[77] In 1703,

---

73 Johnson, Cloth as Money, p. 197; Webb (Jr.), Toward the Comparative Study of Money.

74 Couto, Os capitães-mores em Angola, p. 223–226.

75 Couto remarks that the word *banzo* was already used in a petition to the Crown by the widow of Captain-General and Governor Manuel Pereira Forjaz, written between 1602 and 1624 stating that a "*banzo de fato* [*banzo* of cloth]" was the number of assorted cloths necessary to buy a slave in the hinterlands. António de Oliveira Cadornega refers to "*fazenda banzada*," the cloths included in *banzos*, as the assorted items needed to buy a slave. Heintze mentions that by 1629, the captain-general and governor of Angola had already attempted to regulate *banzos*. Cadornega, História geral das guerras angolanas, Vol. 1, p. 143; Couto, Os capitães-mores em Angola, p. 223; Heintze, Fontes para a História de Angola, Vol. 1, p. 115.

76 Couto, Os capitães-mores em Angola, p. 228–229; Margarido, Algumas formas da hegemonia africana in: Santos (ed.), I Reunião internacional de História de África.

77 According to Ferreira, *banzos* were impossible to regulate because each "*cabeça*" or concrete slave was worth a specific *banzo*, calculated according to at least four factors. First, the relative distance of the *pumbos* or official slave fairs where they were purchased from Luanda and the other Atlantic ports and productive centers of useful currencies. Second, the individual tastes of each trading partner and local ritual practices and clothing fashions. Due to the fact that some useful currencies, such as cloths or beads, were used in courtship and funeral rituals, their worth largely depended on

for instance, the Municipal Council of Luanda clashed with the captain majors who roamed the hinterlands or were in charge of districts, pinning the "*ruin of commerce*" and the minor rebellions that regularly took place in their jurisdictions on their habit of "*lançar banzos* [fixing *banzos*]" and then imposing them on vassal or independent *sobas* by force.[78]

On June 23, 1703, the Overseas Council deliberated on the municipal council's complaints, ruling in favor of the merchant interests it represented.[79] The court dictated that itinerant captain-majors without an established jurisdiction had four months to return to Luanda, determining that slave fairs were to be overseen by scribes appointed by the municipal council. A previous ruling of the Overseas Council, from June 7, 1703, had determined that the merchants in Luanda were to fix the composition of *banzos* sent to the hinterlands with the Luso-African traders and *pumbeiros* and that Portuguese authorities were not to interfere in the process. However, as Couto remarks, the value of *banzos* in *réis* steadily rose until the 1760s, a fact that he attributes to the scarcity of slaves resulting from epidemics, but that can also be attributed to the fact that the inflated nominal sale prices of the goods that composed the *banzos* concealed rising interest rates, or to other Atlantic-wide economic factors.[80] It is in this troubled context, when widespread worries about the rising value of *banzos* in *réis* resulted in captain majors or African partners being scapegoated for it, that the Royal Edict of January 11, 1758, liberalized the internal

---

these social and cultural factors. Third, how each *cabeça* was appraised. According to Ferreira, even if an official *banzo* could be fixed for "*peças da Índia* [male slaves], *molecoens* [large, young, male slaves—from the Kikongo *muleke*], *molequez* [young, male slaves] of six, and five palms, *moleconas* [large, young, female slaves], *molecas* [young, female slaves] of six, and five palms, *negras de cria* [breastfeeding female slaves], *negros barbados* [old, male slaves] and *negras talabardeiras* [old female slaves]," no "two persons would agree on the same price" or classification for a given *cabeça*. Fourth, on the agreed length of the measure standards used to measure cloths (e.g., "*beirames*," "*quivacos*"). These measure standards were based on anthropometrics and varied from region to region. Couto, Os capitães-mores em Angola, p. 229; Ferreira, Documento N.º 4, in: Couto, Os capitães-mores em Angola, p. 310–312; Heintze, Fontes para a História de Angola, Vol. 1, p. 123; Thompson, The Making of Quilengues, p. 234–235.

78 Couto, Os capitães-mores em Angola, p. 224–225; Harvey, Politics, Commerce, and Colonization, p. 38–39.

79 Couto, Os capitães-mores em Angola, p. 225.

80 According to a royal letter from November 14, 1761, *banzos* worth 40$000 *réis* in Luanda were then worth double in the hinterlands. Moreover, the values of the trade goods that composed them were three times higher in Luanda than in Lisbon. For instance, "13 knives" were worth $345 *réis* in Lisbon, $800 *réis* in Luanda and 1$300 *réis* in hinterland fairs, and a piece of "*zuarte liso*" cloth was worth 3$600 *réis* in Lisbon, 6$000 *réis* in Luanda and 12$000 *réis* in hinterland fairs. Couto, Os capitães-mores em Angola, p. 226–227; Miller, The Significance of Drought; Miller, Way of Death, p. 309.

Fig. 7 Portrait of a Woman from Loango by Louis Ohier de Grandpré (1786–87). A slave trading captain active on the coast of Angola, Louis-Marie Joseph Ohier (1761–1846), the Count of Grandpré, was aware of how much his ignoble trade depended on shifting tastes and fashions. In this drawing, a woman from Loango showcases imported cloths and trade beads. OHIER, Discription du costume des noirs de la côte d'Angola (Public Domain).

slave trade in Angola, Benguela, and their dependencies.[81] As Miller summarizes, soon after its promulgation, António de Vasconcelos received orders from Lisbon to assemble all *banzos* in Luanda and to restrict the inclusion of Asian cloths illicitly supplied by Brazilian merchants,[82] Brazilian spirits, and French and British trade

81 Ley para ser livre, e franco o commercio de Angola.

82 According to Roquinaldo Ferreira, Asian cloths, also known as "*fazendas de negro* [Black's cloths]," included "*calameda, durante, taffeta,* and *zuarte*" from the Portuguese colonies of Goa, Damão, and Díu. As Cátia Antunes and Jelmer Vos explain, after Luso-African merchants were barred from the raffia cloth-producing areas under BaKongo jurisdiction in the aftermath of the Battle of Mbwila (1665), Asian cloths were introduced in Angola as an alternative currency. Ever since,

goods in these packages.[83] This "impractical" measure, which proved impossible to implement, was designed to protect Lisbon-backed traders who could only access more expensive European fabrics and spirits.[84]

When Sousa Coutinho succeeded António de Vasconcelos, he immediately focused on another component of the *banzos*, the salt blocks mined in Kissama.[85] Issuing a *bando* prohibiting mineral salt from entering the Portuguese-controlled fairs through Massangano and Ambaca, instead favoring the Benguela maritime salt that had started being extracted under a monopoly contract on November 13, 1761.[86] More importantly, Sousa Coutinho brought the administration of fairs under the jurisdiction of the Board of Commerce established by the Royal Charter of November 14, 1761, preventing the city council of Luanda from having the final say in the regulation of the internal slave trade or the composition of *banzos*.[87] At this point, the board began directly appointing the regulated fairs' scribes, tasking them with the impossible task of enforcing the fixed prices set in Luanda and verifying the contents of the *banzos* traded in the hinterlands.[88] All these measures proved ineffective and highly unpopular with Luso-African merchants and *pumbeiros*, who had the habit of taking advantage of the 'contraband' goods offered by BaKongo, Vili, or Teke *quibucas* or the Dembos and other Mbundu intermediaries to compose their *banzos* whenever these options were available.[89]

6.4 Sousa Coutinho's Ambitious Reforms and Their Limits

Complementing his efforts in establishing and reopening slave fairs, on September 16, 1764, Sousa Coutinho issued an Ordinance of the Fair Scribes comprising

---

merchants from Bahia and Rio de Janeiro had attempted to import Asian textiles directly to Luanda without European mediation, despite this practice being forbidden. For an exhaustive list of Asian fabrics used in the Angolan slave trade by the end of the seventeenth century and their worth in *réis*, see Virgínia Rau. ANTUNES and VOS, Port Cities and Commodities, in: CURRY-MACHADO et al. (eds.), The Oxford Handbook of Commodity History, p. 134, 136; FERREIRA, Dinâmica do comércio intracolonial, in: FRAGOSO et al. (eds.), O Antigo Regime nos Trópicos, p. 350–366; RAU, Prefácio, O "Livro de Rezão," p. 47.

83 MILLER, Way of Death, p. 584–585.

84 Ibid., p. 583–584; FERREIRA, Dinâmica do comércio intracolonial, in: FRAGOSO et al. (eds.), O Antigo Regime nos Trópicos.

85 MILLER, Way of Death, p. 585.

86 Ibid.; AHU, CU, Angola, Box 51, D. 4639.

87 COUTO, Os capitães-mores em Angola, p. 206–207; FERREIRA, Feiras e presídios, p. 22–24; MILLER, Way of Death, p. 583.

88 COUTO, Os capitães-mores em Angola, p. 227–228; MILLER, Way of Death.

89 VELLUT, Le Royaume de Cassange, p. 119.

sixteen articles.[90] This was the first of a series of ordinances and *bandos* meant to clarify the jurisdiction of scribes, captain majors, ordinary judges, and other minor office holders and establish its limits *vis-à-vis* the heads of the independent African polities and vassal *sobas*. According to its first article, the captain majors and scribes were to stop quarreling over "*matters of jurisdiction*," the former "*respecting*" the scribes and supporting them in upholding the "*economic government*" of the fairs, "*public Peace*," and the "*Security of Commerce*." The second article prescribed the adoption of a similar outlook and spirit of cooperation to scribes, reminding them that their office had been created to "*avoid disorders, thefts*," and commercial fraud and that the captain majors kept the monopoly on coercion and legitimate violence. Regarding the limits of the scribes' jurisdiction, the fourth article clarified that whenever the "*Merchants, or Pumbeiros committed offenses involving deaths, wounds, thefts, violence,* [or] *false imprisonment of free Blacks*," they were to immediately send them to the captain majors of their district for him to process their cases "*according to his Ordinance, and Royal Laws*." Regarding the jurisdiction of neighboring *dembos* and *sobas*, articles six, twelve, thirteen, and fourteen advised captain majors and scribes to employ "*sweetness and politeness*" to attract them to commerce and counter the allure of the "*Quibucas traveling to Loango or the Lands to the North of this hinterland*." Moreover, article fourteen ordered them never to "*interfere in the Govêrno particular* [private Government] *of the Sobas, Dembos, or* [other] *Potentates*" and to leave them free to observe their norms, which were nevertheless described as "*irregularities*."

Besides clarifying jurisdictions, the remaining articles of the Ordinance of the Fair Scribes focused on three pressing issues. First, its third, eighth, and fifteenth articles dealt with the dreaded "*reviros*" or "*travessias*."[91] This abusive commercial practice was one of the most significant threats to the credit-based system of the major West Central African commercial trade routes that siphoned slaves to Luanda and, later, to the trade routes ending in Benguela.[92] There were two moments in the slave-trading process when the parties receiving trade goods bought on credit in Luanda could betray their partners' trust.[93] The first moment was after African partners used the *banzos* trusted by Luso-African merchants or *pumbeiros* to obtain rights over dependents or slaves in the African prestige spheres of exchange. When in possession of the slaves they had promised in return for the *banzos*, African partners could be tempted to trade them on the spot to a third party for additional trade goods and abscond from Portuguese jurisdiction. The second moment was

90 AHU, CU, Angola, Box 50, D. 4585.

91 Ibid.; Miller, Way of Death, p. 276.

92 AHU, CU, Angola, Box 50, D. 4585; Miller, Way of Death, p. 579, 596, 621; Silva, The Atlantic Slave Trade p. 66; Silva Porto, Introdução, in: Santos (ed.), Viagens e apontamentos, p. 58–59.

93 Silva, The Atlantic Slave Trade p. 66.

when *pumbeiros* and other itinerant commercial representatives returned to Luanda with the slaves they had obtained with *banzos* entrusted to them by Luso-African slave merchants. These *banzos* comprised trade goods and useful currencies that the Luso-African slavers often obtained from Lisbon-backed merchants on credit. If their *pumbeiros* or commercial representatives failed to deliver on their promises, taking the slaves to other Atlantic ports or anchorages, the Luso-African slave merchants were forced to default on their loans, having their assets forfeited in the process.[94] Wayward *pumbeiros* then used several strategies to cover up *travessias* and *reviros*, often involving elaborate schemes and extensive networks of accomplices.[95]

Second, the fifth and sixteenth articles of the Ordinance of the Fair Scribes regulated how deceased merchants' estates were to be distributed.[96] These articles stipulated how captain majors were to act as judges of orphans with the assistance of the scribes of the fairs, hoping to avoid the many cases of abuse that took place when Luso-African merchants or *pumbeiros* died.[97] Articles five and sixteen replied directly to a request made by the Conference of Commerce on July 10, 1764.[98] Then, the Conference demanded that scribes be allowed to "*seal the doors of the merchant's compounds*" as soon as they died until the captain majors proceeded to write an inventory of their assets as judges of orphans. Sousa Coutinho incorporated this demand into the fifth article of his ordinance, adding in the sixteenth that scribes were to send a list of all the "*brands*" of the slaves of deceased Luso-African merchants and *pumbeiros* to "*avoid that captain majors sold a part of their estate.*"[99] However, the fact is that Sousa Coutinho had to get the approval of the Board of Royal Conscience and Military Orders to interfere with the jurisdiction and procedure of the judges of orphans. Writing to the secretary of state of the overseas and the navy, Francisco Xavier de Mendonça Furtado, on October 31, 1767, Sousa Coutinho expressed his frustration about this fact.[100] Then, he lamented that a new law of June 17, 1766, reforming the procedure to be followed by judges of orphans, was being ignored because the Board of Royal Conscience had not ordered captain majors to observe it.[101] This suggests that captain majors also resisted abiding by articles five and sixteen of the ordinance, perhaps mentioning Sousa Coutinho's lack of jurisdiction over the regulated matters.

---

94 Miller, Way of Death, p. 276–277, 306.

95 AHU, CU, Angola, Box 50, D. 4585; Miller, Way of Death, p. 579, 596, 621; Silva, The Atlantic Slave Trade p. 66; Silva Porto, Introdução, in: Santos (ed.), Viagens e apontamentos, p. 58–59.

96 AHU, CU, Angola, Box 50, D. 4585.

97 Miller, Way of Death, p. 583.

98 Delgado, O governo de Sousa Coutinho em Angola I, p. 21.

99 AHU, CU, Angola, Box 50, D. 4585.

100 AHU, CU, Angola, Box 52, D. 4804.

101 Ibid.; Delgado, O governo de Sousa Coutinho em Angola I, p. 21.

Third, the third, sixth, and ninth articles of the Ordinance of the Fair Scribes sought to restrain the interference of captain majors and scribes in the commercial transactions of Luso-African merchants and *pumbeiros*.[102] While these articles assured that the scribes were allowed to denounce the fraudulent management of assets by *pumbeiros* and commercial representatives and persecute together with the captain major those who "*got paid by their own hands*," article three stressed that the captain majors were barred from "*distributing*" the slaves that came to the fairs or interfering in the arrangement of bundles of trade cloths. Together, these articles addressed some of the criticisms put forward by Ferreira in 1762, abandoning the project of fixing the composition of *banzos* (e. g., in terms of the relative quantity of each useful currency or trade good) but remaining neutral about the possibility of establishing a ceiling for their total value in *réis*. However, as happened regarding articles five and sixteen, captain majors seem to have resisted these measures. Consequently, on February 24, 1765, Sousa Coutinho issued a new ordinance comprising thirty-one articles regulating the activities of captain majors, ordinary judges, scribes, and the administration of justice in the Angolan hinterlands.[103] The sixth article of this new ordinance reminded captain majors of the prohibition to engage in the slave trade,[104] pinning on their "*unruly greed*" the "*ruin of the fairs*."[105] It ordered captain majors to respect the Ordinance of the Fair Scribes, "*under no circumstance distributing the cabeças* [slaves] *and wax*," abstaining from interfering in the composition of *banzos* or other strictly commercial affairs. In cases when "*immediate action*" was needed, they could decide in a provisory manner and submit their resolutions to be reviewed by the captain-general and governor. Moreover, the eighth article of the ordinance clarified that the captain majors' custom of exchanging useful currencies for cloth with their soldiers was considered a form of trade and thus also prohibited. By 1765, soldiers still received stipends in cloths or uniforms, which they needed to exchange for other trade goods and staples. As Sousa Coutinho describes, captain majors took advantage of cloths' oscillating value to cheaply rebuy the wages they paid to their subordinates with other useful currencies, then profited from the arbitrage opportunities presented by transferring the cloths to where they fetched higher prices.

102 AHU, CU, Angola, Box 50, D. 4585.

103 AHU, CU, Angola, Box 51, D. 4624; Coutinho, Documento N.º 6, in: Couto, Os capitães-mores em Angola; Couto, Os capitães-mores em Angola, p. 233–234; Delgado, O governo de Sousa Coutinho em Angola I, p. 25–26.

104 This was in keeping with the law of August 29, 1720, which forbade all military officers with the rank of captain or higher from engaging in the slave trade. Couto, Os capitães-mores em Angola, p. 237.

105 Coutinho, Documento N.º 6, in: Couto, Os capitães-mores em Angola, p. 326–327.

In 1762, to avoid similar problems stemming from the payment of military wages in cloth, the Portuguese Crown planned to introduce a new series of metallic coins known as *macuta* (pl. *macutas*) in the Captaincy of Angola.[106] These coins were minted in copper or silver, substituting a previous series of copper coins introduced into circulation in 1693.[107] In the last decade of the seventeenth century, metallic currency had been introduced in the Captaincy of Angola to counter the inflation of prices paid in official *libongo* cloths and the associated deflation of military wages, paid by *ouvidores gerais* with *libongo* supplied by the holders of the slave duty contract of Angola.[108] However, copper *macutas* soon flooded the market in Luanda, quickly losing value because they were not accepted in the prestige spheres of exchange of the African hinterlands.[109] Moreover, metallic currencies tended to be hoarded, a practice known as "*estanque* [draining]," or transferred to Brazil, quickly leaving circulation.[110] The solution adopted by the contract holders was to continue paying military wages in "*fato* [clothes]" while accepting *letras dos direitos* backed by slaves to be auctioned in Brazil as payment for the slave export duties.[111]

---

106 The name *macuta* alludes to *makuta*, a bundle of 10 *libongo* or *kundi* raffia cloths. Delgado, O governo de Sousa Coutinho em Angola I, p. 33; Garcia, Descrição das moedas de Angola, p. 185.

107 The first series consisted of 20, 10, and 5 *réis* copper coins. The second series consisted of silver coins of 12, 10, 8, 6, 4, and 2 *macutas*, respectively worth 600, 500, 400, 300, 200, and 100 *réis*, and copper coins of 1, ½, ¼, and one *pano*, respectively worth 50, 25, 12.5, and 5 *réis*. Half-*macutas* were also known as "*mitiar*," and quarter-*macutas* as "*equipaga*" or "*kipaka*." As Ralph Delgado describes, 12.000$000 *réis* worth of silver *macutas* were transferred to Angola in 1768, and an additional 20.000$000 *réis* worth of silver *macutas* in 1770. Delgado, O Governo de Sousa Coutinho em Angola I, p. 33; Garcia, Descrição das moedas de Angola, p. 182–187.

108 According to Silva Corrêa, in 1694, 700 *réis* worth of *libongo* (140 cloths each worth five *réis*) were paid per month to the soldiers of the Luanda garrison. When Captain-General and Governor Henrique Jacques de Magalhães, in office between 1694 and 1697, first sought to introduce the new metallic currency, he reduced wages to 200 *réis*, causing a riot that resulted in *Ouvidor Geral* Francisco Lopes da Silva being expelled from Luanda by the mutineers. Cadornega, História geral das guerras angolanas, Vol. 2, p. 534–540; MMA XII, D. 186; Silva Corrêa, História de Angola, Vol. 1, p. 320–322.

109 Cadornega, História geral das guerras angolanas, Vol. 2, p. 539; Dias, Os Portugueses, p. 185–187; Miller, Capitalism and Slaving.

110 Delgado, O governo de Sousa Coutinho em Angola I, p. 33–34.

111 *Letras dos direitos* were divided into subcategories according to the slave duties they were connected to; because these varied considering the privileges of the exporters, so did the worth of *letras dos direitos*. As Miller relates, *letras* resulting from the payment of *direitos velhos* (old duties) entitled their payees to 4$000 *réis* per *cabeça* exported to Brazil, while *letras* resulting from the payment of *direitos novos* (new duties) entitled their payees to 7$000 *réis* per *cabeça*. These values amounted to 15 to 25 percent of the initial funds realized from the auctioning of slaves in Brazil and were paid to the payees in bullion as soon as the first, healthier individuals were sold. As explained in the second chapter, soldiers were paid with the funds raised with *letras dos direitos*. Contract holders used these funds to buy cloths or uniforms to transfer to Angola and Benguela and comply with

By the 1760s, this practice, first tolerated as a practical way of dealing with the lack of metallic currencies or other currencies accepted outside of the regional West Central African monetary system, had evolved into a complex mechanism geared towards extracting wealth.[112] It was complemented by other forms of bills of exchange and the issuing of *livranças* by the contract holders at the beginning of their contracts to cover all their expenses in West Central Africa, which then circulated as unofficial fiduciary money. Because these personal bills of credit were backed by nothing but the contract holder's reputation, they were a form of 'bad money' that, in keeping with Gresham's Law, quickly drove 'good money,' such as *macutas* or bills of exchange backed by the funds raised by auctioning of slaves in Brazil, out of the currency market.

To illustrate how different kinds of paper money enabled the credit system at the base of the Angolan slave trade to operate, Delgado offers the following hypothetical scenario.[113] By the 1760s, somebody interested in investing in the Angolan leg of the Atlantic slave trade would arrive in Luanda with 10$000 *réis* worth of *cruzados* (or any other metallic currency).[114] They would leverage this sum by using the bullion to buy 20$000 *réis* worth in *livranças* issued by the contract holders or *letras de risco* issued by Brazilian shipping companies,[115] then use this high-risk paper money to

---

their obligation of supplying the *ouvidor geral* of Luanda with useful currencies to pay military wages. According to Silva Corrêa, by 1694, soldiers were paid 140 *libongo* worth five *réis* per month and a sack of manioc flour (totaling 700 *réis*). Captain-generals and governors of Angola also received *letras dos direitos*, using this secure paper money to pay a portion of the salaries of their direct subordinates, such as the secretaries of the government. Delgado, O governo de Sousa Coutinho em Angola I, p. 33–37; Miller, Capitalism and Slaving, p. 44; Silva Corrêa, História de Angola, Vol. 1, p. 321.

112 Delgado, O governo de Sousa Coutinho em Angola I, p. 37–40; Menz, A Companhia de Pernambuco; Menz, As "geometrias" do tráfico; Miller, Way of Death, p. 299–300, 310–312, 442, 561–562.

113 For a detailed account of the financial and economic aspects of the Angolan leg of the Atlantic slave trade during the last decades of the seventeenth century based on the accounting books of António Coelho Guerreiro, see Virgínia Rau and Miller. See Miller for an alternative hypothetical scenario focused on a Brazilian captain arriving in Angola with a load of Brazilian spirits. Miller, Capitalism and Slaving, p. 45–46; Rau, Prefácio, O "Livro de Rezão."

114 Delgado, O governo de Sousa Coutinho em Angola I, p. 38.

115 *Letras de risco* [high-risk bills of exchange] differed from *letras seguras* [secured bills of exchange] in several aspects. As Miller clarifies, the latter were issued by established Angolan shippers against accounts they held in Brazil, specifying the bankers or merchants who were to act as drawees and when the payees could realize the sums. The former were issued by Brazilian shipping companies or ship captains who assumed the role of drawees. They depended on the safe arrival of concrete shipments of slaves to Brazil and specified no date to realize the sums promised to the payees. Due to the risks associated with the middle passage (e. g., piracy, shipwreck, mutinies, epidemics), holders of *letras de risco* earned a premium of up to 30% of the note's face value when the cargo backing them was sold. While *letras seguras* were either reserved or used to transfer wealth out of

buy the useful currencies and trade goods needed to compose *banzos* in the markets of Luanda.[116] They would then head to the hinterland *pumbos* with these *banzos* or trust a *pumbeiro* or Luso-African merchant to go to *pumbos* or official slave fairs in their stead.[117] If they were lucky enough to survive or were not conned by their associates with *reviros* and *travessias*,[118] the hypothetic slave trader would find themselves in Luanda with a coffle of slaves intended for sale in Brazil. Then, they would draw *letras dos direitos* as a payee to pay the slave export duties to the contract holders.[119] Personal bills of credit backed with the sale of slaves could be used to pay Brazilian intermediaries for the transfer of the slaves to Brazil, their feeding along the middle passage, and their posterior handling.[120] Once in Brazil, the slaves

---

Angola, *letras de risco* circulated as fiduciary currency on par with less desirable personal bills of credit such as *livranças*. Miller, Capitalism and Slaving, p. 44.

116 According to Miller, these personal bills of credit "ranked at the very bottom" of the "hierarchy of commercial paper generally circulating in Luanda" because they "bore no date by which the obligation they represented had to be discharged" and were "little more than personal IOUs." Delgado, O governo de Sousa Coutinho em Angola I, p. 38; Miller, Way of Death, p. 561–562.

117 As Sousa Coutinho remarked in a letter he wrote to the Captain Major of Cambambe on November 25, 1771, by then, Luanda-based merchants were also free to send their representatives and "*Pumbeiros descalços* [barefoot *pumbeiros*]" to "faraway *Pumbos*." However, he points out that this was a risk they willingly accepted and that the captain major was not obligated to protect those who chose to trade outside official fairs. Sousa Coutinho, Carta para Iozé Thomás Vás Vieira.

118 Silva Corrêa provides an extensive list of everything that could go wrong during this leg of the transaction. Silva Corrêa, História de Angola, Vol. 1, p. 35–57.

119 Miller, Way of Death, p. 558–560.

120 In a letter from June 17, 1774, Sousa Coutinho claimed that for a *peça da Indía* to be auctioned in Brazil, if the Luso-African slave trader respected all regulations and was invested in their wellbeing, they would have to incur the following expenses, totaling a minimum of 22$660 *réis* (this value does not take into account the price of daily rations on both sides of the Atlantic). 1. "*Expenses in the African Ports*:" baptism—300 *réis*, daily meals until shipping—35 *réis*, "*Loincloths or cloths with which they cover* [themselves]"—900 *réis*, supplies for the middle passage—2$000 *réis*, "*Extra for the med*[icine]"—300 *réis*, "*Passage if* [they] *arrive alive*"—6$000 *réis*, "[Payment] *to a sailor to ensure they reach* [Brazil] *alive*"—800 *réis*, custom duties on "African harbors"—9$000 *réis*. 2. "*Expenses in the Brazilian Harbors*:" "*Food rations for each day of delay*"—60 *réis*, "*Baeta* [cloths], *hats and pipes and tobacco*"—1$600 *réis*, customs "*in Rio de Janeiro and Bahia*"—1$760 *réis*. As for the price that *Peças da Indía or* bills of exchange backed by their sale in Brazil could fetch, these were 30$000 *réis* in Luanda and 40$000 in Benguela. This meant that Luso-African slave traders operating in the Luanda-Kasanje connection could expect to make less than 7$500 *réis* off of each *peça da Indía* if they found no way of cutting corners. Female slaves "*picked as if a Peça da India*" were worth 25$000 *réis* in each of these harbors, the same as "*moleques* [young male slaves]." As for "*molecas* [young female slaves]," they would fetch 18$000 *réis* in Benguela and 20$000 *réis* in Luanda. Since all expenses were adjusted, the profit margins from selling these enslaved persons should not vary much from those obtained by selling *peças*. According to Sousa Coutinho, the price differences were related to the preferences of certain kinds of buyers (e. g., plantation owners, miners, and those in search of domestic or urban slaves) for slaves from a given

were auctioned and paid for with bullion, which was used to reimburse the payees of all the *letras* and personal bills of credit drawn by the slave trader (according to a pre-established priority scale that privileged the payment of tax-related bills), any surplus being used to buy Brazilian trade goods, which were then shipped to Luanda. The hypothetical slave trader would use some of these goods to compose *banzos*, exchanging others for *livranças* of the contract holders, and then repeat the cycle.[121] When they planned to leave Angola and move their acquired wealth to Portugal or Brazil, they would invest in *letras seguras* or secured bills of exchange and use them to raise a sum in bullion or colonial trade goods in Brazil.[122] Throughout this process, contract holders repeatedly exchanged worthless bills of credit for *cruzados* and secure paper money that was quickly converted to bullion in Brazil. Lisbon-based merchants and Brazilian shipping companies received payment for their wares and services similarly, the latter also taking advantage of the system to pay for slaves with *letras de risco*. All then proceeded to transfer the wealth obtained in Brazil to Lisbon, either by exporting bullion or Brazilian slave-produced commodities such as sugar and tobacco to Portugal.[123] In the meantime, as Miller concludes, all liabilities associated with the middle passage and the hinterland slave trade remained with the Luso-African slave traders, who were the only ones ever owning slaves or losing money upon their deaths.[124]

In 1769, Sebastião José de Carvalho e Melo expressed his opinion about this complex ad hoc system, comparing the issuing and circulation of *livranças* or personal bills of credit as fiduciary currency to the crimes of minting and circulating "*false currency*" and denouncing the Jesuits as the instigators of this practice, going so far as to blame the Company of Jesus for the introduction of cloth currencies to the Captaincy of Angola.[125] As a drastic solution, Carvalho e Melo argued for the end of the slave duty contract, which came to pass on August 5, 1769, when the issuing of personal bills of credit was also forbidden by royal edict.[126] At this point, the Board of Finance substituted the personal bills of credit of the contract

---

region. See Aldair Rodrigues for an analysis of the racial and other stereotypes that influence these preferences. ANTT, CLNH, Fol. 45, D. 10; Delgado, O governo de Sousa Coutinho em Angola I, p. 38; Rodrigues, African body marks.

121 Menz, A Companhia de Pernambuco; Menz, As "geometrias" do tráfico; Delgado, O governo de Sousa Coutinho em Angola I, p. 37–40; Miller, Way of Death, p. 299–300, 310–312, 442.

122 Miller, Capitalism and Slaving, p. 44.

123 Menz, A Companhia de Pernambuco; Menz, As "Geometrias" do tráfico.

124 Miller, Capitalism and Slaving; Miller, Way of Death, p. 299–300, 310–312, 442.

125 Carvalho e Melo, Documento N.º 8, in: Couto, Os capitães-mores em Angola, p. 368–372; Delgado, O governo de Sousa Coutinho em Angola I, p. 37–40.

126 Sousa Coutinho was tasked with seizing the assets of the last holders of the slave duty contract of Angola, using them to pay 92.980$884 *réis* worth of unbacked *livranças*, thus ending their circulation as fiduciary money. Delgado, O governo de Sousa Coutinho em Angola I, p. 37–40.

holders circulating as fiduciary money for bills of exchange of its own and pushed for the introduction of silver *macutas* to pay military wages, forwarding the Crown's control over Luanda's currency market.[127] All these reforms took place under the auspices of the powerful *Erário Régio* (1761–1832), which reclassified the slave duties of Angola as 'public' revenues.[128] As discussed in the third chapter, the Justice Board was also essential for this transition to happen peacefully, as soldiers knew that mutiny against the new payment system would be punished by summary execution.[129]

Sousa Coutinho's attempts to abolish local uses and customs predicated on the circulation or consumption of useful currencies and to control the production and circulation of salt as a currency in the Angolan hinterlands must be understood as parallel efforts to these monetary reforms. The uprooting of African normative systems through the issuing of police legislation went hand in hand with the regulation of local currency markets and attempts to block or control exchanges in African prestige spheres of exchange. In other words, all these different sets of reforms had in common that they targeted currencies that were used as social currencies in West Central Africa, be they the *livranças* that oiled the cogs of the Angolan slave trade or the cloths, salt, and Brazilian spirits that enabled Mbundu and BaKongo corporate kin groups to accumulate wealth in people. These currencies stood in the way of the absolutist state because they were used by Lisbon-backed merchants, Brazilian shipping companies, Luso-African merchants and *pumbeiros*, and Africans to "create, maintain, and otherwise reorganize relations between people" that escaped the state's control.[130] Therefore, the attempts to disassemble the pre-capitalist economic systems they were embedded in and associated normative spheres cannot be reduced to the unfolding of a purely economic agenda or as part of a "civilizational mission" grounded on conversion—as Jean and John Comaroff argue was the case in nineteenth-century South Africa.[131] They were episodes in the history

---

127 The captain-general and governor took immediate measures to ensure that the military received their uniforms at discount prices, requesting that the Secretariat of the Overseas and the Navy assume the role of supplying them henceforward. AHU, CU, Angola, Box 54, D. 4972, D. 4976, Box 55, D. 4992; MILLER, Way of Death, p. 596.

128 Thornton remarks that by the 1770s, taxes on the export of slaves made up 88% of the total revenue of Angola. ANTT, Contadoria da Junta da Fazenda Real do Reino de Angola; BENAVENTE, A Extinção do Erário Régio; DANTAS DA CRUZ, Pombal e o Império Atlântico; RODRIGUES, Os homens do Erário Régio; THORNTON, A History of West Central Africa, p. 290.

129 MILLER, Way of Death, p. 558.

130 GRAEBER, Debt, p. 130.

131 See Cristina Nogueira da Silva and Miguel Bandeira Jerónimo for an analysis of the "civilizational mission" trope in the Portuguese Empire. BANDEIRA JERÓNIMO, The "Civilising Mission" of Portuguese Colonialism; COMAROFF and COMAROFF, Beasts, Banknotes and the Colour of Money; COMAROFF and COMAROFF, Of Revelation and Revolution, Vol. 2, p. 171; FERGUSON, The

of absolutist state formation in Angola and part of a concerted push towards a new hierarchy of sources of law that encompassed other Pombaline reforms described in the first chapter, from the issuing of the Law of August 18, 1769, to the reform of the University of Coimbra, in 1772.[132] Instead of being predicated on theological or even moral grounds, Sousa Coutinho's reforms were justified as the forwarding of public order, predicated on a new understanding of sovereignty, and backed up with threats of legitimate violence.

In this spirit, the first article of the Ordinance of February 24, 1765, ordered captain majors to persecute Mbundu *mutambis* [sacrifices to the dead] that "*scandalize the People and disturb Public order*," denouncing Catholic Priests who failed to eradicate them.[133] Shortly before promulgating the ordinance, on January 9, 1765, Sousa Coutinho had issued a *bando* decreeing the abolition of "*entambes* [burial ceremonies]" and Mbundu marriage ceremonies in Luanda.[134] Four years later, on January 10, 1769, he would issue an even more ambitious *bando*, decreeing the abolition of *entambes* and *mutambis* in the whole Captaincy, also ordering the closure of "*quicumbis*," shrines he described as public "*whorehouses*," and the "*quibamgos* [shrines]" of idols.[135] Not coincidentally, in all these social events and cross-cultural spaces, useful currencies such as cloth, Brazilian spirits, livestock, and other trade goods were exchanged or consumed to maintain or establish social relations with the living and the dead. As for salt, the second article of the 1765 ordinance allowed religious tithes to be paid in "*salt rocks*" as was "*customary*."[136] However, whenever possible, Sousa Coutinho sought to regulate its value. In 1771, he went as far as abusively acting on behalf of the Municipal Council of Massangano. He decreed that each rock of mineral salt circulating in the district would be worth 80 *réis* and established a ceiling on the local price of trade goods.[137] This use of police laws

---

Bovine Mystique; Nogueira da Silva, "Missão civilizacional" e codificação de "usos e costumes;" Nogueira da Silva, A dimensão imperial do espaço jurídico português.

132 Silva (ed.), Colleção de legislação portugueza (1763–1774), p. 407–415.

133 Coutinho, Documento N.º 6, in: Couto, Os capitães-mores em Angola, p. 324; Delgado, O governo de Sousa Coutinho em Angola I, p. 27–28.

134 Delgado, O governo de Sousa Coutinho em Angola I, p. 27–28.

135 The context of these regulations is further explored in Part III. Ibid.; AHU, CU, Angola, Box 54, D. 4897.

136 Coutinho, Documento N.º 6, in: Couto, Os capitães-mores em Angola, p. 325.

137 Sousa Coutinho established the following price ceilings, which doubled as conversion rates for useful currencies: one salt rock was worth sixty "*Cacusso*" dry fish; five salt rocks were worth a measure of "*folhinha*," "*Linhajem*," or "*Cré*" cloths or a female turkey; ten salt rocks were worth a flask of Brazilian spirits, or a male turkey, kid, sheep, or ram, and were equivalent to one "*beirame*;" fifteen salt rocks were worth a flask of wine, and were equivalent to three "*folhinhas*;" twenty salt rocks were worth a flask of Portuguese brandy or a flask of olive oil, and were equivalent to two "*beirames*." *Beirames* were a standard measure of Indian cotton cloth. Bluteau, Beirame, in: Moraes Silva (ed.), Diccionario da língua portugueza, Vol. 1, p. 176; Conceipção et al., Carta

to breach municipal autonomy arguably stems from Sousa Coutinho's awareness that the privilege the ordinary judge and municipal councilors of Massangano had of fixing commodity prices in salt amounted to them having indirect control over the currency market of the village that stood at the "entrance" to the eastern hinterlands.[138] While this fact already warranted his direct intervention, the rising inflation of prices paid in salt also threatened the viability of the nearby Nova Oeiras Royal Foundry, one of his flagship projects, forcing him to take immediate action or lose control over its tightly regulated social environment.[139]

In the same vein, the tenth, eleventh, and twelfth articles of the Ordinance of February 24, 1765, regulated the hearings of "*Mucanos*" in a way that both clarified the jurisdiction captain majors had over Mbundu pleas, stipulated what sources of law they could resort to, and forbade the circulation of African useful currencies as emoluments.[140] The tenth article admitted that "*jurisdictional certainty*" and clarity about "*jurisdictional limits*" were now "*of absolute need*." Captain majors had to be aware of the "*different modalities*" through which they exerted their jurisdiction and could no longer "*confuse*" under the designation of *mucanos* "*freedom cases*," the summary punishment of crimes against the "*public tranquility*," the adjudication of regular legal processes, and the arbitration of "*irregular*" pleas. As Sousa Coutinho clarified, captain majors had been entrusted with adjudicating freedom cases in their districts by the Royal Charter of March 15, 1698; punishing crimes against Public order according to extant military regulations as military officers; adjudicating regular legal processes as ordinary judges, according to the *Philippine Ordinances* (1603) and other extant statutory laws and regulations; but had no right to "*use Gentilic Laws*" to arbitrate any "*irregular*" pleas brought to them by either Portuguese *moradores*, Luso-African merchants, or Africans under their jurisdiction. However, the following articles explained that they could still intervene in Mbundu and other African legal disputes, taking advantage of the monopoly on legitimate violence they held as the highest-ranking military officers of their districts to uphold the *Ordre public* and protect rustic Blacks from the 'abuses' of Luso-African merchants and *pumbeiros* and African despots.

---

que o Senado da Camara de Massangano; SOUSA COUTINHO, Forma do bando, q. S. Ex.ª mandou p.ª se publicar em Massangano.

138 ALFAGALI, Blacksmiths of Ilamba, p. 37–38.

139 See Crislayne Alfagali and Delgado for a history of the Nova Oeiras iron foundry. ALFAGALI, Blacksmiths of Ilamba; CONCEIPÇÃO et al., Carta que o Senado da Camara de Massangano; DELGADO, O Governo de Sousa Coutinho em Angola III; SOUSA COUTINHO, Forma do bando, q. S. Ex.ª mandou p.ª se publicar em Massangano; THORNTON, A History of West Central Africa, p. 291.

140 COUTINHO, Documento N.º 6, in: COUTO, Os capitães-mores em Angola, p. 328–329.

According to Sousa Coutinho, the irregular pleas presented to the captain majors were often based on the "*rights of Quituxe and Opanda*."[141] The first consisted in determining who was to pay compensation for "*calamitous occurrences*," such as "*fires, the ruin of houses,* [and] *the loss or fall of trees*"—a clear reference to the imposition of penalties after sorcery accusations against suspects of causing these 'calamitous' disasters had been preestablished through divination. The second consisted in adjudicating adultery charges and all matters related to bride payments according to Mbundu normative systems or, as Sousa Coutinho put it, "*determining the obligations that Blacks had towards their amigas* [concubines]" and upholding the rules of "*concubinage*." After the tenth article disambiguated all these different kinds of pleas, the eleventh determined that captain majors had to respect different command and jurisdictional hierarchies in each case,[142] repeating that they should never "*govern themselves according to barbarous Laws*" or extort emoluments from "*the miserable Blacks to* [arbitrate] *cases of Opanda, Quituxe, and other barbarities*." Finally, the twelfth article determined that in all irregular pleas "*not included in His Majesty's Laws*," or that the "*Justice of this same Lord*" precluded from being heard, captain majors should punish wrongdoers as military officers so that the "*Blacks*" under their jurisdiction were not, due to "*their miserable ignorance*," "*exposed to the vengeance*" of others. However, captain majors had to explain to the supplicants "*the irregularity of their pleas*" and were forbidden from receiving emoluments. In practice, recognizing this exception amounted to using a Portuguese doctrinal understanding of '*Ordre public*' as a benchmark to render all the normative systems that interfaced in the captain majors' jurisdiction comparable according to a single standardized scale.[143] In other words, the urgent need to maintain social stability for the continuation of the slave trade justified the ad hoc adjudication of irregular pleas based on African normative systems. This was even though such systems were considered incompatible with Portuguese legal principles under the commensuration regime proposed by Sousa Coutinho.

Articles ten to twelve sought to provide the jurisdictional clarity Leitão had claimed was a prerequisite for slave fairs such as Cassange to function, entrusting the captain majors with disambiguating each plea brought before them, separating regular from irregular ones, and acting accordingly. The seventeenth and eighteenth articles dealt with some of the pending issues already mentioned, the former

141 Ibid.

142 As discussed in the third chapter, the twentieth-second article of the ordinance also stipulated that the Justice Board would adjudicate captain majors' final reviews and ascertain whether they had respected its articles. AHU, CU, Angola, Box 51, D. 4624; Coutinho, Documento N.º 6, in: Couto, Os capitães-mores em Angola, p. 332; Couto, Os capitães-mores em Angola, p. 68–70.

143 Sunstein, Incommensurability and Valuation in Law, p. 784.

stipulating that the captain major of Encoge was to send all those caught trading "*contraband*" goods with BaKongo *quibucas* back to Luanda to be punished by the *provedor da Real Fazenda*, and the latter prohibiting captain majors from bartering with the cloths that continued to be paid as military wages to soldiers in most *presídios*.[144] Finally, the fifteenth article established the external limits of the captain major's and the ordinary judge of Massangano's jurisdiction, decreeing that they were not to "*interfere*" in the "*domestic Government of Potentates, Sobas and their Vassals and Sons*"—not even to stop the "*execution of the barbarous Laws between us reproached*." In conclusion, the article stated that the prohibition of "*extorting*" fees from Black subjects to pay for the adjudication of cases pertaining to "*what they could not have done*" (e. g., sorcery), and decided according to the divinations "*in which the Gentilic laws are based*," was only valid for the "*Officers of His Majesty*" acting within their jurisdictions, not for African rulers—the latter were free to continue adjudicating sorcery accusations according to their "*Gentilic laws*."[145] However, the Ordinance of February 24, 1765, failed to define the precise limits of personal jurisdiction, taking them for granted. This meant that, despite Sousa Coutinho striving for jurisdictional clarity, one of the critical issues Leitão identified as being at the origin of countless disputes at the fair of Cassange, namely determining who had jurisdiction over Luso-African merchants and *pumbeiros* in hinterland fairs under direct African control, was left unresolved.

Articles thirteen and fourteen addressed one other critical issue Leitão had already identified in his demands. Namely, the *jaga*'s adjudication of sorcery accusations through the *ndua* ordeal.[146] Sousa Coutinho tackled this issue while respecting the limits imposed by the fifteenth article of the 1765 ordinance and taking into consideration the fact that if the *jaga* stopped condemning those accused of sorcery and punishing them and their dependents with death penalties commuted to slavery, business would surely flounder at the slave fair of Cassange. Therefore, in the spirit of articles ten, eleven, twelve, and fifteen, Sousa Coutinho focused his efforts on policing the behavior of Portuguese officeholders. Article thirteen forbade captain majors from committing the "*terrible abuse*" of conceding "*licenses*" for accused "*Blacks to go to the lands of Kasanje and take the Judua* [*ndua*] *oath to purify themselves of the stain of being Feiticeiros*," also prohibiting captain majors from taking the "*Fazenda* [wealth] *of the accused*," either in collaboration with the "[*jaga* of] *Kasanje or by splitting it with the Scribe*" of the fair of Cassange.[147] In

144 Coutinho, Documento N.° 6, in: Couto, Os capitães-mores em Angola, p. 330–331.

145 In other words, African rulers were not to be censored for charging fees and payments to compensate them for adjudicating cases of sorcery accusations involving ordeals or any other in keeping with African norms.

146 Sebestyén, Vansina (eds.), and Leitão, Angola's Eastern Hinterland, p. 337–338.

147 Coutinho, Documento N.° 6, in: Couto, Os capitães-mores em Angola, p. 330.

the same vein, article fourteen forbade the scribes of the fair from writing down "*the certificates, which they usually write down, to those who have taken that drink, in which the* [*indua*] *oath consists*," and ordered all captain majors to confiscate these certificates whenever they came upon them. It further stated that scribes who continued to write *indua*-ordeal certificates were to be denounced to the captain-general and governor and punished for the "*practice of a barbarous custom, offensive to the Christian Religion and its Purity*."

Both articles prove that, by then, captain majors and scribes were circumventing the third, sixth, and ninth articles of the Ordinance of the Fair Scribes, which forbid them from interfering in commerce, as well as its fifth and sixteenth articles, that regulated their function in case merchants or *pumbeiros* died, by doubling as agents of the *indua* ordeal supervised by the *jaga* of Kasanje.[148] In other words, just as captain majors used the opportunity presented by the arbitration of *mucanos* according to Mbundu norms to illicitly enrich themselves, Portuguese authorities at Cassange and nearby *presídios* had found creative ways of profiting from the *ndua* ordeal, going as far as adjusting to this purpose the bureaucratic procedures imposed on them by enlightened captain-general and governors. Unsurprisingly, as Miller remarks, during this period, the "*houses of charms*" mentioned by Leitão provide the "best-known example" of a West Central African court of arbitration being turned into a "tribunal converted to creating slaves for sale." These new slaves came from the ranks of "accused thieves, witches, and sorcerers from rural areas."[149]

The "*ndua* poison ordeal," however, proved to be more than just an enslaving mechanism.[150] As Miller points out, it was also a critical political and statecraft tool, turning the fair of Cassange into a prestigious "judicial centre"[151] and enabling the *jaga* to resist the destabilizing tendencies brought forward by his subjects trading directly with BaKongo *quibucas* or wayward Luso-African merchants and *pumbeiros*.[152] According to Miller, by the early decades of the eighteenth century, the *jagas* of Kasanje were already looking for ways to increase their political power

---

148 AHU, CU, Angola, Box 50, D. 4585; Miller, Way of Death, p. 123.

149 Miller, Way of Death, p. 123; Sebestyén, Vansina (eds.), and Leitão, Angola's Eastern Hinterland, p. 337–338.

150 Miller, Way of Death, p. 123.

151 As Leitão remarked, by 1756, the ordeal was already so respected and sought after as a means of settling disputes that people came from "*all the realms of Portugal in these kingdoms, and from the Libolo nation, from Quissama* [Kissama], *from the Dembos and from the kingdoms* [sic] *of Congo*." Sebestyén, Vansina (eds.), and Leitão, Angola's Eastern Hinterland, p. 339.

152 Miller claims that for West Central Africans, one of the most enticing and socially destabilising aspects of European trade was that Luso-African merchants and *pumbeiros* accepted to exchange prestige goods in "any social context," offering their wares to "minor lineages," "warlords," "gunmen who threatened older communities of farmers," "provincial lords who challenged old royalty" and all kinds of parvenus. Therefore, the arbitration of sorcery accusation at the public courts of

and expand their wealth at the expense of internal rivals.[153] In the process, they must have realized that since, according to *ijila* of the *kilombo*, enslaved war prisoners were "more suitable for retention" as soldiers "than for sale," their capture tended to reinforce the direct followings of lesser titleholders and *makota* in charge of military detachments. Contrariwise, persons enslaved through judicial means, especially those accused of sorcery, were easily alienated. Moreover, the Mbangala rulers could claim a share of the wealth that resulted from their condemnation as emoluments or fees and encourage the ordeal to target their internal rivals. Internal purges, made possible by the Luso-African slave fair, also occurred during the chaotic transition periods between the death of an incumbent *jaga* and the installation of a new Mbangala ruler. As Miller explains, these periods were marked by violent succession struggles when all internal factions clashed, often in a bloody civil war, hoping to secure the title of *kulashingo* (whom the Portuguese titled *jaga*) for their favorite candidate and privileged access to the fair.[154] This struggle excluded the *makota* of Lunda ancestry, who were part of Kasanje but, as official protectors of the office of *kulashingo*, were ritually excluded from vying for control of the Mbangala throne and having a ruler elected from their ranks.[155] During these transition periods, Cassange was closed to traders, and all the caravans to the west were withheld.[156] As soon as the war between factions concluded and a new *jaga* was successfully enthroned, the slave fair was reopened, and the prisoners captured from the ranks of the losers were traded as slaves with the Luso-African merchants and *pumbeiros*.

As Martin Chanock describes, these developments resonate with what would happen in much of Central Africa during the nineteenth century.[157] In that context, what he defines as "heterogeneous conquest and slaving states" adapted similar ordeals as centralizing political and statecraft tools.[158] While Chanock focuses on polities that emerged after the abolition of the Atlantic slave trade, the Kingdom of Kasanje fits his definition as an early conquest state. Just as the conquest states that later emerged in Central Africa, as discussed in the previous chapter, Kasanje evolved through the "amalgamation" of pre-existing chiefdoms and the creation

---

African rulers can be also understood as attempts to reign in these wayward subjects. MILLER, Way of Death, p. 97, 223; VELLUT, Le Royaume de Cassange, p. 132.

153 MILLER, Way of Death, p. 121–123.

154 Ibid., p. 128.

155 MILLER, Kings and Kinsmen, p. 191–192; MILLER, Kings, Lists, and History in Kasanje, p. 52–53.

156 MILLER, Way of Death, p. 128.

157 Notably, in the Kingdom of Kazembe. Basing himself on the reports of Portuguese explorers Francisco José de Lacerda e Almeida (1753–1798) and António Cândido Pedroso Gamito (1806–1866), Chanock describes how the "*mwavi*" or "*moave*" ordeal was used in "cases of sorcery" and "adultery cases where the offense was denied." CHANOCK, Law, Custom, and Social Order, p. 87–88.

158 Ibid.

of a "new kind of judicial authority and a new kind of enforceable custom" out of improvised elements and what could be salvaged from previous normative systems.[159] Moreover, Chanock's description of the social and moral effects of assembling "large numbers of slaves and slave wives in owner's villages" not only aptly portrays the tense environment of "slaving states" but also of Luso-African slave fairs, where many enslaved persons waited long periods for the completion of coffles and for the remaining debts of the slavers to be settled. There, "vital social norms held only tenuously," and "the golden age of consensual judgment and compensatory settlement" gave way to "ordealing" as the heads of corporate kin groups and political officers had no interest in organizing lengthy and costly palavers to settle disputes involving alienable slaves.[160] According to Chanock, in these milieux characterized by an "atmosphere of malevolence," the detection of the "responsibility for death and misfortune" increasingly fell to ordeals.[161] A shared, 'cross-cultural' belief in sorcery provided the framework for these developments.

As MacGaffey and Thornton claim was the case for the nineteenth-century Kongo, in the Luanda-Kasanje connection, "the slave trade itself" was thought of in terms of sorcery.[162] "Folk opinions" about the functioning of the trade were expressed employing the idiom of *feitiçaria*, *kindoki*, and *uanga*, giving rise to sorcery rumors and accusations that created the need for "ritual means such as initiation, divination, and various ordeals" to disambiguate the "morally ambiguous" use of these forms of power.[163] Behind these "ritual means," MacGaffey concludes, "lay the secular realities of political power—the ability to mobilize wealth, violence, and oratorical support in local competition." Therefore, as Miller remarks, the *ndua* ordeal owed a great share of its success to the *jaga*'s ability to "seize defendants declared guilty and hand them over to their accusers as slaves" and to the fact that local Portuguese authorities collaborated in this process and that Luso-African merchants and *pumbeiros* were "ready buyers" of the accused.[164] Moreover, as further discussed in the next chapters, Sousa Coutinho's efforts to extirpate rival ordeals and ritual means of disambiguation inside Portuguese jurisdictions also favored the *ndua* ordeal. The fact that the Luso-African merchants and *pumbeiros* simultaneously profited from the *jaga*'s monopoly of violence, which allowed the *ndua* ordeal to operate and serve as an enslaving mechanism, and were threatened by it, being liable to be accused of being sorcerers just as Grizante had, presented

159 Ibid., p. 20, 22.
160 Ibid., p. 88–89.
161 Ibid.; Sebestyén, Vansina (eds.), and Leitão, Angola's Eastern Hinterland, p. 339.
162 MacGaffey, Kongo Political Culture, p. 12; Thornton, Cannibals, Witches, and Slave Traders.
163 MacGaffey, Kongo Political Culture, p. 12.
164 Miller, Way of Death, p. 223.

them with another double bind.[165] Sousa Coutinho proposed no definitive solution to this problem, simply seeking to counter the *jaga*'s power to disambiguate sorcery accusations in areas where the Portuguese had a de facto monopoly on physical violence.

On July 29, 1775, Captain-General and Governor António de Alencastre, in office between 1772 and 1779, issued a new Ordinance of the Scribes of the Fairs of Cassange, Haco and Beja (1775) comprised of thirteen articles.[166] Its first article confirmed that scribes only had jurisdiction over the "*economic government*" of fairs, being tasked with upholding "*public Peace*" and enforcing contracts. The second, seventh, and eleventh articles clarified that they were tasked with avoiding "*travessias*." The fifth article ordered them to prevent Luso-African merchants and *pumbeiros* from using their "*own hands*" to collect their debts as this practice led to "*thefts, beatings, deaths, and other iniquities that ruin Fairs, and depopulate the hinterlands*." The fourth and twelfth articles regulated the procedures scribes should follow when merchants died; the sixth determined that they had to submit bi-annual reports about the state of commerce; the ninth forbade them to coerce porters to work for free; the eighth and tenth recommended them to keep good terms with nearby "*Dembos and Potentates*;" and the thirteenth ordered them to register the ordinance in their record books. Less ambitious than Sousa Coutinho's, Alencastre's ordinance does not mention the *ndua* ordeal or sorcery accusations. In all, the only significant innovation was that its first article determined scribes had to assemble a jury "*of truthful Witnesses*" to mediate commercial disputes, forwarding their deliberation to the captain-general and governor for him to confirm or command otherwise.

6.5 Policing the Slave Fair of Cassange

José de Almeida e Vasconcelos, the Baron of Mossâmedes and Captain-General and Governor of Angola between 1784 and 1790, was the first to attempt to reach a more definitive solution to the problems arising from the lack of jurisdictional clarity in Cassange. On July 26, 1789, he sent an embassy to the Kingdom of Kasanje, demanding the *jaga* accept a new treaty between the two kingdoms.[167] According to the fifth point of this treaty, the Mbangala ruler was henceforth "*forbidden,*

165 Miller remarks that Luso-African merchants and *pumbeiros* frequenting slave fairs under the jurisdiction of independent *dembos* faced a similar situation during the second half of the eighteenth century. Then, a "law of *kitushi*" or "*quituxe*" became customary which mandated that the penalty for very small offenses was "*loss of civil status or enslavement*." Ibid.

166 Lencastre, Documento N.º 9, in: Couto, Os capitães-mores em Angola, p. 373–376.

167 Vellut, Le Royaume de Cassange, p. 119–120.

[from] *sequestering, finning or extorting the Merchants,*" and using the "*snares, and stratagems with which, making use of his Gentilic Laws, he has harassed them.*"[168] Moreover, in the body of the new treaty, the Baron of Mossâmedes proposed that in case any of the merchants or other Portuguese subjects "*committed a transgression against the government and the Laws of the Jaga,*" the Mbangala ruler had them stand before the captain major of Ambaca.[169] Still, according to the treaty, the captain majors would have the scribe of the *presídio* examine the merchants' guilt, write appropriate indictment booklets, and send the booklets and the prisoners to Luanda for adjudication. It is impossible to determine how realistic the *jaga* found the proposal of persecuting Luso-African merchants and *pumbeiros* in Luanda for the infringement of *ijila*, perhaps being evident to him that such a rule would, in practice, exempt them from abiding by the *kilombo*'s norms and regulations. In any case, on December 19, 1789, *Jaga* Kitamba kya Shiba agreed to sign a version of this treaty, which the Portuguese exaggeratedly framed as a "*termo de fidelidade, e Vassalagem* [bill of fidelity and vassalage]."[170] In the final text of the renegotiated treaty, Kitamba kya Shiba promised to pay "*ganda* [tribute]"[171] to the captain-general and governor, to return runaway slaves, stop extorting the merchants and *pumbeiros* with "*fantastical crimes*" such as "*Cabellos* [*caballo*]"[172] and "*Upandas* [*Opanda*]," and help secure the western roads leading to Cassange.[173] Furthermore, he promised to establish a price ceiling for the *banzos* exchanged for *peças da Indía* in Cassange: 28 *beirames*, the *beirame* being a standard measure of Indian cotton cloth of varying lengths.[174]

Complementing this treaty on the domestic front, Manuel de Almeida e Vasconcelos, captain-general and governor of Angola between 1790 and 1797, issued a new ordinance regulating the fair of Cassange.[175] According to it, the Luso-African

---

168 Almeida e Vasconcelos, De S. Ex.ª para o Potentado Iaga Cassangi.

169 Ibid., p. 569.

170 Miller, Kings, Lists, and History in Kasanje, p. 79; Ximenes, Bahia e Angola, p. 112–113.

171 According to Parreira, Mbundu *sobas* usually paid the *ganda* to the captain-general and governor's envoys when he visited them to rally their forces for war. Before the Portuguese conquest, the *sobas* paid it to the commanders of Mbundu armies. The *ganda* comprised one, two, or more slaves. Parreira, Dicionário glossográfico, p. 48.

172 In 1851, Adrião Acácio da Silveira Pinto defines "*caballo*" as "*gentilic crimes.*" Pinto, Regimento do Chefe do Districto de Talla-Mugongo, in: Carvalho (ed.), O Jagado de Cassange.

173 Parreira, Dicionário glossográfico, p. 107; Ximenes, Bahia e Angola, p. 112–113.

174 According to Silveira Pinto, governor-general of Angola between 1848 and 1851, the length of the *beirame* varied between 1.7 and 2 meters, depending on "*the hinterlands where one trades.*" Bluteau, Beirame, in: Moraes Silva (ed.), Diccionario da língua portugueza, Vol. 1, p. 176; Pinto, Regimento do Chefe do Districto de Talla-Mugongo, in: Carvalho (ed.), O Jagado de Cassange, p. 147; Ximenes, Bahia e Angola, p. 112–113.

175 Almeida e Vasconcelos, Sendo proposto pela praça desta Capital.

slave fair now had a director under the direct jurisdiction of the captain major of Ambaca, the former being tasked with administering ordinary justice as a deputy of the latter. Furthermore, the third article of the ordinance determined that, contrary to scribes, directors could use coercive means if peaceful ones proved insufficient. In such cases, those accused of severe misdeeds were to be arrested and sent, together with their indictment booklets, to the *presídio* of Ambaca. Once there, the ordinance determined, the accused were to be incarcerated by the captain major until they could be forwarded to Luanda to stand before the Board of Justice. With the new ordinance, Manuel de Almeida e Vasconcelos also clarified that the director had to appoint an "*impartial*" merchant as his scribe and that, besides persecuting economic misdeeds, he was supposed to intervene when "*Whites, or pumbeiros*" took part in "*killings, maiming, violence, illegal arrests*" and the punishment of "*free persons*." Finally, the seventh article stipulated that the director had to guarantee that the merchants didn't impose deals and always respected the uses and customs of Kasanje. This respect was due, the captain-general and governor explained, because "*the economic government of his Lands*" still belonged to the *jaga*, and the Portuguese authorities could only "*punish the Blacks*" who broke the treaty's terms.

In Manuel de Almeida e Vasconcelos' words, the treaty was "*the only Law*" that the director could "*force them to observe*," and he was not to interfere "*with the ones that stem from their barbarity*."[176] No mentions are made of any form of Natural law or *Ius gentium*. Agreeing with Sousa Coutinho, the captain-general and governor believed that respecting the boundaries between the Portuguese and African normative systems was crucial for forwarding the twin objectives of introducing a policed form of government in Angola and ensuring the circulation of slaves.[177] Not caring to intervene in the intricate doctrinal debate inaugurated by Father Miguel Garcia and Father Gonçalo Leite and continued by Father Luis de Molina and Father Manuel Ribeiro Rocha, Manuel Almeida e Vasconcelos upheld, in a 1794 letter instructing the new captain major of Encoge on how to adjudicate freedom cases, that "*all those who are born slaves, or that were made slaves by the Barbarians, by any means and due to any cause, according to Gentilic laws and the contrary not being proved, should be sentenced as slaves*."[178] Setting the technical intricacies and moral subtleties of Father Rocha's argument momentarily aside, the captain-general and governor's pragmatism rested on accepting an empirical fact—the Portuguese could neither police independent African polities nor force them to respect their municipal laws. Therefore, they had to depend on African rulers and their normative systems to uphold and justify the enslavement of free Africans

176 Ibid.

177 Couto, Os capitães-mores em Angola, p. 166–167.

178 Ibid.

'ransomed' at slave fairs. While it is not accurate to describe the normative ordering proposed by Manuel Almeida e Vasconcelos as a form of "classic legal pluralism" typical of later indirect rule,[179] his proposal moved in the direction of reifying the limits of cultural groups and normative systems together, a clear break from the jurisdictional paradigm of the Portuguese *Antigo Regime*.[180] Moreover, the captain-general and governor tied the future of the Angolan slave trade to these reified divisions, making them highly relevant to the economy. All that was left to do was to persuade African rulers to police their hinterlands and stop them from interfering in Portuguese jurisdictions. Meanwhile, their "*Gentilic laws*" would ensure slaves were delivered to Luso-African merchants and *pumbeiros*.[181] On November 17, 1790, to conclude his reform of the fair of Cassange, Manuel Almeida e Vasconcelos sent an embassy to Kasanje, asking the *jaga*'s help in "*bringing back to the Feira bad merchants and pumbeiroz* [sic]" and in "*arresting them if they disobeyed the Orders that the Director gave them*," regardless of whether they were "*white or black*."[182]

A couple of years later, complaints against the directors of the fair of Cassange started to be voiced. On April 4, 1792, the Luso-African merchants established at the market undersigned a letter addressed to the captain major of the *presídio* of Ambaca complaining about Manoel de Sousa de Andrade, an ensign that had

---

179 This was the case because the superstructure of a colonial state with territorial, jurisdictional, and sovereignty claims over the Kingdom of Kasanje and other African polities was absent. In the case of Kasanje, Governor Adrião Acácio da Silveira Pinto was the first to attempt to establish a district envisioned according to a liberal conception of territorial jurisdiction that included it as one of its four divisions. The district was to be named Talla-Mugongo, created by *portaria* [governmental decree] number 290 on August 16, 1851. However, the occupation of Kasanje proved difficult, and the new district would only be 'pacified' in 1911–12. FERNANDES, A feira de Cassanje; FORD, Sovereignty; PINTO, Regimento do Chefe do Districto de Talla-Mugongo, in: CARVALHO (ed.), O Jagado de Cassange; WHEATLEY, Legal Pluralism as Temporal Pluralism, in: EDELSTEIN et al. (eds.), Power and Time.

180 For a critique of anachronic uses of the concept of "legal pluralism," see Tamar Herzog. As she remarks was the case for an extended period in Europe's past, during most of the Portuguese *Antigo Regime*, there was no "reason to assume that, [...] «different sorts of people» necessarily sent us to differences in ethnicity or culture" and that a "single law" would be "typical to a group, as several types of laws could easily coincide within the same community." HERZOG, The Uses and Abuses of Legal Pluralism; MERRY, Legal Pluralism.

181 COUTO, Os capitães-mores em Angola, p. 166–167.

182 On December 4, 1769, Sousa Coutinho issued two *bandos* regulating the "*Angolan hinterlands against vagrants, Blacks that live estranged from their sobas, sobetas, quilambas, and quimbares, réus da Justiça* [defendants in court], *and deserters from the troops*." Previous treaties had demanded that African rulers assist in upholding these regulations, destined to ensure that all who sojourned in the hinterlands were under the direct jurisdiction of either a Portuguese or African authority. AHU, CU, Angola, Box 54, D. 4962; ALMEIDA E VASCONCELOS, Carta de S. Ex.ª ao Jaga Cassange em resposta da embaixada.

been recently appointed to the new position.[183] In their opinion, Andrade "*lacked the proper knowledge and understanding of the uses, and Gentilic Rites of the Jaga, necessary to persuade and convince him*" to lower the price ceiling of the *banzos* exchanged for "*peças*."[184] According to their letter, the *jaga* had raised it to 30 *beirames*, two more than the maximum of 28 *beirames* he had publicly agreed upon two years earlier.[185] As was customary, the price ceiling of the *banzos* paid for other enslaved persons was calculated and inflated accordingly: the price ceiling of the *banzo* asked for a "*molecão* [pubescent male person]" reached 25 *beirames*; those of the *banzos* asked for a "*molecão de seis palmos* [male child]" or a "*molecona de peito atacado* [pubescent female person]" reached 22 *beirames*; and the price ceilings for the *banzos* asked for all other enslaved persons reached 15 *beirames*.[186] The *beirame*, however, was only used as a currency of account, as *banzos* still consisted of a bundle of trade goods—during this period, often including the Asian cloths, Brazilian spirits, gunpowder, and guns that Lisbon-backed merchants had tried in vain to exclude from them in the 1760s.[187] Therefore, the undersigned merchants hoped that a new director could influence the *jaga* to either lower the price ceiling or accept alternatively composed *banzos* as having the desired estimated worth in *beirames*. This could be achieved through renegotiating the trade goods included in *banzos*,[188] or the length of the "*calibamba*," one of the official measures used in Cassange to measure the fabrics they included.[189] More than 180 years after it was established, the Luso-African slave fair was still the stage where political disputes over the regional regime of commensuration were played out, the merchant's letter proving that arguments over measuring standards, the

---

183 Portela et al., Directorio para o Capitão Chagas; Vellut, Le Royaume de Cassange.

184 Portela et al., Directorio para o Capitão Chagas.

185 Ibid., Vellut, Le Royaume de Cassange, p. 120; Ximenes, Bahia e Angola, p. 112–113.

186 Portela et al., Directorio para o Capitão Chagas.

187 Ferreira, Dinâmica do comércio intracolonial, in: Fragoso et al. (eds.), O Antigo Regime nos Trópicos; Vellut, Le Royaume de Cassange, p. 120.

188 According to the Luso-African merchants, before the *jaga* changed these equivalencies in 1792, a *calibamba* of fabrics with "*the Arma Portugueza*" [Portuguese Seal] was worth six *beirames* in Cassange, and the same measure of "*granadeira*" fabric two *beirames*. A "*quizambo* [*kizambo*]" of Asian cloths, such as "*tafetá*" and "*zuarte*," was worth two *beirames*, also being measured with the *calibamba*. As for "*missanga* [colored-glass beads]," a measure of "*thirty threads of large*" ones was worth a *beirame*, the same value being attributed to a flask of gunpowder or an anker of Brazilian spirits. Portela et al., Directorio para o Capitão Chagas.

189 The other local measure also used in trade, the "*kizambo*," was probably a Mbundu standard. It was named after a Kimbundu word designating a "*piece of cloth big enough to dress a person*." Ferreira, Dinâmica do comércio intracolonial, in: Fragoso et al. (eds.), O Antigo Regime nos Trópicos, p. 350; Pinto, Regimento do Chefe do Districto de Talla-Mugongo, in: Carvalho (ed.), O Jagado de Cassange; Portela et al., Directorio para o Capitão Chagas.

composition of composite currencies, and the price ceiling of slaves could not be settled without acknowledging "*the uses, and Gentilic Rites of the Jaga.*"[190]

On August 20, 1792, in reaction to the undersigned letter of April 4, 1792, Manuel Almeida e Vasconcelos got rid of the inexperienced ensign and appointed the merchants' favorite substitute for his position, Captain Francisco das Chagas Veiga, as the new director of the fair of Cassange.[191] According to both the merchants and the captain-general and governor, Veiga was "*experienced in that hinterland*" and was thus in an excellent position to "*acquire the trust and friendship of the Jaga*" and convince him to lower the price ceiling of *banzos*.[192] As Jean-Luc Vellut makes plain, in 1792, the merchants of Cassange's complaint was not an isolated event but an episode in an ongoing economic crisis that was aggravated by the aftermaths of the Haitian (1791–1804) and French (1789–1799) Revolutions and that resulted in a diplomatic tug-of-war between Kasanje and Angola that the Portuguese ultimately lost.[193] Roquinaldo Ferreira concludes that this crisis ended in 1794, when the Luso-African merchants finally accepted the price ceiling of 30 *beirames* for a *banzo* exchanged for a *peça*.[194] This happened after Manuel Almeida e Vasconcelos' plans to evacuate the merchants and their assets from Kasanje militarily failed.[195] This evacuation plan had been a desperate attempt to escape from the double bind imposed by the *jaga* on Luso-African merchants and their Lisbon-based

190 This situation would only change after 1851 when Governor Silveira Pinto issued an "*Ordinance for the District Chief of Talla-Mugongo*" that included a section describing the duties of the subordinate officer in charge of the Cassange division. This ordinance was imposed on Kasanje after two military campaigns against the *jaga* in 1850–51, led by Portuguese infantry Major Francisco de Salles Ferreira (c. 1820–1857). This resulted in the Portuguese de jure annexing Kasanje's territory to the colony of Angola. The 1851 ordinance determined that the length of the "*calibamba* of the fair of Cassange" was to be decided by the chief of the new district after hearing all the settled merchants, the *jaga*, and the corporal in charge of the Cassange division. After the General Government approved it, the reformed *calibamba* was to be provided to all the new merchants settling in the fair of Cassange, together with a certified *covado* (0.66 meters), for 250 *réis* each. In other words, merchants were forced to pay for an exemplar of the new measures. Pinto, Regimento do Chefe do Districto de Talla-Mugongo, in: Carvalho (ed.), O Jagado de Cassange; Portela et al., Directorio para o Capitão Chagas; Rau, Prefácio, O "Livro de Rezão," p. 47.

191 Almeida e Vasconcelos, Ordem da nomeação do Capitão Francisco das Chagas Veiga.

192 Ibid.; Portela et al., Directorio para o Capitão Chagas.

193 Ferreira, Dinâmica do comércio intracolonial, in: Fragoso et al. (eds.), O Antigo Regime nos Trópicos, p. 372; Vellut, Le Royaume de Cassange.

194 Basing himself on documents kept by the National Archives of Angola, Luanda, Vellut argues that, on the contrary, the conflict ended on March 7, 1793, when the "regime of fixed prices" was abandoned. Ferreira, Dinâmica do comércio intracolonial, in: Fragoso et al. (eds.), O Antigo Regime nos Trópicos; Vellut, Le Royaume de Cassange, p. 121.

195 Ferreira, Dinâmica do comércio intracolonial, in: Fragoso et al. (eds.), O Antigo Regime nos Trópicos, p. 122–123; Vellut, Le Royaume de Cassange.

Luanda sponsors. By 1793, as Vellut remarks, the capital invested in the credit-based exchanges taking place in the prestige spheres of exchange of Kasanje was "immense," enough to cause "the most serious damage" to the finances of Brazilian and Portuguese trading companies.[196] Faced with such a delicate situation, Manuel Almeida e Vasconcelos preferred not having to trust the *jaga*'s diligence in speeding up exchanges or to hope for a succession struggle not to provide the opportunity for a new Mbangala sovereign to start negotiations with the Portuguese with a clean slate.[197] However, after the military column entrusted with evacuating Cassange was routed in Lundo, Manuel Almeida e Vasconcelos was forced to opt for a different solution. He sent Francisco Honorato da Costa (?–1816), a former factor of the Pernambuco Company heavily indebted in Cassange, as a diplomatic envoy to the *jaga*, asking the Mbangala ruler to cooperate in recovering the Luso-African capital, trade goods, and slaves invested in Kasanje.[198] Honorato da Costa then assumed the position of director of Cassange, which he kept until 1804, doing his best to recover bad debts and the capital he had invested in the region.[199] However, shortly after Miguel António de Mello became captain-general and governor of Angola in 1797, he opted to disinvest in the Luso-African fair in favor of the slave market of Ambaca, believing that the slow removal of trade goods circulating on credit would gradually achieve Manuel Almeida e Vasconcelos' objectives.[200] Moreover, Mello actively attempted to break the *jaga*'s monopoly on trade with the Lunda Commonwealth.[201]

---

196 Vellut, Le Royaume de Cassange, p. 122.

197 As Miller remarks, newly elected *jagas* might not be inclined to honor the debts of their predecessors and rivals, committing what the Portuguese must have perceived as a monumental act of *reviro*. In the early nineteenth century, Portuguese merchants began withdrawing from Cassange, frustrated by the unwillingness of successive *jagas* to settle their outstanding debts. Miller, Way of Death, p. 626–627.

198 Francisco Honorato da Costa arrived in Luanda in 1777 and soon adopted the trading practices of Lisbon-backed merchants. This involved offering trade goods on credit to Luso-African merchants and *pumbeiros* headed for the Kasanje hinterlands. According to Miller, Costa had a poor track record as an administrator for the Pernambuco Company. Additionally, he was "beholden to the governor because he was himself under suit for debts." Miller, Way of Death, p. 576, 626–627; Vellut, Le Royaume de Cassange, p. 122–123.

199 Miller, Way of Death, p. 630.

200 Ibid., p. 626–627.

201 Miguel Mello entrusted Honorato da Costa (then acting from a slave fair in Mucari) with attempting to make official contact with the Lunda Commonwealth. As a result, the latter not only established direct commercial links with the *mwaant yaav* in 1804–05 but sent two of his *pumbeiros*, Pedro João Baptista and Anastacio Francisco, to the court of Kazembe, becoming the first known Portuguese to have made the transcontinental crossing. Ibid., p. 288, 628, 630–631; Bontinck, Le Voyage des pombeiros; Thornton, A History of West Central Africa, p. 312–313.

In the meantime, the ever-present tension arising from the high ambiguity levels and the atmosphere of malevolence reigning in slave fairs and slave-operated *arimos* constantly resurfaced. On November 21, 1791, José de Seabra da Silva (1732–1813) wrote a letter to Manuel de Almeida e Vasconcelos.[202] In its alarmed pages, he reports that Sousa Coutinho's attempts to curtail the influence of the *jaga* of Kasanje had failed. A prodigal child, Seabra da Silva had a genuinely meteoric career, becoming an adjunct secretary of state under the Marquis of Pombal when he was still under forty.[203] After serving for years as Pombal's right-hand man and being instrumental in implementing his absolutist reforms, one morning, without explanation, he was suddenly arrested and exiled to the Portuguese *presídio* of Pungo Andongo.[204] By then, Pungo Andongo was Angola's remotest and deadliest *presídio*, not far from the fair of Cassange. As Seabra da Silva relates, the "*renowned, infamous, and barbarous oath of Endua* [*ndua*]" was still "*practiced by White Moradores* [settlers] *from inside the Dominions of His Majesty*" who traveled from "*Massangano, Cambambe, Pedras* [Pungo Andongo], [...] *Ambaca,* [...] *and Muxima*" to submit to it.[205] This "*great injury to the Portuguese Name and the Christian Faith*," he continued, was based on a "*thousand brutal and superstitious suppositions*" and was impossible to explain in "*all its extension*." According to Seabra da Silva, from within Portuguese domains, "*large groups of free Blacks, and Slaves*" left on a fourteen-day trip to the court of the *jaga* of Kasanje. Once there, they "*drank a Poison artfully but coarsely prepared by a Black Impostor appointed by the Jaga*" to disambiguate the sorcery charges against them.

To curtail the considerable influence and prestige of the *ndua* ordeal for good, Seabra da Silva advocated that the practice of sending slaves or free Blacks to Kasanje be publicly forbidden, recommending the penalty of "*having all their assets Confiscated*" and being forced to serve in "*Galleys for all their Lives to the Whites, or Blacks, who instigated or participated in such an abomination*."[206] However, in his opinion, the captain majors were the ones to blame for the popularity of the ordeal because they self-interestedly supported similar "*oppressions*." Seabra da Silva argued that Africans under Portuguese jurisdiction were otherwise eager to abandon their normative systems, seeking "*Refuge in the Dominions of His Majesty*." In keeping with his biased interpretation, they only failed to "*embrace the Laws and Religion*" of the Portuguese and "*benefit from Civil Laws that are as soft as theirs are barbarous*" because the religion practiced in Portuguese *presídios* and districts was "*indistinguishable in practice*" from theirs. Seabra da Silva's eyewitness account

202 Seabra da Silva, Carta de José de Seabra da Silva.
203 Gorjão-Henriques, José de Seabra da Silva e a sua família, p. 99–101.
204 Ibid.
205 Seabra da Silva, Carta de José de Seabra da Silva, p. 79.
206 Ibid.

of how the *jaga* of Kasanje had turned the fair of Cassange into a judicial center suggests that, by 1792, the normative ordering of the Angolan hinterlands depended not only on a delicate '*pax Lusitana*' but on the generalized threat of being accused of being a sorcerer and having the accusation arbitrated by the Mbangala ruler.[207] While enlightened captain-general and governors sought to establish a monopoly on disambiguation using '*Ordre public*' or public tranquility as a standard and entrusting captain majors and the Justice Board with backing it with legitimate violence, the Mbangala ruler relied on the *ndua* ordeal to disambiguate between social and anti-social uses of *uanga* and separate the guilty from the innocent, also backing its rulings with state-sanctioned violence. Both orderings were bound to clash, but because the Portuguese were interested in continuing to ransom slaves from Kasanje, they agreed to limit their policies and frame slave fairs as the interface of separate spheres of influence, normative systems, and sovereignties—expecting the *jaga* to abide by their rules of engagement. However, the resurgence of jurisdictional conflicts suggests that the Mbangala did not share this vision. To conclude this chapter, we explore now how the Mbangala might have understood the fair and situated the Luso-African merchants and Portuguese in the extensive networks established by perpetual kinship that scaffolded West Central African regional inter-polity order.[208]

6.6 A Seat at the 'Cannibal's Feast'

In 1850, Portuguese infantry Major Francisco de Salles Ferreira (c. 1820–1857) led a punitive expedition from Pungo Andongo to the "*hinterlands of Bondo*" with the official intent of deposing the *ndala quissua* of Mbondo and installing a puppet ruler in his stead.[209] These were the same valleys Leitão had once described as lying outside Natural law.[210] Once there, he received an undersigned letter from the merchants of the fair of Cassange, complaining that Jaga Mbumba a Kinguri (?–1873) was abusively submitting them to his jurisdiction.[211] According to the signatories,

207 Luiz Felipe de Alencastro introduced the concept of "*pax Lusitania*" in his doctoral dissertation, using it to describe the outcome of the balance of interests of all parties involved in the Angolan slave trade (e.g., different corporations, religious orders, mercantile interests). I argue that a comparable '*pax* Mbangala' rested on a cross-cultural willingness to submit to the *ndua* ordeal. Alencastro, Le commerce des vivants; Ohata, Brazilian Civilization's Missing Link.

208 Heintze, Translocal 'Kinship' Relations in : Freitag and von Oppen (eds.), Translocality.

209 Ferreira, Memoria sobre o sertão de Cassange.

210 Sebestyén, Vansina (eds.), and Leitão, Angola's Eastern Hinterland, p. 335–336.

211 Miller, Kings, Lists, and History in Kasanje, p. 75; Neves, Memória da expedição a Cassange p. 123.

not only was the Mbangala ruler arbitrating "*quituxes*" involving them, he also forced them to pay compensation if they were found guilty by his court.[212] Furthermore, the merchants added that Mbumba a Kinguri issued *ijila* forbidding them to collect timber and cut wood, draw fresh water from wells and rivers, and "*send banzos* [...] *to the hinterlands*" without paying him tribute first. These complaints echoed those expressed by the merchants based in Cassange in 1792, proving that the Luso-Africans settled there were experiencing the same jurisdictional conflicts as before and that the struggle to control the commensuration regime in place in the Luanda-Kasanje connection had not been definitively won by the enlightened captain-general and governors of the last decades of the eighteenth century.[213] Spurred by this letter, Ferreira marched with his expeditionary force to Cassange, arriving there on July 22, 1850.[214] Once he arrived, the major sent a message to the *jaga* demanding a meeting at the fair. Faced with the latter's unwillingness to comply with his summons because of his *ijila*, Salles Ferreira interpreted this action as an "*insult to the Portuguese Flag*" and used this fabricated *casus belli* as a pretext to raze Mbumba's *kilombo*, install a puppet ruler in his place, and substitute the director of Cassange.[215]

Ferreira claimed he was informed about the Kingdom of Kasanje's history, uses, and customs during his military campaigns by the *makota* of Lunda origin who supported him.[216] In 1853, paraphrasing and adapting the *malunda* and *musendo* narrated by these *makota*, Ferreira wrote an official report relating his rendition of the uses and customs of the African kingdom. The report on the oral traditions of Kasanje that Ferreira then submitted to the recently reinstated Overseas Council (1851–1868)[217] was later published in the first volume of the *Annals of the Overseas*

---

212 Neves, Memória da expedição a Cassange p. 123.

213 Almeida e Vasconcelos, Ordem da nomeação do Capitão Francisco das Chagas Veiga.

214 Neves, Memória da expedição a Cassange p. 123.

215 Mbumba a Kinguri escaped with thousands of supporters to the eastern bank of the Kwango. A couple of months later, he had already managed to slay the new director in battle, assassinate the loyalist *jaga*, and regain control of the fair of Cassange. In response, Ferreira was tasked by the governor of Angola to capture Mbumba a Kinguri, install a new loyalist *jaga*, and formally annex Kasanje as a vassal kingdom. While another puppet ruler was indeed installed on April 26, 1851, Mbumba a Kinguri escaped once more, continuing to harass the Portuguese until 1857. Ibid., p. 123–139; Ferreira, Memoria sobre o sertão de Cassange; Miller, Kings, Lists, and History in Kasanje, p. 75.

216 AHU, SEMU, Angola, Box 823 (1798–1895), D. 117.

217 After its reinstitution by the liberals (1851–1868), this council was an advisory, fiscal, and coordinating board composed of seven permanent voting members (councilors) and seven substitutes. It was part of the Portuguese Secretary of State of the Navy and Overseas Affairs until 1868, when it was replaced by the Overseas Advisory Board (1868–1911). Beginning in 1854, the Overseas Council edited volumes to make its archive accessible to a broader audience. By then, it was presided over by Bernardo de Sá Nogueira de Figueiredo, the Marquis of Sá da Bandeira (1795–1876).

Council (1867).[218] Together with the commentaries of Ferreira's contemporaries António Rodrigues Neves, David Livingstone (1813–1873), and Francisco Travassos Valdez (1825–1892),[219] his account offers invaluable information about the different forms of groupwork performed by Mbangala intellectuals at a time when the regional trade in enslaved Africans was giving way to trade in commodities such as wax and ivory.[220] Furthermore, although Ferreira fails to elaborate on it, his mention of the "*terrible and mortal oath*" of "*Undua* [*indua*]" confirms that, still in the early 1850s, it existed and kept its centrality in the normative ordering of the middle Kwango Valley and the eastern borders of the Angolan colony.[221] This chapter concludes by exploring how the Portuguese traditionally fit into the regional inter-polity order according to the *makota* who informed Ferreira.

As Vellut emphasizes, the fair of Cassange was unlike the other slave fairs established under the close surveillance of Portuguese *presídios* because the *jaga* and the *Makita*, the political title holders who acted as electors of new *jagas*, controlled most of the exchanges.[222] Moreover, as he explains, on the African side, two kinds of exchanges occurred at the fair.[223] On the one hand, the heads of corporate kin groups exchanged goods in the prestige spheres where rights over women and dependents were traded, swapping them between themselves and with the Luso-African merchants and *pumbeiros*. On the other, Cassange was on the receiving

---

Ibid.; Conselho Ultramarino (1851–1868); Henrique, O acesso ao arquivo colonial português; Santos, Macau e o Oriente, Vol. 1, p. 37.

218 Ferreira, Memoria sobre o sertão de Cassange; Heintze, The Extraordinary Journey of the Jaga, p. 67–101.

219 In his report, Neves introduces himself as a "*mobile captain*" detached from Ambriz. Passing through Cassange in 1852, David Livingstone was hosted by Neves, whom he described as an "honest" and very caring man. Valdez had been one of the arbiters of the Anglo-Portuguese Mixed Commission in Luanda and Cape Town, and he wrote extensively about the Portuguese African and Asian colonies. Livingstone, Missionary travels and researches in South Africa, Vol. 2, p. 369; Neves, Memória da expedição a Cassange; Valdez, Africa Occidental, Vol. 1, p. 147–148.

220 Carvalho, O Jagado de Cassande; Miller, The Confrontation on the Kwango, in: Santos (ed.), I Reunião internacional de História de África.

221 Ferreira, Memoria sobre o sertão de Cassange, p. 27.

222 According to Thornton, by the 1850s, the Kingdom of Kasanje had a "central administration" composed of a "Council of State" that included the *sobas* Gunza a Bangela, Rabunda, Ndala Maunyo, and a *tendala*, all owning "slave-worked estates" and other important independent sources of revenue. The titleholder of the "Kituxe ka Kilwaje" office commanded its "central army." Several *makita* acted as electors of new *jagas*, representing the interests of three different factions. Finally, the ancestor cults of previous *jagas* gave rise to alternative clientele networks, each radiating from their burial site where their *kilombo* used to be. These cults also constituted important power bases. Fernandes, A feira de Cassanje; Vellut, Le Royaume de Cassange, p. 128; Thornton, A History of West Central Africa, p. 329.

223 Vellut, Le Royaume de Cassange, p. 129.

end of long-distance "tributary commerce" coming from the courts of the principal Lunda titleholders from the East of the Kwango and Chokwe and Songo polities who had contributed to the political formation of the original proto-Mbangala warbands. The former included the *mwaant yaav*, the head of the Lunda Commonwealth, and several other Lunda lords established on the east bank of the Kwango, such as *malundo*, the ruler of the Shinje.[224] The *jagas* prioritized ensuring the monopoly on eastern trade routes[225] while guaranteeing that their dependents did not accumulate excessive power and wealth over people by using the prestige goods brought by the Luso-African merchants. Besides instrumentalizing the *ndua* ordeal and imposing a regime of commensuration of Mbangala design, successive *jagas* performed this complicated balancing act by sponsoring the work of "Kasanje intellectuals" who fashioned regional histories in the form of *malunda* and *musendo*.[226] These oral narratives situated the *jaga*'s office concerning other regional title holders and a shared matrix of cultural heroes and legendary ancestors.[227] As Thornton summarizes, by the early 1850s, the rewritten history of Kasanje accommodated its privileged relations with the Lunda Commonwealth and rationalized the elective system of new *jagas* based on a rotation of candidates appointed by three main internal factions.[228] The political tributes received and reciprocated at Cassange can be understood as a performative rendering and constant renegotiation of the regional inter-polity networks that the *malunda* and *musendo* of Mbangala intellec-

---

224 Miller, Kings and Kinsmen, p. 137; Miller, Way of Death, p. 26–27, 214–215; Thornton, A History of West Central Africa, p. 307–308; Vansina, Government in Kasai before the Lunda; Vansina, It Never Happened; Vellut, Le Royaume de Cassange, p. 129.

225 See Miller and Thornton for an account of how this monopoly was breached during the first decades of the nineteenth century. Miller, The Confrontation on the Kwango, in: Santos (ed.), I Reunião internacional de História de África; Miller, Way of Death, p. 214–217; Thornton, A History of West Central Africa, p. 329–332.

226 Miller, Kings and Kinsmen, p. 21; Thornton, A History of West Central Africa, p. 189.

227 Miller, Kings and Kinsmen, p. 21.

228 As explained in the previous chapter, *malunda* and *musendo* are constantly refashioned to accommodate new groups and allies into the complex lattice of myths, corporate kin groups, and political offices that constituted the institutional underbelly of the Kingdom of Kasanje. Therefore, the oral traditions about the establishment and political system of Kasanje collected by Ferreira in 1850–1851 differ markedly from those collected by Father Antonio Giovanni Cavazzi da Montecuccolo in the 1660s. In the 1850s, as Thornton sums up, Mbangala historians connected the establishment of Kasanje to the migration of "Kinguri kia Bangala" or "Kulaxingo' from Lunda and the successive accretion into the Mbangala polity of a first group of migrants from Libolo led by "Ngunga," and a second group of migrants from Matamba lead by "Kalunga." The three factions entitled to rotate electing a new *jaga* out of their ranks were said to have originated from the followers of each of these mythical ancestors. Cavazzi, Thornton (trans.) MSS Araldi, Modena, Book 1, Chap. 3; Thornton, A History of West Central Africa, p. 327–329.

tuals described in terms of perpetual kinship and positional succession.[229] While the Portuguese did not figure in these, they were referred to in a revised description of the "*Kissembula*" ritual narrated to Ferreira in 1850–1851 (this ritual was first mentioned by Samuel Purchas and Andrew Battel in 1625).

According to Ferreira, the most memorable of Mbangala uses and customs was the final enthronement ritual of new *jagas*, which he claimed to have successfully proscribed in 1850.[230] Called the "*Sambamento*," Ferreira portrays it as an elaborate state ceremony involving the sacrifice of a human victim who was given the title of "*nicango*." In keeping with his report, this ritual would take place after an "*electoral college, which is composed of the Macotas, Cazas, Catondo, and Tendalla*" had agreed on a contender for the *jaga* title, selected out of three electable families and after a series of other minor rituals, such as the circumcision of the candidate, had been adequately dealt with. Without the *sambamento*, Ferreira affirms, the Mbangala would not consider the *jaga* to be "*in full possession of his sovereignty*." As reported by Ferreira, the *nicango* had to be a stranger with no kinship ties to the new *jaga* and the *makita*. Furthermore, he had to be kidnapped in the Nsongo region to be sacrificed. Once caught, Ferreira continues, he was brought to the encampment of the new *jaga*, where he was "*catered to, and even his orders* [were] *fulfilled as if they had originated from the jaga*." When the right moment came for the *nicango* to be slaughtered, the *makota* told Ferreira that he was brought before the newly elected ruler. The electee waited for him in front of his household, seated on a ceremonial "*iron stool*." Ferreira describes this stool as being a "*palmo* [foot] *tall and* [having] *a circular, concave seat, with a hole in the center*." During the *Sambamento*, the *makota* explained, the "*Bansacuco* [first wife of the *jaga*]" and the *jaga*'s "*concubines*" stood immediately next to him, as well as the "*Cassange Cagongue*," a ritual operator tasked with playing the "*gongue*." The *gongue* or *ngonge*, also known as *lunga*, was a sacred Mbangala metal instrument "*formed by two metal bells united at their top by an iron arch*," which was played with a "*mallet*" the size of a "*palmo comprido* [long foot]."[231] Surrounding this inner group, the electors, *makota*, and the general populace stood in expanding, concentric circles.

Once the *Cassange Cagongue* started striking the bells of the *gongue*, Ferreira continued, the *jaga* was supposed to use a "*crescent-shaped cleaver*" to "*open the nicango in the back*," rip out his heart, bite it, and throw it away, "*to be burned at a later stage*."[232] After this climax was reached, Ferreira continues, the *makota* would

---

229 Heintze, Translocal 'Kinship' Relations in: Freitag and von Oppen (eds.), Translocality.

230 Ferreira, Memoria sobre o sertão de Cassange, p. 28.

231 Bracks Fonseca, Queen Njinga of Ndongo and Matamba; Ferreira, Memoria sobre o sertão de Cassange, p. 28; Henriques, Njinga a Mbande e Aimé Césaire; Neves, Memória da expedição a Cassange p. 116–118.

232 Ferreira, Memoria sobre o sertão de Cassange, p. 28–29.

"*take the body of the nicongo* [sic], *and pour all the blood that* [was] *gushing from the hole where the heart once was over the belly of the jaga.*" Then, as the fresh blood dripped through the central hole of the iron stool, the *makita* would rub their hands with it and anoint "*their chests and beards, screaming a lot, exclaiming that the jaga is great.*" Once the first stage of the ceremony was completed, Ferreira claims, the body of the *nicango* was taken away to be skinned, butchered, and cooked together with an "*ox, dog, chicken, and other animals.*" When ready, this meal would be served to the enthroned *jaga*, the *makota*, the other title holders, and all the gathered populace. Finally, according to Ferreira's report, all those who were "*disgusted*" by the banquet were "*immediately sold off as slaves, as well as their entire families.*" He also reported that it "*was customary to send to the Director of the fair of Cassange a leg of the nicango*" that he had the chance of politely refusing while paying an anker of spirits and cloths "*as tribute*" to the *jaga*. Once in the past, Ferreira recounts, a director had, considering "*the offer too repugnant,*" refused to acknowledge it and pay this tribute. The new *jaga* of Kasanje found this gesture so offensive that he tried to "*force*" the director of Cassange to "*eat the flesh of the nicango* […] *as his rightful subject.*" In the end, Ferreira concludes, this diplomatic impasse was settled only when the "*director satisfied the customs,*" paying full tribute.[233]

As Ferreira relates, by the 1790s, when the first directors of the fair of Cassange were appointed, the merchants and *pumbeiros* established in Kasanje had to pay a tribute called "*malucu aquitamba*" to the *jaga*.[234] If we read the oral tradition about the *Kissembula* ritual collected by Ferreira in 1850–1851 as a *malunda* that used the office of the director of Cassange to describe, by metonymy, the position of all Luso-African merchants and *pumbeiros* concerning the *jaga*, this payment, which the Portuguese sources register as a 'fee,' was understood by the Mbangala as a symbolic tribute that confirmed the subordination of the Luso-Africans to the *jaga*, securing their exemption from *ijila* for only as long as they paid it.[235] After almost a century had passed since Sousa Coutinho started a campaign of

233 Writing on November 10, 1797, the retired Colonel Paulo Martins Pinheiro de Lacerda describes a similar ritual taking place amongst the "*Quimbangalas* [Mbangala]" from the southern plateau of Benguela. He described how the Mbangala would eat a "*Macongo*" whenever a new "*Sova of theirs is enthroned.*" This "*Macongo*" would be the first "*miserable black*" the "*Quindures*" caught "*on the road.*" According to Pinheiro de Lacerda, *quindures* were the "*oldest*" "*slaves of the State,*" who were also the electors of the new Mbangala leader. After they picked a "*Macongo,*" he continued, they would offer them in sacrifice to the new *Sova*, who would cut "*their head with a small axe, and skin them like a piglet.*" Afterward, the sacrificed human would be chopped in pieces and cooked with "*dog meat, cat meat, a chicken, a kid, a ram, pig meat, a mouse, and all living beings they can seize.*" When the stew was ready, it was served to everybody, including small children. PINHEIRO DE LACERDA, Notícia da Cidade de S. Filipe de Benguela; PURCHAS, Purchas his Pilgrimage, p. 699.

234 FERREIRA, Cross-Cultural Exchange, p. 48–49.

235 Ibid.

jurisdictional clarification and disambiguation, which his successors continued to wage by imposing new ordinances and forcing the rulers of Kasanje to sign treaties, ambiguity still reigned at the Luso-African slave fairs, which remained at the center of the political and ideological disputes over the regime of commensurability that underpinned the slave trade and the regional inter-polity order. As the Comaroffs' argue was the case in nineteenth-century South Africa, on the easternmost borders of Angola, attempts to retain control of the limits of (in)commensurability also remained central to the chiefs' and the heads of corporate kin groups' resistance against colonial encroachment.[236]

236 Comaroff and Comaroff, Of Revelation and Revolution, Vol. 2, p. 174; Graeber, Debt, p. 148–164.

III. Establishing Limits, Negotiating Belonging

Introduction

The chapters grouped in this part explore the personal and institutional challenges posed by the disturbingly close relationship between the power to harm others through *uanga*, *kindoki*, or *feitiçaria* and physical proximity, domesticity, and intimacy. They outline how these have been addressed by Africans, Luso-Africans, and the Portuguese in West Central Africa since the establishment of Luanda until the end of the eighteenth century. As further unpacked in the following paragraphs, the paradoxical nature of human relationships, which are always equally threatening and possibly rewarding, is likely experienced by members of all cultures in all historical periods, giving rise to different institutional solutions, legal remedies, and socially prescribed ways of ritually dealing with the anxiety and insecurity this duality causes.[1] While the chapters grouped in Part Two surveyed how slavers and those who had jurisdiction over slave fairs exploited ambiguity and profited from the power to disambiguate, the ones included in this part focus on the more

1 See Geschiere for an overview of the vast literature on this topic. For a discussion about the relationship between proximity and supernatural danger in the European context, see Robin Briggs and J. Favret-Saada. Focusing on contemporary South Africa, Isak Niehaus has explored decades of archival evidence about sorcery accusations, which he refers to as "witchcraft accusations" in keeping with the Anglophone convention established by E. Evans-Pritchard. He concludes that these accusations usually target spouses, neighbors, and cognates—the targets shifting according to historical circumstances. Focusing on Mozambique, Harry West has historicized the dynamics of *uwami* [sorcery] in the Mueda Plateau since the early twentieth century, noting that despite all the innovations brought about by Portuguese settler-colonialism, the Mozambican liberation struggle, independence, subsequent socialist one-party rule, and neoliberalism, *uwami* has always "festered in the intimate spaces among kin." Clifton Crais and Adam Ashforth also focus on the intrinsic connection of sorcery (or witchcraft) and kinship. See Yvonne Maggie and the volume edited by Nicolau Parés and Roger Sansi-Roca for an overview of how proximity generates fears of sorcery in the Lusophone Black Atlantic and Brazil. ASHFORTH, Madumo; ASHFORTH, Witchcraft Justice, and Human Rights in Africa, p. 5–38; ASHFORTH, Witchcraft, Violence, and Democracy; BRIGGS, Witches and Neighbours; CRAIS, The Politics of Evil; EVANS-PRITCHARD, Witchcraft, Oracles, and Magic; FAVRET-SAADA, Désorceler; FAVRET-SAADA, Les Mots, la mort, les sorts; MAGGIE, Medo do Feitiço; NIEHAUS, The ANC's Dilemma, p. 93–118; NIEHAUS, Witchcraft and a Life in the New South Africa; NIEHAUS, Witchcraft, Power and Politics; NIEHAUS, Witch-Hunting and Political Legitimacy, p. 498–529; SANSI-ROCA and PARÉS, Sorcery in the Black Atlantic; WEST, "Governem-se vocês mesmos!" p. 347–368; WEST, Creative Destruction and Sorcery of Construction, p. 13–31; WEST, Ethnographic Sorcery; WEST, Kupilikula, p. 178–179; WEST, Sorcery of Construction and Socialist Modernization, p. 119–150.

personal side of the drama caused by what Peter Geschiere defines as "the dark side of kinship"—a common simile for *uanga, kindoki* or *feitiçaria*.[2]

According to Geschiere, in Anglophone Africa, as in other regional contexts, vernacular conceptualizations of the forces or processes that came to be lumped under the catch-all designations of "witchcraft" and anti-witchcraft afford a framework to think through and attempt to reshape the "interface" between "intimate relations within the house and the outside world" or an "intimate inner circle and an uncertain outside."[3] While James Sweet, Kalle Kananoja, Roquinaldo Ferreira, and Timothy Walker have already approached some of the Inquisitorial and missionary sources explored in the following chapters, they nevertheless opted to frame their analyses as histories of African therapeutic knowledge and cultural and religious practices and beliefs.[4] Although spiritual and therapeutic aspects are essential in anti-sorcery rituals and divinations, these performances also serve as a link between the private or domestic normative sphere of the household, family, or other close-knit corporate groups (e. g., associations, cults, garrisons) and the public forums where commerce and exchanges take place, and conflicts are resolved. As a result, they are also fundamentally judicial or forensic acts.

In the South American domains of the Portuguese and Spanish Crowns, the household ("*casa grande*"), which consisted of the extended family under the authority of its patriarch or matriarch,[5] was the most "relevant" and "immediate" normative sphere for most settlers and the Amerindians and diasporic Africans under their direct control or tutelage.[6] While the same can be said to be true regarding West Central African households, due to the epidemiological limits to White settlement, the nonexistence of voluntary White female migration, and the hegemony of BaKongo, Mbundu, and Ovimbundu normative systems regarding the circulation

---

2 Geschiere, The Modernity of Witchcraft; Geschiere, Witchcraft as the Dark Side of Kinship, p. 43–61; Geschiere, Witchcraft, Intimacy, and Trust, p. 23.

3 Geschiere, Witchcraft, Intimacy, and Trust, p. 16–17.

4 Ferreira, Cross-Cultural Exchange, p. 179–188; Kananoja, Healing Knowledge in Atlantic Africa, p. 26–49; Sweet, Recreating Africa; Walker, Doctors, Folk Medicine and the Inquisition.

5 As Romina Zamora remarks, in Spanish South America's urban "*casas pobladas*," the *oeconomic* power often rested with mothers. Zamora, The Domestic Sphere, in: Duve and Herzog (eds.), Latin America Law in Global Perspective, p. 220–222.

6 In the aftermath of Gilberto Freyre's *Casa Grande e Senzala* [The Masters and the Slaves] (1933), the bibliography on Brazilian *casas grandes* is too extensive to cover in a footnote. See Marshal Eaking for an introduction to this historiography. For an introduction to the historical debates about the connection between household management (*Oeconomia*), *patria potestas*, and "police power" in North America, see Markus Dubber and Neil Websdale. Dias Paes, Esclavos y tierras; Dubber, The Police Power; Eakin, Becoming Brazilians, p. 1–26; Freyre, The Masters and the Slaves; Hespanha, Fazer um império com palavras, in: Barreto Xavier and Nogueira da Silva (eds.), O governo dos outros, p. 91; Websdale, Policing the Poor.

of women in marriage and the establishment of kinship and clientage networks, the normative and social patterns that can be observed in the archives vary significantly from those described by scholars of South America.[7] Discussing how the domestic norms that governed the "normative sphere" of the Brazilian "*casas grandes*" were translated as municipal bylaws or recognized as the biding uses and customs of local communities, Romina Zamora argues that this "normative translation" was facilitated by the fact that the same individuals ("*homens bons*") often accumulated the "roles of *pater familias*, master, and lord" also being socially active as neighbors and parishioners.[8] The presence of *homens bons* in municipal councils and lay brotherhoods and their preferential access to offices with a jurisdictional role thus guaranteed the continuity between these institutions' normative framework and their standpoints, assuring a seamless interface between the domestic and public spheres.[9]

However, in the Captaincy of Angola, Benguela, and their dependencies, municipal institutions and lay brotherhoods were sparse and understaffed, as discussed in the chapters gathered in Part One. Moreover, unlike the Brazilian *casas grandes*, the households of Portuguese and Luso-African *moradores* were barely racially segregated, even if enslaved Africans destined for the Atlantic slave trade were kept in separate compounds. Furthermore, while the urban households of Luanda and Benguela depended on rural plantations and farmsteads established by their *moradores* near the main riverbanks (the *arimos*), this did not result in a clear division of social and normative spheres as was seen between *casas grandes* and *senzalas* in Brazilian society or between *casas pobladas* and *haciendas* in Spanish South America.[10] These two factors, the lower levels of racial segregation amongst African, Luso-African, and Portuguese elites and the hegemony of African normative systems regarding critical areas of the *oeconomic* government of West Central African households, exposed Portuguese and Luso-African soldiers, missionaries,

---

7 Barreto Xavier and Nogueira da Silva, Introdução, in: Barreto Xavier and Nogueira da Silva (eds.), O governo dos outros, p. 40; Curto, The Donas of Benguela, in: Bergamo, Pantoja and Silva (eds.), Angola e as angolanas, p. 99–120; Margarido, Algumas formas da hegemonia africana in: Santos (ed.), I Reunião internacional de História de África, p. 383–406; Oliveira, Slave Trade and Abolition; Pantoja, A diáspora feminina, p. 555–572; Pantoja, Inquisição, degredo e mestiçagem em Angola, p. 117–136; Pantoja, Personagens entre mares Atlânticos, p. 136–149.

8 Zamora, The Domestic Sphere, in: Duve and Herzog (eds.), Latin America Law in Global Perspective, p. 222, 231.

9 Hespanha, Fazer um império com palavras, in: Barreto Xavier and Nogueira da Silva (eds.), O governo dos outros, p. 83–84.

10 Dias Paes, Esclavos y tierras; Freudenthal, Arimos e fazendas; Freyre, The Masters and the Slaves; Zamora, The Domestic Sphere, in: Duve and Herzog (eds.), Latin America Law in Global Perspective, p. 220–249.

moradores, and all kinds of sojourners to the dangers of intimacy and the "the dark side of kinship:" *uanga, kindoki* or *feitiçaria.*[11]

As already explored in the first chapter, the Mbundu and members of neighboring "*nations*" believed that significant breaches in their moral and social orders, as those evidenced by accidents, misfortune, or mysterious diseases, either happened "*by the impulse of the Indelles or Sandes, who are the souls of their deceased or by the meleficio* [evil deeds] *of feiticeiros*"—the breaching of *ijila* or prohibitions by the victims being a third explanatory option.[12] This meant that ordeals and divinations were an essential part of therapeutic processes and a significant incentive to the cult of the ancestors and territorial spirits and the upholding of *ijila*. It also meant they were crucial "responsibility allocation" mechanisms central to the arbitration of conflicts.[13] Even when ordeals and divinations determined that no sorcery was involved in a given case, they performed an essential judicial function, being two of the remedies readily available to West Central Africans, Luso-Africans, and the Portuguese to restore public 'trust' after private or intimate tragedies had taken place.[14] As the chapters grouped in Part Three argue, the other remedy was the public destruction of *iteke, indeles,* and *feitiços*—the physical objects Africans, Luso-Africans, and the Portuguese associated with sorcery or 'idolatry.' This 'iconoclasm' (or, from an African perspective, ritual cleansing) was often backed by the imposition of European religious and social norms and, during the second half of the eighteenth century, the enforcement of police regulations.

Nevertheless, during most of the period under consideration, the imposition of Portuguese norms, statutory laws, and police regulations remained hampered by two constraints. First, before the 'Law of Good Reason' of August 18, 1769, imposed a hierarchy of sources of law, local uses and customs directly influenced by BaKongo,

11 The dangers posed by sorcery were also acutely felt by Afro-Brazilians and other diasporic Africans and Afrodescendents, being central to many domestic dramas in the Americas and the Caribbean. While the normative solutions they adapted did not find their way into municipal bylaws or became biding uses and customs, they regularly resurfaced in the White settler's courts and tribunals. Calainho, Metrópole das mandingas; Davis, Judges, Masters, Diviners, p. 925–984; Diana, Witchcraft, Poison, Law, p. 235–264; Geschiere, The Modernity of Witchcraft; Geschiere, Witchcraft as the Dark Side of Kinship, p. 43–61; Geschiere, Witchcraft, Intimacy, and Trust, p. 23; Heywood and Thornton, Central Africans; Mello e Souza, O diabo e a terra de Santa Cruz; Sansi-Roca and Parés, Sorcery in the Black Atlantic; Santos, Bolsas de mandinga; Sweet, "Not a thing for white men to see," in: Curto and Lovejoy (eds.), Enslaving Connections, p. 139–148; Sweet, Domingos Álvares; Sweet, Recreating Africa; Thornton, Africa and Africans in the Making of the Atlantic World; Vanhee, Central African Popular Christianity, in: Heywood (ed.), Central Africans and Cultural Transformations, p. 243–264

12 José da Silva, Continuação da viagem ao sertão de Benguella, continuada do N.º 2.º, p. 54.

13 Geschiere, Responsibility versus Responsibilization, in: Denian, Fumanti and Lynteris (eds.), Anthropology and Responsibility.

14 Geschiere, Witchcraft, Intimacy, and Trust.

Mbundu, Mbangala, and Ovimbundu normative systems often prevailed over royal enactments and ordinances—a tendency that was hard to invert.[15] It is telling that despite the *Philippine Ordinances* decreeing the punishment of diviners and ordeal providers with public flogging, permanent exile to Brazil, and a 3$000 *réis* fine in favor of the denouncer, the possibility of punishing African ritual operators in this manner was never seriously entertained by Angolan authorities, not even after 1769.[16] Second, West Central African households, military corporations, lay brotherhoods, trading compounds, and other intimate or domestic spheres were mixed-race or predominantly Black spaces. This meant that African solutions were often adopted to address the spiritual dangers and nefarious consequences of 'cross-cultural' proximity and intimacy, especially in life-threatening situations and acute crises.[17] This happened even though ordinances, treaties, and police regulations were often explicitly framed according to the personality principle, requiring that these be the sole law ("*Ius proprium*") applied to metropolitan Portuguese and Luso-African *moradores* and merchants considered White.[18] Due to this deeply ingrained practice, as the ninth chapter explores, some captain-general and governors came to predicate the success of police regulations on social segregation and White settlement or the writing down and clear-cut systematization of African uses and customs, neatly demarcating the other's *Ius proprium*.

In conclusion, no analysis of the complex 'normative fabric' of the Captaincy of Angola, Benguela, and their dependencies would ever be complete without considering how Portuguese and African jurisdictions related not only to sorcery and the danger posed by physical proximity but also to anti-sorcery ordeals and divinations, linking the evolution of this fraught relationship with the history of the introduction of police laws and regulations and projects to reform the administration of justice. Contrary to the chapters grouped in Part Two, which traced the evolution of doctrines about legitimate enslavement and the limits of Natural law and *Ius gentium* from the beginning of the sixteenth century until the last decades of the

15 Barreto Xavier and Nogueira da Silva, Introdução, in: Barreto Xavier and Nogueira da Silva (eds.), O governo dos outros, p. 21–30; Herzog, Colonial Law, in: Tellkamp (ed.), A Companion to Early Modern Spanish Imperial Political and Social Thought, p. 105–127; Hespanha, Fazer um império com palavras, in: Barreto Xavier and Nogueira da Silva (eds.), O governo dos outros, p. 92–100; Saavedra, Jurisdictional Autonomy and the Autonomy of Law, p. 325–337; Silva (ed.), Colleção de legislação portugueza (1763–1774), p. 407–415; Wehling and Wehling, Direito e Justiça.

16 Ord. Fil., Book V, Tit. 3, § 2.

17 As the ninth chapter explores, these racial categories increasingly gained relevance during the second half of the eighteenth century, remaining fluid.

18 On the principle of personality, see Peter Oestmann. Hespanha, Fazer um império com palavras, in: Barreto Xavier and Nogueira da Silva (eds.), O governo dos outros, p. 91; Oestmann, Legal Layers, Legal Spheres, Legal Systems, p. 11–12.

eighteenth, correlating it with the history of Portuguese conquest and the development of the Atlantic slave trade, the following chapters will focus primarily on the eighteenth-century transition from the jurisdictional, poli-synodal paradigm of the *Antigo Regime* to the police state one.[19] They approach ad hoc solutions to the 'trust' issues raised by living amongst possible sorcerers, considering that different Portuguese and Luso-African individuals and corporations had dissimilar approaches to the judicial mechanisms and remedies developed by the Mbundu and adjacent peoples to deal with the same moral, social, and normative challenges. Moreover, they take social and cultural pluralism seriously by acknowledging that referring to populations as BaKongo, Mbundu, Ovimbundu or Mbangala creates a misleading sense of unity that misrepresents the social and linguistic plurality of the kingdoms and chiefdoms where these language-defined groups were either more numerous or more powerful. Not only individuals circulated between cultural areas and polities due to enslavement, marriage, or because of their specialized occupations and trade, but titles, institutions, and political and religious innovations also circulated—with some forms of African "groupwork" such as cults, secret societies, and shrine complexes cutting across different political and language groups.[20]

---

19 Hespanha, As vésperas do Leviathan; Subtil, Espaço político e organização, p. 88–116; Subtil, Estado de polícia, p. 15–40; Subtil, O Terramoto Político.

20 Kodesh, Beyond the Royal Gaze; Miller, Worlds Apart, in: Madeira Santos (ed.), Actas do seminário, Vol. 1, p. 232–233; Schoenbrun, The Names of the Python, p. 3–12.

7. Sorcery and the Dangers of Intimacy

7.1 Opening the Door to African Otherness

Three years after the founding of Luanda (1576), the seat of the General Government of the Portuguese Captaincy of Angola, the Jesuits who had accompanied Paulo Dias de Novais (1510–1589) in his return to West Central Africa wrote an optimistic yearly report.[1] They reported that their mission had progressed despite the untimely deaths of Father Garcia Simões, their previous superior, and Brother Cosme Gomez. Father Baltazar Barreira and Brother Fructuoso Ribeiro had recently arrived as substitutes, with the enthusiastic Father Barreira acting as Jesuit superior and Dias de Novais' right-hand man. Moreover, their "*church was small but well stocked with ornaments and altarpieces*," and a "*hundred souls had been baptized*." Finally, they announced, a "*great door*" had been "*opened for the salvation of those peoples*" due to the "*generalized destruction of Idols*" which had taken place in the land of a "*gentile*" called "Manicorimba [*Mani* Corimba]," an "*important fidalgo of the Kingdom of Angola* [Ndongo]."[2] The Jesuits reported that this iconoclastic campaign had been long postponed "*because the Devil had stalled*" Father Garcia Simões "*with threats and bouts of war*."[3] But now, "*fifteen public houses*" storing a "*great sum of feitiços*" to whom the locals were "*very affectionate*," as well as the "*heads of snakes, feet and nails of men, and birds, teeth of leopards, and many other similar things*," had been burned down, together with a "*great number* [of idols] *that* [were dispersed] *through the pathways, bushes, and in their homes*." The "*joy with which all the populations offered their idols and feitiços & helped to burn them*," together with the enthusiasm the subjects of *Mani* Corimba showed in "*visiting the* [communal] *crosses and preparing for baptism*" gave the Jesuits great hopes.[4] However, the missionaries were soon to realize that the conquest of Ndongo, the massive intake of enslaved

---

1 MMA III, D. 42.

2 *Mani* Corimba was one of the rulers of the marshes known as "*Ensaca of Cassanze* [Kasanze]," immediately to the West of Luanda. As discussed in the previous chapter, he was thus a tributary of the Kingdom of Kongo, not Ndongo. MMA VII, D. 7, p. 20; Sousa, Mapa das regiões circunvizinhas de Luanda, in: Heintze (ed.), Fontes para a História de Angola, Vol. 1, p. 158–165.

3 MMA III, D. 42.

4 As mentioned in the previous chapter, these were the people whom Captain-General and Governor João Correia de Sousa, in office between 1621 and 1623, illegitimately enslaved and transferred en masse to Brazil, much to the dismay of the Jesuits. MMA VII, D. 7, D. 20; Sousa, Mapa das regiões circunvizinhas de Luanda, in: Heintze (ed.), Fontes para a História de Angola, Vol. 1, p. 158–165; Thornton, A History of West Central Africa, p. 129.

war prisoners, and the 'door' opened by their violent proselytizing let all kinds of subjects inside their domestic sphere and the expanded fold of Christianity, some of them posing serious threats to the patriarchal hetero normative order they were trying to establish.[5]

After three years had passed, Father Barreira reported the baptism of *Soba* Songa, together with his sons and nobles, to the father general of the Company of Jesus.[6] Using the same celebratory tone as his predecessors, he presented *Soba* Songa as a powerful "*relative of the King of Angola* [*ngola*]."[7] According to the Jesuit superior, despite his proficiency in burning "*idols and feitiços*," it was to Father Baltasar Afonso, one of his companions, to whom God had "*given a special gift against the Idols of the land, and the instruments of their idolatry*."[8] During their trip to the lands of *Soba* Songa to perform his baptism, Father Afonso separated from the main group to take "*revenge against the demons, who were still in some of the straw huts of Christians*." Father Barreira then transcribes Father Afonso's letters to give the father general an idea of the "*demons*" he had found in the villages of baptized Africans, describing how the Jesuit missionary dealt with them.

In the transcribed sections, Father Afonso claims to have confronted a "*great feiticeiro, who used the clothes of a woman, and for a woman was taken while being a man*," confessing that this was the "*ugliest and most frightening thing*" that he had seen in all his life.[9] According to the Jesuit, "*all were afraid of him, and nobody dared to talk to him because he was taken as a god of water and health*." When they were brought to Father Afonso with their hands tied behind their back, the priest "*was astonished, and all were amazed to see something so deformed*:" they had come "*dressed as a priest of the old law, with a headdress made of his hair, with so many long michembos* [sic] *that he looked like the devil*." Father Afonso asked them if they were a "*man or a woman*," but according to the Jesuit, they "*didn't want to answer*." Frustrated, the missionary ordered them "*to cut off his hair, which looked like a woolen fleece, and to take off the clothes he was wearing, leaving him in men's clothes*." After this, Father Afonso claims that they "*confessed that he had been born a man, but that the devil had told his mother to make him a woman otherwise he would die, and that until now he had been a woman*." The Jesuit priest concludes the story of this forced 'gender realignment,' claiming in the name of his prisoner that, from then on, "*because he was telling the truth, he wanted to be a man*."

---

5 Almeida, A narrativa etnográfica na literatura missionária, in: Pantoja and Thompson (eds.), Em Torno de Angola, p. 20–21.

6 MMA XV, D. 101.

7 Ibid.; Heywood and Thornton, Central Africans, p. 100.

8 MMA XV, D. 101, p. 272–274.

9 Ibid., p. 273.

Father Afonso then ordered his prisoner to "*bring all his feitiços*," which were "*so many that all were amazed*," and to "*discover*" all "*the feiticeiros of the nearby libatas* [villages], *especially those of one of the principal nobles, named Manicafanze* [*Mani* Kasanze]."[10] While it is unclear if Father Afonso understood he was taking advantage of his prisoner's insider knowledge or their skills as a diviner to 'discover' sorcerers, the Jesuit continues his narrative by describing how they took him to a great "*goat*" that served for years as *Mani* Kasanze's "*feitiço*" as well as to several "*houses of feitiços*" which Father Afonso proceeded to burn immediately. Afterward, he ordered the goat to be killed, butchered, and served boiled to the *Mani* Kasanze and everyone who had accepted baptism.[11] Father Afonso's letter ends with him claiming that a massive thunderstorm struck the village when he was preparing to leave, allowing the Jesuit to spend four more days burning "*idols*"—and benefiting, in all likelihood, from being taken for a new kind of rain priest. Father Afonso's encounter with a person who might be anachronistically framed as queer, gender fluid, intersex, or transgender has been explored by scholars such as Luiz Mott and James Sweet to help establish an archive of "homosexuality" or homosocial desire in West Central Africa under Portuguese influence.[12] Similar passages about cross-dressers or gender-bending ritual specialists are familiar in Jesuit reports or other primary sources about the Captaincy of Angola and several Captaincies in Brazil where enslaved Africans shipped from Luanda had been resettled, including Bahia, Minas Gerais, Paraíba, and Pernambuco.[13]

In his digest of the global yearly reports received by the Company of Jesus between 1604 and 1606, Father Fernão Guerreiro narrates a "*mission through the lands of Christian sobas, or lords*" which took place between 1605 and 1606.[14] As he relates, when the Jesuits reached the lands of *Soba* "Casanha [Kasanze]," whom he describes as a "*powerful soba with four small sobas under his rule*," despite "*all having been baptized*" during the trip previously described by Fathers Barreira and Afonso, "*not one person was able to bless themselves*."[15] Moreover, the priests found not one but

---

10 Ibid.

11 Ibid., p. 274.

12 See Francisco Miguel and Marc Epprecht for a discussion of the pitfalls and epistemological opportunities afforded using contemporary concepts such as "queer" or "transgender" to explore the early colonial African archives. See Alan Bray on the concept of "homosocial desire" and its applicability to the Early Modern period. Bray, Homosexuality in Renaissance England; Epprecht, Hungochani; Miguel, Séculos de silêncio, p. 111–134; Mott, Escravidão, homossexualidade e demonologia; Mott, Feiticeiros de Angola, p. 85–104; Sweet, Recreating Africa, p. 50–57, 72–76.

13 Mott, Escravidão, homossexualidade e demonologia; Mott, Feiticeiros de Angola, p. 85–104; Mott, O calundu-Angola de Luzia Pinta, p. 73–82; Mott, Rosa Egipcíaca; Mott, Transgressão na calada da noite, p. 57–84; Sweet, Recreating Africa.

14 Guerreiro, Relação anual das coisas que fizeram os padres da Companhia de Jesus, Vol. 2, p. 413.

15 Ibid., p. 414.

"*several* [persons] *whom they call chibados and who are the greatest feiticeiros, who being men carry themselves as women, always shaved; sitting like women, and talking as women.*" "*Chibados*," Father Guerreiro concluded, "*take it as a great offense to be addressed as men; have husbands as every other woman, and in the evil sin are the same devils*" as women.

Two later sources return to the topic of Father Guerreiro's "*greatest feiticeiros*," providing clues about their role in Mbundu and neighboring societies. The first is António de Oliveira Cadornega's (1623–1690) *General History of the Angolan Wars* (1681).[16] Cadornega wrote that there was a "*lot of sodomy*" amongst the Mbundu; some "*dressed as women, whom they call using the local name quimbandas* [Kimbundu: sing. *kimbanda*, pl. *yimbanda*]" were "*fine feiticeiros*."[17] The second is the published version of Friar Antonio Giovanni Cavazzi's account of the Kingdoms of Kongo, Ndongo, and Matamba, the *Historical Description of the Three Kingdoms of Kongo, Matamba, and Angola* (1687).[18] When discussing the "*idolatry and sacrifices*" of the Mbangala of the Kingdom of Kasanje, at the southeastern borders of Matamba and east of Ndongo, Friar Cavazzi identifies the "*Ganga-ya-Chibanda* [*kimbanda*]" as the "*chief of sacrifices*," remarking that they "*display, as a sign of the talent, which their diabolical ministry obliges them to have, female clothing, manners, and bearing*," being "*commonly called the great Mother*."[19] Moreover, Friar Cavazzi also describes the cult of an "*idol*," which consisted of a "*huge, live goat*" called "*Ganga-n-zumba*" in the Kingdom of Ndongo and the Captaincy of Angola.[20] Depicting it as "*covered*

---

16 Cadornega, História geral das guerras angolanas, Vol. 1–3.

17 Cadornega, História geral das guerras angolanas, Vol. 3, p. 259; Miller, Kings and Kinsmen, p. 302.

18 Friar Cavazzi's *Historical Description of the Three Kingdoms of Kongo, Matamba, and Angola* was highly influential and underwent several editions. It was also reprised and abridged in many edited volumes of travel and missionary accounts. According to Francisco Leite Faria, the first edition, published in Bologna (1687), was quickly followed by an edition in Milan (1690), both in the original Italian and a third one in Munich (1694), in German. These were followed by an abridged edition in Italian (Parma, 1691), edited by Aurelio degli Anzi, and a French translation by Jean-Baptiste Labat (Paris, 1732). A second German edition (Munich, 1794) and an abridged edition in French (Paris, 1828; 1842) were based on Labat's translation. The first abridged edition in German was edited by H. Külb (Regensburg, 1863). Between 1931 and 1937, Friar Cavazzi's work was published as a serial pamphlet in Rome by the review *Il Massaia*. The first Portuguese translation dates from 1965, done by Friar Graciano Maria de Leguzzano. Almeida, A narrativa etnográfica na literatura missionária, in: Pantoja and Thompson (eds.), Em Torno de Angola, p. 15; Cavazzi, Istorica descrizione de' tre' Regni Congo, Matamba et Angola; Faria, João António Cavazzi, in: De Leguzzano (ed.), Descrição histórica dos três Reinos, p. xi–lviii.

19 Cavazzi, Istorica descrizione de' tre' Regni Congo, Matamba et Angola, p. 218.

20 In the description of "*Gentilic Rites of Angola*" (1720) which can be found in the 31st volume of the *Holy Office* series edited by Prosecutor Manuel da Cunha Pinheiro, it is claimed that the Mbundu worshiped "*the devil in the figure of a goat, to whom they call cacuto, many gathering around it*

by the darkest Shroud, with a very long beard, [and] *so deformed that it looked like a Demon,*" the Capuchin claimed the goat was tended by a "*Husband*" and a "*Wife*" *xinguilas* [spirit mediums], both called "*Ganga-n-zumbi* [*nganga nzambi*]," who boasted "*of foretelling future events using* [the goat], *and of healing the sick, always accompanying their functions with holocausts and prayers.*"[21]

As described in the first chapter, the Mbundu regarded *yimbanda* as healers and diviners, opposing their socially approved, constructive power, termed *umbanda* in Kimbundu, with nefarious *uanga*, the power of anti-social *aloji* [sorcerers].[22] Moreover, the Mbundu conceptualized the origin and nature of *umbanda* and the social role of *kimbanda* differently from how the BaKongo understood *banganga* (sing. *nganga*) and their *minkisi* to operate.[23] While the latter, as Georges Balandier and John Thornton describe, manipulated material elements into assemblages called "*iteke*" (sing. *kiteke*) capable of bidding "*minkisi*" (sing. *nkisi*) spirits, Mbundu *kimbanda* seem to have embodied and performed, through animal sacrifices and the adoption of specific gender-coded norms and behaviors, a privileged relationship with spiritual entities as the root of their *umbanda* power.[24] Such a portfolio of activities might have conflicted with that of the *nganga nzambi*, explaining perhaps why the *kimbanda* tormented by Father Afonso had no qualms denouncing a rival *nganga nzambi*. From the point of view of Fathers Afonso, Barreira, and Guerreiro, who probably brought the lessons learned by the Jesuits in the Kingdom of Kongo to bear on their first 'cross-cultural' encounters with the Mbundu, *yimbanda* thus presented a particularly vexing challenge. As their reports to the Jesuit father general make clear, faced with these ritual operators, the Jesuits realized that the burning of Mbundu "*quiteles*"[25]—which they characterized as 'idols'—and "*feitiços*" was

---

at night, with much noise of atabaques [possession drums] *in their senzallas* [quarters]." Ibid., p. 231–232; ANTT, TSO, CG, Sr. 25, Fol. 272.

21 Cavazzi, Istorica descrizione de' tre' Regni Congo, Matamba et Angola, p. 231–232; Sweet, Recreating Africa, p. 154.

22 Rodrigues de Areia, Estrutura magico-religiosa, p. 36–38.

23 Ibid., p. 34, 44.

24 See also Wyatt MacGaffey's extensive writings on BaKongo *minkisi*. Balandier, Le Royaume de Kongo, p. 254–255; MacGaffey, Aesthetics and Politics, p. 63–75; MacGaffey, Astonishment and Stickiness, p. 137–150; MacGaffey, Constructing a Kongo Identity, p. 159–180; MacGaffey, Crossing the River, in: Heintze and von Oppen (eds.), Angola on the Move, p. 221–242; MacGaffey, Fetishism Revisited, p. 172–184; MacGaffey, Franchising Minkisi, p. 148–157; MacGaffey, Religion and Society; MacGaffey, The Personhood of Ritual Objects, p. 45–61; Thornton, A History of West Central Africa, p. 45–46.

25 The list of "*Gentilic Rites of Angola*," edited by Prosecutor Pinheiro, describes Mbundu "*idols*" as "*various images to which they call Quiteles, to which they pay cult saying; this is my son, this is my Father, this my Brother, and as if living they offer them sustenance.*" According to John Thornton, the Mbundu referred to their shrines as "*iteke* (sing. *kiteke*)" while naming the "otherworldly being" that the shrines were dedicated to as "*kilunda*," "*kilundu*," or "*nzambi* [pl. *jinzambi*]." It was the *iteke*,

not enough to cleanse an area of African religious manifestations and the "*priest*[s] *of the old law*."[26] This forced them to redirect their iconoclastic fury towards the bodies, gendered public persona, and social relationships mediated by the Mbundu *yimbanda* and other spirit mediums.

Compared to burning *iteke* and *quiteles*, this task was infinitely more daunting for several reasons. First, while local populations seem to have contributed to the burning of *iteke* and *quiteles*, likely framing the process as an anti-*kindoki* or anti-*uanga* cyclical purge, the Jesuits could not count on local collaboration against the *yimbanda* unless they convinced their constituencies that they could substitute them as successful rainmakers and healers.[27] This often left the priests at the mercy of the elements.[28] Second, changing and supervising behavior is more demanding than destroying shrines and burning their material contents. As evidenced by the *kimbanda*'s coerced snitching of rival ritual operators to Father Afonso, promoting a culture of gossip and denunciation was the immediate response to the need to regulate behaviors understood by the Portuguese as socially threatening. The Ordinance of the Holy Office of the Inquisition of 1613, which allowed the Inquisition of Lisbon to appoint officials of the Holy Office in Luanda, created an

---

not the *kilunda*, that the Jesuits designated as 'idols.' Joseph Miller refers to *kilunda* as *malunga* [sing. *lunga*], pointing out that besides these "wooden figurines," Mbundu figurines called *mukishi* were also referred to as 'idols' by the missionaries. These often occurred in "male-female pairs," had no connection with the ancestors, "claimed adherents only in a specified geographical region," and were often associated with "political chiefs." *Mukishi* communicated with the living through *xinguilas*. In *Samuel Purchas His Pilgrimes* (1625), Samuel Purchas bases himself on Andrew Battel's accounts to describe several "*mokisso*" or "*Mokeso*:" one as having "*more then three Tunnes of Elephants Teeth piled over him,*" the other as being the "*Grave*" of "*old Lord Shillambasa* [sic]," with "*a hundred tame Peacockes*" kept around it and a "*great store of Copper, Cloth, and many other things laid upon*" it. ANTT, TSO, CG, Sr. 25, Fol. 272; Miller, Kings and Kinsmen, p. 46–47, 59, 256–257; Purchas, Purchas His Pilgrimes, Vol. 6, p. 381–382; Thornton, Conquest and Theology, p. 255; Thornton, Religious and Ceremonial Life, in: Heywood (ed.), Central Africans and Cultural Transformations, p. 76.

26 MMA XV, D. 101, p. 273.

27 Thornton argues that the Jesuit's success at uprooting the cult of a given *kilunda* depended on a "co-revelation" taking place when its *kiteke* or shrine was destroyed. In the case of entities connected with rain, this "co-revelation" would be the coming of rain—understood as a supernatural event by the Jesuit and the Mbundu alike. Thornton mentions the case of Father Pedro Tavares, who was told by his Mbundu interlopers that before a cross was erected in Quionzo, "*not a drop of rain had fallen on the lands of the Soba*" but after "*it rained*." In his letter to the head of the Jesuit college in Luanda narrating a mission in Bengo, Father Tavares mentions forcefully removing several 'idols' related to rain. MMA VIII, D. 14; Thornton, Conquest and Theology, p. 255–256.

28 On September 7, 1619, Friar Manuel Baptista (1559–1620), then bishop of Congo and Angola, wrote a letter to the Portuguese king complaining about the fact that the Mbundu "*ask for Sun, and rain to the prelates and priests, as they ask to the feiticeiros, complaining when they don't give it to them as if it was within their reach*." MMA VI, D. 123, p. 383.

institutional mechanism capable of collecting and processing the ensuing influx of denunciations—now essential historical sources.[29] Third, because the *yimbanda*'s capability to incorporate or interact with spirits was mental or spiritual (despite its sacrificial and performative prompts), it was harder to assess if persons already fully integrated into Portuguese domestic spaces and jurisdictions still possessed it.[30] As the early Jesuit reports prove, African villages that the missionaries considered Christianized after wooden figurines and other material elements had been burnt, a communal cross erected, and a mass baptism performed could still harbor *yimbanda* determined to disrupt Roman Catholic norms and accepted forms of hetero-affective domesticity acting from inside the community.

Fatefully, the Jesuits shared their anxiety regarding spiritual threats coming from within the community with their Mbundu interlocuters and European peers and superiors, who might remain unconcerned about what the Jesuit in Ndongo framed as sodomy and cross-dressing[31] but were highly responsive to the possibility of

---

29 During the last decades, much scholarship on the Lusophone Black Atlantic has used inquisitorial records to reconstruct the diaspora and Creolization of African practices and beliefs, which accompanied the forced migration of enslaved Africans, including ritual specialists, to the Americas. While helpful to situate some of the practices and beliefs described in this chapter on a broader framework, this literature focuses more on the cultural, religious, social, and therapeutic aspects of ordeals and divinations because outside of West Central Africa, at plantations and in other settler-colonial contexts, their normative dimension often comes second. For the same reason, these judicial or forensic interventions are usually framed as forms of resistance, a framework with limited heuristic value if applied to interpret the cases in the Captaincy of Angola and its dependencies. ANTT, TSO, CG, Sr. 34, D. 335; Calainho, Jambacousses e gangazambes, p. 141–176; Calainho, Metrópole das mandingas; Castelnau-L'Estoile, Páscoa Vieira diante da Inquisição; Kananoja, Pai Caetano Angola, p. 18–37; Marcussi, Estratégias de mediação simbólica, p. 97–124; Mello e Souza, Inferno Atlântico; Mott, Feiticeiros de Angola, p. 85–104; Mott, O calundu-Angola de Luzia Pinta, p. 73–82; Nogueira, Relações sociais e práticas mágicas na capitania do ouro, p. 181–203; Precioso, Catarina Juliana e sua sociedade de culto, p. 68–127; Reis, Domingos Sodré, um sacerdote africano; Ribeiro da Silva, A Inquisição em África, in: Silva and Mateus (eds.), As Inquisições Modernas, p. 177–234; Sansi-Roca and Parés, Sorcery in the Black Atlantic; Santos, Africans, Afro-Brazilians, p. 49–63; Santos, Bolsas de Mandinga; Souza, O diabo e a terra de Santa Cruz; Sweet, Recreating Africa.

30 The same can be said of other ritual specialists who incorporated spiritual entities such as the "*Singhile* or *Singilla* [*xinguilas*]" and "*ngombos*" whom Friar Cavazzi identified in Kasanje and Kongo, respectively. Cavazzi, Istorica descrizione de' tre' Regni Congo, Matamba et Angola, p. 77, 223–224; Parreira, Dicionário glossográfico, p. 113.

31 While the Jesuits never cite Deuteronomy 22:5, this biblical passage is probably at the root of their hostility towards the African social convention they construed as 'cross-dressing.' The Revised Standard Version of the bible provides the following translation from Hebrew: "*A woman shall not wear anything that pertains to a man, nor shall a man put on a woman's garment; for whoever does these things is an abomination to the Lord your God.*" For a discussion of how this passage has been interpreted and its probable original meaning, see Harold Vedeler. Vedeler, Reconstructing Meaning in Deuteronomy 22:5, p. 459–476.

spiritual powers being used for anti-social or selfish ends. The difference was that Africans framed these abuses as *kindoki* or *uanga* and the Europeans as heresy, simony, Judaizing practices, or Judaism, as already discussed in the previous chapter.[32] Nevertheless, this convergence of anxieties about the dangers of physical proximity and intimacy prompted the 'cross-cultural' adoption of shared solutions, either of European or African origin.

7.2 Patterns of Non-recognition, Recognition, Adoption, and Rejection

As Madeira Santos describes, during the Early Modern period, the same "legal principles that regulated the hierarchy between ius commune and iura propria" in the Portuguese Kingdom "provided the legal framework necessary for the validity of indigenous *direitos* [legal systems/rights]" to persist within the Portuguese Empire.[33] She explains that this framework allowed "indigenous institutions" such as arbitration bodies or fiscal systems to be coopted in Goa, Brazil, and West and East Central Africa without challenging the overall consistency of the Portuguese

32 In 1665, when Father Manoel Fernandes Curado, then dean of Angola, sought to discredit Canon Simão de Medeiros and Canon Miguel de Castro, two BaKongo priests of the Diocese of Congo and Angola who ensured that its see and cathedral remained in Mbanza Kongo instead of Luanda, he wrote to the Crown accusing them of "*making sacrifices to idols, as the gentiles of the land*," being "*schismatic because of some* [doctrinal] *errors they introduced*," and being "*sorcerers, as magic is their only esteemed science*." Moreover, he accused them of simony and of "*the public sale*" of positions in their chapels and jurisdictions to "*persons of the Hebraic nation*" and of having "*killed with feitiçarias and poison*" the previous bishops. These charges were taken seriously by the Overseas Council, which found evidence that Canon Medeiros and Canon Castro were guilty of "*divine and human lese-majesty*," forwarding the charges against them to the Board of Royal Conscience to adjudicate their secular crimes and the Inquisition of Lisbon for the spiritual ones. To the accusations of Dean Curado, the council members added that the canons had sided with the Dutch and advised their constituencies to "*cut the throat of all whites*" if a "*Castilian armada*" came to conquer West Central Africa. Moreover, they introduced several "*errors in the Ecclesiastical government*" because they appointed BaKongo clergy. Finally, the council members added that the canons sided with the *Mwene* Kongo and admonished Luso-African soldiers not to fight against him because he was a Christian. These accusations were written down on August 12, 1665, a few months before the Battle of Mbwila of October 29, 1665. Therefore, sorcery accusations and the fear of internal enemies played a crucial role in fabricating a *casus belli* against the Kongo. MMA XII, D. 235, D. 236.

33 Hespanha, Fazer um império com palavras, in: Barreto Xavier and Nogueira da Silva (eds.), O governo dos outros, p. 67–100; Santos, O Império Português face às instituições indígenas, in: Palomo, Stumpf and Barreto Xavier (eds.), Monarquias ibéricas em perspectiva comparada, p. 275–276.

normative regime.[34] In keeping with her model of 'normative imbrication,' the Portuguese great councils and courts, such as the Overseas Council (1643–1833), the India Council before it (1604–1614), or the Board of Royal Conscience and Military Orders (1532–1833), enabled this co-option whenever it proved convenient by approving or tolerating different ad hoc processes that relied on what Madeira Santos defines as "institutional connectors." She completes her model by proposing a typology of different institutional connectors. In keeping with it, these can be classified as "direct and encompassing" connectors when they presuppose the incorporation of "local administrative systems" into the imperial structure (e. g., land tenure systems, fiscal systems, succession rules, and inheritance norms). As "bifrontal" connectors when they entail the creation of "in-between offices" that participate in the "colonial and indigenous political cultures." As "catalyst" connectors when they presuppose the institutionalization of new forms of relationality (e. g., through treaties, royal charters, granting of privileges). Finally, as "indirect or informal" connectors when they rely on individual actors' practices and accumulated normative knowledge to mediate the relationship and translate between different normative systems (e. g., the circulation of learned judges and magistrates).[35] Building on her previous work on how Enlightened captain-general and governors of Angola attempted to reform what she defines as "in-between" jurisdictions in West Central Africa, Madeira Santos' model of normative imbrication and typology of institutional connectors clarify how the Portuguese Crown relied on "indigenous institutions," the fostering of vernaculars, and on establishing a constellation of regional centers to maintain its delicate hegemony over a 'poly-centric' empire.[36] Nevertheless, they fail to address several critical theoretical challenges.

First, Madeira Santos' model does not address the fact that the composite nature of the Portuguese Empire and the high level of autonomy that each person with jurisdiction had within its protean framework also created the possibility for different groups, corporations, or individuals to adopt shifting and often opposing

---

34 Santos, O Império Português face às instituições indígenas, in: Palomo, Stumpf and Barreto Xavier (eds.), Monarquias ibéricas em perspectiva comparada, p. 276–277.

35 Madeira Santos refers to the "*amos*" system and the "*Mucano* court," already explored in the previous chapters, as examples of "encompassing" institutional connectors. According to her, captain majors, "*mani-quitanda*," "*tendala* [interpreters]," and the *dembos* all occupied "in-between" offices, performing the role of "bifrontal" institutional connectors. Finally, she argues that Luso-African "vassalage treaties" functioned as "catalyst" institutional connectors. Ibid., p. 292–298.

36 Cardim et al., Polycentric Monarchies, in: Cardim et al. (eds.), Polycentric Monarchies, p. 3–8; Sánchez, Spanish Theories of Empire, in: Tellkamp (ed.), A Companion to Early Modern Spanish Imperial Political and Social Thought, p. 17–52; Santos, Administrative knowledge, p. 539–556; Santos, De "antigos conquistadores" a "angolenses," p. 195–222; Santos, Entre deux Droits, p. 817–848; Santos, Um governo "polido" para Angola.

strategies concerning African normative systems.[37] These ranged from outright hostility to open embrace, so a model that focuses on normative imbrication and purely additive processes misses several nuances. Second, it fails to consider the full consequences of not all African normative systems being compatible, with the extreme example being the *ijila* of the Mbangala *kilombo* and the Mbundu kinship-based norms described in the previous chapter. This allowed individual or corporative actors to adopt different strategies regarding conflicting African norms or Luso-African customs, covertly endorsing some by selectively persecuting others. Third, Madeira Santos' model does not account for the difficulty different groups or actors had in evaluating how other actors positioned themselves, making establishing 'trust' a challenge even for different Portuguese jurisdictions and authorities. Fourth, it doesn't pay sufficient attention to what happened at the micro-scale. Households or the inner spheres of local corporations were also spaces where privileged individuals (e. g., the *pater familias*, the slave master, the superior, the steward, the first wife, and the head of the corporate kin group) often assumed jurisdictional roles.[38] This chapter argues that these spaces were also traversed with tensions and riddled with trust issues. They could become the stage of bitter conflicts between individuals who adopted opposing strategies regarding African norms and institutions. As exposed in the following pages, the public spillover of these conflicts intensified social anxiety about the danger posed by internal enemies, further aggravated by the widespread fear of sorcery.

A folder of letters the Capuchin Prefect Lourenço de Lucca addressed to the prosecutor of the Inquisition of Lisbon[39] in 1716 can help us clarify these points

---

37 Hespanha, Fazer um império com palavras, in: Barreto Xavier and Nogueira da Silva (eds.), O governo dos outros, p. 91–100.

38 As Romina Zamora argues, this was also the case for South America during the same period, where the "domestic normative sphere" was the most "relevant in people's lives." Zamora, The Domestic Sphere, in: Duve and Herzog (eds.), Latin America Law in Global Perspective, p. 220.

39 See Fabiana Schleumer, José Horta, Marco Nunes da Silva, Sônia Siqueira, and Sweet on the role of the prosecutor of justice of the Inquisition of Lisbon and the content of the judicial documents, notes, and letters contained in his notebooks. On the topic of the impact of the Portuguese Inquisition in Africa, see also Filipa Silva, Francisco Bethencourt, Philip Havik, Tahinan Santos, and Toby Green. Bethencourt and Havik, A África e a Inquisição Portuguesa, p. 21–27; Green et al., African Voices from the Inquisition; Green, Inquisition; Havik, La Sorcellerie, l'acculturation et le genre, p. 99–116; Havik, Walking the Tightrope, in: Williams (ed.), Bridging the Early Modern Atlantic World, p. 173–192; Horta, A Inquisição em Angola e Congo, p. 387–415; Horta, Africanos e portugueses, p. 301–321; Ribeiro da Silva, A Inquisição em África, in: Silva and Mateus (eds.), As Inquisições Modernas, p. 177–234; Ribeiro da Silva, A Inquisição em Cabo Verde, Guiné e S. Tomé e Príncipe; Ribeiro da Silva, A Inquisição nas Ilhas, p. 157–173; Santos, Inquisição Portuguesa na África, p. 229–245; Schleumer, Nas bordas do Rio Kwanza, p. 13–28; Siqueira, A disciplina da vida colonial, p. 497–571; Siqueira, O momento da Inquisição; Sweet, Recreating Africa.

before proposing a revised version of Madeira Santos' model that acknowledges the complexity they introduce. As described in the previous chapters, at this stage, the institutional and jurisdictional layout of the Captaincy of Angola had already assumed the shape they would retain until the second half of the eighteenth century. Moreover, Italian Capuchins had taken the lead in criticizing the social and cultural innovations that had stemmed from the 'space of correlation' between African cosmological categories and Roman Catholic beliefs created during the first decades of the Portuguese presence in West Central Africa, adopting a discourse on African sorcery more aligned with the central European *imaginaire* of diabolical pacts and witchcraft.[40] On October 22, 1716, Friar de Lucca wrote one of the letters included in the folder, explaining that most of the other documents related to a trip he had made the previous August to the Village of Massangano and its whereabouts to "*satisfy*" his duties as commissar of the Holy Office of Lisbon.[41] Exceptionally, the folder also includes a letter he wrote before leaving Luanda on June 3, 1716. In it, he wrote that in Luanda, there was a "*Synagogue House, where the children* [were] *circumcised, both those of the white and those of the black*." There were more "*Jews than Christians*," the former living unimpeded and thus proceeding with their "*diabolical Judaized feichicherias* [sorceries]." Moreover, "*almost all the white and black women in their illnesses* [...] *fetch*[ed] *a feichichero* [sorcerer] *so that with their diabolical feichicherias* [sorcery] *they find them health through the Devil*." In conclusion, Friar de Lucca claimed that, "*if all these* [abuses] *were not remediated with punishment*," Luanda "*would be in a few years worse than an assembly*" of sorcerers.

The reason why he took no immediate action, he clarified, was because he could not "*punish*" the sorcerers, as "*he needed others to back him up*."[42] His foreigner status and the fact that the Capuchin mission was an apostolic prefecture under the jurisdiction of the *Propaganda Fide* did not create the perfect conditions for the commissar of the Inquisition of Lisbon to collaborate with local secular authorities.[43] Given the setbacks caused by Portuguese institutional distrust for rival Europeans, he warned that the danger was great of Luanda "*losing the Faith, and his Majesty losing the Kingdom* [of Angola] *because if these feichicherios multiply, they can pervert both*."[44] Besides mobilizing elements from two important discursive tropes to convey a sense of imminent danger and internal threat, namely that of

40 Fromont, Collecting and Translating Knowledge Across Cultures, in: Bleichmar and Mancall (eds.), Collecting Across Cultures, p. 141; Fromont, The Art of Conversion; Fromont, Under the sign of the cross, p. 109–123; Paiva, Bruxaria e Superstição.

41 ANTT, TSO, IL, Sr. 30, CP 86, Book 279, p. 38–39v.

42 Ibid., p. 39v.

43 De Leguzzano, Ao Leitor, in: De Leguzzano (ed.), Descrição Histórica dos Três Reinos, p. v–ix.

44 ANTT, TSO, IL, Sr. 30, CP 86, Book 279, p. 40.

the witches' sabbat and "blood libel" against Jews,[45] Friar da Lucca uses them to scapegoat African 'sorcerers' and women for the lack of institutional cooperation, trying to overcome his relative marginalization within the Captaincy of Angola by directing attention to this internal threat. While these first two tropes never resurface in the testimonies he collects when visiting Massangano, the themes of institutional mistrust and African ritual specialists and women being at the root of social disintegration are constantly referred to. After arriving at the Capuchin Hospice of Our Lady of Conception in Massangano, Friar de Lucca started receiving "*denunciations and complaints*," assisted by the local Vicar António de Almeida, who acted as a scribe.[46] The first denunciation was from the Luís Baptista Thomas Captain Major of Massangano, whom Friar de Lucca summoned before his tribunal on August 4th.

Captain Major Thomas was twenty-eight years old and born and raised in Lisbon, where he had also married.[47] According to his testimony, he had heard from his friend Colonel Pedro Borges Madureira, a married *morador* of Massangano, that Lieutenant Pasqual Rodrigues de Queiroga, originally from the Algarve, Portugal, but who had married in Luanda, had procured the services of a "*black gentilic feiticeiro*" to determine the cause of the illness that plagued his *compadre* Sergeant Major João de Moura da Silva, born and raised in Lisbon but who had married an African woman from the village. To ascertain the illness' cause, Captain Major Thomas con-

45 In his report of a mission to Bengo in 1631, Father Tavares claims that after he removed a rain "*idol*" from the courtyard of "*Soba Jióllo*," a "*white man*" he describes as a "*poor Hebrew*" came to intercede with him asking for the devolution of the 'idol.' Father Tavares threatened him with a denunciation to the Inquisition, to which he supposedly replied that Father Tavares was free to "*burn the idol*." Throughout the report, Father Tavares insinuates that Jews were responsible for administering Roman Catholic sacraments in a wrong manner or for-profit and advocating for idolatry. These and similar accusations built on the trope of Jews being an internal enemy and profited from a thematic association between the elements of the 'blood libel' against Jews and circulating tropes about African cannibalism (especially of the Mbangala). For an introduction to blood libel—the mythical complex about Jews kidnapping Christian children to sacrifice in a reenactment of the passion of Christ and consume their blood, Jewish men menstruating, and other associated beliefs, see E. M. Rose. Kathryn T. McClymond, and Magda Teter. For how the othering of Jews overlapped with the othering of colonized populations, see Claudia Bruns. See Silvia Federici for a critique of how witchcraft accusations and the trope of the witches sabbath enabled colonial dispossession and Laura Mello e Souza and José Paiva for its impact in the Portuguese-speaking world. Bruns, Antisemitism and Colonial Racisms, in: Vogt (ed.), Colonialism and the Jews in German History, p. 25–55; Federici, Caliban and the Witch; McClymond, Blood Libel, in: McClymond (ed.), Ritual Gone Wrong, p. 65–105; Mello e Souza, A feitiçaria na Europa Moderna; MMA VIII, D. 14; Paiva, Bruxaria e Superstição; Rose, The Murder of William of Norwich; Teter, Blood Libel.

46 ANTT, TSO, IL, Sr. 30, CP 86, Book 279, p. 41.

47 Ibid., p. 42.

tinued, the *feiticeiro* performed the "*Bollungo* [*mbulungo*] *oath*"[48] in Sergeant Major Silva's household, concluding that he was only "*suffering from Zumbi.*" This "*illness*" has been examined by Miller, Sweet, and, more recently, Ferreira and Kananoja.[49] Sweet describes it as a common ailment in West Central Africa, claiming that a "*nganga nzambi*" was the "*priest of the spirits*" who specialized in curing it.[50] The *nganga nzambi* is described in a list of "*Gentilic Rites of Angola*" (1720) edited by Prosecutor Manuel da Cunha Pinheiro of the Inquisition of Lisbon.[51] According to this document, they also performed "*a lot of feiticerias*" to "*give and take lives*" and "*attract hatred, or love,*" being frequented by "*several whites of the land.*" Sweet then points to the testimony of Friar Joseph of Modena before the Inquisition of Lisbon in 1721, who claimed that "*Zumbi*" was an "*illness that comes naturally* [but which] *the feiticeiro attributes to diabolical art, saying that the sick person is suffering from the soul of one of his dead relatives.*"[52]

To appease these spirits, Father Joseph clarified that "*the sick person*" had to "*give many edible things to the feiticeiro, who says that the soul of the dead person requests these things and that because he was not given the referred things, the dead person entered the body of the sick person.*"[53] In keeping with Miller, who bases his analysis on his collection of contemporary oral traditions and Friar Cavazzi's accounts,[54] "*Zumbi*" resulted from neglected Mbundu ancestors, called "*nzumbi* [pl. *jinzumbi*]" in Kimbundu, seeking revenge and compensation from their kin.[55] *Jinzumbi*, Miller argues, "harmed only their relatives, an offended spirit always belonging to the same lineages as the person afflicted." While he agrees that a "*nganga a nzumbi*" was called to handle the affair together with other "specialized lineage members," Miller states that only *xinguilas* were capable of dialoguing with the disgruntled *nzumbi* spirit and ascertaining its terms and conditions. Focusing on the second half of the seventeenth century, Ferreira explores the report of the Jesuit Father Manuel Ribeiro of his mission to the hinterlands of Luanda in 1672–1673 and the denunciations of Catarina Borges and Gregório Pascoal Gaspar to the Inquisition

---

48 The *mbulungo* ordeal is further unpacked in the following pages.

49 Ferreira, Cross-Cultural Exchange, p. 179–188; Kananoja, Healing Knowledge, p. 28–29, 40–42; Miller, Kings and Kinsmen, p. 254–255; Sweet, Recreating Africa, p. 154–155.

50 Sweet, Recreating Africa, p. 154–155.

51 ANTT, TSO, CG, Sr. 25, Fol. 272.

52 ANTT, TSO, IL, Sr. 30, CP 94, Book 287, p. 372v–373.

53 Ibid.

54 As already mentioned, Friar Cavazzi associated the "*Ganga-n-zumba*" with the cult of a "*huge, live goat*" who supposedly had the same name, but which the list of "*Gentilic Rites of Angola*" compiled by Prosecutor Pinheiro identified as "*cacuto*" instead. ANTT, TSO, CG, Sr. 25, Fol. 272; Cavazzi, Istorica descrizione de' tre' Regni Congo, Matamba et Angola, p. 121–124, 231–232.

55 Miller, Kings and Kinsmen, p. 254–255.

of Lisbon (1698).[56] Father Ribeiro reported that, the subjects of "*Dembo Caculo Cacahenda* [*Dembo* Kakulu ka Kahenda]" believed in the "*teachings*" of a "*doctor*" called "*Gangazumba* [*nganga a nzumbi*]" who claimed that "*when they dreamt of the dead, it was the souls that appeared to them, asking sacrifices to their gods.*"[57] As for Borges and Gaspar, Ferreira remarks that the former admitted performing a ceremony in which a "soul would appear to her" and that the latter affirmed that "when someone died, a malign spirit would enter their minds."[58] Finally, Kananoja explores several other denunciations to the Inquisition of Lisbon from the 1710s and 1720s, remarking that "*zumbi*" was a widespread ailment, mentioning the case of a Portuguese soldier who believed he was tormented by the spirit of his deceased wife, buried back in Europe.[59] He points to a passage in Cadornega's *General History of the Angolan Wars*, where the retired ordinary judge claims that "*zumbi is a thing that causes* [the Mbundu] *to take great care.*"[60] According to Cadornega, when people "*dreamed about some deceased*" person, they "*imagined they were coming to ask them something*" or "*to take them as companions*" and had to pour libations at their "*imbillas, which are their mausoleums,*" or slowly perish.

Therefore, as Captain Major Thomas' denunciation relates, the diagnosis reached by the "*black gentilic feiticeiro*" pointed back to Sergeant Major Silva's household, or adopted African corporate kin group, as the origin of the illness that tormented him, proving that cross-cultural intimacy raised issues that required the adoption of African normative remedies, regardless of which *Iura propria* the principle of personality determined each group should follow.[61] According to another of Captain Major Thomas' acquaintances, Ensign Pasqual da Motta Telles, born and raised in Lisbon but married in Massangano, Lieutenant Queiroga had also taken the oath himself, together with the members of his "*household,*" having only then

---

56 Ferreira, Cross-Cultural Exchange, p. 179, 182; MMA XIII, D. 114.

57 *Dembo* Kakulu ka Kahenda was a powerful, independent territorial lord. For information on his state archive, see Santos and Vieira. MMA XIII, D. 114., p. 258; Santos, Écrire le pouvoir en Angola, p. 767–795; Santos, Escrever o Poder, in: Heintze and von Oppen (eds.), Angola on the Move, p. 173–181; Vieira, As cartas do Dembo Caculo Cacahenda, p. 41–54; Vieira, O Dembo Caculo Cacahenda.

58 Ferreira, Cross-Cultural Exchange, p. 182.

59 Kananoja, Central African Identities, p. 203–205; Kananoja, Healing Knowledge, p. 41–42

60 Cadornega, História geral das guerras angolanas, Vol. 3, p. 262.

61 As Romina Zamora remarks, "theoretical knowledge" and "practical solutions to everyday problems" were both "necessary components of casuistic systems," in this case, the life and death situation forcing those involved to embrace African normative knowledge and practices. ANTT, TSO, IL, Sr. 30, CP 86, Book 279, p. 42; Duve, What is Global Legal History? p. 73–115; Zamora, The Domestic Sphere, in: Duve and Herzog (eds.), Latin America Law in Global Perspective, p. 223.

imposed it on the sergeant major and his "*female slaves*."[62] By proceeding in this manner, Captain Major Thomas concluded, Lieutenant Queiroga had hoped to prove that he was not causing the illness of his *compadre*, an extreme but necessary measure because rumors had begun circulating that he was to blame for it given the fact that he carried a "*certain kind of feitiços made with Bambos, which are small deer horns filled with poisons*."[63]

When Ensign Telles was heard by Friar da Lucca two days later, he confirmed that he had "*heard from Gebuga, a slave of the Licenciado Francisco Telles Barreto*,"[64] that Lieutenant Queiroga had sent the "*Tandalla* [*tendala*] *Manuel Antonio*," also a slave of Barreto, to "*call a black sorcerer*" to administer the "*oath of the Land, to which they call, Bollungo*."[65] Moreover, he added that the oath was public and other persons, "*whiter than himself*," could testify to its result.[66] According to Ensign Telles' version, the rumors about Lieutenant Queiroga had been spread by Sergeant Major Silva's daughters, who had told Father João Moratto, the chaplain of San Benedetto of Parlermo's Chapel at the local Capuchin Hospice, that the lieutenant had brought a "*frog and a tortoise under his jacket*" to their house to do his "*feitiçarias*" under their father's bead. The ensign concluded by remarking that Lieutenant Queiroga had told him that "*he feared neither poisons nor feitiços; because having gone to Luangola* [sic], *he took their master feiticeiros' medicines, having two Xillo* [amulets] [full] of *wicked things and Mbundu ironies* [sic]."[67] Moreover, having been told not to accept water to clean his face from anyone, he always washed it with water "*from a pot with water and twigs*" that he had "*inside the house where he slept*."[68] In sum, according to Ensign Telles, sorcery suspicions and accusations were bitterly exchanged between Lieutenant Queiroga and Sergeant Major Silva's daughters and wife.

On August 8, 1716, Friar de Lucca summoned Father Moratto, recording his version of events.[69] The latter confirmed that the denounced "*never washed his face if not with the water of Mbundu leaves and grasses he had in his house*."[70] However,

---

62 ANTT, TSO, IL, Sr. 30, CP 86, Book 279, p. 42.

63 Ibid., p. 42v.

64 The title of *Licenciado* refers to someone who had obtained an intermediate grade between a bachelor's and a doctorate from a university.

65 ANTT, TSO, IL, Sr. 30, CP 86, Book 279, p. 43v.

66 Ibid., p. 42.

67 References to horns or wooden whistles filled with herbs abound in the primary sources. According to Friar Joseph of Modena's testimony from 1720, these "*small trumpets filled with poisonous herbs*" could be "*blown by a feiticeiro against any person, even if many Leagues away, and there* [they] *kill them through diabolic power*." ANTT, TSO, IL, Sr. 30, CP 86, Book 279, p. 42, CP 94, Book 287, p. 322v; Kananoja, Healing Knowledge, p. 37.

68 ANTT, TSO, IL, Sr. 30, CP 86, Book 279, p. 42.

69 Ibid., p. 44v–45.

70 Ibid., p. 45–45v.

according to Father Moratto, Lieutenant Queiroga was a true friend of Sergeant Major Silva, having pledged to cure him even if he had to use "*the superstitions of the devil.*" And indeed, the chaplain claimed, he did, thus causing great harm to his friend's soul, household, and community. According to Father Moratto, Lieutenant Queiroga's first step had been to summon his slave "*Luzia*" and another slave belonging to his *compadre*, telling them to go "*see what the black sorcerer divined.*" This first ritual operator, Father Moratto explained, was not the one who later administered the *mbulungo* ordeal,[71] being an expert in "*saquellar* [spirit possession] *and summoning the devil.*" His verdict, the chaplain concluded, was that the sergeant major was tormented by the "*zumbo* [*zumbi*] *of the nurses of his children,*" convincing both men that Sergeant Major Silva's mother-in-law and wife were the ones responsible for neglecting their ancestors' spirits. The rumors against Lieutenant Queiroga began spreading, Father Moratto claimed, when Luzia and the other slave warned his *compadre*'s wife about the possession ritual organized by Lieutenant Queiroga. Then, faced with the accusation of being responsible for the sergeant major's ailment, the women from his household retaliated by publicly accusing the lieutenant of being the sorcerer who caused it. When António Fernandes, another *morador* from Massangano, was summoned by Friar de Lucca three days later, he confirmed Father Moratto's version, adding the crucial detail that after Lieutenant Queiroga had called a "*feiticeiro*" to determine if his friend was plagued by a "*Zumbi from his Household,*" the chaplain, in collusion with the Sergeant Major Silva's daughters, had publicly claimed that "*since the accused had said that* [Queiroga] *would call a feiticeiro,*" he "*would summon another magico* [magician] *who had more understanding than*" Lieutenant Queiroga's "*feiticeiro.*"[72] In other words, the ritual operator responsible for overseeing the *mbulungo* ordeal. In keeping with this version, therefore, it was Father Moratto who had called for the *mbulungo* ordeal to be administered to exonerate Sergeant Major Silva's wife, daughters, and mother-in-law—not Lieutenant Queiroga to clear his good name and restore the lost trust between *compadres*. In any case, the ordeal was necessary to attribute responsibility and restore trust, stopping cross-accusations.

In conclusion, according to the testimonies collected by Friar da Lucca at the Capuchin Hospice of Massangano during August 1716, members of different corporations not only recognized the intimate spheres of their households and garrison as particularly exposed to sorcery and other forms of spiritual affliction associated with kinship and physical proximity but also accepted that Mbundu institutions and normative solutions could prevent, identify the causes, and address these ailments, also affording them some degree of control over their inner circles and

71 The ninth chapter explores the *mbulungo* and other judicial ordeals and oaths further.

72 ANTT, TSO, IL, Sr. 30, CP 86, Book 279, p. 46.

what transpired from them to the public forums of the village. This overall agreement, however, did not preclude the adoption of different, at times oppositional strategies regarding specific practices and rituals, all agreeing on the efficacy of the *mbulungo* oath, except the Capuchin inquisitors and the captain major—if his denunciation to the Inquisition of Lisbon was made in good faith. Moreover, the spheres of intimacy from which different groups perceived threats could originate varied substantially. On the one hand, Portuguese soldiers appear to have been distrustful of the hetero-affective environment of the households of Europeans married to African women, believing they exposed them to spiritual threats such as disgruntled Mbundu *jinzumbi* and sorcery. While there is much scholarship about the economic and social rewards Europeans gained from these unions,[73]

---

73 Vanessa Oliveira provides a good overview of this literature regarding the Captaincy of Angola and describes the different modalities of marriage. She argues that marriage ensured the "basic infrastructure" foreign merchants and soldiers needed to establish themselves in West Central Africa—health care, accommodation, food preparation, laundry, and easier access to porters, translators, and pre-established social networks. Oliveira explains that during the Early Modern period, most marriages were either "common-law unions" or celebrated through the Mbundu ceremony of "*lambamento*" or similar Ovimbundu rituals, with Catholic marriages remaining a small minority. The children born within Catholic wedlock were considered "*filhos legítimos* [legitimate children]" and all the other "*filhos naturais* [children born in the state of Nature]," all entitled to a share of assets of their parents (if not the product of "an adulterous or sacrilegious relationship") in keeping with the *Philippine Ordinances*. Oliveira concludes that the African women entering these partnerships also profited from accessing the trade and social opportunities presented by the settler's society, being nevertheless exposed to adultery and promiscuity charges that could result in them being subjected to ordeals. For overviews of similar processes elsewhere in Africa, see Catherine Coquery-Vidrovitch and the volume edited by Mariana Candido and Adam Jones. For more detailed analyses of Angolan case studies, see Candido and José Curto. See Arlindo Caldeira, Eugénia Rodrigues, and Philip Havik for a survey of similar processes in São Tomé and Príncipe, Mozambique, and Portuguese Guinea, respectively, and Carina Ray, Emily Osborn, and Pernille Ipsen for detailed descriptions of mixed households in other African contexts. Finally, see also Miller on Luso-African families as corporate kin groups. Caldeira, Mulheres, sexualidade e casamento em São Tomé e Príncipe; Candido and Jones, African Women in the Atlantic World; Candido, Aguida Gonçalves da Silva, p. 33–54; Candido, An African Slaving Port; Candido, Concubinage and Slavery in Benguela, in: Hunt and Ojo (eds.), Slavery in Africa and the Caribbean, p. 66–84; Candido, Engendering West Central African History, p. 7–36; Candido, Strategies for Social Mobility, in: Campbell and Elbourne (eds.), Sex, Power and Slavery, p. 272–288; Candido, Wealth, Land, and Property in Angola; Candido, Women in Angola, in: Spear (ed.), Oxford Research Encyclopedia of African History; Candido, Women, Family, and Landed Property, p. 136–161; Coquery-Vidrovitch, African Women; Curto, The Donas of Benguela, in: Bergamo, Pantoja and Silva (eds.), Angola e as angolanas, p. 99–120; Havik, Women and Trade in the Guinea Bissau Region, p. 83–120; Ipsen, Daughters of the Trade; Miller, Way of Death, p. 246–250; Oliveira, Slave Trade and Abolition, p. 28–32; Osborn, Our New Husbands are Here; Ray, Crossing the Color Line; Rodrigues, Portugueses e africanos nos Rios de Sena; Vedeler, Reconstructing Meaning in Deuteronomy 22:5, p. 459–476.

this darker side of being included in Mbundu corporate kin groups has yet to be consistently explored, perhaps because, as Geschiere argues, historians and social scientists tend to assume a purely "positive view of intimacy" and kinship.[74]

On the other hand, Father Moratto and the daughters and female slaves of Sergeant Major Silva seem to have been distrustful of the homo-affective bonds that structured the local garrison, hinting at the fact that some of its members might be adepts of ritual practices that clashed with mainstream Mbundu norms and sensibilities. The result was a generalized breakdown of trust that led to the circulation of rumors, creating the need to publicize the consulting of diviners, the taking of judicial oaths, and announce the results of these forensic procedures to restore peace within the intimate spheres of the garrison and each soldier's household, and normalize the interface between these intimate circles and the public sphere. In other words, the 'public ritual' aspect of ordeal taking was crucial to stopping the circulation of rumors.

However, Friar de Lucca seems to have understood that all these increasingly radical attempts to reestablish trust were evidence of the same creeping moral decay that he had warned the prosecutor of the Inquisition of Lisbon about when describing the situation in Luanda. Therefore, the adoption of Mbundu remedies in the quest to ascertain the ultimate cause of Sergeant Major Silva's ailment and restore his wife's or Lieutenant Queiroga's tarnished reputations were equally framed as 'diabolic' acts inspired by African sorcerers. This reduction of various forms of normative knowledge and practices to commensurable sins attributes a false sense of unity to the beliefs and convictions of the *moradores* of Massangano and projects coherence, if not coordination, to their conflicting actions. A reduction that not only masks the plurality of strategies adopted regarding African normative systems and the underlying social pluralism that helps explain them but also characterizes African societies as culturally monolithic, denying the existence of a vast gamut of possible normative solutions and ways of addressing the challenges posed by sorcery and the dangers of intimacy.

It is essential to keep Friar de Lucca's interpretative biases in mind when Friar Cavazzi's lists of BaKongo and Mbundu "*Sacerdoti* [ministers]" and "*Giuramenti* [oaths]" and Mbangala "*idolatries*," and "*sacrifices*" are further explored in the following pages and chapters.[75] As Friar de Lucca, Friar Cavazzi believed that the Capuchins had failed to attain a complete victory against the "*tyranny of the common Enemy* [the devil]" due to "*the occult stratagems of certain Ministers, who, by inciting the ancient errors, endeavor in all their power to maintain the religion, or*

74 Geschiere, Witchcraft, Intimacy, and Trust, p. 23.

75 Cavazzi, Istorica descrizione de' tre' Regni Congo, Matamba et Angola, p. 69–116, 208–247.

rather the Sect of the Adversary."[76] Christianized BaKongo nobles, he continued, "*in secret foment*[ed], *encourage*[d], *and with all industry protect*[ed] *the false Priests, Stregoni* [sorcerers], *and Fattucchieri* [sorcerers]" and "*everywhere there was an occult minister of Satan, breaking all reasonable provisions, to diminish the good fruits and progress of the holy faith*." Accepting that this vision of a common 'demonic' front against Roman Catholicism is merely an operative fiction,[77] it becomes clear that all the ritual operators, institutions, and customs described by Friar Cavazzi belong, in fact, to a complex constellation of often clashing African normative systems. This creates the need to reconceptualize our model of how different Portuguese, Europeans, and Luso-Africans related to the plural normative knowledge of the African societies and groups they interacted with daily.[78] As Lieutenant Queiroga and Sergeant Major Silva's case proves, a revised model needs to account for different strategies being adopted even by members of the same household or corporation, focusing not only on processes of 'normative imbrication' and 'institutional co-option' but also on the intricate normative patterns these individual choices formed.

When exploring how contemporary African state officials deal with the paradoxes posed by customary law, Olaf Zenker and Markus Hoehne have proposed an interpretative grid abstract enough to assist us in complementing Madeira Santos' model without incurring anachronism.[79] Hoehne and Zenker argue that there are "four principal modes" by which contemporary states address customary law in Africa: "ignorance, awareness, recognition, and rejection."[80] While "ignorance" entails the non-recognition of African normative knowledge, which can stem from a "true lack of knowledge or a more or less intentional pretense of not knowing," the other three modes entail some form of acknowledgment. Father Barreira's strategic option to leave out some crucial details about Mbundu rules regarding the exchange of enslaved Africans in Mbundu *itanda*, whose consequences were explored in detail in the fourth chapter, offers an excellent example of "ignorance" as a mode of relating to African normative knowledge.[81] As for "awareness," Hoehne and Zenker

---

76 Ibid., p. 69–70.

77 See Jorge Cañizares-Esguerra on how the rhetoric of a battle against a "common enemy" attributed coherence to the different forms of violent proselytism and territorial conquest undertaken by agents and corporations belonging to the Iberian Empires in Africa, America, and India. Cañizares-Esguerra, Puritan Conquistadors.

78 Marcussi, Uma "caça às bruxas," p. 1–2.

79 Zenker and Hoehne, Processing the paradox, in: Zenker and Hoehne (eds.), The State and the Paradox, p. 1–40.

80 Ibid., p. 22.

81 MMA III, D. 54.

explain, it consists of several strategies that have in common an official acknowledgment of customary law that does not entail an "accommodation or recognition" of customary law within the realms of "state law and legal practice."[82] If transposed to the early modern Captaincy of Angola, awareness aptly describes situations when individuals known to play a critical role in African normative systems were endowed with authority within the Portuguese system but not as a recognition of their *other* functions—for instance, the appointment of Mbundu diviners or ordeal specialists as bailiffs which is explored in the following pages. This differs from the adoption of what Madeira Santos defines as "bifrontal" institutional connectors because a given incumbent, not necessarily their office, was situated "in-between" normative systems.[83] In other words, the same office occupied by a Portuguese person would not be an instance of "awareness," as Hoehne and Zenker define it.[84]

According to Hoehne and Zenker's model, the modality "recognition" can be further subdivided into "deference," "delegation," and "incorporation."[85] These registers vary since deference only entails the recognition of the "limited normative autonomy of communities by granting them a private space," delegation entails the recognition that their normative systems are legal ones but "still denies them full autonomy," and incorporation entails the co-option of "certain parts or aspects of customary law into state law." Deference aptly describes how the captain-general and governors of Angola who collaborated with Mbangala warrior bands related to the *ijila* and rituals of their *kilombo*, never recognizing them as valid normative principles and rules but deferring to them for military cooperation—an instance of what Madeira Santos defines as them acting as "indirect or informal" normative connectors.[86] In contrast, an excellent example of how delegation was central to the institutional and normative reforms of Captain-General and Governor Sousa Coutinho is the delimitation of a "*domestic Government of Potentates, Sobas and their Vassals and Sons*" where the captain majors and other Portuguese authorities were not to gain access or interfere as determined by the Ordinance of February 24, 1765—an instance what Madeira Santos defines as a "catalyst" institutional con-

82 Zenker and Hoehne, Processing the paradox, in: Zenker and Hoehne (eds.), The State and the Paradox, p. 22–23.

83 Santos, O Império Português face às instituições indígenas, in: Palomo, Stumpf and Barreto Xavier (eds.), Monarquias ibéricas em perspectiva comparada, p. 276–277.

84 Zenker and Hoehne, Processing the paradox, in: Zenker and Hoehne (eds.), The State and the Paradox, p. 22–23.

85 Ibid., p. 23.

86 Santos, O Império Português face às instituições indígenas, in: Palomo, Stumpf and Barreto Xavier (eds.), Monarquias ibéricas em perspectiva comparada, p. 276–277.

nector.[87] Finally, the "*Mucano*" hearings described in the first chapter are clear examples of incorporation—an instance of what Madeira Santos defines as "direct and encompassing" institutional connectors.[88]

After establishing this typology, Hoehne and Zenker introduce dynamism into their model by recognizing that these different modalities simply provide "the rules of the game," leaving enough leeway for state agents to play "with the rules themselves."[89] Following Tom de Herdt and Jean-Pierre Olivier de Sardan's exploration of "practical norms" and the "game of the rules" in Sub-Saharan Africa, they argue that concrete "patterns of practice" always depend as much on official norms and openly stated strategies as on the fulfillment of mundane needs and practical norms.[90] Moreover, embracing practical norms can also entail different modes of relating to African customary law, varying from ignorance, awareness, recognition, and rejection.[91] According to Hoene and Zenker, contemporary state officials and bureaucrats get much of their work done by exploring the opportunities posed by combining different modes of relating to African customs at the levels of official and practical norms, namely, by adopting a strategy at one level and a different one at another. For example, African customs can be recognized at a practical level when appointing 'traditional' authorities for official positions, while, at the same time, only awareness of African customary law is expressed at the official level because these authorities are addressed as ordinary citizens. The following pages explore if evidence of similar dynamics can be found in the inquisitorial records, also paying attention to the fact that Portuguese and Luso-African jurisdictions interfaced with different African normative systems (e.g., those of the Bakongo, Mbangala, Mbundu, or Ovimbundu), creating the possibility of them playing the game of the rules by adopting dissimilar strategies at the official and practical levels *vis-à-vis* each one of them.

87 Coutinho, Documento N.º 6, in: Couto, Os capitães-mores em Angola, p. 330; Santos, O Império Português face às instituições indígenas, in: Palomo, Stumpf and Barreto Xavier (eds.), Monarquias ibéricas em perspectiva comparada, p. 276–277.

88 Santos, O Império Português face às instituições indígenas, in: Palomo, Stumpf and Barreto Xavier (eds.), Monarquias ibéricas em perspectiva comparada, p. 276–277.

89 Zenker and Hoehne, Processing the paradox, in: Zenker and Hoehne (eds.), The State and the Paradox, p. 24–25.

90 De Herdt and Olivier de Sardan, Real Governance and Practical Norms; Zenker and Hoehne, Processing the paradox, in: Zenker and Hoehne (eds.), The State and the Paradox, p. 24–25.

91 Zenker and Hoehne, Processing the paradox, in: Zenker and Hoehne (eds.), The State and the Paradox, p. 24–25.

7.3 Patterns of Practice in the Hinterland Districts and *Presídios*

On May 24, 1765, a company of lay brothers of the Brotherhood of Our Lady of Assumption of Ambaca gathered in the house of Father José de Barros Correia, presbyter of the Chapter of St. Peter and scribe of the Portuguese *presídio* of Ambaca.[92] The news that Manuel de Pedro, also known as "Cambongue," had been recently spotted walking free in the fortress of Our Lady of Assumption had brought them there in haste. Pedro was a slave of their Brotherhood, whom the assembled lay brothers had recently passed judgment on, determining that he was to be sold off to Brazil.[93] Subsequently, they had him delivered to António Gonçalves da Costa, the *Almoxarife da Real Fazenda* of Ambaca, to be brought before Father José de Matos, the canon-treasurer responsible for the "*fábrica da Igreja* [church council]" of the Chapter of Luanda.[94] Father Matos was accountable for managing the church's property, so the lay brothers asked him to dispose of Pedro according to their ruling.[95] Since that didn't happen, on May 24, in a state of panic, the lay brothers requested Father Correia to write a complaint to the Inquisition of Lisbon, expressing their anxiety about Pedro returning to Ambaca "*without any other Signal of having been punished*," except for the fact that he had "*been extinguished* [sic] *as a Christian*."[96] Clearly, the lay brothers did not understand Pedro's ex-communication as sufficient punishment, fearing it would instead enhance his prestige.[97]

As the brothers of the Brotherhood of Our Lady of Assumption of Ambaca explain in the documents annexed to their complaint, they had found Pedro guilty of being a "*feticero*," "*magician*," and "*superstitious*" person involved in divination or the "*taking of indicios* [omens]."[98] According to them, and to the testimonies they annexed to their complaint,[99] Pedro was an "*unruly, drunken, thief*" who charged

---

92 The brothers included Pedro Correia da Silva, the vicar president of the Brotherhood; António Bezerra, the judge of the Brotherhood; Gaspar Vandunen Medeiros, the scribe of the Brotherhood; Manuel dos Santos, its treasurer; and António Soares Ferreira, João Pinto da Silva, and António Gonçalves da Costa, all stewards. ANTT, TSO, IL, Sr. 28, D. 13970, p. 1.

93 Ibid., p. 5, 7.

94 ANTT, TSO, IL, Sr. 28, D. 13970, p. 5; Hair, Portuguese Documents on Africa, p. 95–96.

95 ANTT, TSO, IL, Sr. 28, D. 13970, p. 5.

96 Ibid., p. 3.

97 Due to the small size and remoteness of the Chapter of Luanda, the vicar general acted as the judicial vicar responsible for reviewing the lay brothers' ruling. He might have had no special training in Canon law. For an introduction to how general vicariates functioned in Brazil, see Aldair Rodrigues. Rodrigues, Clergy, Society, and Power Relations in Colonial Brazil, p. 40–67; Torres, Memorias, p. 279.

98 ANTT, TSO, IL, Sr. 28, D. 13970, p. 3, 5.

99 The witnesses who swore oaths were Domingos Palha Torres, a 54-year-old resident of the *presídio*, António João, a 36-year-old soldier of its garrison, and António Soares Ferreira, a 75-year-old

"*emoluments*" as a "*Bailiff and feitisseiro* [sic]," being responsible for several deaths that he had caused through the magical "*arts*" he publicly performed.[100] In sum, the lay brothers argue that he was "*good for nothing*" and, because of his "*depraved life*" and "*bad customs*," set a bad "*example to the other slaves*." Therefore, they had initially recommended to Father Matos that Pedro be shipped to "*Pernambuco, or any other Place in Brazil*" and sold there to a new master. Seeing him walking free in Ambaca, the lay brothers confessed they felt that "*their lives were in great danger because the feteceiro* [sic] *would continue to mock them and take revenge on the Community*."[101] It was distinguished members of the local Luso-African elite that made this claim, as their surnames Bezerra, Vandunem, and dos Santos and their ability to mobilize the efforts of the scribe and the *Almoxarife da Real Fazenda* of Ambaca prove.[102] As Miller remarks, by the eighteenth century, Luso-African "familial factions" recognizable from the use of surnames such as these and "Machado, Correia Leitão, Matozo de Andrade" or "Ornellas" had established a kaleidoscopic "web of alliances and feuds" that was unpredictable and impenetrable to the "eyes of outsiders."[103] Nevertheless, it structured the critical social and commercial relations between Luanda, the *arimos* at the bars of the major rivers that supplied its food, the *presídios* of the hinterlands, and remote slave fairs and *pumbos*. Moreover, the "clan loyalties" that structured each Luso-African familial faction extended to different African partners, patrons, and clients, being consolidated through marriages or common law unions and regular gift exchanges, finding institutional expression in the deliberations of the Municipal Councils of Luanda and Massangano, as well as of the councils of the *Santa Casas da Misericordia* and other lay brotherhoods where these Luso-African elites were represented.[104]

However, the Luso-African brothers of the Brotherhood of Our Lady of Assumption of Ambaca were not the only faction active in the *presídio*. Ambaca was first established by Captain-General and Governor Bento Banha Cardoso in 1614 at the site of Ango, near the River Lucala.[105] Four years later, Captain-General and Governor Luís Mendes de Vasconcelos moved the settlement to its definitive location, in a

---

sexton of the Church of Our Lady of Assumption, all of them originally from Ambaca. Ibid., p. 9–11.

100 Ibid., p. 7.

101 Ibid., p. 5.

102 See Jill Dias and Beatrix Heintze for a brief history of how the strategies of Ambaca's elites evolved during the nineteenth century. Dias, Estereótipos e realidades sociais, in: CNCDP (ed.), Construindo o passado angolano, p. 597–623; Heintze, A lusofonia no interior da África Central na era pré-colonial, p. 179–207; Heintze, Pioneiros Africanos; Vellut, New Perspectives on the Ambaquista Network, p. 327–329.

103 Miller, Way of Death, p. 249.

104 Ibid., p. 249–251.

105 Cadornega, História geral das guerras angolanas, Vol. 3, p. 434.

site known as Licondo do Ouro or Condeça, between the Rivers Lucala and Lutete, providing it with a rammed earth fortification and a permanent garrison.[106] Then, it occupied a strategic military position in the Mbundu heartlands, established at one day's march from the mobile capital of the *ngola* of Ndongo in the former territory of the "*soba Kaita ka Balanga*," whom Vasconcelos had defeated with the help of Mbangala mercenaries.[107] When Cadornega's *General History of the Angolan Wars* (1681) was written, the *presídio* of Ambaca had no more than fifteen *moradores*.[108] The district was composed of several *sobas* who were supposed to relate to Portuguese authorities and the Luso-Africans according to the "*termo de undamento* [vassalage treaty]" their predecessors had signed with the representatives of the Portuguese Crown.[109] Its garrison had "forty soldiers" commanded by a captain major, a lieutenant, an ensign, and several sergeants and corporals, and included an artillery captain, a scribe, and an *almoxarife*.[110] These regular troops were assisted by irregular Mbundu "*guerra preta* [Black war]" regiments, commanded by *quilambas* or *tendalas*, and the "*Songos* [Mbangala regiments]" of *jaga* Cabucu,[111] commanded by several "*quilambas and Macotas*."[112] As Jan Vansina explains, by the eighteenth century, this small military outpost had grown into one of the most important Portuguese *presídios* in West Central Africa because it overlooked the slave caravans coming to Luanda from the slave fair of Lucamba, situated at a day's

---

106 Cadornega, História geral das guerras angolanas, Vol. 3, p. 162–163; Thornton, A History of West Central Africa, p. 117; Vansina, Ambaca Society and the Slave Trade, p. 1–27.

107 Cadornega, História geral das guerras angolanas, Vol. 1, p. 155–156, Vol. 3, p. 162–163; Heintze, The Extraordinary Journey of the Jaga, p. 67–101; Thornton, A History of West Central Africa, p. 117.

108 Cadornega, História geral das guerras angolanas, Vol. 3, p. 164.

109 Mbundu *sobas* were expected to provide *corvée* labor, rally irregular troops in times of war, and pay tribute or taxes, either in kind or slaves, according to the terms of their vassalage treaty. According to Sousa Coutinho, captain majors had the habit of distributing specific chores to *sobas* and their subjects so that "*there was a soba for fixing the Church, another to fix his* [the captain major's] *residence, another* [to fix] *the fortress, another to supply timber, another water, another* [palm] *oil for the guards and jail corps, another to man the canoes, another* [to supply] *porters to help the military garrison,* [and] *the quilambas for the postal service*." Couto, Os capitães-mores em Angola, p. 124–133, 245–256; Heintze, Luso-African Feudalism, p. 111–131; Hespanha, A constituição do Império português, in: Fragoso et al. (eds.), O Antigo Regime nos Trópicos, p. 171; Vansina, Ambaca Society and the Slave Trade, p. 10.

110 Cadornega, História geral das guerras angolanas, Vol. 3, p. 164.

111 Cadornega refers to this *jaga* both as "*Jaga Cabuco Candonga*" and "*Jaga Cabucu e Calanda*." Ibid., p. 164–165, 244–245.

112 Cadornega provides a list of sixteen *quilambas* serving in the "*captainship of Ambaca*," including Dom Joseph, to whom he added the title "*Manimuto hita a lunga*," explaining that a "*manimuto*" was a "war title" and "*hita a lunga*" meant "*he who gather the troops*." Ibid.

travel away, and from the further-inland fair of Cassange.[113] By 1703, John Harvey remarks that Ambaca had one hundred and three soldiers.[114] However, the walls of its fortress had crumbled to the ground, and the troops had become "integrated into the hinterland societies"—never wearing military uniform and freely pursuing their private interests. These were directly tied to the trans-Atlantic slave trade. By 1765, Vansina estimates, about 10.000 enslaved Africans passed through the *presídio* and its hinterlands yearly, creating a massive need for supplies and free African porters' labor.[115]

Therefore, besides the familial factions represented in its lay brotherhood, which could count on their privileged connections with Luanda and communicate directly with the Inquisition of Lisbon, members of the garrison of Ambaca also had high stakes in overseeing all matters related to the enslavement of Africans, the logistics of coffles, the arbitration of 'cross-cultural' conflicts, and the arbitration of sorcery accusations and other pressing judicial matters (e. g., thefts, adulteries, debt settlements). As discussed in the second chapter, the top civil and military authority of Ambaca was its captain major, who was responsible for administering ordinary justice and settling disputes between African *sobas*.[116] Just as the lay brothers, the captain majors of Ambaca were usually local-born, often of mixed Portuguese and Mbundu ancestry, and therefore, as Vansina argues, a "genuine part of the social fabric."[117] Because of the constant shortage of porters and supplies, the near-monopoly that captain majors in charge of garrisons had over extracting free and *corvée* labor from the African *sobas* was bitterly resented by the Luso-African merchants and the other *moradores* of Ambaca.[118] To aggravate matters, since the payment of "heavy fines" and even enslavement were often imposed on those found guilty of serious misdeeds, all understood the administration of ordinary justice to be highly profitable and tended to resent their peers with jurisdiction.[119] Therefore, the accusation against Pedro might be a symptom of latent conflicts of interest if he acted as a "*Bailiff*" of the captain major of Ambaca, perhaps in collusion with

---

113 Vansina, Ambaca Society and the Slave Trade, p. 1–27.

114 Harvey, Politics, Commerce, and Colonization, p. 22–24.

115 Thornton, A History of West Central Africa, p. 117; Vansina, Ambaca Society and the Slave Trade, p. 1–27.

116 Vansina, Ambaca Society and the Slave Trade, p. 1–27.

117 Ibid., p. 8.

118 Elias Alexandre da Silva Corrêa provides an eyewitness account of how captain majors abused their ability to demand porters from the *sobas* under their jurisdiction to auction their services to Luso-African merchants for the highest bid. Ibid., p. 1–27; Couto, Os capitães-mores em Angola, p. 230–237; Silva Corrêa, História de Angola, Vol. 1, p. 35–37.

119 Silva Corrêa, História de Angola, Vol. 1, p. 94; Vansina, Ambaca Society and the Slave Trade, p. 1–27.

a local *soba*.[120] As Ferreira, Kananoja, and Selma Pantoja argue, at least since the seventeenth century, similar instrumentalizations of the Holy Office were common in Luanda, where the competition between wealthy families and influential individuals to assume coveted positions in the colonial hierarchy, especially that of captain major, often led to crossed denunciations of idolatry and sorcery.[121]

Choosing an African ritual operator to act as bailiff would not be unheard of, although that kind of recognition of African normative systems seems to have occurred at the practical, not official, level (contrary, for instance, to the official recognition of *tendalas* as interpreters or *quilambas* as military commanders). Soon after the Lent of 1714, in the district of Golungo, several military officers, clerics of minor orders, slaves, *tendalas*, and *quilambas* denounced Captain Major Luís Maia to the Holy Office.[122] All testimonies shared a narrative core, describing events directly witnessed by the accusers or rumors circulating in the *arimos* of the district. Only a few provide details that are unconfirmed by the other testimonies. As Captain Miguel Marques de Almeida, Cleric António Matos de Bibar, and all other testimonies heard by the inquisitors agreed, Captain Major Maia had forced two Black men to take the Mbundu "*oath called bolungo* [*mbulungo*]" because he believed them to be "*feiticeiros*." One of these men was called Cuzanguella, a free worker at the *arimo* of the *Santa Casa* of Massangano; the other was called António and was an enslaved worker at the *arimo* of the *morador* João Correa Dias. The oath had confirmed them both as guilty and, according to a slave called Sebastião who claimed to be an eyewitness of these events because he was in jail with the victims, Captain Major Maia determined that they were to be drowned in the river, one being immediately thrown by his men "*with a rock* [tied] *to his neck*" the other being "*delivered to his kinsmen with the obligation that they should kill him*." Sebastião and Cleric Matos de Bibar claimed that Father Joseph de Camargo Veiga assisted Captain Major Maia in organizing the *mbulungo* ordeals, together with

---

120 Three other explanations for Pedro being referred to as "*Bailiff*" were that he was a bailiff of the vicar general of the Diocese of Congo and Angola or of a vicar forane, the bailiff of a local tax-farmer, or an 'informal' bailiff of one of the high officers residing in Luanda (e. g., captain-general and governor, *ouvidor geral*) in charge of procuring slaves and conducting business. However, because he was a slave of the lay brotherhood, only the first two options seem likely.

121 Ferreira remarks that in 1733, Antonio da Fonseca Coutinho, then *mestre de camp* of the regiment of Luanda, was "*accused by his political enemies of using witchcraft to murder*" Paulo Caetano de Albuquerque, captain-general and governor of Angola between 1726 and 1732. This denunciation to the Holy Office happened after Coutinho attempted a putsch to be appointed interim captain-general and governor. Couto, Os capitães-mores em Angola, p. 59; Ferreira, Cross-Cultural Exchange, p. 164–177; Kananoja, Healers, Idolaters, and Good Christians, p. 451; Marcocci and Paiva, História da Inquisição Portuguesa; Pantoja, Inquisição, degredo e mestiçagem em Angola, p. 117–136; Pantoja, Personagens entre mares Atlânticos, p. 136–149.

122 ANTT, TSO, IL, Sr. 30, CP 94, Book 287, p. 47–60.

his scribe, and that the ordeal itself was administered by the "*feiticeiro*" António a Quizanga and the *Sobas* Mussungo-a-Posse and Anganbambe. When called to witness, *Quilamba* Bango Bango clarified that Quizanga was a *quimbar* who only administered the *mbulungo* privately at the household of Captain Major Maia. He added that the public oaths were always performed under the jurisdiction of the *sobas* by their own "*surgeons*." Sebastião further claimed that Pellosia, the captain major's lover, also helped organize these private oaths, having often been subject to them to prove that she remained faithful to him.

Besides organizing these public oath-takings with the collaboration of *Sobas* Mussungo-a-Posse and Anganbambe, the four *quilambas* called as witnesses, Bango Bango, Bango-a-Sungue, Balufo-a-Loango, and Diogo Andrade, agreed that it was a well-known rumor that Captain Major Maia had a "*surgeon*" from Massangano "*open up a black* [woman] *seven months pregnant to take the child from her belly to make ungoentos* [unguents]" for himself.[123] Moreover, they agreed that he had buried alive a fully dressed "*moleque* [young male slave]" to "*always be victorious over his enemies*." Besides, they continued, he was adept at using "*ambundo* [Mbundu] *oaths*" and "*ambundu* [Mbundu] *divinations*,"[124] even "*sacalando* [being possessed by spirits] *in his house*." *Quilamba* Bango Bango added that the "*sacalamentos* [possession cults]" were performed inside his household with the assistance of Father Camargo. Soldier Valentim Correa confirmed that when he was tasked to verify if Captain Major Maia had the habit of "*chingular* [*xinguilar*]," he had snuck into his courtyard and found him dressed with a "*penacho* [feather headdress], *two onça* [leopard] *skins, with a small axe in his hand, sitting on a small stool, with his black slave named Agueda chinguilando* [in trance]."[125] Moreover, Bango-a-Sungue reported that he "*buried feitiços in his household, lands, and courtyard, so that through these feitissarias, no one should cause him harm, nor imprison or punish him for the maleficios* [evil deeds] *that he committed in the district*." Besides noting that a priest was once again involved in performing private *mbulungo* oaths, two crucial pieces of information can be retained from these testimonies. First, the *quilambas* and other witnesses clearly distinguished between Mbundu oaths and divinations and other practices attributed to Captain Major Maia. Second, all agreed there was a substantial difference between the public ordeal performed

123 Ibid.

124 *Quilamba* Bango Bango claimed that Captain Major Maia had ordered *soba* Mussungo to have two cocks fight in his court to "*know through magic arts if he or Lieutenant General Domingos da Cunha were to Govern this District* [Golungo]." Ibid.

125 Auxiliar Correa also claimed that Captain Major Maia used "*some powders*" to magically treat the letters he sent to Captain General and Governor António de Saldanha de Albuquerque Castro e Ribafria, in office between 1709 and 1713, to "*turn the heart of the Governor*" in his favor. Ibid.

by authorized specialists at the courts of *sobas* and those privately held in Maia's household.

As Alexandre Marcussi remarks when exploring what he describes as a "central African witch hunt" that took place in Massangano in 1717, the difference between *mbulungo* oaths performed in private and those performed before *sobas* in public courts was essential to Mbundu normative systems.[126] The latter's results were considered a sort of second-instance confirmation of the former's and thus both definitive and binding.[127] The documents analyzed by Marcussi contain the testimonies collected by Friar Joseph of Modena at the Capuchin Hospice of Massangano on behalf of Friar de Lucca on June 10 and 11, 1717.[128] The documents relate that several *quimbares* from Carinda, an *arimo* in the fertile riverine lands close to the village, accused Domingos Aganga Aquilonga and his wife Izabel Camassa Caganga of being disciples of the famous 'sorcerer' João Congo Aquilombo and using "poison and *feitiço*" to kill "many people and their kinsfolk."[129] As Marcussi clarifies, Aquilombo had been publicly accused of being a *muloji*, having then been sent by the ecclesiastical authorities of Massangano to the public jail of Luanda, where he had perished before facing trial.[130] Soon after his death, rumors started spreading that the *aloji* network he was part of would soon take revenge[131] by sacrificing their kin and neighbors to be consumed by the surviving cannibalistic *aloji* during their nocturnal assemblies—a pattern that Geschiere describes as common in other contemporary African contexts.[132]

Several accused were forced to take the *mbulungo* oath at the court of nearby *Soba* Quiagonga, including Fernando Lungariambamba, who had already been cleared from the charges of being a "*feiticeiro*" by the ecclesiastical justice of Massangano, and Lourenço Quituque, who had already taken the *mbulungo* privately "four or five times."[133] Basing himself on Friar Cavazzi, Macussi points out that only

---

126 ANTT, TSO, IL, Sr. 30, CP 93, Book 286, p. 134–141; Marcussi, Uma "caça às bruxas," p. 8–9.

127 Marcussi, Uma "caça às bruxas," p. 8–9.

128 Ibid., p. 4.

129 Ibid.; ANTT, TSO, IL, Sr. 30, CP 93, Book 286, p. 134–141.

130 As Kananoja remarks, a 1703 provision determined that ecclesiastical prisoners would be sent to the public jail in Luanda until an *aljube* [ecclesiastical prison] was built. Kananoja, Healing Knowledge, p. 40–41; Marcussi, Uma "caça às bruxas," p. 4.

131 Pedro Quibuca Quiagola, Fernando Lungariambamba, Manoel Aganga, Antóni Aquilombo, and Lourenço Quituque were also accused of being "*feiticeiros*" and part of this network by their families and close neighbors. ANTT, TSO, IL, Sr. 30, CP 93, Book 286, p. 134–141; Marcussi, Uma "caça às bruxas," p. 4.

132 Geschiere, Witchcraft and Modernity, in: Parés and Sansi-Roca (eds.), Sorcery in the Black Atlantic, p. 233–258; Geschiere, Witchcraft as the Dark Side of Kinship, p. 43–61; Geschiere, Witchcraft, Intimacy, and Trust.

133 ANTT, TSO, IL, Sr. 30, CP 93, Book 286, p. 134–141; Marcussi, Uma "caça às bruxas," p. 4–8.

the *mbulungo* oaths held before *Soba* Quiagonga seem to have been considered final, not the ones performed semi-privately in Carinda.[134] Friar Cavazzi argued that the BaKongo diviners called "Ngombo" performed two kinds of divination, one private, the other public, to ascertain who had been responsible for a given death. According to him, the private divinations held by the *ngombo* involved "*invoking the devil*" as an "*oracle*," who then pointed out names of "*innocent friends*" of the deceased to seed distrust in the community.[135] Public divinations, Friar Cavazzi continued, involved "*the Ngombo having his drum played to gather all the neighbors in an open place*," being possessed by the "*devil*" and ordering the accused to be taken to a secluded place to "*drink a beverage prepared by the same Ngombo*." Whoever "*resist*[ed] *the violence of this drink being considered innocent, by vomiting it*." All others were "*subjected to capital punishment*."[136] Assuming there is a proximity between BaKongo and Mbundu beliefs and institutions and considering the patterns of practice observed in the inquisitorial records, Macussi argues that a similar judicial hierarchy existed between private *mbulungo* ordeals and those performed at the *sobas*' courts.[137]

The case against Captain Major Maia in Golungo seems to confirm Macussi's argument, as all testimonies added a final accusation. According to Captain Almeida, Captain Major Maia had promoted a "*black called Paulo Luiz to captain of bolungos giving him a bastão* [staff] *for this end*."[138] Captain João Alvaro Roiz confirmed this information, adding that acting as "*capetam bulungueiro* [captain of *mbulungo*]," Paulo Luiz had resisted being arrested by the bailiffs whom Vicar António da Costa Vieira had sent to detain him and bring him before ecclesiastical justice, inflicting upon them a "*lot of strikes*" with the help of his underlings. Captain Roiz concluded that Paulo Luiz was not afraid of the general vicar because the captain major stood by his acts. Sebastião, the sexton of the Church of Our Lady of *Desterro*, added that Paulo Luiz was the "*son*" or subject of *Soba* Itonde, who backed him up and legitimized his oath-giving. Sexton Sebastião said that because of this double institutional support, Paulo Luiz "*boasted of being captain of bollungos and giving bolungos*

---

134 Cavazzi, Istorica descrizione de' tre' Regni Congo, Matamba et Angola, p. 77–78; Marcussi, Uma "caça às bruxas," p. 8–9.

135 Friar Cavazzi seems to have testified to the dire consequences of the paradox of intimacy breeding spiritual danger and *kindoki* accusations, making sense of it by framing the escalation of conflicts as both the result and evidence of 'demonic' intervention. The Capuchin friar often commented on the alleged "*lack of love*" of the Mbundu and related peoples "*towards their kin*" and the "*mutual coldness between parents and children, and brothers and sisters.*" He called it a "*great defect that Nature abhors attributing even to wild beasts*." Cavazzi, Istorica descrizione de' tre' Regni Congo, Matamba et Angola, p. 67–68, 77–78.

136 Ibid., p. 77–78.

137 Marcussi, Uma "caça às bruxas," p. 8–9.

138 ANTT, TSO, IL, Sr. 30, CP 94, Book 287, p. 47–60.

[*mbulungo* ordeals] *publicly in the district*." In conclusion, Captain Major Maia was accused of unofficially creating an 'in-between' office backed by the military muscle at his command and recognized as a legitimate authority by *Soba* Itonde. This allowed him to vie for control of the two instances of *mbulungo* ordeal taking. First, the private ordeal he organized in collusion with Father Veiga and second, the public one Paulo Luiz administered with the backing of *Soba* Itonde. Captain Major Maia thus gained a significant advantage over his local rivals by appointing a legitimate *mbulungo* oath giver as a bailiff, unofficially recognizing Mbundu norms and institutions. His frustrated rivals and denouncers to the Inquisition of Lisbon included Mbundu *quilambas* and *tendalas* and soldiers and clerics who might have belonged to the Luso-African familial factions, which coopted these subalternate offices to further their interests and profit directly or indirectly from the slave trade.

The brothers of the Brotherhood of Our Lady of Assumption of Ambaca who accused Pedro might have felt equally frustrated. The fact that he had allegedly killed several persons with his magical "*Arts*" before being denounced suggests that Pedro had the unofficial backing and recognition of at least one powerful Portuguese military authority as well as privileged connections with a *soba* who legitimized and authorized his public performances.[139] By the last decades of the eighteenth century, the patterns of practice evidenced in these inquisitorial records had become so well known that they were discussed in the lectures of the Royal Academy of Sciences of Lisbon. Luís António de Oliveira Mendes (1750–1817) explained in an academic lecture he presented to the Academy in 1793 that captain majors "*often incorporated themselves with the Sova* [sic], *helping him to adjudicate*," and, "*after interrogating witnesses*," usually condemned "*debtors, and the adulterous*" to slavery, sharing the profits with their African partners.[140] Oliveira Mendes, however, did not wholly condemn these practices, basing his approving account of

---

139 Captain majors, however, did not always have the upper hand in similar disputes. Schleumer explores a denunciation from the *Presídio* of Cambambe, 1753, in which Captain Major Julião da Nobrega was victimized by an alleged "Black *feiticeiro*" called João Fernandes Zanba. In this case, Zanba supposedly acted on behalf of *morador* Francisco Rodrigues de Azevedo, a wealthy *arimo* owner, and lived in the compound of one of the garrison's captains, Pais Souto. Most of the accusatory witnesses were also soldiers. ANTT, TSO, IL, Sr. 28, D. 13970, p. 5, 7; SCHLEUMER, Nas bordas do Rio Kwanza, p. 13–28.

140 Oliveira Mendes was a Brazilian-born jurist who had studied at the University of Coimbra and served for years as a lawyer at the *Casa da Suplicação*. According to his lecture, the African subjects of each *presídio* had the custom of "*choosing their Judge, whom they call Sovas* [*sobas*], *to judge them.*" Besides the *soba*, Oliveira Mendes proceeded, each *presídio* had a captain major, a "*son of the land, a black passing for a soldier, to whom, as a payment,*" the Portuguese Crown offered "*a new uniform every year*." EUGÊNIO, Os relatos de Luiz Antônio de Oliveira Mendes, p. 201–231; MELLO PEREIRA, A escravidão e o acesso à terra, p. 181–231; MENDES, Memória a respeito dos escravos, p. 18–19.

how Luso-African captain majors interacted with Mbundu normative systems on two misleading premises. First, he claimed Mbundu customs were in keeping with *Ius gentium* and echoed the same normative principles found in ancient Roman law, so there was no scandal in using them as subsidiary norms.[141] Second, he assumed that the personality principle guaranteed that no Portuguese, Luso-Africans, or Christianized Africans were subjected to African norms during arbitrations. Either ignoring or strategically choosing to ignore that neither of these premises was true, the jurist proceeded to argue in favor of imbricating into the Portuguese normative system what he believed to be the five modes of enslavement the Mbundu *sobas* recognized as legitimate, thus producing yet one more apology for the legality of the Angolan leg of the Atlantic slave trade.[142]

Moreover, Oliveira Mendes' academic lecture ignored one issue that the testimonies against Captain Major Maia raised, which is still to be explored, namely that some of his Mbundu accusers were appalled not only by his ambitious attempt to control private and public *mbulungo* ordeal taking in the district of Golungo but also by his adoption of what they perceived as inhuman practices which could only be attributed to the dreaded Mbangala *jagas* of old. Namely, the murder of a pregnant woman to use the unborn baby to make unguents, which sounds like an outsider's description of the rituals of the *maji a samba* warrior's cult described in the fifth chapter,[143] and the burial of a live young male slave to "*always be victorious over his enemies*," which echoes the rituals prescribed by the *ijila* of the Mbangala *kilombo* during the burials of "*valorous soldiers*."[144] Moreover, Captain Major Maia's *dissaquelas*, as described by his denouncers, had more similarities with Mbangala possession rituals than with Mbundu ones, which were mediated by figurines or

141 Oliveira Mendes claimed that some Mbundu norms regarding marriage and adultery echoed the *Lex Iulia* issued in 100 BC, while others related to thefts echoed the *Lex Aquilia* (c. 286 BC). He also claimed that Mbundu "*fathers*" had the right to deliver "*their children, wives, and nephews*" as slaves to avoid being punished with slavery after being condemned judicially, which could be related to some passages of the *Duodecim Tabulae*. Finally, he argued that Mbundu penalties followed the same principle as the *lex Talionis*. The extent to which these comparisons shed light on Mbundu normative systems is dubious at best. MENDES, Memória a respeito dos escravos, p. 17–20.

142 As described in Oliveira Mendes' academic lecture, these were being condemned for adultery, being enslaved instead of one's father, uncle, or husband, being blamed for theft, being captured during a war, and, finally, having wrongly enslaved a free person. ibid.

143 See also Friar Cavazzi's unsubstantiated claim that the *jagas* "*had all pregnant women slaughtered*" ostensibly not to "*delay the marching of their armies*" but, in truth, to have the "*children served at their tables*." CAVAZZI, Istorica descrizione de' tre' Regni Congo, Matamba et Angola, p. 245; CAVAZZI, THORNTON (trans.) MSS Araldi, Modena; MILLER, Kings and Kinsmen, p. 165–167.

144 These were the "*Quixilla quitanù*" or "*Quixilla quitanu*," the "*Quixilla Cuim*," and the "*Quixilla Cuim ne moxi*" already discussed in the fifth chapter. ANTT, TSO, IL, Sr. 30, CP 94, Book 287, p. 47–60; CAVAZZI, THORNTON (trans.) MSS Araldi, Modena, Book 1, Chap. 3, 5.

were site-specific, as discussed in the following pages.[145] Contrariwise, as Andrew Battel had informed Samuel Purchas in the early 1600s, the Mbangala worshiped no images.[146] If a *jaga* wished to "*sacrifice to the Divell*," he "*sitteth upon a stoole*" being assisted by a "*man Witch*" on each side, "*fortie or fiftie women*" who sang and danced around them holding "*wilde horses*" tails, and a "*great store of Petes, Ponges, and Drummes, which they always play*." These ceremonies, Purchas concluded, culminated with the *jaga* being offered his "*Casengala, which is a weapon like a hatchet*" used to perform human sacrifices.

Half a century later, Friar Cavazzi described the *dissaquelas* of Mbangala *xinguilas* in similar terms, explaining that the "*spirits of one, or another Jaga*" possessed the *xinguila*, answering the questions of the *jagas* who organized the ceremony, as "*if omniscient*," and requesting human sacrifices—usually of young male slaves.[147] In one of the drawings that accompany volume A of *Manoscritti Araldi* representing a male and female *xinguila*, both are depicted marked with a white kaolin called *mpemba*, wearing cloths around their waists, and with the male *xinguila* wielding an axe in his right hand.[148] Considering these elements, the accusations against Captain Major Maia can be read as evidence that he adopted some Mbangala beliefs and practices.[149] These not only clashed with the moral and normative ideals of his Mbundu constituency but also could not as easily be assimilated into the normative fabric of the Captaincy of Angola by being construed as echoes of *Ius gentium* doctrines or received Roman law, as already discussed in the fifth chapter. The fact that Portuguese and Luso-African officers with jurisdiction adopted Mbangala customs deemed against all forms of Natural law posed a particular challenge to the Enlightened captain-general and governors of Angola, who had limited options apart from official ignorance and rejection when relating to this specific African normative system. However, official hostility towards one set of norms often amounted to an unofficial endorsement of another, giving rise to a zero-sum game in which persecuting Mbangala uses and customs amounted to favoring Mbundu ones, and vice-versa.

---

145 ANTT, TSO, IL, Sr. 30, CP 94, Book 287, p. 47–60.

146 Purchas, Purchas His Pilgrimes, Vol. 6, p. 386.

147 Cavazzi, Istorica descrizione de' tre' Regni Congo, Matamba et Angola, p. 225–228.

148 Sweet, Recreating Africa, p. 141.

149 The fact that Captain Major Francisco Gomes Pereira, head of the Golungo district, was also denounced to the Holy Office in 1732 because he "*divined through* [the intervention of] *black feiticeiros*" and had a "*black women, his slave, called Maria who was xinguiladora* [*xinguila*]" suggests that some of the patterns of practice adopted by Captain Major Maia were either rather common or had become unofficially associated with the office of Captain Major of Golungo. Precioso, Catarina Juliana e sua sociedade de culto, p. 116–117.

7.4 Telling the "*Wasps from the Bees*"[150]

In 1791, José de Seabra da Silva, with his reputation fully restored and acting as a minister of the Portuguese Kingdom, wrote an official letter to Captain-General and Governor Manuel de Almeida e Vasconcelos.[151] In its pages, he remarked that as soon as one left Luanda behind and entered "*its neighboring hinterlands, many remnants of Gentilic barbarism were still found in Religion, the Laws, and the Customs*" of the Luso African *moradores*. These "*Laws*," he concluded, were unacceptably cruel, resulting in extortionary practices and the unjust enslavement of freeborn Africans.[152] It was customary that any "*Morador acting against a Miserable Black debtor, who fails to pay them immediately*," had the right to "*take their Wife*" and "*use her as a Slave while awaiting payment*." Furthermore, Seabra da Silva maintained that debtors were "*often forced to go to the House of the Scribe with the creditor and write a Termo de Escravidão* [enslavement writ]," being "*immediately branded*" as slaves of their creditors. Moreover, according to him, porters who had the bad luck of damaging a fraction of their cargoes were obliged to pay compensation for the whole cargo, and the heads of families were obliged to pay for the crimes of their "*Parentes* [kin]" and neighbors, even if they were not involved in them. Matters escalated so quickly, Seabra da Silva denounced, that heads of families often had to enslave their dependents or sign their enslavement writs to atone for crimes others had committed. These customs were aggravated, Seabra da Silva argued, by the fact that *moradores* demanded slaves as payment for debts that amounted to only a fraction of a slave's value and that they disposed of African pawns as if they were slaves, selling them off before their kin had had the chance to ransom them back by repaying the original debts.[153] As for the captain majors, the minister of the kingdom accused them of 'abusing' their power during wartime, condemning to slavery African allies who arrived too late to the battlefield or left too early, and also of extracting undue *corvée* labor from their independent African neighbors.

In Seabra da Silva's opinion, all these practices were genuinely scandalous. They proved the dire need for police regulations to prevent *moradores* and captain majors

150 Purchas and Battel were the first to use this metaphor to contrast the Mbundu and the Mbangala. PURCHAS, Purchas His Pilgrimes, Vol. 6, p. 384.

151 SEABRA DA SILVA, Carta de José de Seabra da Silva, p. 175.

152 Ibid., p. 176–178.

153 This merchant practice, known in West Africa as "panyarring," a Creole term based on the Portuguese *penhorar* [seize] and *penhor* [pawn], had already been denounced by John Atkins (1685–1757) as highly disruptive. Nevertheless, Atkins argued it enabled merchants "*to carry on* [the] *Slave-trade with Europeans*." See Lovejoy for a comparative reassessment of the custom of 'panyarring' in West Africa. ATKINS, A Voyage to Guinea, p. 150–151; LOVEJOY, Pawnship, Debt, and 'Freedom' in Atlantic Africa, p. 55–78.

from acting as slave masters outside of the private spheres of their households, establishing the cruel norms and institutions of slavery as local uses and customs. According to the minister, this 'scandal' was exacerbated by the fact that "*bad uses and customs*" contrary to Portuguese laws were not only upheld by African vassals, "*Barbarians, barbarously educated, only attached to Their Gentilic superstitions*," but also by legitimate Portuguese authorities who accepted them as binding.[154] This situation originated, he continued, from "*the sordid convenience of the White Moradores, and the audacity of Captain Majors, who are the Judges, and who are interested in maintaining these abuses and oppressions, derived from Gentilic Laws*." In the end, Seabra da Silva concluded, the economic interest that captain majors had in arbitrating African cases according to African norms also resulted in the application of the "*laws*" of the "*Black Jagas* [Mbangala] *and Black Gingas* [subjects of the Kingdom of Matamba]" as biding uses and customs. As explored in the previous chapter, Seabra da Silva was also very critical of the *moradores* from "*Massangano, Cambambe, Pedras* [Pungo Andongo], [...] *Ambaca*, [...] *and Muxima*" sending their slaves and dependents to the court of the *jaga* of Kasanje to submit to the "*barbarous oath of Endua* [*ndua*]."[155] Considering that the *ndua* oath rivalled in social prestige and judicial reputation with the public *mbulungo* oaths taken at the courts of powerful Mbundu *sobas* and that both responsibility allocation mechanisms addressed the same fundamental issues raised by the dark sides of intimacy, proximity, and kinship, the question remains if by proposing a criminalization of the *ndua* ordeal Seabra da Silva was not unwittingly promoting the *mbulungo* as a viable alternative.

While Seabra da Silva's indirect endorsement of rival ordeals seems unintentional, as the minister naively upheld that Africans under Portuguese jurisdiction were eager to abandon their normative systems, captain majors and other local agents were less likely to share this romantic view.[156] In 1750, João Pereira da Cunha, a former captain major of Ambaca and member of the Order of Christ, entered the prison of the Inquisition in Lisbon, together with Catarina Juliana, his mistress, and ten of their slaves.[157] Kananoja explains that these prisoners were kept under

154 Seabra da Silva, Carta de José de Seabra da Silva, p. 176.

155 Seabra da Silva argued in favor of confiscating the assets and forcing all "*Whites, or Blacks, who instigated or participated in such abominations*" to serve in the galleys for life. Ibid., p. 79.

156 Ibid.

157 According to Daniel Precioso, Juliana was born and baptized in Luanda in the 1710s, being the daughter of Paulo Eugênio and Juliana Salvador, Christianized enslaved Africans from Luanda. While still enslaved to Cipriano da Silva, she had a "natural daughter" from Cunha, who had died when she was eight months old. Cunha bought her in the aftermath, manumitting her immediately after. ANTT, TSO, IL, Sr. 28, D. 5067, D. 6948, D. 9691, D. 13836; Kananoja, Healers, Idolaters, and Good Christians, p. 443–465; Kananoja, Healing Knowledge in Atlantic Africa, p. 26–49; Precioso, Catarina Juliana e sua sociedade de culto, p. 72–75, 114–117.

custody for several years while their lawsuits were slowly adjudicated.[158] According to him, in 1717, Cunha had been deported to Angola as a "*degredado*" and had slowly risen in the ranks of the colonial army until he managed to secure the much-coveted position of captain major of Ambaca.[159] While he occupied this position, Cunha was very apt at extracting *corvée* labor from local *sobas* and managed to send back to Luanda an entire shipment of slaves every fortnight, doubling the monthly average of his predecessors. The testimonies of Cunha's neighbors and subordinates that were gathered by the prosecutor of the ecclesiastical court of the Diocese of Congo and Angola in 1746 suggest that Cunha organized possession ceremonies in his compound, owning as he did several slaves who were *xinguilas*, including his mistress Juliana.[160] Furthermore, according to the evidence gathered by a canon in Ambaca, Cunha cooperated with *Soba* Domingos of Mucori, who "*assisted the capitão-mor in his magical arts*."[161]

In Kananoja's opinion, Cunha, Juliana, and their African slaves and collaborators were involved in a healing cult.[162] According to him, jealousy of their successful slave-trading enterprise and Cunha's ability to recruit porters motivated idolatry and sorcery accusations of their neighbors and subordinates. However, their therapeutic activities had a judicial impact, if by no other reason, than because they ruled out sorcery rumors and speculation about possible origins of illnesses. One of Cunha's claims in his defense was that while serving as captain major of Ambaca, he had managed to suppress the *mbulungo* ordeal[163] and the traditional Mbundu "*upanda* [adultery]" hearings, which, as Vansina explains, made regular use of the private version of this ordeal.[164] Therefore, Cunha's endorsement of *xinguilas* can be understood as a powerplay like Captain Major Maia's, probably resulting in his control over some of the cases previously settled through private *mbulungo* oath-taking.[165] Such a maneuver would significantly contribute to his performance

---

158 Cunha died on 17 March 1751, and Catarina died on 21 October 1763, both before they could hear their verdict. However, in the end, both were proven innocent and given Catholic burials. Kananoja, Healers, Idolaters, and Good Christians, p. 455, 464.

159 Ibid., p. 452.

160 Ibid., p. 443–465; ANTT, TSO, IL, Sr. 28, D. 9691; Kananoja, Healing Knowledge in Atlantic Africa, p. 26–49.

161 Kananoja, Healers, Idolaters, and Good Christians, p. 446.

162 Ibid., p. 454–455, 459.

163 According to Daniel Precioso, who analyzed Catarina's inquisitorial process and correspondence, the inquisitors also accused her of taking part in "*bulungo*" oaths. Still, even under torture, Catarina only admitted to being a *xinguilas*. Precioso, Catarina Juliana e sua sociedade de culto, p. 68–127.

164 Kananoja, Healers, Idolaters, and Good Christians, p. 450; Vansina, Ambaca Society and the Slave Trade, p. 10–11.

165 Despite Cunha's claim, some accusers claimed that Juliana performed private *mbulungo* ordeals, suggesting that Cunha might have only persecuted the public ones sponsored by Mbundu *sobas*.

Fig. 8 A Mbangala Xinguila. Cavazzi, Alamandi (trans.), Istorica descrizione de' tre' regni Congo, Matamba, et Angola, p. 199 (Public Domain).

as a slave provider at the expense of the other local factions.[166] However, despite alarming his Mbundu constituency, Cunha's possession rituals don't seem to have abided by Mbangala norms, complicating Seabra da Silva's claim that the traditions of the *jagas* were the sole alternative to mainstream Mbundu norms. They thus force us to consider an additional source of normative pluralism and associated anxieties and needs for disambiguation mechanisms, namely the existence of different cohorts of spiritual entities who could manifest through the same ritual operators.

As Kananoja remarks, Juliana claimed she had become a *xinguila* after being afflicted by two spirits, "*Kibuku* and *Muta*," being cured in a possession ritual based on a dance performance called "*calundúz*,"[167] which she then became adept at per-

---

This interpretation strengthens the thesis that he was attempting a powerplay similar to Captain Major Maia. Precioso, Catarina Juliana e sua sociedade de culto, p. 117.

166 As Vansina highlights, adultery trials involving the *mbulungo* often resulted in the enslavement of those found guilty or of subordinates or pawns of their corporate kin group in their stead. By substituting these for *dissaquelas*, Cunha tapped into this vital source of enslaved Africans. Vansina, Ambaca Society and the Slave Trade, p. 10–11.

167 A lot has been written about Brazilian *calundús*, some authors tracing their genealogy back to Angolan possession rituals, others focusing only on their novelties and innovations. This Creole

forming and organizing.[168] According to Daniel Precioso, despite Juliana referring only to "*Quibuco* [*Kibuku*] and *Mottâ* [*Muta*]" in her confession, her accusers agreed that she was also an adept of the entity "*Gangazumba*."[169] *Calundús* were referred to as "*Quilundo*" in an unsigned manuscript Lino d'Assumpção transcribed from the collection of Jesuit papers (c. 1702–1719) found at their old college in Évora, Portugal, and published in 1875.[170] The manuscript related that, when someone "*suffered from an illness that affected their understanding, it is said they have Quilundos*."[171] The author specified that suffering from "*Quilundos*" differed from suffering from "*Ndelles or Nzumbi*" since the afflicted were targeted not by their ancestors' spirits but by "territorial deities" who claimed to be "*the Authors of their lives*."[172] To appease the illness these entities caused as punishment for being neglected and to "*reduce to obedience*" the afflicted, a "*Nganga of Quilundos*" was called, being responsible for mediating with the spiritual entity and organizing a "feast" with plenty of food "*and thanksgiving*." It was this 'feast' honoring spiritual entities that Juliana metonymically referred to as "*calundúz*." The manuscript also explains that this *nganga* would prescribe to the patients "*their eating regimes, or what not to eat, which they call Quigillas* [*ijila*—prohibitions] *and strictly obey*." Spirits, the manuscript's author concludes, could be told apart by the illnesses they caused. Edema was called "*the Cassuto affliction*" and attributed to *cacuto*, the "*goat with a large beard*." As for an unspecified "*Quiluno affliction*," it was said to be caused by an "*idol*" of the same name and cured by sacrificing "*emcombas* [sic] and chickens" to it.

In the second half of the seventeenth century, Friar Cavazzi had already identified several territorial spirits, classifying "*Haviez* [*Navieza*]," "*Quilondo*," and "*Cas-*

---

institution is beyond the scope of this chapter. Marcussi, Estratégias de mediação simbólica, p. 97–124; Mello e Souza, O diabo e a terra de Santa Cruz; Mott, O calundu-Angola de Luzia Pinta, p. 73–82; Precioso, Catarina Juliana e sua sociedade de culto, p. 68–127; Sweet, Recreating Africa.

168 Kananoja, Healing Knowledge, p. 36.

169 Precioso remarks that the "idols" "*Tulariam Bandê*," "*Alutá*," and the twins "*Quitari Quia Cuvimba*" and "*Pingi*" were also mentioned by some of the accusers but not all. Precioso, Catarina Juliana e sua sociedade de culto, p. 98–99, 107.

170 Sweet attributes the authorship of this manuscript to Bishop Luís Simões de Brandão, doctor in Canon law from the University of Coimbra, and bishop of Congo and Angola between 1702 and 1719. According to Jaime de Gouveia, Bishop Simões de Brandão was often accused of being directly involved in the slave trade. Gouveia, D. Luís Simões Brandão (1702–1719); Lino D'Assumpção, Exploração à Africa, p. 371–374; Sweet, Recreating Africa, p. 254.

171 Lino D'Assumpção, Exploração à Africa, p. 372.

172 Thornton and Linda Heywood remark that in the "Kimbundu speaking area," the "shrines of territorial deities" were associated with specific sites such as "high places, watercourses, and uncultivated areas." Ibid., p. 373; Thornton, Religious and Ceremonial Life, in: Heywood (ed.), Central Africans and Cultural Transformations, p. 76.

suto" as important Mbundu "*idols*" and associating the first with the "*provinces*" of Kissama and Libolo, and the latter with the province of "*the two Ganguelas of the Kingdom of Matamba.*"[173] *Navieza* was also mentioned by Friar Serafino da Cortona in 1656, being referred to together with "*Ganzambumbo*" as the main "*idol*" of the "*King* [*Soba*] *of Maupungo* [Pungo Andongo]."[174] According to Friar Serafino, the other "*idols*" worshipped in the area of Pungo Andongo were "*Muegilla, Muchiua,* [and] *Nabua-uà-imbangi*," to whom "*several trees were consecrated*," and the less-famous "*Badè, Lambria, Caaolo, Cangongo, or Cagnongo, Canguise, Dalabanga, Bunghi, Aqueza,* [and] *Muta-calombo*." According to Friar Cavazzi, the Mbangala paid homage to *Navieza* and his wife "*Cassumba*" by building a "*house*" to the first and a "*side shrine*" to the second, filling them "*with many calabashes*." One of these, "*dedicated to the Idol*," was filled "*with a lot of feathers and hair*." There, they sacrificed "*goats, chickens, and other animals*," performed dances, sang, and feasted for "*eight days straight*" to obtain good health.[175] *Navieza* and *Cassumba*, the Capuchin friar argued, originated from the Ganguelas region, being associated with the bubonic plague.[176] A third 'idol,' "*Ibundo*," was worshiped in Libolo and Friar Cavazzi remarked his *xinguilas* always carried an "*arch, knife, and a small axe*."[177] As for "*Cassuto*," he was worshiped in Matamba together with his wife, "*Inquixì*." Their shrines had a "*very large calabash*" called "*iaco*" that was filled with "*bones, goat casks and tails, chicken feet, and paws of sacrificed dogs mixed with oil and other ingredients*." It was used to cure the illnesses of the afflicted.[178] Regarding the "*twenty idols*" of Pungo Andongo, Friar Serafino explained in a December 9, 1658, report that they were evoked to "*cure diseases, ask for rain, divine future events, obtain good luck in war & similar things*."[179]

The entities worshiped by Juliana and Cunha were different from these mostly benevolent territorial spirits associated with illnesses and healing. According to Friar Cavazzi, "*many* [West Central African] *gods* [were] *believed to be meek, joyful, and merciful*," such as the ones described in the previous paragraphs, while "*others* [were] *believed to be strict, severe, and cruel*."[180] The Mbangala, Friar Cavazzi argued, preferred to worship the latter because they "*were not ashamed to attribute to these*

---

173 Cavazzi, Istorica descrizione de' tre' Regni Congo, Matamba et Angola, p. 232–233.

174 MMA XII, D. 9.

175 Friar Cavazzi also claimed that these "*Jagas*" brought the bodies of their dead to the shrine of *Cassumba* if they were women or to the house of *Navieza* if they were male. Cavazzi, Istorica descrizione de' tre' Regni Congo, Matamba et Angola, p. 232–233.

176 Ibid., p. 240.

177 Ibid., p. 234.

178 Ibid., p. 233–234.

179 MMA XII, D. 78, p. 196.

180 Cavazzi, Istorica descrizione de' tre' Regni Congo, Matamba et Angola Congo, Matamba et Angola, p. 241.

pretend divinities [their] *unchecked passions*." They were "*Muta, Catombo, Equitopope, Cabola, Muengo, and Essuquico*," and "*Quibondo*." The latter was considered the cruelest, a "*homicidal, treacherous, and ruthless*" deity who often caused his *xinguilas* to be devoured by "*wild beasts*." Paradoxically, Friar Cavazzi's claim that the Mbangala worshiped 'idols' or territorial spirits goes directly against the description of their uses and customs by Battel and Purchas and his description of the normative system of the Kingdom of Kasanje. It can be interpreted as further evidence that upon settling, the Mbangala warbands gradually adopted the political institutions of their Mbundu subjects.[181] However, it also suggests that Friar Cavazzi used the abstract opposition between Mbundu and Mbangala normative systems and beliefs as a heuristic device to sort out spirits according to their perceived ethical attributes and supernatural abilities. In that case, his claim that the Mbangala worshiped a given territorial spirit simply reinforces its anti-social nature and opposition to mainstream Mbundu values and norms.

Writing in the last decades of the eighteenth century, Raimundo Cunha Matos (1776–1839), a Portuguese soldier who became the interim Governor of São Tomé and Príncipe between 1817 and 1817, referred to the following entities as "*the main gods*" of the Mbundu: "*Quibuco, Matumba Calumbo, and Lamba Lianquita*." According to him, "*Quibuco*" was the "*god of wealth*," "*Mutacalumbo the* [god] *of hunting*," and "*Lamba Lianquita que god of thunder, and therefore,* [...] *of all the most feared*."[182] Instead of highlighting the anti-social demeanor of these spirits by associating them with the Mbangala, Cunha Matos pointed to their association with profit and violence, opening the possibility that their increasing popularity was associated not with the spread of Mbangala beliefs and practices but with the disruptive impact of the Atlantic slave trade. In other words, the higher incidence of their afflictions and subsequent *calúndus* was another facet of the normative disruption the inhumane traffic caused.[183]

---

181 Miller defends this thesis, arguing, for instance, that "*muta a kilombo*" was a political title originally from Libolo given to an officer "entrusted" by the king of Libolo "with control of certain supernatural powers." In keeping with this hypothesis, the title became a territorial spirit as the Mbangala gradually adopted local institutions after settling in Kasanje. Contrariwise, in *Folk Tales of Angola* (1894), Héli Chatelain considered "*Muta Kalombo*" one of the three original "*genni, or demons*" of Mbundu mythology, being the "*king or governor*" of the forest and in control of "*the chase and of the paths*." The other "*genni*" were the "*Kituta or Kianda*," who ruled over water and were "*fond of great trees and hilltops*," and the "*Lemba*," to whom pertained "*the mysterious province of generation*." While Chatelain's folklorist reinterpretation of his sources reads as dated, it suggests that a Mbundu 'version' of *Muta Kalombo* evolved parallel with the Mbangala one, regardless of their origins. See the next paragraphs for Vansina's take on "*Muta Kalombo*." CHATELAIN, Folk-Tales of Angola, Vol. 1, p. 11; MILLER, Kings and Kinsmen, p. 94, 101, 253–255.

182 CUNHA MATOS, Compêndio histórico, p. 337.

183 SEABRA DA SILVA, Carta de José de Seabra da Silva, p. 175.

In 1750, João Pedro Macollo was also delivered to the Holy Office jail in Lisbon.[184] His case can help us understand how Cunha's practices clashed with Mbangala and other Mbundu customs. It also enables us to explore the idea that they showed the influence of the Atlantic slave trade on spiritual beliefs and related norms. Macollo was accused of idolatry and sorcery, eventually dying in the aftermath of the Lisbon Earthquake (1755) before he could hear his verdict.[185] According to his accusers, he was one of the *xinguilas* of Cunha's entourage,[186] being suspected of worshiping several Mbundu "*idols*," including those of "*Macongo*," "*Muta Calombo*," and "*Vunji*."[187] As Vansina explains, *Muta Kalombo* and similar spiritual entities were not communitarian "ancestor spirits" but "personal spirits" associated with "hunting, warfare and fire," who were mainly "venerated" by the entrepreneurial *empacasseiros* who manned the garrisons of inland *presídios* such as Ambaca.[188] The spread of the worship of anti-social spirits amongst *empacasseiros*, Vansina argues, was a consequence of the societal disruption and anomie caused by the expansion of the transatlantic slave trade.[189]

To understand the social impact such a development had, it must be considered that *empacasseiros* were originally large game hunters whom Miller associates with Mbundu *kibinda* [pl. *yibinda*].[190] *Yibinda* were "master hunters" with a "Mbundu initiated status."[191] According to Miller, this entailed the "possession of supernatural powers" obtained "through the manipulation of carved figures, animal horns, or plants." These substances allowed *yibinda* to "deal with large wild animals."[192] As such, these master hunters were a crucial element of the community, protecting it from dangerous beasts, mediating between the "visible world of the living and the invisible world of the supernatural," and obtaining the wild game and "certain animals believed necessary to divine the intentions of lineage spirits."[193] If we accept

184 ANTT, TSO, IL, Sr. 28, D. 10120; Kananoja, Healing Knowledge, p. 36–37.

185 ANTT, TSO, IL, Sr. 28, D. 10120.

186 Kananoja analyses the inquisitorial processes of two other Africans accused of participating in Cunha's possession ritual, Filipe Dias Chaves and Dala á Tango, noting that the former also possessed several elements of material culture he associated with *Muta Kalombo* and the later objects he associated with *Muta* [*Kalombo*?] or with no particular spirits. Kananoja, Healing Knowledge, p. 37–38.

187 ANTT, TSO, IL, Sr. 28, D. 10120; Kananoja, Healers, Idolaters, and Good Christians, p. 453; Kananoja, Healing Knowledge, p. 36–37.

188 Couto, Os capitães-mores em Angola, p. 256–261; Vansina, Ambaca Society and the Slave Trade, p. 1–27.

189 Vansina, Ambaca Society and the Slave Trade, p. 1–27.

190 Miller, Kings and Kinsmen, p. 300–302.

191 Ibid., p. 52–53.

192 Ibid., p. 52–53, 160.

193 Ibid., p. 51–53.

that the Portuguese recruited the *empacasseiros* from the ranks of Mbundu *yibinda*, the former's abandonment of the traditional *yibinda*'s ethos in favor of the worship of new anti-social spirits and their full embrace of the opportunities presented by the Atlantic slave trade must have been perceived as severe threats by the Mbundu heads of corporate kin groups and *sobas*. Acting according to their self-interest and the cruel dictates of the slave trade, there would be little difference between these upsetting *empacasseiros* and the *jagas* of old, making it difficult to distinguish between the *wasps and the bees*.

Considering the existence of different groups of 'territorial' spirits and these new, 'personal' ones, deeply entangled with the Atlantic slave trade, allows us to return to Lieutenant Queiroga's and Sergeant Major Silva's case with fresh eyes. His wife and daughters' distrust of Lieutenant Queiroga's disturbing practices and charms can thus be reframed as the reaction of ordinary Mbundu commoners to the new spiritual techniques brought into their midst by the entrepreneurial *empacasseiros* and soldiers who manned the garrison of Massangano. The possibility of contrasting sets of spirits possessing or being worshiped by the same kind of ritual specialists, either *yibinda* or *xinguilas*, confronted Mbundu, Portuguese, and Luso African observers with the same problem the Jesuits once faced when they first encountered *yimbanda*. Namely, it made it impossible to determine if the entities they interacted with were pro-social or anti-social, opening the possibility of living, working, or consorting with a dangerously ambitious individual, if not with a sorcerer. In conclusion, the physical proximity and intimacy with individuals who occupied offices until recently considered the ethical and moral pillars of Mbundu communities had become problematic, as personal ambitions and jealousies incentivized by the Atlantic slave trade led everyone to question and mistrust their true intentions.

The same could be said of the Portuguese and Luso-African who occupied 'in-between' offices, from captain majors to the bailiffs, chaplains, and scribes who assisted them. As the cases detailed in this chapter highlight, captain majors could explore their ability to appoint bailiffs and recruit *empacasseiros* to unofficially recognize and adopt anti-social institutions and practices that furthered their economic interests. In their households, they could even become adept at Mbangala possession rituals and ceremonies or sponsor *xinguilas* and *mbulungo* ordeals, attempting to unofficially institute these practices as the 'practical norms' of their jurisdictions. The following chapters delve into how the Portuguese authorities, Luso-African *moradores*, and Mbundu subjects dealt with the generalized crisis of trust this caused.

8. West Central African Grammars of Affect

8.1 Conflicting Understandings of Love and Charity

Elias Alexandre da Silva Corrêa argues in *History of Angola* (c. 1787–1799) that Portuguese "*magistrates*" in West Central Africa were responsible not only for "*safekeeping the Conquest*" and ensuring that the Crown's vassals "*prospered*" but also for "*introducing the Law of Jesus Christ and perpetuating the examples of excellent piety, and fatherly love*" offered by the "*Loving Sovereigns*" of the Portuguese Kingdom.[1] With a tint of irony, he described these "*magistrates*" as "*Demigods of the Republic,*" in whom "*science and justice compose a perfect bouquet of virtues, topped by the crown of love and respect.*"[2] As discussed in the first chapter, Silva Corrêa then proceeds to portray the Captaincy of Angola, Benguela, and their dependencies as horrible places entirely destitute of grace and even beyond the pale of Natural law, blaming this paradoxical situation on the climate and the corrupting influence of the Atlantic slave trade. However bleak his assessment of the state of the administration of justice (*jurisdictio*) may be, it still confirms that 'love' and 'charity' remained central to the "jurisdictional culture" of the Portuguese even during the modernizing reforms of the second half of the eighteenth century that introduced the new commissarial boards in the 1760s (the Boards of Justice, Commerce, and Finance) and several new police regulations in West Central Africa.[3] Silva Corrêa was a privileged eyewitness of their impact, dedicating a chapter of his *History of Angola* to display his takes on "*Policing.*"[4] In it, he identifies the social relationships that the new "juridical grammar and technology" was supposed to "organize, arrange, and rearrange"—to use Tamar Herzog's terms.[5] This chapter argues that the captain-general and governors of Angola attempted to reshape these relationships by intervening in how major lifecycle events (e. g., births, initiations, marriages, funerals) were celebrated and the lived environments of Luanda were occupied and experienced by African, Luso-African, and Portuguese subjects.

---

1 Silva Corrêa, História de Angola, Vol. 1, p. 179.

2 Ibid., p. 77.

3 Cardim, O poder dos afectos; Duve, How is Law Produced? in: Duve and Herzog (eds.), Latin America Law in Global Perspective, p. 57; Herzog, What is Legal History, in: Duve and Herzog (eds.), Latin America Law in Global Perspective, p. 47; Hespanha, A cultura jurídica europeia, p. 150–152.

4 Silva Corrêa, História de Angola, Vol. 1, p. 77–84.

5 Herzog, What is Legal History, in: Duve and Herzog (eds.), Latin America Law in Global Perspective, p. 46.

In Silva Corrêa's view, such a reorganization did not necessarily involve the subordination of love and charity to different virtues or values but instead surveying social fields where African understandings of these virtues persisted or the Atlantic slave trade had corrupted Christian values beyond recognition. This could be then followed by uprooting the former and amending the latter. If, as António Hespanha argues, past juridical "texts referring to love are predicated on (and construct and disseminate) a different grammar of feelings" from the ones of the present, then it is safe to say that Silva Corrêa's *History of Angola* describes not one, but two distinct grammars of love and affect, one of Portuguese and one of Mbundu or Luso-African conception, dramatizing their many conflicts and surprising concurrences.[6] Adopting this perspective allows us to view the introduction of police regulations in Angola in a different light, considering the period under analysis more according to its terms, not projecting into the past later concepts such as "civilizing mission" or racialized understandings of social relations in Angola.[7] In other words, to conceive of enlightened reforms in West Central Africa not only as rationalizing and bureaucratizing efforts but also as attempts to impose a Portuguese grammar of affects and feelings.[8]

This perspective also allows us to frame the introduction of police regulations in the Captaincy of Angola not as a purely ideologically driven project but as an attempt to overcome the anti-social threats posed by the generalized lack of 'trust' described in the previous chapter. It recognizes the Mbundu and other Africans as the prime movers and their creative normative solutions to the anomie caused by the Atlantic slave trade and the problems raised by the 'dark side' of kinship and intimacy as the status quo ante the Portuguese police regulations were forced to react against and, at best, amend.[9] In other words, agreeing with Alfredo Margarido,

---

6 Hespanha, A cultura jurídica europeia, p. 65.

7 See Cristina Nogueira da Silva and Miguel Jerónimo Bandeira on the adoption of the trope of the "civilizing mission" in the Portuguese Empire. On the use of "civilization" to describe the demilitarization of the administration of justice in Angola during the nineteenth century, see João Figueiredo. See Arlindo Barbeitos for an introduction to the history of racism and race relations in Angola. Bandeira Jerónimo, The 'Civilising Mission' of Portuguese Colonialism; Barbeitos, A "raça" e o racismo, p. 13–50; Barbeitos, A "raça" ou a ilusão de uma identidade definitiva, in: Gonçalves (ed.), O racismo ontem e hoje, p. 139–148; Barbeitos, Angola/Portugal; Figueiredo, A Questão das "Ouvidas," p. 81–104; Nogueira da Silva, "Missão civilizacional" e codificação de "usos e costumes," p. 899–921; Nogueira da Silva, A dimensão imperial do espaço jurídico português, p. 187–207.

8 See Tyrone S. Palmer on contemporary Black grammars of affect. Palmer, "What Feels More Than Feeling?" p. 31–56; Palmer, Affect and Affirmation, in: Seigworth and Pedwell (eds.), The Affect Theory Reader, Vol. 2, p. 122–140; Palmer, Otherwise than Blackness, p. 246–283.

9 For instance, Portuguese police regulations addressed some of the social issues that African 'cults' or 'secret societies,' such as the *Lemba* drum of affliction, already addressed. Such an understanding avoids framing African institutions as forms of "resistance" against Portuguese police regulations

this hypothesis acknowledges that African affects, rather than Portuguese ones, textured the daily lives and structured the domestic spheres of Portuguese and Luso-African *moradores* and sojourners, influencing their uses and customs and resulting in a clash of worldviews and grammars of affect that is brilliantly captured in the pages of Silva Corrêa's *History of Angola*.[10] This chapter begins by unpacking his lively descriptions of daily life in Luanda. It then explores how the captain-general and governors of Angola attempted to reform the behaviors of their subjects by policing how lifecycle events were celebrated. It also pays attention to other "liminal" and "liminoid" phases and events, when norms and hierarchies were temporarily dissolved or reversed before being reconfirmed, and new institutions and practices could more easily be imposed.[11]

As Victor Turner explains, Arnold van Gennep was the first to use the concepts of "*limen*" and "liminal phase" to investigate life-cycle events.[12] He was particularly interested in analyzing "rites of passage," the celebrations that mark an individual's or a cohort of individuals' transition from one social or legal status to another, or significant seasonal changes in agrarian societies.[13] He described the former as "life crises" and the latter as communitarian ones, proposing that the rituals associated with them had a tripartite structure including "separation," "transition," and "incorporation" phases. It is the "transition" phase that van Gennep and Turner define as "liminal" and marked by "symbols of reversal or inversion of secular things, relationships, and processes." According to Turner, liminal periods are a "free and experimental region of culture, a region where not only new elements but also new combinatory rules may be introduced."[14] While Turner focuses on how innovations are introduced by 'autochthonous' agents during liminal periods, this chapter argues that they also presented external Portuguese reformers with opportunities due to the uncertain status and openness to meaningful change of those undergoing them. Turner also proposes distinguishing between "liminal" phases and "liminoid." As he explains, "liminoid" rites of passage occur in secularized societies and are often

---

when they were, in fact, anterior and alternative to these. See Herzog on the dangers of projecting "resistance" where it is not to be found. HERZOG, What is Legal History, in: DUVE and HERZOG (eds.), Latin America Law in Global Perspective, p. 54; JANZEN, Lemba, 1650–1930; SHAW, Memories of the Slave Trade.

10 MARGARIDO, Algumas formas da hegemonia africana in: SANTOS (ed.), I Reunião internacional de História de África, p. 383–406.

11 ABRAHAMS, Foreword, in: TURNER (ed.), Ritual Process, p. v–xii; TURNER, Liminal to Liminoid, p. 53–92.

12 TURNER, Liminal to Liminoid, p. 56–57, 61; TURNER, The Ritual Process, p. 94–95; VAN GENNEP, The Rites of Passage.

13 TURNER, Liminal to Liminoid, p. 56–57; VAN GENNEP, The Rites of Passage.

14 TURNER, The Ritual Process, p. 56.

optional and with less personal or cosmological impact.[15] This chapter considers ritualized interactions such as paying tithes, taxes, and tributes and taking part in arbitrations and judicial ordeals tendentially "liminoid" because of their optional nature in keeping with the framework proposed by Turner (e. g., taxes might be mandatory, but tax evasion has no cosmological impact and often little personal one).[16]

Silva Corrêa's chapter on policing starts by criticizing the housing in Luanda, which he described as entirely composed of "*cadaverous buildings*" or "*humble, dark, and sordid*" straw huts of "*sad architecture*" and as windowless as "*prisons*."[17] He then considered the open-air dumpsters that dotted the streets and the backyard compounds where slaves were kept "*submerged in filth and mixed with those suffering from serious illnesses*."[18] Criticizing the inability of magistrates to impose stricter public hygiene rules, he noted how this failure led to a higher incidence of preventable diseases. Silva Corrêa then criticized the "*quitandas* [open-air markets]," the practices of "*quitandeiras* [female street vendors]," and the habit *moradores* had of letting their pigs and dogs live freely in the streets.[19] Finally, he turned his atten-

---

15 Contrariwise, according to Turner's model, "liminal" rites of passage and celebrations take place in societies where, for cosmological reasons, the continuity of the group or the survival of the individual is understood to be predicated on moments of ritual separation, transition, and incorporation. Both modalities must be understood as ideal types that define the extreme limits of the spectrum of concrete rites of passage. ABRAHAMS, Foreword, in: TURNER (ed.), Ritual Process, p. xi; TURNER, Liminal to Liminoid, p. 53–92.

16 Roman Catholic festivals such as All Hallows Eve, All Saints Day, and Saint James Day can also be described as liminoid. John Thornton remarks that these were important celebrations in West Central Africa, especially in the Kingdom of Kongo, where BaKongo beliefs and normativities profoundly impacted them. The same can be said of annual celebrations of local lay brotherhoods such as the *Nossa Senhora do Rosário dos Homens Pretos* (1628) and the processions of Corpus Christi and other public rituals associated with chapels' patrons in Luanda and the hinterlands of Angola. However, their study is beyond the scope of this chapter. CADORNEGA, História geral das guerras angolanas, Vol. 3, p. 21–22, 118–122; FONSECA, Religião e liberdade; THORNTON, Religious and Ceremonial Life, in: HEYWOOD (ed.), Central Africans and Cultural Transformations, p. 71–90.

17 On Captain-General and Governor Francisco Inocêncio de Sousa Coutinho's urbanist reforms (1764–1772) and later attempts to intervene in the built environment of Luanda, see António Tomás, Ralph Delgado, Roquinaldo Ferreira, and Susana Ferraz. DELGADO, O Governo de Sousa Coutinho em Angola I, p. 19–56; DELGADO, O Governo de Sousa Coutinho em Angola III, p. 7–48; FERRAZ, Espaço público de Luanda; FERREIRA, Slavery and the Social and Cultural Landscapes of Luanda, in: CAÑIZARES-ESGUERRA et al. (eds.), The Black Urban Atlantic, p. 185–206; SILVA CORRÊA, História de Angola, Vol. 1, p. 78–80; TOMÁS, In the Skin of the City, p. 32–42.

18 SILVA CORRÊA, História de Angola, Vol. 1, p. 78–83.

19 For a detailed account of Luanda's urban *quitandas* and the activities of *quitandeiras*, see Arlindo Caldeira, José Venâncio, and Vanessa Oliveira. See Ferreira for the municipal council's failed attempts to regulate *quitandas* in the 1770s. CALDEIRA, Luanda in the 17th Century, p. 72–104; FERREIRA, Slavery and the Social and Cultural Landscapes of Luanda, in: CAÑIZARES-ESGUERRA

tion to how the Portuguese, Luso-African, and Mbundu celebrated their life-cycle events, from "*Engagements, to Entambes, or funerals*," also describing how wealthy "*Ladies*" celebrated major Roman Catholic feasts, such as weddings and baptisms, in a decadent and luxurious manner.[20] Silva Corrêa concluded by commenting on how women dressed, what makeup they used to paint their faces, and what clothes male "*blacks*" and "*whites, fuscos, and civilized molatos* [sic]" used, noting that all communicated through African languages, the men "*speaking Portuguese, and flirting in Kimbundu*."[21]

From this description, it becomes clear that social and intimate relations that Silva Corrêa believed should be guided by a Roman Catholic understanding of charity[22] and a Neo-Scholastic grammar of love[23] were governed by Mbundu affects expressed in local idioms and through African or Luso-African practices. Of all forms of love, "*profane love*" captures most of Silva Corrêa's attention.[24] As he

---

et al. (eds.), The Black Urban Atlantic, p. 192–193; Oliveira, African Women and Commerce in the Atlantic World; Oliveira, Slave Trade and Abolition, p. 40–55; Venâncio, A economia de Luanda.

20 Silva Corrêa, História de Angola, Vol. 1, p. 82–84.

21 See Ferreira and Linda Heywood on the generalized adoption of Kimbundu as a *lingua franca* during the eighteenth century. The following chapter briefly exposes Sousa Coutinho's attempts to impose Portuguese as a *lingua franca*. Heywood, Portuguese into African, in: Heywood (ed.), Central Africans and Cultural Transformations, p. 103–105; Ferreira, Slavery and the Social and Cultural Landscapes of Luanda, in: Cañizares-Esguerra et al. (eds.), The Black Urban Atlantic, p. 185–206.

22 As discussed in the second chapter, in keeping with medieval Christian theology, there were seven "corporal works of mercy:" feeding the hungry, giving water to the thirsty, clothing the naked, sheltering the homeless, visiting the sick, visiting the imprisoned and ransoming the captive, and burying the dead. These provided a blueprint for the action of all officeholders with jurisdiction, from municipal judges to captain majors or the *provedores* of the *Santa Casa*. Therefore, during this period, the policing of Luanda's housing, hygienic measures destined to prevent epidemics, and regulating how slaves were kept and how free persons dressed were understood first and foremost as charitable acts. Guimarães Sá and Rodrigues, Introduction, in: Guimarães Sá and Rodrigues (eds.), The Confraternities of Misericórdia, p. 11.

23 As Hespanha explains, following St. Thomas Aquinas' *Summa Theologica*, Portuguese jurists and canonists understood "*amor* [love]" to be expressed through a variety of human affects, including "familial love, which arises from […] within the natural family," "filial or parental love, based on birth," "love by contrition, promoted by a common childhood and upbringing," "love by affinity, based on common undertakings," "love by vassalage, which arises from the institutions of government of the republic," "love by co-citizenship, which exists between the patricians of the same republic," "love by comradeship, which is woven between comrades in arms." All these created binding obligations, and a hierarchy between different "forms of love" could be established, with "love towards God, and through him, to all of their creatures" at the top of the list. Hespanha, A cultura jurídica europeia, p. 150–151.

24 Silva Corrêa, História de Angola, Vol. 1, p. 92.

described it, in Luanda, the "*fire of sensuousness, stoked by the fiery environment, devoured human nature,*" and the "*heads of families welcomed the growth of their wealth through the children of their slave women.*" In his opinion, it was privileging "*profane love*" over other forms of love that led "*Single men, free from the Vows of marriage, to dedicate their homesteads to slave women,*" mothers to "*forfeit their children,*" and fathers to "*shamelessly*" adopt the children of other men. At the center of these unruly displays of affection stood an "*Idol that attract*[ed] *the general esteem of the people*:" kola nuts.[25] According to Silva Corrêa, kola nuts were not only consumed and forced on slaves as an important stimulant,[26] being a "*gift as generalized as tobacco, because they are offered in all occasions, and eaten,*" but also substituted "*tea, being shared by all persons gathered in an assembly, or during a match.*"[27] Moreover, as Arlindo Caldeira remarks, their aphrodisiac properties were also esteemed by Europeans and Africans alike.[28]

According to Silva Corrêa, the generalized use and exchange of kola nuts "*oblige*[d] *oneself to buy them for these offerings, the custom being respected by all, from those of the lowest classes to those of the most qualified ones.*"[29] Kola nuts, he continued, mediated all affective and social relationships, "*being given from hand to hand during meetings, either arranged, or fortuitous ones, signifying nothing more than friendship, or social recognition,*" according to the size of the gift. Moreover, kola nuts provided "*the Alphabet used to express the passions of love,*" as "*love correspondence was not easy to maintain through writing in Angola*" and it took

---

25 Ibid., p. 140–141.

26 Silva Corrêa remarked that those born and raised in West Central Africa said that "*the juice*" of kola nuts helped "*to nourish; because when they eat a leg of kola in the morning, they forget to have lunch.*" A "*leg of kola*" is a row of several nuts. A kola fruit consists of several 'legs,' and each nut has three to four segments. In a letter from 1575, Father Garcia Simões had already remarked that the Mbundu would "*claim they maintain themselves a whole day with one kola.*" On Kola nuts being fed to slaves forced to march, see Joseph Miller. Miller, Way of Death, p. 383; MMA III, D. 21, p. 133; Silva Corrêa, História de Angola, Vol. 1, p. 141.

27 Silva Corrêa, História de Angola, Vol. 1, p. 141.

28 Caldeira, Luanda in the 17th Century, p. 93.

29 The cultural significance of kola nuts in Angola is evident in António de Oliveira Cadornega's remark in 1681 that "*collas* [kola nuts], *which are very tasty, being by nature bitter, are eaten by all the Portuguese from Angola; and some are particularly fond of them, especially the women, daughters of this land, that* [prefer them] *to the best morsels of good sweets.*" The generalized consumption of kola nuts was also noted by the medical doctor José Pinto de Azeredo (1763–1807) during the same period as Silva Corrêa, who described kola nuts as a "*solid and bitter fruit, which all inhabitants permanently use, chewing it whenever they want to drink water.*" According to Azeredo, "*its use had become a luxury, and in all gatherings, they offer pieces they call legs, with the same pageantry we offer snuff.*" Azeredo, Ensaios sobre algumas enfermidades d'Angola, p. 46; Cadornega, História geral das guerras angolanas, Vol. 3, p. 201–202; Silva Corrêa, História de Angola, Vol. 1, p. 140–141.

time for the newly arrived to become fluent, let alone gallant, in Kimbundu.[30] Silva Corrêa explained that kola nuts were "*a treat that lightens the spirit of those who receive it*," uniting and bounding "*in friendship those who exchange it reciprocally*." If a kola fruit was sent whole to somebody, it signified "*affection, friendship, or the beginning of a legitimate affair*," if sent with one leg missing, it "*signified a new love*" seeking recognition; if sent with a bit "*bitten off and sent on its side*," it solicited an illegitimate carnal affair. The addressees could then either return a "*kola leg with a missing bit*" to propose a meeting, a kola fruit "*with a bite*" but without separating the bitten bit off, as a "*signal of the most steadfast desire of a strong and deep-rooted love*," a kola fruit "*with several bits separated*" as a signal of "*longing*," an intact kola fruit, as a sign of unrequited love, or fail to return the gift as a sign of "*despise*." This "*A, B, C was intelligible and accessible to muster by all nations*," Silva Corrêa concluded, and no "*European, American, or Asian man would ever consider not getting used to eating kola*" if they intended "*to become lovers*."

In sum, kola nuts signaled affection and functioned as a powerful antidote to the lack of trust and social anomie described in the previous chapter. It prevented sorcery rumors and accusations by cementing Mbundu, Luso-African, and Portuguese relationships. Being adopted at the practical level, its ritualized consumption was barely recognized at the official one. Moreover, much like God's love and the love of the Portuguese monarch were supposed to ground the administration of justice (*jurisdictio*), distributing kola nuts and the ambiance of benevolence and goodwill created by this act were a prerequisite for any public gathering where disputes were arbitrated and settled according to African norms. Finally, there is evidence that African rulers expressed their bonds with their subjects through the ritual use of kola nuts. Writing a letter to the Jesuit Provincial on October 20, 1575, Father Garcia Simões had already noted that kola was "*a fruit used by whites and blacks*," the latter "*always bringing it in their mouths*" and using its juice to "*draw certain patterns on their chests and arms*."[31] Kola nuts had to be used to invite the Mbundu to any gathering or "*feast*," he continued, and of all victuals, they were the ones that could never "*go missing in any household*." Finally, Father Simões claimed that the *ngola* of the Kingdom of Ndongo used to "*make circles on the body of* [his subjects] *with kola juice*." When they failed to perform their duties, he would "*erase some of those circles*," a form of symbolic chastisement that was promptly understood by all and that forced the rebuked subjects to protest their loyalty. In conclusion, as Silva Corrêa makes clear, aligning Mbundu or other African normative systems with Portuguese grammars of love implied first surveying and then substituting all these different usages of kola nuts. Such an ambitious reform project, however, could

---

30 Silva Corrêa, História de Angola, Vol. 1, p. 142–143.

31 MMA III, D. 21, p. 133.

only start there. Silva Corrêa pointed out that, besides courtship, several life cycle celebrations and political rituals followed Mbundu norms and grammars of affect. Moreover, he argued that the "*vast majority of whites* [...] *following their inclination towards an idle and licentious life*" loved "*gentilic rites that* [were] *in keeping with the objects of their desires*."[32]

Silva Corrêa then turned his attention to the Luso-African uses and customs he understood to "*hurt Christian charity*" in a chapter dedicated to "*Religion*," or love towards God; from the initiation rituals that prepared nubile women for Mbundu weddings, which he describes as the "*auctioning*" and "*purchase*" of "*feminine virginity*," to "*Entâmes* [funerals]" and "*Chinguilamentos* [possession rituals], *or feitiçarias,*" that were "*mixed with the most devout, and serious, acts of Christianity*."[33] These rituals, according to him, were performed by "*Gangas* [*banganga*]" and tolerated by "*Parish priests*," "*dilacerating the body of the Church*." According to Silva Corrêa, Bishop Alexandre da Sagrada Família, who was entrusted with the vicariate government of the Diocese of Congo and Angola on February 15, 1784, while bishop of Malaca, had posed the only substantial opposition to this situation.[34] However, in Silva Corrêa's opinion, the most severe threats to "*Christian Charity*" came not from Mbundu beliefs and practices but from the Atlantic slave trade.[35] According to him, "*the commerce of slaves* [was] *too precious for its foundation to be ruined with the Holy doctrine of the Apostles*," so effective evangelization was put on hold where it was "*incompatible with* [Mbundu] *Laws, and gentilic customs*." In other words, according to Silva Corrêa, the "*flowing of slaves would cease if this important kernel of Christianity was established amongst the blacks: Charity*." Therefore, "*State*" interests related to the slave trade, and opposed to a Christian understanding of charity, dictated that enslaved Africans destined for Brazil were summarily catechized before baptism and that "*the Captain majors from Presídios*" were allowed to arbitrate "*Mocanos*."[36] This meant, Silva Corrêa explained, that captain majors "*sentenced*" Mbundu "*oral Disputes*" in a form that granted "*their subjects the freedom of exerting their customs*; *despite these being predicated on inhumanity, avarice, and vain caprices of superiority*."[37] Because "*the sale of captives*" was the "*object of most convenience*," he argued that "*Loss of Freedom*

32 Silva Corrêa, História de Angola, Vol. 1, p. 87.

33 Ibid., p. 88–90.

34 Bishop Alexandre da Sagrada Família, *née* Alexandre José da Silva Garrett, had been asked to direct the vacant see of Congo and Angola until a fit replacement was found. He would never occupy his post as bishop of Malaca, resigning from this position due to this feud with José de Almeida e Vasconcelos. Torres, Memorias, p. 273–294.

35 Silva Corrêa, História de Angola, Vol. 1, p. 93.

36 Ibid., p. 93–94, 98.

37 Ibid., p. 93–98.

[was] *the penalty for the most insignificant misdeeds*," even noncriminal ones, all being "*arbitrated according to the fantasy of barbarous* [Mbundu] *Legislators*." Greed, Silva Corrêa concluded, also led Christian "*Lords of Arimos*" to treat their slaves as a "*foreign republic*" allowing them to profess "*paganism without remorse*," tax farmers to force unbaptized Africans to "*pay one-tenth of their harvest to a God, who they don't know*," and Brazilian shipowners to allow the "*lack of Charity*" to "*reign in their* [slave] *yards*" and aboard their slave ships.

In conclusion, Silva Corrêa's *History of Angola* provides an overview of the social fields, liminal periods, and life cycle celebrations that were regulated by conflicting grammars of love and charity, identifying two limits to the reforms introduced by the enlightened captain-general and governors of Angola. First, pre-existing Mbundu institutions and norms regulated the relationship between the intimate spheres of West Central African households and corporations and the public sphere, where marriages, funerals, and other important events were celebrated. Second, the institutions of slavery predicated on the doctrine of ransom and the othering and segregation of African normative systems. Regarding the latter, Silva Corrêa promptly noted that the traffic of slaves depended on "*Paganism being kept in all its purity*" in the Angolan hinterlands, opposing the enlightened reforms to the conversion efforts of the past centuries—a topic further discussed in the next section.[38] The following pages explore in more detail specific regulations and reforms, noting how these two limits conditioned them and how they entailed the non-recognition, recognition, adoption, or rejection of Mbundu and Luso-African uses and customs at the official and practical levels—beginning with birth and early childhood rites, proceeding with weddings and funerals, and concluding by exploring the ritualized payment of tributes and taxes.

8.2 Eating the 'Salt of God' and Shipload Baptisms

The first book-length catechism written in Kimbundu was edited by the Italian Jesuit Francisco Pacconio (1589–1641) in the 1620s and published posthumously as *Gentio de Angola sufficientemente instrudo nos mysterios de nossa sancta fé* [Gentile from Angola sufficiently instructed in the mysteries of our holy faith] (1642).[39]

---

38 Ibid., p. 93.

39 As Festo Mkenda notes, Father Pacconio's catechism had four editions in total. The second one was published in Rome, titled *Gentilis Angollae fidei mysteriis Lusitano olim idiomate…* (1661), and had an additional Latin column added by Capuchin Friar Antonio da Monteprandone. The third and fourth ones were published in Lisbon. The third was a reprint of the second, ordered by Queen Maria I (1784). The fourth was a version of the first, commissioned by Francisco de Salles Ferreira, titled *Explicações de doutrina christã em Portuguez e Angolense, para uso das missões do*

As noted by John Thornton, Father Pacconio's catechism was likely circulated as a manuscript for several years before being printed.[40] It was based on his extensive missionary experience in the *presídios* of Cambambe and Massangano and the "linguistic work" of his predecessors who had been active in the Jesuit Mission of the Kingdom of Kongo.[41] These Jesuits were familiar with the BaKongo religious system, seeking to address the theological issues that they believed undermined the version of Christianity that emerged from D. João I of Kongo's voluntary conversion in the late fifteenth century.[42] As explored in the fourth chapter, this event resulted in the opening of what Cecile Fromont describes as a "space of correlation," enabling the commensuration of Portuguese and BaKongo cosmologies, facilitating conversion, and giving rise to new religious practices and doctrinal innovations.[43]

Father Pacconio's catechism aimed to create a similar 'cross-cultural' discursive space in the conquered areas of the Kingdom of Ndongo. Organized as a series of dialogues meant to guide European missionaries through converting Kimbundu speakers, it exposes the basic tenets of the Christian faith and Roman Catholic dogmas in Kimbundu, pointing out common misconceptions stemming from a BaKongo understanding of Christian sacraments and doctrine. Therefore, its formulaic answers to objections and frequently asked questions assume an underlying continuity exists between BaKongo and Mbundu normative systems and beliefs, failing to register significant differences between the Kingdoms of Kongo and Ndongo institutional cultures.[44] The eighth dialogue, in which the "*seven sacraments are declared*," opens with a discussion of baptism, which Father Pacconio claims the Mbundu called, following the BaKongo, "*curià mongoa üa Nzambi* [eating the salt of God]."[45] Describing it as the "*first sacrament*" and as necessary "*to enter the*

---

interior de Angola [Explanations of Christian doctrine in Portuguese and Angolan, for use in the missions of the interior of Angola] (1885). Mkenda, Jesuits in Africa, p. 64, 66; Pacconio, Gentio de Angola.

40 Thornton, Conquest and Theology, p. 252.

41 Previously, a *Cartilha da doutrina christã em lingoa do Congo* [A primer of Christian doctrine in the language of Kongo] had been composed by the Jesuits in 1556, building on the notes of Father Cornélio Gomes, *née* Diogo Gomes (the *Mwene Kongo* had sent Gomes as ambassador to Lisbon before being ordained). Moreover, as Thornton remarks, Father Pacconio's catechism was prepared for publication by Father António do Couto, a Jesuit "born and raised in Kongo." Ibid., p. 248, 252; Mkenda, Jesuits in Africa, p. 64–65.

42 Mkenda, Jesuits in Africa, p. 64–65; Thornton, Afro-Christian Syncretism, p. 53–77; Thornton, Conquest and Theology, p. 252; Thornton, Religious and Ceremonial Life, in: Heywood (ed.), Central Africans and Cultural Transformations, p. 71–90; Thornton, The Kingdom of Kongo and the Counter Reformation, p. 40–58.

43 Fromont, The Art of Conversion; Fromont, Under the sign of the cross, p. 109–123.

44 Thornton, Religious and Ceremonial Life, in: Heywood (ed.), Central Africans and Cultural Transformations, p. 71–90.

45 Pacconio, Gentio de Angola, p. 33–34.

Catholic Church," it explains that only priests were allowed to baptize, except in cases of imminent death, when any Christian could perform the sacrament on adults or children, in the first case after repentance of past sins. If baptism was performed during this risky liminal period, Father Pacconio concluded, "*it was not necessary to toss salt in the mouth*" of the baptized, declaring that water alone was essential to perform the sacrament and that the BaKongo and Mbundu "*were wrong in calling baptism, eating the salt of God*."[46]

While it is unclear when and why the rite of feeding a few grains of salt to neophytes became central to how West Central Africans conceived of the sacrament of baptism,[47] Carlos Cardoso and James Sweet connect the custom to the conversion of Kongo, Sweet remarking that of all the "misrepresentations that plagued the relationship between Europe and Central Africans," this one was "the most significant."[48] In the Kingdom of Kongo, according to a letter written by Father Cristóvão Ribeiro on July 31, 1548, and a coeval document titled "*The Mission of the Jesuit in the Congo*" (1548), the missionaries had the habit of "*baptizing adults and children without any instruction*," resulting in the converts, when inquired about their new faith, having nothing to say except that they "*had eaten some salt*."[49] Regarding slaves about to be shipped to the Americas, by 1618, this practice had become so widespread that the Board of Royal Conscience and Military Orders issued a consultation on the subject to the *Desembargo do Paço*, insisting that "*overseas prelates*" were supposed to ensure that the "*baptisms of adult blacks*" were "*truthful*" and abided by what the *Philippine Ordinances* (1603) stipulated on this important

46 Ibid., p. 38–39.

47 As Matthieu Pignot notes, "giving salt to catechumens at their admission" was an essential rite of incorporation in the Late Antique African Church. While he admits that "the origins of the rite are obscure" and is unsure whether it was "a specific African rite," Pignot notes that mentions of this salt sacrament abound in Augustinian writings, resurfacing in early medieval sources. In the seventh volume of *De Baptismo Contra Donatistas* (c. 400), St. Augustine of Hippo mentions a "catechumeno sacramentum" that J. R. King translates as "sacrament of the catechumen." As Philip Schaff notes in a footnote to this passage, this sacrament is also mentioned in the Canons of Hippo (393) and confirmed by the Council of Carthage (397) as "the sacrament of salt." In *De Peccatorum Meritis et Remissione* (411), St. Augustine mentions that while "*not the body of Christ*," this salt "*is holy, more holy than the food whereby our bodies are sustained, because it is a sacrament*." According to his Confessions (397–400), St. Augustine had himself been "seasoned with salt" soon after birth, having received salt on the tongue to signal his incorporation as a catechumen. I thank Leslie Carr-Riegel and Armando Guevara Gil for these references. AUGUSTINUS, A Treatise on the Merits and Forgiveness of Sins, in: SCHAFF (ED.), Nicene and Post-Nicene Fathers, Series 1, Vol. 5, p. 61; AUGUSTINUS, On Baptism, Against the Donatists, in: SCHAFF (ED.), Nicene and Post-Nicene Fathers, Series 1, Vol. 4, p. 460; CRAMER, Baptism and Change, p. 117–118; PIGNOT, The Catechumenate in Late Antique Africa, p. 102–108.

48 CARDOSO, Comer o Sal; SWEET, Recreating Africa, p. 195–197.

49 MMA II, D. 67; D. 76; MMA XV, D. 64.

matter.[50] In the report that Captain-General and Governor Fernão de Sousa left to his children (c. 1625–1630), he claims that after sending a letter asking the ruler of Loango to convert to Catholicism following the example of the *Mwene Kongo*, the former had answered him that he "*was not interested in eating the salt at the present moment*" and convert following the example of his BaKongo neighbors.[51] As for "*the Kongolose*," Thornton remarks that, by the first decade of the eighteenth century, they "*always wanted their children baptized*," exhausting traveling priests with demands and shouts of "*Nganga, nganga, sant mungwa* [Father, Father, holy salt]!"[52] Sometimes, Thornton concludes, a single priest baptized more than one thousand children daily by distributing grains of salt, some claiming to have baptized up to 50.000 persons in a single mission.[53]

In time, as Cardoso explains, the Kikongo expression "*Ku-dià Mungwa*," which is often recorded in Portuguese sources as "*curia munguae*," "*Cudia mungua*" or "*ocudiâmungua*," all translated as "eating the salt," came to signify "to be baptized" not only in BaKongo and Kimbundu-speaking areas but also in adjacent ones.[54] Friar Cavazzi testifies to this spread in the 1680s, mentioning in the manuscript "*Evangelical Mission to the Kingdom of Kongo*" that when attempting to convert a Mbangala military commander called Bartolomeo, the latter replied that Mbangala "*women when they are pregnant eat victuals with salt, and similarly the child they hold in their womb receives his part* [of salt] *so that it is not necessary for you,*

50 The *Philippine Ordinances* determined that whoever acquired an adult "*slave from Guinea*" was forced to have them baptized within six months after their purchase or lose any *dominium* over their freedom. Slaves older than ten years could refuse baptism, exempting their masters from this obligation. Younger slaves had no choice but to be baptized and had to be so within one month of their purchase. Those "*born from slaves*" were to be baptized at the same time as customary for freeborn children, or their masters would suffer the same penalties. Andrade e Silva (ed.), Colleção chronologica da legislação portugueza (1613–1619), p. 335; Ord. Fil. Book V, Tit. XCIX, § 1–2.

51 Sousa, O extenso relatório do governador a seus filhos, in: Heintze (ed.), Fontes para a História de Angola, Vol. 1, p. 228.

52 Thornton, The Kongolese Saint Anthony, p. 149–150.

53 Ibid.; Thornton, Religious and Ceremonial Life, in: Heywood (ed.), Central Africans and Cultural Transformations, p. 84.

54 This belief persisted well until the twentieth century. Writing in 1951, the *spiritan* missionary and ethnographer Carlos Estermann (1896–1976) lamented this fact, decrying the expression as a "*debasement made by the ignorant who take a secondary rite for the essential part*" and confirming that, by the mid-twentieth century, this "*secondary rite*" was still in use in the Ovimbundu heartlands of central Angola. In 1972, Cardoso verified the adoption of the term in several neighboring languages, documenting its wide dissemination in Kimbundu and Chokwe-speaking areas. Cardoso, Comer o sal, p. 68–69; Estermann, A terminologia cristã, p. 358–364; Macedo, Escrita e conversão na África Central do Século XVII, p. 81; Sweet, Recreating Africa, p. 196.

Father, to baptize them."[55] Commenting on this enigmatic answer, the Capuchin friar noted that "*they commonly call baptism eating salt, and if anyone were to administer it without salt, it would be a great error because they would think they have not been baptized*" and act accordingly. In *Historical Description of the Three Kingdoms of Kongo, Matamba, and Angola* (1687), Friar Cavazzi also mentions the practice of referring to baptism as "*Curia Mungua,*" arguing it was an "*error of many consequences.*"[56] For instance, he tells the story of a dying child who had recently been baptized *in extremis* by a Catholic BaKongo just with salt and, therefore, had died barred from "*Paradise.*" Aware of this possibility, Friar Cavazzi explained that the Capuchins had sought to substitute the designation of baptism in Kimbundu for "*Lusùculù Languisi*" or "*sacred bath*" but to no avail. According to him, "*eating the salt*" was so popular that during a capuchin mission to the Kongo province of Mbata, people would even line up, "*impatient and complaining,*" waiting to eat the salt, attributing to it "*the essence of baptism.*"

James Sweet argues that this popularity stemmed from the BaKongo belief that salt is a "repellent of evil people and spirits" and the framing of Christian baptism as a powerful ritual to ward off evil and *kindoki*.[57] Alternatively, Sweet remarks that individual BaKongo could also have believed that eating the salt and Christian baptism was central to the *kindoki* of Europeans, gladly accepting the sacrament to become powerful "like the other whites" by gaining access to the source of their spiritual power. He describes that "Father Miguel da Silva," a BaKongo priest who was denounced to the Inquisition of Lisbon in the early 1700s, performed hundreds of salt baptisms using only salt and no baptismal water. As for the slaves about to be embarked on ships bound for the Americas, Sweet explains that they were given a Christian name, fed a bit of salt, and washed with water on their heads—the bare minimum required by the *Philippine Ordinances*.[58] According to him, this "three-step process" was interpreted by the slaves as a form of sorcery intended either to prevent them from rebelling or having sex during the middle passage or to protect them from illnesses. In any case, the resonance of salt baptisms with BaKongo and Mbundu rituals and beliefs made them a powerful ideological tool in ensuring the compliance of slaves immediately before and during their hellish Atlantic journeys.

Writing in the early 1840s, José Joaquim Lopes de Lima (1797–1852) also associated the spread of the custom of "*eating the salt*" with the popularity of the "*baptismos de carregação* [ship-load baptisms]" both amongst slave owners bent on saving money and the Mbundu and BaKongo who readily accepted and even

55 Cavazzi, Thornton (trans.) MSS Araldi, Modena, Book 3, Chap. 3.

56 Cavazzi, Istorica descrizione de' tre' Regni Congo, Matamba et Angola, p. 425–426.

57 Sweet, Recreating Africa, p. 195–196.

58 Ibid.; Ord. Fil. Book V, Tit. XCIX, § 1–2.

sought the salt's supposed virtues.[59] According to him, during these collective rituals, priests or missionaries would simultaneously baptize hundreds or even thousands of converts.[60] In the early decades of the nineteenth century, Lopes de Lima explained, the "*ship-load baptisms*" that included the distribution of "*sal bento* [holy salt]" were particularly popular in the Mbundu hinterlands of Luanda, so much so that "*whole villages*' would run to the missionaries and form lines begging for "*that salt, which they believe is a feitiço of the good god capable of preserving them from the trickery of the evil god.*"[61] This evidence suggests that 'eating the salt' had also become a kind of anti-sorcery ritual in the Mbundu cultural area, or at least a popular way of creating an ambiance of trust and goodwill, much like distributing and consuming kola nuts, explaining both its popularity and the local habit of demanding the missionaries for successive baptisms.

However, contrary to the exchange and consumption of kola nuts, the practical recognition of 'eating salt' as a form of Roman Catholic baptism—which persisted despite official hostility towards the practice—had legal consequences besides the spiritual and theological ones already mentioned. First and foremost, the persistence of salt baptisms and the high likelihood of only salt being administered during these rituals, thus nullifying the canonical validity of the sacrament, left hundreds, if not thousands, of West Central Africans in limbo regarding their status as Christians and subsequent obligations. These ranged from paying tithes to honoring monogamous marriages and burying the dead in consecrated ground. Moreover, as discussed in the following pages, it was of legal consequence if Mbundu rituals were practiced by unbaptized subjects (thus being framed as superstitious gentilic or heathen customs) or by baptized subjects subject to accusations of heresy or apostasy.[62]

As for the Mbundu uses and customs associated with birth and the first years of life that the Jesuits rejected as heathen or rebuked as heretic if celebrated by baptized Christians, these are thoroughly described in the document "*Gentilic rites,*

---

59 Lopes de Lima and Bordalo, Ensaios sobre a statistica das possessões portuguezas, Vol. 3, p. 158.

60 According to Charles Boxer, the Jesuits were fond of mass baptisms, usually performed on January 25 to celebrate Saint Paul's conversion. However, in a collective letter of the members of the Jesuit College of Luanda to the captain-general and governor of Angola from November 2, 1678, the priests explained that because baptized adults tended to return to "*idolatry*" and commit "*many mistakes,*" thus becoming "*heretics,*" they opted only to baptize children. This, because according to the Jesuits, since being a heretic was worse than being heathen, in such circumstances, baptism was a disservice to the Africans. This policy might have contributed to tightening the association between Christian baptism and Mbundu childhood rites. Boxer, A Igreja militante, p. 124; MMA XIII, D. 192, p. 458–462.

61 Lopes de Lima and Bordalo, Ensaios sobre a statistica das possessões portuguezas, Vol. 3, p. 158.

62 Heywood, Portuguese into African, in: Heywood (ed.), Central Africans and Cultural Transformations, p. 100.

and superstitions, of the gentilic blacks from the Kingdom of Angola" (c.1702–1719), which Sweet attributes to Bishop Luís Simões de Brandão of Congo and Angola.[63] According to this work, Mbundu women preferred to "*give birth outside of their houses*" because of the "*superstitious belief*" that, on the contrary, the "*earth,*" which they "*venerated and respected as an Idol, called euchila oxi*" would cause harm to them and their babies.[64] Then, the newborns were immediately "*given a name, in keeping with the omens, with which the child had been born.*" Those born "*with the umbilical cord between the neck and breast*" were called "*Mugingas,*" "*with their face down*" were called "*Mufalamas,*" "*with their feet first*" were called "*Mussundas,*" with their upper teeth out were called "*Queza,*" with their lower teeth out were called "*Mazenzemena,*" the older twins were called "*Caculo*" and the younger "*Cabaça,*" and, finally, those born "*showing their rears first*" were called "*Bungus*" and immediately killed.[65] After this ceremony, Bishop Brandão continued, the Mbundu fed the newborn a "*piece of meat or fish*" in a ritual called "*Hacu,*" following the food fed to their fathers during their "*Hacu.*"[66] Then, after a while, when the mother and baby were "*free from the risk of delivery,*" the Mbundu celebrated the "*Sango.*" This was a "*luxurious ceremony*" when the father played with the baby in the public yard. From birth until the baby was weaned, the father could not "*cohabitate with women,*" and no "*bird meat*" could be fed to the newborn. Otherwise, the Mbundu believed the child would die. When the first teeth came in, Bishop Brandão concluded, the "*Cazumba*" feast was celebrated, during which the children would be paraded around, receiving gifts from friends and relatives.

This list suggests that, by identifying all these Mbundu celebrations, Bishop Brandão believed to be taking the first step towards their eradication, lacking the means to impose their prohibition. Moreover, it opens up the possibility that salt baptisms were recognized by BaKongo and Luso-African priests at the practical level in an unsanctioned attempt to substitute Mbundu birth and early childhood rites, such as the *hacu* or *sango* ceremonies, for equally propitiating rituals of Christian inspiration. Such an approach would allow them to exploit the personal fragility

---

63 Sweet, Recreating Africa, p. 254.

64 Lino D'Assumpção, Exploração à Africa, p. 371.

65 Friar Cavazzi claimed that, if born with a "*considerable time interval between each other,*" twins were called "*Nzima*" and "*Nzfusí,*" meaning "*civet cat*" and "*wild cat,*" respectively. According to him, such an occasion would warrant special rites and dances. The Capuchin friar also described other early childhood rites from the Kingdom of Kongo. See Wyatt MacGaffey for an account of beliefs about twins being embodied "*Simbi*" water spirits in Kongo. Cavazzi, Istorica descrizione de' tre' Regni Congo, Matamba et Angola, p. 113–115; MacGaffey, Twins, Simbi Spirits, and Lwas in Kongo and Haiti, in: Heywood (ed.), Central Africans and Cultural Transformations, p. 211–226.

66 Lino D'Assumpção, Exploração à Africa, p. 371.

and normative laxness associated with liminal moments to impose a solution based on a European grammar of affect.[67]

8.3 Weddings and Funerals

In 1784, a feud erupted between Captain-General and Governor José de Almeida e Vasconcelos (1737–1812) and Bishop Alexandre da Sagrada Família.[68] As João Carlos Feo Cardoso (1798–1868) recounts in his chronicle of the lives and times of the captain-generals and governors of Angola, this feud was first triggered by a minor dispute.[69] According to Cardoso, at some point in 1784, "*some blacks and mulatos of both sexes*" were caught by the bailiffs of the general vicar in the outskirts of Luanda "*in the act*" of "*celebrating the Lembamento and Quicumbi*."[70] According to Cardoso, the first ritual was "the wedding of the Blacks." In his account, it included the payment of a bride price and the performance of an eight-day initiation at a "*casa do uso*," where the new bride would be groomed by a "*Black who pretends to be a feiticeiro*." Cardoso claims that this ritual operator would begin by completely undressing the bride, then anointing her with several ointments, and consecrating her to an "*Iteque*" to bless her future union and ensure she had "*many children*." The second ritual, Cardoso argued, consisted of the final celebration of the Mbundu marriage, when the bride was honored with "*vile songs, ludicrous gestures, and dances*" and addressed as "*Quicumbe*."[71] It was during this second leg of the ritual, which lasted for three days and was an open, public event, that the unnamed

67 Hespanha, A cultura jurídica europeia, p. 65; Turner, Liminal to Liminoid, p. 53–92; Turner, The Ritual Process.

68 Selma Pantoja remarks that similar feuds were quite common, as captain-general and governors and bishops often headed opposing factions, one favoring the interests of locally born Luso-Africans, the other the *filhos de mar em fora*. As an example, she analyses the conflict between Bishop Manoel de Santa Catarina, in office between 1722 and 1731, and Captain-General and Governor Paulo Caetano de Albuquerque, in office between 1726 and 1732, over the appointment of Father João Teixeira as schoolmaster of the Chapter of Luanda. In this conflict, the *ouvidor geral* sided with Albuquerque, while the municipal judge with Bishop Manoel de Santa Catarina. AHU, CU, Angola, Box 74, D. 6275; Lopes de Lima and Bordalo, Ensaios sobre a statistica das possessões portuguezas, Vol. 3, p. 158; Monteiro, D. Frei Alexandre da Sagrada Família; Pantoja, Entre Luanda e Rio de Janeiro, in: Pantoja and Thompson (eds.), Em torno de Angola, p. 87–110; Silva Corrêa, História de Angola, Vol. 2, p. 153–157; Torres, Memorias, p. 273–294.

69 Torres, Memorias, p. 273–294.

70 Ibid., p. 274.

71 According to Óscar Ribas, contemporary Kimbundu speakers refer to girls experiencing their menarche or first menstruation as *kikumbi*, not to brides. The Portuguese expression *quicúmbi*, which also designates teenage girls, originates from Kimbundu term *kikumbi*. Ibid.; Ribas, Ilundo, p. 91.

"*blacks and mulatos*" were caught by the bailiffs of the bishop and subsequently imprisoned.[72]

The conflict between Bishop Alexandre da Sagrada Família and José de Almeida e Vasconcelos arose when Captain João Ribeiro and the Chief Physician José Rodrigues petitioned the captain-general and governor for his intervention in the immediate release of the prisoners, alleging that the "*Bishop was unfair, bloodthirsty, and a usurper of Royal Authority*."[73] This was the case, the signatories argued, because maintaining "*public sossego* [peace/rest]" was a royal prerogative (e.g., a form of *imperium*), and only the captain-general and governor and his delegates were entitled to intervene if it happened to be threatened. Agreeing with the petitioners, whom Cardoso claims were the lovers of some of the arrested Black women, José de Almeida e Vasconcelos asked Bishop Alexandre da Sagrada Família to order the general vicar to immediately release the whole group, sowing the first seeds of their long-lasting enmity. As would happen with other disputes between the captain-general and governor and the bishop, the matter over who had jurisdiction over the prisoners and if serious canonical offenses had been committed hinged on them being baptized—and on the validity of this sacrament. Moreover, the public wedding celebrations that marked the end of courtship and the social recognition of the new status of the bride and groom were the focus of the contention, not the Mbundu institution the Portuguese framed as marriage or the custom of *alembamento* and the paying of bride prices per se.[74]

This suggests that the crux of the matter was the bishop's attempt to ban a Mbundu wedding celebration that was adopted by Luso-African *moradores* and unofficially recognized by secular Portuguese authorities by imposing his jurisdiction over the poor free Black residents of Luanda who took part in it. In other words, because, as Silva Corrêa reported ironically, the "*canes of penance only stroke the backs of poor Black men or women*," Bishop Alexandre da Sagrada Família seems to have hoped to reach the powerful Portuguese and Luso-Africans by punishing their Mbundu associates and lovers.[75] Therefore, by invoking the royal prerogative of maintaining peace, Captain Ribeiro and Chief Physician Rodrigues perhaps intended not to

---

72 Torres, Memorias, p. 274.

73 Ibid.

74 As discussed in the fourth chapter, since the early years of the conquest of the Kingdom of Ndongo, the Jesuits wrote about the Mbundu institution they framed as marriage, strategically distancing it from the Roman Catholic one. As for the *alembamento*, as Alfredo de Sousa remarks, the Portuguese started interfering with it as soon as they participated in prestige spheres of exchange where rights over women were swapped by introducing new currencies and contributing to the inflation of bride prices. MMA III, D. 55; Sousa, Estruturas Socio-Económicas e Dialéctica de Culturas em África, p. 53.

75 Silva Corrêa, História de Angola, Vol. 1, p. 90.

subordinate Christian love and charity to an abstract ideal of *Ordre public* or public tranquility but to resist ecclesiastic encroachment in local domestic spheres where, as Silva Corrêa also noted, patterns of behavior were regulated by Mbundu grammars of love which enabled men like themselves to forge lasting alliances with Luso-African "familial factions."[76] Their bet seems to have paid off, likely because José de Almeida e Vasconcelos was keen on reasserting his office's authority over public space in Luanda. As Silva Corrêa remarks, Bishop Alexandre da Sagrada Família had also feuded with the subaltern Governor of Benguela Pedro José Correia de Quevedo because the latter jailed a cleric who had publicly offended him after the subaltern governor refused to grant him immediate passage to Luanda.[77] In this case, the outcome was the subaltern governor's temporary ex-communication by the bishop, which, according to Silva Corrêa, significantly undermined his authority and "*consumed public order*." Therefore, José de Almeida e Vasconcelos' reassertion of his jurisdiction can be understood not as an endorsement of Mbundu institutions or the marriage strategies of Luso-African familial factions but as a reconfirmation of the boundaries between secular and ecclesiastic jurisdiction for reasons of state.

According to Roquinaldo Ferreira, the "*alembamento*" and the "initiation ritual" known as "*quicumbe*" were only two of the ceremonies performed during Mbundu "traditional weddings," the first consisting of a gathering between the two families to "negotiate the payment of the bride's dowry [sic]," the second preparing her to "have a liaison or sex with men."[78] Ferreira explains that the "*quicumbe*" ritual lasted for "eight days," during which future brides would be secluded and anointed with an "*untura* [cream]" by a "sorcerer." Basing himself on the testimony of António Soares to the Inquisition of Lisbon, collected on December 20, 1699, Ferreira adds that this rite was followed by three days of festivity in which the bride celebrated together with "other black men and women."[79] Half a century before, Bishop Brandão had remarked that the Mbundu celebrated a ceremony called "*caulama*," which seems similar to the "*quicumbe*," as Ferreira describes it.[80] According to Bishop Brandão,

---

76 See Miller and Vanessa Oliveira on Luso-African "familial factions" and marriage strategies. Miller, Way of Death, p. 249; Oliveira, African Women and Commerce in the Atlantic World; Oliveira, Slave Trade and Abolition.

77 Delgado, A Famosa e Histórica Benguela, p. 15; Silva Corrêa, História de Angola, Vol. 2, p. 127.

78 Ferreira, Cross-Cultural Exchange, p. 185.

79 Writing in 1847, Joaquim Menezes repeats Cardoso's description of the *alembamento* and *quicumbe* rituals, adding that "*they have greatly contributed to the prostitution and bigamy of the whites with black and parda women*" contributing to the low rate of Christian weddings "*between these races*." This confirms that Mbundu grammars of love regulated most hetero-affective relationships in Angola until the 1840s. Ibid.; Menezes, Demonstração geographica e politica, p. 204.

80 The Portuguese word *alembamento* (also *lembamento* in the sources) derives from the Kimbundu expression "*kilembu* [bride price]" and refers to the gifts exchanged during courtship or to Angolan forms of "traditional marriage" more broadly. See Kiame Tomalela for current debates about the

the Mbundu sent their "*maiden daughters*" to a "*house where they* [were] *kept apart for a whole month*" when they got their menarche, for them to be anointed with the dye of "*tacula* [*Pterocarpus tinctorius* Welw.]," a redwood with ceremonial significance.[81] After this month, the initiated women would be paraded, drums played, and all would share a banquet.[82] In Bishop Brandão's opinion, the *caulama* prepared young women to "*go live in a climate different from their natural one*" and was believed to "*avoid monstrous births*." The exoticizing and dehumanizing elements of later depictions of *alembamento* and *quicumbe* are absent from this description, being unclear if the *caulama* is a separate coming-of-age rite not associated with marriage or part of the same complex of rituals.[83] The list of "*Gentilic Rites of Angola*" (1720), edited by Prosecutor Manuel da Cunha Pinheiro of the Inquisition of Lisbon, added male circumcision to this complex,[84] remarking that even of the sons "*of baptized parents*" underwent it because otherwise "*no black women would consent to cohabit with them physically*."[85] Bishop Brandão's neutrality regarding the *caulama* rite suggests that, at this period, the public celebrations that

---

word's possible origin and correct spelling. FERREIRA, Cross-Cultural Exchange, p. 185; LINO D'ASSUMPÇÃO, Exploração à Africa, p. 372; TOMALELA, O alambamento.

81 In 1884, the botanist Francisco Melo Breyner, Count of Ficalho, described *tacula* (also known as "*lucula*" or "*hula*") as "*well known by the Portuguese*." As described by him, it could be found in "*every market or quitanda*" and was one of the "*most important items of commerce*" in West Central Africa. A red powder was obtained from *tacula* through friction, used "*as a very effective tonic medicine*" and "*in the confection of their mysterious feitiços*." Moreover, according to Ficalho, in the last decades of the nineteenth century, body "*paintings with tacula*" had a "*superstitious meaning*" being used in all the "*major acts of life*." Children had their bodies "*painted several times, as soon as they were born*." Brides were "*kept for eight days in a special hut, at the care of the nganga, or of an old woman specialized in this rite*" who painted their whole naked bodies with *tacula* to initiate them in their new social obligations. Due to the use of *tacula*, Ficalho claimed these huts were known as "*the house of paint*." LINO D'ASSUMPÇÃO, Exploração à Africa, p. 372; MELO BREYNER, Plantas úteis da África Portuguesa, p. 144–145.

82 LINO D'ASSUMPÇÃO, Exploração à Africa, p. 372.

83 MENEZES, Demonstração geographica e politica, p. 204; TORRES, Memorias, p. 274.

84 Miller highlights the role of Mbundu circumcision camps in establishing "cross-lineage groups" of men who "shared experiences" and "retained limited ties throughout their lives." Because boys lived with their fathers' corporate kin groups until adulthood but then dispersed to live with those of their mother's brothers, these ties enabled them to access a network of contacts that spanned several villages and eased trade, hunting, and travel. These homo-affective networks also facilitated the diffusion of the cult of the anti-social personal spirits described in the previous chapter. MILLER, Kings and Kinsmen, p. 51.

85 Bishop Brandão also mentions a ritual that Mbundu men and women performed when establishing a new household to ensure good health. It involved "*the men, the women, and their children*" simultaneously holding the sticks that would serve as the four pillars of the new house and was called "*Ximbicar*." ANTT, TSO, CG, Sr. 25, Fol. 272; LINO D'ASSUMPÇÃO, Exploração à Africa, p. 371–372.

signaled the conclusion of Mbundu marriages were officially tolerated. However, contrary to him, Bishop Alexandre da Sagrada Família opted to take a more active stand against the Mbundu public displays of affection attended by Luso-African and Portuguese *moradores* and soldiers.

According to Silva Corrêa, whose ingrained misogyny transpires in his framing of the *alembamento* as the auctioning of a woman's "*feminine virginity*" by their "*infamous progenitors*," local "*Catholics*" were the "*most Liberal and less scrupulous merchants of this shameless commodity*," frequenting "*without remorse the elegant celebration of these abominable nuptial*" arrangements to satisfy the "*their sensuality*."[86] According to his biased take, "*once this purchase* [was] *concluded, the indecent merchandise* [was] *not transferred to the hands of their owner without undergoing a purification*," which consisted of the bride being "*locked in the darkroom of a house, where she exists naked for 40 days or 3 months, if she is freeborn, being maintained by her buyer*." While secluded, Silva Corrêa continued, the bride would be "*daily anointed with shreds or shavings of Tacula wood, or Quissuêca, moistened with water*," the first producing a red pigment, the latter a yellow one, "*to whiten her skin*." This "*superstition*," Silva Corrêa remarked, was meant to avoid giving birth to "*Mossunda*," babies born with their feet first. Meanwhile, the "*parents of the anointed*" would "*sing, dance, and happily eat in the room next to her*" for the duration of the rite of passage. Finally, at the end of the bride's seclusion at the "*Caza do uzo*," Silva Corrêa claimed that the "*merchandise was delivered to the merchant*." If the groom "*deflowered*" the bride, there would be a public celebration accompanied by the firing of muskets and "*indecent dances*." Otherwise, he argued, the bride price would be returned to the "*purchaser*," and no celebrations would occur.

As for Roman Catholic weddings, Silva Corrêa argued that they also abided by the "*uses of the* [Angolan] *fatherland*," so while "*the hymns resounded in the abodes*" of Luanda's churches, outside the "*Guingôma and the batuque*" drums gathered the Luso-African and African neighbors, awaiting the bride to perform her dance.[87] In this case, he continued, it was the godmother who taught the bride how to have heterosexual intercourse. Following the nuptial night, Silva Corrêa concluded, the groom would offer "*20 to 30 dobras* [between 256$000 and 384$000 *réis*]" to the bride's family if he confirmed her 'virginity,' an offer ritually counter-gifted with a gift of a "*sweet egg pudding or scrambled eggs*." After this exchange, the bride's family would take the sheets from the couple's room and parade them through the streets demanding "*Quizallêlo* [wedding gifts]" from their neighbors, with "*sound celebrations, and rounds of dance*," ending with the bride taking a ritual bath. Silva

86 Silva Corrêa, História de Angola, Vol. 1, p. 88–89.
87 Ibid.

Corrêa speculated that Bishop Alexandre da Sagrada Família's failure to "*uproot*" these and similar Luso-African celebrations led him to abandon Angola.[88]

However, the next decisive episode in the feud between Bishop Alexandre da Sagrada Família and José de Almeida e Vasconcelos, which occurred in October 1878, did not involve the *alembamento* and *quicumbe* rituals but instead, a funeral.[89] While Alexandre was taking confessions, performing a collective wedding, and a mass baptism at the parish of St. John the Baptist, a small community situated on the Island of Cazanga immediately south of Luanda, the bishop received a letter from his secretary informing him that the vicar forane of the Dande district, Friar Amaro de Souza had just sent "*some prisoners*" to Luanda, to be judged by the general vicar.[90] According to the same letter, some prisoners were accused of being "*caught celebrating a Mutambe*." The Friar had also ordered the arrest of *Soba* Ilamba and his "*sergeant major*" or "*Tendalla*," accusing them of hosting the ceremony.[91] By then however, it would turn out, the *soba* and his *tendalla* had already escaped, perhaps with the help of António Bernardo, the corporal in charge of the prison where Friar Souza had the Captain Major of Dande Paulo Marques take them.[92] According to some witnesses, this prison was nothing more than a "*tronco* [stocks]," where the prisoners were arrested and further tortured with thumbscrews.[93] According to Silva Corrêa, Friar Souza had been banished from the Province of Lisbon to the Convent of St. Joseph in Luanda with a "*dishonorable recommendation*."[94] After having regained the trust of his superior due to his politeness and considerable "*skill in crafting* [paper] *flowers and other womanly pastimes*," Bishop Alexandre da Sagrada Família appointed him to the vacant parish that included the *arimos* of the Convent in Dande. Once at the parish of Dande, in collaboration with Captain Major Paulo Marques, Friar Souza "*visited, pronounced, arrested, demanded emoluments, and condemned*" his parishioners "*at will*," making a considerable profit and causing a lot of unrest.

According to the description provided by Cardoso, the "*Mutambe*" or "*Tambe*" in which the prisoners were involved was the Mbundu funerary rite described by Silva Corrêa as *entambe*.[95] According to Cardoso, the celebration lasted for eight days and involved a lot of drinking, dancing, and singing, the veneration of an "*Iteque*,"

---

88 Ibid., p. 91.

89 Silva Corrêa, História de Angola, Vol. 2, p. 154–157; Torres, Memorias, p. 274.

90 Silva Corrêa, História de Angola, Vol. 2, p. 154; Torres, Memorias, p. 276–277, 279.

91 Torres, Memorias, p. 276–277.

92 Ibid., p. 276–277, 279; AHU, CU, Angola, Box 74, D. 6275.

93 AHU, CU, Angola, Box 74, D. 6275.

94 Silva Corrêa, História de Angola, Vol. 2, p. 154–155.

95 Silva Corrêa, História de Angola, Vol. 1, p. 82–84; Torres, Memorias, p. 277.

and the slaughtering and eating of a whole pig.[96] During the festivities, Cardoso explains, all circumcised men and women would announce their social status, and the surviving spouse of the deceased would have to remain lying down in a "*small hut*" built for this purpose, with a "*broken plate, calabash, and pipe*" laid next to their mat. At the end of this period, he concludes, the spouse would throw the skull of the slaughtered pig into a nearby river, thus appeasing the "*Zumbi*" spirit of the deceased and concluding the ritual.[97] Prosecutor Pinheiro's list of "*gentilic rites*" from 1720 briefly mentions the "*Tambes*" of Luanda, simply noting them as loud celebrations punctuated with "*atabaquez and Engomas* [drums], *and other instruments*" and where food and drink were shared indiscriminately between Whites and Blacks.[98] António de Oliveira Cadornega has little to add to this description, confirming that "*baptized Christians*" also participated in "*emtambis*."[99] However, he provides more information about the period of "*dôs*" or "*dós*," a liminal time tightly regulated by the *Philippine Ordinances*.[100]

In the Portuguese Kingdom, "*dós*" were the clothes used to signal mourning, and nobody was allowed to wear them for more than a month, even when a close relative died.[101] After this period, or in the case of the death of a more distant relative, only a "*cloak of dó* [pity]" could be used, and the same rules applied to the servants and slaves of the bereaved. Failure to comply with these rules, the *Philippine Ordinances* stipulated, would result in a two-year exile to Africa and a twenty *cruzado* fine, ten for the denouncer and ten for the local municipal council. In Luanda, however, baobab-bark cloths dyed black, known as *licondos,* were used by widows and widowers.[102] According to Cadornega, these were believed to protect the wearer from the "*zumbis*" of the deceased until the moment came when the mourner would leave their house, crawling to the nearest river, where another widow or widower would use a knife to cut the cord that secured the *licondos* to their waist.[103] After this ritual, the mourners would end the period of "*dôs*" by washing in the river to free themselves from the danger of being molested by the

96 Torres, Memorias, p. 277.

97 In 1847, Menezes confirmed that "*mutambi*" rituals were still daily in Luanda despite being persecuted and dispersed with "*the usual beatings*." Moreover, a "*lot of European whites* [used to] *take part in this savage entertainment*," characterized by an "*impudent debauchery and repulsive sensuousness*." Ibid.; Menezes, Demonstração geographica e politica, p. 204–205.

98 ANTT, TSO, CG, Sr. 25, Fol. 272.

99 Cadornega, História geral das guerras angolanas, Vol. 3, p. 369.

100 Ord. Fil. Book V, Tit. C, § 1–3.

101 Namely, the ecclesiastical garments "*capuz, tabardo, and loba cerrada*"—a black hood, an ecclesiastic tabard, and a penitential robe. Ibid.

102 Cadornega, História geral das guerras angolanas, Vol. 3, p. 265–266.

103 Ord. Fil. Book V, Tit. C, § 1–3.

"*zumbi*" of the deceased.[104] Writing at the beginning of the eighteenth century, Bishop Brandão noted that as soon as "*widowers or widows*" took the body of their former spouses to the grave, they were taken to a river where their "*belts*" were cut and their bodies washed and anointed with "*several herbs*" to prevent the deceased from "*killing them with their Nzumbi.*"[105] After this ceremony, he continued, "*emcombos* [*sic*] *and chickens*" were killed to offer to those present who had assisted with their "*macanzas* [instruments]." In keeping with his version, only then would the bereaved be secluded for eight days in their houses, wearing an "*aliconde*," which Bishop Brandão describes as having a hood. According to him, during this period, they could have heterosexual intercourse with either the widows or widowers who visited them (depending on their gender) and used only broken plates to eat, broken cups to drink, and broken pipes to smoke—all to be discarded afterward. At the end of this liminal period, the bishop claimed that the bereaved would finally leave their homes. Then, if they crossed paths with another widow or widower, the latter would offer them kola nuts or tobacco as apotropaic gifts. Light mourning would last for up to a year, after which the bereaved offered the relatives of the deceased a white or colorful cloth to ask permission to stop mourning. In the 1680s, Friar Cavazzi remarked that in case of the death of close relatives, "*the Catholic women of Angola and Congo*" would undergo this ritual after a whole year of seclusion and wearing *licondos*, or a month in case of distant ones. He frames this prolonged mourning as superstition, not as a display of affection.[106]

As for the actual burying of the dead, Bishop Brandão claimed that before the body was shrouded, their spouses would lay on top of it, performing a ritual called "*Cubandama.*"[107] Then, those in charge of opening the grave would charge an "*emcombo* [*sic*]" or a chicken if the deceased was a commoner, eating it, together with "*what else there is to eat*," in sight of the "*hunbilla* [grave]" where a "*curiri*" or makeshift bed decorated with mats awaited the corpse. If the deceased had been notable or a noble, Bishop Brandão claimed, "*some people would be killed at the day of their death*," usually, the "*ones that had been in their immediate service*," to be buried in the same grave as their master. Once the grave was closed, the bishop continued, a broken vessel was left on top of it to be filled with drinks for

---

104 See Pantoja on how *entambes* were prescribed to appease disgruntled *zumbi*. She explores a denunciation of Captain Major Antônio de Freitas of the *presídio* of Benguela to the Inquisition of Lisbon in 1722. According to the account, the captain major had performed an *entambe* at his residence to appease the *zumbi* of his deceased wife. Pantoja, Inquisição, degredo e mestiçagem em Angola, p. 124–127.

105 Lino D'Assumpção, Exploração à Africa, p. 373–374.

106 Cavazzi, Istorica descrizione de' tre' Regni Congo, Matamba et Angola, p. 125.

107 Lino D'Assumpção, Exploração à Africa, p. 373.

the deceased. Graves would be cleaned every year, Bishop Brandão concluded, occasioning a banquet and a night of slumber next to them.

Returning to the impending crisis between Bishop Alexandre da Sagrada Família and José de Almeida e Vasconcelos, Cardoso recounts that, as soon as the bishop reached Luanda on October 15, 1878, he received an official letter from the captain-general and governor, demanding the immediate release of the prisoners, the termination of Friar Souza's commission as a vicar forane, and that he be punished for usurping the "*Royal rights and the Authority*" that had been entrusted to him, as governor of Angola, "*to preserve public order.*"[108] According to Cardoso and Bishop Alexandre da Sagrada Família, José de Almeida e Vasconcelos had been informed about the case by a letter that a group of Black *moradores* from Dande had sent him, demanding the release of the prisoners and accusing Friar Souza of being a "*bloodthirsty wolf*" committing all kinds of "*extortions and abuses.*"[109] As Cardoso and Silva Corrêa narrate, the conflict only seems to have de-escalated when the commissioned vicar returned to his convent, and *Soba* Ilamba and his *tendalla* escaped imprisonment.[110] Bishop Alexandre da Sagrada Família wrote a long message to the captain-general and governor in reply to the accusations, which Cardoso fully transcribes.[111]

In its pages, the bishop declares that the prisoners were, in fact, under his jurisdiction, according to the "*sacred Canons*" and the "*Portuguese Ordinances,*" because, by a testimony made under oath by Corporal Bernardo, *Soba* Ilamba and "*all his Banza* [village]" were "*Baptized Christians.*"[112] In the bishop's account, it was the fact that these Christians were burying the "*corpses of Christians in the profane places that they call monturo* [literally trash heaps]" that forced Friar Souza to intervene, not the celebration of the *entambe* per se.[113] Aggravating matters, he continued, nobody awaited permission of the Church to be exempted from "*Ecclesiastical burial,*" and "*the corpses of those publicly excommunicated*" had been buried by the *soba* "*in holy cemeteries and Churches because they were left unguarded.*"[114] Therefore, Bishop Alexandre da Sagrada Família concluded what was at stake was not a disturbance of public order caused by an African festivity but the violation of the articles of the *First Constitutions of the Archdiocese of Bahia* (1707) regulating Roman Catholic

---

108 Torres, Memorias, p. 277–278.

109 Ibid., p. 287–290; AHU, CU, Angola, Box 74, D. 6275.

110 Silva Corrêa, História de Angola, Vol. 2, p. 155–156; Torres, Memorias, p. 287–290.

111 It is also annexed to the official letter Friar Alexandre da Sagrada Família wrote to the Secretary of State of the Navy and the Overseas Martinho de Melo e Castro after arriving in Lisbon in 1788, following his resignation. AHU, CU, Angola, Box 74, D. 6275.

112 Torres, Memorias, p. 282.

113 Ibid.; AHU, CU, Angola, Box 74, D. 6275.

114 AHU, CU, Angola, Box 74, D. 6275.

burials.[115] He added that the penalties for such an offense were excommunication and paying a fine of fifty *cruzados* while in custody.[116] Aggravating matters, Bishop Alexandre da Sagrada Família argued that *Soba* Ilamba had a standing debt with the council of the Church of St. Anna of Dande because he had recently used "*sacred ground*" to bury corpses and then failed to pay the due emoluments.[117]

After reasserting his jurisdiction over the prisoners, the bishop explained to José de Almeida e Vasconcelos what he believed were the real motives behind the letter against Friar Souza.[118] According to Bishop Alexandre da Sagrada Família, the *moradores* who signed it "*encouraged the Blacks of their arimos not to pay*" the emoluments that were due for burying their deceased on consecrated grounds, protecting them whenever they decided to "*thrash the Bailiffs of the Church.*"[119] Furthermore, the bishop continued, they lived in "*perpetual concubinage*" and had impeded Friar Souza from celebrating Christian weddings in their farmsteads and villages, arguing that, since the vicar forane allowed "*the slaves and free Blacks of his Convent to live emancebados* [in concubinage]," he had no right to impose Christian rites on them. Moreover, three of the *moradores* had already been excommunicated. One of the signatories, Manoel Antunes, had been previously arrested by Captain Major Marques for possessing "*what they call milongos and we call feitiços*" and being a "*poisoner and assassin*"—having also escaped from jail, burning it in the process.[120] The bishop concluded that their testimony could have no standing in any court because they were all "*evil Blacks*" without "*soul, conscience, or honor*" and "*renowned perverts, to whom the most moderate exercise of the legitimate authority*

---

115 Torres, Memorias, p. 282; Vide, Constituições primeiras do Arcebispado da Bahia.

116 According to Bishop Alexandre da Sagrada Família, he had, in fact, recently issued a pastoral graciously reducing the fine to ten *cruzados*. Nevertheless, accusatory witnesses reported that Friar Souza had the habit of imprisoning persons in the *arimo* of the convent, using slaves' "*limbambos and chains.*" Allegedly, he kept them arrested until their relatives paid the fines of "*fifty, one hundred, or two hundred cruzados.*" AHU, CU, Angola, Box 74, D. 6275; Torres, Memorias, p. 282.

117 In a letter to the Chapter of Luanda annexed by the canons to a petition they directed to Queen Maria I of Portugal, the successor of the *soba* of Ilamba that Friar Souza punished, tells his version of the events. According to him, his predecessor had refused to pay Friar Souza the "*cahidos* [fallen]" that previous *sobas* had failed to pay, agreeing only to pay the *cahidos* for the burials that took place while he was in office. It was this refusal, according to the new *soba*, that had triggered his predecessor's arrest and torture. "*Cahidos*" is how the new *Soba* Ilamba referred to the emoluments due for burying the dead in the consecrated ground. AHU, CU, Angola, Box 73, D. 6250; Torres, Memorias, p. 282.

118 Torres, Memorias, p. 287–290.

119 Ibid., p. 283–284; AHU, CU, Angola, Box 74, D. 6275.

120 Silva Corrêa defines "*Milongos*" as "*Medicine, or feitiços composed of several herbal composites.*" It is unclear if this 'jail' was a simple stock with chains or a more elaborate structure. AHU, CU, Angola, Box 74, D. 6275; Silva Corrêa, História de Angola, Vol. 1, p. 89, Vol. 2, p. 155; Torres, Memorias, p. 283–285.

of the Church causes great abhorrence."[121] Furthermore, as Bishop Alexandre da Sagrada Família pointed to the governor in a somewhat threatening way, despite having already been excommunicated, they could still be persecuted as "*heretics*."[122] Finally, he added, Corporal Bernardo, whom the bishop believed was collaborating with the *moradores* and had helped *Soba* Ilamba to escape, was well known for keeping at least one un-baptized concubine in a polygynous household.

Considering Bishop Alexandre da Sagrada Família's claims, it appears that Antunes and Corporal Bernardo cooperated with *Soba* Ilamba in the administration of justice,[123] perhaps having reached an agreement similar to the one between Captain Major Luís Maia and *Sobas* Mussungo-a-Posse and Anganbambe, described in the previous chapter.[124] As Silva Corrêa confirms, by then, the population of Luanda often made use of the services of "*Moêne-Bengo*," a "*feiticeiro who assists in adjudicating*" cases and is based very nearby, on the margins of the Bengo River.[125] Therefore, it is not unlikely that the "*milongos*" that Antunes owned were the substances used in private *mbulungo* oaths and that his judicial activities were mischaracterized as poisoning by Captain Major Paulo Marques, Friar Souza, and Bishop Alexandre da Sagrada Família.[126] If this was the case, the captain major's cooperation with Friar Souza might have been more self-interested than the bishop admits in his letter. By assisting the vicar forane and giving him access to the prison of the nearby district of the Bar of the Dande, Captain Major Marques might have been trying to instrumentalize him to dispose of Antunes, Corporal Bernardo, and the current *Soba* Ilamba, his direct rivals, when it came to arbitrating conflicts according to Mbundu norms. It is worth mentioning that as captain major of a regular district, Captain Major Paulo Marques had no fixed stipend and no garrison to command, thus was severely limited in his efforts to extract porters and *corvée* labor from local populations, and depended a great deal more on the emoluments that he could charge as an ordinary judge or arbiter.[127]

About fifteen years before these events unfolded, Captain-General and Governor Francisco Inocêncio de Sousa Coutinho had faced similar situations, opting to address them by issuing a *bando* and writing an official letter to the canons of the

---

121 AHU, CU, Angola, Box 74, D. 6275; Torres, Memorias, p. 281.

122 Torres, Memorias, p. 287–290.

123 Bishop Alexandre da Sagrada Família briefly mentions that *Soba* Ilamba might have resisted paying tithes, arguing that his *sobado* was exempt from the obligation. However, he immediately dismisses this as the reason for the conflict. AHU, CU, Angola, Box 74, D. 6275.

124 The following chapter explores the consequences of vicars forane's jurisdiction overlapping with those of captain majors and African ritual operators. ANTT, TSO, IL, Sr. 30, CP 94, Book 287, p. 47–60; Torres, Memorias, p. 283–285.

125 Silva Corrêa, História de Angola, Vol. 1, p. 87.

126 Torres, Memorias, p. 283–285.

127 Couto, Os capitães-mores em Angola, p. 230–237, 244; Mello, Relação dos officios civis, p. 291.

diocese, when the bishop's seat was *Sede vacante*.[128] Perhaps because no bishop of Congo and Angola was present, tilting the balance of power in Sousa Coutinho's favor, the captain-general and governor gave precise orders to the canons, disregarding their jurisdictional autonomy. Moreover, in the first article of his Ordinance of February 24, 1765, regulating the activities of captain majors, Sousa Coutinho explicitly forbade captain majors from assisting "*any parish priests, vicars forane, or pastoral visitors*" who decided to "*correct*" misdeeds by "*extorting one or several peças d'India*."[129] These "*misdeeds*," the captain-general and governor continued, included burying the "*dead bodies of Gentiles*" outside of "*sacred grounds*" and refusing to pay tithes. In such cases, Sousa Coutinho determined that captain majors should inform him to "*promote*" the wayward priests' punishment or "*determine their expulsion*" from the Captaincy of Angola. These precedents might help explain why Bishop Alexandre da Sagrada Família was now keen to reaffirm his ecclesiastical jurisdiction.

Sousa Coutinho's "*Bando that forbids Entambes, and other Barbarities*" was issued on January 10, 1769, and only targeted the "*Gentilic vices*" that tainted "*the purity of Customs*" in the cities of Luanda and Benguela.[130] According to it, these celebrations were a "*core of disorder, public dissolution, Theft, and scandalous superstitions*" practiced by "*the Black, and to which the Whites*" adhered. Sousa Coutinho claims that he had hoped that "*family Fathers would proscribe from their houses such an unruly custom*," but, contrariwise, after a first *bando* from December 1768 prohibited *entambes* in Luanda, the Luso-African *moradores* started celebrating them in their rural *arimos* or ordering their slaves to do it in their stead. Faced with the recalcitrant attitude of the Luso-African *patres familias*, the captain-general and governor determined that those responsible for organizing *entambes* should be immediately arrested, together with their "*households or senzala* [African quarters]," and sent to Luanda to "*work in the Royal factories*." Sousa Coutinho concludes the *bando*, which he ordered to be translated in Kimbundu before it was publicly read, explaining that a "*clear and decisive experience had demonstrated that only the power of His Majesty*" exerted "*through their Governors is armed with the necessary strength to curtail such dissolute, barbarous, and Diabolic customs*." On August 1768, the captain-general and governor had already sent a letter to the Chapter of Luanda imposing rules destined to "*curtail the unruly ambition of the Parish priests of the Kingdom*."[131] According to the document, the Parish Priests of Ambaca had a habit "*of extorting*

---

128 AHU, CU, Angola, Box 54, D. 4897; AHU, CU, Angola, Box 53, D. 4860.

129 Coutinho, Documento N.º 6, in: Couto, Os capitães-mores em Angola, p. 324.

130 AHU, CU, Angola, Box 54, D. 4897.

131 AHU, CU, Angola, Box 53, D. 4860.

from the Blacks who died thirty or more léguas" away "two *Beirames*" of cloth[132] to "*bury them in consecrated soil,*" asking twofold or fourfold this price of "*Sobas, Quimbares, and other elite members of Peoples or Families.*" As for those who had passed away closer to Ambaca, Sousa Coutinho continued, sometimes the priests refused to bury them in consecrated ground because they claimed that "*they had not taken the sacrament*" of communion "*during the last Lent.*" Moreover, their bailiffs demanded an exorbitant "*Teleco* [subsistence allowance]" to render their services to the families of the deceased.[133] Adding insult to injury, the captain-general and governor concluded that when the Mbundu were forced to bury their dead in deconsecrated ground because of long distances or excessive demands, the priests found ways to charge them penalties.

According to Sousa Coutinho, these and other 'abuses' reduced "*the miserable Blacks to a state of permanent affliction,*" aggravated by their "*poverty and brutality.*"[134] On the contrary, he continued, the priests should "*conduct them with charity, and through Love bring them much more softly to Christianity,*" a duty they failed to perform, he concluded, because their own profitable "*businesses*" occupied them. Therefore, he ordered the canons of Luanda to put an end to these abuses, concluding that demanding that someone carry a dead body "*for more than a légua*" in "*such a climate*" should be considered the "*true crime,*" and that no penalties should be charged in the hinterlands of Angola and Benguela for burying the dead in deconsecrated ground. In conclusion, Sousa Coutinho's police regulations insisted on respecting the boundaries separating the urban environments of Luanda and Benguela and their immediate outskirts (the riverine *arimos* that supplied both settlements) from the hinterlands, also differentiating the seats of jurisdictions, such as *presídios* and the village of Massangano, from their remote dependencies. Within these limits, a Christian grammar of love and charity was to regulate all social relations, any threat to it being an insult to the Crown and its delegates, first

132 Bluteau, Beirame, in: Moraes Silva (ed.), Diccionario da língua portugueza, Vol. 1, p. 176; Ximenes, Bahia e Angola, p. 112–113.

133 In a letter to Sebastião José de Carvalho e Mello, the future Marquis of Pombal, from 1765, Sousa Coutinho explains that Mbundu "*telecos*" were like Portuguese "*hospedagens,*" the subsistence allowances due to traveling officials. According to Sousa Coutinho, even though he had outlawed them in 1765, the ecclesiastical bailiffs from Ambaca charged "*a chicken*" to sit down when dealing with the family of a deceased person, "*another for them to spend the night*" at their village and one "*pot to spit*" plus a "*lamb or a pig*" and "*two beirames for themselves, and two for the parish priests*" to return with the dead body. While the charging of these payments had no grounding in the articles of the *First Constitutions of the Archdiocese of Bahia,* it echoes the tributes asked during the Mbundu burials described by Bishop Brandão in the early eighteenth century. AHU, CU, Angola, Box 51, D. 4648, Box 53, D. 4860; Lino D'Assumpção, Exploração à Africa, p. 373.

134 See Hespanha for an analysis of the privileges this degraded status afforded them. AHU, CU, Angola, Box 53, D. 4860; Hespanha, Imbecillitas.

and foremost, even if coming from the ministers of the Roman Catholic Church. From this perspective, when Sousa Coutinho took the opportunity to ban the "*houses they call do uzo, or Quicumbis*" in the same *bando* he forbade *entambes*, he described these as the places where "*Black women go to, under Diabolic invocation, and the rudest, and most Gentilic superstitions, before the presence of Swindlers, and ridiculous Idols, to receive the preparation and training for Prostitution.*"[135] The public celebration of Mbundu weddings was thus not the focus of Sousa Coutinho's reforms. Instead, it was a Mbundu institution that he believed threatened the spread of a Christian grammar of love that he actively supported.[136] In his view, this threat was due to the promotion of Black prostitution, which, like all forms of prostitution, was considered a crime and harshly punished by the *Philippine Ordinances*.[137]

When José de Almeida e Vasconcelos was faced with Bishop Alexandre da Sagrada Família's threat to persecute Antunes and the other *moradores* as heretics, *Soba* Ilamba for not paying his debts to the Church, and Corporal Bernardo for polygamy and concubinage, he might have equally perceived it as an intrusion into his jurisdiction. Proceeding with care, in response to the bishop's allegations and threats, the governor decided to send the artillery Captain José da Fonseca, together with his scribe Bernardo José Ribeiro and the interpreter Lieutenant Tavares, to the Dande district, instructing them to enquire about the past acts of Friar Souza and write a comprehensive "*devassa* [inquest]."[138] This inquest, the captain-general and governor ruled, was then to be "*judged in his presence, by a Board constituted by the General Vicar, Manoel Dantas Lima, the Municipal Judge of Luanda, José Francisco de Oliveira* [...] *and the Lawyer, Domingos Placido.*" According to Cardoso and Silva Corrêa, Bishop Alexandre da Sagrada Família was greatly offended by this decision, immediately resigning from the position of bishop, handling the management of the diocese to the Chapter, and thus forcing his general vicar to resign and delaying the creation of this commissarial board.[139] In the bishop's words, by creating this ad hoc tribunal, the captain-general and governor of Angola had "*with thundering noise overstepped his jurisdiction,*" causing a shameful "*fight between the two swords*"

135 AHU, CU, Angola, Box 54, D. 4897.

136 As Silva Corrêa remarked, Sousa Coutinho even sponsored the "*dowries*" of many Luso-African brides to make Christian marriage a more palatable institution to his White subjects. Silva Corrêa, História de Angola, Vol. 2, p. 30.

137 The next chapter discusses Sousa Coutinho's takes on prostitution in greater detail. Ord. Fil. Book V, Tit. XXXII, § 1–7.

138 Torres, Memorias, p. 291.

139 In a letter to Queen Maria I of Portugal, the canons of the Chapter of Luanda referred to this board as a "*Junta Criminal* [Criminal Board]," highlighting the breach in Friar Souza's ecclesiastical privileges being adjudicated by it represented. Ibid., p. 291–293; AHU, CU, Angola, Box 73, D. 6250; Silva Corrêa, História de Angola, Vol. 2, p. 156–157.

of justice.[140] As he remarks, by including in it the general vicar, José de Almeida e Vasconcelos was "*forcing* [the bishop's] *court, and even himself, to be a witness and accomplice in injuring the Diocese*" of Congo and Angola, turning its bishop into a mere "*clerk of the governor*."[141] In the end, Cardoso concludes, there were so many inconsistencies in Captain Fonseca's inquest that, when the board finally convened, it declared the inquest null, deciding nevertheless to ship Friar Souza to Brazil as punishment for all the unrest he had caused.[142]

As is clear by now, this jurisdictional dispute also hinged on determining the original cause of the arrests and ascertaining if *Soba* Ilamba and the members of his village had been properly baptized. If their baptism could not be considered valid, Friar Souza would have had no legal ground to demand emoluments or, for that matter, to impose Christian wedding rites on them. The same could be said of the Luso-African *moradores* of Dande and the "*Blacks and mulatos*" of Luanda, whom the general vicar could not rebuke for celebrating a Mbundu wedding if they were not Christians—despite Sousa Coutinho's *bando* from 1765, an oral edict which could be interpreted as no longer extant after his term in office ended in 1772.[143] A third dispute between Bishop Alexandre da Sagrada Família and Municipal Judge Oliveira focused on this crucial point. By accepting all baptisms as equally valid and not distinguishing salt baptisms from regular baptisms celebrated by the Presbyters of the Chapter of Luanda, the bishop welcomed a maximalist understanding of the Catholic sacrament that significantly extended the size of his flock and the limits of his jurisdiction. Unsurprisingly, the municipal judge was not happy with this solution and, according to Lopes de Lima, formally enquired Bishop Alexandre da Sagrada Família about the Canon law validity of "*Baptisms administered while in Mission to persons who become Neophytes while living amongst infidels, with no other means of continuing to learn the catholic Faith*."[144] Perhaps sensing a trap, the bishop refused to answer immediately. Instead, still according to Lopes de Lima, Bishop

---

140 AHU, CU, Angola, Box 74, D. 6275.

141 Moreover, Bishop Alexandre da Sagrada Família was greatly offended because "*Black women*" were heard as witnesses. He argued that they had been called to testify at the request of Captain João Ribeiro and the Chief Physician of Luanda. He believed "*Black women*" also advocated for *Soba* Ilamba and against Friar Souza. Ibid.

142 The canons of the Chapter of Luanda would then annex a copy of Captain Fonseca's inquest to the petition they sent to Queen Maria I of Portugal requesting the appointment of a new bishop of Congo and Angola. AHU, CU, Angola, Box 73, D. 6250; Torres, Memorias, p. 291–293.

143 AHU, CU, Angola, Box 54, D. 4897; Torres, Memorias, p. 274.

144 Miguel António de Mello (1766–1826), captain-general and governor of Angola between 1797 and 1802, also narrates this episode in a letter he wrote to Secretary of State of the Navy and the Overseas Rodrigo de Sousa Coutinho (1755–1812) on February 3, 1800. Lopes de Lima and Bordalo, Ensaios sobre a statistica das possessões portuguezas, Vol. 3, p. 158–159; Mello, Carta a D. Rodrigo de Sousa Coutinho.

Alexandre da Sagrada Família opted to pose this vexing question to the theologians of the University of Coimbra and the Archbishop of Bahia, the metropolitan bishop responsible for overseeing the Diocese of Angola and Congo.[145]

According to Lopes de Lima, while the professors never cared to reply to Alexandre's query, the archbishop, unwilling to or incapable of providing a better answer, simply cited a previous report of his private theologian on the conversion of Amerindians.[146] This theologian had previously argued that "*Baptism should not be denied to Pagans for the simple reason that* [...] *the Neophytes*" were at risk of "*returning to Idolatry due to the lack of Masters.*" If this unsubstantiated answer was deemed good enough in South America, the archbishop suggested, it would have to make do in West Central Africa. However, as Lopes de Lima remarks, it provided no solution to the practical problems Municipal Judge Oliveira and the captain-general and governors of Angola had to deal with. Several *presídios* and districts were poorly secured and precariously occupied, and disputes over the obligations of Mbundu, who had only been baptized with salt, could quickly escalate into full-blown rebellions.[147] A more sensible solution, from their perspective, was thus to respect the boundaries determined by Sousa Coutinho, only imposing police regulations and strict obeyance of Canon law where the secular harm of justice could be felt.

Outside these limits, the tendency was to gather as much information as possible on African uses and customs related to death and funerals if it was relevant to train future missionaries or understand the mechanisms of enslavement and state succession. In *Historical Description of the Three Kingdoms of Kongo, Matamba, and Angola*, Friar Cavazzi had already dedicated several pages to the funerary rites of the three kingdoms, also contrasting them with those of the Mbangala.[148] As he described it, while the BaKongo preserved some of their "*gentilic rites,*" they followed Christian customs, having the "*very notable*" habit of offering alms for the deceased even if they had been "*their worst enemy.*" However, in non-Christianized areas of Kongo, Friar Cavazzi claimed that "*two or three concubines*" were sacrificed to accompany the dead.[149] As for Matamba, the Capuchin friar described how bodies were preserved and buried either in caves or deposited in houses, being guarded by sentinels so that cannibals did not steal their flesh before their bones could be transferred to wooden coffers. In the case of the Mbangala, Friar Cavazzi claimed

145 Lopes de Lima and Bordalo, Ensaios sobre a statistica das possessões portuguezas, Vol. 3, p. 158–159.

146 Ibid.

147 Couto, Os capitães-mores em Angola, p. 105–108; Torres, Memorias, p. 277–278.

148 Cavazzi, Istorica descrizione de' tre' Regni Congo, Matamba et Angola, p. 116–128.

149 Ibid., p. 118–119.

they referred to their graves as "*Imbila,*" and their funerals were called "*Tambo.*"[150] The *tambo* ritual, he remarked, lasted for eight days, during which the deceased sat on a chair to receive homage. While it lasted, the ritual was accompanied by dances and the sacrifice of "*animals and men.*" A *xinguila* was tasked with asking the deceased to reveal the 'ultimate' cause of their death. All these rituals, the Capuchin friar concluded, were accompanied by a "*funereal crying that was more apt to provoke laughter than compassion,*" the "*Blacks*" not "*shedding a single tear*" and being adept at dissimulating their lack of 'sincere' love.[151] While he never mentions it, it transpires from Friar Cavazzi's description that his focus was the rituals performed by the elites on the passing of nobles or chiefs, as commoners would probably lack the means to perform these rites or sacrifice slaves.

As for the Ovimbundu funerary rites, the Naturalist Joaquim José da Silva describes them in detail in his report on the journey José de Almeida e Vasconcelos ordered him to make to the hinterlands of Benguela in 1785.[152] Similar reports were produced by the expeditions to the southern shores of Benguela ordered by the captain-general and governor in 1785–1786, all meant to prepare for the conquest or further occupation of these territories.[153] According to José da Silva, amongst the Ovimbundu, as soon as a "*Sôva* [*soma*] *dies, days before the people know about his death, the Quindures* [nobles] *and other notables from the Lombe* [chief's court], *have* [his corpse] *hanging from the neck with a thin rope until it breaks.*"[154] As soon as this happened, he claimed, the *quindures* would pick up the detached skull, "*comb*" its hair, and "*decorate it with the best props.*" Only then, José da Silva concluded, would they announce the death and, accompanied by the skull, inform the one elected as the *soma*'s successor of his new office.[155] After this, the new *soma* would be brought to the "*Songo* [village]" where he was kept hidden until the funeral of his predecessor was publicly celebrated in a rite called "*Intambi.*" José da Silva's attention to succession rules and the funerary ceremonies that preceded the public *intambi* contrasts with contemporary descriptions of long-conquered provinces, where the emphasis is placed on the latter. This suggests that the Portuguese had little concern for how people expressed their love for deceased chiefs, being more

---

150 Ibid., p. 119–123.

151 Ibid., p. 125, 127–128.

152 José Da Silva, Continuação da viagem ao sertão de Benguella, continuada do N.° 2.°, p. 49–60; José Da Silva, Extracto da viagem, que fez ao sertão de Benguella no anno de 1785, p. 97–100; José Da Silva, Viagem ao sertão de Benguella, continuada do N.° 1.°, p. 86–98.

153 See Delgado's annexes for a transcription of these reports. Delgado, Ao Sul do Cuanza, p. 555–575; Figueiredo, Falling into History, p. 1–21; Matos, "Terras Desertas e Selvagens," p. 106–128.

154 José Da Silva, Continuação da viagem ao sertão de Benguella, continuada do N.° 2.°, p. 49–51.

155 José Silva notes that the *quindures* were free to pick whomever they supposed best, as the "*sons of the Sôva had no right whatsoever to the Sôvado* [estate]" being excluded from the *lombe*. Ibid., p. 50.

interested in how dynastic succession was managed, possibly to be better equipped to explore latent conflicts.[156]

The "*Intambi proper*," José da Silva described, consisted of "*crying the passing away*" of the *soma* in the "*most barbarous and horrible manner*."[157] Before it started, the skull of the old *soma* was put in a basket called "*Gonga*" and kept in a "*house*" with those of his predecessors so that their "*Indelles*" or spirits could be invoked to help in state matters. The decapitated body would be buried wrapped in a black bull's leather hide. The *intambi* consisted of a loud celebration accompanied by storytelling, heavy drinking, and the slaughter of cattle for a public banquet.[158] It ended with the depositing of the skulls of all the sacrificed beasts upon the grave where the body had been buried. The *intambi* of commoners, José da Silva explained, were scaled down "*according to their wealth*," followed by a divination ritual meant to determine the ultimate cause of the death—even if they had died in war or been murdered.[159] According to him, a "*Quizambula or Zambulador*" would be fetched from a "*faraway land*" to divine the cause, it being essential that he came "*from another jurisdiction*" so that his verdict could be trusted. José da Silva claimed that the same custom was followed in Loango and other places of the Captaincy of Angola. After the *zambulador* divined the cause of death, if a sorcerer had been identified, a sorcery accusation would be brought before the court of the *soma*, who would ask another *zambulador* for confirmation. In case the accusation was confirmed, the "*miserable réu* [defendant] *would be delivered to the relatives of the deceased to be killed or sequestered* [enslaved], *their assets being shared between the accusers, including the profit made with the sale*" of the defendant. If these measures were not taken, José da Silva remarked, the "*Sandes*" or spirits of the ancestors would "*appear in horrible dreams*" to relatives of the deceased, "*sternly reprimanding them for letting the killer live in peace*."[160] In conclusion, the naturalist claimed that a lot of "*Mucano*" or criminal accusations were triggered by the "*divinations of Quizambulas*" in the aftermath of *intambi*, proving that in

156 The fifth chapter briefly describes Mbangala funerary rites. Francisco de Salles Ferreira, Major António Rodrigues Neves, and Augusto Fortunato da Costa Cândido also wrote about the topic in the 1840s–50s. By the end of the nineteenth century, Captain Henrique de Carvalho would reprise and complete their descriptions with his proto-ethnographic accounts. This chronology suggests that peaks in Portuguese interest in the funerary and succession rituals of African elites and rulers correlated with expansionary moments. AHU, CARTM, Sr. 1, D. 1340; AHU, SEMU, Angola, Box 823 (1798–1895), D. 117; Carvalho, O Jagado de Cassange, p. 282–283; Ferreira, Memoria sobre o sertão de Cassange, p. 26–28; Neves, Memória da expedição a Cassange.

157 José Da Silva, Continuação da viagem ao sertão de Benguella, continuada do N.º 2.º, p. 51.

158 Ibid., p. 52–53.

159 Ibid., p. 54–55.

160 Ibid., p. 56.

the hinterlands of Benguela, it was impossible to restore an ambiance of 'trust' and goodwill until divination rituals and subsequent judicial hearings were held.

Writing twelve years later, the retired Colonel Paulo Martins Pinheiro de Lacerda confirmed that no Ovimbundu "*took death as nature's pension, to which all living beings are destined*," believing instead that death always resulted from "*feitiços*."[161] According to him, as soon as "*someone died*," the "*Sova* [*soma*] *orders two blacks to hold the corpse, tie it to a stick, and, together with the great many that accompanied them, so that the deceased can show them who made them feitiço*," the group would "*carry the corpse on their backs to several libatas* [villages] *of their country*." As soon as the corpse found a "*door to his liking*," they would "*refuse to move on*," and all the members of the "*Quicumba*" or family that lived there would be sequestered until a "*trial*" was held. If the head of the household accused of being a sorcerer were found guilty, Pinheiro de Lacerda concluded, they would be "*burned alive, and everything else is sold, to eat, and drink, and dress, and they claim that so says their laws*." Due to this, the retired colonel insisted on a cynical reading of Ovimbundu funerary rites and the arbitrations that followed them. He concluded that the deceased only "*stopped*" in front of the household of wealthy persons, "*so they have something to steal*," failing to consider how this rite could also function as a social levelling mechanism or to punish those whose riches had been acquired through anti-social means (e.g., by participating in the Atlantic slave trade).

8.4 Taxes, Plagues, and Other Misfortunes

On August 6, 1765, the Board of Justice convened in Luanda to summarily adjudicate seven cases.[162] One involved the "*dizimeiro* [tithe farmer]" Ignácio Mendes Machado, who had been awarded the tax farming contract of the district of Ambaca.[163] Presided over by Sousa Coutinho, after hearing Machado and consulting his "*devassa* [inquiry]," the Board ruled that Machado was not guilty of collecting tithes with "*violence, extortion, and prejuízo* [damage] *to the People*" of Ambaca. Machado had also been accused of "*obliging the Blacks from the said district, either with beatings or with imprisonment, to carry for him what he* [had] *collected from*

161 Pinheiro de Lacerda, Notícia da cidade de S. Filipe de Benguela, p. 486–491.

162 Besides the cases discussed in the following paragraphs, the Board adjudicated: the case of José Lemos Landim, who was absolved of accusations of theft, the case of the "*Black João de Bastos*" from Massangano, absolved of the allegation of falsifying measuring standards, and the case of Roque Vieira de Lima, condemned to a year of exile to the *presídio* of Encoge. ANTT, MR, EXP, Sr. 34, F. 605, p. 50–55.

163 ANTT, MR, EXP, Sr. 34, F. 605, p. 53.

them" as payment. In his defense, the tax farmer alleged that he took no extraordinary measures when collecting tithes, even allowing a "*two or three days*" delay in payments—payments which, he added, "*greatly Disgusted the Blacks.*" Considering all, the commissars reasoned that the tithe collection proceeded as "*smoothly*" as possible, freeing Machado and releasing him from any charges. Similarly, the Board reviewed the condemnation of Manoel Rodrigues Serrão, another tithe farmer accused of collecting "*more than was due, harassing, arresting, and whipping the Blacks of the district of Ambaca who were uncertain if they had to pay.*"[164] While Serrão was condemned in the first instance to three years of exile to "*any port of Brazil,*" on August 6, the Board decided to absolve him, accepting his argument that he exerted no extraordinary violence, as all he needed to impose the payment of tithes was to request the assistance of the captain major of Ambaca.[165] Contrariwise, during the same session, the Board condemned Pedro Matos Coutinho and Pedro Lourenço de Andrade for charging undue emoluments in a coercive manner.[166] Coutinho had been accused of receiving gifts on behalf of the captain major of Ambaca, António Manoel Lisboa, and also allowing the soldiers from the *presídio* to collect quantities exceeding "*seven beirames*" of cloth when they were "*sent on a deligência* [official mission]." For this, the commissars condemned him to pay a fine of 60$000 *réis* and the costs of the trial. As for Andrade, he stood accused of soliciting gifts from all who needed a "*despacho* [executive order]" of Captain Major Lisboa, with whom he cohabited. In keeping with the evidence gathered during the "*devassa* [inquiry]" that preceded the hearing, Andrade even asked *beirames* of cloth of the prisoners of the jail of Ambaca, claiming that he could intercede with the captain major to obtain their freedom. For this, Andrade was condemned to be perpetually ostracized from Ambaca under the penalty of being exiled to the furthest *presídio* of Angola for five years if he was ever seen again walking its streets.

The opposite destinies of Machado, Serrão, Coutinho, and Andrade illustrate three complementary aspects of Sousa Coutinho's simplification of tax collection practices in Angola and Benguela, which singled out tithes as the primary contribution and general-purpose tax.[167] First, this reform presupposed the universal enforcement of tithe-paying was logistically and politically feasible.[168] Second, it

---

164 ANTT, MR, EXP, Sr. 34, F. 605, p. 53–54.

165 Coutinho, Documento N.º 6, in: Couto, Os capitães-mores em Angola, p. 323–338; Coutinho et al., Documento N.º 3, in: Couto, Os capitães-mores em Angola, p. 306–309.

166 ANTT, MR, EXP, Sr. 34, F. 605, p. 51–52.

167 AHU, CU, Angola, Box 51, D. 4624.

168 Regarding the logistical dimension of these reforms, it is worth noting that, as José Curto remarks, the effective collecting of capitation taxes (tithes or any other) hinged on statistical information that was only beginning to be collected. See Curto, Domingues da Silva, and José Venâncio on the history of the second half of the eighteenth-century censuses. See Heywood and Thornton on how

assumed that tithes could be simultaneously framed as capitation and income taxes as well as political tributes that signaled subjection to the Portuguese monarch.[169] Third, it presumed that abolishing Mbundu, Ovimbundu, and other African customary tributes that intermediary authorities could easily pocket was possible.[170] Therefore, tithes could be framed as political tribute implying the recognition of Portuguese sovereignty, rendering other political tributes of Mbundu origin redundant. It is also worth mentioning again that, as stated in the second article of the Ordinance of February 24, 1765, in Angola, tithes that "*were due according to Divine law*" were to be paid "*to the royal Treasury*" on account of the theocratic privileges and rights of patronage conceded by the Holy See to the Portuguese monarch.[171]

As the following paragraphs show, none of the abovementioned conditions were easy to meet. Sousa Coutinho's tax reforms also hinged on downplaying the spiritual dimension and religious grounding of tithes to allow their levying from non-practicing Christian populations as long as they were baptized,[172] leaving open the question of the validity of salt or mass baptisms.[173] Concomitantly, the abolition of

---

African rulers calculated and levied taxes. The tributary system of the Kingdom of Kongo is briefly discussed in the fourth chapter. Regarding the political dimension, as Sousa Coutinho notes in the second article of the Ordinance of February 24, 1765, several "*persons*" had the privilege of not paying tithes, a custom that he referred to as a "*barbarous abuse*" that needed to be "*eradicated*." The success of his reforms thus depended on the captain-general and governor's ability to confront local elites. Coutinho, Documento N.º 6, in: Couto, Os capitães-mores em Angola, p. 324; Curto, The Population of the Lower Kwanza Valley, p. 95–117; Heywood and Thornton, African Fiscal Systems as Sources for Demographic History, p. 213–228; Silva, The Early Population Charts, p. 107–124; Venâncio, Espaço e dinâmica populacional em Luanda, p. 67–97.

169 Coutinho, Documento N.º 6, in: Couto, Os capitães-mores em Angola, p. 324.

170 In the second and third articles of the Ordinance of February 24, 1765, Sousa Coutinho specifically mentions "*telecamentos, ingaus, and mocendos*" that were abusively charged as "*hospedagens* [subsistence allowances]," abolishing these and other abuses and ordering captain majors to destroy the private jails used by tithe collectors to imprison debtors. As discussed in the previous chapters, *corvée* labor and porter service were also extracted from local populations, either legitimately, according to the terms of their vassalage treaties and local uses and customs, or abusively by coercive means. Coutinho, Documento N.º 6, in: Couto, Os capitães-mores em Angola, p. 324–325; Couto, Os capitães-mores em Angola, p. 129–130; Delgado, O Governo de Sousa Coutinho em Angola I, p. 25–26.

171 Coutinho, Documento N.º 6, in: Couto, Os capitães-mores em Angola, p. 324.

172 Due to its paradoxical nature (both religious tribute and secular tax), Linda Heywood describes the "*dízimo*" [tithe] as an "absurd tax" when levied on the income of non-practicing or only nominally Christian populations, while Curto opts to describe it as a combination of the "hut tax," a later institution, "and the religious tithe." Heywood, Portuguese into African, in: Heywood (ed.), Central Africans and Cultural Transformations, p. 110; Couto, Os capitães-mores em Angola, p. 133; Curto, The Population of the Lower Kwanza Valley, p. 97.

173 In his correspondence with some captain majors, Sousa Coutinho insisted on this, especially in hinterland contexts where the power balance did not favor the Portuguese. For instance, on

Mbundu and other tributes unofficially charged by Portuguese officers implied the non-recognition of any spiritual or religious dimensions to them and the framing of their levying as an abuse against *miserabiles personae*.[174] Therefore, in practice, Sousa Coutinho's reforms imposed a tendentially secular understanding of taxation on the Mbundu, Ovimbundu, and other African, Luso-African, and Portuguese populations of the Captaincy of Angola, Benguela, and their dependencies when such an understanding was still only shared by a small elite minority in the Kingdom of Portugal.[175]

This understanding predicated the obligation of contributing with one-tenth of the yearly yield of fields, livestock, and fisheries on purely political grounds,[176]

December 26, 1771, he repeated to Captain Major Feliciano Pinto da Costa Vianna of Encoge that "*only the Blacks who are baptized Christians should pay*" tithes. However, even in Encoge, where the power of nearby independent *dembos* overshadowed the Portuguese, Sousa Coutinho determined that it was up to the missionaries residing with the *Dembos* "*Ambuela*" and "*Cahenda* [*Kakulu ka Kahenda*]" to determine which "*libatas* [villages]" were deemed Christianized. Of these, some would pay tithe directly to the missionaries as their *Congrua portio*; the other would pay tithes to the Portuguese Crown, incentivizing them to perform salt baptisms and inflate the number of nominally Christian villages. Simultaneously, *Dembo* Ambuela levied taxes on the slaves traded in the nearby Portuguese *pumbos* of "*Emquemque de Cabamba, Insona de Mubulo, and Insona de Muene quinsima*." HEYWOOD, Portuguese into African, in: HEYWOOD (ed.), Central Africans and Cultural Transformations, p. 109–110; SOUSA COUTINHO, Carta para Feliciano Pinto da Costa Vianna, p. 359–360, 417–418.

174 HESPANHA, Imbecillitas.

175 As Daniel Alves and Francisco Ribeiro da Silva explain, tithes over several fixed and non-fixed incomes ("*décimas*" or "*dizimos*"), were also the most important direct tax collected by the Crown in the Portuguese Kingdom. After 1640, these tithes were levied as a war tax to support the ongoing conflict against Spain. This tax was parallel to the religious tithe levied on different incomes, evolving over the years as different exemptions and privileges were granted to various groups. In the Portuguese Kingdom, the collection of *décimas* was usually coordinated by *corregedores*, municipal judges, or *provedores*, with the help of the municipal scribes and several informants. After the amount due from each contributor was stipulated, payments were due on St. John's Day and Christmas Day. According to Alves, despite their secular nature, the tithes levied by the Crown never entirely lost their semantic and normative association with ecclesiastic tithes during the *Antigo Regime*. This situation would only change when liberals sought to base their tributary regime on physiocratic or political-economic principles, abolishing tithes on December 16, 1872, and imposing an *ad valorem* tax in their stead. ALVES, Os dízimos no final do Antigo Regime, p. 13–14; RIBEIRO DA SILVA, A sustentação financeira do Estado e da Corte, in: AMORIM et al. (eds.), IV Congresso histórico de Guimarães, Vol. 1, p. 582–583.

176 Besides tithes, the primary sources of public revenue were the duties levied on slaves and ivory at the custom houses of Luanda and Benguela, the revenues obtained by the auctioning of the salt monopolies, the proceedings obtained by auctioning one-fifth of all slaves captured in war (the 'royal fifth'), and the "*subsídio dos molhados*" or "*subsídios literários*," a tax charged on alcoholic beverages and fresh cut meat (one *real* for each "*arratel*" [c. 0,459 kg.] of meat and ten *réis* for each "*canada*" [1,3945 liters] of spirits) destined to finance public education. Other than these taxes,

not even assuring local populations that by replacing the tributes or sacrifices they customarily offered to ensure rain, harvests, game, public health, the regular flow of seasons, and the warding off of *uanga* or other forms of sorcery, the agents of the Portuguese Crown or the Roman Catholic Church would take on the obligation of caring for these basic personal and social needs. Aggravating matters, during this period, alms collecting was often violently imposed by unscrupulous "*esmoleiros* [alms collectors]" on African populations in exchange for indulgences that probably meant little to them and failed to address the gaps in spiritual services opened by the ongoing secularization of tributes and taxes.[177]

---

the Luanda, Massangano, and Benguela municipal councils had the jurisdictional autonomy to raise and collect municipal taxes (*fintas*) and fees—for instance over exported slaves (the "*direitos novos* [new duties]" of 3$000 *réis* established by Captain-General and Governor Salvador Correia de Sá e Benevides in 1648) and alcohol (in 1626, a temporary tax of 2$000 *réis* paid in raffia cloths for each wine "*pipa* [cask]" was levied to pay for the fortification of Luanda). Municipal taxes also included empire-wide taxes such as the "*meias-anatas*," a tax introduced in 1631 consisting of half the first yearly stipends of civil and military officeholders, and exceptional levies such as the one gathered for the dowry of Catarina de Bragança, Queen of England (1638–1705). As Arlindo Caldeira remarks, the imposition of these taxes was always met with resistance in Luanda, leading to threats of rebellion and their tacit suspension. On the different normative groundings of taxes (direct and indirect), duties, fees, and tributes, see Ribeiro da Silva. See Oliveira on the taxes paid in Luanda's markets. Caldeira, Dimensão sociopolítica, p. 27–59; Oliveira, Slave Trade and Abolition, p. 44; Ribeiro da Silva, A sustentação financeira do Estado e da Corte, in: Amorim et al. (eds.), IV Congresso histórico de Guimarães, Vol. 1, p. 585–623.

177 As elsewhere in the Portuguese Empire, alms collecting was conducted in Angola by lay brotherhoods, such as the *Santa Casas*, mendicant orders, such as the Capuchins and Franciscans, and the commissars of the Court and Board of the Bull of the Holy Crusade (1591–1851). The bulls of the holy crusade were a series of bulls issued throughout the centuries to the monarchs of Portugal and Spain (1089–1914), conceding indulgencies, exemptions (e.g., from fasting, pilgrimage, abstinence), and privileges to their subjects in exchange for a series of acts of contrition and the payment of alms. Initially, the proceeds were destined to finance the reconquest of the Peninsula or successive crusades. However, by the second half of the eighteenth century, the alms were destined to repair churches and finance other religious activities and missions. Encyclics would be regularly issued from Rome to the local dioceses explaining the indulgencies, other spiritual benefits and exemptions granted by each new bull, and the spiritual and material contributions required. The Court and Board of the Bull of the Holy Crusade were headed by an "apostolic commissary general" appointed by the Pope and nominated by the Portuguese Crown, several ecclesiastic commissars, and a general treasurer who kept a treasury separated from the Public Treasury where he collected the alms sent by the treasurers of the bull of the crusade of each diocese. The Court and Board employed several secular commissars in each diocese to collect alms. In the Diocese of Congo and Angola, tithe collectors were often also tasked with collecting alms. Boletim do Conselho Ultramarino. Legislação Antiga (1755–1834), Vol. 2, p. 205; Figueiredo, Os esmoleiros do Rei; Ribeiro da Silva, A sustentação financeira do Estado e da Corte, in: Amorim et al. (eds.), IV Congresso histórico de Guimarães, Vol. 1, p. 585–623.

In other words, just as police regulations presupposed the substitution or suppression of lifecycle-event celebrations framed by a Mbundu grammar of affects, reforms of the tax-collecting and tributary systems also hinged on imposing a different affective and normative understanding of what happened during the act of tax or tribute collecting and what kind of bonds or relationships it forged between subjects, sovereigns, and spiritual entities or ancestors. According to this new understanding, the tributes and taxes levied in the Captaincy of Angola and its dependencies were not part of a broader moral economy grounded on generalized gift exchange, the recognition of different forms of love, and African normative systems but wholly alienated from them and thus free to become the arrow-tip of un-reciprocal extraction and colonial exploitation.[178]

The first attempt to abolish tributes based on Mbundu normative systems and institutions and streamline the collection of tributes in the Captaincy of Angola dated from 1620 when Garcia Mendes Castello Branco proposed reforming its tributary regime, arguing for the "*aforamento* [lease]" of *sobados* as its basis.[179] According to his scheme, each *sobado* could be leased to tax farmers for 100$000 *réis*, 150$000 *réis*, or 200$000 *réis* yearly, depending on its wealth and extension. Tax farmers would be obliged not to collect more than the *sobas* used to pay to the *ngola* of Ndongo as tribute, and in "*the same kind, never forcing them to pay anything else*." These Luso-African tributes based on the ones paid to the *ngola* of Ndongo were known as *baculamentos* and stipulated on the vassalage treaties signed by each conquered *soba*.[180] According to Aida Freudenthal and Beatrix Heintze, they were usually paid with slaves or cattle collected by a *quilamba* doubling as *baculador*.[181] After 1630, a *Book of Baculamentos* was kept in Luanda, registering the obligations of each of the 202 *sobas* that composed the body politic of the Captaincy.[182] In Castello Branco's opinion, all other "*gifts or pensions paid to any persons of whatever status*" should be abolished. Portuguese captains were to stop sending "*macunces* [ambassadors]" with additional demands.[183] However, as Captain-General and

178 Curto, The Population of the Lower Kwanza Valley, p. 95–117.

179 Cordeiro (ed.), Da Mina ao Cabo Negro segundo Garcia Mendes Castello Branco, p. 13–15.

180 ANTT, MR, EXP, Sr. 34, F. 605, p. 290–292; Green, Baculamento or encomienda? p. 310–336; Heintze, Der Portugiesisch-Afrikanische Vasallenvertrag in Angola, p. 195–223; Heintze, Fontes para a História de Angola, Vol. 1, p. 115; Heintze, Luso-African Feudalism, p. 111–131; Santos, Escrever o poder, in: Heintze and von Oppen (eds.), Angola on the Move, p. 173–181.

181 Freudenthal, Sobas, conquistadores e peças d'Índias, in: Pantoja and Thompson (eds.), Em torno de Angola, p. 72, 77; Heintze, Fontes para a História de Angola, Vol. 1, p. 115.

182 Freudenthal, Sobas, conquistadores e peças d'Índias, in: Pantoja and Thompson (eds.), Em torno de Angola, p. 71; Livro dos baculamentos.

183 Castello Branco specified that *sobas* should pay with "*cloths*," except for those of Kissama, which were to pay with salt rocks. According to his project, the proceeds from the lease of *sobados* would be used to pay soldiers' stipends. A similar tributary system would be impossible in Benguela,

Governor Fernão de Sousa, in office between 1624 and 1630, commented on the report of his time in government he wrote for his sons, besides the "*baculamento*" tribute captain majors of *presídios* collected from *sobas* on behalf of the Crown, "*efuta, loanda, and vestiduras*" were also abusively imposed on Africans.[184] While Fernão de Sousa's ordinance tasked him with abolishing these practices, only in 1638, during the tenure of Captain General and Governor Francisco de Vasconcelos da Cunha, was the tributary regime of the Captaincy of Angola formally regulated, with tithes, not *baculamentos*, assuming the complex role of income taxes as well as political tributes levied on the general population (*sobas*, however, continued to pay *baculamentos*, as stipulated by their vassalage treaties, being exempted from tithes in 1650).[185]

To assess the impact of these developments, it is essential to understand the nature of the tribute previously paid to the *ngola* of Ndongo, what kind of reciprocity it entailed between payers and their ruler, and what moral community recognized itself through its ritualized payment. In keeping with contemporary ethnographic descriptions and the Mbundu and Mbangala oral traditions collected by Miller in the 1960s, the *ngola* [pl. *jingola*] title first emerged in association with a "lineage symbol," referring to a "small piece of iron," a "sacred relic of descent groups" to which the Mbundu attributed the powers of corporate kin group headmen known as "*malemba dya ngola* [uncles of the *ngola*]."[186] As such, *jingola* existed alongside other "lineage symbols" or sources of power, for instance, the *mulemba* trees associated

---

where, according to an anonymous manuscript from 1617–1622, the Ovimbundu "*recognized no king*" and "*paid no tribute, contrary to the Gentiles of Angola*." Cordeiro (ed.), Benguella e seu sertão por um anonymo, p. 19; Cordeiro (ed.), Da Mina ao Cabo Negro segundo Garcia Mendes Castello Branco, p. 13–16.

184 According to Beatrix Heintze, the *loanda* was a tribute paid to the *ngola* of Ndongo, which the *baculamentos* substituted. At the same time, *efuta*, *infuta*, or *futa* were "gifts given by an inferior to a superior in recognition of their superiority." Heintze provides no additional information about *vestiduras*. Writing in the second half of the eighteenth century, Silva Corrêa also mentions the tribute called "*Ganda*," consisting of "*one, two, or more slaves*" *sobas* paid to commanders of armies when they rallied for war. Green, Baculamento or encomienda? p. 310–336; Heintze, Der Portugiesisch-Afrikanische Vasallenvertrag in Angola, p. 211–212; Heintze, Fontes para a História de Angola, Vol. 1, p. 115, 119; Livro dos baculamentos; Silva Corrêa, História de Angola, Vol. 2, p. 49; Sousa, O extenso relatório do governador a seus filhos, in: Heintze (ed.), Fontes para a História de Angola, Vol. 1, p. 264.

185 According to Carlos Couto, during this period, Christianized *sobas* were made responsible for stipulating the tithes to be collected in the areas under their jurisdiction and proceeding with their levying. It was then that the religious tax assumed the role of a political tribute. An ad hoc "*Junta de Fazenda* [Board of Finance]" was created in Luanda to regulate the payments. A few years later, this Board began stipulating the tithes according to each jurisdiction's estimated number of huts and cattle heads. Couto, Os capitães-mores em Angola, p. 127.

186 Miller, Kings and Kinsmen, p. 58, 63–70.

with the "*malemba dya ngundu* [uncles of the matrilineage],"[187] or the territorial authority emblems known as *malunga* [sing. *lunga*] held by some *malemba dya ngundu*.[188] According to Miller, the holders of the *lemba dya ngundu* position were responsible for performing the public seasonal rites assuring "bounteous harvests," guaranteeing the "fertility of the lineage women," "rains," and attracting "plentiful supplies of game."[189] *Malemba dya ngundu* were supposed to achieve these goals by serving as an "intermediary between the living lineage members and dead occupants of the same position" and between them all and territorial spirits. *Makota* [elders] served as their political advisors while *xinguilas*, *banganga nzambi*, or other possession-ritual specialists facilitated their communication with deceased past title-holders.[190] The white kaolin *pemba*, the red powder made from "*takula* [*Pterocarpus tinctorius* Welw.]," and *mulemba* trees were associated with these rites of passage.[191] The *mulemba* was "always planted in front of his dwelling in the village" and assumed to facilitate contact with the ancestors, so *malemba dya ngundu* always arbitrated conflicts under its cool shade. As for *malunga*, as described by Miller, they assumed many shapes but usually were a "human figure carved from wood."[192] *Malunga* entities were said to have come from the Atlantic Ocean, associated with water, and believed to help the *lemba dya ngundu* of *malunga*-holding corporate kin groups to "call the rains" and divine subterranean water sources. Contrarily to *mulemba* and *pemba*, which afforded ritual and political power only over the members of the *malemba dya ngundu*'s corporate kin groups, the Mbundu believed *malunga* to afford ritual and political power over all those residing on a given territory, usually the banks of a river or lake. Because they controlled "land and rain," *malemba dya ngundu* could levy tributes, being made responsible in case of draughts or famines.

Jingola incorporated many traits previously attributed to *mulemba* trees or *malunga*, consisting first of an "iron object of defined shape, a hammer, a bell, a hoe, or a knife," and more recently of a "rusty piece of metal."[193] According to Miller, they were held by an important "lineage official" called "*malemba dya ngola*,"

187 The title of *lemba* [uncle] of a Mbundu *ngundu* [corporate kin group] referred to a position within the perpetual kinship and positional successions system described in the sixth chapter, not to an individual who happened to be the biological uncle of a set of nephews. Ibid., p. 46–48.

188 Ibid., p. 46–47, 59; Miller, Imbangala Lineage Slavery (Angola), in: Miers and Kopytoff (eds.), Slavery in Africa, p. 210–211.

189 Miller, Kings and Kinsmen, p. 46–48.

190 According to Friar Cavazzi, in BaKongo areas, "*Ganga Itiqui*" were the ones responsible for collecting "*sacrifices and victims from the hands of*" those who offered them. Cavazzi, Istorica descrizione de' tre' Regni Congo, Matamba et Angola, p. 71.

191 Miller, Kings and Kinsmen, p. 46–48.

192 Ibid., p. 60–62.

193 Ibid., p. 63.

Fig. 9 The Style of West Central African Courts, According to the Capuchin Friar Giovanni Cavazzi. Cavazzi, Alamandi (trans.), Historische Beschreibung Der In dem untern Occidentalischen Mohrenland ligenden drey Königreichen, Congo, Matamba, und Angola, p. 250 (Source: gallica.bnf.fr / Bibliothèque Nationale de France).

assisting him in arbitrating cases or "divining the justice of each party's cause" and also mediating between the "living and dead members of the descent group." Crucially, contrary to the offices associated with *mulemba* trees, which could only propagate and move to distant territories by "lineage fragmentation" (an event symbolized by the planting of a *mulemba* tree in the new village using a cut from the *mulemba* of the old village), and those associated with *malunga*, which remained fixed to a body of water, offices associated with *jingola* were mobile, thus affording political and spiritual stability to migrating groups and facilitating the creation of long-distance alliances.[194]

Because of these advantages, Miller argues that the adoption of *jingola* as a preferential authority symbol and source of power eventually led to the establishment of Mbundu proto-states, as "senior *malemba dya ngola* could grant similar but subordinate titles to other corporate kin groups by awarding them portions of their own *jingola*" thus establishing a new hierarchy of political titles expressed in the

194 Ibid., p. 64–65.

kinship terms of perpetual genealogies (e. g., father-son, as related to the shared *ngola*).[195] According to this interpretation, the holder of the *ngola a kiluanje* office, whom the Portuguese first encountered as ruler of Ndongo,[196] was simply a "great *ngola*" heading what Miller describes as a "hierarchical centralized political institution" based on his sacred relic—a rusty piece of iron.[197] Miller claims that it was controlling and taxing the salt production of Kissama and overseeing the iron-rich valley of the Nzongeji River that afforded the *ngola a kiluanje* an economic basis for the consolidation of their power and eventual ascendency over other Mbundu *malemba dya ngola*, as iron allowed the forging of weapons and tools and salt was central to the function of the prestige spheres of exchange where rights over women and dependents were brokered.[198] From this, it becomes clear that by adopting and adapting the tributary regime of Ndongo and claiming a monopoly over salt production in the salt pans of Benguela, the Portuguese embedded several layers of Mbundu normative knowledge into their taxation system, capitalizing on the legitimacy of the previous tributary system but unwittingly generating expectations regarding the kind of relationship established between those who paid and those who received tithes and *baculamentos*.

In conclusion, Mbundu tributes were intimately connected to the apotropaic and thaumaturgic abilities of the *malemba dya ngundu* and *malemba dya ngola* (*e. g.*, rainmaking, ensuring harvests, game, and fertility) and their material symbols and sources of power (e. g., wooden figurines, iron objects, *mulemba* trees, *pemba* kaolin, or *takula* powder). Moreover, their payment was conceived of as gift-giving, establishing reciprocity between giver and receiver modeled according to kinship norms (e. g., the obligations of fathers towards sons or uncles towards nephews and

195 Ibid., p. 68.

196 Miller argues that a holder of the "*ndambi a ngola*" office, a "son" or subaltern office created by the *ngola a kiluanje*, took the throne of Ndongo in the 1540s, pushing the latter to contact the Portuguese in the Kingdom of Kongo. In keeping with this theory, when Paulo Dias de Novais replied to this call, he met a *ndambi a ngola* as the head of Ndongo, not the *ngola a kiluanje* who had expressed the will to receive the Portuguese, explaining the hostile reception he and the missionaries who accompanied him received. Ibid., p. 83.

197 Ibid., p. 74–78.

198 According to this interpretation, later marriages and conquests consolidated the position of *ngola a kiluanje* as the head of Ndongo. Ibid., p. 76–82.

vice-versa)[199] and deeply connected with seasonal rites of passage.[200] Therefore, tributes were central to how Mbundu corporate kin groups established and policed the boundaries of their moral communities, legitimizing the administration of justice and enabling the divination of sorcerers, adulterers, thieves, and other wrongdoers—either under the shade of a *mulemba* tree or at the court of a *soba* that was a *malemba dya ngola*. This system presupposed a very different grammar of affect from the one grounding the *imperium* and *dominium* of the Portuguese monarch over West Central Africa and his claim to collect tithes and tributes.

When narrating his mission to the Angolan hinterlands in 1672–73, Father Manuel Ribeiro captured some of these aspects of Mbundu tributes, describing how they offered the "*primisias das colheitas* [first harvests] *to their idols*."[201] According to him, as soon as they "*harvested the fruits of their fields, the whole Banza* [village], *grownups and children alike would disappear into the woods with axes, and cleavers, and carve into the trunk of any tree the figure of a man.*" This figure, which sounds similar to the *malunga* described by Miller, would be "*painted on the face with black ink*" and dressed with a "*cloth around the waist*," becoming their new "*quiteque, or idol, to whom they attribute the fruits, they harvested in their lands*."[202] Then, Father Ribeiro continued, with much "*music, dancing, and frolicking*," the wooden figure would be "*taken to a place*" where it "*was offered the first fruits, that they harvested in their fields, and the barns where these dizimos* [tithes] *were collected were their stomachs*."[203] These communal banquets, the Jesuit concluded, were the sum of "*their sacrifices and gentilic rites*" as they recognized "*no other God*." "*Quiteques*" were deemed responsible for there being "*rain in the fields, and the sun to bless them*," were supposed to guide hunters in finding "*shelter in the wild*," provide "*remedies*"

---

199 Catarina Madeira Santos describes how the obligation to reciprocate was at the root of two common strategies employed by Portuguese and Luso-African merchants to exploit Mbundu *sobas*: "*fazer ocamba* [to make *ocamba*]" and "*dar emfuca* [to give *emfuca*]." The first consisted of offering and forcing the acceptance of gifts to demand counter-gifts, usually in slaves, and the second consisted of using the idiom and normative framing of gift-giving to offer trade goods on credit. As she remarks, both originated conflicts that constantly gave rise to *mucano* hearings. SANTOS, Esclavage africain, p. 127–148.

200 As Freudenthal remarks, the *loandas* paid to the *ngola* of Ndongo were levied during the *cacimbo* (the winter dry season that followed harvest). They consisted of "foodstuff (sorghum, palm oil, beans, honey, salt), livestock (kids, chickens, cows), *moleques* [young slaves] or *peças* [slaves], *almadias* [canoes], and ivory tooth." FREUDENTHAL, Sobas, conquistadores e peças d'Índias, in: PANTOJA and THOMPSON (eds.), Em Torno de Angola, p. 72.

201 MMA XIII, D. 114, p. 265.

202 If Father Ribeiro is describing the seasonal rites of passage of a *malunga*-holding corporate kin group, then it appears the wooden figurines that temporarily embodied the entities were ritually renewed each season. Ibid.

203 Ibid., p. 266–268.

for sicknesses, assure "*nobles*" divined "*good omens before wars*" and guarantee that "friends" received "*good advice*."[204]

As for the propitiating or apotropaic dimension of Mbundu tributes, which approximated them to European sacrifices, Sousa Coutinho himself testified to this, describing in his *bando* forbidding "*Entambes*" how, during an epidemic that followed the "*war against the Maungos*," the Mbundu erected "*some dreadful lodges called Quibangos, in public spaces, and on Royal highways, so that travelers could worship*" and pay tribute to their "*idols*."[205] Given the reciprocal nature of the relationships mediated by Mbundu tributes, by grafting their tributary and taxation system to previous ones, Portuguese authorities were obliged to assure rain, plentiful harvests, fertility, health, and justice in the eyes of their African and Luso-African subjects and vassals—just as the Jesuits and Capuchins were forced to assume the role of the *banganga* they persecuted, ensuring rain instead of the so-called idols they burned, and *yimbanda* they persecuted. However, as the following pages and the next chapter discuss, the Portuguese did not even assume they were obliged to provide West Central Africans access to Roman Catholic sacraments when they received their tithes, greatly disturbing their subjects, as Ignácio Machado argued.[206]

As already noted, by the time Silva Corrêa wrote his *History of Angola*, the "*Gentiles under the jurisdiction of Presídios were forced, under severe penalties* […] *to pay the tithe of their harvest to a God they know nothing about*" except for the "*Apostolic zeal of the titularies of the* [tax farming] *contract*."[207] Moreover, as he wrote ironically, the yield of these taxes grew "*not according to the size of the population but the ambition of the tax farmers and the impiousness and ruthlessness of their large and*

204 Lino d'Assumpção transcribes excerpts from a report written by Father Pedro Tavares at "*the beginning of the second half of the seventeenth century*" about a mission to Ndongo. According to the Jesuit, he had found in a "*yard an idol made of wood, the size of a man, anointed with many herbs, the mouth full of manioc flour and palm wine, sitting atop a high pyramid*." This "*idol*," to which the Mbundu symbolically offered their harvests, was next to a "*very gross and hollow stake, filled inside with many feiticeirias exhaling an infernal smell*" and to a "*straw hut, covered in mats*" where they "*spoke with the devil*." As described by Father Tavares, these "*idols*" were next to the "*Inibielas*," or cemetery graves, where they built tiny "*houses*" with "*holes*" to feed the dead. This description suggests that ancestors and a territorial spirit were simultaneously offered tribute to guarantee good harvests. Lino d'Assumpção, Exploração à Africa, p. 356.

205 AHU, CU, Angola, Box 54, D. 4897.

206 In a letter from December 6, 1754, Captain-General and Governor António Alvares da Cunha noted *that* Mbundu farmers were required to pay the same amount of tithe regardless of the yield of their fields and even where rains and harvests failed, causing a generalized feeling of revolt. In other words, in their eyes, the Portuguese failed to ensure rain and harvests and required tribute all the same. ANTT, MR, EXP, Sr. 34, F. 605, p. 53; Couto, Os capitães-mores em Angola, p. 129.

207 Silva Corrêa, História de Angola, Vol. 1, p. 94.

small Delegates."[208] According to Silva Corrêa, tax farming contracts were auctioned every three years, and those over households and their harvests were separated from those over ocean fisheries (Luanda) or lake (Muxima and Golungo) and river fisheries (Bar of Dande). Outside of the jurisdictions covered by these contracts, tithes were directly collected by captain majors as agents of the Royal Treasury[209] and by the *provedor da Real Fazenda* in the district of Luanda. This had been a result of Sousa Coutinho's reform from November 14, 1766, which determined that all the "*arimos, lands, fisheries, and cattle, as well as properties situated in the district of Luanda, not under the jurisdiction of captain majors*" were to be appraised by the *provedor da Real Fazenda* who would then be responsible for keeping a book of records and coordinating the collection of tithes.[210] By the late 1790s, when *sobas* were not vassals (thus not paying *baculamentos*), their populations were exempt from tithes.[211] In this case, friendly *sobas* still paid *loandas* to the captain-general and governors of Angola, not to the Crown, as a goodwill gesture. Tithes of perishable goods and produce were paid with currency, and those covering non-perishable goods in kind, usually every three years instead of annually, thus amounting to thirty percent of the harvests of that year.[212] The currency used to pay tithes varied according to the customs of each jurisdiction, causing several problems and conflicts worsened by the imposition of additional emoluments and *corvée* labor (e. g., the obligation to serve as porters of their tithes).

According to Captain-General and Governor António Álvares da Cunha, in office between 1753 and 1758, by the time he took office, where salt circulated as currency, tithe farmers collected "*two salt rocks twice per year*" from each Mbundu household, each worth 100 *réis*.[213] Moreover, they also abusively charged "*two chickens*" from each household as "*sustento and tellecamentos* [subsistence allowances]." Aggravating matters, he continued, tithe collectors considered the "*separate hut*" of each wife in a polygynous marriage a separate household, at times multiplying thirty or fifteen times the tithe collected from "*Quilambas*" and other notables or doubling the one collected to commoners. In areas such as Ambaca, where salt was not readily available, Álvares da Cunha explained that tithe farmers charged "*a*

---

208 Ibid., p. 163, 166.

209 When acting as tithe collectors, if captain majors received no fixed stipend (those heading districts, for instance), they received twelve percent of the total amounts levied as compensation for their efforts, giving rise to all sorts of abuses. Ibid., p. 166.

210 Previously, as Delgado explains, the big property owners of the district of Luanda used to sponsor the bidding for the tithe contract fraudulently, then having the contractor artificially lower the value of their tithes. Delgado, O governo de Sousa Coutinho em Angola I, p. 29.

211 Silva Corrêa, História de Angola, Vol. 1, p. 166.

212 Ibid., p. 164.

213 Couto, Os capitães-mores em Angola, p. 129.

covado and a half [0.9 m.] *of Baeta or one eight of a cloth of serafina*" worth fifteen "*tustões* [1$500 *réis*]" instead of the four rocks of salt worth a "*cruzado* [400 *réis*]" per year. By the time of Silva Corrêa's writing, tithes were collected in Ambaca and Cambambe in "*páos de fio*," a conventional measure of raw spun cotton that could be sold as a cash crop for one "*tostão* [100 *réis*]" of yarn.[214] However, the tithe collectors attributed an arbitrary value to the *pau de fio*, profiting from speculating in the emerging commodities market. Faced with this practice, Sousa Coutinho issued a *portaria* [ordinance] on May 9, 1769, decreeing that salt would be the preferred currency to pay tithes, but to little effect.[215]

After years of exposing similar abuses to the Secretary of State of the Navy and the Overseas Martinho de Melo e Castro, Captain-General Manuel de Almeida e Vasconcelos, in office between 1790 and 1797, finally received a royal ordinance regulating the levying of tithes on June 6, 1796, when Rodrigo de Sousa Coutinho (1755–1812),[216] was secretary of state of the navy and the overseas.[217] The ordinance stipulated that tithes were to be levied on "*prédios rústicos* [rural properties]" with cattle, varying in value according to their appraisal, while each household constituted by a "*head of the family, their sons, single or married, under the power of the father, and its slaves*," was to pay a fixed amount of 200 *réis* per year. As for the cash crops increasingly used to pay tithes, six years before, on October 7, 1791, Manuel de Almeida e Vasconcelos had ordered all captain majors to send to Luanda the measures used during tithe collecting so that these could be inspected and harmonized. A standard was adopted for the *pau de fio*, defining it as the amount of raw spun cotton worth one *tostão*, and the "*dishes of beeswax*," which were also used to pay tithes, were regulated as weighing one Portuguese pound.

From the point of view of the captain-general and governor of Angola and the secretary of state of the navy and overseas, these measures sorted out most of the problems caused by using tithes as capitation and income taxes, transforming them into an effective tool to impose cash crops and the export of beeswax. Combined with the repressive measures towards those who charged undue emoluments or tributes according to Mbundu uses and customs dispensed by the Board of Justice,

214 Silva Corrêa, História de Angola, Vol. 1, p. 164.

215 Delgado, O governo de Sousa Coutinho em Angola I, p. 30.

216 Rodrigo de Sousa Coutinho was the son of Francisco Inocêncio de Sousa Coutinho and the godson of Sebastião José de Carvalho e Melo. He had a degree in law from the University of Coimbra, was an anglophile, and an avid reader of Adam Smith and the Physiocrats. According to Jeremy Adelman, Rodrigo de Sousa Coutinho rose to be the most influential Portuguese statesman of the first decade of the nineteenth century, being responsible for the "vision" of a "Great Empire" that shaped Portuguese "imperial policy" during this period. Adelman, Sovereignty and Revolution, p. 127–128; 220–222.

217 Couto, Os capitães-mores em Angola, p. 131–132.

they transformed the tributary system of the Captaincy of Angola, Benguela, and their dependencies, frustrating Mbundu and Ovimbundu expectations regarding any reciprocity resulting from the payment of taxes or tributes. If the paying of tributes was a liminal period in Kinbumdu-speaking and other African societies, as evidenced by its association with seasonal rites of passage, the Portuguese explored the fragility associated with this moment not only to impose new tributes and taxes predicated on different grammars of affect but also to exploit their subjects economically. However, separating tithes from their religious origins was impossible. Soon, the issue of determining whether African groups without access to Roman Catholic sacraments and institutions could legitimately be required to pay them resurfaced. Confronted with "*countless requests and questions addressed to the Board of Finance about the levying of ecclesiastic tithes*," Miguel António de Mello, captain-general and governor of Angola between 1797 and 1802, decided to spend two months systematizing the "*infinite papers and ledger books of orders related to them*" concluding that it would be best for public finances and public rest if tithes were abolished.[218]

According to Mello, tithes "*distressed the population*," and it was not "*honest to collect them, from those who live in Paganism, when tithes are levied to maintain the Church and its Ministers, to which they don't belong*."[219] Even when African populations embraced Christian "*Dogmas*," Mello continued, the Portuguese failed them by not providing access to "*priests or temples*." Moreover, he concluded, the profit was not worth it. If all tithes had been collected in the previous ten years (1787–1797), the total collected would have amounted to 101.413$061 *réis* according to his estimate, of which 12.169$567 *réis* would have to be deducted to pay the services of collectors and treasurers. In the end, António de Mello argued, this sum paled compared to the 1.620.108$000 *réis* collected as export duty taxes over *cabeças* (slaves regardless of their age and gender), so he recommended an additional tax of 800 *réis* per *cabeça* to compensate for the abolishment of tithes to support the Roman Catholic Church in the Captaincy of Angola. Rodrigo Sousa Coutinho rejected Mello's proposal because the secretary of state of the navy and the overseas worried it would negatively impact the economy of Brazil by raising the price of slaves.[220] Tithes would continue to be levied despite, as Mello convincingly argued, the "*majority of the Peoples of Angola being Christians only in name, but neither in acts nor in exterior demonstrations*" of affection, still acting according to the African grammars of love, charity, sadness, and joy briefly described in this chapter.[221]

---

218 AHU, CU, Angola, Box 87, D. 6986.

219 Ibid.

220 Couto, Os capitães-mores em Angola, p. 133.

221 AHU, CU, Angola, Box 87, D. 6986.

9. The Impact of Unfinished Projects

9.1 Accelerating Religious Reform and Assimilation

As soon as Friar Alexandre da Sagrada Família reached Lisbon in 1788, the former vicar Bishop of Congo and Angola wrote a report to the Secretary of State of the Navy and the Overseas Martinho de Melo e Castro informing him of the motives for his recent resignation.[1] However, more than justifying his past actions or arguing in defense of his vicar forane against the 'abuses' of Captain-General and Governor José de Almeida e Vasconcelos, in this letter, Friar Alexandre da Sagrada Família exposed the pastoral plan he had devised for the Diocese of Congo and Angola, delving into an epistolary genre that was usually reserved for former captain-general and governors—the political testament. Similar reports and letters abound in the archives. Listing the officeholders' achievements and service records, they were crucial to their career strategies or obtaining favors and privileges from the Crown in exchange for past long-term personal and financial investments.[2] This was often done by contrasting what their authors had accomplished with what they understood still needed to be done, thus also listing flaws and justifying shortcomings. Therefore, final reports and political testaments delve deep into failure to harness what Catherine Alexander describes as its "positive generativity."[3] One aspect of the 'folk doctrines' about West Central Africa that has gone unexplored so far is that they also provided the perfect 'alibi' for arguing in favor of the intrinsic merits of failed projects. By pinning the blame on the extreme conditions of West Central Africa, the authors of political testaments could salvage their projects' credibility,

---

1 See the previous chapter for information about the jurisdictional conflict that led to his resignation. AHU, CU, Angola, Box 74, D. 6275.

2 Their more mundane counterparts were the hundreds of petitions addressed by minor officeholders, soldiers, and Luso-African *moradores* to captain-general and governors, requesting minor boons (e. g., land grants) and the official recognition of past services for career purposes. Usually, more significant services to the Crown were acknowledged by granting the authors of successful petitions membership in the Military Orders of Aviz, St. James of the Sword, and Christ. Apart from social prestige, this membership granted them access to a yearly stipend and privileged jurisdiction. As Francisco Bethencourt explains, "purity of blood" was central to the success of petitions, excluding New Christians and most "mixed-race people" from accessing these rewards. BETHENCOURT, Managing Diversity in the Portuguese Empire, p. 1–23; GUARDA, Angolan Slave Trade in the early 18th century, in: POLÓNIA and ANTUNES (eds.), Mechanisms of Global Empire Building, p. 59–76; OLIVAL, As Ordens Militares na historiografia portuguesa p. 97–108.

3 ALEXANDER, Writing failure, p. 8–30.

promise, and potential from the clutches of ridicule and disappointment.[4] This potential turns final reports into carefully crafted "objects of failure"[5]—documentary traces that have a lingering or continuous impact on the agents who can access them, either in personal or institutional archives or through their publication.[6] While contemporary ethnographical and sociological literature has engaged with the nonlinear temporality of failure, the deferred impact of accounts of failure in the history of the Captaincy of Angola, Benguela, and their dependencies during the second half of the eighteenth century and the nineteenth century remains underexplored.[7]

As Alexander, Timothy Carroll, David Jeevendrampillai, and Aaron Parkhurst remark, failure can be "highly productive" even when framed by those who admit to it in purely negative terms, enabling them to pass their guilt to others, scapegoating vulnerable groups and proposing a "reorganization of social relations" for the future.[8] Therefore, paradoxically, failures often have a more lasting impact than punctual or partial successes, which recurring problems and unfixed issues can

4 See Judith/Jack Halberstam, Jessica Greenberg, and Sarah Muir for a critique of contemporary politics of disappointment and pessimism. GREENBERG and MUIR, Disappointment, p. 307–323; HALBERSTAM, The Queer Art of Failure.

5 ALEXANDER, Writing failure, p. 25.

6 A historical analysis of how access to final reports and political testaments narrating failed projects evolved from the early years of Portuguese settlement in West Central Africa to the last decades of the eighteenth century is beyond the scope of this book. However, it is worth mentioning a widening of the audience with access to these documentary traces from the time when Captain-General and Governor Fernão de Sousa, in office between 1624 and 1630, wrote his *Extensive Report of the Governor to his Sons* to when most of the reports and letters analyzed in this section were produced (c. 1770–1800). No longer addressed primarily to members of their noble households or the Overseas Council, where elites served according to patrimonial principles, but to the Secretariat of State of the Navy and the Overseas, where access to information was brokered according to merit, it is safe to assume that later documents had more impact, conditioning the actions of whole groups of bureaucrats and planners instead of a few influential individuals. However, in the transition period under analysis, the older modes of making failure known and thus harnessing its generative potential were also present. See João Figueiredo for a detailed analysis of how documents attesting to the failures and unfinished projects of the elites of the *Antigo Regime* were later published in print and politically leveraged by the liberal elites of the nineteenth century. FIGUEIREDO, Política, escravatura e feitiçaria em Angola.

7 See also Jacques Derrida and Mark Fisher for a critique of linear conceptions of history and an account of the haunting presence of unfulfilled promises or "past futures." ALEXANDER, Writing failure, p. 22; APPADURAI, Introduction, p. xxi–xxvii; CARROLL et al., The Material Culture of Failure; DERRIDA, Specters of Marx; FISHER, Ghosts of My Life; HALBERSTAM, The Queer Art of Failure, p. 87–122.

8 ALEXANDER, Writing failure, p. 8–30; CARROLL et al., Introduction, in: CARROLL et al., (eds.), The Material Culture of Failure, p. 1–20.

quickly overshadow.[9] This chapter concludes Part Three by exploring how several failed projects of two senior statesmen and one ecclesiastical authority addressed the challenges delineated in the previous chapters. Namely, Friar Alexandre da Sagrada Família's assimilationist pastoral plan, Francisco Inocêncio de Sousa Coutinho's plan to base the White settler-colonization in the Captaincy of Angola and Benguela on a radical form of racial patriarchy, and António de Mello's attempt to further the interests of commerce by having the "*Direitos* [laws/rights] *of the Souvas* [*sobas*]" of West Central Africa written down and the style of the *mucanos* hearings systematized.[10] It argues that these visions of the future had a bearing on subsequent policies despite their immediate failure or limited success and implementation.

In the words of Friar Alexandre da Sagrada Família, his time in Luanda was marked by painful failure. A "*long-standing deprivation of Workers*" brought the diocese to a standstill, leaving many "*Bush parishes*" and even some *presídios* without a priest and affecting the religious life of Luanda, Benguela, and Massangano.[11] Only three Capuchin missionaries staffed the missions in the Kingdom of Kongo, the Kingdoms of Matamba and Kasanje were left without a single missionary, and the Chapter of Luanda was composed of twelve prebendary canons either too sickly or too entitled to travel outside the capital.[12] Regarding the regular orders, Friar Alexandre da Sagrada Família remarked that their numbers dwindled and their hospices were empty, a situation the regulars attributed to the Crown's refusal to let them take Luso-Africans and free Blacks as novices but that the former bishop understood as a sign of resignation.[13] In sum, the "*diocese was long lost*," the "*hinterland churches, built with fragile materials,* [were] *slowly falling apart*," and the "*church chalices of most of them* [had] *disappeared*." "*If the sacred paraments*" also ended up "*in the hands of Blacks, who could hold back the tears*?"—the friar dramatically asked the secretary of state, claiming that the paraments would end

9 I argue that self-ascribed 'successes' and 'failures' were understood by the authors of reports and political testaments not as binary outcomes but as ideal opposites that delineated a continuous spectrum of possibilities. Moreover, I take these as emic classifications, not analytical categories, and I am aware of the subjects' political and social motivations when strategically constructing their objects of failure and success. Moreover, by only focusing on self-ascribed 'failures' and limiting the analysis to emic understandings, I seek to avoid anachronic judgments—in other words, avoid ascribing failure or success to policies according to their later historical impact. ALEXANDER, Writing failure, p. 25; APPADURAI, Introduction, p. xxi–xxvii; CARROLL et al., Introduction, in: CARROLL et al. (eds.), The Material Culture of Failure, p. 7–9.

10 MELLO, Carta de oficio do Governador.

11 In his words, due to the lack of priests, "*thousands of* [baptized] *Slaves were left unconfessed*" every year in Luanda and Benguela during Lent. AHU, CU, Angola, Box 74, D. 6275.

12 Friar Alexandre da Sagrada Família claims they would sue him in the *ouvidor geral*'s court if he dared to touch their privileges. Ibid.; AHU, CU, Angola, Box 71, D. 6118.

13 AHU, CU, Angola, Box 74, D. 6275.

up being used to "*adorn their concubines*." As for the church's "*Sacred Images*," Friar Alexandre da Sagrada Família continued, they were either being "*eaten by bugs*" or "*mistaken for idols in their houses, serving as the object, not of religious adoration, but of profane idolatry*." "*The Devil was worshiped even in the Images of Jesus Christ*," and the Angolan hinterlands were a "*bushland filled with all sorts of beasts,* [...] *all baptized monsters*," where the "*Blacks, the many Mulatos, and the few whites that were there* [were] *as black in their customs as the Blacks*." Moreover, according to Friar Alexandre da Sagrada Família, contrarily to the BaKongo, the Mbundu and Ovimbundu insisted on having their children baptized for "*entirely profane reasons*," rendering the "*baptism sterile and* [riddled] *with all the errors and rites of paganism*."[14] As for the Luso-African and European Whites and mixed-race *moradores* of *presídios*, they were "*infected by the same vices, errors, and superstitions, Casas de uso, Tambes* [*entambes*], *xinguilamentos, Indua oaths, or similar ones, the worshiping of idols, and* [...] *Judaic circumcision*," freely and publicly committing "*polygamy, adultery, and incest*."[15]

Facing this bleak scenario (which is a perfect rendition of the 'folk doctrine' about West Central Africa), Friar Alexandre da Sagrada Família identified a culprit and devised a long-term pastoral plan. According to him, apart from the lack of priests, the "*extreme imbecility of Black women*" was at the root of most of these "*moral scandals*," standing in the way of Canon law "*matrimonies*" that would provide an example for the community.[16] However, as discussed in the previous chapters, Mbundu and other African and Luso-African marriage agreements were central to establishing alliances with the "familial factions" that brokered access to patronage, credit, and commercial networks in the Angolan hinterlands, enabling both the newly arrived men and long-established *moradores* to participate in the Atlantic slave trade.[17] Moreover, African marriage arrangements and rites permitted the accumulation of dependents as a form of 'wealth in people.'[18] Therefore, Friar Alexandre da Sagrada Família faced considerable resistance when he attempted to impose Canon law marriages and all the religious observances required to access

---

14 Ibid.; AHU, CU, Angola, Box 71, D. 6118.

15 See the previous chapter for a discussion of these rituals. AHU, CU, Angola, Box 74, D. 6275.

16 Friar Alexandre da Sagrada Família's misogyny and racial hatred against Black women are evident in several passages of this letter.

17 Miller, Way of Death, p. 249.

18 In his letter, friar Alexandre da Sagrada Família mentions the case of a White Portuguese *morador* who had baptized seventy-five sons from different mothers, having many more to whom he had not conceded the privilege. This enabled him to accumulate wealth in dependents, if the children were born of enslaved mothers or establish political alliances with several Mbundu corporate kin groups if the children were born of free mothers. See the fourth chapter for a discussion of the 'wealth in people' concept. Miers and Kopytoff, Slavery in Africa; AHU, CU, Angola, Box 74, D. 6275.

them.[19] In his words, he first reacted by bringing back the custom of imposing "*pecuniary fines*" on those who skipped sacraments, mass, and confession, tasking the church's bailiffs with collecting them. However, he argued, many resisted by brutalizing his deputies. Nevertheless, only a few destitute "*Blacks*" were made responsible for these abuses, being brought before the secular arm of justice to be whipped or sent to work in the galleys. In response to this, Friar Alexandre da Sagrada Família gave to "*many missionaries the powers of Vigario da Vara* [vicar forane], *as the Prelates of old used to give to their parishioners so that they could pursue with correction what they could not correct with persuasion*." His plan to snatch victory from the jaws of defeat was thus to establish a network of vicariates forane, perhaps like the ones established in South American dioceses, consolidating his episcopal authority over the territory.[20] Lacking armed muscle, vicars forane were left to their own devices, probably forging alliances with captain majors, sergeant majors, or even *quilambas* who felt excluded from the existing arrangements of Luso-African familial factions.

According to Aldair Rodrigues, in Brazil, each vicar forane headed an ecclesiastical judicial county, having jurisdiction over the members of their parishes and acting in parallel with the ecclesiastical tribunal ("ecclesiastical auditorium") run by the general vicar at the seat of the diocese.[21] Following the Ordinance of the Ecclesiastical Auditorium (1704) of the Archdiocese of Bahia, vicars forane were ideally "*Lettrados* [learned persons]," preferably bachelors in Canon law, or at least "*persons of good judgment, prudence, virtue, and exemplary behavior*."[22] They were bound to uphold the *First Constitutions of the Archdiocese of Bahia* (1707).[23] Vicars forane could conduct "*devassas* [inquiries]" and receive denunciations, adjudicating summarily cases involving "*sacrileges*" committed in sacred places and were able to reconsecrate "*polluted churches*" (except those which the bishop had

---

19 AHU, CU, Angola, Box 74, D. 6275.

20 See José Pedro Paiva, Pollyana Muniz, and Michelle Britto for a global analysis of "peripheral diocesan justice" in the overseas bishoprics of the Portuguese Empire during the Early Modern period. See Aldair Rodrigues for an overview of how a network of vicariates forane was established in Minas Gerais and São Paulo between 1745 and 1800. As he remarks, since vicars forane were direct representatives of the ecclesiastical authority, they had greater jurisdiction than pastoral visitors. Moreover, because of a royal decree from 1646, at least in South America, bishops were granted the privilege of directly appointing their vicars forane instead of presenting their names to the Board of Royal Conscience and Military Orders for confirmation. This also seems to have been the case in the Captaincy of Angola. Ibid.; Paiva et al., A justiça infra-diocesana no Império Português p. 211–247; Rodrigues, Clergy, Society, and Power Relations in Colonial Brazil, p. 59–62.

21 Rodrigues, Clergy, Society, and Power Relations in Colonial Brazil, p. 41.

22 Vide, Regimento do Auditório Ecclesiastico, p. 90.

23 Ibid., p. 91; Vide, Constituições primeiras do Arcebispado da Bahia.

consecrated).[24] Their inquiries were to be adjudicated by the general vicar, who also reviewed their adjudications against those who disobeyed their (legitimate) orders.[25] Vicars forane had ample Canon law jurisdiction over matters related to marriage and burials in consecrated spaces. They also had jurisdiction over "*all those who usurp* [the bishop's] *jurisdiction*," regardless of their being secular or ecclesiastic authorities. Consolidating a network of ecclesiastical tribunals headed by vicars forane, in tandem with the revival of the "*old custom*" of charging pecuniary fines, would give Friar Alexandre da Sagrada Família access to a revenue stream that was vital for any future projects as the Crown, not the Church, collected tithes in West Central Africa.[26] Therefore, his pastoral plan must be recognized as more ambitious than simply providing the future Bishops of Congo and Angola the means to interfere with Mbundu lifecycle event celebrations and "*correcting*" those who adopted African grammars of affect. Indeed, Friar Alexandre da Sagrada Família also sought to reform the financial grounding of the diocese by extending the ecclesiastical judicial system and making it 'profitable.' Considering this, the long list of failures and the catastrophic description of the state of West Central African churches he portrayed can be read as a rhetorical preamble to this ambitious project.

Captain majors and other secular authorities who also depended on their broad jurisdiction and the emoluments they charged to make a living probably met Friar Alexandre da Sagrada Família's project with skepticism. As did José de Almeida e Vasconcelos and all subsequent captain-generals and governors equally invested in imposing the hierarchy of sources of law proposed by 'The Law of Good Reason' of August 18, 1769, and preserving the flow of enslaved Africans from hinterland slave fairs and *pumbos*.[27] As Captain-General and Governor Sousa Coutinho had pointed out in the tenth article of his Ordinance of February 24, 1765, a lot of *mucano* hearings held by captain majors arbitrated disputes related to Mbundu marriages and *opanda* [adultery] charges, thus falling under the jurisdiction of the vicars forane commissioned by the bishop if one or both spouses were baptized, even if only with 'salt.' While Sousa Coutinho barred captain majors and ordinary

---

24 Regarding the desecration of sacred images denounced by Friar Alexandre da Sagrada Família as a common occurrence, not only did the vicars forane had jurisdiction over the abusers, but also the Inquisition of Lisbon, according to the Ordinance of 1774. Cosme da Cunha, Regimento do Santo Officio, p. 114; Vide, Regimento do Auditório Ecclesiastico, p. 91–92.

25 Vide, Regimento do Auditório Ecclesiastico, p. 91–92.

26 AHU, CU, Angola, Box 74, D. 6275.

27 As discussed in the first section of the first chapter, the new hierarchy of sources of law privileged the *leis pátrias* [laws of the fatherland] and royal enactments and ordinances over other sources of law, including Canon law and all forms of revived Roman law. Couto, Os capitães-mores em Angola; Silva (ed.), Colleção de legislação portugueza (1763–1774), p. 407–415; Wehling and Wehling, Direito e Justiça.

judges from adjudicating these (with no apparent success), neither he nor his successors could prohibit "*any parish priests, vicars forane, or pastoral visitors*" who decided to adjudicate them, simply asking captain majors to inform their superiors if parishioners committed abuses, for instance by "*extorting one or several*" slaves as compensation for their services or as a fine.[28] Complicating matters, the jurisdiction vicars forane had over those who 'usurped' the jurisdiction of the bishop of Congo and Angola also enabled them to persecute all those who administered or facilitated the taking of "*Juramentos de Indua* [*ndua* oaths], *or similar ones*" commonly used to assist settling adultery charges.[29] As the previous sections described, this lot included not only captain majors and slave fair scribes but also members of the clergy. Thus, the stage was set for jurisdictional conflicts like the one that had led to the former bishop's resignation, as energetic vicars forane could ruthlessly compete to adjudicate cases both with secular Portuguese jurisdictions, African *sobas*, and other arbitrators, together with the African or Luso-African ritual operators that often assisted them.

Friar Alexandre da Sagrada Família described African judicial ordeals as poisonings if they involved the ingestion of emetic beverages and, in keeping with the Ordinance of the Portuguese Inquisition of 1774, as "*superstitions*" if not.[30] In 1720, the *mbulungo* or *golungo* ordeal had already been described by the list of "*Gentilic Rites of Angola*" edited by the Inquisition of Lisbon's Prosecutor Manuel da Cunha Pinheiro as an "*oath of the blacks, tolerated and still endorsed by whites, especially those filhos da terra* [locally born]" which was "*used to know who committed, or not, a given crime.*"[31] Before exploring what earlier sources tell us of the many judicial ordeals and divinations that were common in the Captaincy of Angola, Benguela, and their dependencies, it is thus worth exploring how the perception inquisitors and ecclesiastical judges and visitors had of these rituals evolved, contrasting it with the new framing of sorcery in the Portuguese Kingdom proposed by the Ordinance of the Portuguese Inquisition of 1774.[32] A document of the late Enlightenment, this ordinance unambiguously states that, after "*two centuries*" of experience, the mixed-court had finally concluded that "*evil spirits, through the pacts they make with Feiticeiros*" could not "*break the Fundamental Laws of the order of Nature,*" "*implicit pacts*" were impossible to prove, and "*explicit pacts*" could only be proven through the untrustworthy "*Judicial Confessions*" of the accused. Given these premises, the ordinance regulated the processes against those accused of the "*crimes of Feiticeria,*" which would henceforward be verbally and quickly

28 Coutinho, Documento N.º 6, in: Couto, Os capitães-mores em Angola, p. 324.
29 AHU, CU, Angola, Box 74, D. 6275.
30 Ibid.; Cosme da Cunha, Regimento do Santo Officio, p. 118–127.
31 ANTT, TSO, CG, Sr. 25, Fol. 272, p. 123.
32 Cosme da Cunha, Regimento do Santo Officio, p. 118–127.

adjudicated. If the accused confessed, or if there were enough accusatory witnesses, they were to be condemned neither for practicing the crimes of sorcery or of heresy but for the "*Crime of Superstition*," being publicly informed that their confessions and the accusatory witnesses' claims were unfounded fantasies. For this crime, the Ordinance of 1774 proposed a five to ten-year exile in Angola as the penalty for nobles, whipping and work in the galleys as the penalty for commoners, perpetual exile in Angola, or work in the galleys, for male clerics, and banishment to the farthest convent of their orders for female regulars. All those who insisted they had special powers obtained through demoniac pacts, either to cause harm, heal, or "*divine contingent futures*," were to be delivered to the All-Saints Royal Hospital in Lisbon to be locked away as lunatics in the "*Mad-persons Prison*."[33]

These regulations lacked any practical applicability in the hinterlands of Angola and Benguela. However, the secularized worldview they propose afforded a re-reading of the West Central African judicial ordeals and divinations long described by Portuguese observers, resituating them fully in the sphere of the administration of justice (*jurisdictio*). It suggested the establishment of an alternative judicial network, such as the one proposed in Friar Alexandre da Sagrada Família's pastoral plan, as an effective means of addressing the normative, social, and personal issues otherwise resolved through divination and ordeals. Moreover, it afforded the framing of those who still held archaic beliefs in the efficacy of ordeals as problematic, introducing the question of how to govern different "temporalities" to the problem.[34] Central to this project is the attribution of what François Hartog defines as a "legal temporality" to African ordeals and divinations, turning them into a "sort of past in the present" or a "present past."[35] In other words, as the existence of demonic pacts was no longer an accepted possibility, and there were no apparatuses ("*dispositive*") in place to frame African beliefs as madness, ordeals were re-framed as survivals of old judicial procedures that could now be persecuted as poisonings

33 The All-Saints Royal Hospital was severely damaged by the Lisbon earthquake of 1755. It remained abandoned and was finally demolished in 1775, shortly after the Ordinance of 1774 was published. Carreira, Lisboa de 1731 a 1833, p. 42–60.

34 As François Hartog remarks, there is vast and multifaced literature on how "different forms of temporality and different regimes of historicity" were brought into sharp contrast in colonial settings. For this chapter, I conceive of temporality as a way of understanding how time is ordered and experienced. For more on different temporalities, "temporal pluralism," and "regimes of temporality," see Dan Edelstein, Hartog, Natasha Wheatley, and Stefanos Geroulanos. For classic critiques of how colonial and imperial powers attempt to manipulate regimes of temporality for their advantage, see Johannes Fabian and Marshall Sahlins. Edelstein et al. (eds.), Power and Time; Fabian, Time and the Other; Geroulanos, The Invention of Prehistory; Hartog, Chronos; Hartog, Regimes of Historicity, p. 36; Sahlins, Islands of History; Wheatley, The Life and Death of States.

35 Hartog, Regimes of Historicity, p. 201.

or the fraudulent exploitation of the credulity of "rustics."[36] This solution can be described as assimilationist in as much as it presupposes not only conversion but also progressive homogenization of normative horizons, grammars of affect, and the shape of the normative fabric of the Captaincy of Angola (e. g., through the establishment of regular parishes, municipal councils, lay brotherhoods). Because of this, Friar Alexandre da Sagrada Família's pastoral plan was at odds with segregationist projects and the demands of the Atlantic slave trade.[37] Moreover, it implied what Natasha Wheatley defines as the creation of a "coeval" community out of "temporally disparate communities" by synchronizing the slow-paced, conservative temporality of African 'rustics' with the faster-paced temporality of the officials of "learned and official law."[38] After all, even the Portuguese Inquisition had moved on after two hundred years of insisting on the same inquisitorial procedures and pointless inquiries.

In the document "*Gentilic rites, and superstitions, of the gentilic blacks from the Kingdom of Angola*" (c.1702–1719), Bishop Luís Simões de Brandão of Congo and Angola had already described the three "*Mbundu oaths used by blacks*" as either poisonings or frauds.[39] According to him, these were: the "*Bulungu Nguenge*" or "*Bulumgu* [*mbulungo*]" ordeal, consisting of the ingestion of an emetic drink that "*clearly offends the brain and can kill*," the "*nguenge*," consisting of tying the hands of the accused with "*palm leaves*" and ascertaining if they could untie them without assistance, and the "*Quilumbu*," consisting of having the accused pick a stone from inside a boiling pot of water. In Bishop Brandão's opinion, all these ordeals were manipulated by "*nganga*," who were thus the true adjudicators of Mbundu complaints. About thirty years before, the *Propaganda Fide* had published Friar Cavazzi's list of "*Giuramenti* [oaths]" administered in the Kingdoms of Kongo, Matamba, and Ndongo.[40] The Capuchin friar introduces it by stressing that these "*Civil and Ecclesiastical pruove* [ordeals]" had been "*in frequent use in ancient times*" and were later "*abused by many Christians, due to their little respect for God and their simplicity*." Because of this 'abuse,' Friar Cavazzi continued, the Church had banned them, but it was "*the most difficult* [task to] *completely eradicate them, even from the*

---

36 On "rustics" and their privileges, see António Hespanha. Foucault, Power/Knowledge, p. 194–128; Hespanha, A cultura jurídica europeia, p. 261–262; Hespanha, As fronteiras do poder, p. 47–105; Hespanha, Imbecillitas; Hespanha, Sábios e rústicos, p. 31–60.

37 As Elias Alexandre da Silva Corrêa noted, the "*flowing of slaves*" depended on "*Paganism being kept in all its purity*" in the Angolan hinterlands, as the slave trade "*would cease*" if "*Christianity was established amongst the blacks*." Silva Corrêa, História de Angola, Vol. 1, p. 93.

38 Hespanha, A cultura jurídica europeia, p. 70, 86, 148, 255, 261–264; Wheatley, Legal Pluralism as Temporal Pluralism, in: Edelstein et al. (eds.), Power and Time, p. 55, 72–73.

39 Lino D'Assumpção, Exploração à Africa, p. 372.

40 Cavazzi, Istorica descrizione de' tre' Regni Congo, Matamba et Angola, p. 88–103.

Fig. 10 The Mbulungo Oath, According to António Oliveira Cadornega. CADORNEGA, História geral das guerras angolanas, Vol. 3 (Public Domain).

hearts of those who have joined our Holy Faith" because they safeguarded "*mutual commerce*." In other words, they restored the ambiance of 'trust,' benevolence, and goodwill necessary for civil coexistence and trade after a domestic or public crisis had shaken it, thus being a form of "groupwork" that was central to the constitution and social reproduction of local communities of "moral belonging."[41]

In Kongo, Friar Cavazzi starts by identifying a *nganga* called "*Nzi*" as the "*Minister of the Devil*" or "*Priest of the Oath*" responsible for administering a simple oath consisting of forcing the accused to ingest a mixture prepared in secret and calling "*the wrath of the gods*" upon themselves if they lied.[42] In some provinces of the kingdom, he continued, there were divinations involving pressing a *nzimbu* shell against the forehead of the accused and ascertaining if it fell on its own (a sign of innocence) or if it remained stuck in place (a sign of guilt). Other divinations or oaths involved drinking specially prepared water: water from a pot where a torch had been previously extinguished, water that had been used to wash a carpenter's hammer (the "*ndefi-a-nzundu*" oath), or water employed to wash the feet of the *Mani* Soyo (the "*ndefi-a-maza-ma-Sonho*" oath). Licking a pestle used to grind corn previously washed in a "*specific lake*" before testifying was also considered an effective oath (the "*ndefi-a-quizu*" oath). However, according to Friar Cavazzi, the

41 KODESH, Beyond the Royal Gaze; SCHOENBRUN, The Names of the Python, p. 3–12.

42 CAVAZZI, Istorica descrizione de' tre' Regni Congo, Matamba et Angola, p. 89–90.

more severe BaKongo judicial ordeals were the "*Ncassa* [*enkasa*] *oath*," using the bark of the tree with the same name, and the "*Nbaù*" ordeal.[43] The *enkasa* oath was a public judicial ordeal that European observers described as similar to the public *mbulungo* oaths.[44] It consisted of the accused drinking a mixture prepared by the "*Sacerdote Ncassa* [*enkasa* priest]" from the powdered bark of *enkasa* and being forced to dance and jump until the accused either vomited it (proving themselves innocent) or fainted or died (proving themselves guilty).[45] The "*Nbaù*" ordeal consisted of forcing the accused to pick up a red-hot iron, innocence being proven if this did not cause a severe skin burn.

When describing the Mbundu oaths and ordeals of the Kingdoms of Matamba and Ndongo, Friar Cavazzi also starts by mentioning that daily oaths evoked the "*spirit of their deceased*," or "*any given Idol*" and that the Mbundu also swore on the "*benedizione* [blessings] *of their King*."[46] To ascertain if the oath to an "*Idol*" had been broken, he claimed that the *nganga* responsible for the "*Idol*" would "*force the accused to drink the water used to wash the head*" of an animal of the kind usually sacrificed to the "*Idol*," obliging them to pay for their performance.[47] It is unclear what effect this water would have on the accused, and how truth was to be established. To ascertain if the oath that invoked the "*king*" was broken, Friar Cavazzi continued, the accused would be summoned before their court and asked to raise the king's arm before an audience. If the task proved impossible, the breaking of the oath was considered proven. The Capuchin friar also mentioned several other "*trivial*" oaths and the custom of "*Ongij-à-Calunga*," which consisted of two persons solemnly swearing never to talk to each other again. According to Friar Cavazzi, it was considered so binding and powerful that specific rituals had to be performed to save their lives if either part broke the silence pact. António de Oliveira Cadornega

---

43 As Kalle Kananoja explains, *enkasa* was used by the BaKongo to "detect" *bandoki* and by the Portuguese as *materia medica* "against *feitiços* and poison" or to treat their gums and teeth (as Friar Cavazzi claims to have done). Francisco Melo Breyner, the Count of Ficalho, identifies *enkasa* as *Erythrophloeum guineense*, now *Erythrophleum suaveolens*, arguing that it was the same tree used to prepare several other "poison ordeals" in West Central Africa. The Portuguese sources also refer to *enkasa* as "*casca de encaça*," "*cassa*," "*emcassa*," "*encace*," and "*incussa*." On its medical properties, ritual uses, and the Portuguese and Luso-African appropriations of the bark of *enkasa*, see Figueiredo and Kananoja. Cavazzi, Istorica descrizione de' tre' Regni Congo, Matamba et Angola, p. 91–92; Figueiredo, Política, escravatura e feitiçaria em Angola, p. 252, 309–310, 552, 568–569; Kananoja, Healing Knowledge, p. 62–63; Lopes de Lima and Bordalo, Ensaios sobre a statistica das possessões portuguezas, Vol. 3, p. 199–200; Melo Breyner, Plantas úteis da África Portuguesa, p. 161–168; Sarmento, Os sertões d'Africa p. 101–102.

44 Melo Breyner, Plantas úteis da África Portuguesa, p. 161–168.

45 Cavazzi, Istorica descrizione de' tre' Regni Congo, Matamba et Angola, p. 91–92.

46 Ibid., p. 93, 98.

47 Ibid., p. 97–98.

also described this pact as "*cungi*," as well as several other judicial ordeals and oaths used in the Angolan hinterlands—all "*demoniacal*" versions of the Portuguese "*oath on the Gospels*," in his opinion.[48] As the BaKongo, Friar Cavazzi continued, the Mbundu also drank the "*water in which their King, or their Priest, had washed their feet*" but only in oaths taken when treason against them was suspected.[49] Moreover, they had a version of the hot iron ordeal, which Friar Cavazzi claims was the oath called "*Chilumbo*" (not the boiling water ordeal mentioned by Bishop Brandão as "*Quilumbo*").[50] It consisted of scrubbing a hot iron against the accused's skin, slowly moving it from their knees to their heels.[51] Cadornega described this "*fire ordeal*" slightly differently, stating that it involved a diviner touching the leg of the accused with a "*red-hot*" knife, and only the guilty would be burned.[52]

Friar Cavazzi also described a boiling water ordeal called "*Giagij*" that consisted of forcing the accused to pick a stone from a pot of boiling water where "*red earth and a piece of calabash used to keep oil*" had also been thrown.[53] Meanwhile, according to Cadornega, the accused had to pick the stone from a cauldron filled with boiling oil while uttering, "*bulungo me coate* [let *mbulungo* catch me]."[54] Friar Cavazzi and Cadornega also offer divergent descriptions of the judicial ordeal referred to by Bishop Brandão as "*nguenge*."[55] According to the Capuchin friar, it was called "*Olungengue*" and consisted of having the accused tied with "*fine but strong strings of palm rope*" that would be strained until their flesh was cut.[56] He explained that those who felt no pain were considered innocent. As for Cadornega, he described this ordeal as the "*palanca*" oath, claiming that it involved the tying of the accused with wet ropes that would contract as they dried, first causing muscular strain and then deep tissue cuts.[57] According to Cadornega, the torture would continue until the tortured person confessed their crimes.

Tellingly, all authors agreed when discussing the *mbulungo* ordeal, evidencing its widespread use and the familiarity Europeans and Luso-Africans had with its functioning and rationale.[58] Friar Cavazzi said its preparation varied due to the

---

48 Cadornega, História geral das guerras angolanas, Vol. 3, p. 262, 318–324.

49 Cavazzi, Istorica descrizione de' tre' Regni Congo, Matamba et Angola, p. 98–99.

50 Ibid., p. 94–95; Lino D'Assumpção, Exploração à Africa, p. 372.

51 Cavazzi, Istorica descrizione de' tre' Regni Congo, Matamba et Angola, p. 94–95.

52 Cadornega, História geral das guerras angolanas, Vol. 3, p. 322.

53 Cavazzi, Istorica descrizione de' tre' Regni Congo, Matamba et Angola, p. 95–96.

54 Cadornega, História geral das guerras angolanas, Vol. 3, p. 319–320.

55 Lino D'Assumpção, Exploração à Africa, p. 372.

56 Cavazzi, Istorica descrizione de' tre' Regni Congo, Matamba et Angola, p. 95.

57 Cadornega, História geral das guerras angolanas, Vol. 3, p. 322–323.

58 Ibid., p. 320–321; Cavazzi, Istorica descrizione de' tre' Regni Congo, Matamba et Angola, p. 93–94; Lino D'Assumpção, Exploração à Africa, p. 372.

"*diversità di riti* [diversity of rites]" in the Kingdoms of Matamba and Ndongo.[59] The beverage could be prepared with "*the meat of a given snake, the pulp of a fruit, or the juice of some plants.*" Some *mbulungo* makers added a "*cut of the root of a banana tree*" to the mix or used the fruit of the "*palm tree called Emba*" instead of the regular *mbulungo* beverage. In the former case, swallowing the root was considered proof of innocence. In the case of the ordeal using the emba fruit, the "*Minister*" in charge of it ate a chunk of the fruit and challenged the accused to eat the remainder—if they accepted and survived, they would be proven innocent. When a beverage was prepared and forced on the accused, Friar Cavazzi argued that they either vomited it, thus proving their innocence, or became "*alienated*" and trembled "*like a paralytic, unable to stand up.*" Then, those offered a "*countermeasure*" would survive, while the others would first become "*stolid, senseless, & unable to dispose of themselves*" and then "*die in a few days.*"

According to the Capuchin friar, "*these indecent procedures of administering justice*" were often manipulated by the "*Judges,*" who used them to "*violently convict the innocent and acquit the criminals*" by withdrawing the antidote and manipulating the dosage of the extracts employed in the brewing of the *mbulungo*. Cadornega states that the *mbulungo* was prepared in an "*icao* [calabash]" by mixing "*hitro,*" the powdered seeds of a fruit called "*quijuluango,*" with an alcoholic corn beverage called "*oallo* [corn beer]."[60] Once brewed, Cadornega explained, a "*ganga*" would gather all those suspected of having committed misdeeds, have them sit in a circle, and then serve them a sip of this mixture. After drinking the *mbulungo*, he claimed, the accused would say "*bulungo me coate,*" which he translates as "*let mbulungo catch me,*" and, if guilty, they would begin to be affected by the *mbulungo*, and either confess their guilt and receive an antidote or be left to die. Finally, both authors refer to a judicial ordeal like the *mbulungo*, which also involved eating a poisonous fruit. The Capuchin friar called it "*Oroncio*" and identified the fruit as "*Nicesso,*" while Cadornega named it "*majongo,*" "*mecefo,*" or "*cajongo*" after the "*tasty fruit that takes the poison inside.*"[61]

Friar Cavazzi explained that he described all these oaths and ordeals to educate future missionaries of the *Propaganda Fide* tasked with eradicating them, writing from the point-of-view of the prefect of the Capuchins' Mission to West Central Africa. However, he concluded his "*oaths*" section by partially admitting his defeat. In his own words, "*even the missionaries*" under his jurisdiction "*veiledly threatened* [their parishioners] *to use these oaths* [...] *to discover the truth,*" stating that they

---

59 Cavazzi, Istorica descrizione de' tre' Regni Congo, Matamba et Angola, p. 93–94.

60 Cadornega, História geral das guerras angolanas, Vol. 3, p. 318–324.

61 António de Oliveira Cadornega also mentions the "*Zenza*" and the "*indua*" ordeals as the official ordeals of the Kingdom of Matamba and the Kingdom of Kasanje, respectively. Ibid.; Cavazzi, Istorica descrizione de' tre' Regni Congo, Matamba et Angola, p. 94.

"*had learned from these Ministers* [e. g., the African ordeal specialists] *the way of practicing them, and the recipes for the beverages*."[62] While Friar Cavazzi reassured his editors and readers that no Capuchin missionary would ever actually perform or organize African judicial ordeals because they "*were contrary to the sanctity of* [Christian] *rites*," the Inquisitorial records explored in the seventh chapter prove that other priests were not as scrupulous. In any case, the tolerance for, and even use of, African oaths, ordeals, and forms of divination that did not explicitly involve entities described by European observers as idols or the evocation of ancestors through *xinguilamentos* was the flipside of them being considered vernacular versions of the medieval European *judicium Dei*, duels, or other trials by ordeal.[63]

By 1687, Friar Cavazzi was ambivalent about letting the missionaries under his jurisdiction entertain the hypothesis of unofficially recognizing Mbundu and BaKongo ordeals as judgments by God in their pursuit of truth because he could not rule out the possibility of them opening the door for diabolical interventions instead. By the time Friar Alexandre da Sagrada Família drafted his pastoral plan, this last possibility was no longer seriously entertained. However, since African ordeals and oaths were framed as 'rustic' or 'archaic' judicial practices and divinations as superstitions, those who practiced them could be persecuted by vicars forane as usurpers of the bishop's jurisdiction if the ordeals had been called for to help settle matters under their delegated jurisdiction—as judicial ordeals most often did (e. g., related to marriages, adultery, and deaths/burials). If not, they could still be arrested and transferred to the secular arm of justice when the ordeals involved practices that could be framed as torture or poisoning. Therefore, Friar Alexandre da Sagrada Família's pastoral plan sought not only to guarantee the financial means to rebuild the abandoned churches of the Captaincy of Angola and its dependencies but also homogenize the temporality of the hinterland parishes with that of the Portuguese

---

62 Cavazzi, Istorica descrizione de' tre' Regni Congo, Matamba et Angola, p. 101.

63 *Judicium Dei* were judicial duels where both parties or their champions fought to prove their innocence. Of Germanic influence, they were shunned by the Catholic Church after Pope Nicholas I (820–867) condemned them in the *Epistola dedicatoria ad Carolum Calvum* (c. 843–850). Other widespread ordeals of Germanic influence included the hot iron and boiling water ordeals. The "bitter water" adultery ordeal had a Hebraic root. While mapping the vast literature on Germanic or Hebraic ordeals is beyond the scope of this chapter, a brief survey of this scholarship confirms the existence of recognizable historical trends. One is the demise of ordeals and oaths as new epistemologies and methods for producing evidence and proof gained traction, culminating in the Enlightenment's abandonment of *judicium Dei*; the other is the concurrent association of ordeals and oaths with 'archaic' judicial practices and traces of the past. Barlett, Trial by Fire and Water; Ho, The Legitimacy of Medieval Proof, p. 259–298; Kerr et al., Cold Water and Hot Iron, p. 573–595; Leeson, Ordeals, p. 691–714; Leeson, Trial by Battle, p. 341–375; Morris, Judicium Dei; Radding, Superstition to Science, p. 945–969; Ziegler, Trial by Fire and Battle.

Church, promoting and accelerating the cultural and normative assimilation of converted Africans and 'rustic' Portuguese or Luso-African *moradores*.

9.2 A Blueprint for Segregation and Racial Patriarchy

Writing ten years before Friar Alexandre da Sagrada Família's arrival in Luanda, former Captain-General and Governor Sousa Coutinho held a different view on the best approach to uphold Christian values and a European grammar of affect in the capital of Angola. In the report he left to his successor António de Lencastre when he finished his tenure, written on November 26, 1772, he confidently stated that he had "*extinguished all the public abuses of Entambes, and other superstitions, which the ignorance of the whites had*" used of to "*take advantage of the rudeness of the blacks.*"[64] Moreover, he also claimed that he had "*burned all* [...] *public Idols*" and made sure that in Luanda, "*at least all the exteriors*"—meaning public spaces and behaviors—"*were Christian.*" Therefore, Sousa Coutinho advised Lencastre not to let "*Entambes, cazas de uzo, and other such nonsense raise their heads again*" as he believed these institutions caused a "*thousand damages to public well-being, to the safety of households, and the honor of families.*" Focusing only on public spaces and the outward behavior of the Portuguese and Luso-African *moradores* and their African associates and dependents allowed Sousa Coutinho to positively assess the impact of his reforms while leaving the thornier *foro interno* issues regarding true conversion and intimate beliefs to be dealt with by the bishops of Congo and Angola. However, he could not help but harbor suspicions and fears that nothing had truly changed behind the public facade of Luanda. In other words, his emphasis on external indicators exacerbated the same paranoia that had once seized the Jesuit missionaries described in the seventh chapter, as the possibility that old habits and customs could at any time resurface from the intimate and domestic spheres of Luanda, Benguela, Massangano and the hinterland *presídios* and *arimos* haunted Sousa Coutinho. He thus came to accept as his worst failure his inability to regulate what happened in the intimacy of domestic spheres and his incapacity to segregate Black subjects from mixed-race and White *moradores*.

Soon after writing his "*Report and Reflections*" to Lencastre, while already in Lisbon, Sousa Coutinho wrote two "*Reports on the Kingdom of Angola and its Conquests,*" on 1773 and 1775, and a "*Broad description of Angola and its Conquests, including Benguela,*" on February 3, 1775.[65] These three documents comment on all his major projects, listing successes while recommending future policies to continue

64 ANTT, CLNH, Fol. 45, D. 1.

65 ANTT, CLNH, Fol. 45, D. 1, D. 2; Coutinho, Memórias do Reino de Angola, p. 173–202.

them "*but much more perfect, and free of all defects.*" They identified the "*countless obstacles of the Weather and the customs of the country*" as the biggest obstacles to be overcome.[66] The first two are deposited in the Public Library of Porto, Portugal, having been edited and published in 1939, while the latter, together with a copy of Lencastre's report, is part of the personal library of his son, Rodrigo de Sousa Coutinho, the first count of Linhares and the godson of Sebastião José de Carvalho e Melo, the Marquis of Pombal. While Rodrigo only finished the first three years of his bachelor's in law from the reformed University of Coimbra (1772–1775), he was accepted as a full member of the Royal Academy of Sciences of Lisbon and had a brilliant diplomatic and political career despite the fall from grace of his godfather and benefactor in 1777.[67] After serving as the Portuguese minister to the Kingdom of Sardinia from 1779 to 1796, Rodrigo returned to Lisbon in 1796 to take on the role of secretary of state of the navy and the overseas. He then served as president of the Royal Treasury from 1801 to 1803, being appointed secretary of state of foreign affairs and war from 1808 to 1812 after advising Prince Regent João (future King João VI of Portugal) to move his court to Brazil in 1807.[68] Sousa Coutinho's reports were part of Rodrigo's political education, undoubtedly having an impact on his outlook when acting as a secretary of state of the navy and the overseas and working in close collaboration with Captain-General and Governor of Angola António de Mello. While the report from 1772 is divided into four different articles (e.g., "*Royal Treasury*," "*Military Discipline*," "*Politics*," and "*Religion and Customs*"), the other documents read more as afterthoughts and comments on this original report, adding extra information about Benguela and the Nova Oeiras iron foundry.[69]

Regarding his economic projects, Sousa Coutinho started by explaining his monetary reforms. He praised the excellent results of the abolition of the "*livranças*" issued by the holders of the Angolan slave duty contract, argued against the auctioning of tax farming contracts over the "*subsídio dos molhados*," the tax charged on

66 ANTT, CLNH, Fol. 45, D. 1.

67 Cardoso, Coutinho, D. Rodrigo de Sousa; Silva, Portrait d'un Homme d'État, Vol. 1, Vol. 2.

68 Despite his brief stay with the Portuguese Royal Court, Rodrigo de Sousa Coutinho profoundly influenced the Kingdom of Brazil. His efforts in promoting industry and mining and his instrumental role in the reforms that facilitated free trade with the British Empire significantly shaped the economic landscape of the Kingdom of Brazil. Cardoso, Coutinho, D. Rodrigo de Sousa; Silva, Portrait d'un Homme d'État, Vol. 1, Vol. 2.

69 The first manuscript deposited at the Public Library of Porto was written in Lisbon on September 17, 1773, but includes a long list of "*Instructions for the new Governor of Benguela*" and a transcription of the "*Broad description of Angola and its Conquests, including Benguela*," written on February 3, 1773, as annexes. The second manuscript, titled "*Report*," was written on September 16, 1773, and is focused only on the New Oeiras Iron Foundry. ANTT, CLNH, Fol. 45, D.1, D. 2; Coutinho, Memórias do Reino de Angola, p. 173–202.

alcoholic beverages and fresh-cut meat, and recommended great care in the issuing and handling of "*letras*" backed by the Board of Finance of Luanda and further reforms in tithe collecting.[70] Considering the iron foundry and the other factories established in Nova Oeiras, Sousa Coutinho recommended that the government of the captaincy should "*buy up to four hundred muleques* [young slaves] *of both sexes, marry them, and establish them at the Factory, the men to* [work] *all the trades of the said* [factory], *as similarly their sons, the women to till the lands that would feed them all*."[71] Regarding military discipline, it is worth mentioning that Sousa Coutinho blamed the "*carneiradas* [malaria fevers]" for decimating the White soldiers, recommending that newcomers should be forbidden to seek assistance or food outside of their garrison as a preventive measure and decrying the merit and uselessness of non-White soldiers.[72] As for "*religion and customs*," besides the recommendation already referred to in the previous paragraphs, Sousa Coutinho only stated that he had "*been happy in all endeavors*." Finally, under the heading 'politics,' he outlined his biopolitical project, briefly describing how he envisioned exerting biopolitical control over the health, reproduction, and sexuality of the White population through pioneering abolitionist measures and the granting of minor offices according, not to the principles of patrimonialism, but a racialized understanding of meritocracy. In his words, because of the "*thefts made by Death*," "*Population* [was] *an object of great care*" in West Central Africa, and it was "*necessary to attach men so that through the result of many marriages, there can be some* [White] *population*" in the Captaincy of Angola. These men, Sousa Coutinho told Lencastre, should be induced to "*marry White women or nearly White ones*," being granted privileged access to "*Civil and Military offices*" if they "*complied*." As for the mixed-race "*Mulatos*," he argued they were all to be manumitted if previously enslaved, no compensation whatsoever being paid to their former masters, who should "*console themselves in the loss of their dominion*" over their former slave's freedom with "*the benefit*" this abolitionist measure brought for "*the Kingdom*." Mixed-race men were then to be taken from their "*ignorant Mothers*" and taught a

---

70 See the sixth chapter for information about *livranças* and *letras* and the eighth chapter for more information on different taxes and tributes. ANTT, CLNH, Fol. 45, D. 1.

71 A sawmill, lime kiln, and brick and tile factories were also established in Nova Oeiras. See Crislayne Alfagali for more details on the iron foundry. In his report, Sousa Coutinho also briefs and advises his successor on the sulfur and pitch mines, about navigation of the River Kwanza, and the trade in copper. Ibid.; Alfagali, Blacksmiths of Ilamba; Coutinho, Memórias do Reino de Angola, p. 204.

72 Sousa Coutinho also commented on the uselessness of the *presídio* of Encoge and listed his fortification efforts, arguing for the need to provide Benguela and other coastal settlements with artillery and troops capable of defending them from European incursions. ANTT, CLNH, Fol. 45, D. 1.

mechanical trade at the expense of the Crown, while mixed-race women were to be married off to White settlers if they were "*nearly Whites*."[73]

Significantly, only after outlining and recommending these biopolitical measures does Sousa Coutinho explain the rationale beyond his reform of the administration of justice in the Captaincy of Angola and Benguela, casting a new light on his Ordinance of February 24, 1765, police regulations and attempts to abolish the municipal council of Massangano.[74] Considering his report to Lencastre, it becomes clear that Sousa Coutinho intended these hinterland offices to be tendentially held by Whites[75] and that his hostility towards both the ordinary judges, municipal councilors, and brothers of the *Santa Casa* of Massangano, and the Luso-African captain majors who headed most of the districts and *presídios* of the hinterlands was informed by his racial prejudice and conviction that mixed-race and Black individuals were less capable and only worthy of the "*charity due to mizeraveis* [miserable people]" and "*mizericordia* [mercy]."[76] Therefore, the better-defined boundaries, hierarchies, and jurisdictional limits Sousa Coutinho advocated for as a solution to the countless cases of jurisdictional abuse and conflict he faced while acting as captain-general and governor of Angola were envisioned by him as organized according to racial and gender lines and depended upon controlling the

---

73 As Sousa Coutinho explained, reforming the ordinances and closely monitoring the performance of judges of orphans and *provedores* would be essential to attaining this goal. Ibid.

74 AHU, CU, Angola, Box 54, D. 4897; Coutinho, Documento N.º 6, in: Couto, Os capitães-mores em Angola, p. 323–338; Delgado, O governo de Sousa Coutinho em Angola III, p. 42.

75 Despite favoring White officers, Sousa Coutinho took into consideration the harshness of the epidemiological environment, keeping most Europeans in Luanda and Benguela and, in his own words, sending "*all those who are useless and unfit for military service*" to be "*honorably buried*" in the pestiferous hinterland *presídios*. Considering that Sousa Coutinho based his assessment of relative merit on racialized prejudices, this can be understood as a "necropolitical" policy that promoted the treatment of Black and mixed-race bodies as expendable. See Achille Mbembe for a definition of "necropolitics" and Carolyn Rouse for how it differs from Foucault's biopolitics. AHU, CU, Angola, Box 53, D. 4823; Mbembe, Necropolitics; Rouse, Necropolitics Versus Biopolitics, p. 360–367; Trigo de Sousa, D. Francisco de Sousa Coutinho, p. 53–54.

76 António Álvares da Cunha, captain-general and governor of Angola between 1753 and 1758, had already complained to Diogo de Mendonça Corte Real Secretary of State of the Navy and the Overseas at the time, about the rebelliousness of the Municipal Council of Massangano using racialized arguments. According to him, after a series of incidents involving Miguel Gomes Brandão, a relative and *protégé* of the municipal judge of Massangano, that had taken place during the Holy Week of 1754, he was forced to send a cavalry squad to arrest him and the judge and restore order. In Álvares da Cunha's words, Massangano, "*once very Rich*," was then "*reduced to be inhabited by very few whites, some mulatos, and a lot of blacks, the latter being the councilmen, and ordinary judges of that miserable village, all composed of feiticeiros*" and African chieftains. The solution proposed by Álvares da Cunha was the re-settlement of Massangano with White couples sent from the Portuguese Kingdom or the Azores. ANTT, CLNH, Fol. 45, D. 1; AHU, CU, Angola, Box 42, D. 3920; Coutinho, Memórias do Reino de Angola, p. 188.

sexuality and reproductive capabilities of women as much as on regulating judicial court styles or secondary rules regarding hierarchies of sources of law. By his own admission, measures such as the creation of "*fixed settlements*" in the hinterlands of Benguela,[77] his use first of the Board of Justice of Luanda as a disciplinary institution, and his treatment of free Blacks as '*personae miserabilae*' all stemmed from the same racialist worldview.[78] In Sousa Coutinho's words, "*the irregularities of the blacks, the vices of the captain majors, the disordered greed of the whites, and the so-called whites, occupied a good part of* [his] *time*," each populational group being targeted by specific biopolitical or "necropolitical" measures.[79] Racially segregated Christian marriage was the institution that he considered crucial not only to (re)produce and police the racial boundaries between these groups but also to sort out all the issues plaguing the economic, judicial, and military administration of the Captaincy of Angola and promote White settlement of the Central African hinterlands.

Laura Doyle has defined "racial patriarchy" as a form of "kinship patriarchy" that aptly describes the ideal society envisaged by Sousa Coutinho for the Captaincy of Angola and its dependencies.[80] According to her, racial patriarchy is a social system in which the "sexual and ancestral economies" are closely linked through the "kin-bordered arrangement of women's mothering," leading to the reproduction of bodies for "either a dominant or a subordinate group" separated by "racial or ethnic boundaries"—in the case at hand one dominant, one intermediary or client, and one subordinate group: Whites, mixed-race "*Mulatos*," and Blacks.[81] It is through

---

77 As Sousa Coutinho explains in his report from September 17, 1773, after settling the White "*vagrants*" in these new settlements and appointing "*Judges and Captain Majors*" to head them and "*parish priests*" to oversee them, he requested White settler "*couples*" from the secretary of state of the navy and the overseas to "*finish this great project*." On Sousa Coutinho's efforts to promote White settlement in the hinterlands of Benguela, see Catarina Madeira Santos. For a discussion of the influence of the Marquis of Pombal's plan to encourage White settlement in Angola on Sousa Coutinho's, see Ana Trigo de Sousa. Coutinho, Memórias do Reino de Angola, p. 174; Santos, Entre deux Droits, p. 817–848; Santos, Um governo "polido" para Angola; Trigo de Sousa, D. Francisco de Sousa Coutinho, p. 114–116.

78 ANTT, MR, EXP, Sr. 34, F. 605, p. 326–328.

79 Mbembe, Necropolitics.

80 Doyle, Bordering on the Body, p. 5.

81 Laura Doyle builds on Claude Meillassoux's and Igor Kopytoff's criticism of strict Western notions of genealogical "lineage" to highlight several forms of structuring and organizing "genealogical descent"—what she calls "ancestral economies." According to Kopytoff, "inflexible kinship-based rules of membership" such as "membership by birth" are sub-optimal for the social reproduction of African groups dependent on different modes of production (e. g., hunting-gathering bands, horticultural, pastoral); therefore, several other more inclusive or flexible ways of incorporating or expelling members from them historically developed. As Kopytoff has pointed out, and as Joseph Miller and Beatrix Heintze have explored in West Central Africa, kinship provided the framework to conceptualize membership not only in corporate kin groups but also in "cross-lineage" or "extra-

the "controlled circulation of women in marriage," she argues, that patriarchal institutions construct and reproduce racial and class boundaries, co-instituting stable gender and racial categories.[82] Doyle's theoretical framework is particularly illuminating if applied as a heuristic to analyze Sousa Coutinho's projects because it enables us to provincialize racial patriarchy as a historically and geographically situated form of kinship patriarchy. In this manner, Sousa Coutinho's project can be contrasted with the West Central African forms of kinship patriarchy that underpinned the rule of African elites and the economic strategies of Luso-African *moradores* against whom White Portuguese settlers competed for economic and political gains.

Sousa Coutinho's failed attempt to regulate White marriage can thus be reframed as an attempt to wrestle control over the "circulation of women" and of mother's procreative functions from African men at the head of Mbundu patriarchal institutions: *malemba dya ngundu* [uncles of the matrilineage], *makota*, *malemba dya ngola* [uncles of the *ngola*], and other perpetual-kinship title-holders the Portuguese referred to as *sobas*, *dembos*, or kings.[83] His measures also targeted the socio-economic strategies of Portuguese and Luso-African *moradores* and the social reproduction of the powerful Luso-African familial factions described in the previous chapters. Both participated in Mbundu and other African patriarchal institutions (e. g., BaKongo, Mbangala, Ovimbundu) to gain access to the prestige spheres of exchange where rights over dependents and women were brokered in the hinterlands, as well as to land and human resources (e. g., militias, porters, canoe rowers, servants) controlled by corporate kin groups. Therefore, Sousa Coutinho's attempt to impose, through regulating Christian marriage, an alternative form of kinship patriarchy based on racialist myths of White supremacy and merit and racial segregation must be understood as a normative, political, and economic project that neatly dovetailed with his restructuring of the hinterland slave fairs, reforms of the credit and monetary system, and police regulations forbidding the

---

lineage" ones such as trading networks or cults (different "communities of moral belonging" in David Schoenbrun's terms). However, other conceptual frameworks or forms of "groupwork" were also available in this region. For example, Mbangala warbands used the concept of cannibalism to think about the incorporation of new members, as discussed in the fifth chapter. See also the sixth chapter for a discussion of the concepts of metaphorical kinship and how "perpetual kinship" and 'positional succession' structured inter-polity relations in the Angolan hinterlands. ANTT, CLNH, Fol. 45, D. 1; Doyle, Bordering on the Body, p. 5; Heintze, Translocal 'Kinship' Relations in: Freitag and von Oppen (eds.), Translocality, p. 179–204; Kopytoff, Introduction, in: Kopytoff (ed.), The African Frontier, p. 41–43; Meillassoux, The Anthropology of Slavery, p. 23–26; Miller, Kings and Kinsmen; Schoenbrun, The Names of the Python.

82 Doyle, Bordering on the Body, p. 5–6.

83 See the previous chapter for more information about these patriarchal institutions. Ibid., p. 21.

celebration of major life cycle events such as Mbundu weddings and funerals. Moreover, as further discussed when analyzing Mello's projects, his attempt to regulate *mucano* hearings was also aimed at reforming the legal and normative framework that grounded the existing kinship patriarchal arrangements, as the Luso-African institution was central to upholding their normative framework.

Proposing a feminist rereading of the works of Claude Lévi-Strauss, Jack Goody, and Igor Kopytoff and Suzanne Miers, Doyle makes three additional points that are relevant to the discussion at hand.[84] First, stressing a point made by Claude Meillassoux and countless Marxist anthropologists, Doyle insists that cultural and normative arrangements regarding marriage are also always economic arrangements reinforcing class structures and being influenced by modes of production.[85] Second, she remarks that the circulation of women in marriage could take two directions, "inside the kin group" or "outside," the first being defined as endogamy and the second as exogamy. Following Goody, Doyle argues that endogamy was often used to "protect the dominant kin group's possession of scarce resources of land or capital."[86] At the same time, exogamy served to "extend" the possession of these resources. Third, Doyle identified "kinship or racial mythologies" as either concurring or contrasting ideologies used to establish and police "kin boundaries" that served rulers' political and economic needs.[87] With these points in mind, we can return to Sousa Coutinho's 'utopic' plans to regulate marriages in the Captaincy of Angola, better expressed in an additional report he penned five years after the ones already discussed, shortly before he died in 1780.[88] There, the former captain-general and governor adds little additional information about how to improve his monetary reforms, the management of the factories in Nova Oeiras, or the collection of tithes and taxes but explores in greater detail the projects of connecting the Captaincy of Angola with the *prazos* of Rios de Senna, situated in the Zambezi

84 Goody, Technology, Tradition, and the State in Africa; Goody, The Development of the Family and Marriage in Europe; Doyle, Bordering on the Body, p. 23–25; Lévi-Strauss, The Elementary Structures of Kinship; Miers and Kopytoff, Slavery in Africa.

85 Claude Meillassoux criticizes "classical anthropology" for not connecting the "normative and formal sides" of kinship to its "basic function:" the "production and reproduction of the immediate essentials of life." Namely, food, shelter, clothes, tools, weapons, and new generations of human beings. According to him, each "mode of production has its own laws of population," affecting domestic communities where the "physical reproduction" of human beings occurs through women's mothering. Doyle, Bordering on the Body, p. 24–25; Meillassoux, Maidens, Meal, and Money, p. xi–xiii; Meillassoux, The Anthropology of Slavery.

86 Doyle, Bordering on the Body, p. 24; Goody, Technology, Tradition, and the State in Africa, p. 30–38; Kopytoff, Introduction, in: Kopytoff (ed.), The African Frontier, p. 41–43.

87 Doyle, Bordering on the Body, p. 24–25.

88 ANTT, CLNH, Fol. 45, D. 4.

River valley in East Africa and establishing White-manned agricultural colonies in its hinterlands.[89]

Sousa Coutinho begins this last report by stating that "*experience strengthened by five years of serious meditation has shown* [...] *that this Kingdom* [of Angola was] *ruined much more by the defects of its economic constitution than by the rigid intemperance of its climate.*"[90] However, the economic constitution the former captain-general and governor had in mind was, first and foremost, the domestic economy of the White *moradores*' households. The "*incomparable vanity of the Regions of the Sun,*" Sousa Coutinho argued, made "*all* [White] *families in general, whether they are the most accredited or the most humble, live encerradas* [cloistered]," avoiding "*even the acts of Religion*" if they couldn't afford "*an excessive number of black women and mulatas to accompany them, and when they lack the gold, silver, and stones they require for adornment.*" These sumptuary tastes impacted weddings because dowries were squandered in "*Damask Beds, Curtains, Plates, useless Slaves, and gilded Hand Chairs*" and other "*luxurious materials*" instead of being used to "*raise their children.*"[91] Moreover, Sousa Coutinho continued, "*the hatred of work*" led White women to spend their days lying in bed, refusing "*to use their hands,*" so that "*for the smallest and most futile work they need to call tailors, because they do not know how to, and do not want to do a single stitch.*"[92] Because of this, he lamented that White men had no access to free social reproductive labor at home, as White women refused to serve "*the Europeans by ironing, washing, or cooking.*" Instead, the most dynamic ones dedicated themselves to small-scale commerce either by "*sending black women, commonly known as Quitandeiras, to sell knick-knacks, fruits, and supplies to Ships or to resell them on the Roads,*" organizing the production and distribution of "*hucálo*' [corn beer]," or "*selling the honor of their most cherished female slaves.*" In conclusion, Sousa Coutinho argued, "*Daughters who are brought up in this defective Religion, in this idleness, and in this vanity*" never came to marry, cherishing luxury and, above all, a "*small, separate Population of prostituted Black women*" they could exploit and financially rely on.[93] In other words, they sought to accumulate wealth in people just like most West Central African men with no

---

89 The *prazos* of Rios de Sena were a Luso-African land-holding vernacular institution unique to East Africa. For a history of its development and the creation of the government of Rios de Sena, see Eugénia Rodrigues. Rodrigues, Portugueses e africanos nos Rios de Sena.

90 ANTT, CLNH, Fol. 45, D. 4.

91 Sousa Coutinho also argued that this preference inflated the dowries required to marry women off, as a dowry sufficient to marry a "*Lady of the First Order in Portugal and Europe*" came "*to be despised*" in Luanda. Ibid.

92 Ibid.

93 The former captain-general and governor also claimed that "*second class*" White women and "*Mulatas*" almost always "*prostituted themselves,*" publicly "*auctioning their honor.*" In this case, contrary to Sousa Coutinho's allegations about the forced prostitution of Black slaves, the selling

intention of relocating somewhere else in the Portuguese Empire. As for White men, Sousa Coutinho continued, being "*brought up in a Serralho* [*seraglio*] *of Black women and Mulatas, who are corrupt and infectious*" rendered them "*incapable of the slightest work,*" "*unhappy*" and short-lived.[94] In other words, he believed this decadent upbringing brought them closer to the Black men he described as lacking in character and afflicted with "*laziness.*"

However, according to Sousa Coutinho, White and mixed-race "*Fathers and Brides*" would undoubtedly opt for better-regulated Christian marriages if they were presented with the choice.[95] According to him, "*Whites, Pardoz, and Fusco natives*" loved "*Black women so much that even when they married Whites, Beautiful ones at that,*" they always kept "*one* [Black woman] *who satisfied them.*" Nevertheless, this exposed them not only to the "*vices,*" corruption, and "*infections*" Sousa Coutinho prejudicially associated with mixed-race unions but also to the dangers of intimacy and physical proximity explored in the first chapter of this part. In his words, because White and mixed-race "*natives*" were also "*full of superstition,*" "*both members of married couples* [were] *afraid of feitiços*" prepared by Black mistresses. Therefore, on top of alleviating the economic and population issues that had so far 'ruined' the Captaincy of Angola, Sousa Coutinho understood Christian marriages as an institution capable of curtailing fears of sorcery, as well as fears related to *zumbi* afflictions and neglected *jinzumbi* or Mbundu ancestors, by avoiding, through sexual and racial segregation, the inclusion of White and mixed-race *moradores* in Mbundu kin groups. In his words, "*the chaste love of marriage not only preserves and enlivens the qualities of the generous soul but prevents the corruption of customs,*" and the "*Laws of Cesar and Augustus*" had long proved the need to "*bring about the ordering of customs through Marriage.*" Even if Luso-African *moradores* cared little about the "*qualities of the generous soul,*" Sousa Coutinho seems to have believed that the fear of *feitiços* would nudge them in the right direction.

Inspired by the *Lex Julia de Maritandis Ordinibus* (18 B.C.) and the *Lex Papia Poppaea* (9 A.D.), the former captain-general and governor proposed practical measures to transform the existing kinship patriarchy into a racial patriarchy. Through Christian marriage, the reproductive capabilities of White and mixed-race women were to be mobilized to serve State interests, further settler colonialism,

---

of women's honor is likely a reference to Mbundu courtship rituals and the *alembamento* paid to their kin groups. See the previous chapter for more details about both. Ibid.

94 The Orientalist reference to the Ottoman seraglio is often repeated in Sousa Coutinho's report. In its pages, he contrasts Middle Eastern sexuality and fantasized promiscuity with an idealized description of Chinese marriage institutions and rules to impose monogamy and punish adultery. See Anne McClintock for an introduction to how Orientalist tropes were used to other the sexuality of African rulers. Ibid.; McClintock, Imperial Leather.

95 ANTT, CLNH, Fol. 45, D. 4.

and reproduce the racial, gender, and class categories that Sousa Coutinho's reforms aimed to uphold. To bring this about he first proposed a set of 'religious' reforms, namely substituting "*useless*" Luso-African priests for missionaries of the Mendicant Orders, "*strictly forbidding all Gentilic customs, such as Entambes, paranymphs during weddings, and the medicines of Blacks*," and expelling "*from the slave quarters the Black prostitutes that are useless and fatal to families*."[96] Second, Sousa Coutinho suggested the manumission of all mixed-race individuals. As previously discussed, he believed that this measure would force mixed-race men to "*learn useful trades*" and put an end to the "*prostitution of Mulatas,*" thus re-introducing mixed-race women into the marriage circuit. Third, he defended the introduction of sumptuary laws to limit the number of domestic slaves to up to "*eight female Slaves*" per family, remove unproductive dependents to the nearby *arimos*, and restrict the use of "*silk, Indian cloths, Silver, Gold*" and other luxurious materials. Fourth, Sousa Coutinho argued that non-married individuals should be denied access to civil or military offices or permission to trade in the hinterlands. Fifth, he demanded the introduction of "*fair penalties*" to punish "*Parents who delayed the marriage of their Children*," arguing that an "*order forcing a Father to marry his legitimate Daughters, and bastard ones by the age of fourteen years, under the threat of severe penalties and justice taking in its hands the task of correcting his negligence*" would not "*offend the Freedom of Marriage*" because fathers could still choose their daughter's grooms. At the end of every year, Sousa Coutinho concluded, all those who were left unmarried because of lack of dowry would be either granted a "*modest endowment*" by the Crown or the usufruct of the privileges and lands of "*unclaimed Chapels*," thus promoting the settlement of White couples in the Angolan hinterlands.

These measures were presented by Sousa Coutinho as essential to secure the future of the African leg of the Atlantic slave trade, complementing his Ordinance of the Fair Scribes of September 16, 1764, and the Ordinance of February 24, 1765.[97] Moreover, he believed they reduced the risks associated with the royal edict of January 11, 1758, that opened up trade to all White Portuguese subjects in "*Angola, Kongo, Loango, and Benguela,* [and] *the adjacent Ports and hinterlands*" in keeping with the Pombaline doctrine of freedom of trade.[98] As the former captain-general and governor explained, while men "*invested in illicit Love become effeminate and set themselves apart from good people, living as Wild Beasts, always startled and fearful*," due to their "*Wives, Husbands never fail to fulfill their obligations.*"[99] Therefore,

---

96 Ibid.

97 AHU, CU, Angola, Box 50, D. 4585; Maxwell, Pombal and the Nationalization of the Luso-Brazilian Economy, p. 608–631.

98 For a discussion of the Marquis of Pombal's economic doctrines and reforms and their impact on Angola, see the sixth chapter. Ley para ser livre, e franco o Commercio de Angola, p. 531–535.

99 ANTT, CLNH, Fol. 45, D. 4.

according to Sousa Coutinho, to bring the White and mixed-race Portuguese and Luso-African itinerant merchants and *pumbeiros* entirely under the Crown's control, it was not only necessary to regulate slave fairs, provide an ordinance to their scribes, and settle them in permanent hamlets under the jurisdiction of a judge but also to marry them to White or mixed-race women. The "*Remedy*" for the "*abuses of Hinterland Trade*," he concluded, "*was in keeping with* [his] *Idea of Marriage*:" married "*Merchants would trade* [while always] *thinking of establishing themselves, as domesticated Animals, that go away but always come back; and not as Wild Ones, that once gone never return*." According to his racial-patriarchal scheme, the motherhood of White and mixed-race women would not only (re)produce the next generation and racial divisions but also produce children who could be used as collateral to enforce good trading practices and debt repayment on their fathers. Thus, racial patriarchy would finally solve the long-standing problems of bad credit and uncollectable debt that negatively affected the Angolan leg of the Atlantic slave trade.

"*Men, once captives of their Wife and Children, would be better governed*," Sousa Coutinho concluded.[100] "*Caring more about accounting*," "*avoiding iniquitous expenses*," they would even be more respectful towards "*the Blacks*" because they could not simply disappear into the African wilderness when things went wrong. Moreover, if "*unequal marriages and the mixture of Bloods*" were carefully avoided, the former captain-general and governor envisaged a slow but sure settler-colonial occupation of the Angolan hinterlands by Whites, eventually realizing the utopic project of connecting the Captaincy with the Government of Rios de Senna, in East Africa. These racially segregated settlements would first co-exist with, and then slowly substitute, the existing matrix of African polities integrated into larger regional inter-polity constellations structured according to the kinship patriarchal institutions described by Heintze.[101] In other words, Sousa Coutinho believed a policy of White supremacist endogamy associated with territorial encroachment and progressive dispossession of African lands would compete with and eventually supplant the exogamic practices and institutions of African heads of corporate kin groups and Luso-African familial factions, which sought to maximize the accumulation of wealth in people. Meanwhile, despite not being central to Sousa Coutinho's argument, his Orientalist tropes of African *seraglios* and Black laziness, together with his exaltation of supposed White racial merits and decrying of the hinterland uses and customs as those of "*Wild Beasts*" added to a racist ideological and mythical substratum that would inform later settler-colonial projects.[102]

---

100 Ibid.

101 HEINTZE, Translocal 'Kinship' Relations in: FREITAG and VON OPPEN (eds.), Translocality, p. 179–204.

102 ANTT, CLNH, Fol. 45, D. 4.

9.3 Promoting Commerce by Reducing Legal Uncertainty

On April 30, 1798, Captain-General and Governor Miguel António de Mello wrote a very long official letter to Rodrigo de Sousa Coutinho, then secretary of state of the navy and the overseas.[103] In its pages, he complained about the subaltern governor of the recently established Government of Benguela, Alexandre José Botelho de Vasconcelos.[104] Mello denounced to the secretary of state that Botelho de Vasconcelos had recently sided with Miguel Antonio Serrão, the regent of the district of Quilengues, Joaquim Vieira de Andrade, former captain major of Quilengues,[105] and Alberto Antonio Pereira, municipal judge of Benguela, to first wage and then justify an illegal and unfair war against the "*Souva* [soba] *of Socoval*."[106] *Soba* Socoval was the most important Ovimbundu ruler of the district, which, according to Estevam Thompson, also included the powerful *sobados* of Quipungo, Huila, Njau, Gambos, Handa, and Humbe, being a traditional supporter of the Portuguese dating back to the mid-seventeenth century.[107] Fourteen years before, it was at the court of *Soba* Socoval that the Naturalist Joaquim José da Silva had sojourned during his scientific expedition to the hinterland of Benguela, collecting the descriptions of Ovimbundu uses and customs discussed in the previous chapters.[108] As Mello recounts, this war had resulted in a "*great injustice being committed against that Souva and all his People, who were arrested, driven out of their lands, reduced to unfair bondage, and, finally, sacked and robbed*."[109] According to him, Serrão was at the heart of this act of aggression, having asked for the military intervention of the governor of Benguela because *Soba* Socoval supposedly refused to pay tithe

103 AHU, CU, Angola, Box 88, D. 7034; Mello, Carta de oficio do Governador.

104 Delgado, A famosa e histórica Benguela, p. 25–39.

105 According to Estevam Thompson, Joaquim Vieira de Andrade and his brothers João and Elias were the most influential and wealthiest slave traders and cattle owners in Quilengues. During his several stints as captain major, Joaquim had gained a reputation as a violent extortionist. Thompson, The Making of Quilengues, p. 218.

106 Delgado, A famosa e histórica Benguela, p. 32; Mello, Carta de oficio do Governador; Mello, Documento n.º 2, in: Delgado (ed.), A famosa e histórica Benguela, p. 444–446.

107 Thompson, The Making of Quilengues, p. 216–217.

108 José Da Silva, Continuação da viagem ao sertão de Benguella, continuada do N.º 2.º, p. 49–60; José Da Silva, Extracto da viagem, que fez ao sertão de Benguella no anno de 1785, p. 97–100; José Da Silva, Viagem ao sertão de Benguella, continuada do N.º 1.º, p. 86–98.

109 A total of forty-five slaves and seventy-nine beasts were paid as royal fifth to the Crown, meaning that at least 225 individuals had been enslaved and 395 cattle heads had been taken as prizes. The royal fifth mainly consisted of old women and children, including a few old men and only three "*peças da Índia*." According to Thompson, before being auctioned, the slaves and cattle that composed the royal fifth were evaluated at 854$600 *réis* and 180$000 *réis*, respectively. AHU, CU, Angola, Box 88, D. 7034; Mello, Carta de oficio do Governador; Thompson, The Making of Quilengues, p. 232–235.

and usurped his jurisdiction by adjudicating "*Mucanos*."[110] However, as Mello's official letter hints at and Thompson explores in detail, the roots of the conflict can be traced back to the longstanding enmity between Vieira de Andrade, a notorious slave trader, and *Soba* Socoval. The former constantly attempted to steal cattle and slaves from the latter and violently enslaved his freeborn subjects.[111]

In his official letter to Rodrigo de Sousa Coutinho, Mello explained the reasoning behind his handling of the 'Socoval affair' and proposed measures to prevent similar cases while acknowledging the limitations of his reforms. Like his predecessors, the captain-general and governor of Angola also wrote a final report at the end of his tenure in 1802, writing several other reports and official letters about the state of the Captaincy of Angola, Benguela, and their dependencies, including plans and projects to improve its economy, tax-collecting, defense, religious administration, and even the humanitarian conditions of the Atlantic slave trade.[112] In accordance with Mello's final report, because José da Silva had successfully reorganized the archives of the Secretariat of the Government of Angola, his successor, Fernando António de Noronha, in office between 1802 and 1806, could easily find his unfinished projects, ideas, as well as the comments and feedback he received from Rodrigo de Sousa Coutinho and other secretaries of state and the central Boards

110 Mello, Carta de oficio do Governador.

111 Two previous "*devassas* [inquiries]" were made during the tenure of Captain-General and Governor Manuel de Almeida e Vasconcelos concerning the alleged harassment of a "*sobeta* [subordinate *soba*]" under the jurisdiction of *Soba* Socoval, Cacombo of Quipuças, and subsequently of *Soba* Socoval by Vieira de Andrade. In the first case, Vieira de Andrade was accused of unlawfully enslaving porters granted to him by Cacombo, helping his 'nephew' usurp his title, and violently raiding his compound. In the second case, Vieira de Andrade was accused of adjudicating *mucanos* concerning *feitiçaria* accusations instead of *Soba* Socoval, usurping his jurisdiction also in other *mucanos* that resulted in the enslavement of the condemned. He was also accused of raiding the latter's court. Serrão, Vieira de Andrade's successor, wrote the second inquiry as soon as he was appointed regent of Quilengues in 1796. Ibid.; AHU, CU, Angola, Box 88, D. 7034; Thompson, The Making of Quilengues, p. 218–256.

112 Miguel Mello also wrote an official letter contradicting the proposals of Alexandre José Botelho de Vasconcelos. In his letter, Mello explained his project for the Government of Benguela. He argued that all jurisdictions headed by captain majors should be abolished. Instead, a different subaltern officer should govern Quilengues, rotating every six months to prevent abuses and promote commerce with the Crown's vassals while upholding "*Royal Justice and Clemency*." AHU, CU, Angola, Box 87, D. 6986, Box 90, D. 7125; Mello, Acerca das riquezas; Mello, Carta do Governador para a Real Junta do Commercio, p. 593–602; Mello, Oficio do Governador e Capitão General de Angola, p. 591; Mello, Oficio em que o Governador e Capitão General reprova a fundação de um convento de franciscanos em Benguela, p. 623–640; Mello, Plano para a organização, p. 189–254; Mello, Relação dos officios civis, p. 281–293; Mello, Relatorio do governo, p. 548–564.

and Councils of Lisbon.[113] Therefore, Mello explained he felt no need to repeat the details of his projects, adjudications, and oral edicts and regulations, simply advising Noronha not to decide on anything before visiting the secretariats and informing himself of the decisions of his predecessors because, in Angola, all petitioners were "*shameless liars*" and present long-settled disputes afresh to new magistrates.[114] Considering its accessibility in the reformed archive and Mello's innovative way of managing his political legacy, his official letter about the illegal war waged against *Soba* Socoval in 1798 must also be understood as a political testament of sorts—thus explaining the expositive, almost didactic style in which it is written.[115] As Rodrigo de Sousa Coutinho, Mello, later Count of Murça, would have a successful career, assuming very influential offices in the Portuguese Empire. He would be the captain-general of the Azores (1806–1810) during the Napoleonic Wars (1803–1815) and, already during the Liberal period, minister and secretary of state of the Treasury, president of the Royal Treasury, and standing minister of Foreign Affairs, all in 1825. In 1826, he would become a peer of the Kingdom and an honorary member of the Royal Academy of Sciences of Lisbon.[116] Moreover, in 1823, Mello started drafting a project for a constitutional charter for the Portuguese Kingdom that he published anonymously in Paris in 1827.[117]

In his final report as captain-general and governor, he identified the "*great thefts*" and "*violence against the people*" committed by captains majors "*and all subjects who live in the hinterlands and hold public office*" as the origin of the "*rebellions of the blacks*" and source of the "*wars that were always very detrimental to the public treasury*."[118] Arguing that "*feirantes* [slave merchants], *captain majors, and other perverse men who had provoked the indignation of blacks*" should be punished before any punitive military intervention took place, Mello listed several cases during his tenure when Portuguese and Luso-Africans officers were to blame for disastrous military interventions, not including the Socoval affair.[119] However,

---

113 Mello, Relatorio do governo, p. 549; Sousa Coutinho, Oficio de Dom Rodrigo de Sousa Coutinho enviando um extracto do protesto do comércio da praça de Luanda, p. 603–605.

114 Mello, Relatorio do Governo, p. 563.

115 AHU, CU, Angola, Box 88, D. 7034; Mello, Carta de oficio do Governador.

116 Pinho da Cruz et al., D. Miguel António de Melo, in: Pinho da Cruz (ed.), Dos Secretários de Estado dos Negócios da Fazenda aos Ministros das Finanças, p. 143–144.

117 In the first title of this project, Mello envisions the "*Portuguese nation*" as being governed by a "*monarchic-representative-hereditary*" government. In keeping with its second article, it included "*Angola, Benguella, and their dependencies*" as one of its territories, thus extending all liberal rights to the subjects residing there. Ibid.; Osório de Castro, Arco-Íris liberal, p. 33–53; Projecto para a reforma da Ley Fundamental.

118 Mello, Relatorio do governo, p. 553.

119 The captain-general and governor reported a conflict involving "*Dembo-Gombe-amuquiana*" and several other *dembos* from Nambo Angongo triggered by the actions of officers Manuel Antonio

Mello mentions only two broadly outlined policy orientations in this report and proposes no concrete measures to avoid future conflicts. First, he highlighted that extant looting regulations only required one-fifth of the slaves and cattle taken during wars and raids to be paid as tribute to the Royal Treasury. The remaining four-fifths would be distributed among the officers and soldiers, which fueled their greed. While claiming that this ancient custom greatly destabilized the peace and harmony in the hinterlands of Angola and Benguela, Mello failed to propose a solution. Second, he argued that the forced "*introduction of* [the Portuguese] *religion and customs*" was decried by West Central Africans as an excuse for the Whites to "*gain lordship over their lands and wealth*," creating a resistance that was opposed to the best interests of commerce. Therefore, he implicitly distanced himself from Francisco Inocêncio de Sousa Coutinho's segregationist project while explicitly condemning the assimilationist one of Friar Alexandre da Sagrada Família. According to Mello, the latter's plan to simultaneously evangelize and establish a commercial outpost in the Port of Mpinda, then part of the independent Kingdom of Soyo, had failed because the *Mani* Soyo cared only "*for the beauty, cheapness, and good taste of commodities,* [...] *not their intrinsic rightfulness* [sic]" or virtue. Hence, he continued to trade with the British and other non-Catholics, being aware that if he allowed a religious establishment to be founded in his lands by Friar Alexandre da Sagrada Família, "*soon we would send to his lands captain majors, and other officers of justice and war, who would dispossess them*."[120] To this plan, Mello contrasted his idea that "*henceforward these peoples should be directed with softness and justice, to try to make them forget the damages, the violence, and the evils that we have oppressed them with now for more than three centuries*."

As transpires from his official letter about the Socoval affair, Miguel António de Mello's plan aimed to minimize legal uncertainty in the hinterlands of Angola and Benguela by establishing secondary rules, primarily through imposing writing and using new archival technologies. He believed the war against the *soba* had been unquestionably unfair and illegal.[121] Either *Soba* Socoval was a vassal, and his supposed crimes had to be dealt with through ordinary judicial means, or he was not. In that case, a War Board would have had to be assembled and consulted to validate the *casus belli* against him. Since neither condition had been met, Mello harbored no

Tavares and Luiz de Miranda Ribeiro. Additionally, there were two military campaigns against the "*Mussuis*" and their *soba* in the hinterlands of Benguela in 1790 and 1793, led by António José da Costa. Mello concluded that the Portuguese officers, not the African rulers, were the instigators and perpetrators. Ibid., p. 553–558.

120 For a description of Friar Alexandre da Sagrada Família to Soyo and an account of his objectives, see the report he wrote to the Secretary of State of the Navy and the Overseas Martinho de Melo e Castro on November 26, 1785. Ibid., p. 558; AHU, CU, Angola, Box 71, D. 6118.

121 MELLO, Carta de oficio do Governador.

doubts about the illegality of the punitive war. However, when informing Rodrigo de Sousa Coutinho about the way he dealt with the affair, he took the opportunity to outline five points to illustrate how he thought similar situations should be addressed and prevented in the future. According to Mello, when news about the ongoing conflicts between Serrão, Vieira de Andrade, and *Soba* Socoval first reached him on January 27, 1798, already after the Municipal Judge Pereira had intervened in the affair, he decided to investigate the matter by posing and answering a series of five questions. What immediately caught his attention was that the municipal judge had started his "*devassa* [inquiry]" about the rebellious acts and crimes attributed to *Soba* Socoval on December 1, 1797, while the slave raid disguised as a punitive war against him had been conducted by Serrão between October and November 1797, at the orders of Governor Botelho de Vasconcelos.[122] In his words, "*the inquiry was undertaken after the* [supposed] *punishment had been carried out, which makes it absurd to have handed down a penalty to a certain person when the crime was uncertain because it was not legally proven*."[123] Faced with such blatant disrespect for legality, before reporting to Rodrigo de Sousa Coutinho, Mello issued an oral edict on March 28, to be publicly announced in the streets of Benguela with a military drum roll.[124] In the official letter that accompanied it, Mello stated for all to hear that all prizes taken during the illegal war against the *soba* were illegitimate, and all *dominion* over the freedom of the enslaved captives and cattle was thus rendered null.[125] In case the enslaved prisoners had been slaves, their title was to be restored to *Soba* Socoval; if freeborn, their 'natural Freedom' was to be restored immediately. The official letter also announced which reparative measures were to be taken and decreed the payment of compensation in case enslaved captives had already been transferred to Brazil or North America or cattle consumed.

As clearly stated in the official letter accompanying the oral edict of March 28, *Soba* Socoval's detractors had accused him of "*disobedience, usurping Jurisdiction, and opposing paying Tithes*."[126] Therefore, the five questions guiding Mello's report to Rodrigo de Sousa Coutinho address these issues. According to the captain-general and governor, the case hinged first on ascertaining what tithes were annually collected in Benguela.[127] Second, on ascertaining if *Soba* Socoval had "*always paid them if he was obliged to* [pay them], *and if this obligation was old, or modern, and why it was introduced in the first place*." Third, on ascertaining if the "*conhecimento de Mucanos* [hearing of Mucanos]" was an exclusive prerogative of captain majors

122 Ibid.; Thompson, The Making of Quilengues, p. 242.
123 Mello, Carta de oficio do Governador.
124 Mello, Documento n.º 2, in: Delgado (ed.), A famosa e histórica Benguela, p. 444–446.
125 Ibid.
126 Ibid.
127 Mello, Carta de oficio do Governador.

or if the *sobas* of their districts had shared jurisdiction. It is worth noting that the original conflict between Vieira de Andrade and *Soba* Socoval was triggered by the former's decision to start adjudicating *mucanos* related to sorcery accusations and land disputes.[128] Fourth, on ascertaining if *Soba* Socoval had "*always adjudicated Mucanos*" and if he was a vassal of the Portuguese Crown.[129] Fifth, on ascertaining if these "*Mucanos*" were the freedom cases that the captain majors and regents adjudicated as ordinary judges or if they referred to customary cases usually arbitrated by *sobas*. In other words, the fifth and final question grappled with the legal uncertainty caused by the loose definition of *mucano*. In the seventeenth century, according to Cadornega, this Portuguese legal term of Kimbundu origin meant both a "*misdemeanor, crime*" or "*fault*," but also a "*legal case*" or the oral arbitration of a quarrel. Francisco Inocêncio de Sousa Coutinho had previously attempted to define it as a "*freedom case*," opting not to officially recognize all other conflicts and forms of conflict resolution that were also referred to by the Kimbundu "*mukano*" and unofficially recognized by Portuguese and Luso-African adjudicators who shared a broader understanding of *mucano*.[130]

However, as Catarina Madeira Santos remarks and Mello was aware of, it was impossible to disentangle freedom cases from other conflicts, such as adultery charges, debt settlements, or sorcery accusations, because the transfer of women, dependents, or slaves or rights over women and dependents as compensation were central to how Mbundu *mukano* and Portuguese or Luso-African *mucanos* worked as conflict resolution mechanisms that sought to restore balance between corporate kin groups through the transfer of social currencies or rights over people between them.[131] For the same reason, the enslavement of the accused and their dependents was a common penalty. For all purposes, Luso-African *mucanos*, Mbundu *mukano*, and similar African and Luso-African arbitration procedures and forms or styles of administering justice were central to the African forms of kinship patriarchy

---

128 Thompson, The making of Quilengues, p. 229.

129 Mello, Carta de oficio do Governador.

130 See the seventh chapter for an introduction to Olaf Zenker and Markus Hoehne's model of how recognition and non-recognition could co-exist and be strategically mobilized by different actors at both official and unofficial levels. Cadornega, História geral das guerras angolanas, Vol. 2, p. 61, 305; Coutinho, Documento N.º 6, in: Couto, Os capitães-mores em Angola, p. 328; Santos, Entre deux Droits, p. 817–848; Zenker and Hoehne, Processing the paradox, in: Zenker and Hoehne (eds.), The State and the Paradox.

131 Madeira Santos remarks that by 1703, a Capuchin missionary stationed at the Bango Aquitamba hospice had already noted that *mucanos* were entangled with the "movement of people, in particular the rights of matrilineal ascendents over [women's] sons, and the transactions arising from marriage and dowries, linked to the movement of women." In his words, *mucanos* concerned "generations," meaning the rights of corporate kin groups. Santos, Entre deux Droits, p. 817–848; Santos, Esclavage africain, p. 127–148.

Francisco Inocêncio de Sousa Coutinho was trying to eradicate and substitute by a racial-patriarchal system. Therefore, there was a significant difference between the 'normative horizons' and expectations of Captain-General and Governor Sousa Coutinho and those of the Portuguese and Luso-Africans who arbitrated *mucanos*. The former ordered those adjudicating freedom cases not to base their decisions on 'Gentilic Laws' but on *Ius gentium* doctrines of just war and *Ius commune* doctrines regarding the legal conditions for enslavement.[132] The latter, however, determined the fairness or equity of enslavement and the transfer of slaves, women, and dependents or rights over them in sight of the outcome of past arbitrations involving entire corporate kin groups. The outcome of these arbitrations could be determined by how the offenses or mischief caused by distant group members had previously been settled, through standing debts, or as the result of African ordeals and divinations that enabled the intervention of ancestors and territorial spirits. All these sources of normativity had no grounding on any legal source recognized as legitimate by 'The Law of Good Reason' of August 18, 1769.[133] However, these complex arbitrations were essential to settling conflicts between Mbundu or other African corporate kin groups, being crucial to stopping feuds and ascertaining the status of their members. This forced captain majors to intervene, making it unclear where the jurisdiction of captain majors and ordinary judges over freedom cases ended—and their right to review or even arbitrate Mbundu conflicts according to "*Gentilic Laws*" and Luso-African uses and customs began.[134]

As already discussed, Captain-General and Governor Sousa Coutinho's solution to this problem was to progressively segregate White settlers from mixed-race Luso-African familial factions and Black subjects and their corporate kin groups, forbidding the use of African judicial ordeals and divinations and reducing *mucano* hearings to the summary adjudications of freedom cases with recurse only to European sources of law.[135] In the last pages of his report on the Socoval affair, Mello proposed a different approach after reasoning through the five guiding questions he posed himself. Regarding the first of his guiding questions, Mello concluded that in Benguela, outside of the village, tithes were regularly collected only in the

132 AHU, CU, Angola, Box 88, D. 7031; Coutinho, Documento N.º 6, in: Couto, Os capitães-mores em Angola, p. 328.

133 Santos, Entre deux Droits, p. 817–848; Santos, Esclavage africain, p. 127–148.

134 Coutinho, Documento N.º 6, in: Couto, Os capitães-mores em Angola, p. 328; Santos, Esclavage africain, p. 127–148.

135 AHU, CU, Angola, Box 88, D. 7031; Coutinho, Documento N.º 6, in: Couto, Os capitães-mores em Angola, p. 330.

presídio of Caconda, the sole district served by a church and a parish priest.[136] Regarding the second guiding question, he concluded that *Soba* Socoval had never had the obligation of regularly paying tithe for three sets of reasons. First, because "*he was Pagan, as were all the Peoples of the hinterland of Benguela and a great part of Angola.*" Second, the Crown had not declared the collection of tithes a "*Royal Prerogative*" in Benguela, and, therefore, it could only be imposed on Catholics who were "*spiritually*" served by the Church.[137] Third, regarding *Soba* Socoval's obligation to pay tithe, Mello considered that he had only been forced to pay tithe once, exceptionally as a punishment for deserting the garrison of the *presídio* of Caconda when it was besieged by hostile *sobas* back in 1796. Regardless of its fairness, Mello concluded, this punishment could not set a valid precedent for the regular collection of tithes in his domain.

By clearly stating his reasoning, Mello endorsed a practical solution to one of the problems posed by 'salt' baptisms in Benguela, framing the obligation to pay tithe as compensation for religious services that could be objectively accessed and not on the canonical validity of sacraments long administered and challenging to confirm. His vision regarding this matter is more explicit in a series of official letters he wrote contesting Governor Botelho de Vasconcelos' project of establishing a Franciscan convent in Benguela.[138] According to Mello, the refusal to accept the ordination of mixed-race and Black priests was the origin of the lack of clergy in Angola and Benguela, together with the low stipends paid to parish priests and canons. In his opinion, this refusal explained why no seminary had been created in the Diocese of Congo and Angola using the properties and wealth confiscated from the Jesuits by the Crown in 1759 and why the Governor of Benguela preferred to sponsor a Franciscan convent rather than a non-segregated Latin grammar school.[139] Moreover, Mello argued that lacking proper language training and a regular stipend, European regular missionaries under the jurisdiction of the *Propaganda Fide* were not only useless but pernicious. They tended to disobey the commands of the bishop of Congo and Angola and parish priests and refused to keep a formal register of Christian baptisms, weddings, and funerals as they ought to following the regulations

---

136 In keeping with the documents Mello annexed to his report, between 1788 and 1796, 873$240 *réis* of tithe had been levied in Caconda by the captain majors. AHU, CU, Angola, Box 88, D. 7034; Mello, Carta de oficio do Governador.

137 It is unclear why Mello argues this was the case after the Crown had been levying tithes in the Captaincy of Angola for over two centuries. Nevertheless, this argument is in keeping with Mello's proposal to abolish tithes discussed in the previous chapter.

138 Mello, Oficio do Governador e Capitão General de Angola, p. 581–592; Mello, Oficio em que o Governador e Capitão General reprova a fundação de um convento de franciscanos em Benguela, p. 623–640.

139 Mello, Oficio em que o Governador e Capitão General reprova a fundação de um convento de franciscanos em Benguela, p. 623–640.

of the *First Constitutions of the Archdiocese of Bahia* (1707), creating uncertainty when determining their canonical validity.[140] By establishing a network of parish priests and enforcing the registry of sacraments, Mello believed most of the issues related to asserting the right to levy tithes would be resolved.

Regarding the third guiding question, Mello concluded that captain majors often adjudicated *mucanos* as ordinary judges, rightfully if they were freedom cases and instructed in keeping with Sousa Coutinho's Ordinance of February 24, 1765, and abusively if they were customary cases arbitrated according to African uses and customs.[141] To *sobas*, he continued, "*was left the hearing of Cases based on their Laws and customs, that by tradition their people keep and observe.*" However, a great "*diversity and confusion*" reigned in Angola, Benguela, and their dependencies because *sobas* "*always* [fought] *for the Right they originally had to judge their peoples.*" Moreover, the captain majors sought to exert their jurisdiction by "*desembargando* [reviewing] *conflicts for the desembargo* [review] *of which they charge exorbitant and unfair costs.*" In other words, even if the provisions of the Ordinance of February 24, 1765, were respected, the understandable aspirations of *sobas* and the fact that captain majors had to review all sorts of cases grounded on "*Gentilic Laws*" during the adjudication of regular freedom cases could still propagate jurisdictional disputes like the one that pitted Serrão and Vieira de Andrade against *Soba* Socoval. Mello's solution was for the Portuguese Crown to "*declare and decide, what is the law of the Souvas of this Conquista*" a task he deemed utopic because he found it difficult to "*clearly establish* [them] *in a way that matters are reduced to certain and transparent principles based on reason and Justice.*"

Regarding the fourth guiding question, Mello concluded that *Soba* Socoval had always had the right to adjudicate *mucanos*, whether these were understood as the arbitration of customary cases or the conflicts that triggered them, and that he was not a formal vassal of the Portuguese Crown.[142] To be so, the captain-general and governor concluded, the *soba* would have had to have signed a treaty of "*obedience and vassalage*" followed by a public *undamento* ceremony.[143] In Mello's opinion, since archival traces of both acts could not be found, it was inconsequential if the governor of Benguela and its municipal judge argued that *Soba* Socoval was

---

140 Accordingly, Mello abolished the Missions Board of Luanda and lobbied for the expulsion of the remaining members of the religious orders. Ibid.; PINHO DA CRUZ et al., D. Miguel António de Melo, in: PINHO DA CRUZ (ed.), Dos Secretários de Estado dos Negócios da Fazenda aos Ministros das Finanças, p. 143–144; VIDE, Constituições primeiras do Arcebispado da Bahia.

141 COUTINHO, Documento N.º 6, in: COUTO, Os capitães-mores em Angola, p. 323–338; MELLO, Carta de oficio do Governador.

142 MELLO, Carta de oficio do Governador.

143 See the seventh chapter for more on the *undamento* ritual and Luso-African "vassal treaties." HEINTZE, Luso-African Feudalism, p. 111–131.

traditionally regarded as a vassal and subject of the Crown, being an "*ally and friend*" instead.[144] Therefore, because they had breached the obligations of friendship due to allies, "*the Whites, and not the Blacks*" deserved to be punished. Furthermore, he clarified that Vieira de Andrade had once before tried to usurp *Soba* Socoval's right to adjudicate *mucanos*. Still, the *soba* had addressed a formal complaint to Manuel de Almeida e Vasconcelos, then captain-general and governor of Angola, who had decided the case in his favor. Regarding the fifth guiding question, Mello began by confirming the official definition of *mucano*, clarifying that, at least since 1699, the "*Cases of Mucanos of Freedom*" were understood to be just one specific kind of *mucano* amongst others and that the Ovimbundu equivalent of *mukano* was "*Obimbo*." According to him, even though the term *mucano* originally referred to all "*cases, or litigations that are orally decided according to the customs of the Country*" and could, therefore, be used to describe the oral and summary adjudication of processes by either captain majors and ordinary judges or the arbitration of conflicts by *sobas*, the first only had jurisdiction over *mucanos* that were "*freedom cases*," according to the Ordinance of February 24, 1765.

As for the *sobas*, Mello explained, they arbitrated several types of *mukano* or *obimbo*, classifiable according to the substantive content of each case.[145] Therefore, in the captaincy of Benguela, *obimbo* could be designated either as "*Obimbo muquiti*" when they involved a violent death, as "*Obimbo biohuanga*" when they involved "*Feiticeria*," as "*Obimbo biatuca*" when they involved debts and peonage, as "*Obimbo buiumunu*" when they involved robbery or thefts, or, finally, as "*Obimbo biombaro*" when they involved injuries or physical offenses. According to Mello, freedom cases were the only *mucanos* captain majors had exclusive jurisdiction over. Therefore, he concluded that since *Soba* Socoval was not arbitrating those, the war against him had been entirely unfounded. In the process of reaching and explaining to Rodrigo de Sousa Coutinho this conclusion, Mello took steps in the direction of systematizing the "*Direitos* [rights/laws] *of the Souvas* [*sobas*]" of Angola and Benguela and thus reducing legal uncertainty. Contrary to Francisco Inocêncio de Sousa Coutinho's proposal to bar captain majors from recognizing the validity of *mucano* complaints and arbitrations based on the "*direitos* [rights/laws] *of Quituxe and Opanda*," Mello accepted those as part of his typology, suggesting that he welcomed their revision by captain majors during freedom cases if these "*direitos*" had been systematized through writing to avoid legal uncertainty.[146] This could be

144 Mello, Carta de oficio do Governador.

145 Ibid.; Ferreira, Cross-Cultural Exchange, p. 99–100.

146 As explained in the sixth chapter, *mucanos* regarding *quituxes* consisted in determining who was to pay compensation for "*calamitous occurrences*," such as "*fires, the ruin of houses,* [and] *the loss or fall of trees*," and "*Opanda*" arbitrations settled adultery charges. Coutinho, Documento N.º 6, in: Couto, Os capitães-mores em Angola, p. 328–329.

gradually achieved by naturalists such as José da Silva collecting proto-ethnographic information to be either published or deposited in the archives of the Secretariats of the Governments of Angola and Benguela.[147] Such a systematization would afford different modalities of settler-colonization of the hinterlands, not based on segregation and the progressive eradication of African normative systems but on their gradual recognition, as written customary law, by the Portuguese legal regime. As the following pages discuss, Mello believed this option would provide a more stable normative grounding for the perpetuation of the Atlantic slave trade.

In his "*Plan for the Organisation, Discipline and Government of the Troops of the Kingdom of Angola*," Mello argues that granting "*the Civil Government of the Presídios and Districts of this Kingdom* [...] *to Captain Majors*" could only lead to "*the Peoples* [of the hinterlands] *being oppressed by them with violence and unheard-of extractions, which are daily and unfortunately renewed*."[148] In his opinion, this had nothing to do with racial predispositions but happened because the government of the "*said Districts came with no stipend*."[149] Men who were removed from their previous positions, where they earned a stable income and regular promotions, and made to serve for three years as captain majors, earning nothing but the uncertain emoluments they could charge as ordinary judges, could be expected to engage in cruel and extortionary practices.[150] Therefore, the solution was to raise these stipends or establish more villages endowed with municipal councils in the interior, "*even if they are neither better settled nor governed than Massangano*." In his opinion, the Royal Charter of July 22, 1766, which ordered the implementation of a similar pattern of occupation in the interior of the Captaincy of Bahia in Brazil, could be used as a model. Complementing the writing down of African "*uses and customs*," the creation of a network of civil jurisdictions was thus proposed by Mello as the definitive solution to the many jurisdictional conflicts and extortions that took place in the hinterlands of Angola and Benguela.[151] Such a solution, however, would only be essayed in the 1860s, when a series of new municipal councils were established.

---

147 José Da Silva, Continuação da viagem ao sertão de Benguella, continuada do N.º 2.º, p. 49–60; José Da Silva, Extracto da viagem, que fez ao sertão de Benguella no anno de 1785, p. 97–100; José Da Silva, Viagem ao sertão de Benguella, continuada do N.º 1.º, p. 86–98.

148 Mello, Plano para a organização, p. 189–254.

149 Miguel Mello believed that racial barriers to access military offices should be dropped, as he was against the "*erroneous*" use of "*diverting the Mulattoes and Blacks who serve in the Loanda troops from* [hinterland] *Posts*," a discriminatory gesture that brought "*them down*" and broke their "*spirit and desires*," discouraging them "*to do well to achieve promotions and honours*." AHU, CU, Angola, Box 88, D. 7031.

150 Mello, Plano para a organização, p. 189–254.

151 Mello, Carta a D. Rodrigo de Sousa Coutinho, p. 274–281.

At which point, the "*juízes de Paz* [judges of peace]" who had substituted the ordinary judges immediately faced the challenge of adjudicating *mucanos*.[152]

On April 30, 1798, Mello wrote to Rodrigo de Sousa Coutinho a memorandum concerning possible reforms of the administration of civil and criminal justice in Angola.[153] This document outlined eight articles, which had been decided upon after extensive discussions with Ouvidor Geral João Alvares de Mello, who had "*more than ten years of experience*" in West Central Africa. The two top magistrates agreed the measures in these articles were the "*future remedies*" needed to address the "*present vices*" of the Captaincy of Angola. As Mello stated in the first article, these would "*restore* [it] *from decadence and darkness*," promote "*Public Peace in the Colony*," and have its "*perfect Administration and Government reconciled with the principles of Justice and Greatest Clemency, inseparable virtues of the Portuguese Throne*." Most of the measures related to competence ranges, the constitution of commissarial boards, and the hierarchy of courts. In his view, these slight adjustments would speed up civil, criminal, and administrative justice in West Central Africa. The second article focused on the constitution of the board that elected the general vicar, the stipend he should receive, and protocol matters (e. g., where each board member should sit during meetings). Focusing more on social than legal issues, the third article addressed the question of *degredados* [convicts] and all the social and judicial problems that the "*continuous sending*" of "*facinorous men from Portugal and Brazil*" caused in the Captaincy of Angola.[154] In the captain-general and governor's opinion, turning West Central Africa into a penal colony was a lousy solution to the demographic challenges posed by high White mortality rates.[155] Instead, as discussed, Mello was open to accepting Black and mixed-race individuals in military, civil, and ecclesiastical offices, according to their merit, and promoting the progressive settlement of the Angolan hinterlands through the establishment of a pattern of municipal councils and parishes like the one in Brazil. The fifth article proposed that the *Relação* of Rio de Janeiro, established by the Ordinance of October 13, 1751, substituted the *Relação* of Bahia (1609) as the second instance court for both civil and criminal cases because it was more accessible.[156] The sixth article asked for clarification regarding the destiny of appeals

---

152 Figueiredo, A Questão das "Ouvidas," p. 81–104.

153 AHU, CU, Angola, Box 88, D. 7031.

154 For more information on *degredados* and penal colonization in the Portuguese Empire, see Anabela Cunha, Timothy Coates, and Selma Pantoja. Coates, Degredados e Órfãos; Cunha, Degredo para Angola, p. 87–104; Pantoja, A diáspora feminina, p. 555–572; Pantoja, Inquisição, degredo e mestiçagem em Angola, p. 117–136.

155 AHU, CU, Angola, Box 88, D. 7031.

156 While Mello's notes suggest that the *Relação* of Bahia had functioned as a court of appeal to Angolan courts in civil matters, Nuno Camarinhas argues that this was never the case, despite the possibility

made by nobles condemned to death in the Captaincy of Angola, if they were only to be adjudicated by the *Casa da Suplicação* in Lisbon, or if the Criminal Board could have its jurisdiction extended to review them.[157] Similarly, the seventh article asked for clarification regarding appeals of the decisions of the Board of Finance of Angola, if they were to continue to be adjudicated by the *Casa da Suplicação*, or if the *Relação* of Bahia could review them. The eighth article proposed that the values of all the civil and criminal competence ranges of *Ouvidores Gerais* and municipal judges should be doubled.

At the center of the document, the fourth and lengthiest article addressed the issue that Mello considered most urgent—namely, reforming the style of the *Mucano* hearings of Luanda and reorganizing the parallel legal system that had these hearings as its upper instance.[158] In Mello's words, he had found in the archives and secretariats of the Captaincy no "*title authorizing Governors to be the Privative Judges*" of *mucanos*, nor any other legal basis other than ancient custom allowing them to "*decide by themselves these causes, without taking as Adjunct one of the Ordinary Magistrates*" or granting the petitioners the right to have their *mucanos* reviewed by higher instances. Therefore, he could not determine what style the legislators intended this court to follow. However, because the sixteenth article of the 1688 Ordinance of the Secretariat of the General Government of Angola ordered an official of this secretariat only to keep a record of the "*resolutions*" of *mucanos* in a dedicated ledged so that "*certificates could be drawn*," Mello assumed that *mucanos* were to be "*known verbally, and summarily, independent of Forensic formalities.*"[159] Mello claimed that "*practice contradicted*" these dispositions. "*Voluminous files, processed in keeping with all the Rules of Direito* [Law]" were created "*by a private Clerk of the Court, but without any costs,*" admitting "*embargoes on the judgments*" and being argued in sight of "*what the Jurisconsults and Roman Emperors had left written in the Pandects of Civil Law*" or the "*customs and Laws of the* [Roman] *Empire*"—which the captain-general and governor believed "*not at all applicable to the Blacks of Africa.*" Moreover, Mello remarked, "*issues very different from the* [legal] *condition of persons*" were being adjudicated, for instance, "*whether a servant had been manumitted by his master cheating his creditors.*" Because of the complexity of these *mucano* files and of not being trained "*in theoretical and practical Jurisprudence*," Mello claimed, past captain-general and governors picked "*an Assistant from the learned men of the land*," who thus assumed in practice the privilege of adjudicating these cases, in the process postponing their regular duties.

---

of Angola becoming part of the judicial district of Bahia being often discussed. CAMARINHAS, Tribunais de Relação.

157 AHU, CU, Angola, Box 88, D. 7031.

158 Ibid.

159 AHU, CU, Angola, Box 88, D. 7031; LANCASTRO, Regimento do Secretario deste Reino, p. 493–496.

Besides delaying the regular course of justice, Mello argued this mishandling of *mucano* hearings had severe economic consequences "*since there were already quite a few trading houses, which were close to defaulting on their debts due to the growing number of slaves they had bought in the hinterlands who had been recognized as free persons by the Court of Liberties.*"[160] This happened, in his opinion, because "*the Proclamations of the Blacks*" bought in the hinterland were "*not given the attention they deserve*" there, as all that the Luso-African slave merchants and *pumbeiros* cared for was the "*price they were sold to their buyers*" by "*Souvas* [*sobas*] *and other Blacks.*" In the captain-general and governor's opinion, the most "*fecund origin and perhaps the main one*" of the slaves sold in Luanda was not Portuguese warfare and punitive raids but "*the customs of the said Blacks, according to which they capture each other, not only in war but as a penalty.*" Therefore, proclamations of freedom should be immediately addressed. Regardless, Mello continued, of Mbundu penalties having been applied to offenses "*that take place in all Nations, either barbarous or civilized,*" such as "*homicide, adultery, and veneficio* [sorcery/poisoning]," or to one of the "*crimes*" which he considered "*for the most part ridiculous, such as, for example, a man suffering from some natural illness in another man's house, being warmed by another man's fire,*" or "*being the neighbor of a man who has fled without paying his creditor*"—in other words, those associated with offenses caused by other members of the corporate kin groups, either living or ancestors, or with the transgression of ritual prohibitions.

Complicating matters, Mello continued, not all Africans enslaved through legal means had been so by the initiative of their African peers. "*Portuguese and naturais* [locally born] *or those naturalized in this Conquest,*" the captain-general and governor continued, "*accommodated themselves with the uses and customs, and barbarous ways of the Gentiles,*" "*forçando liberdades* [forcing freedoms]" through "*unjust and reproved means*"—meaning, promoting the enslavement of free Africans either through African arbitrations, or the adjudication of *mucanos* according to African sources of law and normative systems.[161] More than two hundred years after the Jesuits who accompanied Paulo Dias de Novais first faced the same issue, Mello was thus confronted with the fact that substituting African institutions and offices for Portuguese ones opened the door for African normative understandings, beliefs, and customs to infiltrate their core and continue to dictate the 'rules of the game' or influence behavior. As discussed in this chapter, both Captain-General and Governor Sousa Coutinho and the vicar Bishop Alexandre da Sagrada Família faced the same challenge. Despite the Christian façade imposed by the former, the mass baptisms favored by the latter, or the references to the "*Pandects of Civil Law*"

160 AHU, CU, Angola, Box 88, D. 7031.

161 Ibid.

in *mucano* rulings criticized by Mello, African normative systems and grammars of affect continued to shape the daily lives of the Portuguese, Luso-African, and African individuals in the Captaincy of Angola. These systems structured their life events and celebrations. They provided remedies to restore social peace when it was disturbed by sorcery and ways to prevent the other dangers associated with intimacy, physical proximity, and kinship. Moreover, as Mello was aware, African normative systems structured a crucial leg of the Atlantic slave trade. Considering this, he proposed a solution that differed from those of his predecessors, neither focused on religious assimilation nor racial segregation—as he believed both would halt the trade in slaves.

According to Mello, to decide "*on the justice or injustice of captivity by our customs and not by those of the Blacks*" would result in "*almost all the so-called slaves*" being by force "*considered free, regardless of the reasons and foundations of Natural Law, and consequently in a short time the Portuguese Trade in this Kingdom would end or be ruined.*"[162] His solution consisted of taking five complementary steps. First, all "*persons enslaved by Whites*" through legal proceedings inspired by African legal systems would be "*considered free.*" The same would apply to all persons enslaved by other Portuguese "*vassals*" of any race who lived "*in the European manner.*" This would equate all Portuguese and Luso-Africans who resorted to African arbitration or the arbitration of *mucanos* in keeping with African norms with "*forçadores de liberdades* [forcers of freedoms]," making them amenable to be punished as such by Portuguese "*Justices.*" This solution differed from the racial patriarchy endorsed by Captain-General and Governor Sousa Coutinho in as much as it proposed to restrict access to the arbitration courts where the members of African corporate kin groups settled their disputes based not on racial criteria but on the level of acculturation or cultural assimilation of individuals. This freed these arbitration courts, and even Portuguese and Luso-African captain majors and ordinary judges, to keep deciding *mukano* or *mucanos* between African subjects in keeping with African norms (the former could even continue using judicial ordeals), and thus producing the enslaved Africans needed to supply the Atlantic market and balance the finances of the Captaincy of Angola.[163] Second, all "*those who have been sold by the Souvas* [*sobas*], *or by their Peoples according to their barbaric customs and Laws*" were to be automatically "*considered legally enslaved.*" Third, the *ouvidor geral* would be entrusted with co-adjudicating the freedom cases heard in the *mucanos* court with the captain-general and governor. Fourth, the *mucanos* that were not related to the legal status of individuals were to be heard by ordinary civil courts, in

---

162 Ibid.

163 It is important to note that Mello favored introducing new taxes over exported slaves to finance the Captaincy of Angola. See the previous chapter for his proposed taxation policies.

keeping with "*Portuguese Laws*," with the option of appealing to the *Relação* of the judicial district. Fifth, the same principles were to be applied in Benguela, where the municipal judge substituted the *ouvidor geral*, and no costs were to be paid by the plaintiffs.

Considering this five-step plan, Mello's request for the Crown to systematize the "*Direitos* [laws/rights] *of the Souvas* [*sobas*]" of Angola and Benguela can be read differently.[164] Such a measure would not only reduce legal uncertainty, dovetailing with his rationalization of archives and other enlightened reforms but also address the same problems discussed in the fifth and sixth chapters, namely that, as Pascoal José de Melo Freire (1738–1798) concluded in 1791, the enslavement of free Africans and the dominion over the freedom of "*Black slaves*" had no basis whatsoever in the civil laws of the fatherland.[165] If, as discussed, the doctrine of ransom was the solution found by Canon law specialists and royalist jurists to justify slavery or similar forms of extreme asymmetrical dependency during the Enlightenment, Mello proposed implementing a legal regime that would accommodate it. While Captain-General and Governor Sousa Coutinho's plans sought to guarantee that slaves would continue to be 'rescued' from outside of Portuguese jurisdiction by associating these limits with racial boundaries (re)produced by regulating marriages and motherhood, Mello suggested that legal and jurisdictional segregation according to ethnically or culturally defined boundaries would have better practical results.[166] Moreover, Mello argued for a different pathway toward assimilation. Not based exclusively on religious conversion and Roman Catholic sacraments, his secular understanding of assimilation foregrounded cultural and normative integration as forms of negotiating belonging. Finally, by recovering the concept of *veneficio* [sorcery/poisoning] to describe sorcery practices amongst the subjects

---

164 Mello, Carta de oficio do Governador.

165 Freire, Meneses (trans.), Instituições de Direito Civil, p. 18.

166 The difference between both visions of the future can be best understood by considering Mahmood Mamdani's analysis of posterior forms of legal and social segregation in South Africa and its neighboring countries. According to his model, the *apartheid* regime was predicated on two different kinds of segregation and forms of rule. The first was based on constructed racial differences, direct rule, and attributing individual citizenship rights to privileged individuals according to their racial status. This racial form of segregation was operational in urban environments. The second was based on constructed ethnic differences, indirect rule, and the attribution of corporate rights to culture-bound groups and corporate subjecthood to their members. This ethnic form of segregation was operational in rural environments. If we adopt this abstract model, keeping in mind possible anachronisms, it transpires that despite their differences, Sousa Coutinho's and Mello's projects, the first based on racial segregation, the latter on ethnic or cultural one, could be articulated. In any case, the solutions devised by these former captain-general and governors inaugurate the conceptual field of later discussions about direct and indirect rule and different forms of segregation. Mamdani, Citizen and Subject; Mamdani, Define and Rule.

of independent African polities, Mello solved an issue that could potentially arise from *mucanos* involving them being reviewed or adjudicated by Portuguese or Luso-African officers.[167]

As already discussed, by this point, the Inquisition of Lisbon no longer attributed the same weight to sorcery and witchcraft charges, framing them instead as either superstitions or madness. By the end of the eighteenth century, Portuguese enlightened penal thought had progressed in the same direction. Following the opinions of Christian Thomasius (1655–1728) and Samuel Stryk (1640–1710) on *crimina magiae*, and Cesare Beccaria's (1738–1794) doctrines on punishment, Melo Freire characterized "*magical arts, feitiçarias, spellcasting, prestidigitation, cursing, enchanting, and everything else under the designation of magic or popularly attributed to the power of demons*" as "*erros da plebe* [plebeian mistakes]."[168] In the twenty-third article of the first title of his "*Instituições de Direito Criminal Português* [Institutions of Portuguese Criminal Law]" (1794), dedicated to "*Criminal Offenses Without Penalty*," Melo Freire claimed that the received Roman and Visigoth regulations and Canon laws on sorcery and divination glossed in the *Afonsine* (1446), *Manueline* (1512), and *Philippine Ordinances* (1603), were "*abrogated due to disuse*" and that "*feiticeiros and enchanters were to be treated not as real delinquents but as superstitious persons* [...] *and fanatics*," being thus "*publicly scorned and instructed*," except those who "*caused damage with the natural means at their disposal*," as he remarked in the thirteenth article of the second title.[169] Framing resolute sorcerers as fanatics allowed Melo Freire to recast their activities as a public crime against the *Ordre public* or public tranquility and, therefore, under the jurisdiction of the Crown instead of framing it as a religious sin under Canon law jurisdiction. Similarly, throughout *Institutions of Portuguese Criminal Law*, he reframed religious

---

167 Pietz, The Problem of the Fetish, p. 39.

168 Most notably, Stryk's skepticism in *Specimen usus moderni pandectarum* (1690–1692) regarding confessions obtained through torture and "*crimina magiae*" and Thomasius' *Theses Inaugurales de Crimine Magiae* (1701). José Subtil and Mário Leite Santos also list the influence of: Augustin Leyser (1683–1752), Christian Thomasius (1655–1728), Cornelis van Bijnkershoek (1673–1743), François-Michel Vermeil (1730–1810), Gabriel Bonnot de Mably ()1709–1785), Hugo Grotius (1583–1645), Jean-Baptiste le Rond d'Alembert (1717–1783), Jeremy Bentham (1748–1832), Johann Brunnemann (1608–1672), Johann Samuel Friedrich Böhmer (1704–1772), Justus Henning Böhmer (1674–1749), Karl Anton von Martini (1726–1800), Montesquieu (1689–1755), Nicolaus Hieronymus Gundling (1671–1729), Samuel von Pufendorf (1632–1694), Samuel Stryk (1640–1710), amongst others, both on Melo Freire's writings and teaching at the University of Coimbra. For an overview of Melo Freire's contribution to the differentiation of Portuguese criminal law as a field, see Alexander de Castro, António Hespanha, and Leite Santos. Castro, "Boa Razão" e codificação penal, p. 105–143; Freire, Instituições de Direito Criminal Português, p. 74; Hespanha, A cultura jurídica europeia, p. 360–361; Santos, Melo Freire, p. 178–179; Subtil, O crime e o castigo, in: Subtil, Atallah and Mota (eds.), Criminalidades, Direito e justiça no Mundo Ibérico, p. 35–64.

169 Freire, Instituições de Direito Criminal Português, p. 74, 95.

crimes such as heresy and blasphemy, as well as moral crimes such as adultery, concubinage, rape, sodomy, bestiality, and masturbation.[170] As José Subtil explains, the former were recast as "social crimes" because of the damage they caused to "social cohesion" and, together with the latter, became *mixti fori* crimes.[171]

In West Central Africa, these innovations opened the door for African *feiticeiros* to continue to be persecuted as public criminals in Portuguese jurisdictions if the substances used in African judicial ordeals or *kindoki, uanga*, or *wanga*—the spiritual source of the anti-social power of sorcerers—were framed as poison and their acts as "*veneficio*," which also meant poisoning.[172] For the same reason, simply accepting penal pluralism as a fact, Portuguese and Luso-African judges and officers with jurisdiction could confirm the enslavement of African sorcerers as a result of arbitrations according to African normative systems without incurring the paradox of confirming African "*superstitions*."[173] In keeping with this view, as Mello remarked, condemning someone to the penalty of slavery for conducting "*veneficios* [sorcery/poisoning]" was simply a barbarous custom, not an unjustified one, as all civilized nations punished anti-social fanatics and poisoners who caused damage with the natural means at their disposal, regardless of the accused framing it as magic or sorcery.[174] In Mello's view, enslavement would be a fitting penalty for all those who did not live "*in the European manner*." This final aspect of his project for the future of the Captaincy of Angola, Benguela, and their dependencies points in two directions that would be central to the economic restructuring of these territories in the aftermath of the legal abolition of the Atlantic slave trade.[175] First, it points to the criminalization of African uses and customs at the root of the 'Dark Continent' myths that would provide an alibi for the effective colonization of

---

170 Subtil, O crime e o castigo, in: Subtil, Atallah and Mota (eds.), Criminalidades, Direito e justiça no Mundo Ibérico, p. 45.

171 Canon law courts were to determine the degree of the blame of heretics (e. g., if they had committed "*simple heresy*" or "*seditious heresy*") and other religious and moral offences, while the Crown's courts were to conduct the process of gathering evidence and determining penalties. Ibid.

172 Rodrigues de Areia, Estrutura magico-religiosa, p. 38–39, 51.

173 Following John Beattie's seminal work, several scholars have remarked that penal pluralism was the norm in *Ancien Régime* societies. For an introduction to the history of penal pluralism in the Portuguese Empire, see Cristina Nogueira da Silva and Fernanda Thomaz. See also Luzia Sebastião for contemporary discussions about penal pluralism in Angola. Beattie, Crime and the Courts in England; Innes and Styles, The Crime Wave, p. 380–435; Nogueira da Silva, A construção jurídica dos Territórios Ultramarinos, p. 55–61; Sebastião, Legalidade penal, costume e pluralismo jurídico; Thomaz, Casaco que se despe pelas costas.

174 AHU, CU, Angola, Box 88, D. 7031.

175 Most notably, after the Decree of December 10, 1836 and the Anglo-Portuguese Treaty of 1842. For an exhaustive analysis of abolitionist legislation in the Portuguese Empire, see Margarida Seixas. Seixas, Abolição da escravidão, in: Homem (ed.), Grandes realizações da história do direito português, p. 5–7; Seixas, Pessoa e trabalho no Direito Português.

Africa during the nineteenth century.[176] Second, it paved the way for the doctrines that justified the adaptation of the Portuguese Penal Code of 1852 to the "*idle nature of the* [African] *natives*."[177] As Cristina Nogueira da Silva remarks, despite the universal applicability of the Penal Code of 1852 in the Portuguese Empire, on July 17, 1854, the Ministry of the Affairs of the Navy and the Overseas requested the recently reinstated Overseas Council (1851–1868) to suggest adjustments and modifications to it before it was published in the "*overseas provinces.*" As a result, the second article of the decree that published the Penal Code in Angola stated that the penalties applied to slaves and "*libertos* [freed slaves]" would always include forced labor as it was better adjusted to their "*indole* [nature]." This influential doctrinal stance, arguably pioneered by Mello, would condition Portuguese penal thought and 'indigenous policies' well into the mid-twentieth century.

---

176 Brantlinger, Victorians and Africans, p. 166–203; Figueiredo, Política, escravatura e feitiçaria em Angola.

177 Nogueira da Silva, A construção jurídica dos territórios ultramarinos, p. 55–61.

Concluding Remarks

In this book, I account for the gritty practicalities of jurisdiction and normative translation in the Captaincy of Angola, Benguela, and their many dependencies during the Early Modern period. More than focusing on jurisdictional jockeying or local claim-making practices, I strove to foreground how Luso-African and African uses and customs, judicial practices, and normative constellations were deeply intertwined with broader theoretical or ideological frameworks. Instead of categorizing these elements into obscure 'black boxes,' such as 'culture,' 'religion,' or 'economy,' I place concrete accounts and events within the evolving dynamics of global interactions and local political imaginations, social conflicts, and power struggles. I found this approach particularly apt to describe a historical period before system differentiation when norms from these overlapping spheres often competed or concurred instead of regulating parallel, semi-autonomous fields of human activity. Additionally, I pay attention to how environmental and ecological conditions, along with technological constraints, created physical limits on the transplant of norms and institutions from Europe, as well as on policing and other forms of religious, social, and cultural control. These limitations, combined with the vitality, resourcefulness, and resilience of African normative systems and Luso-African legal cultures, allowed Africans to maintain a significant influence over key normative areas during this period despite the substantial disruptions caused by the Atlantic slave trade and the increasing rates of European colonial dispossession. Overall, the chapters address a central question: how did the Portuguese and West Central Africans translate their rich, complex, non-overlapping multinormative orders 'on a shoestring'? By this, I mean in the (almost) absence of learned magistrates, jurists, or dedicated African practitioners while the Atlantic slave trade was either funding or profoundly disrupting local institutional life.

This question led me to propose the existence of 'folk doctrines' regarding African otherness and to survey their normative impact. These 'doctrines' postulated West Central Africa's exclusion from Natural law and God's grace, creating many conceptual challenges but easing the conscience of unscrupulous slavers and Portuguese officers. Then, to redefine the slave fairs where the political struggle for control over the local 'regime of commensuration' took place as crucial juridical and sociocultural arenas. Finally, to explore how seasonal and personal events, from acute 'trust' crises triggered by sorcery accusations to regular rites of passage, structured and unstructured the domestic normative spheres of West Central African subjects. This allowed me to reframe Enlightened reforms and police regulations as attempts to socialize them into a European 'grammar of affect.'

All these attempts to repurpose or craft new heuristics capable of doing better justice to the historical, geographical, and socio-cultural specificities of early modern West Central Africa would not have been possible without the momentous contribution of António Manuel Hespanha (1945–2019) to the fields of institutional history and the history and theory of law—fields often opposed to theoretical innovation. In keeping with Hespanha's radically honest and transparent understanding of historiography, I maintain that my theoretical solutions are provisory and somewhat unsatisfactory attempts to make sense of persistent issues and unanswered questions in terms that are closer to the worldviews and experiences of early modern West Central Africans, Luso-Africans, and Portuguese settlers and sojourners—or at least to how their lived-worlds and perspectives can be reconstructed from the information gleaned from legal and archival sources.

The central riddle that historians of West Central African institutions and normative systems and regimes are bound to reencounter, regardless of their focus being colonial or imperial legal cultures or African normative orders, is how to account for the prevalence of sorcery beliefs and accusations, as well as anti-sorcery divinations, ordeals, and other creative institutional solutions that Africans have found to the ontological and social problems posed by the 'dark side' of kinship and the existence of evil. This is evidenced not only by the contemporary ethnographies of Peter Geschiere, Jean and John Comaroff, and countless other social and cultural anthropologists and ethnographers they inspired but also by the historical and genealogical studies that explore the paths opened by the hugely influential works of William Pietz and James Sweet on fetishism and divination in the Early Modern Black Atlantic.

As the chapters grouped in Part One explain, the incredibly rich and deep-rooted West Central African normative thesaurus regarding *kindoki*, *uanga*, *wanga*, and *feitiçaria* not only posed problems and established limits to the reforms of enlightened captain-general and governors of Angola but also afforded a 'cross-cultural' space of 'correlation' that enabled normative translation and gave rise to local vernaculars of Portuguese institutions. In other words, a shared understanding of sorcery was just as crucial to the development of Luso-African uses, customs, and styles of administering justice as the better-explored malleability and adaptability of Portuguese *Ius commune* doctrines and the jurisdictional form of government and juridical culture of the *Antigo Regime*. Bringing the latest scholarship on the Portuguese Empire into dialogue with the West Central African historiography of Jan Vansina, John Thornton, Joseph Miller, Linda Heywood, Wyatt MacGaffey, and many of their disciples and colleagues, this book drafts a first approach to how its *Antigo Regime* society adapted to a world with 'sorcerers.' In a domain where White Europeans suffered immensely from the harshness of the weather and the epidemiological environment, and the brutal institutions of slavery often prevailed over those structured by gentle affects such as love, charity, or religious piety, the administration of justice (*jurisdictio*) frequently seemed impossible to European observers. Yet, it is worth mentioning again that African normative systems, in all their resilience, creativity, and resourcefulness, not only filled in the gaps influencing Luso-African normativities but remained hegemonic in most domestic and public spheres well into the nineteenth century. This, while also operating as a constant source of inspiration for new institutional and normative solutions to the problems resulting from the social anomie caused by the Atlantic slave trade. In other words, birthing West Central African vernaculars and decisively shaping colonial legal cultures. All this richness transpires from the analyzed sources. Still, it would remain invisible in any legal history of Angola that strictly focuses on what happened in courtrooms or what remains registered on written claims and petitions.

As the economic, religious, legal, and political systems increasingly differentiated during the last decades of the eighteenth century, these Luso-African normative solutions of African inspiration became increasingly suspect, recast as 'superstitions' and 'abuses.' This coincided with the rise of a novel understanding of sovereignty and the power of the Portuguese monarch to legislate, which marked the transition of the Captaincy of Angola, Benguela, and their dependencies towards a 'police state' paradigm. As explored in the chapters grouped in Part Two, system differentiation did not imply that significant innovations or reforms in one dimension stopped impacting the other or that sorcery beliefs and related normativities no longer served as conceptual bridges allowing Europeans and West Central African subjects to make sense of the complexities of the Atlantic slave trade. In fact, Africans and Luso-Africans not only understood and made sense of this inhuman traffic and the circulation of new commodities, trade goods, and currencies it occasioned by using the vocabulary and '*imaginaire*' of *feitiçaria*, *kindoki*, *uanga*, and *wanga*, but the legitimacy of the *dominium* masters had over the freedom of slaves (and the financial stability of the Portuguese Crown and trading companies) became impossible to disentangle from sorcery beliefs and anti-sorcery practices. If, at first, it had been the conversion and Christianization of 'gentiles' who allegedly believed in nothing but *feitiços* and 'idols' that legitimized their conquest and enslavement, it was the 'right' to 'ransom' the victims of sorcery accusations, 'cannibalism,' and anti-sorcery ordeals that provided a solid ideological alibi for the traffic in human flesh during the last decades of the eighteenth century. A continuous line can thus be traced between early Jesuit accounts of African institutions, the Second-Scholastic doctrinal and theological discussions about the legitimate conditions of enslavement held at the Universities of Coimbra and Évora, and the post-1772 attempts by royalist jurists to 'accommodate' the increasingly uncomfortable institutions of slavery within their systematizations of the Portuguese 'laws of the fatherland.' This continuity reflects the omnipresence of European (mis)readings of African beliefs and practices associated with sorcery, the dangers posed by kinship, physical proximity, and intimacy, and the sacrifices and ritual restrictions related to the cult of ancestors, territorial spirits, and powerful political leaders.

However, the last four decades of the eighteenth century were characterized by the introduction of critical institutional novelties and reforms in the Captaincy of Angola, Benguela, and their dependencies, as also occurred in the other domains that composed the Portuguese Empire. From the expulsion of the Jesuits in 1759 to the establishment of new commissarial boards in 1761, the abolition of the slave duty contract in 1769, and the subsequent introduction of metallic currencies, many of these eroded the foundations of the jurisdictional form of government, introducing new forms of bureaucratic and biopolitical management to West Central Africa and promising a rationalization of financial and human resources. Portuguese reformers were forced into a paradoxical position regarding sorcery beliefs and anti-sorcery institutions within this new paradigm. On the one hand, as mentioned, the ideological, normative, and moral groundings of the Atlantic slave trade came to be predicated on the continued existence of African normative spheres that European observers could frame as dominated by irrational beliefs in sorcery and the inhuman treatment of those accused of practicing it. It was this framing that justified the 'ransom' of enslaved Africans in the hinterland markets. On the other hand, the 'gentle' eradication of similar beliefs and practices was one of the ideological cores of the Enlightenment, justifying the introduction of police laws and canonical regulations that, as several contemporaries noted, if fully abided by West Central Africans, would put a stop to the Atlantic slave trade ruining Lisbon merchants and Brazilian planters. Different solutions were proposed to this puzzle as the chapters grouped in Part Three explore. These ranged from the delimitation of racially segregated social or physical spaces where different grammars of affect regulated White and Black behavior and institutions, to more assimilationist approaches that insisted on uprooting African normative systems and formatting local sensibilities according to Christian ones. While never implemented systematically, these projects had a tremendous impact during the nineteenth century, when similar institutional and socio-political problems triggered by beliefs in sorcery and the dangers posed by intimacy and kinship brought back discussions about the relative merits of assimilation, racial segregation, and the need to 'codify' or write down African uses and customs. But these stories are better left for a second volume.

Acknowledgments

Sorcery and Jurisdiction in Angola was a long time in the making. I could have neither begun nor completed writing it without the support of my outstanding partner, Maria Elena Indelicato, and the joy and motivation our children, António Figueiredo and Beatriz Alinta Figueiredo, provide us. I also take this opportunity to express my love and deepest gratitude to my parents, Hermano Figueiredo and Maria de Lourdes Figueiredo, and my sister, Alda Figueiredo. In many regards, this book is indebted to the directors of the Käte Hamburger *Kolleg* "Einheit und Vielfalt im Recht" (EViR), Peter Oestmann and Ulrike Ludwig. Their scientific vision and inspiring leadership afforded the multiple encounters and fruitful collaborations that decisively shaped its writing over the last two years. The archival work and secondary readings that ground it were made possible by the pioneering research project "LEGALPL—Legal Pluralism in the Portuguese Empire (18th-20th centuries)," led by Cristina Nogueira da Silva and Ângela Barreto Xavier and hosted by the Research Center on Law and Society (CEDIS) of NOVA Law School of Lisbon, in partnership with the Institute of Social Sciences (ICS) of the University of Lisbon. I am deeply grateful for their guidance and generosity during the difficult times of COVID-19 when access to archival documents and some of the most commonplace, taken-for-granted academic activities seemed almost impossible to perform. I am equally thankful for the funding from the German Federal Ministry of Education and Research (BMBF) and the Portuguese Science and Technology Foundation (FCT) through the PTDC/DIR/OUT/30873/2017 grant.

Over the years, many colleagues have shaped my arguments and claims in this volume. Immediately after finishing my PhD, Joel Andrade and Helder Macedo challenged me to present a keynote at the colloquium "História Cultural e Sensibilidades" (2016) in Caicó, Brazil, which provided me with the opportunity to start working on the linguistic arguments that shape the first chapter. This event also allowed me to dialogue with Durval Albuquerque Júnir, Evandro dos Santos, Juciene Andrade, Lourival Andrade Júnior, and many other Brazilian colleagues who contributed to my understanding of how Angolan influences came to shape and be shaped by broader Atlantic dynamics. Soon after, the fantastic team assembled by Nogueira Silva and Barrêto Xavier eased my introduction to key debates and ongoing discussions regarding the structure of the Portuguese Empire during the *Antigo Regime*, its interaction with local normative systems and institutions, and how colonial circumstances shaped the translation of normative knowledge and legal history. I am particularly thankful to Anabela Brizido, Fernanda Thomaz, Luís Cabral de Oliveira, Maria da Conceição Neto, Nuno Camarinhas, Pedro Cardim,

Ricardo Roque, and Yamê Paiva, to our consultants Lauren Benton and Thomas Duve, and to the colleagues who joined us for our final conference, Felipe Oliveira, João Azevedo, Jorge Silva Santos, Karolyne Mendes, Luisa Stella Coutinho, Margarida Seixas, Maysa Souza, and Michelle Britto. During this period, I was lucky to become more familiar with António Manuel Hespanha's (1945–2019) writings and intellectual legacy through the close guidance of some of his brightest former students. Tragically, I never met Portugal's foremost legal historian personally, as our project started only a few months before his departure. During my stay in Lisbon, I also accrued a massive debt of gratitude to the many archivists and functionaries who kept the Historical Archive of the Army (AHE), the Historical Overseas Archive (AHU), and the National Archive of the Torre do Tombo (ANTT) open to the public—as well as many other archives that I consulted but did not inform the writing of this volume. Their sense of duty and ability to adapt to extreme working conditions enabled me to research during the pandemic.

I owe a lot to all former fellows of EViR, starting with Armando Guevara Gil, whom I thank for his feedback on a very early draft of the first three chapters; Leslie Carr-Riegel, whom I thank for carefully editing my English and for sharing her knowledge of European *Lex mercatoria* and prizetaking with me; and Sebastian Spitra, whom I thank for his comments on the first draft of my introduction and ongoing discussions about colonial law, Indigenous normative orders, and legal pluralism. I am also thankful for the insightful comments and instigating conversations I had the opportunity to have during my stay in Münster with Alexey Tikhomirov, Andrea Nicolas, Clara Harder, Cecilia Cristellon, Daniel Witte, Dieter Gosewinkel, Dorothea Schulz, Éva Jakab, Eva Schlotheuber, Felix Brahm, Ferdinando Mazzarella, Giacomo Mariani, Gregor Albers, Gundula Gahlen, Heikki Pihlajamäki, Hillard von Thiessen, Hesi Siimets-Gross, Jan Matthias Hoffrogge, Ido Shahar, Jakub Urbanik, Kaveh Yazdani, Kostadin Karavasilev, Lena Klos, Marco Cavarzere, Marie Seong-Hak Kim, Matthias Bähr, Mia Korpiola, Nora Markard, Nordert Oberauer, Olaf Zenker, Olga Kozubska, Quentin Verreycken, Radhika Singha, Raquel Gil Montero, Salvatore Marino, Salvatore Marino, Susanne Lepsius, Ulrich Falk, Vera Teske, Yurii Zazuliak and Sarah Albiez-Wieck. While writing *Sorcery and Jurisdiction in Angola*, I also co-organized one spring school with Felix Brahm, one international conference with Mariana Armond Dias Paes, and two international conferences with Sebastian Spitra, which will result in an edited volume. Such productivity would have never been possible without the exceptional organizational skills of my co-organizers and the constant, unwavering support of EViR's core team: Andre Dechert, Nadine Konrad, Claudia Lieb, Lennart Pieper, and Kathrin Schulte. Together with my brilliant fellow research associates, Benjamin Seebröker and Sophia Mösch, they make everything seem possible. Moreover, they made Münster feel like home for me and my family. I am also thankful for the support of Ben Riepe, Emily Todt, Henrik Wilkens, Marla Kaminsky, Nele Aßmann,

Ralf Bureck, and Selina Krause, to whom I wish the brightest of futures. Finally, I sincerely thank Artur José Felgueiras de Carvalho, Amílcar da Costa Mendes, and Fábio Maia Almeida for their generous hospitality during my visits to Angola over the years. I hope their warmth and affection for their country shines through the pages of this book.

Münster, 26.01.2025.

Abbreviations

AHM	*Arquivo Histórico Militar*
AHU	*Arquivo Histórico Ultramarino*
ANTT	*Arquivo Nacional Torre do Tombo*
Art.	Article
BLR3	Bantu Lexical Reconstructions 3
c.	Circa
CARTM	*Cartografia Manuscrita*
CG	*Conselho Geral do Santo Ofício*
CGR	*Campanhas da Guerra da Restauração*
Chap.	Chapter
CLNH	*Conde de Linhares*
Cod.	Codex
CP	*Cadernos do Promotor*
CR.	Congregation of Clerics Regular
C.R.S.A.	Holy and Apostolic Order of Regular Canons of St. Augustine
CS	Comparative series
CU	*Conselho Ultramarino*
D.	Document (if on footnotes)
D.	Dom (if before a proper name)
Div.	*Divisão*
ed./eds.	Editor/Editors
EXP	*Expediente Geral*
F.	*Folio*
Fol.	*Folder*
GANG	*Governo Geral de Angola*
IL	*Inquisição de Lisboa*
MMA	*Monumenta Missionaria Africana*
MO	*Marqueses de Olhão*
MR	*Ministério do Reino*
MSS	Manuscripts
NU	*Núcleo Ultramarino*
O. Carm.	Order of the Brothers of the Blessed Virgin Mary of Mount Carmel
OFMCap	Order of Friars Minor Capuchin
OP	The Dominican Order of Preachers
Ord. Fil.	*Ordenações Filipinas*
p.	Page or page range.

Par.	Paragraph
PcE	*Portugal e campanhas na Europa*
Pl.	Plural
Pr.	Father (Priest)
Pt.	Part
SEMU	*Secretaria de Estado da Marinha e do Ultramar*
SENEG	*Secretaria de Estado dos Negócios Estrangeiros e da Guerra*
Sing.	Singular
SJ	The Society of Jesus
Sr.	*Series*
St.	Saint
Tit.	Title
TSO	*Tribunal do Santo Ofício*
v	Verso
Vol.	Volume

Symbols

$	Unicode standard stand-in for the Portuguese *cifrão,* written with two vertical lines
§	Section
*-(…)	Starred form

Glossary of Untranslated Words

Adivinho Fortune teller, diviner, or seer. In West Central Africa, it might also refer to the ritual operators who prepare and administer ordeals and oaths.

Alcaide Originally the commander of a fortress, stronghold, or castle. In the West Central African context, the head of a prison and its bailiffs and jailors.

Almotacé Inspector of weights and measures in charge of setting prices. He had jurisdiction over matters related to the purity of foodstuff, the water supply, and rationing in times of crisis.

Almoxarife da Real Fazenda Collector, foreman, and treasurer of the Royal treasury.

Angolense A person born in the Captaincy of Angola and its dependencies.

Arimo Farmstead or farmland cultivated using Mbundu agricultural practices.

Autos de undamento Vassalage treaties inspired by Mbundu customs. Listed the obligations of vassal *sobas,* including the tribute *(baculamento)* they were supposed to pay.

Baculamento Political tribute paid by vassal *sobas,* inspired by Mbundu customs.

Bando Oral edict solemnly announced in the streets, often accompanied by *toque de caixa* [military drum rolls].

Banzo A commodity or currency bundle traded for one enslaved person.

Beirame A standard measure of Indian cotton cloth of varying lengths.

Brasílico A person born in Brazil.

Bruxaria Witchcraft.

Cabeça Accounting unit used to tally slaves regardless of their traits (e. g., age, sex, physical condition). Literally 'head.'

Casa da Suplicação The final-instance judicial court of the Portuguese Crown. Its jurisdiction included the whole Kingdom of Portugal and all its overseas domains.

Casa do uso A dwelling where Mbundu female initiation rites took place. Literally, 'house of the custom.'

Casa grande Patriarchal household; literally 'large house.'

Compadre How parents refer to the godfather of their children. Figuratively, a trusted or close friend.

Corregedor Inspector-General, magistrate.

Cruzado Gold or silver coin of varying fixed value.

Curandeiro Healer. In West Central Africa, it might also refer to anti-sorcery experts.

Degredado Deported convict.

Dembo Mbundu political title recognized by the Portuguese. Semi-independent or independent Mbundu rulers settled in the Dembos district area. Also referred to as Ndembu in English literature.

Desembargador Magistrate, judge of a second instance court *(Relação).*

Desembargo do Paço The higher court of justice, it also administered the Portuguese judicial system and handled matters of grace.

Direito Refers to the Law, to what is right, and to a right or rights.

Dissaquela Possession ritual.

Empacasseiro Master hunters who served the Portuguese as soldiers and scouts. The Portuguese *empacasseiro* was derived from the Kinbundu word for the red buffalo: *mpakasa.*

Engenho Sugar cane mill, machinery used to prepare the sugar cane derivatives: sugar and alcohol.

Estatutos Statutes.

Estrangeirado Foreignized. Used as a name to refer to expatriate or exiled intellectuals who criticized what they perceived as Portuguese backwardness compared to other European nations during the Portuguese Enlightenment.

Feitiçaria Sorcery. In English translations of Portuguese sources, it is also rendered as 'witchcraft.' However, *feitiçaria* is not to be confused with the Portuguese *bruxaria.*

Feitoria Large commercial establishment or trading post, usually headed by a *feitor* or foreman appointed by the Crown.

Fidalgo High noble, literally 'the son of someone.'

Filho de mar em fora A person born in the Kingdom of Portugal. Literally, 'son from overseas.'

Fusco Mixed-race person.

Guerra preta Irregular army, raised, disciplined, and paid according to African norms. Literally 'Black war.'

Homem bom A community member who held social significance, either due to owning property or engaging in non-manual occupations, could participate in electing members of the municipal councils and be elected.

Intendentes Inspectors, managers, and caretakers.

Irmandade da Santa Casa da Misericórdia Lay brotherhood under the direct patronage of the Portuguese Crown. It coordinated medical assistance and most charitable acts.

Jaga Political title attributed by the Portuguese to the leaders of Mbangala warbands and the head of the Kingdom of Kasanje.

Juiz do cível Judge of the civil court.

Légua Portuguese route unit. It could refer to a league of 18 to the degree (6.173 m) or to a league of 20 to the degree (5.555 m).

Letra Bill of exchange.

Letra do tesouro Bill of exchange backed by the Royal Treasury.

Letras dos direitos Bill of exchange backed by the taxes on the export of slaves.

Libambo Coffle, chains with handcuffs used to secure slaves. Literally 'mob.'

Livranças Personal bill of credit.

Morador A person who lived in a settlement, *presídio,* or *arimo* and identified as a Portuguese subject.

Mucano Oral arbitration, complaint, guilt, condemnation, possibly from the Kikongo *bagi-a-nkano,* a Kikongo expression that also designated the place where the *Mwene* Kongo adjudicated cases.

Mulato Mixed-race person.

Mwene Lord, Bakongo title. At the origin of the Portuguese title *muene* (lord).

Ordenança Order, military regulation, soldier.

Osoma Chief, Ovimbundu title.

Ouvidor Judge appointed by the *donatário.* judge of law.

Ouvidor Geral Crown judge, the superintendent of other *ouvidores.*

Pardo Mixed-race person.

Presídio A military post, garrisoned place, or fortified settlement under the jurisdiction of the Portuguese Crown.

Procurador Authorized representative, trustee.

Provedor Person in charge of ensuring the rights of vulnerable or dependent groups and the management of legacies or chapels, the head of a charitable association or brotherhood. Literally 'purveyor' or 'provider.'

Provedor da comarca Head of the *provedores* of the judicial district.

Provedor da Real Fazenda Provedor of the Royal Treasury.

Pumbeiro Slave merchant who traded at *pumbos,* unofficial slave fairs named after the slave fair at Mpumbu, contemporary Pool Malebo. *Pumbeiros* differed from Luso-African merchants because they travelled barefoot, being either free Africans or slaves. By not wearing shoes, *pumbeiros* exempted themselves from abiding by Portuguese ordinances, bylaws, and laws forbidding the entrance of Whites and Blacks with shoes in the hinterlands while being answerable to jurisdictional claims by *sobas* and other African authorities. *Pumbeiros* were also known as *funantes, funadores, enviados* or *certanejos.*

Pumbo Unofficial slave fair. See *pumbeiro.*

Quadrilheiro Soldier in charge of night patrols and policing.

Quimbar Europeanized African.

Real Accounting currency of the Portuguese empire (plural: *réis).*

Real Fazenda Royal Treasury.

Relação Second instance court.

Relação Eclesiástica Second instance Canon law tribunal.

Senzala Slave quarters. From the Kimbundu *sanzala* [hamlet].

Soba Chief, Portuguese adaptation of a Mbundu title.

Sobado Chieftaincy.

Superintendente Overseer, superintendent.

Tabelião Public notary.

Tendala Military commander, if Mbundu or Mbangala title; Translator or interpreter, if Portuguese title.

Xinguila Ritual specialist specialized in invoking the spirits or being possessed.

Bibliography

Archival Sources

Arquivo Histórico Ultramarino
Conselho Ultramarino (03.24.1530–03.08.1833):
Series 1, Angola (04.22.1602–1837).
Box 2; Box 6; Box 18; Box 19; Box 23; Box 28; Box 30; Box 39; Box 42; Box 47; Box 50; Box 51; Box 52; Box 53; Box 54; Box 55; Box 66; Box 67; Box 71; Box 74; Box 76; Box 87; Box 88; Box 90.
Governo Geral de Angola (02.12.1676–1975).
Codex 1643.
Secretaria de Estado da Marinha e Ultramar (1833–1911):
Box 823, Angola (1798–1895).
Cartografia manuscrita:
Angola (1655–1975).

Arquivo Nacional Torre do Tombo
Conde de Linhares (1501–1930).
Folder 7; Folder 45; Folder 47; Folder 49; Folder 52.
Marqueses de Olhão (1494–1877):
Núcleo ultramarino (02.09.1611–08.16.1829):
Box 8.
Ministério do Reino (1736–1910):
Expediente geral (1700–1908):
Series 34, Informações dos governadores e magistrados das Ilhas adjacentes e Ultramar. Negócios do Ultramar.
Tribunal do Santo Ofício (1536–1821):
Conselho Geral do Santo Ofício (1569–1821);
Series 25, Obras sobre a acção e defesa da Inquisição;
Series 34, Regimentos (1552–1778).
Inquisição de Lisboa (1536–1821):
Series 20, Inquirição de Testemunhas (1596–1597);
Series 28, Processos (1536–1821);
Series 30, Cadernos do Promotor (1541–1802).

Arquivo Histórico Militar
Divisões:

Portugal e campanhas na Europa:
Campanhas da Guerra da Restauração (1640–1668).
Box 1.
Secretaria de Estado dos Negócios Estrangeiros e da Guerra (1736–1756):
Box 3.

Source Collections

Monumenta Missionaria Africana (MMA)

Brásio, António (ed.). *Monumenta missionaria africana.* África Ocidental (1471–1531), series 1, Vol. 1. Lisbon, 1952.

Brásio, António (ed.). *Monumenta missionaria africana.* África Ocidental (1532–1569), series 1, vol 2. Lisbon, 1953.

Brásio, António (ed.). *Monumenta missionaria africana.* África Ocidental (1570–1599), series 1, Vol. 3. Lisbon, 1953.

Brásio, António (ed.). *Monumenta missionaria africana.* África Ocidental (1469–1599), series 1, Vol. 4. Lisbon, 1954.

Brásio, António (ed.). *Monumenta missionaria africana.* África Ocidental (1600–1610), series 1, Vol. 5. Lisbon, 1955.

Brásio, António (ed.). *Monumenta missionaria africana.* África Ocidental (1611–1621), series 1, Vol. 6. Lisbon, 1955.

Brásio, António (ed.). *Monumenta missionaria africana.* África Ocidental (1622–1630), series 1, Vol. 7. Lisbon, 1955.

Brásio, António (ed.). *Monumenta missionaria africana.* África Ocidental (1631–1642), series 1, Vol. 8. Lisbon, 1960.

Brásio, António (ed.). *Monumenta missionaria africana.* África Ocidental (1647–1650), series 1, Vol. 10. Lisbon, 1965.

Brásio, António (ed.). *Monumenta missionaria africana.* África Ocidental (1656–1665), series 1, vol 12. Lisbon, 1981.

Brásio, António (ed.). *Monumenta missionaria africana.* África Ocidental (1666–1885), series 1, Vol. 13. Lisbon, 1982.

Brásio, António (ed.). *Monumenta missionaria africana.* África Ocidental. Suplemento (sécs. XV, XVI, XVII), series 1, Vol. 15. Lisbon, 1988.

Published Primary Sources

Almeida e Vasconcelos, Manuel de, Carta de S. Ex.ª ao Jaga Cassange em resposta da Embaixada, que este remeteu ao mesmo Exmo Senhor (17 de Novembro de 1790), in: Arquivos de Angola: Publicação Oficial 2 (1936) 14, p. 579–580.

Almeida e Vasconcelos, Manuel de, De S. Ex.ª para o Potentado Iaga Cassangi, com a Embaixada que lhe enviou (26 de Julho de 1789), in: Arquivos de Angola: Publicação Oficial 2 (1936) 14, p. 567–570.

Almeida e Vasconcelos, Manuel de, Ordem da nomeação do Capitão Francisco das Chagas Veiga, para Director da Feira de Cassange nomeado, e requerido pelos negociantes desta praça para cujo exercício parte (20 de Agosto de 1792), in: Arquivos de Angola: Publicação Oficial 1 (1936) 6.

Almeida e Vasconcelos, Manuel de, Sendo proposto pela praça desta capital para Director da Feira de Cassange Paulo Jozé de Loureiro, foi Sua Ex.ª servido confirmar esta eleição, expedindo-o com o Regimento seguinte (6 de Outubro de 1790), in: Arquivos de Angola: Publicação Oficial 2 (1936) 14, p. 573–577.

Andrade e Silva, José Justino de (ed.), Collecção chronologica da legislação portugueza. Compilada e annotada por José Justino de Andrade e Silva, bacharel formado em Direito (1603–1612), Lisbon, 1854.

Andrade e Silva, José Justino de (ed.), Colleção Chronologica da Legislação Portugueza Compilada e annotada por José Justino de Andrade e Silva, bacharel formado em Direito. (1613–1619). Lisbon, 1855.

Andrade e Silva, José Justino de (ed.), Collecção chronologica da legislação portugueza. Compilada e annotada por José Justino de Andrade e Silva, bacharel formado em Direito. (1657–1674), series 2. Lisbon, 1856.

anonymous, Projecto para a reforma da Ley Fundamental da Monarquia Portuguesa. Paris, 1827.

Assis Júnior, António de, Dicionário de Kimbundu-Português. Linguístico, botânico, histórico e corográfico. Luanda, 1949.

Atkins, John, A Voyage to Guinea, Brasil, and the West-Indies; in His Majesty's Ships the Swallow and Weymouth. London, 1737.

Augustinus, Aurelius, City of God. London, 2003.

Azeredo, José Pinto de, Ensaios sobre algumas enfermidades d'Angola. Lisbon, 1799.

Bluteau, Raphael, entry "Beirame," in: Diccionario da lingua portugueza composto pelo Padre D. Rafael Bluteau, reformado, e accrescentado por Antonio de Moraes Silva natural do Rio de Janeiro, Vol. 1, edited by Antonio de Moraes Silva, Lisbon, 1789, p. 176.

Bluteau, Raphael, entry "Feitiço," in: Vocabulario Portuguez & Latino, Vol. 4, edited by Raphael Bluteau, Coimbra, 1728, p. 66.

Bluteau, Raphael, entry "Idolatria," in: Vocabulario Portuguez & Latino, Vol. 4, edited by Raphael Bluteau Coimbra, 1728, p. 30–34.

Boletim do Conselho Ultramarino. Legislação Antiga (1446–1754), Vol. 1. Lisbon, 1867.

Boletim do Conselho Ultramarino. Legislação Antiga (1755–1834), Vol. 2. Lisbon, 1867.

Brito, Domingos de Abreu, Um inquérito à vida administrativa e económica de Angola e do Brasil em fins do século XVI, segundo o manuscrito inédito existente na Biblioteca Nacional de Lisboa pelo Licenciado Domingos de Abreu e Brito. Publicação revista e prefaciada por Alfredo de Albuquerque Felner. Coimbra, 1931.

Cadornega, António de Oliveira, História geral das guerras angolanas por António de Oliveira de Cadornega, capitão reformado e cidadão de S. Paulo da Assunção, natural de Vila Viçosa (1680). Anotado e corrigido por José Matias Delgado, Vol. 1. Lisbon, 1940.

Cadornega, António de Oliveira, História geral das guerras angolanas por António de Oliveira de Cadornega, capitão reformado e cidadão de S. Paulo da Assunção, natural de Vila Viçosa (1680). Anotado e corrigido por José Matias Delgado, Vol. 2. Lisbon, 1940.

Cadornega, António de Oliveira, História geral das guerras angolanas por António de Oliveira de Cadornega, capitão reformado e cidadão de S. Paulo da Assunção, natural de Vila Viçosa (1680). Anotado e corrigido por José Matias Delgado, Vol. 3. Lisbon, 1942.

Caetano, Marcelo, As reformas pombalinas e post-pombalinas respeitantes ao Ultramar. O novo espírito em que são concebidas, in: António Baião, Hernani Cidade and Manuel Murias (eds.), História da expansão portuguesa no mundo. Lisbon, 1941, p. 251–260.

Caetano, Marcelo, O Conselho Ultramarino. Esboço da sua história. Lisbon, 1967.

Cardoso, An.^{to} Ferr.^{o}, Relação dos rendimentos certos e incertos que no collegio desta cidade de Loanda do Reino de Angolla tinhão os padres da Companhia de Jezus, in: Arquivos de Angola: Publicação Oficial 2 (1936) 14, p. 541–554.

Carneiro, Manoel Borges, Mappa chronologico das leis, e mais disposições de Direito Portuguez, publicadas desde 1603 até 1817. Lisbon, 1816.

Carta de doação a Paulo Dias de Navais e a seus herdeiros, da capitania e governança de trinta e cinco leguas de terra na costa do Reino de Angola, para o sul do Rio Coanza, e para o interior até onde podesse entrar; e, bem assim, em dias de sua vida sómente, das terras situadas entre os Rios Dange e Coanza (6 de Setembro de 1571), in: Arquivos de Angola: Publicação Oficial 2 (1936) 13, p. 451–462.

Carvalho e Melo, Sebastião José, Documento N.º 8, 1769, Julho. Importância dos domínios africanos para a coroa, in: Carlos Couto (ed.), Os capitães-mores em Angola no século XVIII. Subsídio para o estudo da sua actuação. Luanda, 1972, p. 368–372.

Carvalho, Henrique A. D. de, O Jagado de Cassande na Provincia de Angola. Lisbon, 1898.

Carvalho, Henrique A. D. de, O Jagado de Cassange. Excerpto. Cerimonias que se observam quando morre o Jaga de Cassange, in: O Occidente 12 (1899) 755, p. 282–283.

Cavazzi, Giovanni Antonio, Istorica descrizione de' Tre' Regni Congo, Matamba et Angola. situati nell'Etiopia Inferiore Occidentale e delle missioni apostoliche esercitateui da religiosi Capuccini. Bologna, 1687.

Cavazzi, Giovanni Antonio, Fortunato Alamandi (trans.), Historische Beschreibung Der In dem untern Occidentalischen Mohrenland ligenden drey Königreichen, Congo, Matamba, und Angola, Und Der jenigen Apostolischen Missionen, so von den PP. Capucinern daselbst verrichtet worden. Munich, 1694.

Cavazzi, Giovanni Antonio, Thornton, John K. (trans), Missione evangelica al Regno de Congo (MSS Araldi, Modena. 3 vols: A, B, C). https://www.bu.edu/afam/people/faculty/john-thornton/john-thorntons-african-texts/ accessed 01/16/2025.

Chatelain, Heli, Folk-Tales of Angola, Vol. 1. Boston, 1894.

Cicero, De Re Publica. De Legibus. London, 1928.

Coimbra, Carlos Dias (ed.), Livros de "Ofícios para o Reino" do Arquivo Histórico de Angola de 1726/1801. Luanda, 1959.

Collecção das leys, decretos e alvarás que comprehende o feliz reinado del rey fidelissimo D. Jozé I nosso senhor, vol 3. Lisbon, 1771.

Conceipção, Ambrozio Iozê da, Antonio Frz. Frango, Antonio de Barros, and Manoel de Araujo Cinza, Carta que o Senado da Camara de Massangano escreveu a Sua. Ex.ª (3 de Dezembro de 1771), in: Arquivos de Angola: Publicação Oficial 3 (1937) 28, p. 325–326.

Constituição da República de Angola. Luanda, 2019.

Cordeiro, Luciano (ed.), Benguella e seu sertão por um anonymo.Viagens, explorações e conquistas dos portuguezes. Collecção de documentos por Luciano Cordeiro (1617–1622). Lisbon, 1881.

Cordeiro, Luciano (ed.), Da mina ao Cabo Negro segundo Garcia Mendes Castello Branco. Viagens, explorações e conquistas dos portuguezes. Collecção de documentos por Luciano Cordeiro (1574–1620). Lisbon, 1881.

Cordeiro, Luciano (ed.), Estabelecimentos e resgates portuguezes na Costa Occidental de Africa por um anonymo. Viagens, explorações e conquistas dos portuguezes. Collecção de documentos por Luciano Cordeiro (1607). Lisbon, 1881.

Cordeiro, Luciano (ed.), Terras e minas africanas segundo Rebello de Aragão. Viagens, explorações e conquistas dos portuguezes. Collecção de documentos por Luciano Cordeiro (1593–1631). Lisbon, 1881.

Cosme da Cunha, João, Regimento do Santo Officio da Inquisição dos Reinos de Portugal, ordenado com o real beneplacito, e regio auxilio pelo Eminentissimo, e Reverendissimo Senhor Cardeal da Cunha, dos Conselhos de Estado, e gabinete de Sua Magestade, e Inquisidor Geral Nestes Reinos, e em todos os seus dominios. Lisbon, 1774.

Coutinho, Antonio de Azevedo, Alexandre Metello de Souza Menezes, and Ignacio Ferreira Souto, Documento N.º 3, 1758, Janeiro, 3. Assento sobre o comércio de Angola, in: Carlos Couto (ed.), Os capitães-mores em Angola no século XVIII. Subsídio para o estudo da sua actuação. Luanda, 1972, p. 306–309.

Coutinho, Francisco Innocencio de Sousa, Memórias do Reino de Angola e suas conquistas, escritas em Lisboa nos anos de 1773–1775, in: Arquivos de Angola: Publicação Oficial 4 (1939) 49, p. 173–202.

Coutinho, Francisco Innocencio de Sousa, Documento N.º 6, 1765, Fevereiro, 24. Regimento dos capitães-mores, in: Carlos Couto (ed.), Os capitães-mores em Angola no século XVIII. Subsídio para o estudo da sua actuação. Luanda, 1972, p. 323–338.

Cunha Matos, Raimundo, Compêndio histórico das possessões de Portugal na África. Rio de Janeiro, 1963 [1848].

Dias, Gastão Sousa, Os portugueses em Angola. Lisbon, 1959.

Estatutos da Universidade de Coimbra do Anno de MDCCLXXII. Livro II, que contém os cursos juridicos das Faculdade de Canones e de Leis., Vol. 2. Lisbon, 1773.

FERNANDES, Ernesto and Anibal RÊGO, História do Direito Português. Súmula das lições proferidas pelo Ex.mo Prof. Doutor Marcelo Caetano ao Curso do 1.º ano Jurídico de 1940–41 na Faculdade de Direito de Lisboa. Lisbon, 1941.

FERREIRA, Francisco de Salles, Memoria sobre o sertão de Cassange, in: Annaes do Conselho Ultramarino 1 (1867), p. 26–28.

FERREIRA, João Alvarez, Documento N.º 4, 1762, Junho, 26. Regularização dos banzos, in: Carlos COUTO (ED.), Os capitães-mores em Angola no século XVIII. Subsídio para o estudo da sua actuação. Luanda, 1972, p. 310–317.

FREIRE, Pascoal José de Melo, Instituições de Direito Civil Português (Tanto Público como Particular). Lisbon, 1966 [1791].

FREIRE, Pascoal José de Melo, Instituições de Direito Criminal Português, in: Boletim do Ministério da Justiça (1966 [1794]) 155–156, p. 44–168.

GUERREIRO, Fernão, Relação anual das coisas que fizeram os padres da Companhia de Jesus nas suas missões do Japão, China, Cataio [...], nos Anos de 1600 a 1609 e do processo da conversão e cristandade daquelas partes. Tiradas das cartas que os missionários lá escreveram, Vol. 1. Coimbra, 1930.

GUERREIRO, Fernão, Relação anual das coisas que fizeram os padres da Companhia de Jesus nas suas missões do Japão, China, Cataio [...], nos Anos de 1600 a 1609 e do processo da conversão e cristandade daquelas partes. Tiradas das cartas que os missionários lá escreveram, Vol. 2. Coimbra, 1931.

GUERREIRO, Fernão, Relação anual das coisas que fizeram os padres da Companhia de Jesus nas suas missões do Japão, China, Cataio [...], nos Anos de 1600 a 1609 e do processo da conversão e cristandade daquelas partes. Tiradas das cartas que os missionários lá escreveram, Vol. 3. Coimbra, 1942.

JEAN-FRANÇOIS DE ROME, La Fondation de la mission des Capuchins au royaume du Congo (1648). Louvain, 1964.

JOSÉ DA SILVA, Joaquim José, Continuação da viagem ao sertão de Benguella, continuada do N.º 2.º pag. 86, in: O Patriota: Jornal Politico Liberal 1 (1813) 3, p. 49–60.

JOSÉ DA SILVA, Joaquim José, Extracto da viagem, que fez ao sertão de Benguella no anno de 1785 por ordem do Governador e Capitão General do Reino de Angola, o Bacharel Joaquim José da Silva, enviado àquelle Reino como Naturalista, e depois Secretario do Governo, in: O Patriota: Jornal Politico Liberal 1 (1813) 1, p. 97–100.

JOSÉ DA SILVA, Joaquim José, Viagem ao sertão de Benguella, continuada do N.º 1.º pag. 100, in: O Patriota: Jornal Politico Liberal 1 (1813) 2, p. 86–98.

LANCASTRO, D. João de, Regimento do Secretario deste Reino (1 de Abril de 1688), in: Arquivos de Angola: Publicação Oficial 2 (1936) 13, p. 493–496.

LENCASTRE, António de, Documento N.º 9, 1775, Julho, 29. Regimento dos escrivães das feiras de Cassange, Haco e Beja, in: Carlos COUTO (ed.), Os capitães-mores em Angola no século XVIII. Subsídio para o estudo da sua actuação. Luanda, 1972, p. 373–376.

Ley para ser livre, e franco o Commercio de Angola, e dos portos, e sertões adjacentes, etc (11 de Janeiro de 1758), in: Arquivos de Angola: Publicação Oficial 2 (1936) 14, p. 531–535.

Ley sobre a arrecadação dos direitos dos escravos, e marfim, que sahirem do Reino de Angola, e pórtos da sua dependencia (25 de Janeiro de 1758), in: Arquivos de Angola: Publicação Oficial 2 (1936) 14, p. 537–540.

Lima, Manuel Dantas, IV, in: Boletim da Sociedade de Geografia de Lisboa 6 (1886) 5, p. 294–300.

Lino D'Assumpção, Exploração à Africa. Nos ineditos da bibliotheca de Évora in: Boletim da Sociedade de Geografia de Lisboa 5 (1875) 6, p. 350–376.

Livingstone, David, Missionary Travels and Researches in South Africa. Including a Sketch of Sixteen Years' Residence in the Interior of Africa, and a Journey from the Cape of Good Hope to Loanda, on the West Coast, Thence Across the Continent, Down the River Zambesi, to the Eastern Ocean, Vol. 2. London, 1857.

Livro dos baculamentos que os sobas deste reino de Angola pagam a sua majestade (1630). Luanda, 2013.

Lopes de Lima, José Joaquim and Francisco Maria Bordalo, Ensaios sobre a statistica das possessões portuguezas na Africa Occidental e Oriental; na Asia Occidental; na China, e na Oceania. Escriptos, Vol. 3. Lisboa, 1844.

Maia, António da Silva, Dicionário Complementar. Português-Kimbundu-Kikongo. Línguas nativas do Centro e Norte de Angola. Luanda, 1964.

Matos, Gregório, Descreve a um amigo desde aquele degredo as alterações, e misérias daquele Reino de Angola, e o que juntamente lhe aconteceu com os soldados amotinados, que o levaram para o campo, e tiveram consigo para os aconselhar no motim, in: João Adolfo Hansen and Marcello Moreira (eds.), Poemas Atribuídos. Códice Asensio-Cunha. São Paulo, 2014, p. 287–289.

Matos, Gregório, Descreve o que realmente se passa no reino de Angola, in: João Adolfo Hansen and Marcello Moreira (eds.), Poemas Atribuídos. Códice Asensio-Cunha. São Paulo, 2014, p. 286.

Mello, Miguel António de, Relatorio do governo de D. Miguel António de Mello (1802), in: Boletim da Sociedade de Geografia de Lisboa 5 (1885) 9, p. 548–564.

Mello, Miguel António de, Carta a D. Rodrigo de Sousa Coutinho (3 Fevereiro de 1800), in: Boletim da Sociedade de Geografia de Lisboa 6 (1886) 5, p. 274–281.

Mello, Miguel António de, Relação do clero regular que existe n'este bispado no dia de hoje pertencente ás religiões que têem conventos n'esta cidade in: Boletim da Sociedade de Geografia de Lisboa 6 (1886) 5, p. 293–294.

Mello, Miguel António de, Relação dos officios civis de justiça e fazenda, economia publica e politica que n'este reino de Angola existem , feita segundo a determinação do aviso de 11 de fevereiro de 1799, in: Boletim da Sociedade de Geografia de Lisboa 6 (1886) 5, p. 281–293.

Mello, Miguel António de, Acerca das riquezas desta colónia, e da possibilidade ou impossibilidade de as aproveitar (30 Julho de 1799), in: Arquivos de Angola: Publicação Oficial 4 (1935) 1.

Mello, Miguel António de, Carta de oficio do Governador para Dom Rodrigo de Sousa Coutinho, expondo a injustiça com que fôra tratado o Soba de Socoval da jurisdição de Quilengues, no Governo da Capitania de Benguela, in: Arquivos de Angola: Publicação Oficial 1 (1936) 6.

Mello, Miguel António de, Carta do Governador para a Real Junta do Commercio, Agricultura, e Navegação e Fabricas do Reyno de Portugal e seus Dominios, propondo medidas mais humanas no tráfico da escravatura (12 de Março de 1799), in: Arquivos de Angola: Publicação Oficial 2 (1936) 14, p. 593–602.

Mello, Miguel António de, Oficio do Governador e Capitão General de Angola, contrariando varias propostas do Governador da Capitania de Benguella (24 de Dezembro de 1798), in: Arquivos de Angola: Publicação Oficial 2 (1936) 14, p. 581–592.

Mello, Miguel António de, Oficio em que o Governador e Capitão General reprova a fundação de um convento de franciscanos em Benguela, propondo novas providências de caracter eclesiástico (17 de Agosto de 1801), in: Arquivos de Angola: Publicação Oficial 2 (1936) 15, p. 623–640.

Mello, Miguel António de, Plano para a organização, desciplina e governo das tropas do Reino de Angola (Fevereiro 3, 1800), in: Arquivos de Angola: Publicação Oficial 2 (1936) 10, p. 189–254.

Mello, Miguel António de, Regimento da alfandega da cidade de São Paulo d'Assumpção Capital do Reino de Angola (21 de Outubro de 1799), in: Arquivos de Angola: Publicação Oficial 2 (1936) 12, p. 359–447.

Mello, Miguel António de, Documento n.º 2. Edital do Ex.mo Snr. General sobre o Soba do Socoval, publicado a toques de Caixas nesta Cidade a 28 de Março de 1798, acompanhado do officio seguinte, in: Ralph Delgado (ed.), A Famosa e Histórica Benguela. Catálogo dos Governadores (1779 a 1940). Benguela, 1940, p. 444–446.

Melo Breyner, Francisco Manuel (Count of Ficalho). Plantas úteis da África Portuguesa. Lisbon, 1957 [1884].

Melo e Castro, Martinho de and Sebastião Francisco Bettamio, Carta do Ministro Martinho de Melo e Castro para o Governador Barão de Mossamedes, referindo-se aos bens deixados aos Jesuitas por Gaspar Alvares, com a obrigação de sustentarem um seminario em Luanda (18 de Fevereiro de 1784), in: Arquivos de Angola: Publicação Oficial 2 (1936) 14, p. 561–566.

Mendes, Luís António de Oliveira, Memória a respeito dos escravos e tráfico da escravatura entre a Costa d'África e o Brazil: apresentada à Real Academia das Ciências de Lisboa, 1793, in: Memorias economicas da Academia Real das Sciencias de Lisboa para o adiantamento da agricultura, das artes, e da industria em Portugal e suas Conquistas, Vol. 4. Lisbon, 1812, p. 1–82.

Menezes, Joaquim Antonio de Carvalho, Demonstração geographica e politica do territorio portuguez na Guiné Inferior, que abrange o Reino de Angola, Benguella, e suas Dependencias. Rio de Janeiro, 1848.

Merêa, Manuel Paulo, Lance de olhos sobre o ensino do Direito (Cânones e Leis), desde 1772 até 1804, in: Boletim da Faculdade de Direito 33 (1957), p. 187–214.

Merêa, Manuel Paulo, O Ensino do Direito em Portugal de 1805 a 1836, in: José Pinto Loureiro (ed.), Jurisconsultos portugueses do século XIX. Lisbon, 1947, p. 149–190.

Merêa, Manuel Paulo, Resumo das lições de História do Direito Português (Feitas no ano lectivo de 1924–1925). Coimbra, 1925.

Molina, Luis de, On Slavery and the Slave Trade. De Iustitia et Iure, Book 1, Treatise 2, Disputations 32–40. Washington, D.C., 2024.

Neves, António Rodrigues, Memória da expedição a Cassange em 1850. Africa Occidental. Lisbon, 1854.

Ofícios para o Reino do Governdor D. Fernando António de Noronha (1802 a 1806), in: Arquivos de Angola: Publicação Oficial 19 (1962) 75–78, p. i–xxviii, 1–209.

Ordenações Filipinas, Livro I, Vol. 1. Lisbon, 1985 [1603].

Ordenações Filipinas, Livros II e III, Vol. 2. Lisbon, 1985 [1603].

Ordenações Filipinas, Livros IV e V, Vol. 3. Lisbon, 1985 [1603].

Pacconio, Francisco, Gentio de Angola sufficientemente instruido nos mysterios de nossa sancta fé. Lisbon, 1642.

Pacheco Pereira, Duarte, Esmeraldo de situ orbis. London, 1937 [1506].

Pigafetta, Filippo and Duarte Lopes, Relatione del reame di Congo et delle circonvicine contrade, tratta dalli scritti e ragionamenti di Odoardo Lopez portoghese per Filippo Pigafetta. Rome, 1591.

Pigafetta, Filippo and Duarte Lopes, Regnum Congo hoc est vera descriptio regni Africani, quod tam ab incolis quam Lusitanis Congus appellatur. Frankfurt, 1598.

Pinheiro de Lacerda, Paulo Martins, Notícia da cidade de S. Filipe de Benguela, e dos costumes dos gentios habitantes daquele sertão, in: Annaes Maritimos e Coloniaes 5 (1845) 12, p. 486–491.

Pinto, Adrião Accacio da Silveira, Regimento do chefe do Districto de Talla-Mugongo, in: Henrique A. D. de Carvalho (ed.), O Jagado de Cassange na provincia de Angola. Lisbon, [1851] 1898, p. 142–152.

Portela, Bernardo Nunes, Manoel Bernardes Pires de Oliveira, Francisco Roiz Barbora, Joao da Costa Feio, Jozé Pinto Barbosa, José de Abreu Castello, Branco Pimentel, Francisco Honorato da Costa, Joao Leite de Faria, Paulo da Silva Rego, Anselmo da Fonseca Coutinho, Manoel Silva, Jozé da Rocha e Regadas, Manoel Francisco, Antonio Roiz Regello, Directorio para o Capitão Chagas com o estabelecimento da nova regulação do commercio (22 Agosto 1792), in: Arquivos de Angola: Publicação Oficial 1 (1936) 6.

Provizão da reformação da infantaria de Angolla (5 de Abril de 1666), in: Arquivos de Angola: Publicação Oficial 2 (1936) 11, p. 309–311.

Provizão sobre a forma que se há observar no provimento dos postos militares (16 de Outubro de 1659), in: Arquivos de Angola: Publicação Oficial 2 (1936) 11, p. 303–304.

Purchas, Samuel, Purchas his Pilgrimage. Or Relations of the World and the Religions Observed in all Ages and Places discovered, from the Creation unto this Present. London, 1614.

Purchas, Samuel, Hakluytus Posthumus or Purchas His Pilgrimes. Contayning a History of the World in Sea Voyages and Lande Travells by Englishmen and others by Samuel Purchas, B.D., Vol. 6. Glasgow, 1904.

Ravenstein, E. G., The Strange Adventures of Andrew Battell of Leigh, in Angola and the Adjoining Regions. London, 1901.

Redinha, José, Etnossociologia do Nordeste de Angola. Lisbon, 1958.

Regimento das fronteiras. Capitulos incluzos na provizam de 16 de Outubro de 1659, in: Arquivos de Angola: Publicação Oficial 2 (1936) 11, p. 305–308.

Regimento do governo deste Reyno de Angolla (12 de Fevereiro de 1676), in: Arquivos de Angola: Publicação Oficial 1 (1936) 5.

Regimento dos capitães móres & mais capitães & officiaes das companhias da gente de pé & de cavallo & da ordem que terão em se exercitarem. Lisbon 1597 [1570].

Regimento dos Ouvidores Geraez deste Reyno de Angolla (23 de Junho de 1651), in: Arquivos de Angola: Publicação Oficial 2 (1936) 11, p. 295–301.

Ribas, Óscar, Ilundo, divindades e ritos angolanos. Luanda, 1958.

Ribas, Óscar, Uanga (Feitiço). Romance folclórico angolano. Luanda, 2009 [1951].

Rocha, Manoel Ribeiro, Ethiope resgatado, empenhado, sustentado, corregido, instruido, e libertado. Lisbon, 1758.

Sarmento, Alfredo de, Os sertões d'Africa (apontamentos de viagem). Lisbon, 1880.

Schaff, Philip (ed.) St. Augustin. The Anti-Pelagian Writings. Edinburgh, 1887.

Schaff, Philip (ed.) St. Augustin. The Writings Against the Manichaens and Against the Donatists. Edinburgh, 1887.

Seabra da Silva, José, Carta de José de Seabra da Silva, em nome de Sua Magestade, para o Governador proteger os Negros sertanejos contra os abuzos das autoridades e de outros individuos, os quais, em parte, descreve, afim-de serem reprimidos (21 de Novembro de 1791), in: Arquivos de Angola: Publicação Oficial 3 (1937) 22, p. 175–180.

Silva, António Delgado da (ed.), Colleção de legislação portugueza (1763–1774). Lisbon, 1829.

Silva, António Delgado da (ed.), Colleção da legislação portugueza desde a ultima compilação das Odenações (1750–1762). Lisbon, 1830.

Silva, António Delgado da (ed.), Supplemento à collecção de legislação portugueza do Desembargador António Delgado da Silva pelo mesmo (1750–1762). Lisbon, 1842.

Silva, Chantal Luís da, L'Évêche du Congo et de l'Angola (1596–1760), in: Revista Anais de História de Além-Mar 4 (2003), p. 295–334.

Silva Corrêa, Elias Alexandre da Silva, História de Angola, Vol. 1. Lisbon, 1937 [c. 1787–1799]

Silva Corrêa, Elias Alexandre da Silva, História de Angola, Vol. 2. Lisbon, 1937 [c. 1787–1799].

Silva Porto, António Francisco Ferreira da, Introdução (Trajectória do comércio do Bié), in: Maria Emília Madeira Santos (ed.), Viagens e Apontamentos de um Portuense em África. 1986, p. 13–216.

Simões, Garcia, De Garcia Simões para o Provincial de São Paulo de Loanda a vinte de outubro de 1575, in: Boletim da Sociedade de Geografia de Lisboa 4 (1883) 7, p. 339–346.

Sousa, Fernão de, A Angola portuguesa e regiões circunvizinhas. Descrição topográfica e histórica da ocupação portuguesa, in: Beatrix Heintze (ed.), Fontes para a História de Angola no século XVII. Memórias, relações e outros manuscritos da colectânea documental de Fernão de Sousa (1622–1635), Vol. 1. Stuttgart, 1985, p. 210–216.

Sousa, Fernão de, História das relações entre a Angola Portuguesa e o Ndongo (1617–Setembro de 1625), in: Beatrix Heintze (ed.), Fontes para a História de Angola no século XVII. I Memórias, relações e outros manuscritos da colectânea documental de Fernão de Sousa (1622–1635), Vol. 1. Stuttgart, 1985, p. 197–201.

Sousa, Fernão de, Mapa das regiões circunvizinhas de Luanda com uma minuciosa descrição, in: Beatrix Heintze (ed.), Fontes para a História de Angola no século XVII. Memórias, relações e outros manuscritos da colectânea documental de Fernão de Sousa (1622–1635), Vol. 1. Stuttgart, 1985, p. 158–165.

Sousa, Fernão de, O extenso relatório do governador a seus filhos (s.d., 1625–1630), in: Beatrix Heintze (ed.), Fontes para a História de Angola no século XVII. Memórias, relações e outros manuscritos da colectânea documental de Fernão de Sousa (1622–1635), Vol. 1. Stuttgart, 1985, p. 217–362.

Sousa, Fernão, Regimento de Fernão de Sousa a Paio de Araújo de Azevedo (27 de Agosto de 1628), in: Beatrix Heintze (ed.), Fontes para a História de Angola no século XVII. Memórias, relações e outros manuscritos da colectânea documental de Fernão de Sousa (1622–1635), Vol. 1. Stuttgart, 1985, p. 207–208.

Sousa Coutinho, Francisco Inocêncio de, Bando sobre as feiras que devem haver nos Certoes de Benguela, e Caconda (23 de Setembro de 1768), in: Arquivos de Angola: Publicação Oficial 1 (1936) 6.

Sousa Coutinho, Rodrigo, Oficio de Dom Rodrigo de Sousa Coutinho enviando um extracto do protesto do comércio da praça de Luanda contra certas providências projectadas pelo Governador Dom Miguel António de Melo (17 de Novembro de 1799), in: Arquivos de Angola: Publicação Oficial 2 (1936) 14, p. 603–605.

Sousa Coutinho, Francisco Inocêncio de, Carta para Feliciano Pinto da Costa Vianna Cap.^{am} mór de Encoje (7 de Março de 1772) in: Arquivos de Angola: Publicação Oficial 3 (1937) 29, p. 417–418.

Sousa Coutinho, Francisco Inocêncio de, Carta para Feliciano Pinto da Costa Vianna Cap.^{am} mór de Encoje (26 de Dezembro de 1771), in: Arquivos de Angola: Publicação Oficial 3 (1937) 29, p. 359–360.

Sousa Coutinho, Francisco Inocêncio de, Carta para Ioaquim Iozê Roiz, Cap.^{am} mór, e Iuiz de Amarante, e do mesmo teor se escreveo aos Cap.^{ens} mores de Beng.^{a}, Caconda, e Novo

Redondo, e p.[a] todos os Iuizes das povoações novas, in: Arquivos de Angola: Publicação Oficial 3 (1937) 28, p. 297–298.

Sousa Coutinho, Francisco Inocêncio de, Carta para Iozé Thomás Vás Vieira Cap.[am] mór Regente de Cambambe (25 de Novembro de 1771), in: Arquivos de Angola: Publicação Oficial 3 (1937) 28, p. 317–319.

Sousa Coutinho, Francisco Inocêncio de, Carta para Iozê Vieira de Araujo Cap.[am] mór da Cidade de Benguela, in: Arquivos de Angola: Publicação Oficial 3 (1937) 29, p. 379–382.

Sousa Coutinho, Francisco Inocêncio de, Forma do bando, q. S. Ex.[a] mandou p.[a] se publicar em Massangano, feito em nome do Iuiz, Vereadores, e mais oficiaaes do Senado da Camara da dita Villa, in: Arquivos de Angola: Publicação Oficial 3 (1937) 28, p. 333–334.

Souza, João da Silva e, Alvará da creação do Governo de Benguela, com separação do de Angola (14 Fevereiro 1615), in: Arquivos de Angola: Publicação Oficial 4 (1938) 41–48, p. 113–114.

Systema, ou collecção dos regimentos reaes, Vol. 5. Lisbon, 1789.

Tavares, Ana Paula and Catarina Madeira Santos (eds.), *Africæ Monumenta.* Arquivo Caculo Cacahenda. Lisbon, 2002.

The Digest of Justinian, Vol. 1. Philadelphia, 1985.

Torres, João Carlos Feo Cardoso de Castelo Branco e, Memorias contendo a biographia do Vice Almirante Luiz da Motta Feo e Torres, a historia dos governadores e capitaens generaes de Angola, desde 1575 até 1825, e a descripção geographica e politica dos reinos de Angola e de Benguella. Paris, 1825.

Valdez, Francisco Travassos, Africa Occidental. Noticias e Consideraçôes, Vol. 1. 1864.

Valdez, Francisco Travassos, Six Years of a Traveller's Life in Western Africa, Vol. 2. London, 1861.

Vandelli, Domingos, Memória sobre a necessidade de uma viagem filosófica feita no reino, e depois nos seus domínios, in: José Luís Cardoso (ed.), Memórias Económicas Inéditas (1780–1808). Lisbon, 1987, p. 33–36.

Vide, D. Sebatião Monteiro da, Constituições primeiras do Arcebispado da Bahia. Feitas, e ordenadas pelo Ilustrísimo e Reverendíssimo D. Sebastião Monteiro da Vide São Paulo, [1707] 1853.

Vide, D. Sebatião Monteiro da, Regimento do Auditório Ecclesiastico do Arcebispado da Bahia, Metropole do Brasil, e da sua Relação, e officiais da justiça ecclesiastica, e mais cousas que tocão ao bom governo do dito Arcebispado, ordenado pelo illustrissimo Senhor D. Sebastião Monteiro de Vide. São Paulo, [1704] 1853.

Literature

Abrahams, R. G., Foreword, in: Victor Turner (ed.), Ritual Process. Structure and Anti-Structure. London, 2011 [1969], p. v–xii.

Abrahão, Juliana Diogo, A conjuração dos degredados em Angola, 1763, in: Crítica Histórica 12 (2021) 24, p. 69–110.

Abreu, Adélio Fernando, Iluminismo e cristianismo em Portugal. Uma abordagem histórica, in: Humanística e Teologia 33 (2012) 2, p. 31–61.

Abreu, Laurinda, O papel das Misericórdias dos 'lugares de além-mar' na formação do Império Português, in: História, Ciências, Saúde—Manguinhos 8 (2001) 3, p. 591–611.

Adelman, Jeremy, Sovereignty and Revolution in the Iberian Atlantic. New Jersey, 2006.

Agamben, Giorgio, State of Exception. Chicago, 2005.

Aidar, Bruno, Governar a Real Fazenda. Composição e dinâmica da Junta da Fazenda de São Paulo, 1765–1808, in: História Económica & História de Empresas 16 (2013) 2, p. 163–217.

Alencastro, Luiz Felipe de, The Apprenticeship of Colonization, in: Barbara L. Solow (ed.), Slavery and the Rise of the Atlantic System. Cambridge, 1991, p. 151–176.

Alencastro, Luiz Felipe de, O trato dos viventes. Formação do Brasil no Atlântico Sul—Séculos XVI e XVII. São Paulo, 2000.

Alencastro, Luiz Felipe de, Mulattos in Brazil and Angola. A Comparative Approach, from the Seventeenth to the Twenty-First Century, in: Francisco Bethencourt (ed.), Racism and Ethnic Relations in the Portuguese-Speaking World. London, 2012, p. 71–96.

Alexander, Catherine, Writing Failure. Knowledge Production, Temporalities, Ethics, and Traces, in: Journal of the Royal Anthropological Institute 29 (2023) 1, p. 8–30.

Alfagali, Crislayne Gloss Marão, Blacksmiths of Ilamba. A Social History of Labor at the Nova Oeiras Iron Foundry (Angola, 18th Century). Berlin, 2023.

Almeida, Carlos, A narrativa etnográfica na literatura missionária sobre o Kongo, séculos XVI a XVIII, in: Selma Pantoja and Andrew S. Thompson (eds.), Em torno de Angola: Narrativas, identidades e as conexões atlânticas. São Paulo, 2014, p. 15–32.

Alves, Daniel Ribeiro, Os dízimos no final do Antigo Regime. Aspectos económicos e sociais (Minho, 1820–1834). Lisbon, 2012.

Amaral, Ilídio do, O consulado de Paulo Dias de Novais. Angola no último quartel do século XVI e primeiro do século XVII. Lisbon, 2000.

Amorin da Costa, A. M., As ciências naturais na reforma pombalina da Universidade. «Estudo de rapazes, não ostentação de príncipes», in: Ana Cristina Araújo (ed.), O Marquês de Pombal e a Universidade. Coimbra, 2014, p. 181–208.

Antunes, Cátia and Jelmer Vos, Port Cities and Commodities. Luanda in the Early-Modern Period, in: Jonathan Curry-Machado, Jean Subbs, William Gervase Clarence-Smith and Jelmer Vos (eds.), The Oxford Handbook of Commodity History. Oxford, 2024, p. 127–144.

Anzoátegui, Víctor Tau, La ley "se obedece pero no se cumple." En torno a la suplicación de las leyes en el Derecho indiano. Quito, 1980.

Appadurai, Arjun, Introduction, in: Social Research: An International Quarterly 83 (2016) 3, p. xxi–xxvii.

APTER, Andrew, Atinga Revisited. Yoruba Witchcraft and the Cocoa Economy, 1950–1951, in: John L. COMAROFF and Jean COMAROFF (eds.), Modernity and its Malcontents. Ritual and Power in Postcolonial Africa. Chicago, 1993, p. 111–128.

ARAÚJO, Ana Cristina, A formação científica e filosófica de Ribeiro Sanches e o seu reformismo pedagógico. Habilitation dissertation, University of Coimbra, Coimbra, 1984.

ARAÚJO, Ana Cristina, A cultura das Luzes em Portugal. Temas e problemas. Lisbon, 2003.

ARAÚJO, Ana Cristina, O Marquês de Pombal e a Universidade. Coimbra, 2014.

ARAUJO, Ana Lucia, The Gift. How Objects of Prestige Shaped the Atlantic Slave Trade and Colonialism. Cambridge, 2023.

ASHFORTH, Adam, Madumo, a Man Bewitched. Chicago, 2000.

ASHFORTH, Adam, Witchcraft, Violence, and Democracy in South Africa. Chicago, 2005.

ASHFORTH, Adam, Witchcraft Justice, and Human Rights in Africa. Cases from Malawi, in: African Studies Review 58 (2015) 1, p. 5–38.

AUSLANDER, Mark, "Open the Wombs!" The Symbolic Politics of Modern Ngoni, in: John L. COMAROFF and Jean COMAROFF (eds.), Modernity and its Malcontents. Ritual and Power in Postcolonial Africa. Chicago, 1993, p. 167–192.

AVRAMESCU, Cătălin, An Intellectual History of Cannibalism. New Jersey, 2009.

BALANDIER, Georges, Le Royaume de Kongo du XVIe au XVIIIe Siècle. Paris, 2013 [1965].

BANDEIRA JERÓNIMO, Miguel, The "Civilising Mission" of Portuguese Colonialism, 1870–1930. London, 2015.

BARBEITOS, Arlindo, A "raça" ou a ilusão de uma identidade definitiva, in: António Custódio GONÇALVES (ed.), O racismo ontem e hoje. Estados poderes e identidades na África Subsariana. Porto, 2005, p. 139–148.

BARBEITOS, Arlindo, Angola/Portugal. Des identités coloniales équivoques. Historicité des représentations de soi et d'autrui. Paris, 2009.

BARBEITOS, Arlindo, A "raça" e o racismo. Algumas incidências sobre Angola, in: Mulemba 6 (2016) 12, p. 13–50.

BARDWELL, Ross Little, The Governors of Portugal's South Atlantic Empire in the Seventeenth Century. Social Background, Qualification, Selection, and Reward. PhD dissertation, University of California, Santa Barbara, 1974.

BARLETT, Robert, Trial by Fire and Water. The Medieval Judicial Ordeal. Oxford, 1986.

BARROS, Edval de Souza, Negócios de tanta importância. O Conselho Ultramarino e a disputa pela condução da guerra no Atlântico e no Índico (1643–1661). Lisbon, 2008.

BASTIAN, Misty L., "Bloodhounds Who Have No Friends:" Witchcraft and Locality in the Nigerian Popular Press, in: John L. COMAROFF and Jean COMAROFF (eds.), Modernity and its Malcontents. Ritual and Power in Postcolonial Africa. Chicago, 1993, p. 129–166.

BAUCON, Ian, Specters of the Atlantic. Finance Capital, Slavery, and the Philosophy of History. Durham, 2005.

BAYART, Jean-François, The State in Africa. The Politics of the Belly. London, 1993.

BAYART, Jean-François, The Illusion of Cultural Identity. Chicago, 2006.

BAYART, Jean-François, Fait Missionnaire and Politics of the Belly. A Foucaultian Reading, in: Peter GESCHIERE, Birgit MEYER and Peter PELS (eds.), Readings in Modernity in Africa. Oxford, 2008, p. 92–98.

BAYART, Jean-François, Historical Regimes of Responsibility in 'the Politics of the Belly,' in: Benjamin RUBBERS and Alessandro JEDLOWSKI (eds.), Regimes of Responsibility in Africa. Genealogies, Rationalities and Conflicts. New York, 2020, p. 21–39.

BEATTIE, J. M., Crime and the Courts in England. Oxford, 1986.

BENAVENTE, Rodrigues M., A extinção do Erário Régio, em 1832, in: Jornal de Contabilidade (2000) 281, p. 238–246.

BENTON, Lauren, Law and Colonial Cultures. Legal Regimes in World History (1400–1900). Cambridge, 2002.

BENTON, Lauren, A Search for Sovereignty. Law and Geography in European Empires. Cambridge, 2009.

BENTON, Lauren, Possessing Empire. Iberian Claims and Interpolity Law, in: Saliha BELMESSOUS (ed.), Native Claims. Indigenous Law against Empire (1500–1920). 2011, p. 19–40.

BENTON, Lauren and Adam CLULOW, Interpolity Law and Jurisdictional Politics, in: Law and History Review 42 (2024) 2, p. 197–209.

BERG, Maxine and Pat HUDSON, Slavery, Capitalism and the Industrial Revolution. Cambridge, 2023.

BERNARDINO, Luís Manuel Brás, A defesa de Angola. A estatégia militar portuguesa no período da grande guerra, do Capitão Gastão Sousa Dias, in: Revista Militar (2014) 2548, p. 403–428.

BETHENCOURT, Francisco, História das Inquisições. Portugal, Espanha e Itália. Lisbon, 1996.

BETHENCOURT, Francisco, Enlightened Reform in Portugal and Brazil, in: Gabriel PAQUETTE (ED.), Enlightened Reform in Southern Europe and its Atlantic Colonies, c. 1750–1830. Farnham, 2009, p. 41–44.

BETHENCOURT, Francisco, Racisms. From the Crusades to the Twentieth Century. New Jersey, 2013.

BETHENCOURT, Francisco, Managing Diversity in the Portuguese Empire, in: e-Journal of Portuguese History 19 (2022) 2, p. 1–23.

BETHENCOURT, Francisco and Philip HAVIK, A África e a Inquisição Portuguesa. Novas perspectivas, in: Revista Lusófona de Ciência das Religiões 3 (2004) 5–6, p. 21–27.

BICALHO, Maria Fernanda, Os Conselhos da Índia e Ultramarino, a Secretaria de Estado e a circulação de saberes no Império Português (séculos XVII e XVIII), in: Reflexos (2022) 5.

BICALHO, Maria Fernanda and Nuno Gonçalo MONTEIRO, As instituições civis da monarquia portuguesa na Idade Moderna. Centro e periferia do Império, in: Federico PALOMO, Roberta STUMPF and Ângela Barreto XAVIER (eds.), Monarquias ibéricas em perspectiva comparada (séculos XVI–XVIII). Dinâmicas imperiais e circulação de modelos político-administrativos. Lisbon, 2018, p. 209–236.

BICALHO, Maria Fernanda and Vera Lúcia Amaral FERLINI (eds.), Modos de governar. Ideias e práticas políticas no Império Português (séculos XVI a XIX). São Paulo, 2005.

Birmingham, David, The Mbundu and Neighbouring Peoples of Central Angola under the Influence of Portuguese Trade and Conquest (1482–1790). PhD dissertation, School of Oriental and African Studies, London, 1964.

Birmingham, David, Speculations on the Kingdom of Kongo, in: Transactions of the Historical Society of Ghana 8 (1965), p. 1–10.

Birmingham, David, The Date and Significance of the Imbangala Invasion of Angola, in: The Journal of African History 6 (1965) 2, p. 143–152.

Blackburn, Robin, The Overthrow of Colonial Slavery (1776–1848). London, 1996 [1988].

Blackburn, Robin, The Making of New World Slavery. From the Baroque to the Modern (1492–1800). London, 1998.

Blackburn, Robin, The Reckoning: From the Second Slavery to Abolition (1776–1888). London, 2024.

Bohannan, Laura and Paul Bohannan, The Tiv of Central Nigeria. London, 1953.

Bohannan, Paul and Laura Bohannan, Tiv Economy. Evanston, 1968.

Bohannan, Paul, The Impact of Money on an African Subsistence Economy, in: The Journal of Economic History 19 (1959) 4, p. 491–503.

Bonciani, Rodrigo Faustinoni, Heresias e rebelião em Angola, fim do século XVI. O processo inquisitorial contra Duarte Nunes Nogueira, in: Revista de Fontes 7 (2020) 12, p. 1–27.

Bonciani, Rodrigo Faustinoni, Inquisição, tráfico de escravos e circulação entre a África, Brasil e Índias Ocidentais, in: José Manuel Santos Pérez, Ana Paula Torres Megiani and José Luis Ruiz-Peinado Alonso (eds.), Redes y circulación en Brasil durante la Monarquía Hispánica (1580–1640). Madrid, 2020, p. 265–289.

Bonciani, Rodrigo Faustinoni, "Minas de almas." Comércio de gente e geopolítica cristã (fim do século XVI), in: Revista de História (2023) 182, p. 1–29.

Bonciani, Rodrigo Faustinoni and Amanda Santos Silveira, Um pombeiro nas origens do Atlântico. O processo contra Aires Fernandes, o Dinga Dinga, in: Afro-Ásia (2021) 64, p. 520–591.

Bontinck, François, Introduction. La fondation de la mission des Capuchins au royaume du Congo (1648). Louvain, 1964, p. vii–xxviii.

Bontinck, François, Le voyage des pombeiros. Essai de reinterpretation, in: Cultures au Zaïre et en Afrique (1974) 5, p. 39–70.

Bontinck, François, Un mausolée pour les Jaga, in: Cahiers d'Études Africaines 20 (1980) 79, p. 387–389.

Bostoen, Koen, A Diachronic Onomasiological Approach to Early Bantu Oil Palm Vocabulary, in: Studies in African Linguistics 34 (2005) 2, p. 113–158.

Bostoen, Koen, Pearl Millet in Early Bantu Speech Communities in Central Africa. A Reconsideration of the Lexical Evidence, in: Afrika und übersee (2007) 89, p. 183–213.

Bouza, Fernando, Pedro Cardim, and Antonio Feros (eds.), The Iberian World (1450–1820). London, 2020.

Boxer, Charles R., Salvador de Sá and the Struggle for Brazil and Angola (1602–1686). London, 1952.

Boxer, Charles R., Race Relations in the Portuguese Colonial Empire (1415–1825). Oxford, 1963.

Boxer, Charles R., Portuguese Society in the Tropics. The Municipal Councils of Goa, Macao, Bahia, and Luanda (1510–1800). Madison, 1965.

Boxer, Charles R., Four Centuries of Portuguese Expansion (1415–1825). A Succinct Survey. Berkely, 1969.

Boxer, Charles R., A igreja militante e a expansão ibérica (1440–1770). São Paulo, 2007 [1978].

Boxer, Charles R., O império colonial português. Lisbon, 1981.

Boxer, Charles R., Um panfleto raro acerca dos abusos da escravidão no Brasil (1764), reimpresso e comentado por Charles R. Boxer, in: IHGB [Brazilian Historical and Geographical Institute] (ed.), Anais do congresso comemorativo do bicentenário da transfêrencia da sede do governo do Brasil da cidade de Salvador para o Rio de Janeiro (1963). Rio de Janeiro, 1967.

Brantlinger, Patrick, Victorians and Africans. The Genealogy of the Myth of the Dark Continent, in: Critical Inquiry 12 (1985) 1, p. 166–203.

Brásio, António, Para a história do Cabido de Angola e Congo, in: Boletim Geral das Colónias 18 (1942) 219, p. 24–56.

Brásio, António, As Misericórdias de Angola, in: STVDIA (1959) 4, p. 106–149.

Braun, Harald Ernst, Erik de Bom, and Paolo Astorri (eds.) (eds.), A Companion to the Spanish Scholastics. Leiden, 2022.

Bray, Alan, Homosexuality in Renaissance England. New York, 1982.

Brett, Annabel S., Liberty, Right and Nature. Individual Rights in Later Scholastic Thought. Cambridge, 1997.

Brett, Annabel S., Changes of State. Nature and the Limits of the City in Early Modern Natural Law. Princeton, 2011.

Briggs, Robin. Witches and Neighbours. The Social and Cultural Context of European Witchcraft. London, 1996.

Brigola, João Carlos Pires, Colecções, gabinetes e museus em Portugal no século XVIII. Lisbon, 2003.

Bronislaw, Malinowski, Argonauts of the Western Pacific. New York, 1961 [1922].

Bruns, Claudia, Antisemitism and Colonial Racisms. Genealogical Perspectives, in: Stefan Vogt (ed.), Colonialism and the Jews in German History. From the Middle Ages to the Twentieth Century. London, 2022, p. 25–55.

Burbank, Jane and Frederick Cooper, Empires in World History. Power and the Politics of Difference. Princeton, 2010.

Cabral de Oliveira, Luís Pedroso de Lima, "He homem pardo, mas para com os nacionaes he branco da terra." Dinâmicas e estratégias sociais e familiares da Luanda setecentista em três processos de habilitação para o Santo Ofício, in: Raízes e Memórias (2013) 30, p. 169–202.

Cagle, Hugh, Imperial Tensions, Colonial Contours. Jesuits, Slavery, and Race within and beyond the Portuguese Atlantic, in: Yolanda Martínez-San Miguel and Santa Arias (eds.), The Routledge Hispanic Studies Companion to Colonial Latin America and the Caribbean (1492–1898). London, 2021, p. 215–230.

Cagle, Hugh and Matthew Crawford, Enlightened Reformism in Iberian Culture and Science, in: Fernando Bouza, Pedro Cardim and Antonio Feros (eds.), The Iberian World (1450–1820). London, 2020, p. 500–519.

Calafate, Pedro, A Escola Ibérica da Paz nas Universidades de Coimbra e Évora (séculos XVI e XVII), in: Revista de Hispanismo Filosófico (2014) 19, p. 119–142.

Calafate, Pedro (ed.) A Escola Ibérica da Paz nas Universidades de Coimbra e Évora (século XVI). Sobre as matérias da guerra e da paz. Coimbra, 2015.

Calafate, Pedro (ed.) A Escola Ibérica da Paz nas Universidades de Coimbra e Évora: (século XVI). Escritos sobre a justiça, o poder e a escravatura. Coimbra, 2015.

Calafate, Pedro, Estudo Introdutório I, in: Pedro Calafate (ed.), A Escola Ibérica da Paz nas Universidades de Coimbra e Évora (século XVI). Sobre as matérias da guerra e da paz. Coimbra, 2015, p. 17–49.

Calafate, Pedro, Plano da obra, in: Pedro Calafate (ed.), A Escola Ibérica da Paz nas Universidades de Coimbra e Évora (século XVI). Sobre as matérias da guerra e da paz. Coimbra, 2015, p. 13–15.

Calainho, Daniela Buono, Jambacousses e Gangazambes. Feiticeiros negros em Portugal, in: Afro-Ásia (2001) 25–26, p. 141–176.

Calainho, Daniela Buono, Metrópole das mandingas. Religiosidade negra e Inquisição Portuguesa no Antigo Regime. Rio de Janeiro, 2008.

Caldeira, Arlindo Manuel, Mulheres, sexualidade e casamento em São Tomé e Príncipe, século XV a XVIII. Lisbon, 1999.

Caldeira, Arlindo Manuel, Luanda in the 17th Century. Diversity and Cultural Interaction in the Process of Forming an Afro-Atlantic City, in: Nordic Journal of African Studies 22 (2013) 1–2, p. 72–104.

Caldeira, Arlindo Manuel, Dimensão sociopolítica do Município de Luanda durante o século XVII, in: Cadernos de Estudos Africanos (2015) 30, p. 27–59.

Calmon, Pedro, A vida espantosa de Gregório de Matos. Rio de Janeiro, 1983.

Camarinhas, Nuno, Juízes e administração da justiça no Antigo Regime. Portugal e o império colonial, séculos XVII e XVIII. Lisbon, 2010.

Camarinhas, Nuno, As residências dos cargos de justiça letrada, in: Roberta Stumpf and Nandini Chaturvedula (eds.), Cargos e ofícios nas monarquias ibéricas. Provimento e venalidade (séculos XVII e XVIII). Lisbon, 2012, p. 161–174.

Camarinhas, Nuno, Administração da justiça em espaços coloniais. A experiência imperial portuguesa e os seus juízes, na época moderna, in: Jahrbuch für Geschichte Lateinamerikas 52 (2015) 1, p. 109–124.

Camarinhas, Nuno, Lugares ultramarinos. A construção do aparelho judicial no ultramar português da época moderna, in: Análise Social 53 (2018) 226, p. 137–160.

CANDIDO, Mariana P., African Freedom Suits and Portuguese Vassal Status. Legal Mechanisms for Fighting Enslavement in Benguela, Angola (1800–1830), in: Slavery & Abolition 32 (2011) 3, p. 447–459.

CANDIDO, Mariana P., Aguida Gonçalves da Silva, une dona à Benguela à la fin du XVIIIe siècle, in: Brésil(s) Sciences humaines et sociales (2012) 1, p. 33–54.

CANDIDO, Mariana P., Concubinage and Slavery in Benguela (c. 1750–1850), in: Nadine HUNT and Olatunji OJO (eds.), Slavery in Africa and the Caribbean. A History of Enslavement and Identity Since the 18th Century. London, 2012, p. 66–84.

CANDIDO, Mariana P., An African Slaving Port and the Atlantic World. Benguela and Its Hinterland. Cambridge, 2013.

CANDIDO, Mariana P., Strategies for Social Mobility. Liaisons between Foreign Men and Slave Women in Benguela (c. 1770–1850), in: Gwyn CAMPBELL and Elizabeth ELBOURNE (eds.), Sex, Power and Slavery. The Dynamics of Carnal Relations under Enslavement. Athens OH, 2014, p. 272–288.

CANDIDO, Mariana P., Engendering West Central African History. The Role of Urban Women in Benguela in the Nineteenth Century, in: History in Africa 42 (2015), p. 7–36.

CANDIDO, Mariana P., Women, Family, and Landed Property in Nineteenth-Century Benguela, in: African Economic History 43 (2015), p. 136–161.

CANDIDO, Mariana P., Women in Angola, in: Thomas SPEAR (ED.), Oxford Research Encyclopedia of African History. Oxford, 2018.

CANDIDO, Mariana P., African Businesswomen in the Age of Second Slavery in Angola, in: Dale W. TOMICH and Paul E. LOVEJOY (eds.), The Atlantic and Africa. Albany, 2021, p. 179–202.

CANDIDO, Mariana P., Wealth, Land, and Property in Angola. A History of Dispossession, Slavery, and Inequality. Cambridge, 2022.

CANDIDO, Mariana P. and Adam JONES (eds.), African Women in the Atlantic World. Property, Vulnerability and Mobility (1660–1880). Woodbridge, 2019.

CANDIDO, Mariana P. and Toby GREEN, How Europe Underdeveloped Africa by Walter Rodney—50 Years On, in: African Economic History 50 (2022) 2, p. 1–3.

CAÑIZARES-ESGUERRA, Jorge, Puritan Conquistadors. Iberianizing the Atlantic, 1550–1700. Stanford, 2006.

CAPELA, José, A burguesia mercantil do Porto e as colónias (1834–1900). Porto, 2010 [1975].

CAPELA, José, Éthique et représentation de l'esclavagisme colonial au Mozambique, in: Isabel Castro HENRIQUES and Louis SALA-MOLINS (eds.), Déraison, esclavage et droit. Les Fondements ideologiques et juridiques de la traite négrière et de l'esclavage. Paris, p. 329–348.

CARDIM, Pedro, Cortes e cultura política no Portugal do Antigo Regime. Lisbon, 1998.

CARDIM, Pedro, O poder dos afectos. Ordem amorosa e dinâmica política no Portugal do Antigo Regime. PhD dissertation, Nova University of Lisbon, Lisbon, 2000.

CARDIM, Pedro, A Casa Real e os órgãos centrais de governo no Portugal da segunda metade de seiscentos, in: Tempo (2002) 13, p. 13–57.

Cardim, Pedro, "Administração" e "governo." Uma reflexão sobre o vocabulário do Antigo Regime, in: Maria Fernanda Bicalho and Vera Lúcia Amaral Ferlini (eds.), Modos de governar. Ideias e práticas políticas no Império Português (séculos XVI a XIX). São Paulo, 2005, p. 45–68.

Cardim, Pedro and Nuno Goncalo Monteiro (eds.), Political Thought in Portugal and its Empire (c. 1500–1800). Cambridge, 2021.

Cardim, Pedro, Tamar Herzog, Jisé Javier Ruiz Ibáñez and Gaetano Sabatini, Polycentric Monarchies. How did Early Modern Spain and Portugal Achieve and Maintain a Global Hegemony? in: Pedro Cardim, Tamar Herzog, Jisé Javier Ruiz Ibáñez and Gaetano Sabatini (eds.), Polycentric Monarchies. How did Early Modern Spain and Portugal Achieve and Maintain a Global Hegemony? Eastbourne, 2014, p. 3–8.

Cardoso, Carlos Lopes, Comer o sal. Lisbon, 1971.

Cardoso, José Luís entry "Coutinho, D. Rodrigo de Sousa," in: Dicionário Biográfico de Cientistas, Engenheiros e Médicos em Portugal, edited by Maria Paula Diogo and Ana Simões, Lisbon, 2022.

Carmo, Marcelo Lunardi, Para a boa administração da justica. A inserção dos juízes de fora e a promoção de mudanças no judiciário da Colônia no final do século XVII, in: CLIO: Revista de Pesquisa Histórica (2019) 37, p. 85–110.

Carneiro, Ana, Ana Simoes, Maria Paula Diogo, Enlightenment Science in Portugal. The *Estrangeirados* and their Communication Networks, in: Social Studies of Science 30 (2000) 4, p. 591–619.

Carreira, Adélia Maria Caldas, Lisboa de 1731 a 1833. Da desordem à ordem no espaço urbano. PhD dissertation, Nova University of Lisbon, Lisbon, 2012.

Carroll, Timothy, David Jeevendrampillai, and Aaron Parkhurst (eds.), The Material Culture of Failure. When Things Do Wrong. London, 2017.

Carroll, Timothy, David Jeevendrampillai and Aaron Parkhurst, Introduction. Towards a General Theory of Failure, in: Timothy Carroll, David Jeevendrampillai and Aaron Parkhurst (eds.), The Material Culture of Failure. When Things Do Wrong. London, 2017, p. 1–20.

Carvalho, Flávia Maria de, Os homens do rei em Angola. Sobas, governadores e capitães mores, séculos XVII e XVIII. PhD dissertation, Universidade Federal Fluminense, Niterói, 2013.

Carvalho, Flávio Rey de, Um Iluminismo português? A reforma da Universidade de Coimbra (1772). São Paulo, 2008.

Cassirer, Ernst, The Philosophy of the Enlightenment. Princeton, 2009 [1951].

Castelnau-L'Estoile, Charlotte de, Páscoa Vieira diante da Inquisição. Uma escrava entre Angola, Brasil e Portugal no século XVII. Rio de Janeiro, 2020.

Castro, Alexander de, "Boa Razão" e codificação penal. Apontamentos sobre a questão penal setecentista em Portugal (1769–1789), in: Revista Brasileira de Estudos Políticos (2015) 111, p. 105–143.

Castro, Alexandre de, Enlightened Absolutism and Legal Culture in Portugal. Rise and Decline of legal Pombalism in the 18th century (1769–1789), in: Zeitschrift der Savigny-Stiftung für Rechtsgeschichte 133 (2016), p. 296–364.

Chanock, Martin, Law, custom, and social order. The colonial experience in Malawi and Zambia. Cambridge, 1985.

Clist, Bernard, Els Cranshof, Gilles-Maurice de Schryver, Davy Herremans, Karlis Karklins, Igor Matonda, Fanny Steyaert, and Koen Bostoen, African-European Contacts in the Kongo Kingdom (Sixteenth–Eighteenth Centuries). New Archaeological Insights from Ngongo Mbata (Lower Congo, DRC), in: International Journal of Historical Archaeology 19 (2015) 3, p. 464–501.

Coates, Timothy Joel, Degredados e órfãos. Colonização dirigida pela coroa no Império Português (1550–1755). Lisbon, 1998.

Coelho, Virgílio, Em busca de Kábàsà. Uma tentativa de explicação da estrutura politico-administrativa do "Reino de Ndongo," in: Maria Emília Madeira Santos (ed.), Actas do Seminário Encontros de Povos e Culturas em Angola. Lisbon, 1997, p. 443–478.

Comaroff, Jean and John L. Comaroff, Of Revelation and Revolution. The Dialectics of Modernity on a South African Frontier, Vol. 2. Chicago, 1997.

Comaroff, Jean and John L. Comaroff, Occult Economies and the Violence of Abstraction. Notes from the South African Postcolony, in: American Ethnologist 26 (1999) 2, p. 279–303.

Comaroff, Jean and John L. Comaroff, Transparent Fictions; or, The Conspiracies of a Liberal Imagination. An Afterword, in: Harry G. West and Todd Sanders (eds.), Transparency and Conspiracy. Durham, 2003.

Comaroff, Jean and John L. Comaroff, Beasts, Banknotes and the Colour of Money in Colonial South Africa, in: Archaeological Dialogues 12 (2005) 2, p. 107–132.

Comaroff, Jean and John L. Comaroff, Cattle, Currencies & the Politics of Commensuration on a Colonial Frontier, in: Wale Adebanwi (ed.), The Political Economy of Everyday Life in Africa. Suffolk, 2017, p. 35–71.

Comaroff, John L. and Jean Comaroff (eds.), Modernity and its Malcontents. Ritual and Power in Postcolonial Africa. Chicago, 1993.

Comaroff, John L. and Jean Comaroff, Introduction, in: John L. Comaroff and Jean Comaroff (eds.), Modernity and its Malcontents. Ritual and Power in Postcolonial Africa. Chicago, 1993, p. xi–xxxvii.

Comaroff, John L. and Simon Roberts, Rules and Processes. The Cultural Logic of Dispute in an African Context. Chicago, 1986 [1981].

Coquery-Vidrovitch, Catherine, African Women. A Modern History. London, 1997.

Costa, Palmira Fontes da and Henrique Leitão, Portuguese Imperial Science (1450–1800). A Historiographical Review, in: Daniela Bleichmar, Paula De Vos, Kristin Huffine and Kevin Sheehan (eds.), Science in the Spanish and Portuguese Empires (1500–1800). Stanford, 2009, p. 35–56.

Couto, Carlos, Os capitães-mores em Angola no século XVIII. Subsídio para o estudo da sua actuação. Luanda, 1972.

Couto, Carlos, Regimento do governo subalterno de Benguela, in: STVDIA 1 (1981) 45, p. 285–294.

Cover, Robert M., The Supreme Court, 1982 Term—Foreword. Nomos and Narrative, in: Harvard Law Review (1983) 97, p. 4–68.

Crais, Clifton, The Politics of Evil. Magic, State Power, and the Political Imagination in South Africa. Cambridge, 2002.

Cramer, Peter, Baptism and Change in the Early Middle Ages (c. 200 –c. 1150). Cambridge, 1993.

Crawford, J. R., Witchcraft and Sorcery in Rhodesia. London, 1967.

Cruz e Silva, Rosa da, As feiras do Ndongo. A outra vertente do comércio no século XVII, in: Maria Emília Madeira Santos (ed.), Actas do Seminário Encontros de Povos e Culturas em Angola. Lisbon, 1997, p. 405–422.

Cruz, Ariane Carvalho da, Militates e militarização no Reino de Angola. Patentes, guerra, comércio e vassalagem (segunda metade do século XVIII). Masters dissertation, Rural Federal University of Rio de Janeiro, Seropédica, 2014.

Cruz, Miguel Dantas da, Um império de conflitos. O Conselho Ultramarino e a defesa do Brasil. Lisbon, 2015.

Cunha, Anabela, Degredo para Angola. Sentença de morte lenta, in: Locus: Revista de História 18 (2012) 2, p. 87–104.

Cunha, Mafalda Soares da, Governo e governantes do Império Português do Atlântico (século XVII), in: Maria Fernanda Bicalho and Vera Lúcia Amaral Ferlini (eds.), Modos de governar. Ideias e práticas políticas no Império Português (séculos XVI a XIX). São Paulo, 2005, p. 69–92.

Cunha, Mafalda Soares da, Maria Fernanda Bicalho, António Castro Nunes, Fátima Farrica, Mello Isabele, Corregedores, ouvidores-gerais e ouvidores na comunicação política, in: João Luís Ribeiro Fragoso and Nuno Gonçalo Monteiro (eds.), Um reino e suas repúblicas no Atlântico. Comunicações políticas entre Portugal, Brasil e Angola nos séculos XVII e XVIII. Rio de Janeiro, 2017, p. 335–370.

Cunha, Norberto Ferreira da, Elites e acadêmicos na cultura portuguesa setecentista. Lisbon, 2000.

Curto, José C., Un butin illégitime. Razzias d'esclaves et relations luso-africaines dans la région des fleuves Kwanza et Kwango, in: Louis Sala-Molins and Isabel Castro Henriques (eds.), Déraison, esclavage et droit. Les fondements idéologiques et juridiques de la traite négrière et de l'esclavage. Paris, 2002, p. 314–327.

Curto, José C., The Story of Nbena (1817–1820). Unlawful Enslavement and the Concept of 'Original Freedom' in Angola, in: Paul E. Lovejoy and David V. Trotman (eds.), Trans-Atlantic Dimensions of Ethnicity in the African Diaspora. London, 2003, p. 43–64.

Curto, José C., Struggling Against Enslavement. The Case of José Manuel in Benguela (1816–1820), in: Canadian Journal of African Studies 39 (2005) 1, p. 96–122.

Curto, José C., Experiences of Enslavement in West Central Africa, in: Social History 41 (2008) 82, p. 382–415.

Curto, José C., Jeribita in the Relations between the Colony of Angola and the Kingdom of Kasanje, in: Anais de História do Além Mar 14 (2013), p. 301–325.

Curto, José C., The Donas of Benguela, 1797. A Preliminary Analysis of a Colonial Female Elite, in: Edvaldo Bergamo, Selma Pantoja and Ana Claudia Silva (eds.), Angola e as Angolanas. Memória, sociedade e cultura. São Paulo, 2016, p. 99–120.

Curto, José C., The Population of the Lower Kwanza Valley (1792–1796), in: Ponta de Lança: Revista Eletrônica de História, Memória & Cultura 12 (2018) 23, p. 95–117.

Dalton, George (ed.) Primitive, Archaic, and Modern Economies. Essays of Karl Polanyi. New York, 1968.

Dantas da Cruz, Miguel, Pombal e o Império Atlântico. Impactos políticos da criação do Erário Régio, in: Revista Tempo 20 (2014), p. 1–24.

Davis, Natalie Zemon, Judges, Masters, Diviners. Slaves' Experience of Criminal Justice in Colonial Suriname, in: Law and History Review 29 (2011) 4, p. 925–984.

De Boeck, Filip, Le «deuxième monde» et les «enfants-sorciers» en République Démocratique du Congo, in: Politique africaine 80 (2000) 4, p. 32–57.

De Herdt, Tom and Jean-Pierre Olivier de Sardan, Real Governance and Practical Norms in Sub-Saharan Africa. The Game of the Rules. London, 2015.

De Heusch, Luc, Le Roi ivre ou l'origine de l'État. Paris, 1972.

De Heusch, Luc, Rois nés d'un coeur de vache. Paris, 1982.

Delgado, Ralph, A famosa e histórica Benguela. Catálogo dos Governadores 1779 a 1940. Benguela, 1940.

Delgado, Ralph, Ao Sul do Cuanza. Ocupação e aproveitamento do antigo reino de Benguela (1483–1942). Lisbon, 1944.

Delgado, Ralph, O governo de Sousa Coutinho em Angola I, in: STVDIA (1960) 6, p. 19–56.

Delgado, Ralph, O governo de Sousa Coutinho em Angola II. Aproveitamento racional do Reino de Benguela, in: STVDIA (1961) 7, p. 49–86.

Delgado, Ralph, O governo de Sousa Coutinho em Angola III, in: STVDIA (1962) 10, p. 7–48.

Delgado, Ralph, História de Angola.Terceiro Período 1648 a 1836, Vol. 3. Lisbon, 197?.

Demaret, Mathieu, Estratégias expansionistas e conflitos políticos em Angola (1575–1641). Lisbon, Portugal, 2009.

Derrida, Jacques, Specters of Marx. The State of the Debt, the Work of Mourning, and the New International. London, 1994.

Diana, Paton, Witchcraft, Poison, Law, and Atlantic Slavery, in: The William and Mary Quarterly 69 (2012) 2, p. 235–264.

Dias Paes, Mariana Armond, Esclavos y tierras entre posesion y titulos. La construcción social del Derecho de propriedad en Brasil (siglo XIX). Frankfurt am Main, 2021.

Dias Paes, Mariana Armond, Registro e colonialismo em Angola, in: Elisabetta Fiocchi Malaspina and Simona Tarozzi (eds.), Historical Perspectives on Property and Land

Law. An Interdisciplinary Dialogue on Methods and Research Approaches. Madrid, 2019, p. 161–176.

Dias Paes, Mariana Armond, Shared Atlantic Legal Culture. The Case of a Freedom Suit in Benguela, in: Atlantic Studies 17 (2020) 3, p. 419–440.

Dias, Jill, Famine and Disease in the History of Angola (c. 1830–1930), in: The Journal of African History 22 (1981) 3, p. 349–378.

Dias, Jill, Mudanças nos padrões de poder do "hinterland" de Luanda. O impacto da colonização sobre os Mbundu (c. 1845–1920), in: Penélope: Fazer e desfazer a história (1994) 14, p. 43–91.

Dias, Jill, Angola, in: Valentim Alexandre and Jill Dias (eds.), O Império Africano (1825–1890). Lisbon, 1998, p. 319–556.

Dias, Jill, Estereótipos e realidades sociais. Quem eram os 'Ambaquistas'? in: Portugueses, CNCDP [National Commission for the Celebration of the Portuguese Discoveries] (ed.), Construindo o passado angolano. As fontes e a sua interpretação. Actas do II Seminário Internacional sobre a História de Angola. Lisbon, 2000, p. 597–623.

Dimmendaal, Gerrit J., Historical Linguistics and the Comparative Study of African Languages. Amsterdam, 2011.

Domingues, Ângela, Viagens de exploração geográfica na Amazónia em finais do século XVIII. Política, ciência e aventura. Coimbra, 1991.

Doré, Andréa, As atuações no Reino do Congo e na Costa da Pescaria. Aproximações para o estudo do Império Português no século XVI, in: Andréa Doré, Luís Filipe Silvério Lima and Luiz Geraldo Silva (eds.), Facetas do Império na história. Conceitos e métodos. São Paulo, 2008, p. 227–243.

Douglas, Mary, Sorcery Accusations Unleashed. The Lele Revisited, 1987, in: Africa: Journal of the International African Institute 69 (1999) 2, p. 177–193.

Doyle, Laura, Bordering on the Body. The Racial Matrix of Modern Fiction and Culture. Oxford, 1994.

Dubber, Markus Dirk, The Police Power. Patriarchy and the foundations of American government. New York, 2005.

Duffy, James, Portuguese Africa. Cambridge MA, 1968.

Duve, Thomas, Was ist „Multinormativität"? Einführende Bemerkungen, in: Rechtsgeschichte—Legal History (2017) 25, p. 88–101.

Duve, Thomas, What is Global Legal History? in: Comparative Legal History 8 (2020) 2, p. 73–115.

Duve, Thomas, Historia del Derecho como historia del saber normativo, in: Revista de Historia del Derecho (2022) 63, p. 1–60.

Duve, Thomas, Legal History as a History of the Translation of Knowledge of Normativity, in: Max Planck Institute for Legal History and Legal Theory Research Paper Series 16 (2022), p. 1–12.

DUVE, Thomas, Legal History as an Observation of Historical Regimes of Normativity, in: Max Planck Institute for Legal History and Legal Theory Research Paper Series (2022) 17, p. 1–10.

DUVE, Thomas, Theorie und Methode der Analyse asymmetrischer Formen von Abhängigkeit. Eine (global)rechtshistorische Perspektive, in: Bonn Center for Dependency and Slavery Studies Working Papers (2022) 5, p. 1–35.

DUVE, Thomas, How is Law Produced? in: Thomas DUVE and Tamar HERZOG (eds.), Latin America Law in Global Perspective. Cambridge, 2024, p. 54–72.

DUVE, Thomas and Tamar HERZOG (eds.), The Cambridge History of Latin American Law in Global Perspective. Cambridge, 2024.

EAKIN, Marshal C., Becoming Brazilians. Race and National Identity in Twentieth-Century Brazil. Cambridge, 2017.

EDELSTEIN, Dan, Stefanos GEROULANOS, and Natasha WHEATLEY (eds.), Power and Time. Temporalities in Conflict and the Making of History. Chicago, 2020.

EHRET, Christopher, History and the Testimony of Language. Berkeley, 2011.

EISENBERG, José, Cultural Encounters, Theoretical Adventures. The Jesuit Missions to the New World and the Justification of Voluntary Slavery, in: History of Political Thought 24 (2003) 3, p. 375–396.

ELLIS, Stephen, The Occult does not Exist. A Response to Terence Ranger, in: Tim KELSALL (ed.), Charlatans, Spirits and Rebels in Africa. The Stephen Ellis Reader. London, 2022, p. 337–353.

ELTIS, David, Precolonial Western Africa and the Atlantic Economy, in: Barbara L. SOLOW (ED.), Slavery and the Rise of the Atlantic System. Cambridge, 1991, p. 97–119.

EPPRECHT, Marc, Hungochani. The History of a Dissident Sexuality in Southern Africa. Montreal, 2004.

ESPELAND, Wendy Nelson and Berit I. VANNBO, Accountability, Quantification, and Law, in: Annual Review of Law and Social Science 3 (2007), p. 21–43.

ESPELAND, Wendy Nelson and Michael SAUDER, Rankings and Reactivity. How Public Measures Recreate Social Worlds, in: American Journal of Sociology (2007) 113, p. 1–40.

ESPELAND, Wendy Nelson and Mitchell L. STEVENS, Commensuration as a Social Process, in: Annual Review of Sociology 24 (1998), p. 313–343.

ESTERMANN, Carlos, A terminologia cristã na Diocese de Nova Lisboa, in: Portugal em África 48 (1951) 11–12, p. 358–364.

ESTORNINHO, Joana de Almeida, A Forja dos Homens. Estudos Jurídicos e Lugares de Poder no Séc. XVII. Lisbon, 2005.

EUGÊNIO, Alisson, Os relatos de Luiz Antônio de Oliveira Mendes sobre a saúde da população escrava. Do trafico na África ao cativeiro no Brasil (1793), in: Ideias 4 (2014) 0, p. 201–231.

EVANS-PRITCHARD, E. E., Witchcraft, Oracles, and Magic among the Azande. Oxford 1976.

FABIAN, Johannes, Time and the Other. How Anthropology Makes its Object New York, 1983.

Fage, J. D., Slavery and the Slave Trade in the Context of West African History, in: The Journal of African History 10 (1969) 3, p. 393–404.

Faria, Leite de, João António Cavazzi. A sua Obra e a sua Vida, in: Graciano Maria de

Leguzzano, Graciano Maria de, Ao Leitor, in: de Graciano Maria de Leguzzano (ed.), Descrição Histórica dos Três Reinos do Congo, Matamba e Angola. Lisbon, 1965, p. v–ix.

Faustino, Gibitá, O comércio de escravos na obra de Antônio de Oliveira de Cadornega, in: Estudos Ibero-Americanos 16 (1990) 1, 2, p. 105–116.

Favret-Saada, J., Désorceler. Paris, 2009.

Favret-Saada, J., Les Mots, la mort, les sorts. Paris, 1977.

Federici, Silvia, Caliban and the Witch. Women, the Body and Primitive Accumulation. London, 2004.

Ferguson, James, The Bovine Mystique. Power, Property and Livestock in Rural Lesotho, in: Man 20 (1985) 4, p. 647–674.

Fernandes, João Manuel A. A. , Luis de Molina. On War, in: Matthias Kaufmann and Alexander Aichele (eds.), A Companion to Luis de Molina. Leiden, 2014, p. 227–256.

Fernandes, Soares, A Feira de Cassanje, in: Geographica 7 (1971) 26, p. 30–41.

Ferraz, Susana, Espaço público de Luanda. Património arquitectónico colonial angolano e português. Masters dissertation, University of Porto, Porto, 2005.

Ferreira, Eugénio, Feiras e presídios. Ensaio de interpetação materialista da colonização de Angola. Luanda, 1958.

Ferreira, Roquinaldo, Dinâmica do comércio intracolonial. Geribitas, panos asiáticos e guerra no tráfico angolano de escravos (século XVIII), in: João Luís Ribeiro Fragoso, Maria Fernanda Bicalho and Maria de Fátima Gouvêa (eds.), O Antigo Regime nos trópicos. A dinámica imperial portuguesa (séculos XVI–XVIII). Rio de Janeiro, 2001, p. 341–378.

Ferreira, Roquinaldo, Cross-Cultural Exchange in the Atlantic World. Angola and Brazil during the Era of the Slave Trade. Cambridge, 2012.

Ferreira, Roquinaldo, Slavery and the Social and Cultural Landscapes of Luanda, in: Jorge Cañizares-Esguerra, Matt D. Childs and James Sidbury (eds.), The Black Urban Atlantic in the Age of the Slave Trade. Philadelphia, 2013, p. 185–206.

Figueiredo, Cecília Maria Fontes, Os esmoleiros do rei. A bula da Santa Cruzada e seus oficiais na Capitania de Minas Gerais (1748–1828). PhD dissertation, Universidade Federal Fluminense, Niterói, 2014.

Figueiredo, Estrela and Gideon F. Smith, Joaquim José da Silva (c. 1755–1810). His Life, Natural History Collecting Activities, and Involvement in the So-Called First Scientific Expedition in the Interior of Angola, in: Candollea 76 (2021) 1, p. 125–138.

Figueiredo, João, Feitiçaria na Angola oitocentista. Razões por detrás de uma suposta maior tolerância administrativa face a crenças locais, in: Mneme—Revista de Humanidades 12 (2011) 29, p. 21–51.

FIGUEIREDO, João, A Questão das "ouvidas," ou a disputa entre autoridades civis e militares pelo julgamento de "causas gentílicas" na Angola de meados do século XIX, in: Cadernos de Estudos Africanos (2015) 30, p. 81–104.

FIGUEIREDO, João, Política, Escravatura e Feitiçaria em Angola (séculos XVIII e XIX). PhD dissertation, University of Coimbra, Coimbra, 2015.

FIGUEIREDO, João, Falling into History. A Case for the Restitution of Mbali Tombstones and the Revival of the Realms of Memory of the Enslaved, in: Postcolonial Studies (2022), p. 1–21.

FISHER, Mark, Ghosts of my Life. Writings on Depression, Hauntology and Lost Futures. Winchester, 2014.

FLIGHT, Colin, Malcolm Guthrie and the Reconstruction of Bantu Prehistory, in: History in Africa 7 (1980), p. 81–118.

FONSECA, Jorge, Religião e Liberdade. Os Negros nas irmandades e confrarias portuguesas (séculos XV a XIX). V. N. Famalicão, 2016.

FORD, Lisa, Sovereignty. Jurisdiction and Indigenous People in America and Australia (1788–1836). Cambridge, 2010.

FOUCAULT, Michel, Power/Knowledge. Selected Interviews and Other Writings (1972–1977). New York, [1972] 1980.

FOUCAULT, Michel, The Birth of Biopolitics. Lectures at the Collège de France (1978–1979). New York, 2008.

FOURCADE, Marion, Cents and Sensibility. Economic Values and the Nature of 'Nature,' in: American Journal of Sociology (2011) 116, p. 1721–1777.

FRAGOSO, Hugo, Na Bahia setecentista, um pioneiro do abolicionismo? in: Revista História 31 (2012) 2, p. 68–105.

FRAGOSO, João Luís Ribeiro, Homens de grossa aventura. Acumulação e hierarquia na praça mercantil do Rio de Janeiro (1790–1830). Rio de Janeiro, 1998.

FRAGOSO, João Luís Ribeiro and Manolo FLORENTINO, O arcaísmo como projeto. Mercado atlântico, sociedade agrária e elite mercantil no Rio de Janeiro (c. 1790 –c. 1840). Rio de Janeiro, 1998.

FREITAS, Judite Antonieta Golçalves de, A burocracia do "eloquente" (1433–1438). Os textos, as normas, as gentes. Cascais, 1996.

FREUDENTHAL, Aida G. N. Faria, Arimos e fazendas. A transição agrária em Angola (1850–1875). Masters dissertation, Nova University of Lisbon, Lisbon, 1989.

FREUDENTHAL, Aida G. N. Faria, Sobas, conquistadores e peças d'Índias (1619–1630), in: Selma PANTOJA and Andrew S. THOMPSON (eds.), Em torno de Angola. Narrativas, identidades e as conexões atlânticas. São Paulo, 2014, p. 69–86.

FREYRE, Gilberto, The Masters and the Slaves. A Study in the Development of Brazilian Civilization. Berkeley, 1986 [1933].

FROMONT, Cécile, Collecting and Translating Knowledge Across Cultures. Capuchin Missionary Images of Early Modern Central Africa, in: Daniela BLEICHMAR and Peter C.

MANCALL (eds.), Collecting Across Cultures. Material Exchanges in the Early Modern Atlantic World. Philadelphia, 2011, p. 134–154.

FROMONT, Cécile, Under the Sign of the Cross in the Kingdom of Kongo. Religious Conversion and Visual Correlation in Early Modern Central Africa, in: RES: Anthropology and Aesthetics (2011) 59/60, p. 109–123.

FROMONT, Cécile, The Art of Conversion. Christian Visual Culture in the Kingdom of Kongo. Chapel Hill, 2014.

FROMONT, Cécile, Common Threads. Cloth, Colour, and the Slave Trade in Early Modern Kongo and Angola, in: Art History 41 (2018) 5, p. 838–867.

FROMONT, Cécile, Nature, Culture, and Faith in Seventeenth-Century Kongo and Angola, in: MAVCOR Journal 6 (2023) 1.

FURTADO, Júnia Ferreira, Evolving Ideas. J. B. d'Anville's Maps of Southern Africa, 1725–1749, in : Imago Mundi, 69 (2017) 2, p. 202–215.

GABRIEL, Manuel Nunes, Padrões da fé. Igrejas antigas de Angola. Luanda, 1981.

GABRIEL, Manuel Nunes, Os Jesuítas na primeira evangelização de Angola. Lisbon, 1993.

GALDINHO DE PAIVA, Yamê, Justiça e poder na América Portuguesa. Ouvidores e a administração da justiça na Comarca da Paraíba (c. 1687 –c. 1799). PhD. dissertation, Nova University of Lisbon, Lisbon, 2020.

GARCIA, Luís Pinto, Descrição das moedas de Angola e São Tomé e Príncipe, in: Nummus 7 (1965) 3, p. 179–215.

GARNSEY, Peter, Ideas of Slavery from Aristotle to Augustine. Cambridge, 1996.

GAY, Peter, The Enlightenment. An Interpretation. The Science of Freedom, Vol. 2. New York, 1966–69.

GEERTZ, Clifford, Agricultural Involution. The Process of Ecological Change in Indonesia. Berkeley, 1963.

GELFAND, Michael, The African Witch. With Particular Reference to Witchcraft Beliefs and Practice among the Shona of Rhodesia Edinburgh, 1967.

GEROULANOS, Stefanos, The Invention of Prehistory. Empire, Violence, and Our Obsession with Human Origins. New York, 2024.

GESCHIERE, Peter, Kinship, Witchcraft and "the Market." Hybrid Patterns in Cameroonian Societies, in: R. DILLEY (ed.), Contesting Markets. Analyses of Ideology, Discourse and Practice. Edinburg, 1992, p. 159–179.

GESCHIERE, Peter, Responsibility versus Responsibilization. Mafiacraft, Witchcraft and the Rise of Conspiracy Thinking Today, in: Melissa DENIAN, Mattia FUMANTI and Christos LYNTERIS (eds.), Anthropology and Responsibility. London, 2023,

GESCHIERE, Peter, Sorcellerie et politique en Afrique. La Viande des autres. Paris, 1995.

GESCHIERE, Peter, Sorcery and the State. Popular Modes of Action Among the Maka of Southeast Cameroon, in: Critique of Anthropology 8 (1988) 1, p. 35–63.

GESCHIERE, Peter, The (Ir)Responsible Witch. Ambiguities among the Maka of Southeast Cameroon, in: Benjamin RUBBERS and Alessandro JEDLOWSKI (eds.), Regimes of Responsibility in Africa. Genealogies, Rationalities and Conflicts. New York, 2020, p. 180–198.

GESCHIERE, Peter, The Modernity of Witchcraft. Politics and the Occult in Postcolonial Africa. Charlottesville 1997.

GESCHIERE, Peter, Witchcraft and Modernity. Perspectives from Africa and Beyond, in: Nicolau PARÉS and Roger SANSI-ROCA (eds.), Sorcery in the Black Atlantic. Chicago, 2011, p. 233–258.

GESCHIERE, Peter, Witchcraft as the Dark Side of Kinship. Dilemmas of Social Security in New Contexts, in: Etnofoor 16 (2003) 1, p. 43–61.

GESCHIERE, Peter, Witchcraft, Intimacy, and Trust. Africa in Comparison. Chicago, 2013.

GESCHIERE, Peter and Cyprian F. FISIY, Witchcraft, Development and Paranoia in Cameroon. Interactions Between Popular, Academic and State Discourse, in: Henrietta L. MOORE and Todd SANDERS (eds.), Magical Interpretations, Material Realities. Modernity, witchcraft and the occult in postcolonial Africa. London, 2001,

GESCHIERE, Peter, Birgit MEYER and Peter PELS, Introduction, in: Peter GESCHIERE, Birgit MEYER and Peter PELS (eds.), Readings in Modernity in Africa. Oxford, 2008, p. 1–7

GLASSMAN, Jonathon, Ethnicity and Race in African Thought, in: William H. WORGER (ed.), A Companion to African History. New York, 2019, p. 199–223.

GOODY, Jack, Technology, Tradition, and the State in Africa. Cambridge, 1971.

GOODY, Jack, The Development of the Family and Marriage in Europe. Cambridge, 1983.

GORJÃO-HENRIQUES, Miguel, José de Seabra da Silva e a sua família. Iconografia e mobilidade social no antigo regime, in: Direito e Justiça 2 (2013), p. 75–155.

GOUVÊA, Maria de Fátima Silva, Conexões imperiais. Oficiais régios no Brasil e Angola (c. 1680–1730), in: Maria Fernanda BICALHO and Vera Lúcia Amaral FERLINI (eds.), Modos de governar. Ideias e práticas políticas no Império Português (séculos XVI a XIX). São Paulo, 2005, p. 179–198.

GOUVEIA, Jaime Ricardo Teixeira, The Creation of a Portuguese Diocese in the Kingdoms of Kongo and Angola in 1596. Imperial Strategies and Religious Implications, in: Hispania Sacra 74 (2022) 150, p. 495–509.

GRAEBER, David, Towards an Anthropological Theory of Value. The False Coin of Our Dreams. New York, 2001.

GRAEBER, David, Debt. The First 5,000 Years. New York, 2011.

GREEN, Toby, Inquisition. The Reign of Fear. London, 2008.

GREEN, Maia, Priests, Witches and Power. Popular Christianity after Mission in Southern Tanzania. Manchester, 2003.

GREEN, Toby, Baculamento or Encomienda? Legal Pluralisms and the Contestation of Power in the Pan-Atlantic World of the Sixteenth and Seventeenth Centuries, in: Journal of Global Slavery (2017) 2, p. 310–336.

GREEN, Toby, A Fistful of Shells. West Africa from the Rise of the Slave Trade to the Age of Revolution. Chicago, 2019.

GREEN, Toby, Philip J. HAVIK, and Fernanda RIBEIRO DA SILVA (eds.), African Voices from the Inquisition. The Trial of Crispina Peres of Cacheu, Guinea-Bissau (1646–1668). 2021.

GREENBERG, Jessica and Sarah MUIR, Disappointment, in: Annual Review of Anthropology 51 (2022), p. 307–323.

GREGORY, Christopher A., Cowries and Conquest. Towards a Subalternate Quality Theory of Money, in: Comparative Studies in Society and History 38 (1996) 2, p. 195–217.

GREGORY, Christopher A., Savage Money. The Anthropology and Politics of Commodity Exchange. London, 1997.

GREGORY, Christopher A., Gifts and Commodities Chicago, 2015.

GREGORY, Christopher A., Savage Money. The Anthropology and Politics of Commodity Exchange. London, 1997.

GROSSI, Paolo, El orden jurídico medieval. Madrid, 1995.

GUARDA, Maria Inês, Angolan Slave Trade in the Early 18th Century. The Atlantic Networks of Rodrigo da Costa de Almeida, in: Amélia POLÓNIA and Cátia ANTUNES (eds.), Mechanisms of Global Empire Building. Porto, 2020, p. 59–76.

GUIMARÃES SÁ, Isabel dos and Lisbeth RODRIGUES, Introduction, in: Isabel dos GUIMARÃES SÁ and Lisbeth RODRIGUES (eds.), The Confraternities of Misericórdia and the Portuguese Diasporas in the Early Modern Period. Leiden, 2023, p. 1–18.

GUTHRIE, Malcolm, Comparative Bantu. An Introduction to the Comparative Linguistics and Prehistory of the Bantu Languages. Farnborough, 1967–1971.

GUYER, Jane I., Wealth in People and Self-Realization in Equatorial Africa, in: Man 28 (1993) 2, p. 243–265.

GUYER, Jane I., Wealth in People, Wealth in Things—Introduction, in: Journal of African History 36 (1995) 1, p. 83–90.

GUYER, Jane I. and Samuel M. Eno BELINGA, Wealth in People as Wealth in Knowledge. Accumulation and Composition in Equatorial Africa, in: The Journal of African History 36 (1995) 1, p. 91–120.

HAIR, P. E. H., Portuguese Documents on Africa and Some Problems of Translation, in: History in Africa 27 (2000), p. 91–97.

HALBERSTAM, Judith, The Queer Art of Failure. Durham, 2011.

HANNULA, Henri, Airton RIBEIRO, Gustavo ZATELLI, Heikki PIHLAJAMÄKI, Comparing Early Modern Colonial Laws. Police Regulation Overseas, in: The Journal for Digital Legal History 2 (2024) 1, p. 1–16.

HARMS, Robert W., River of Wealth, River of Sorrow. New Haven, 1981.

HART, Herbert Lionel Adolphus, The Concept of Law. Oxford, 1976.

HARTOG, François, Chronos. The West Confronts Time. New York, 2022.

HARTOG, François, Regimes of Historicity. Presentism and Experiences of Time. New York, 2015.

HARVEY, John Whitney, Politics, Commerce, and Colonization in Angola at the Turn of the Eighteenth Century. Masters dissertation, Nova University of Lisbon, Lisbon, 2012.

HAVIK, Philip J., Women and Trade in the Guinea Bissau Region. The Role of African and Luso-African Women in Trade Networks from the Early 16th to the Mid 19th Century, in: Studia (1994) 52, p. 83–120.

Havik, Philip J., La Sorcellerie, l'acculturation et le genre. La Persécution religieuse de l'Inquisition portugaise contre les femmes africaines converties en Haut Guinée (XVIIe siècle), in: Revista Lusófona de Ciência das Religiões 3 (2004) 5–6, p. 99–116.

Havik, Philip J., Walking the Tightrope. Female Agency, Religious Practice, and the Portuguese Inquisition on the Upper Guinea Coast (Seventeenth Century), in: Caroline A. Williams (ed.), Bridging the Early Modern Atlantic World. People, Products, and Practices on the Move. Farnham, 2009, p. 173–192.

Heintze, Beatrix, Der Portugiesisch-Afrikanische Vasallenvertrag in Angola Im 17. Jahrhundert, in: Paideuma: Mitteilungen zur Kulturkunde 25 (1979), p. 195–223.

Heintze, Beatrix, Luso-African Feudalism in Angola? The Vassal Treaties of the 16th to the 18th Century, in: Revista Portuguesa de História 18 (1980), p. 111–131.

Heintze, Beatrix, Fontes para a História de Angola no século XVII. Memórias, relações e outros manuscritos da colectânea documental de Fernão de Sousa (1622–1635), Vol. 1. Stuttgart, 1985.

Heintze, Beatrix, António de Oliveira de Cadornega e a sua "História geral das guerras angolanas." Um historiador e etnógrafo do sec. XVII, natural de Vila Viçosa, in: Callipole (1995/1996) 3/4, p. 75–86.

Heintze, Beatrix, Pioneiros africanos. Caravanas de carregadores na África Centro-Ocidental (1850–1890). Lisbon, 2004.

Heintze, Beatrix, A lusofonia no interior da África Central na era pré-colonial. Um contributo para a sua história e compreensão na actualidade, in: Cadernos de Estudos Africanos (2005) 6–7, p. 179–207.

Heintze, Beatrix, Contra as teorias simplificadoras. O 'Canibalismo' na Antropologia e História de Angola, in: Manuela Ribeiro Sanches (ed.), Portugal não é um país pequeno. Contar o "Império" na pós-colonidade. Lisbon, 2006, p. 215–228.

Heintze, Beatrix, The Extraordinary Journey of the Jaga through the Centuries. Critical Approaches to Precolonial Angolan Historical Sources, in: History in Africa 34 (2007), p. 67–101.

Heintze, Beatrix, Exploradores alemães em Angola (1611–1954). Apropriações etnográficas entre comércio de escravos, colonialismo e ciência. Frankfurt am Main, 2010.

Heintze, Beatrix, Translocal 'Kinship' Relations in Central African Politics of the 19th Century, in: Ulrike Freitag; and Achim. Von Oppen (eds.), Translocality. The Study of Globalising Processes from a Southern Perspective. 2010, p. 179–204.

Henrique, Sónia Pereira, O acesso ao arquivo colonial português na segunda metade do século XIX. O Boletim e Annaes do Conselho Ultramarino, in: Boletim do Arquivo da Universidade de Coimbra 32 (2019) 1, p. 111–147.

Henriques, Isabel Castro, A invenção da antropofagia africana, Actas dos VI Cursos Internacionais de Verão de Cascais (1999). Cascais, 2000, p. 51–80.

Henriques, Isabel Castro, Njinga a Mbande e Aimé Césaire. Independência e universalidade. Luanda, 2013.

HERBERT, Eugenia W., Red Gold of Africa. Copper in Precolonial History and Culture. Madison, 1984.

HERZOG, Tamar, A Short History of European Law The Last Two and a Half Millennia. Cambridge, MA, 2018.

HERZOG, Tamar, António Manuel Hespanha according to Tamar Herzog, in: Práticas da História (2019) 9, p. 133–138.

HERZOG, Tamar, Colonial Law. Early Modern Normativity in Spanish America, in: Jörg Alejandro TELLKAMP (ed.), A Companion to Early Modern Spanish Imperial Political and Social Thought. Leiden, 2020, p. 105–127.

HERZOG, Tamar, The Uses and Abuses of Legal Pluralism. A View from the Sideline, in: Law and History Review (2023), p. 1–12.

HERZOG, Tamar, What is Legal History and How Does it Relate to Other Histories, in: Thomas DUVE and Tamar HERZOG (eds.), Latin America Law in Global Perspective. Cambridge, 2024, p. 39–53.

HESPANHA, António Manuel, História das instituições. Epocas medieval e moderna. Coimbra, 1982.

HESPANHA, António Manuel, Sábios e rústicos. A violência doce da razão jurídica, in: Revista Crítica de Ciências Sociais (1988) 25–26, p. 31–60.

HESPANHA, António Manuel, As vésperas do Leviathan. Instituições e poder político. Portugal, séc. XVII. Coimbra, 1994.

HESPANHA, António Manuel, A constituição do Império Português. Revisão de alguns enviesamentos correntes, in: João Luís Ribeiro FRAGOSO, Maria Fernanda BICALHO and Maria de Fátima GOUVÊA (eds.), O Antigo Regime nos trópicos. A dinámica imperial portuguesa (séculos XVI–XVIII). Rio de Janeiro, 2001, p. 163–188.

HESPANHA, António Manuel, Luís de Molina e a escravização dos negros, in: Análise Social 35 (2001) 157, p. 937–960.

HESPANHA, António Manuel, As fronteiras do poder. O mundo dos rústicos, in: Seqüência (2005) 51, p. 47–105.

HESPANHA, António Manuel, Governo, elites e competência social. Sugestões para um entendimento renovado da história das elites, in: Maria Fernanda BICALHO and Vera Lúcia Amaral FERLINI (eds.), Modos de governar. Ideias e práticas políticas no Império Português (séculos XVI a XIX). São Paulo, 2005, p. 39–44.

HESPANHA, António Manuel, Direito comum e direito colonial, in: Panóptica (2006) 3, p. 95–116.

HESPANHA, António Manuel, A Note on Two Recent Books on the Patterns of Portuguese Politics In the 18th Century, in: e-Journal of Portuguese History 5 (2007) 2, p. 1–9.

HESPANHA, António Manuel, Depois do Leviathan, in: Almanack Braziliense (2007) 5, p. 55–66.

HESPANHA, António Manuel, A política perdida. Ordem e governo antes da modernidade. Curitiba, 2010.

HESPANHA, António Manuel, Imbecillitas. As bem-aventuranças da inferioridade nas sociedades de Antigo Regime. São Paulo, 2010.

HESPANHA, António Manuel, Entrevista a António Manuel Hespanha por Pedro Cardim, in: Análise Social 46 (2011) 200, p. 430–445.

HESPANHA, António Manuel, A cultura jurídica europeia. Uma síntese do milénio. Coimbra, 2012.

HESPANHA, António Manuel, Caleidoscópio do Antigo Regime. São Paulo, 2012.

HESPANHA, António Manuel, Uncommon Laws. Law in the Extreme Peripheries of an Early Modern Empire, in: Zeitschrift der Savigny-Stiftung für Rechtsgeschichte: Germanistische Abteilung 130 (2013) 1, p. 180–204.

HESPANHA, António Manuel, Como os juristas viam o mundo (1550–1750). Direitos, estados, coisas, contratos, ações e crimes. Lisbon, 2015.

HESPANHA, António Manuel, Fazer um império com palavras, in: Ângela Barreto XAVIER and Cristina Nogueira da SILVA (eds.), O Governo dos outros. Poder e diferença no Império Português. Lisbon, 2016, p. 67–100.

HESPANHA, António Manuel, Filhos da terra. Identidades mestiças nos confins da expansão portuguesa. Lisbon, 2019.

HESPANHA, António Manuel, Thirty Years of Studies on Prosopography of Portuguese Early Modern Jurists, in: Rechtsgeschichte—Legal History 27 (2019), p. 22–50.

HESPANHA, António Manuel, L'Administration d'une «ombre d'empire». L'organisation des «Portugais» en Afrique et en Asie, in: Godicheau FRANÇOIS and Mathieu GRENET (eds.), Raison administrative et logiques d'empire (XVIe–XIXe Siècle). Rome, 2021, p. 291–335.

HESPANHA, António Manuel and Catarina Madeira SANTOS, Os poderes num império oceânico, in: António Manuel HESPANHA and Catarina Madeira SANTOS (eds.), História de Portugal. Lisbon, 1998, p. 351–366.

HEYWOOD, Linda M., Portuguese into African. The Eighteenth-Century Central African Background to Atlantic Creole Cultures in: Linda M. HEYWOOD (ed.), Central Africans and Cultural Transformations in the American Diaspora. Cambridge, 2002, p. 91–116.

HEYWOOD, Linda M. (ed.) Diáspora Negra no Brasil. São Paulo, 2008.

HEYWOOD, Linda M., Slavery and Its Transformation in the Kingdom of Kongo (1491–1800), in: The Journal of African History 50 (2009) 1, p. 1–22.

HEYWOOD, Linda M. and John K. THORNTON, African Fiscal Systems as Sources for Demographic History. The Case of Central Angola (1799–1920), in: Journal of African History 29 (1988) 2, p. 213–228.

HEYWOOD, Linda M. and John K. THORNTON, Central Africans, Atlantic Creoles, and the Foundation of the Americas (1585–1660). Cambridge, 2007.

HILL, Benjamin and Henril LAGERLUND (eds.), The Philosophy of Francisco Suárez. Oxford, 2012.

HILTON, Anne, The Jaga Reconsidered, in: The Journal of African History 22 (1981) 2, p. 191–202.

HILTON, Anne, The Kingdom of Kongo. Oxford, 1985.

Ho, H. L., The Legitimacy of Medieval Proof, in: Journal of Law and Religion 19 (2004) 2, p. 259–298.

Hochstrasser, T. J. and P. Schröder (eds.), Early Modern Natural Law Theories. Contexts and Strategies in the Early Enlightenment. 2003.

Hogendorn, Jan and Marion Johnson, The Shell Money of the Slave Trade. Cambridge, 1986.

Honwana, Alcinda Manuel, Espíritos vivos, tradições modernas. Possessão de espíritos e reintegração social pós-guerra no Sul de Moçambique. Lisbon, 2003.

Hoover, J. Jeffrey, The Seduction of Ruwej. Reconstructing Ruund History (The Nuclear Lunda, Zaire, Angola, Zambia). PhD dissertation, Yale University, New Haven, 1978.

Höpfl, Harro and Martyn P. Thompson, The History of Contract as a Motif in Political Thought, in: The American Historical Review 84 (1979) 4, p. 919–944.

Horta, José Augusto N. Silva, A inquisição em Angola e Congo. O inquérito de 1596–98 e o papel mediador das justiças locais, in the proceeding of: Arqueologia do estado. Primeiras jornadas sobre formas de organização e exercício dos poderes na Europa do Sul, séculos XIII–XVIII, Vol. I. Lisbon, 1988, p. 387–415.

Horta, José Augusto N. Silva, Africanos e portugueses na documentação inquisitorial de Luanda e Mbanza Kongo (1596–1598), in the proceeding of: Seminário Encontro de Povos e Culturas em Angola. Lisbon, 1997, p. 301–321.

Hudson, Michael, Foreword, in: Schurtz, Heinrich, An Outline of the Origins of Money. Chicago, 2004, p. xv–xxviii.

Hufendiek, Rebekka, Emotions, Habits, and Skills. Action-Oriented Bodily Responses and Social Affordances, in: Fausto Caruana and Italo Testa (eds.), Habits. Pragmatist Approaches from Cognitive Science, Neuroscience, and Social Theory. Cambridge, 2020, p. 100–119.

Innes, Joanna and John Styles, The Crime Wave. Recent Writing on Crime and Criminal Justice in Eighteenth-Century England, in: Journal of British Studies 25 (1986) 4, p. 380–435.

Ipsen, Pernille, Daughters of the Trade. Atlantic Slavers and Interracial Marriage on the Gold Coast. Philadelphia, 2015.

Irigoin, Alejandra and Regina Grafe, Bargaining for Absolutism. A Spanish Path to Nation-State and Empire Building, in: Hispanic American Historical Review 88 (2008) 2, p. 173–209.

Ismard, Paulin, Benedetta Rossi, and Cécile Vidal (eds.), Les Mondes de l'esclavage. Une histoire comparée. Paris, 2021.

Janzen, John M., Lemba (1650–1930). A Drum of Affliction in Africa and the New World. New York, 1982.

Johnson, Marion, Cloth as Money. The Cloth Strip Currencies of Africa, in: Textile History 11 (1980) 1, p. 193–202.

Johnson, Marion, Cotton Imperialism in West Africa, in: African Affairs 73 (1974) 291, p. 178–187.

JUNIOR, Nelson de Campos Ramos, Mediador das luzes. Concepções de progresso e ciência em António Nunes Ribeiro Sanches (1699–1783). Masters dissertation, University of São Paulo, São Paulo, 2013.

KANANOJA, Kalle, Healers, Idolaters, and Good Christians. A Case Study of Creolization and Popular Religion in Mid-Eighteenth Century Angola, in: The International Journal of African Historical Studies 43 (2010) 3, p. 443–465.

KANANOJA, Kalle, Central African Identities and Religiosity in Colonial Minas Gerais. PhD dissertation, Åbo Akademi University, Turku, 2012.

KANANOJA, Kalle, Pai Caetano Angola. Afro-Brazilian Magico-Religious Practices, and Cultural Resistance in Minas Gerais in the Late Eighteenth Century, in: Journal of African Diaspora Archaeology and Heritage 2 (2013), p. 18–37.

KANANOJA, Kalle, Healing Knowledge in Atlantic Africa: Medical Encounters (1500–1850). Cambridge, 2021.

KARPIK, Lucien, Valuing the Unique. The Economics of Singularities. Princeton, 2010.

KAUFMANN, Matthias, Slavery between Law, Morality, and Economy, in: Matthias KAUFMANN and Alexander AICHELE (eds.), A Companion to Luis de Molina. Leiden, 2014, p. 183–226.

KAUFMANN, Matthias and Alexander AICHELE (eds.), A Companion to Luis de Molina. Leiden, 2014.

KERR, Margaret H., Richard D. FORSYTH, Michael J. PLYLEY, Cold Water and Hot Iron. Trial by Ordeal in England, in: The Journal of Interdisciplinary History 22 (1992) 4, p. 573–595.

KLEIN, Herbert, The Atlantic Slave Trade to 1650, in: Stuart B. SCHWARTZ (ed.), Tropical Babylons. Sugar and the Making of the Atlantic World (1450–1680). Chapel Hill, 2004, p. 201–236.

KODESH, Neil, Beyond the Royal Gaze. Clanship and Public Healing in Buganda. Charlottesville, 2010.

KOPYTOFF, Igor, Introduction, in: Igor KOPYTOFF (ED.), The African Frontier. The Reproduction of Traditional African Societies. Bloomington, 1987, p. 3–86.

KOSKENNIEMI, Martti, Vitoria and Us. Thoughts on Critical Histories of International Law, in: Rechtsgeschichte—Legal History 22 (2014), p. 119–138.

KURY, Lorelai, Homens de ciência no Brasil. Impérios coloniais e circulação de informações (1780–1810), in: História, Ciências, Saúde—Manguinhos 11 (2004), p. 109–129.

LAVIÑA, Javier and Michael ZEUSKE (eds.), The Second Slavery. Mass Slaveries and Modernity in the Americas and in the Atlantic Basin. Zürich, 2014.

LEESON, Peter T., Trial by Battle, in: Journal of Legal Analysis 3 (2011) 1, p. 341–375.

LEESON, Peter T., Ordeals, in: The Journal of Law and Economics 55 (2012) 3, p. 691–714.

LEITÃO, José Augusto Duarte, A missão do P.e Baltasar Barreira no Reino de Angola (1580–1592), in: Lusitania Sacra, 2 (1993) 5, p. 43–91.

LEVI, Joseph Abraham, Padre Giovanni Antonio Cavazzi, (1621–1678). Nos reinos do "Congo, Matamba e Angola." Primeiros contactos europeus com a África in: Estudos Portugueses e Africanos 33–34 (1999) 1–2, p. 29–47.

LÉVI-STRAUSS, Claude, The Elementary Structures of Kinship. London, 1969 [1949].

LINNAEUS, Carl, The God-Given Order of Nature, in: Emmanuel Chuckwudi EZE (ED.), Race and the Enlightenment. A Reader. 1997 [1735], p. 10–14.

LOVEJOY, Paul E., Interregional Monetary Flows in the Precolonial Trade of Nigeria, in: The Journal of African History 15 (1974) 4, p. 563–585.

LOVEJOY, Paul E., Polanyi's "Ports of Trade." Salaga and Kano in the Nineteenth Century, in: Canadian Journal of African Studies 16 (1982) 2, p. 245–277.

LOVEJOY, Paul E., Transformations in Slavery. A History of Slavery in Africa. Cambridge, 2000 [1983].

LOVEJOY, Paul E., Pawnship, Debt, and 'Freedom' in Atlantic Africa During the Era of the Slave Trade. A Reassessment, in: The Journal of African History 55 (2014) 1, p. 55–78.

LUONGO, Katherine, If You Can't Beat Them, Join Them. Government Cleasings of Witches and Mau Mau in 1950s Kenya, in: History in Africa 33 (2006), p. 451–571.

LUONGO, Katherine, Motive Rather than Means. Legal Genealogies of Witch-Killing Cases in Kenya, in: Cahiers d'Études Africaines 48 (2008) 189–190, p. 35–57.

LUONGO, Katherine, Witchcraft and Colonial Rule in Kenya (1900–1955). Cambridge, 2011.

MACEDO, José Rivair, Escrita e conversão na África Central do século XVII. O catecismo Kikongo de 1624, in: História Revista 18 (2014) 1.

MACEDO, José Rivair, Jagas, canibalismo e "guerra preta." Os Mbangalas, entre o mito europeu e as realidades sociais da África Central do século XVII, in: História (São Paulo) 32 (2013) 1, p. 53–78.

MACGAFFEY, Wyatt, Fetishism Revisited. Kongo "Nkisi" in Sociological Perspective, in: Africa: Journal of the International African Institute 47 (1977) 2, p. 172–184.

MACGAFFEY, Wyatt, Religion and Society in Central Africa. The BaKongo of Lower Zaire. Chicago, 1986.

MACGAFFEY, Wyatt, The Personhood of Ritual Objects. Kongo "Minkisi," in: Etnofoor 3 (1990) 1, p. 45–61.

MACGAFFEY, Wyatt, Dialogues of the Deaf. Europeans on the Atlantic Coast of Africa, in: Stuart B. SCHWARTZ (ED.), Implicit Understandings. Observing, Reporting, and Reflecting on the Encounters Between Europeans and Other Peoples in the Early Modern Era. Cambridge, 1994, p. 249–267.

MACGAFFEY, Wyatt, Aesthetics and Politics of Violence in Central Africa, in: Journal of African Cultural Studies 13 (2000) 1, p. 63–75.

MACGAFFEY, Wyatt, Kongo Political Culture. The Conceptual Challenge of the Particular. Bloomington, 2000.

MACGAFFEY, Wyatt, Astonishment and Stickiness in Kongo Art. A Theoretical Advance, in: RES: Anthropology and Aesthetics (2001) 39, p. 137–150.

MACGAFFEY, Wyatt, Twins, Simbi Spirits, and Lwas in Kongo and Haiti, in: Linda M. HEYWOOD (ed.), Central Africans and Cultural Transformations in the American Diaspora. Cambridge, 2002, p. 211–226.

MacGaffey, Wyatt, Crossing the River. Myth and Movement in Central Africa, in: Beatrix Heintze and Achim von Oppen (eds.), Angola on the Move. Transport Routes, Communications and History. Frankfurt am Main, 2008, p. 221–242.

MacGaffey, Wyatt, A Note on Vansina's Invention of Matrilinearity, in: The Journal of African History 54 (2013) 2, p. 269–280.

MacGaffey, Wyatt, Franchising Minkisi in Loango. Questions of Form and Function, in: RES: Anthropology and Aesthetics (2014/2015) 65/66, p. 148–157.

MacGaffey, Wyatt, Constructing a Kongo Identity. Scholarship and Mythopoesis, in: Comparative Studies in Society and History 58 (2016) 1, p. 159–180.

MacGaffey, Wyatt, A Central African Kingdom. Kongo in 1480, in: Koen Bostoen and Inge Brinkman (eds.), The Kongo Kingdom. The Origins, Dynamics and Cosmopolitan Culture of an African Polity. Cambridge, 2018, p. 42–59.

Madeira Santos, Maria Emília, Em busca dos sítios do poder na África Centro Ocidental. Homens e caminhos, exércitos e estradas (1483–1915), in: Beatrix Heintze and Achim. Von Oppen (eds.), Angola on the Move. Transport Routes, Communications and History. Frankfurt am Main, 2008, p. 26–34.

Maggie, Yvonne, Medo do Feitiço. Relações entre Magia e Poder no Brasil. Rio de Janeiro, 1992.

Mamdani, Mahmood, Citizen and Subject. Contemporary Africa and the Legacy of Late Colonialism. New Jersey, 1996.

Mamdani, Mahmood, Define and Rule. Native as Political Identity. Cambridge, MA, 2012.

Marcocci, Giuseppe, A consciência de um império. Portugal e o seu mundo (Sécs. XV -XVII). Coimbra, 2012.

Marcocci, Giuseppe and José Pedro Paiva, História da Inquisição Portuguesa (1536–1821). Lisboa, 2013.

Marcussi, Alexandre Almeida, Estratégias de mediação simbólica em um calundu colonial, in: Revista de História (2006) 155, p. 97–124.

Marcussi, Alexandre Almeida, Uma "caça às bruxas" centro-africana. Os juramentos do *bolungo* em Massangano (Angola) em 1717, in: Revista de História da UEG 11 (2022) 1, p. 1–27.

Margarido, Alfredo, Algumas formas da hegemonia Africana nas relações com os Europeus, in: Maria Emília Madeira Santos (ed.), I Reunião internacional de história de África. Relação Europa-África no 3º quartel do Século XIX. Lisbon, 1989, p. 383–406.

Marquese, Rafael de Bivar and Fábio Duarte Joly, Panis, Disciplina, et Opus Servo. The Jesuit Ideology in Portuguese America and Greco-Roman Ideas of Slavery, in: Enrico Dal Lago and Constantina Katsari (eds.), Slave Systems. Ancient and Modern. Cambridge, 2009, p. 214–230.

Marques-Guedes, Armando and Maria José Lopes (eds.), State and Traditional Law in Angola and Mozambique. Lisbon, 2007.

Martin, Phyllis, M., Power, Cloth and Currency on the Loango Coast, in: African Economic History (1986) 15, p. 1–12.

Martin, Phyllis, M., The Kingdom of Loango, in: Alisa LaGamma (ed.), Kongo. Power and Majesty. New Haven, 2015, p. 47–86.

Martino, Enrique and Schmidt, Mario, Introduction, in: Schurtz, Heinrich, An Outline of the Origins of Money. Chicago, 2004, p. 1–24.

Martins, Manuel Alfredo de Morais, Contacto de culturas no Congo Português. Achegas para o seu estudo. Lisbon, 1958.

Marwick, Max (ed.) Witchcraft and Sorcery. Selected Readings. London, 1970.

Marwick, Max, Postscript. The Decline fo Witch-Beliefs in Differentiated Societies, in: Max Marwick (ed.), Witchcraft and Sorcery. Selected Readings. London, 1970, p. 379–382.

Mary, Douglas (ed.) Witchcraft Confessions and Accusations. London, 1970.

Mary, Douglas, Introduction. Thirty Years after Witchcraft, Oracles and Magic, in: Mary, Douglas (ed.), Witchcraft Confessions and Accusations. London, 1970, p. i–xxxviii.

Matos, Paulo Pereira Oliveira, "Terras desertas e selvagens." A região ao Sul de Benguela no imaginário português (1750–1840). Masters dissertation, University of Lisbon, Lisbon, 2023.

Maurer, Bill, Primitive and Nonmetallic Money, in: Stefano Battilossi, Youssef Cassis and Kazuhiko Yago (eds.), Handbook of the History of Money and Currency. Singapore, 2018, p. 1–18.

Mauricio, Domingos, A Universidade de Évora e a escravatura, in: Didaskalia 7 (1977) 1, p. 153–200.

Mauss, Marcel, The Gift. Forms and Functions of Exchange in Archaic Societies. London, 1974 [1925].

Maxwell, Kenneth R., Pombal and the Nationalization of the Luso-Brazilian Economy , in: The Hispanic American Historical Review 48 (1968) 4, p. 608–631.

Maxwell, Kenneth, Pombal, Paradox of the Enlightenment. Cambridge, 1995.

Mbembe, Achille, Necropolitics. Durham, 2019.

McClintock, Anne, Imperial Leather. Race, Gender and Sexuality in the Colonial Contest. London, 1995.

McClymond, Kathryn T., Blood Libel. Ritual Misrepresentation, in: Kathryn T. McClymond (ed.), Ritual Gone Wrong. What We Learn from Ritual Disruption. Oxford, 2016, p. 65–105.

McManus, Stuart M., Martín de Azpilcueta on Trade and Slavery in Jesuit Legal Manuscripts from Iberian Asia, in: Manuela Bragagnolo (ed.), The Production of Knowledge of Normativity in the Age of the Printing Press. Leiden, 2024, p. 352–370.

McNally, David, Blood and Money. War, Slavery, Finance, and Empire. Chicago, 2020.

Meillassoux, Claude, Maidens, Meal, and Money. Capitalism and the Domestic Community. Cambridge, 1981.

Meillassoux, Claude, The Anthropology of Slavery. The Womb of Iron and Gold. Chicago, 1991.

Mello e Souza, Laura de, Desclassificados do ouro. A pobreza mineira do século XVIII. Rio de Janeiro, 1982.

Mello e Souza, Laura, O Diabo e a Terra de Santa Cruz. Feitiçaria e religiosidade popular no Brasil Colonial. Rio de Janeiro, 1986.

Mello e Souza, Laura de, A feitiçaria na Europa Moderna. São Paulo, 1987.

Mello e Souza, Laura de, Inferno Atlântico. Demonologia e colonização (século XVI–XVIII). São Paulo, 1993.

Mello e Souza, Marina, Alianças e embates entre religiões. Missões católicas em terras centro-africanas (século XVII) in: Jacqueline Hermann and William de Souza Martins (eds.), Poderes do sagrado. Europa católica, América ibérica, África e Oriente portugueses (séculos XVI–XVIII). Rio de Janeiro, 2016, p. 361–382.

Mello Pereira, Magnus Roberto de, A escravidão e o acesso à terra nas concepções de Luís Antônio de Oliveira Mendes (1792–1821), in: Afro-Ásia (2021) 63, p. 181–231.

Meneses, Maria Paula, Corpos de violência, linguagens de resistência. As complexas teias de conhecimentos no Moçambique contemporâneo, in: Revista Crítica de Ciências Sociais 80 (2008), p. 161–194.

Meneses, Maria Paula, Feitiçaria e modernidade em Moçambique. Questionando saberes, direitos e políticas. Coimbra, 2008.

Meneses, Maria Paula, Os saberes feiticeiros em Moçambique. Realidades materiais, experiências espirituais. Coimbra, 2019.

Menz, Maximiliano M., A Companhia de Pernambuco e Paraíba e o funcionamento do tráfico de escravos em Angola (1759–1775–80), in: Afro-Ásia (2013) 48, p. 45–76.

Menz, Maximiliano M., As "Geometrias" do tráfico. O comércio metropolitano e o tráfico de escravos em Angola (1796–1807), in: Revista de História (2012) 166, p. 185–222.

Menz, Maximiliano M. and Gustavo Acioli Lopes, A população do Reino de Angola durante a era do tráfico de escravos. Um exercício de estimativa e interpretação (c. 1700–1850), in: Revista de História (2018) 177, p. 1–35.

Merry, Sally Engle, Legal Pluralism, in: Law & Society Review 22 (1988) 5, p. 869–896.

Mesaki, Simeon, Witch-Killing in Sukumaland, in: R. G. Abrahams (ed.), Witchcraft in Contemporary Tanzania. Cambridge, 1994, p. 71–86.

Meyer, Birgit and Peter Pels (eds.), Magic and Modernity. Interfaces of Revelation and Concealment. Stanford, 2003.

Miers, Suzanne and Igor Kopytoff (eds.), Slavery in Africa. Historical and Anthropological Perspectives. Madison, 1977.

Miguel, Francisco Paolo Vieira, Séculos de silêncio. Contribuições de um antropólogo para uma história da "homossexualidade" no Sul de Moçambique (séc. XVI–XX), in: Revista Brasileira de História da Ciência 41 (2021) 86, p. 111–134.

Miguel, Gabriel de Souza, Que se abram os sertões. Um projecto político de centralização e *livre comércio* para o tráfico de cativos e a escravização em Angola (1753–1772). Masters dissertation, Universidade Federal Rural do Rio de Janeiro, Seropédica, 2021.

Miller, Jon, Spinoza and Natural Law, in: Jonathan A. Jacobs (ed.), Reason, Religion, and Natural Law. From Plato to Spinoza. Oxford, 2012, p. 201–221.

Miller, Joseph C., The Imbangala and the Chronology of Early Central African History, in: The Journal of African History 13 (1972) 4, p. 594–574.

Miller, Joseph C., Imbangala Lineage Slavery (Angola), in: Suzanne Miers and Igor Kopytoff (eds.), Slavery in Africa. Historical and Anthropological Perspectives. Madison 1977, p. 205–234.

Miller, Joseph C., Kings, Lists, and History in Kasanje, in: History in Africa 6 (1979), p. 51–96.

Miller, Joseph C., Capitalism and Slaving. The Financial and Commercial Organization of the Angolan Slave Trade, According to the Accounts of Antonio Coelho Guerreiro (1684–1692), in: The International Journal of African Historical Studies 17 (1984) 1, p. 1–56.

Miller, Joseph C., A Marginal Institution on the Margin of the Atlantic System. The Portuguese Southern Atlantic Slave Trade in the Eighteenth Century, in: Barbara L. Solow (ed.), Slavery and the Rise of the Atlantic System. Cambridge, 1991, p. 120–150.

Miller, Joseph C., Angola in the Sixteenth Century—Um mundo que o português encontrou, in: Alfred Hower and Richard A. Preto-Rodas (eds.), Empire in Transition. The Portuguese World in the Time of Camões. Gainesville, 2017 [1983],

Miller, Joseph C., Kings and Kinsmen. Early Mbundu States in Angola. Oxford, 1976.

Miller, Joseph C., Requiem for the "Jaga," in: Cahiers d'Études Africaines 13 (1973) 49, p. 121–149.

Miller, Joseph C., Thanatopsis, in: Cahiers d'Études Africaines 18 (1978) 69, p. 229–231.

Miller, Joseph C., The African Past Speaks. Essays on Oral Tradition and History. Hamden Conn. Folkstone, 1981.

Miller, Joseph C., The Confrontation on the Kwango. Kasanje and the Portuguese (1836–1858), in: Maria Emília Madeira Santos (ed.), I Reunião internacional de história de África. Relação Europa-África no 3° quartel do séc. XIX—Actas. Lisbon, 1989, p. 535–572.

Miller, Joseph C., The Significance of Drought, Disease and Famine in the Agriculturally Marginal Zones of West-Central Africa, in: Journal of African History 23 (1982) 1, p. 17–61.

Miller, Joseph C., Way of Death. Merchant Capitalism and the Angolan Slave Trade. Madison, 1988.

Miller, Joseph C., Worlds Apart. Africans' Encounters and Africa's Encounters with the Atlantic in Angola, before 1800, in: Maria Emília Madeira Santos (ed.), Actas do Seminário "Encontros de Povos e Culturas em Angola." Lisbon, 1997, p. 227–280.

Miller, Joseph C. and Dauril Alden, Out of Africa: The Slave Trade and the Transmission of Smallpox to Brazil (1560–1831), in: The Journal of Interdisciplinary History 18 (1987) 2, p. 195–224.

Miller, Joseph C. and John K. Thornton, The Chronicle as Source, History, and Hagiography. The "Catálogo dos Governadores de Angola," in: Paideuma: Mitteilungen zur Kulturkunde 33 (1987), p. 359–389.

MILLER, Joseph C. and John K. THORNTON, A Crónica como fonte, história e hagiografia. O catálogo dos governadores de Angola, in: Revista Internacional de Estudos Africanos (1990) 12–13, p. 9–55.

MILLS, Charles W., The Racial Contract. Ithaca, 1997.

MIRANDA, Ana, Musa Praguejadora. A vida de Gregório de Matos. Rio de Janeiro, 2014.

MKENDA, Festo, Jesuits in Africa. A Historical Narrative from Ignatius of Loyola to Pedro Arrupe. Leiden, 2022.

MONCADA, Luíz Cabral de, Um 'iluminista' português do século XVIII. Luíz António Verney. São Paulo, 1941.

MONTEIRO, John, Negros da terra. Índios e bandeirantes nas origens de São Paulo. São Paulo, 1994.

MONTEIRO, Luis Nuno Sardinha, A Pioneering Treatise on Naval Strategy. Fernando Oliveira's Art of Wat at Sea (1555), in: Naval War College Review 68 (2015) 4, p. 94–107.

MONTEIRO, Nuno Gonçalo, Governadores e capitães-mores do Império Atlântico Português no século XVIII, in: Maria Fernanda BICALHO and Vera Lúcia Amaral FERLINI (eds.), Modos de governar. Ideias e práticas políticas no Império Português (séculos XVI a XIX). São Paulo, 2005, p. 93–115.

MONTEIRO, Nuno Gonçalo, The Patterns of Portuguese Politics in the 18th Century or the Shadow of Pombal. A Reply to António Manuel Hespanha, in: e-Journal of Portuguese History 5 (2007) 2, p. 1–6.

MONTEIRO, Nuno Gonçalo, Pombal's Government. Between Seventeenth-Century Valido and Enlightened Models, in: Gabriel PAQUETTE (ed.), Enlightened Reform in Southern Europe and its Atlantic Colonies (c 1750–1830). Farnham, 2009, p. 321–338.

MONTEIRO, Ofélia Milheiro Caldas Paiva, D. Frei Alexandre da Sagrada Família. A sua espiritualidade e a sua poética. Coimbra, 1971.

MOORE, Henrietta L. and Todd SANDERS (eds.), Magical Interpretations, Material Realities. Modernity, Witchcraft and the Occult in Postcolonial Africa. London, 2001.

MOORE, Sally Falk, Law as Process. An Anthropological Approach. Hamburg, 2000 [1978].

MOORE, Sally Falk, Reflections on the Comaroff Lecture, in: American Ethnologist 26 (1999) 2, p. 304–306.

MORRIS, Colin, Judicium Dei. The Social and Political Significance of the Ordeal in the Eleventh Century. Cambridge, 2016.

MORTON, Adam, But are they Right? The Prospects for Empirical Conceptology, in: Journal of Cognition and Culture 6 (2006) 1, p. 159–163.

MOTT, Luiz, Escravidão, homossexualidade e demonologia. São Paulo, 1988.

MOTT, Luiz, Rosa Egipcíaca. Uma santa africana no Brasil. Rio de Janeiro, 1993.

MOTT, Luiz, O calundu-angola de Luzia Pinta. Sabará, 1739, in: Revista do IAC (1994) 1, p. 73–82.

MOTT, Luiz, Transgressão na calada da noite. Um sabá de feiticeiras e demônios no Piauí colonial, in: Textos de História 14 (2006) 1, p. 57–84.

MOTT, Luiz, Feiticeiros de Angola na América Portuguesa vítimas da Inquisição, in: Revista Pós Ciências Sociais 5 (2012) 9/10, p. 85–104.

MOUTINHO, Ermelinda, Coletar, preparar, remeter, transportar. Práticas de História Natural nas Viagens Filosóficas portuguesas (1777–1808), in: Revista Brasileira de História da Ciência 4 (2011) 2, p. 125–138.

MOUTINHO, Ermelinda, Terra, água e ar nas viagens científicas portuguesas (1755–1808), PhD dissertation, State University of Campinas, Campinas, 2006.

MUDIMBE, V. Y., The Idea of Africa. Bloomington, 1994.

MUDIMBE, Valentin., The Invention of Africa. Gnosis, Philosophy, and the Order of Knowledge. Bloomington 1988.

MULDOON, James, Popes, Lawyers, and Infidels. The Church and the Non-Christian World (1250–1550). Philadelphia, 2015.

MYRUP, Erik Lars, To Rule from Afar. The Overseas Council and the Making of the Brazilian West (1642–1807). PhD dissertation, Yale University, New Haven, 2006.

NAFAFÉ, José Lingna, Lourenço da Silva Mendonça and the Black Atlantic Abolitionist Movement in the Seventeenth Century. Cambridge, 2022.

NEVES, Marcelo, Ideas in Another Place? Liberal Constitution and the Codification of Private Law at the Turn of the 19th Century in Brazil, in: María Rosario POLOTTO, Thorsten KEISER and Thomas DUVE (eds.), Derecho privado y modernización. América Latina y Europa en la primera mitad del siglo XX. Frankfurt am Main, 2015, p. 47–81.

NEWSON, Linda A. and Susie MINCHIN, From Capture to Sale. The Portuguese Slave Trade to Spanish South America in the Early Seventeenth Century. Leiden, 2007.

NG, Kwai Hang and Xin HE, The Institutional and Cultural Logics of Legal Commensuration. Blood Money and Negotiated Justice in China, in: American Journal of Sociology 122 (2017) 4, p. 1104–1143.

NIEHAUS, Isak, Witch-Hunting and Political Legitimacy. Continuity and Change in Green Valley, Lebowa (1930–1991), in: Africa 63 (1993) 4, p. 498–529.

NIEHAUS, Isak, The ANC's Dilemma. The Symbolic Politics of Three Witch-Hunts in the South African Lowveld (1990–1995), in: African Studies Review 41 (1998) 3, p. 93–118.

NIEHAUS, Isak, Witchcraft in the New South Africa. From Colonial Superstitions to Postcolonial Reality? in: Henrietta L. MOORE and Todd SANDERS (eds.), Magical Interpretations, Material Realities. Modernity, Witchcraft and the Occult in Postcolonial Africa. London, 2001, p. 184–205.

NIEHAUS, Isak, Witchcraft, Power and Politics. London, 2001.

NIEHAUS, Isak, Witchcraft and a Life in the New South Africa. Cambridge, 2013.

NOGUEIRA DA SILVA, Cristina, O modelo espacial do estado moderno, Reorganização territorial em Portugal nos finais do Antigo Regime. Lisbon, 1998.

NOGUEIRA DA SILVA, Cristina, "Missão civilizacional" e codificação de "usos e costumes" na doutrina colonial portuguesa (séculos XIX–XX), in: Quaderni Fiorentini per la Storia del Pensiero Giuridico Moderno 33–34 (2004–05) 2, p. 899–921.

Nogueira da Silva, Cristina, A dimensão imperial do espaço jurídico português. Formas de imaginar a pluralidade nos espaços ultramarinos, séculos XIX e XX, in: Rechtsgeschichte—Legal History (2016) 23, p. 187–207.

Nogueira da Silva, Cristina, A construção jurídica dos territórios ultramarinos portugueses no século XIX. Modelos, doutrinas e leis. Lisbon, 2017.

Nogueira da Silva, Cristina, Ângela Barreto Xavier, Pedro Cardim (eds.), António Manuel Hespanha. Entre a História e o Direito. Coimbra, 2015.

Nogueira, André, Relações sociais e práticas mágicas na capitania do ouro. O caso do negro angola Pai Caetano (Vila Rica, 1791), in: Estudos Afro-Asiáticos (2005) 27, p. 181–203.

Nussbaum, Martha C., Plato on Commensurability and Desire, in: Proceedings of the Aristotelian Society, Supplementary Volumes 58 (1984), p. 55–96.

Oestmann, Peter, Legal Layers, Legal Spheres, Legal Systems. Legal Pluralism as a Problem in Legal History, in: EViR working papers (2023) 3, p. 1–51.

Ohata, Milton, Brazilian Civilization's Missing Link, in: Mediations 23 (2007) 1, p. 195–218.

Olival, Fernanda, As Ordens Militares na historiografia portuguesa (séculos XVI–XVIII). Notas de balanço, in: Penélope: Fazer e desfazer a história 17 (1997), p. 97–108.

Oliveira Marques, A. H. de, Daily Life in Portugal in the Late Middle Ages. Madison, 1971.

Oliveira, Ingrid Silva de, Textos militares e mercês numa Angola que se pretendia "reformada." Um estudo de caso dos autores Elias Alexandre da Silva Correa e Paulo Martins Pinheiro de Lacerda. PhD dissertation, Universidade Federal Fluminense, Niterói, 2015.

Oliveira, Vanessa S., Slave Trade and Abolition. Gender, Commerce, and Economic Transition in Luanda. Madison, 2021.

Olivier, Roland and Anthony Armore, Medieval Africa (1250–1800). Cambridge, 2001.

Osborn, Emily Lynn, Our New Husbands are Here. Households, Gender, and Politics in a West African State from the Slave Trade to Colonial Rule. Athens OH, 2011.

Osório de Castro, Zília, Arco-Íris liberal, in: Revista de História das Ideias 37 (2019) 2, p. 33–53.

Pacheco, Luís, Paulo Costa, Fernando Oliveira Tavares, História económico-social de Angola. Do período pré-colonial à independência, in: População e Sociedade 29 (2018), p. 82–98.

Paiva, José Pedro, Bruxaria e superstição num país sem caça às bruxas (1600–1774). Lisbon, 1997.

Paiva, José Pedro, Dioceses e organização eclesiástica, in: Carlos Moreira Azevedo (ed.), História Religiosa de Portugal. Lisbon, 2000, p. 187–199.

Paiva, José Pedro, Os bispos de Portugal e do Império (1495–1777). Coimbra, 2006.

Paiva, José Pedro, Pollyanna Gouveia Mendonça Muniz, Michelle Britto, A justiça infradiocesana no Império Português (c. 1514–1755). Raízes do modelo, normativas, ação e geografia da rede, in: Revista Portuguesa de História (2022) 53, p. 211–247.

Pallaver, Karin, Introduction. Money, Colonialism and African Societies, in: Karin Pallaver (ed.), Monetary Transitions. Currencies, Colonialism and African Societies. London, 2022, p. 1–30.

Palmeirim, Manuela, Do "Culture Heroes" Exist? A Dialogue With Luc de Heusch on the Limits of the Structuralist Approach to Myth, in: SAGE Open 6 (2016) 2, p. 1–9.

Palmer, Tyrone S., "What Feels More Than Feeling?" Theorizing the Unthinkability of Black Affect, in: Critical Ethnic Studies 3 (2017) 2, p. 31–56.

Palmer, Tyrone S., Otherwise than Blackness. Feeling, World, Sublimation, in: Qui Parle 29 (2020) 2, p. 246–283.

Palmer, Tyrone S., Affect and Affirmation, in: Gregory J. Seigworth and Carolyn Pedwell (eds.), The Affect Theory Reader, Vol. 2. Durham, 2023, p. 122–140.

Palomo, Federico, Ângela Barreto Xavier, and Roberta Stumpf (eds.), Monarquias ibéricas em perspectiva comparada (séculos XVI–XVIII). Dinâmicas imperiais e circulação de modelos político-administrativos. Lisbon, 2018.

Pantoja, Selma, A diáspora feminina. Degredadas para Angola no século XIX (1865–1898), in: Análise Social 34 (2000) 151/152, p. 555–572.

Pantoja, Selma, Inquisição, degredo e mestiçagem em Angola no século XVIII, in: Revista Lusófona de Ciência das Religiões 3 (2004) 5–6, p. 117–136.

Pantoja, Selma, Personagens entre mares atlânticos. Visões de Luanda setecentista, in: Revista de História Comparada 7 (2013) 1, p. 136–149.

Pantoja, Selma, Entre Luanda e Rio de Janeiro. O padre, o bispo e o coronel, in: Selma Pantoja and Andrew S. Thompson (eds.), Em torno de Angola. Narrativas, identidades e as conexões atlânticas. 2014, p. 87–110.

Parreira, Adriano, Dicionário glossográfico e toponímico da documentação sobre Angola (séculos XV–XVII). Lisbon, 1990.

Parreira, Adriano, Economia e sociedade em Angola na época da rainha Jinga século XVII. Lisbon, 1990.

Pateman, Carole, The Sexual Contract. Stanford, 1988.

Pateman, Carole and Charles W. Mills, Contract and Domination. Cambridge, 2007.

Pedroza, Manoela, Archaic Institutions and Economic Growth, in: Études rurales (2020) 205, p. 22–44.

Pels, Peter, The Magic of Africa. Reflection on a Western Commonplace, in: African Studies Review 41 (1998) 3, p. 193–209.

Pels, Peter and Oscar Salemink (eds.), Colonial Subjects. Essays on the Practical History of Anthropology. Ann Arbor, 1999.

Pels, Peter and Oscar Salemink, Introduction. Five Theses on Ethnography as Colonial Practice, in: History and Anthropology 8 (2010) 1–4, p. 1–34.

Pereira, Joana Dias and Rui Henriques, História do mutualismo nas ex-colónias portuguesas. Lisbon, 2022.

Pereira, Luena Nunes, Families, Churches, the State, and the Child Witch in Angola, in: Roger Sansi-Roca and Nicolau Parés (eds.), Sorcery in the Black Atlantic. Chicago, 2011, p. 187–208.

Peres, Fernando da Rocha, Gregório de Mattos e Guerra. Uma Re-Visão Biográfica. Salvador, 2017.

Peres, Fernando da Rocha, Negros e mulatos em Gregório Matos, in: Afro-Ásia (1967) 4–5, p. 59–75.

Pich, Roberto Hofmeister, Second Scholasticism and Black Slavery (Continuation and End), in: Veritas 65 (2019) 1, p. 1–13.

Pich, Roberto Hofmeister, Probabilismo e escravidão negra, in: Humanidades: Revista de la Unisersidad de Montevideo (2020) 8, p. 17–67.

Pich, Roberto Hofmeister, Alfredo Santiago Culleton, Alfredo Carlos Storck, Second Scholasticism and Black Slavery. Some Philosophical Assessments, in: Patristica et Mediaevalia (2015) 36, p. 3–15.

Piersen, William D., White Cannibals, Black Martyrs. Fear, Depression, and Religious Faith as Causes of Suicide among New Slaves, in: Journal of Negro History 62 (1977) 2, p. 147–159.

Pietz, William, Bosman's Guinea. The Intercultural Roots of an Enlightenment Discourse, in: Comparative Civilizations Review (1982) 11, p. 1–22.

Pietz, William, The Problem of the Fetish, I, in: RES: Anthropology and Aesthetics (1985) 9, p. 5–17.

Pietz, William, The Problem of the Fetish, II. The Origin of the Fetish, in: RES: Anthropology and Aesthetics (1987) 13, p. 23–45.

Pietz, William, The Problem of the Fetish, IIIa. Bosman's Guinea and the Enlightenment Theory of Fetishism, in: RES: Anthropology and Aesthetics (1988) 16, p. 105–124.

Pietz, William, The Problem of the Fetish. Chicago, 2022.

Pignot, Matthieu, The Catechumenate in Late Antique Africa (4th–6th Centuries). Augustine of Hippo, His Contemporaries and Early Reception. Leiden, 2020.

Pihlajamäki, Heikki, The Westernization of Police Regulation. Spanish and British Colonial Laws Compared, in: Heikki Pihlajamäki and Thomas Duve (eds.), New Horizons in Spanish Colonial Law. Contributions to Transnational Early Modern Legal History. Frankfurt am Main, 2015, p. 97–124.

Pimenta de Brito, Maria Madalena Carrusca, Fernão Pérez (1531?–1595?). Do domínio de um homem sobre outro homem. PhD dissertation, University of Lisbon, Lisbon, 2019.

Pinho da Cruz, Mário, João Paulo Sabino, and João Manuel Madrina, D. Miguel António de Melo de Abreu Soares de Brito Barbosa e Palha Vasconcelos Guedes, conde de Murça, in: Mário Pinho da Cruz (ed.), Dos Secretários de Estado dos Negócios da Fazenda aos Ministros das Finanças (1788–2006). Uma Iconografia. Lisbon, 2006, p. 143–144.

Pinto, Paulo Jorge de Sousa, Em torno de um problema de identidade. Os "Jaga" na História do Congo e Angola, in: Mare Liberum (1999–00) 18/19, p. 193–243.

Piot, Charles D., Of Persons and Things. Some Reflections on African Spheres of Exchange, in: Man 26 (1991) 3, p. 405–424.

Polanyi, Karl, The Great Transformation. The Political and Economic Origins of our Time. Boston 2001.

Porter, Jean, Nature as Reason: A Thomistic Theory of the Natural Law. Grand Rapids, 2005.

Postma, Johannes Menne, The Dutch in the Atlantic Slave Trade (1600–1815). Cambridge, 1990.

Precioso, Daniel, Catarina Juliana e sua sociedade de culto: rituais e práticas religiosas na Angola setecentista, in: Afro-Ásia (2021) 63, p. 68–127.

Puntoni, Pedro, Uma pax monetaria? Impasses do sistema monetário português no tempo dos Filipes (1580–1640), in: Topoi (Rio de Janeiro) 21 (2020) 43.

Radding, Charles M., Superstition to Science. Nature, Fortune, and the Passing of the Medieval Ordeal, in: The American Historical Review 84 (1979) 4, p. 945–969.

Rademakers, F. W., N. Nikis, T. De Putter, P. Degryse, Copper Production and Trade in the Niari Basin (Republic of Congo) during the 13th to 19th Centuries. ce: Chemical and Lead Isotope Characterization, in: Archaeometry 60 (2018) 6, p. 1251–1270.

Radulet, Carmen M., O Cronista Rui de Pina e a "Relaçao do Reino do Congo." Lisbon, 1992.

Raminelli, Ronald, Viagens ultramarinas. Monarcas, vassalos e governo à distância. São Paulo, 2008.

Randles, William Graham Lister, L'Ancien Royaume du Congo des origines à la fin du XIXe Siècle. Paris, 2013 [2002].

Ranger, Terence, Scotland Yard in the Bush. Medicine Murders, Child Witches and the Construction of the Occult. A Literature Review, in: Africa: Journal of the International African Institute 77 (2007) 2, p. 272–283.

Rau, Virgínia, A Casa dos Contos. Lisbon, 2009 [1951].

Rau, Virgínia, Prefácio, O "Livro de Rezão" de António Coelho Guerreiro. Dundo, 1956, p. 11–78.

Ray, Carina E., Crossing the Color Line. Race, Sex, and the Contested Politics of Colonialism in Ghana. Athens, OH, 2015.

Rebelo da Silva, José Alberto Teixeira, A Academia Real das Ciências de Lisboa (1779–1834). Ciências e hibridismo numa periferia europeia. PhD dissertation, University of Lisbon, Lisbon, 2015.

Rego, António da Silva, Portuguese Colonization in the Sixteenth Century. A Study of the Royal Ordinances (Regimentos). Johannesburg, 1965.

Reis, João José, Domingos Sodré, um sacerdote africano. Escravidão, liberdade e candomblé na Bahia do século XIX. São Paulo, 2008.

Ribeiro da Silva, Filipa, A Inquisição em África. Agentes, Acções, Informantes e Vítimas (1536–1821), in: Marco Antônio Nunes da Silva and Susana Bastos Mateus (eds.), As

Inquisições modernas. Poder político, religião e sociedade entre a Europa e o Atlântico. Salvador, 2020, p. 177–234.

Ribeiro da Silva, Filipa, A Inquisição em Cabo Verde, Guiné e S. Tomé e Príncipe (1536–1821). Contributo para o estudo da política do Santo Ofício nos territórios africanos. Masters dissertation, Nova University of Lisbon, Lisbon, 2002.

Ribeiro da Silva, Filipa, A Inquisição nas ilhas de Cabo Verde e São Tomé e Príncipe, in: Revista Lusófona de Ciência das Religiões 3 (2004) 5–6, p. 157–173.

Ribeiro da Silva, Filipa, A sustentação financeira do estado e da corte. Fiscalidade em Portugal nos finais do Antigo Regime, in: Norberta Amorim, Isabel Pinho and Carla Passos (eds.), IV Congresso histórico de Guimarães. Do absolutismo ao liberalismo. Guimarães, 2009, p. 585–623.

Ribeiro da Silva, Filipa, Dutch and Portuguese in Western Africa. Empires, Merchants and the Atlantic System (1580–1674). Leiden, 2011.

Rocha, Daiane de Oliveira, Administração e poder local. Uma análise do Terreiro Público de Luanda (Angola, século XVIII). BaHons dissertation, Universidade Federal Rural do Rio de Janeiro, Seropédica, 2014.

Rodney, Walter, African Slavery and Other Forms of Social Oppression on the Upper Guinea Coast in the Context of the Atlantic Slave Trade, in: Journal of African History 7 (1966) 3, p. 431–443.

Rodney, Walter, How Europe Underdeveloped Africa. London, 2018 [1972].

Rodrigues de Areia, Manuel Laranjeira, Estrutura magico-religiosa de uma trilogia tradicional nas populações de Angola. Lisboa, 1974.

Rodrigues, Aldair, Clergy, Society, and Power Relations in Colonial Brazil: On the Vicar Forane (*Vigário da vara)* (1745–1800), in: e-Journal of Portuguese History 13 (2015) 1, p. 40–67.

Rodrigues, Aldair, African Body Marks, Stereotypes and Racialization in Eighteenth-century Brazil, in: Slavery & Abolition 42 (2021) 2, p. 315–344.

Rodrigues, Eugénia, Portugueses e africanos nos Rios de Sena. Os Prazos da Coroa em Moçambique nos séculos XVII e XVIII. Lisbon, 2013.

Rodrigues, Manuel Benavente, Os homens do Erário Régio, in: Pecvnia (2011) 13, p. 59–81.

Rodrigues, Miguel Geraldes, Between West Africa and America. The Angolan Slave Trade in the Portuguese and Spanish Atlantic Empires (1560–1641). PhD dissertation, European University Institute, Fiesole, 2019.

Roldão, Cristina, José Augusto Pereira, and Pedro Varela, Tribuna Negra. Origens do Movimentos Negro em Portugal (1911–1933). Lisbon, 2023.

Rood, Daniel B., The Reinvention of Atlantic Slavery. Technology, Labor, Race and Capitalism in the Greater Caribbean. Oxford, 2017.

Rosa, Teresa da Fonseca, O Iluminismo e a expulsão dos jesuítas do Império Português. As reformas pombalinas e o plano de estudos menores, in: Revista de História Regional 19 (2014) 2, p. 361–383.

ROSE, E. M., The Murder of William of Norwich. The Origins of the Blood Libel in Medieval Europe. Oxford 2018.

ROSENTHAL, Caitlin, Accounting for Slavery. Masters and Management. Cambridge, MA, 2018.

ROUSE, Carolyn M., Necropolitics Versus Biopolitics. Spatialization, White Privilege, and Visibility during a Pandemic, in: Cultural Anthropology 36 (2021) 3, p. 360–367.

RUBBERS, Benjamin and Alessandro JEDLOWSKI, Introduction. Regimes of Responsibility in Africa. Towards a New Theoretical Approach in: Rubbers, Benjamin and Alessandro Jedlowski (eds.), Genealogies, Rationalities and Conflicts. New York, 2020, p. 1–20.

RUSSELL-WOOD, A. J. R., Fidalgos and Philanthropists. The Santa Casa da Misericórdia of Bahia (1550–1755). London, 1968.

RUSSEL-WOOD, A. J. R., Iberian Expansion and the Issue of Black Slavery. Changing Portuguese Attitudes (1440–1770), in: American Historical Review 83 (1978), p. 16–42.

RUTHERFORD, Blair, To Find an African Witch. Anthropology, Modernity, and Witch-Finding in North-West Zimbabwe, in: Critique of Anthropology 19 (1999) 1, p. 89–109.

SAAVEDRA, Manuel Bastias, Jurisdictional Autonomy and the Autonomy of Law. End of Empire and the Functional Differentiation of Law in 19th-Century Latin America, in: Rechtsgeschichte—Legal History (2018) 26, p. 325–337.

SAHLINS, Marshall, Islands of History. Chicago, 1985.

SALAS, Victor and Robert FASTIGGI (eds.), A Companion to Francisco Suárez. Leiden, 2015.

SALDANHA, António Vasconcelos, Conceitos de espaço e poder e seus reflexos na titulação régia portuguesa, in: Jean AUBIN (ED.), La Decouverte, le Portugal et l'Europe. Paris, 1990, p. 105–130.

SALDANHA, António Vasconcelos, Iustum imperium: dos tratados como fundamento do império dos portugueses no Oriente. Estudo de História do Direito Internacional e do Direito Português. Lisbon, 1997.

SALGADO, Graça (ed.) Fiscais e meirinhos. A administração no Brasil Colonial. Rio de Janeiro, 1985.

SALVADOR, José Gonçalves, Os cristãos-novos e o comércio no Atlântico Meridional (com enfoque nas Capitanias do Sul, 1530–1680). São Paulo, 1978.

SÁNCHEZ, Manuel Herrero, Spanish Theories of Empire. A Catholic and Polycentric Monarchy, in: Jörg Alejandro TELLKAMP (ed.), A Companion to Early Modern Spanish Imperial Political and Social Thought. Leiden, 2020, p. 17–52.

SANDERS, Todd, Save our Skins. Structural Adjustment, Morality and the Occult in Tanzania, in: Henrietta L. MOORE and Todd SANDERS (eds.), Magical Interpretations, Material Realities. Modernity, Witchcraft and the Occult in Postcolonial Africa. London, 2001,

SANSI-ROCA, Roger, The Fetish in the Lusophone Atlantic, in: Nancy Priscilla NARO, Roger SANSI-ROCA, and David H. TREECE (eds.), Cultures of the Lusophone Black Atlantic. New York, 2007, p. 19–40.

SANSI-ROCA, Roger, Feitiço e fetiche no Atlântico moderno, in: Revista de Antropologia 51 (2008) 1, p. 123–153.

SANSI-ROCA, Roger, Fetishes and Monuments. Afro-Brazilian Art and Culture in the 20th Century. New York, 2009.

SANSI-ROCA, Roger and Nicolau PARÉS (eds.), Sorcery in the Black Atlantic. Chicago, 2011.

SANSI-ROCA, Roger and Nicolau PARÉS, Introduction. Sorcery in the Black Atlantic, in: Roger SANSI-ROCA and Nicolau PARÉS (eds.), Sorcery in the Black Atlantic. Chicago, 2011, p. 1–18.

SANTOS, Catarina Madeira, Entre deux Droits. Les Lumières en Angola (1750 –c. 1800), in: Annales HSS (2005) 4, p. 817–848.

SANTOS, Catarina Madeira, Um governo "polido" para Angola. Reconfigurar dispositivos de domínio (1750 –c. 1800). PhD dissertation, Nova University of Lisbon, Lisbon, 2005.

SANTOS, Catarina Madeira, De "antigos conquistadores" a "angolenses." A elite colonial de Luanda no contexto da cultura das Luzes, entre lugares da memória e conhecimento científico, in: Cultura: Revista de História e Teoria das Ideias 24 (2007), p. 195–222.

SANTOS, Catarina Madeira, Escrever o poder. Os autos de vassalagem e a vulgarização da escrita entre as elites africanas Ndembu, in: Beatrix HEINTZE and Achim VON OPPEN (eds.), Angola on the Move. Transport Routes, Communications and History. Frankfurt am Main, 2008, p. 173–181.

SANTOS, Catarina Madeira, Luanda. A Colonial City between Africa and the Atlantic, Seventeenth and Eighteenth Centuries, in: Liam Matthew BROCKEY (ed.), Portuguese Colonial Cities in the Early Modern World. New York, 2008, p. 249–272.

SANTOS, Catarina Madeira, Écrire le pouvoir en Angola. Les archives Ndembu (XVIIe–XXe siècles), in: Annales HSS 64 (2009) 4, p. 767–795.

SANTOS, Catarina Madeira, Administrative Knowledge in a Colonial Context. Angola in the Eighteenth Century, in: The British Journal for the History of Science 43 (2010) 4, p. 539–556.

SANTOS, Catarina Madeira, Esclavage africain et traite atlantique confrontés: transactions langagières et juridiques (à propos du tribunal de mucanos dans l'Angola des XVIIe et XVIIIe siècles), in: Brésil(s) Sciences humaines et sociales 1 (2012) 1, p. 127–148.

SANTOS, Catarina Madeira, O Império Português face às instituições indígenas (Estado da Índia, Brasil e Angola, séculos XVI–XVIII), in: Federico PALOMO, Roberta STUMPF and Ângela Barreto XAVIER (eds.), Monarquias ibéricas em perspectiva comparada (séculos XVI–XVIII). Dinâmicas imperiais e circulação de modelos político-administrativos. Lisbon, 2018, p. 271–303.

SANTOS, Isaú, Macau e o Oriente no Arquivo Histórico Ultramarino Vol. 1. Macau, 1996.

SANTOS, Mário Leite, Melo Freire. Sistemática e autonomização do Direito Criminal Português, in: Direito e Justiça 7 (1993), p. 163–190.

SANTOS, Rui, A nuvem por Juno? O tema da fisiocracia na historiografia do pensamento económico português, in: Análise Social 28 (1993) 2, p. 423–443.

SANTOS, Tahinan Da Cruz, Inquisição Portuguesa na África. Denunciações do Reino do Congo e Angola no Século XVII, in: Revista Cadernos de Clio 2 (2011) 1, p. 229–245.

Santos, Vanicléia Silva, Africans, Afro-Brazilians and Afro-Portuguese in the Iberian Inquisition in the Seventeenth and Eighteenth centuries, in: African and Black Diaspora: An International Journal 5 (2012) 1, p. 49–63.

Santos, Vanicléia Silva, Bolsas de Mandinga no Atlântico (séculos XV a XVIII). PhD dissertation, University of São Paulo, São Paulo, 2008.

Sarró, Ramon, Manuela Palmeirim, Of Alien Kings and Perpetual Kin. Contradiction and Ambiguity in Ruwund (Lunda) Symbolic Thought, in: Etnográfica 13 (2009) 1, p. 225–226.

Saunders, A. C. de C. M., A Social History of Black Slaves and Freedmen in Portugal (1441–1555). Cambridge, 1982.

Schadeberg, Thilo C., Historical Linguistics, in: Derek Nurse and Gérard Philippson (eds.), The Bantu Languages. London, 2003, p. 143–154.

Schleumer, Fabiana, Nas bordas do Rio Kwanza. Inquisição, administração portuguesa e artes mágicas em Angola, in: Africana Studia (2018) 30, p. 13–28.

Schmoll, Pamela G., Black Stomachs, Beautiful Stones. Soul-Eating among Hausa in Niger, in: John L. Comaroff and Jean Comaroff (eds.), Modernity and its Malcontents. Ritual and Power in Postcolonial Africa. Chicago, 1993, p. 193–220.

Schoenbrun, David L., Crafting Early African Histories with Jan Vansina, in: History in Africa 45 (2018), p. 99–112.

Schoenbrun, David L., Words, Things, and Meaning. Linguistics as a Tool for Historical Reconstruction, in: Gerrit J. Dimmendaal and Rainer Vossen (eds.), The Oxford Handbook of African Languages. Oxford, 2020, p. 961–972.

Schoenbrun, David L., The Names of the Python. Belonging in East Africa (900 to 1930). Madison, 2021.

Schwartz, Stuart B., Sugar Plantations in the Formation of Brazilian Society. Bahia (1550–1835). Cambridge, 1985.

Schwartz, Stuart B., A Commonwealth within Itself. The Early Brazilian Sugar Industry (1550–1670), in: Stuart B. Schwartz (ed.), Tropical Babylons. Sugar and the Making of the Atlantic World (1450–1680). Chapel Hill, 2004, p. 158–200.

Schwartz, Stuart B., Burocracia e sociedade no Brasil Colonial. O Tribunal Superior da Bahia e seus desembargadores (1609–1751). São Paulo, 2011 [1973].

Schweighöfer, Stefan, Die Begründung der normativen Kraft von Gesetzen bei Francisco Suárez. Münster, 2018.

Scott, James Brown, The Spanish Origin of International Law. Oxford, 1934.

Scott, James C., The Moral Economy of the Peasant: Rebellion and Subsistence in Southeast Asia. New Haven, 1976.

Scott, James C., Weapons of the Weak: Everyday Forms of Peasant Resistance. New Haven, 1985.

Scott, James C., State Simplifications. Nature, Space, and People, in: Nomos 38 (1996), p. 42–85.

Scott, James C., Seeing Like a State. How Certain Schemes to Improve the Human Condition Have Failed. New Haven, 1998.

Sebastião, Luzia Bebiana de Almeida, Os problemas penais do Sul e o pluralismo cultural, in: Revista Portuguesa de Ciência Criminal 23 (2013) 4, p. 491–546.

Sebastião, Luzia Bebiana de Almeida, Legalidade penal, costume e pluralismo jurídico. A experiência angolana. O(s) Direito(s) e os facto(s). PhD dissertation, University of Coimbra, Coimbra, 2015.

Sebestyén, Evá, Jan Vansina (eds.), and Leitão, Manoel Correia, Angola's Eastern Hinterland in the 1750s. A Text Edition and Translation of Manoel Correia Leitão's "Voyage" (1755–1756), in: History in Africa 26 (1999), p. 299–364.

Seinecke, Ralf, The Plural Turn. Legal Pluralism in Historical Legal Studies, in: EViR working papers (2024) 13, p. 1–76.

Seixas, Margarida, Abolição da escravidão, in: António Pedro Barbas Homem (ed.), Grandes realizações da história do direito português. Lisbon, 2016, p. 5–7.

Seixas, Margarida, Pessoa e trabalho no Direito Português (1750–1878). Escravo, liberto e serviçal. Lisbon, 2016.

Shaw, Rosalind, Cannibal Transformations. Colonialism and Commodification in the Sierra Leone Hinterland, in: Henrietta L. Moore and Todd Sanders (eds.), Magical Interpretations, Material Realities. Modernity, Witchcraft and the Occult in Postcolonial Africa. London, 2001, p. 50–70.

Shaw, Rosalind, Memories of the Slave Trade. Ritual and the Historical Imagination in Sierra Leone. Chicago, 2002.

Silva Rego, António da, Les Missions portugaises. Aperçu général. Lisbon, 1958.

Silva, Andrée Mansuy Diniz, Portrait d'un homme d'État. D. Rodrigo de Souza Coutinho, Comte de Linhares (1755–1812), Vol. 1. Lisbon, 2002.

Silva, Daniel B. Domingues da, The Early Population Charts of Portuguese Angola (1776–1830). A Preliminary Assessment, in: Anais de História de Além-Mar 16 (2015), p. 107–124.

Silva, Daniel B. Domingues da, The Atlantic Slave Trade from West Central Africa (1780–1867). Cambridge, 2017.

Silva, Marta Fernandes da, A escravidão no discurso de Manoel Ribeiro Rocha. Um homen em seu tempo (Brasil, século XVIII), in: Revista Nordestina de História do Brasil 3 (2021) 6, p. 1–42.

Simões Junior, Mario Francisco, A Secretaria de Estado do Ultramar. Origem, Organização e Expedientes (1736–1750), in: Revista Angelus Novus 8 (2017) 13, p. 73–92.

Simon, William Joel, Scientific Expeditions in the Portuguese Overseas Territories (1783–1808) and the Role of Lisbon in the Intellectual-Scientific Community of the Late Eighteenth Century. Lisbon, 1983.

Siqueira, Sônia Aparecida de, A disciplina da vida colonial. Os regimentos da Inquisição in: Revista do Instituto Histórico e Geográfico Brasileiro 157 (1996) 392, p. 497–571.

Siqueira, Sônia Aparecida de, O momento da Inquisição. João Pessoa, 2013.

Slenes, Robert W., The Great Porpoise-Skull Strike. Central African Water Spirits and Slave Identity in Early-Nineteenth-Century Rio de Janeiro, in: Linda M. Heywood (ed.),

Central Africans and Cultural Transformations in the American Diaspora. Cambridge, 2002, p. 183–210.

Soares, Mariza de Carvalho, O marfim nos acordos de compensação entre o Congo e Portugal (1512–1526), in: José Augusto N. Silva Horta, Carlos Almeida and Peter Mark (eds.), African Ivories in the Altantic World (1400–1900). Lisbon, 2021, p. 317–338.

Sommar, Mary E., The Slaves of the Churches. A History. Oxford, 2020.

Sousa, Alfredo de, Estruturas socio-económicas e dialéctica de culturas em África—II, in: Análise Social 2 (1964) 5, p. 17–65.

Souza Correa, Sílivo Marcus de, A antropofagia na África Equatorial. Etno-História e a realidade do(s) discurso(s) sobre o real, in: Afro-Ásia (2008) 37, p. 9–41.

Souza e Mello, Marcia Eliane Alves de, As Juntas das Missões ultramarinas. Gênese e evolução, in: Amazônia em Cadernos (2001–2002) 7–8, p. 49–69.

Souza e Mello, Marcia Eliane Alves de, Fé e império. As Juntas das Missões nas Conquistas Portuguesas. Manaus, 2007.

Souza, Evergton Sales, Estruturas eclesiásticas da monarquia portuguesa. A Igreja diocesana, in: Federico Palomo, Roberta Stumpf and Ângela Barreto Xavier (eds.), Monarquias ibéricas em perspectiva comparada (séculos XVI–XVIII). Dinâmicas imperiais e circulação de modelos político-administrativos. Lisbon, 2018, p. 513–542.

Spicksley, Judith, The Decline of Slavery for Debt in Western Europe in the Medieval Period, in: Simonetta Cavaciocchi (ed.), Serfdom and Slavery in the European Economy (11th to 18th Centuries). Firenze, 2014, p. 465–486.

Spicksley, Judith, Contested Enslavement. The Portuguese in Angola and the Problem of Debt (c. 1600–1800), in: Itinerario 39 (2015) 2, p. 247–275.

Stewart, Pamela J. and Andrew Strathern, Witchcraft, Sorcery, Rumors, and Gossip. Cambridge, 2003.

Strathern, Marilyn, The Gender of the Gift. Problems with Women and Problems with Society in Melanesia. Berkeley, 1988.

Subtil, José Manuel, Os ministros do rei no poder local, ilhas e ultramar (1772–1826), in: Penélope: Fazer e desfazer a história (2003) 27, p. 37–58.

Subtil, José Manuel, O terramoto político (1755–1759). Memória e poder. Lisbon, 2006.

Subtil, José Manuel, Estado de polícia, revolução e estado liberal (1760–1865). "Em homenagem a António Manuel Hespanha," in: cadernos do Arquivo Municipal (2020) 14, p. 15–40.

Subtil, José Manuel, Espaço político e organização do poder no Antigo Regime em Portugal, in: Revista do Instituto de Estudos Brasileiros (2022) 83, p. 88–116.

Subtil, José Manuel, O crime e o castigo. Alteridade entre as Luzes e o Liberalismo (Portugal, 1750–1841), in: José Manuel Subtil, Cláudia C. Azeredo Atallah and Maria Sarita Mota (eds.), Criminalidades, direito e justiça no mundo ibérico. Buenos Aires, 2022, p. 35–64.

Subtil, José Manuel, Cláudia C. Azeredo Atallah and Maria Sarita Mota, Criminalidades no mundo ibérico. Uma introdução, in: José Manuel Subtil, Cláudia C. Azeredo Atallah and Maria Sarita Mota (eds.), Criminalidades, direito e justiça no mundo ibérico. Buenos Aires, 2022, p. 17–32.

Sunstein, Cass R., Incommensurability and Valuation in Law, in: Michigan Law Review (1993) 92, p. 779–861.

Süssekind, Flora, Satire and Temporal Heterogeneity, in: Mario J. Valdés and Djelal Kadir (eds.), Literary Cultures of Latin America. A Comparative History. Oxford, 2004, p. 241–257.

Sweet, David G., Black Robes and "Black Destiny." Jesuit Views of African Slavery in 17th-Century Latin America, in: Revista de Historia de América (1978) 86, p. 87–133.

Sweet, James, Recreating Africa. Culture, Kinship, and Religion in the African-Portuguese World (1441–1770). Chapel Hill, 2003.

Sweet, James, "Not a Thing for White Men to See." Central African Divination in Seventeenth Century Brazil, in: José C. Curto; and Paul E. Lovejoy (eds.), Enslaving Connections. Changing Cultures of Africa and Brazil During the Era of Slavery. New York, 2004, p. 139–148.

Sweet, James, Domingos Álvares. African Healing and the Intellectual History of the Atlantic World. Chapel Hill, 2011.

Tassinari, Tomás Motta, Notas sobre a justificativa da escravização de Ambundos segundo Baltasar Barreira. Da *accomodatio* jesuítica ao planeta cultural (1583), in the proceeding of: VII Encontro Internacional de História Colonial, Natal,2018.

Teles, Edgar Alexandre Pinto, Das jóias negras do império às jóias da terra. Iluminismo, economia e reforma em Angola (1780–1810). Masters dissertation, Nova University of Lisbon, Lisbon, 2015.

Ter Haar, Gerrie and Stephen Ellis, The Occult Does Not Exist. A Response to Terence Ranger, in: Africa 79 (2009) 3, p. 399–412.

Teter, Magda, Blood Libel. On the Trail of Antisemitic Myth. Cambridge, MA, 2020.

Thomas, Keith, Religion and the Decline of Magic. Studies in Popular Beliefs in Sixteenth- and Seventeenth-Century England. London, 1971.

Thomaz, Fernanda, Casaco que se despe pelas costas. História do colonialismo, justiça e agências africanas em Moçambique. Juiz de Fora, 2022.

Thomaz, Luís Filipe Ferreira Reis, De Ceuta a Timor. Lisbon, 1994.

Thompson, Estevam C., The Making of Quilengues. Violence, Enslavement and Resistance in the Interior of Benguela (1600–1830). PhD dissertation, York University, York, 2021.

Thornton, John K., A Resurrection for the Jaga, in: Cahiers d'Études Africaines 18 (1978) 68, p. 223–227.

Thornton, John K., New Light on Cavazzi's Seventeenth-Century Description of Kongo, in: History in Africa 6 (1979), p. 253–264.

Thornton, John K., Early Kongo-Portuguese Relations. A New Interpretation, in: History in Africa 8 (1981), p. 183–204.

Thornton, John K., The Kingdom of Kongo. Civil War and Transition (1641–1718). Madison, 1983.

THORNTON, John K., The Development of an African Catholic Church in the Kingdom of Kongo (1491–1750), in: The Journal of African History 25 (1984) 2, p. 147–167.

THORNTON, John K., The Correspondence of the Kongo Kings (1614–1635). Problems of Internal Written Evidence on a Central African Kingdom, in: Paideuma: Mitteilungen zur Kulturkunde 33 (1987), p. 407–421.

THORNTON, John K., The Art of War in Angola (1575–1680), in: Comparative Studies in Society and History 30 (1988) 2, p. 360–378.

THORNTON, John K., Africa and Africans in the Making of the Atlantic World (1400–1800). Cambridge, 1998.

THORNTON, John K., The Kongolese Saint Anthony. Dona Beatriz Kimpa Vita and the Antonian Movement (1684–1706). Cambridge, 1998.

THORNTON, John K., The Origins and Early History of the Kingdom of Kongo (c. 1350–1550), in: The International Journal of African Historical Studies 34 (2001) 1, p. 89–120.

THORNTON, John K., Religious and Ceremonial Life in the Kongo and Mbundu Areas (1500–1700), in: Linda M. HEYWOOD (ED.), Central Africans and Cultural Transformations in the American Diaspora. Cambridge, 2002, p. 71–90.

THORNTON, John K., Cannibals, Witches, and Slave Traders in the Atlantic World, in: The William and Mary Quarterly 60 (2003) 2, p. 273–294.

THORNTON, John K., Religião e vida cerimonial, in: Linda M. HEYWOOD (ED.), Diáspora negra no Brasil. São Paulo, 2008, p. 81–100.

THORNTON, John K., Firearms, Diplomacy, and Conquest in Angola. Cooperation and Alliance in West Central Africa (1491–1671), in: Wayne E. LEE(ed.), Empires and Indigenes. Intercultural Alliance, Imperial Expansion, and Warfare in the Early Modern World. 2011, p. 167–192.

THORNTON, John K., A Cultural History of the Atlantic World (1250–1820). Cambridge, 2012.

THORNTON, John K., Afro-Christian Syncretism in the Kingdom of Kongo, in: The Journal of African History 54 (2013) 1, p. 53–77.

THORNTON, John K., The Kingdom of Kongo and the Counter Reformation, in: Social Sciences and Missions 26 (2013), p. 40–58.

THORNTON, John K., Conquest and Theology. The Jesuits in Angola (1548–1650), in: Journal of Jesuit Studies 1 (2014), p. 245–259.

THORNTON, John K., King Afonso I of Kong: The Making of an African Christian King and his Kingdom, in: Dana L. ROBERT (ED.), African Christian Biography. Pietermaritzburg, 2018, p. 107–111.

THORNTON, John K., A History of West Central Africa to 1850. Cambridge, 2020.

THORNTON, John K. and Linda M. HEYWOOD, The Treason of Dom Pedro Nkanga a Mvemba against Dom Diogo, King of Kongo (1550), in: Kathryn Joy MCKNIGHT and Leo J. GAROFALO (eds.), Afro-Latino Voices. Translations of Early Modern Ibero-Atlantic Narratives. Indianapolis, 2015.

Tierney, Brian, Natural Rights. Studies on Natural Rights, Natural Law, and Church Law (1150–1625). Cambridge, 1997.

Tinhorão, José Ramos, Os Negros em Portugal. Uma presença silenciosa. Lisbon, 2019 [1988].

Tomalela, Kiame Leonel Nkanga, O alambamento e a relevância jurídica da promessa de casamento em Angola, in: JuLaw (2020).

Tomás, António, In the Skin of the City. Spatial Transformation in Luanda. Durham, 2022.

Tomich, Dale W. (ed.), Slavery and Historical Capitalism during the Nineteenth Century. London, 2017.

Tomich, Dale W. and Paul E. Lovejoy (eds.), The Atlantic and Africa. Albany, 2021.

Tonda, Joseph, La Violence de l'imaginaire des enfants-sorciers, in: Cahiers d'Études Africaines (2008) 189–90, p. 325–343.

Topa, Francisco, Entre a "Terra de gente oprimida" e a "Terra de gente tostada." Luíz Félix da Cruz e o primeiro poema 'angolano,' in: Literatura em Debate 7 (2013) 13, p. 122–147.

Trigo de Sousa, Ana Madalena Rosa Barros, D. Francisco de Sousa Coutinho em Angola. Reinterpretação de um Governo (1764–1772). Masters dissertation, Nova University of Lisbon, Lisbon, 1996.

Tsing, Anna Lowenhaupt, Friction. An Ethnography of Global Connection. Princeton, 2005.

Tuomela, Raimo, On Radical Conceptual Revolutions in Social Science, in: Journal for General Philosophy of Science / Zeitschrift für allgemeine Wissenschaftstheorie 22 (1991) 2, p. 303–320.

Turner, Victor, Witchcraft and Sorcery. Taxonomy versus Dynamics, in: Africa 34 (1964) 4, p. 314–325.

Turner, Victor, Liminal to Liminoid, in Play, Flow, and Ritual. An Essay in Comparative Symbology, in: Rice Institute Pamphlet—Rice University Studies 60 (1974) 3, p. 53–92.

Turner, Victor, The Ritual Process. Structure and Anti-Structure. Ithaca, 1991 [1969].

Urbanik, Jakub, On the Uselessness of it All. The Roman Law of Marriage and Modern Times in: Fundamina 20 (2014) 2, p. 946–960.

Urbano, Francisco Castilla, The Debate of Valladolid (1550–1551). Background, Discussions, and Results of the Debate between Juan Ginés de Sepúlveda and Bartolomé de las Casas, in: Jörg Alejandro Tellkamp (ed.), A Companion to Early Modern Spanish Imperial Political and Social Thought. Leiden, 2020, p. 222–251.

Van Gennep, Arnold, The Rites of Passage. London, 1960 [1909].

Vanhee, Hein, Central African Popular Christianity and the Making of Haitian Vodou Religion, in: Linda M. Heywood (ed.), Central Africans and Cultural Transformations in the American Diaspora. Cambridge, 2002, p. 243–264.

Vansina, Jan, De la tradition orale. Essai de méthode historique. Tervuren, 1961.

Vansina, Jan, Long-Distance Trade-Routes in Central Africa, in: Journal of African History 3 (1962) 3, p. 376–390.

Vansina, Jan, Foundation of the Kingdom of Kasanje, in: The Journal of African History 4 (1963) 3, p. 255–374.

Vansina, Jan, Oral tradition. A study in historical methodology. London, 1965.

Vansina, Jan, Kingdoms of the Savanna. Madison, 1966.

Vansina, Jan, More on the Invasion of Kongo and Angola by the Jaga and the Lunda, in: The Journal of African History 7 (1966) 3, p. 421–429.

Vansina, Jan, Bantu in a Crystal Ball, II, in: History in Africa 7 (1980), p. 293–325.

Vansina, Jan, Is elegance proof? Structuralism and Africa History, in: History in Africa (1983) 10, p. 307–348.

Vansina, Jan, Paths in the Rainforests. Toward a History of Political Tradition in Equatorial Africa. Madison, 1990.

Vansina, Jan, Government in Kasai before the Lunda, in: The International Journal of African Historical Studies 31 (1998) 1, p. 1–22.

Vansina, Jan, It Never Happened. Kinguri's Exodus and Its Consequences, in: History in Africa 25 (1998), p. 387–403.

Vansina, Jan, Raffia Cloth in West Central Africa (1500–1800), in: Maureen Fennell Mazzaoui (ed.), Textiles. Production, Trade and Demand. Aldershot, 1998, p. 261–282.

Vansina, Jan, Ambaca Society and the Slave Trade (c. 1760–1845), in: The Journal of African History 46 (2005) 1, p. 1–27.

Vansina, Jan, On Ravenstein's Edition of Battell's Adventures in Angola and Loango, in: History in Africa 34 (2007), p. 321–347.

Vec, Miloš, Multinormativität in der Rechtsgeschichte, Berlin-Brandenburgische Akademie der Wissenschaften Jahrbuch 2008. Berlin, 2009, p. 155–166.

Vedeler, Harold Torger, Reconstructing Meaning in Deuteronomy 22:5. Gender, Society, and Transvestitism in Israel and the Ancient Near East, in: Journal of Bible Studies 127 (2008) 3, p. 459–476.

Vellut, Jean-Luc, Notes sur le Lunda et la frontière luso-africaine, in: Etudes d'Histoire africaine 3 (1972), p. 61–66.

Vellut, Jean-Luc, Le Royaume de Cassange et les réseaux luso-africains (ca. 1750–1810), in: Cahiers d'Études Africaines 15 (1975) 57, p. 117–136.

Vellut, Jean-Luc, New Perspectives on the Ambaquista Network, in: The Journal of African History 45 (2004) 2, p. 327–329.

Venâncio, José Carlos, Espaço e Dinâmica Populacional em Luanda no Século XVIII, in: Revista de História Econômica e Social 14 (1984), p. 67–97.

Venâncio, José Carlos, A economia de Luanda e hinterland no século XVIII. Lisbon, 1996.

Vieira, Daiana Lucas, As cartas do Dembo Caculo Cacahenda. Um pouco da história dos Dembos e da relação deste com as autoridades portuguesas situadas em Angola (1780–1850), in: Veredas da História 7 (2014) 1, p. 41–54.

Vieira, Daiana Lucas, O Dembo Caculo Cacahenda. A História de uma região e de uma chefatura (1780–1860). PhD dissertation, Universidade Federal de Juiz de Fora, Juiz de Fora, 2014.

Volavka, Zdenka, Crown and Ritual. The Royal Insignia of Ngoyo. Toronto, 1998.

von Thiessen, Hillard, Normenkonkurrenz Handlungsspielräume, Rollen, normativer Wandel und normative Kontinuität vom späten Mittelalter bis zum Übergang zur Moderne, in: Hillard von Thiessen and Arne Karsten (eds.), Normenkonkurrenz in historischer Perspektive. 2015, p. 241–286.

von Thiessen, Hillard, Das Zeitalter der Ambiguität. Vom Umgang mit Werten und Normen in der Frühen Neuzeit. Göttingen, 2021.

von Thiessen, Hillard, Concurrence and Competition of Norms (*Normenkonkurrenz*) in the Age of Ambiguity. A concept for the analysis of normative orders in early modern Europe in inter-epochal and interdisciplinary perspective, in: Ulrike Ludwig (ed.), Conceptual Forum Concurrence of Norms and Cultural Ambiguity. Münster, 2023, p. 6–51.

Walker, Timothy, The Role and Practices of the *Curandeiro* and *Saludador* in Early Modern Portuguese Society, in: História, Ciências, Saúde—Manguinhos 11 (2004), p. 223–237.

Walker, Timothy, Doctors, Folk Medicine and the Inquisition. The Repression of Magical Healing in Portugal during the Enlightenment. Leiden, 2005.

Webb (Jr.), James L. A., Toward the Comparative Study of Money. A Reconsideration of West African Currencies and Neoclassical Monetary Concepts, in: The International Journal of African Historical Studies 15 (1982) 3, p. 455–466.

Websdale, Neil, Policing the Poor. From Slave Plantation to Public Housing. Boston, 2001.

Wehling, Arno, Uma solução setecentista ousada e inovadora para a escravidão no Brasil, in: História (São Paulo) 34 (2015) 2, p. 146–164.

Wehling, Arno and Maria José Cavalheiro de Macedo Wehling, Direito e justiça no Brasil Colonial. O Tribunal da Relaçâo do Rio de Janeiro (1751–1808). Rio de Janeiro, 2004.

West, Harry G., Kupilikula. Governance and the Invisible Realm in Mozambique. Chicago, 2005.

West, Harry G., Ethnographic Sorcery. Chicago 2007.

West, Harry G., «Governem-se vocês mesmos!» Democracia e carnificina no Norte de Moçambique, in: Análise Social 18 (2008) 2, p. 347–368.

West, Harry G., Creative Destruction and Sorcery of Construction. Power, Hope and Suspicion in Post-War Mozambique, in: Political and Legal Anthropology Review 20 (2008) 1, p. 13–31.

West, Harry G., Sorcery of Construction and Socialist Modernization. Ways of Understanding Power in Postcolonial Mozambique, in: American Ethnologist 28 (2008) 1, p. 119–150.

West, Harry G. and Todd Sanders (eds.), Transparency and Conspiracy. Durham, 2003.

Wheatley, Natasha, Legal Pluralism as Temporal Pluralism. Historical Rights, Legal Vitalism, and Non-Synchronous Sovereignty, in: Dan Edelstein, Stefanos Geroulanos and Natasha Wheatley (eds.), Power and Time. Temporalities in Conflict and the Making of History. Chicago, 2020, p. 53–79.

Wheatley, Natasha, The Life and Death of States. Central Europe and the Transformation of Modern Sovereignty. Princeton, 2023.

Whiteley, Peter M., Ming Xue, Ward C. Wheeler, Revising the Bantu Tree, in: Cladistics 35 (2019) 3, p. 329–348.

WILLIAMS, Eric, Capitalism & Slavery. Chapel Hill, 2021 [1944].

WILLIS, Roy, Translator's Introduction, in: Luc DE HEUSCH, The Drunken King or the Origin of the State. Bloomington, 1982, p. vii–xiv.

WILSON, Monica Hunter, Witch-Beliefs and Social Structure, in: Max MARWICK (ED.), Witchcraft and Sorcery. Selected Readings. London, 1970, p. 252–263.

WINNEBECK, Julia, Ove SUTTER, Adrian HERMANN, Christoph ANTWEILER, and Stephan CONERMANN, On Asymmetrical Dependency. Bonn, 2021.

WISSENBACH, Maria Cristina Cortez, Ritos de magia e sobrevivência: sociabilidades e práticas mágico-religiosas no Brasil (1890–1940). PhD. dissertation, Universidade de São Paulo, São Paulo, 1997.

WISSENBACH, Maria Cristina Cortez, Práticas religiosas, errância e vida cotidiana no Brasil (finais do século XIX e inícios do XX). São Paulo, 2018.

WOLFE, Patrick, Traces of History. Elementary Structures of Race. London, 2016.

WRIGLEY, C. C., Myths of the Savanna, in: The Journal of African History 15 (1974) 1, p. 131–135.

XAVIER, Ângela Barreto, Religion and Empire in Portuguese India. Conversion, Resistance, and the Making of Goa. Albany, 2022.

XAVIER, Ângela Barreto and Cristina NOGUEIRA DA SILVA (eds.), O Governo dos outros. Poder e diferença no Império Português. Lisbon, 2016.

XAVIER, Ângela Barreto and Cristina NOGUEIRA DA SILVA, Introdução. Construção da alteridade no Império Português. Temas e problemas, in: Ângela Barreto XAVIER and Cristina Nogueira da SILVA (eds.), O Governo dos outros. Poder e diferença no Império Português. Lisbon, 2016, p. 21–66.

XAVIER, Ângela Barreto and Fernanda OLIVAL, O padroado da coroa de Portugal. Fundamentos e práticas, in: Federico PALOMO, Roberta STUMPF and Ângela Barreto XAVIER (eds.), Monarquias ibéricas em perspectiva comparada (séculos XVI–XVIII). Dinâmicas imperiais e circulação de modelos político-administrativos. Lisbon, 2018, p. 123–160.

XAVIER, Ângela Barreto and Nuno Gonçalo MONTEIRO, António Manuel Hespanha. O passado é um país estranho, in: Análise Social 55 (2020) 235 (2), p. 473–479.

XIMENES, Cristiana Ferreira Lyrio, Bahia e Angola. Redes comerciais e o tráfico de escravos (1750–1808). PhD dissertation, Universidade Federal Fluminense, Niterói, 2012.

ZAGORIN, Perez, Hobbes and the Law of Nature. Princeton, 2009.

ZAMORA, Romina, The Domestic Sphere, in: Duve, Thomas and Tamar Herzog (eds.), Latin America Law in Global Perspective. Cambridge, 2024, p. 220–249.

ZENKER, Olaf and Markus Virgil HOEHNE, Processing the Paradox. When the State Has to Deal with Customary Law, in: Olaf ZENKER and Markus Virgil HOEHNE (eds.), The State and the Paradox of Customary Law in Africa. London, 2018, p. 1–40.

ZERON, Carlos Alberto de Moura Ribeiro, Linha de fé. A Companhia de Jesus e a escravidão no processo de formação da sociedade colonial (Brasil, séculos XVI e XVII). São Paulo, 2011.

Zeron, Carlos Alberto de Moura Ribeiro, Les Jésuites et le commerce d'esclaves entre le Brésil et l'Angola à la fin du XVIe siècle, in: Hebrard, Jean (ed.), Brésil quatre siècles d'esclavage. Paris, 2012, p. 65–83.

Zeron, Carlos A. de M. R., Vieira em movimento. Subjacências da distinção entre tapuias, tupis e negros, in: Estudos Avançados 33 (2019) 97, p. 171–192.

Zeron, Carlos Alberto de Moura Ribeiro The Concept of Justice Shared in Portuguese America and the Disputes over its Application to Slavery, in: Conermann Stephan, Paes Mariana Dias, Roberto Hofmeister Pich and Paulo Cruz Terra (eds.), Current Trends in Slavery Studies in Brazil. Berlin, 2023, p. 289–332.

Zeron, Carlos Alberto de Moura Ribeiro and Camila Loureiro Dias, A Igreja e a escravidão no Mundo Atlântico. Notas historiográficas sobre a doutrina católica no Mundo Moderno e Contemporâneo, in: Portuguese Studies Review 25 (2017) 2, p. 85–106.

Ziegler, Vickie L., Trial by Fire and Battle in Medieval German Literature. New York, 2004.

Online Resources

Almeida, Carlos, Christianity in Kongo, Oxford Research Encyclopedias. Oxford, 2021 https://doi.org/10.1093/acrefore/9780190277734.013.641.

Balanço geral da receita e despesa da Fazenda Real no Reino de Angola, Arquivo Nacional da Torre do Tombo. Lisbon, 2023. https://digitarq.arquivos.pt/details?id=8959944 accessed 01.16.2025.

Bonciani, Rodrigo Faustinoni, Poder régio em mutação. Expansão atlântica e alianças ibéricas no fim do século XV, in: Nuevo Mundo Mundos Nuevos (2014). DOI: https://doi.org/10.4000/nuevomundo.66538.

Bostoen, Koen and Yvonne Bastin, Bantu Lexical Reconstruction, Oxford Research Encyclopedias. Oxford, 2016. DOI: https://doi.org/10.1093/oxfordhb/9780199935345.013.36.

Bostoen, Koen, The Bantu Expansion, Oxford Research Encyclopedias. Oxford, 2018. DOI: https://doi.org/10.1093/acrefore/9780190277734.013.191

Bracks Fonseca, Mariana, Queen Njinga of Ndongo and Matamba, Oxford Research Encyclopedias. Oxford, 2022. DOI: https://doi.org/10.1093/acrefore/9780190277734.013.997.

Camarinhas, Nuno, entry "Juiz de Fora," in: E-Dicionário da Terra e do Território no Império Português. Lisbon, 2015. DOI: https://doi.org/10.15847/cehc.edittip.2015v008.

Camarinhas, Nuno, entry "Juiz de Vintena," in: E-Dicionário da Terra e do Território no Império Português. Lisbon, 2015. DOI: https://doi.org/10.15847/cehc.edittip.2015v007.

Camarinhas, Nuno, entry "Tribunais de Relação," in: E-Dicionário da Terra e do Território no Império Português. Lisbon, 2015. DOI: https://doi.org/10.15847/cehc.edittip.2015v010.

Conselho Ultramarino (1530–1833), Arquivo Histórico Ultramarino. Lisbon, 2023. https://digitarq.ahu.arquivos.pt/details?id=1119329 accessed 01.16.2025.

Conselho Ultramarino (1851–1868), Arquivo Histórico Ultramarino. https://digitarq.ahu.arquivos.pt/details?id=1119335 accessed 01.16.2025.

Contadoria da Junta da Fazenda Real do Reino de Angola, Arquivo Nacional da Torre do Tombo. Lisbon, 2023. https://digitarq.arquivos.pt/details?id=8959795 accessed 01.16.2025.

D'Anville, Jean-Baptiste Bourguignon, Royaumes de Loando, Congo, Angola, Benguela, c.1725. Paris, 1730. https://gallica.bnf.fr/ark:/12148/btv1b8595614f accessed 01.16.2025.

Dembos (1677–1920), Arquivo Histórico Ultramarino. Lisbon, 2023. https://digitarq.ahu.arquivos.pt/details?id=1157639 accessed 01.16.2025.

Edricson, Bantu Zones. 2007. https://commons.wikimedia.org/wiki/File:Bantu_zones.png accessed 01.16.2025.

Etnografiska Museet, Dyna (inventory number: 1889.04.4166) (CC Licence). Stockholm, 2025. https://collections.smvk.se/carlotta-em/web/object/1360138 accessed 01.16.2025.

Fernandes, Filipe Marques, entry: "Freire, Pascoal de Melo," in: Dicionário de Historiadores Portugueses. Da Academia Real das Ciências ao final do Estado Novo. Lisbon, 2016. https://dichp.bnportugal.gov.pt/historiadores/historiadores_melo_freire7.htm accessed 01.16.2025.

Gonzales, Rhonda M., Historical Linguistics. Words and Things, Oxford Research Encyclopedias. Oxford, 2018. https://doi.org/10.1093/acrefore/9780190277734.013.361.

Gouveia, Jaime Ricardo de, entry "D. Luís Simões Brandão (1702–1719)," in: Religion-AJE. Religião, administração e justiça eclesiástica no Império Português (1514–1750). Coimbra, 2024. https://www.uc.pt/fluc/religionAJE/instrumentos_trabalho/biografias_bispos_congo_angola accessed 01.16.2025 accessed 01.16.2025.

Lei n.º 3820 de 11 de Novembro de 2021. Luanda, 2021. https://sic.gov.ao/wp-content/uploads/2021/10/codigo-penal-angolano-lei-no-3820-de-11-de-novembro_2021-05-08-06-18-59-864.pdf accessed 01.16.2025 accessed 01.16.2025.

Ohier, Louis-Marie Joseph, Discription du costume des noirs de la côte d'Angola (Public Domain). https://permalinkbnd.bnportugal.gov.pt/records/item/84904-discription-du-costume-des-noirs-de-la-cote-d-angola accessed 01.16.2025.

Oliveira, Vanessa S., African Women and Commerce in the Atlantic World, Oxford Research Encyclopedias. Oxford, 2023. https://doi.org/10.1093/acrefore/9780199366439.013.1180.

Saavedra, Manuel Bastias, Gerd Bender, Peter Collin, Thomas Duve, Christian R. J. Pogies; Luca von Bogdandy; Johanna Wolf, and Alexandra Woods, Historical Regimes of Normativity. Part 3, https://doi.org/10.17176/20210923-163541-0.

Saavedra, Manuel Bastias, Gerd Bender, Peter Collin, Thomas Duve, Christian R. J. Pogies; Luca von Bogdandy; Johanna Wolf, and Alexandra Woods, Why "Historical Regimes of Normativity"? https://doi.org/10.17176/20210705-141843-0.

Schadeberg, Thilo and Yvonne Bastin, entry "bàd," in: Bantu Lexical Reconstructions 3, Vol. edited Tervuren, 2024. https://www.africamuseum.be/en/research/discover/human_sciences/culture_society/blr/results_any?Index=14 accessed 01.16.2025.

SCHADEBERG, Thilo and Yvonne BASTIN, entry "bàndà," in: Bantu Lexical Reconstructions 3, Vol. edited Tervuren, 2024. https://www.africamuseum.be/en/research/discover/human_sciences/culture_society/blr/results_any?Index=91 accessed 01.16.2025.

SCHADEBERG, Thilo and Yvonne BASTIN, entry "dòg," in: Bantu Lexical Reconstructions 3, Vol. edited Tervuren, 2024. https://www.africamuseum.be/en/research/discover/human_sciences/culture_society/blr/results_any?Index=1100 accessed 01.16.2025.

SCHADEBERG, Thilo and Yvonne BASTIN, entry "gàngà," in: Bantu Lexical Reconstructions 3, Vol. edited Tervuren, 2024. https://www.africamuseum.be/en/research/discover/human_sciences/culture_society/blr/results_any?Index=1332 accessed 01.16.2025.

TUKI, entry "Wanga," in: MobiTUKI, Taasisi ya Uchunguzi wa Kiswahili Salaam (TUKI) University of Dar es Salaam, Dar es Salaam, 2000. https://swahili-dictionary.com/swahili-english/wanga_wanga accessed 01.16.2025.

List of Figures

Index

Names

Places